The Victorian Country House

THE VICTORIAN COUNTRY HOUSE

Revised and Enlarged Edition

MARK GIROUARD

Yale University Press

New Haven and London

To Dorothy

Half title page. Looking down on Tyntesfield. Somerset.
Frontispiece. The porch and oriel at Bestwood Lodge. Nottinghamshire (S. S. Teulon, 1862–4), as photographed in 1867.

Copyright © 1979 by Mark Girouard
Fourth Printing 1990

Designed by Dorothy Girouard

Filmset in Monophoto Bembo by BAS Printers Limited, Over, Wallop, Hampshire.
Printed in Yugoslavia by ČGP Delo by arrangement with Papirografika

Library of Congress Cataloging in Publication Data

Girouard, Mark, 1931-
   The Victorian country house.

   Includes index.
    1. Country homes—Great Britain.   2. Architecture, Victorian—Great Britain.   I. Title.
NA7562.G5 1979   728.8'3'0942   79-64077
ISBN 0-300-02390-1
ISBN 0-300-03472-5 (pbk.)

PREFACE

THIS is a new and enlarged edition of a book first issued in 1971. Much new material has been published since the first edition; in particular there have been valuable monographs on Butterfield, Norman Shaw and J. L. Pearson, by Paul Thompson, Andrew Saint and Anthony Quiney, as well as numerous relevant articles in *Country Life* and other periodicals. The original text has accordingly been revised, corrected and slightly expanded; two new sections on individual houses have been added (Harlaxton and Tyntesfield) as well as extra plans and thirty-two pages of colour. I am especially grateful to Jill Allibone for providing unpublished information about Harlaxton, Salvin and Devey, and to Gordon Barnes for similar information about Henry Woodyer. The first of the two new houses, Harlaxton Manor, was omitted from the original edition because this was planned as a sequel to Christopher Hussey's *English Country Houses: Late Georgian*. As Harlaxton is at least as much a Victorian house as a late Georgian one, and Christopher Hussey's book has long been out of print, there seemed no point in continuing to omit it. In the first edition footnotes were integrated with the text; they have now been removed to the back of the book except for a selection which I thought might especially interest or amuse the general reader.

The book deals with country houses rather than houses in the country, that is to say with houses built as the centres of sizeable country estates, with all their appurtenances of parks, lodge gates and tenantry. It excludes, accordingly, all Victorian vicarages and all the innumerable houses, in the Home Counties and elsewhere, built for prosperous Victorian middle-class clients, who liked the amenities of country life but were not prepared to set up as full-scale country gentry. These more modest houses form a coherent architectural group, in many ways a more likeable and original group than the grander houses, and one containing more of high architectural quality, especially in the later Victorian period. Yet Victorian country houses, because of their size, their complexity and their social background, the occasional masterpieces and many curiosities among them, and the mixture of piety, snobbery, romanticism, idealism and pretentiousness that contributed to their making, form a fascinating collection. Seldom can so much money and such exhaustive study have produced a group of buildings that, as private houses, became so soon and painfully obsolete. Remarkably few big Victorian country houses are still privately lived in; and it is largely thanks to the English system of private education that so many remain in existence at all.

I must record my gratitude to all the owners, public and private, who welcomed me to their houses and gave me the freedom of their knowledge and papers, and to the librarians and archivists who patiently dealt with my inquiries, especially John Harris and the staff of the Drawings Collection at the R.I.B.A. Peter Ferriday read and criticized the original manuscript; and among the many people who gave information or advice were my father, John Cornforth, Jill Franklin, Charles Handley-Read, Peter Howell, Priscilla Metcalf, John Newman, Phoebe Stanton, Virginia Surtees, Nicholas Taylor, Paul Thompson and David Walker.

ACKNOWLEDGEMENTS

MANY of the accounts of individual houses in this book are based on articles originally published in *Country Life*. I am grateful to I.P.C. Magazines Ltd. for allowing me to make use of this copyright material. The articles have all been revised, and in some cases substantially rewritten, but some contain additional material and illustrations for which there was no room in the book. The relevant articles are as follows: Adcote: CXLVIII (22 October, 1970) 56–9; Bayons: CXXVII (3 March, 1960) 430–3; Bear Wood: CXLIV (17 and 24 October, 1968) 964–7, 1060–3; Brodsworth: CXXXIV (3 and 10 October, 1963) 804–7, 876–9; Cardiff: CXXIX (6 and 13 April, 1961) 760–3, 822–5; Carlton: CXLI (26 January, 2 and 9 February, 1967) 176–80, 230–3, 280–3; Castell Coch: CXXXI (10 and 17 May, 1962) 1092–5, 1174–7; Cragside: CXLVI (18 and 25 December, 1969) 1640–3, 1694–7; Crossleys of Halifax: CXLVIII (24 September, 1970) 756–60; Highclere: CXXV (18 June, 1959) 1378–81; CXXVI (13 August, 1959) 18–21; Horsted: CXXIV (7 and 14 August, 1958) 276–9, 320–3; Humewood: CXLIII (9 and 16 May, 1968) 1212–15, 1282–5; Kelham: CXLI (18 and 25 May, 1967) 1230–3, 1302–5; Ken Hill: CXLII (21 and 28 December, 1967) 1654–8, 1704–7; Kinmel: CXLVI (4 and 11 September, 1969) 542–5, 614–17; Merevale: CXLV (13 and 20 March, 1969) 598–601, 662–5; Milton Ernest: CXLVI (23 October, 1969) 1042–6; Peckforton: CXXXVIII (29 July and 5 August, 1965) 284–7, 336–9; Scarisbrick: CXXIII (13 and 20 March, 1958) 506–9, 580–3; Shadwell: CXXXVI (2 and 9 July, 1964) 18–21, 98–102; Standen: CXLVII (26 February, 5 March, 1970) 494–7, 554–7; Treberfydd: CXL (4 and 11 August, 1966) 276–9, 322–5.

Photographs were supplied or are reproduced by kind permission of the following: (arabic numbers refer to black and white plate numbers, Roman numerals refer to colour plates) Elizabeth Aslin, *Nineteenth Century English Furniture* (by courtesy of Faber & Faber) 238, 239; James Austin 175, 176, 177, 179; by courtesy of E. C. Barnes Esq. 183, 187; Alfred Barry, *Sir Charles Barry* 105; by courtesy of the Headmaster of Bearwood 259; John Bethell XIII, XXII, XXIII, XXIV, XXVIII; Hunter Blair, *Marquess of Bute* 260; British Crown Copyright 120, 121, 125, 325; by courtesy of the Trustees of the British Museum 95; *Building News* 9 (26 June, 1874), 11 (4 July, 1875), 290 (8 Nov. 1872), 333 (20 Feb. 1874), 380 (9 July, 1886), 389 (7 July, 1882); *Builder* 6 (10 June, 1865), 7 (15 March, 1873), 8 (10 Feb. 1866), 37 (12 March, 1864), 38 (29 Oct. 1853), 278 (8 June, 1867), 280 (14 Jan. 1871), 384 (1 Dec. 1888), 412 (9 Aug. 1874), 416 (9 Aug. 1874); by courtesy of John Cresswell-Turner 307; Country Life 10, 16, 21, 22, 23, 24, 26, 28, 29, 32, 33, 34, 46, 49, 50, 52, 55, 59, 64, 67, 69, 73, 74, 75, 76, 77, 78, 79, 80, 82, 83, 84, 85, 87, 88, 89, 90, 91, 92, 93, 94, 96, 97, 98, 99, 100, 101, 102, 103, 106, 107, 108, 109, 110, 111, 112, 113, 114, 115, 116, 117, 118, 119, 126, 129, 130, 133, 134, 135, 136, 137, 138, 139, 140, 141, 142, 143, 144, 145, 146, 147, 151, 152, 153, 154, 155, 156, 157, 158, 160, 161, 162, 163, 165, 166, 167, 168, 169, 170, 173, 178, 180, 181, 182, 184, 185, 186, 188, 189, 190, 191, 192, 193, 194, 195, 196, 197, 198, 199, 200, 203, 204, 205, 206, 207, 208, 209, 210, 211, 212, 213, 214, 215, 216, 217, 218, 220, 221, 222, 223, 224, 225, 226, 227, 228, 241, 242,

243, 244, 246, 248, 249, 250, 251, 252, 253, 255, 256, 257, 258, 261, 264, 266, 267, 269, 270, 271, 272, 274, 275, 276, 285, 288, 289, 291, 292, 293, 294, 296, 297, 298, 299, 300, 301, 302, XXVI, 304, 305, 306, 308, 309, 310, 311, 312, 313, 314, 315, 324, 326, 327, 328, 329, 330, 331, 332, 334, 335, 336, 337, XXIX, 339, 340, 341, 342, 343, 344, 345, 346, 347, 348, 349, 350, 351, 353, 354, 355, 356, 357, 358, 359, 360, 361, 362, 363, 364, 365, 366, 367, 368, 369, 370, 371, 372, 373, 374, 375, 376, 377, 378, 393, 395, 396, 400, 402, 403, 411, 415, 419 (Earl of Dunraven collection), 420, 423, 424; Courtauld Institute 4, 127; C. T. D'Eyncourt, *Eustace* (1851) (by courtesy of George Clive Esq.) 20; Department of the Environment XII; Eastlake, *Gothic Revival* 31, 36, 39, 40, 43; Elvetham Hall 41; English Life Publications 27, 414; 1851 Exhibition: Jury Reports III 159; Miss Fitzsimon 245, 247; John Freeman 86; Gardiner, *Sir William Harcourt* (1923) 404; Mark Girouard XXXII, 390, 405, 410; W. Godfrey, *Work of George Devey* 53; by courtesy of Myles Hildyard Esq. 219; Irish Tourist Board 422; Jarrold & Sons, Norwich 201, 202; by courtesy of the University of Keele, Library Photographic Department 14; A. F. Kersting 44, XXX; Lucinda Lambton X, XVI, XVII, XVIII, XIX, XX, XXI, XXVII; by courtesy of Sir Stephen Lycett Green 352; by courtesy of Mrs Mackeson-Sandbach 399; Sir John Millais 2; Milner Field Sale Catalogue 407; Morris, *Views of Seats* (III, 67), 417; National Monuments Record 5, 17 (Bedford Lemere), 30, 48 (Batsford), 58 (Bedford Lemere), 122, 123, 124, 262, 268, 277, 279, 283 (Bedford Lemere), 284 (Bedford Lemere), 286 (Bedford Lemere), 287, 295 (Bedford Lemere), 379, 388; 398, 401 (Bedford Lemere), 406, 409 (Bedford Lemere), 413 (Bedford Lemere), 425; by courtesy of Ian Nairn 385; National Trust front jacket illustration, II, XXXIII; by courtesy of the Penoyre Golf and Country Club 408; Edward Piper IV, XIV, XV, 236, 240, XXV, XXXI; Pullan, *Designs of William Burges* (1883) 265; by courtesy of the late Sir Geoffrey Raikes 148, 149, 150; Patrick Rossmore 12, 15, 51, 281, 282, 317, 318, 319, 320, 321, 322, 323, 391, 397; Royal Institute of British Architects 13, 19, 25, 41, 42, 45, 54, 56, 61, 81, VII, VIII, IX, 128, 131, 132, XI, 263, 273, 316, 392, 394, 418; Russell Read I, 60, 62, 63, 65, 66, 68, 70, 71, 72, V, VI; Walter Scott, Bradford 1, 3; by courtesy of Mrs J. F. Silcock frontispiece, 387; by courtesy of Lord Somerleyton (from the 1861 Sales Catalogue) 18 and endpapers; by courtesy of Paul Thompson 164, 171, 172; Jeremy Williams 421; Victoria & Albert Museum 35, 47, 104, 392, 427; Wagner-Rieger, R. *Historismus und Schlossbau* (Franz Windisch-Graetz) 426; by courtesy of Mrs John Walter 254; Owen H. Wicksteed 57; by courtesy of Lord Wraxall half-title page, 229, 230, 231, 232, 233, 234, 235, 237.

CONTENTS

I. INTRODUCTION

1. A Great Victorian Gentleman   2
2. The Upper Classes Adapt to their Circumstances   4
3. The Men who Built the Country Houses   7
4. A Country House Analysis   8
5. A Run Round the *Nouveaux-riches*   10
6. Victorian Gentlemen: the Ideal   13
7. The Victorian Gentleman's House   15
8. The Building of a Country House   16
9. The Choice of an Architect   17
10. Materials Old and New   19
11. Technology and the Country House:
    Plumbing, Heating and Ventilation   22
12. Gas and Electricity   24
13. Other Services   25
14. Technology, Comfort, Snobbery
    and Aesthetics   26
15. The Country House Plan   27
16. The Servants' Wing   29
17. Nuances and Drawbacks of Victorian Planning   31
18. The Historical Development
    of the Plan: William Burn   31
19. The Male Domain   34
20. The Conservatory   38
21. The Great Hall   43
22. The Picturesque versus the Functional: Pugin   46
23. Barry, Blore, Burn and Salvin   48
24. The Battle of the Styles   52
25. The High-Victorian Years   53
26. Muscularity   54
27. Texture, Colour and Ruskin   57
28. High-Victorian Attitudes: the Pugin Tradition   59
29. High-Victorian Attitudes:
    the Picturesque Tradition   61
30. The Revolt of the Goths   66
31. The Architect as Artist   67
32. Artistic Houses and Artistic People   68
33. Kerr and Stevenson   69
34. Five Architects   70
35. The Old English Style   71
36. Leys Wood   73
37. 'Queen Anne'   74
38. Shaw: Composition and Planning   75
39. The Hall Revived   78
40. Philip Webb   79
41. Clouds   80
42. Shaw's Contemporaries: Ernest George   82
43. George Devey: a Postscript   83
44. The First Steps to Neo-Georgian   84

2. VICTORIAN COUNTRY HOUSES

1. Harlaxton Manor, Lincolnshire	1831–8	90
2. Bayons Manor, Lincolnshire	1836–42	103
3. Scarisbrick Hall, Lancashire	1837–45	110
	(and 1862–8)	
4. Merevale Hall, Warwickshire	1838–44	120
5. Highclere Castle, Hampshire	1840–50	130
6. Prestwold Hall, Leicestershire	1842–4	138
7. Osborne, Isle of Wight	1844–8	147
8. Peckforton Castle, Cheshire	1844–50	154
9. Treberfydd, Breconshire	1848–52	164
10. Horsted Place, Sussex	1850–4	172
11. Milton Ernest Hall, Bedfordshire	1853–8	179
12. Woodchester Park, Gloucestershire	c. 1854–68	188
13. Shadwell Park, Norfolk	c. 1856–60	194
	(and 1840–2)	
14. The Crossleys of Halifax and their Buildings		205
15. George Devey in Kent:		213
Betteshanger	1856–61, 1882	
St Alban's Court	1875–8	
16. Kelham Hall, Nottinghamshire	1858–61	224
17. Brodsworth Hall, Yorkshire	1861–70	236
18. Tyntesfield, Somerset	1863–6	243
19. Humewood Castle, County Wicklow	1866–70	252
20. Bear Wood, Berkshire	1865–74	263
21. Cardiff Castle, Glamorganshire	1868–85	273
22. The *Nouveau-riche* style		291
23. Cragside, Northumberland	1869–84	305
24. Kinmel Park, Denbighshire	1868–74	318
25. Beauvale Lodge, Nottinghamshire	1871–3	329
26. Castell Coch, Glamorganshire	1872–9	336
27. Carlton Towers, Yorkshire	1873–7	346
28. Adcote, Shropshire	1876–81	359
29. Ken Hill, Norfolk	1879–80	366
30. Wightwick Manor, Staffordshire	1887–93	375
31. Standen, Sussex	1891–4	381

3. CATALOGUE

England and Wales	392
Ireland	426
Scotland	430
Abroad	431
Map	434
Biographical Notes on Architects	436
Notes to the Text	444
General Index	455
Subject Index	467

1.INTRODUCTION

1. A Great Victorian Gentleman

'Gone, one of Britain's noblest gentlemen', ran the opening line of a poem in the *Manchester Guardian* commemorating the death of the Duke of Westminster in 1899. Another paper described him as 'one of the finest illustrations ever beheld of what a nobleman should be'. *The Times* called him 'a fine example of the great noble who, while following the same pursuits and amusements as other Englishmen of wealth and leisure, devotes a great part of his time to the service of those less fortunate than himself'.[1]

On the death of his father in 1869 he had inherited an income of £37,000 a year from his country property and £115,000 from town property in London. His London income rose to over £250,000 in the next thirty years. A great part of this vast income went in charity. He was a good and conscientious man who thought of himself as 'not so much a private millionaire as the head of a great public institution or trust'. His park at Eaton Hall was always open to the public, and, during his life, on the Eaton Hall estate alone he built 48 farmhouses, 360 cottages, 8 schools, 7 village halls and 3 churches. He was as generous with his time as his money. At various times he was President of the Royal Agricultural Society, the Chester Cottage Improvement Society, the Metropolitan Drinking Fountain and Cattle Trough Association, the Hampstead Heath Protection Society, the Gardeners' Royal Beneficent Institution, five London hospitals and the United Committee for the Preventing of Demoralizing of Native Races by the Liquor Traffic.[2]

As his principal seat he inherited Eaton Hall in Cheshire, an enormous building designed for his grandfather in what was considered by 1870 the ignorant and frivolous Gothic of late Georgian days. He made it serious, and even more enormous, at a cost of about £600,000. His architect was Alfred Waterhouse, who had gained his reputation with the new Town Hall in Manchester a few years previously. Much thought was given to the choice of artists to embellish the new house. The glass and mosaics in the sumptuous private chapel were by another Manchester artist, Frederic Shields. Shields worked for eleven years on the chapel and considered the commission 'the opportunity for which my whole longings and aims had fitted me . . . my soul kindled and flamed with the subject accepted'.[3] The walls of the drawing room were decorated with huge paintings of the Canterbury Pilgrims, by Stacy Marks, R.A. In another room the same artist painted a series of bird pictures incorporated in an artistic setting designed by Gertrude Jekyll. ('The Duke's manner was grave, but kind and courteous', Marks wrote in his autobiography.[4]) In the centre of the front quadrangle was a life-size

1. (preceding pages) Eaton Hall, Cheshire (Alfred Waterhouse, 1870–82). The garden front.

2. The first Duke of Westminster, by Sir John Millais.

3. Eaton Hall, Cheshire. The staircase.

equestrian statue of the Duke's medieval ancestor and namesake Hugh Lupus, Earl of Chester. At one time he had his doubts about Lupus, whose moral character he found left much to be desired; he considered commissioning instead 'a King–Saint on horseback—perhaps St. Oswald', but was reassured by the thought that Lupus 'would be rather commemorative of an epoch than an individual'. The commission was offered to Landseer, who turned it down, and was finally carried out by Watts, who refused to take any money for it: 'I should like', he wrote, 'in an affair of such importance, to work for the dignity of art alone.'

The Duke was one of the greatest of Victorian sportsmen. As a young man he had been Master of the Cheshire Hunt; in later life he owned the largest and most successful racing stables in England. He won the Derby five times, and innumerable other races as well. Yet he disapproved of betting and refused to put money on his horses. He was a superb shot. His moors in Scotland, with their four shooting lodges, provided some of the best deer-stalking and salmon and sea trout fishing in the world. The season's bag of pheasants at Eaton Hall, which in his father's time had averaged about 1,000, was up to 4,000 by the 1880s and between 5,000 and 6,000 by the 1890s.* His combination of sporting and philanthropic interests was considered

* A casual invitation 'Care to come out and see if we can pick up a pheasant or two?' resulted in a bag of 1,000 pheasants shot in two hours, according to Lord Ernest Hamilton, *Old Days and New* (London, 1924), p. 137.

entirely suitable to his position. *The Times* wrote in his obituary that he 'could pass from the race courses to a missionary meeting without incurring the censure of even the strictest'.

In the great clock tower of Eaton, 183 feet high, was a carillon of twenty-eight bells which could play twenty-eight tunes and played them remorselessly every quarter of an hour through the night.[5] They played 'Home, Sweet Home' whenever the Duke came to Eaton. He married twice and had fifteen children. Although his first wife was notoriously unfaithful, no hint of scandal ever seems to have touched his own life, before or after marriage. When he did not have a house party at Eaton, he lived quietly with his family in the moderate dimension of the private wing built to one side of the main house. Even his entertaining was done 'on a truly royal scale but with no more beating of drums and flourish of trumpets than if he had been the local rector entertaining the *élite* of the village'.[6] Reading his life one gets the impression that he built and maintained the splendour of Eaton, the fifty indoor servants and forty gardeners as much because of what he considered the duties of his position as because he enjoyed it. He was disappointed in his sons, who acquired a regrettable taste for gambling: 'their affection for him was strongly tinged with respectful awe'. But his daughters and grandchildren found him a delightful companion. George Wyndham the Tory politician (who was no fool) called him not only 'that kind heart and chivalrous gentleman' but 'the nicest man I have ever known'.[7]

2. *The Upper Classes Adapt to their Circumstances*

THE VICTORIAN country house was built for the Victorian country gentleman, and I have started this book with a description of the *beau-ideal* of a Victorian gentleman, inflated by the possession of £300,000 a year until all the most admired qualities of his species can be examined over life size. Although he is the direct ancestor of any public spirited country landowner today, the specifically Victorian atmosphere of earnestness, unencumbered wealth, and almost unbelievable deference, makes him seem very remote. It is not surprising that Eaton Hall, his architectural setting, was largely demolished in 1961. But if one reads Sir Gilbert Scott's *Secular and Domestic Architecture* (1857) one at once finds oneself in the same world.

Providence has ordained the different orders and gradations into which the human family is divided, and it is right and necessary that it should be maintained . . . The position of a landed proprietor, be he squire or nobleman, is one of dignity. Wealth must always bring its responsibilities, but a landed proprietor is especially in a responsible position. He is the natural head of his parish or district—in which he should be looked up to as the bond of union between the classes. To him the poor man should look up for protection; those in doubt or difficulty for advice; the ill disposed for reproof or punishment; the deserving, of all classes, for

4

consideration and hospitality; and *all* for a dignified, honourable and Christian example . . . He has been blessed with wealth, and he need not shirk from using it in its proper degree. He has been placed by Providence, in a position of authority and dignity, and no false modesty should deter him from expressing this, quietly and gravely, in the character of his house.[8]

Victorian gentlemen didn't just happen, they were beautifully adapted to meet the circumstances of their time. These had been potentially explosive. In the 1830s the upper classes were not only very rich, but getting richer. Some had been intelligent enough to exploit, or lucky enough to benefit from, the Industrial Revolution; enclosures had swollen their income from land; the agricultural depression that followed the Napoleonic Wars was over. They were in virtual control of the government, the armed forces and the church, and bought and sold livings, seats in parliament and commissions with the equanimity of people dealing with their own property. But their situation was not at all a comfortable one. The working classes in town and country were wretchedly poor and discontented, and there was real danger of an explosion from beneath. The game laws—the whole terrible paraphernalia of man traps and transportation—were vigorously imposed; a feeling of *après moi le déluge* helped to produce the inane extravagances of the dandies; there was no shortage of aristocrats arrogant to the bourgeoisie and bloody minded to the poor. The middle classes, serious-minded, hard-working, and steadily increasing in numbers and wealth, resented aristocratic frivolity and worldliness, especially in combination with aristocratic monopoly of power. Carlyle and many others fulminated against the upper classes and fulminated with time on their side, for the growing urbanization and industrialization of England meant that an aristocracy based on land had no hope of preserving a monopoly of power.

The upper classes were sensitive enough to realize the dangers, to adapt themselves, to accept encroachments on their preserves and to survive with their slowly lessening power made bearable by their great wealth and prestige. Between 1830 and 1860 there was a gradual change in the tone of their life, which enabled Charles Kingsley, writing his 'preface to the undergraduates of Cambridge' in the 1862 edition of *Alton Locke*, to give them an encouraging pat on the back:

Before the influence of religion, both Evangelical and Anglican; before the spread of those liberal principles, founded on common humanity and justice, the triumph of which we owe to the courage and practical sense of the Whig party; before the example of a Court, virtuous, humane and beneficent; the attitude of the British upper classes has undergone a noble change. There is no aristocracy in the world, and there never has been, as far as I know, which has so honourably repented, and brought forth fruits meet for repentance; which has so cheerfully asked what its duty was, that it might do it . . . The whole creed of our young gentlemen is becoming more liberal, their demeanour more courteous, their language more temperate. They enquire after the welfare, or at least mingle in the sports of the working man, with a simple cordiality which was unknown thirty years ago.

When Hippolyte Taine was in England in the 1860s he was equally impressed by the way the upper classes had changed: 'they realize that they must set their house in order'. He found no hostility between the upper and middle classes. 'One of the greatest industrialists in England . . .' told him that 'it is not our aim to overthrow the aristocracy: we are ready to leave the government and high offices in their hands'. An aristocracy was trained to rule and lead—they had a quality of dash and style. 'But we do absolutely insist that all positions of power be filled by able men. No mediocrities and no nepotism. Let them govern but let them be fit to govern.'[9]

They had advantages on their side. The wave of European unrest, which culminated in 1848 with revolutions abroad and the Chartists at home, convinced both middle and upper classes that men of property should stand together.★ Quite apart from political dangers, the mid-nineteenth century was an age of frightening change to most of those living in it. The growth of knowledge and technology was undermining all accepted beliefs and values. But if man were descended from apes and Genesis was a fairy story, at least the stately homes of England were still stately, something solid and traditional to fall back on. Moreover, to the English merchant or industrialist, working twelve hours a day, disciplining and denying himself, fighting for survival in the commercial jungle, there was increasingly present the vision of a quiet harbour at the end—an estate in the country, a glistening new country house with thick carpets and plate-glass windows, the grateful villagers at the doors of their picturesque cottages, touching their caps to their new landlord, J.P., High Sheriff perhaps, with his sons at Eton and Christ Church and his clean, blooming daughters teaching in the Sunday school.

English manufacturers were prepared to hate and do battle with an upper class that kept them in the cold and looked down on them—like Millbank in Disraeli's *Coningsby* (1844), who 'brought up his only boy with a due prejudice against every sentiment or justification of an aristocratic character'. But a serious church-building aristocracy who took the middle classes into partnership, told them that they were the backbone of England, became patrons of their societies and even married their daughters—or at least their granddaughters—was a different matter. By mid-Victorian days the aristocracy had been placed on such a pinnacle of deference that even the unregenerate members felt compelled to adapt at least their public face to the image expected of it. Gladstone, with his solid Liverpool background, approached Dukes with a kind of ecstatic veneration for their order—even when they were young Dukes and he was an elder statesman. On a lower level one can feel the unctuous joy with which G. G. Scott (as quoted on p. 4) rolled out the rotund phrases '. . . different orders and gradations', 'Providence, authority and dignity', 'dignified, honourable and Christian example'. So spoke England's most prosperous architect, whose mother's family, as he told the readers of his autobiography, was indirectly connected with several good families in England, 'among others with that of Lord Northampton, with the Adbys, and with the Gordons of Stocks'.[10]

★ 'At no period of our history have the upper and middle classes been more united.' MS. Diary of W. S. Dugdale, Merevale Hall, Warwicks. (see pp. 120–9), 11 Apr. 1848.

6

3. The Men who Built the Country Houses

ONCE a Victorian merchant, manufacturer or professional man had made a sufficient fortune he was faced with the dilemma of whether or not to set out to establish his family in the landed gentry. Not all who had the means took the plunge; it was, after all, a debatable advancement to cease being a great man in Manchester, Halifax or Newcastle and to take up a doubtful position as one of the new rich knocking at the door of county society. A socially ambitious wife, or a son educated at public school, often effected the change. A country estate would be bought, if possible with a country house on it already, to supply a mature landscape and a deferential surrounding population. If no country house property was available an estate had to be built up from scratch, and a completely new house built. Even if the property came complete with a house, it often seemed too modest or old fashioned to its new proprietors; and a grand new mansion, with generous entertainments for the neighbours held within it, was a useful means of accelerating acceptance by the county.

It was in this spirit that Lady Charlotte Guest embarked on the expensive remodelling of Canford in 1848. Kept out of polite society through her mother's second marriage to a drunken clergyman, she had married Sir John Josiah Guest, the Welsh ironmaster, and used his great wealth with skill and determination to establish

7

4. *The House Builders* by Frank Dicksee. Sir W. E. and Lady Welby-Gregory with the model of Denton Manor, Lincolnshire, designed by A. W. Blomfield, 1884.

their social position. The Canford property in Dorset was bought in 1846, and rebuilding started shortly afterwards. On 24 February 1849 she confided to her diary:

> Merthyr does not seem to take the interest I thought he would in what is going on. He feels, I know, bitterly, the expense which he has been almost unconsciously led into ... What leads to the children's comfort and happiness and fitting consideration with their neighbours, may be more than money's worth to them, of course in moderation ... His interest is less keen. There is this large house building at vast expense, and he takes no pleasure in it.[11]

There was nothing new about the transformation of urban and industrial wealth into country property. It was the way in which the English upper classes had recruited new members since the late Middle Ages. In some respects the rewards to be gained were growing smaller. The landed interest was gradually losing its power throughout the nineteenth century;[12] and the pressure of new families eager to buy pushed up the price of land so that it demonstrably ceased to be, what had long been taken for granted, the best and most secure form of investment. Land which had been selling for thirty years' purchase in 1840 was up to forty years' by 1860,[13] and an investment returning $2\frac{1}{2}$ per cent was not tempting to a businessman, even before the agricultural depression of the 1880s shattered the illusion that if low-yielding it was at least safe. Yet the power of the landowning classes remained great enough, and the prestige and pleasures of country house ownership so tempting that more and more new recruits invested in country estates, as the increasing momentum of industry and commerce produced more and more capital.

The latter was a process that benefited old as well as new families, for minerals and ground rents from growing towns helped to swell many a country landowner's income. Some members of well-established families, like the Duke of Westminster or the Marquess of Bute, became so immensely rich that they rebuilt or remodelled their houses out of sheer *joie de richesse*. But in any case the changing requirements of the nineteenth century called for more bedrooms, greater variety of living accommodation, and more elaborate servants' wings. Many houses were extensively added to, and it was always tempting for country house owners to go one step further and remodel completely, particularly if their houses were in the unfashionable manner of the eighteenth or early nineteenth century. The prosperity of mid-Victorian agriculture gave them the means to build even without any supplement from industry or town property; but perhaps in some cases they built beyond their incomes to keep up with their richer neighbours.

4. *A Country House Analysis*

AN ANALYSIS of the building dates of 500 country houses either built or remodelled between 1835 and 1889 is summarized in the accompanying graph. The houses all had estates of at least several hundred acres attached—that is to say they were country houses

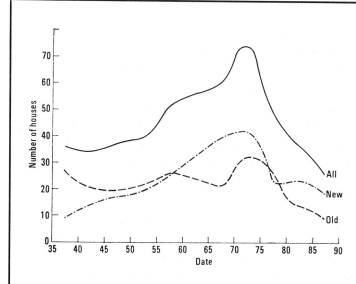

Fig. 1. Graph showing the chronological dispersion of a sample of 500 Victorian country houses.

rather than houses in the country, for it was difficult to be accepted as a country gentleman without an estate of reasonable size. The number analysed in five year batches starts at thirty-six, and after a slight dip in 1840–4 climbs steadily to a peak of seventy-four in 1870–4. After that it falls precipitously to its lowest point of twenty-six in 1885–9. Within the combined total the new families[14] show a steady growth, starting well below the old families, passing them in 1860–4, and climbing away from them to their peak in 1870–4. The old families are less consistent, but maintain an up-and-down progress until they too reach their peak in 1870–4. From then on both old and new decline rapidly; the new retain their superiority, however, and in 1885–9 the ratio of new to old is approximately 2 to 1, as compared to the ratio of old to new of 3 to 1 in 1835–9.

On the whole, the figures are what one would expect. The steady increase in houses built by new families represents the growth of Victorian industry and commerce. The 1870s, with industry and agriculture booming and British prestige at its height, were the golden age of Victorian country house building, as of most other aspects of Victorian life. The country house boom was brought to an abrupt end by the agricultural slump of 1879–94, when disastrous harvests and the influx of cheap American corn, South American beef, and Danish bacon reduced many rent rolls by a half or a third. The decline had started in the half-decade 1875–9, which just caught the beginning of the slump; it is especially noticeable in houses built by new families, suggesting that astute businessmen saw trouble ahead, and kept out of the market (but also that they were feeling the pinch of continental competition). They remained cautious until the end of the period under review, in spite of the possibility of buying estates at bargain prices; the prestige of owning land had suffered a knock from which it took a long time to recover, and it seemed safer and easier to the urban rich to rent country houses than to buy them.★

★ e.g. *The Times*, 14 Oct. 1887: 'The truth is, we suppose, that for purposes of sport capitalists prefer to rent rather than buy, while for purposes of investment they mistrust the security which land offers in present circumstances in England.'

5. *A Run Round the Nouveaux-riches*

THE SENSATIONAL expansion of Victorian industry could never have taken place without railways, which opened up national and (in combination with ships, especially steamships) international markets, and directly or indirectly provided the means of paying for many Victorian country houses. George Hudson, the railway king of early Victorian days, went bankrupt before he could build a country house; the son of a later railway tycoon G. G. Glyn, Lord Wolverton, whose father's peerage commemorated the railway town he had created in Buckinghamshire, was substantially if rather gloomily housed by Waterhouse at Iwerne Minster (1878). Enormous fortunes were made (and sometimes lost) by the great contractors who despatched their armies of labourers to build railways in England and all over the world, and then used them to convey labour and materials for other kinds of contracting work undertaken on an equally international scale. Sir Morton Peto and his partner E. L. Betts, whose railway activities extended from Folkestone to Buenos Aires and Mongolia, erected lavish if unattractive country houses at Somerleyton (1844–51; Pl. 202) and Preston Hall (1850) before crashing with Overend and Gurney in 1866. The more lasting dynasty founded by Thomas Brassey bought or built country houses for itself in Sussex, Kent, Oxfordshire and Northamptonshire.[15] The building Cubitts, who had erected most of late Georgian London, extended their operation over the whole country in the railway age and were the contractors for many of the great Victorian country houses, including Thomas Cubitt's own Italianate mansion at Denbies near Dorking (1850). The large shipping lines were later arrivals; it was not until the 1870s and 1880s that, for instance, Ismay of the White Star Line built Dawpool near Liverpool (1882), and the Yorkshire Wilsons were found at Warter Priory (c. 1878) and Tranby Croft.

Improved communication and new markets encouraged the expansion of industries which had been established well before Victorian times. Cotton, wool, iron and brewing all benefited. Among cotton palaces much the most amazing was Somers Clarke's Wyfold (1872–6) for E. Hermon, M.P. for Preston, with its frenetically tangled French Gothic skyline and picture gallery crammed with the works of the brassier Victorian painters. But on the whole 'cottentot grandees'[16] tended to be more remarkable for wealth than taste or even panache; Orchardleigh (1855), Old Warden (1872) and Nutfield (1870–4) are large but dismal houses. The fact that these are all in the south suggests that their builders were anxious to get as far away as possible from the scene where their money had been made. Wool tycoons had more local pride (and the Yorkshire gentry, whose own fortunes were frequently based on wool, were less exclusive than their Lancashire counterparts); the younger Titus Salt, for instance, ensconced himself at Milner Field (c. 1873–4), a Wagnerian Gothic retreat in the woods above Saltaire, his father's model town and mill where alpaca fabric had been developed and made famous.

The long-established iron industries of Wales and Coalbrookdale supplied the wherewithal for Sir John Guest to remodel Canford and Rebecca Darby to build Adcote (1877). The new Cleveland iron fields produced the purely Victorian

phenomenon of Middlesbrough, with houses in its vicinity built by Bolckows, Vaughans, Peases and Bells, the last discriminating patrons of Philip Webb at Washington Hall and Rounton Grange (1872–6; Pl. 411). In the second half of the Victorian period engineering firms produced a new crop of country houses, such as Norman Shaw's Cragside for Sir William Armstrong (1870–85), financed from the world-famous armaments and engineering works in Newcastle, and Ken Hill (1879), a consequence of Green's Economizer, an ingenious engineering device for reusing steam from boilers.

All this expansion of activity generated banking houses, factories, warehouses, offices and docks, and led to the prosperity of the great Victorian cities. The City of London continued, as in earlier centuries, to be a major source of recruits for county families, led by banking dynasties such as the Barings, Rothschilds, Curries (of Glyn Mills), Lubbocks, Smiths and Huths, but including other kinds of financiers like Sir Francis Goldsmid of Moccatta and Goldsmid, the bullion brokers, whose pride in being Jewish and rich was made quite clear by the enormous house he built above the Cirencester–Cheltenham road at Rendcomb, with a massive marble statue of King Saul in the vestibule. Bristol still fertilized the West Country with grand new mansions, but was overtaken in size and wealth by Liverpool, which provided the resources for even larger and architecturally more discriminating ones, notably G. G. Scott's Hafodunos for the Sandbachs (1861–6; Pl. 399) and Nesfield's superb Cloverley for the Heywoods (1862–70; Pl. 40). From Manchester the multitudinous branches of the Philips family went out to build in Wales, Kent and Warwickshire, as well as in Staffordshire, where the family originated.[17] But Birmingham, a city of many but on the whole small businesses, played little role in the country house world during the period with which I am dealing.

5. Wyfold Court, Oxfordshire (G. Somers Clarke, 1872–6). Cotton.

6. Rendcomb,
Gloucestershire (P. C.
Hardwick, 1863–5).
Bullion Broking.

7. Milner Field,
Yorkshire (Thomas
Harris, 1873). Wool.

8. Tyntesfield,
Somerset (John
Norton, 1863–6).
Guano.

9. Rousdon, Devon
(George and
Vaughan, 1874).
Biscuits.

Guano, the dried droppings of sea birds collected from islands off South America, was one basis of the wealth of the merchant banking dynasty of Gibbs, the builders of Tyntesfield (1863–6); the Garratts of Bishops Court (1860–4) had been City of London tea merchants; pianos paid for Abbotsfield where Wagner stayed and Patti sang, designed by Owen Jones about 1872 for Lukey Collard, of Collard and Collard, the leading Victorian piano makers. Peek Frean biscuits financed Sir Henry Peek's Rousdon (1874); London and Nottingham hosiery provided the Morleys with Breadsall Priory in Derbyshire (1861) and Hall Place in Kent (1871–2); china clay produced a horrible house at Bodnant for the Pochins (c. 1881); Portuguese copper mines an extravagant French chateau at St Leonard's Hill for the Barrys (c. 1875; Pl. 283); Droitwich salt mines the even more extravagant Chateau Impney for John Corbett, the son of a barge owner (1868–80; Col. Pl. XXIV). A quick run round the Victorian new rich can end suitably enough with an ostrich-feather manufacturer,[18] P. Saillard, for whom George and Peto designed the huge and florid Buchan Hill in their best Harrington Gardens manner (1882–3; Pl. 51); his fortunes presumably rose and fell with the fashion for his merchandise, for his house was sold in the 1920s and he never made the haven to which all Victorian new rich aspired, *Burke's Landed Gentry*.

6. *Victorian Gentlemen: the Ideal*

WITH a few exceptions the new families entered country life anxious to please and be accepted, ready to conform to their new neighbours' idea of how a gentleman should behave, and full of veneration and respect for the historic country families. If, by their activity in building a new country house in the park, and a new church, parish hall, almshouses, school and model cottages at the end of the drive, they placed a pressure on their neighbours to do the same, it was unlikely to be a deliberate one. Yet the idea of what a gentleman should be was changing from what it had been in the eighteenth and early nineteenth centuries, as the upper classes unconsciously worked out a code of conduct that would distinguish them from the middle classes, yet remain acceptable both to themselves, their admirers and their critics.

One tradition sufficiently historic, serious minded, romantic, dashing and aristocratic was to be found in Christian chivalry. Walter Scott had already made the trappings of chivalry fashionable. In the 1820s Kenelm Digby described at inordinate length its history and ideals in his best-selling *Broadstone of Honour*[19] (Burne-Jones's favourite bedside book). The early Victorian knight galloped onto the field, his bible the *Broadstone of Honour*, his political expression the Young England party, his escapade the Eglinton tournament. He was faithful to God, reverent to women, courteous in his language, modest in his demeanour, lacking in arrogance to his inferiors, and a shield and support to his tenantry—who would respond, it was hoped, with touching loyalty and devotion. He endeavoured to combine the most creditable aspects of the Arthurian knight and the feudal baron. There could be something more than a little absurd about this mixture of chivalry and Old England, neatly satirized in the lines:

> Oh! flog me at the old cart tail
> I surely should enjoy
> That fine old English punishment
> I witnessed as a boy.

Its more idiotic or fancy-dress aspect soon went out of fashion; but, suitably adapted, it provided a code of conduct which was still active when the sons of the gentry went out to be killed in the trenches in 1914.

The chivalrous Christian gentleman of mid-Victorian days (of whom the Duke of Westminster was a prime example) had more than a touch of the knight about him but he was more practical, domestic and ponderous—the result of a good admixture of Evangelical or High Church seriousness caught from the middle classes. A treasury of Christian gentlemen is to be found in the novels of Charlotte M. Yonge—favourite reading for the more serious young officers in the 1850s. *The Heir of Redclyffe* contains the type in its most and least attractive aspects: Sir Guy Morville, gay, generous, impetuous, with his efforts at self-discipline, his tremendous repentances for what seem to us very trivial faults, his self-denials—'I have promised never even to look on at a game of billiards'—in short his 'serious ascetic temper, coupled with very high animal spirits'; and the intolerable young prig Philip Morville with his 'grand, sedate, gracious way', his readiness to put others right, his inevitable habit of 'leading the discussion to bear upon the duties and prospects of landed proprietors, and dwelling on the extent of their opportunities for doing good'.

To Young England knightliness and Charlotte M. Yonge earnestness must be added the toughness idealized by Thomas Hughes in the two *Tom Brown* books, and by Charles Kingsley in his many novels and essays. It was a quality increasingly emphasized in the 1850s and 1860s, the toughness of the 'old English squire' as glorified in the early nineteenth century,[20] leavened with elements of chivalry and Christianity. The kind of hero that resulted was a bearded and whiskered giant standing six foot two in his socks, a superb sportsman, a fearless rider, ready to give a thrashing (in fair fight, with his fists) to any contemptible sneak he found maltreating an animal or a child. Tom Brown expressed the creed in schoolboy form before he went to Rugby: 'I want to be A1 at cricket and football, and all the other games . . . I want to leave behind me . . . the name of a fellow who never bullied a little boy, or turned his back on a big one.' (He did not want to be A1 at Latin and Greek.) Tennyson beautifully expressed the consensus and put this and most other qualities of a Victorian gentleman into Sir Walter Vivian in the *Princess* (1847):

> No little lily-handed Baronet he,
> A great broad-shouldered genial Englishman,
> A lord of fat prize-oxen and of sheep,
> A raiser of huge melons and of pine
> A patron of some thirty charities,
> A pamphleteer on guano and on grain,
> A quarter-sessions chairman, abler none;
> Fair-hair'd and redder than a windy morn.

A 'little lily-handed Baronet' might, one suspects, have had more visual sensibility than Sir Walter. In the scale of values of a Victorian gentleman neither intellectual nor aesthetic qualities ranked especially high—hence Matthew Arnold's famous classification of upper-, middle- and lower-class England, into Barbarians, Philistines and Populace. Even for a serious as opposed to a purely sporting landowner art tended to take a low place. In Charlotte M. Yonge's *Heartsease* (1855) little Lord St Erme, when turned down by Theodora Martindale, sells all the pictures and sculptures he has collected in Italy in order to build schools and a church for his tenantry. This is the result of a promise that 'I will be content to toil as the knights of old, hopelessly, save that if you hear of me no longer as the idle amateur, but as exerting myself for something serviceable, you will know it is for your sake.' One is left with the impression that it is both ungodly and unmanly to be a virtuoso.

The contrast between the Victorian Christian Gentleman and the Regency Man of Taste is marked. The Man of Taste was personally involved with his house as an expression of his sensibility. The series of lavish early nineteenth-century monographs on country houses is one result of this: Sezincote (1818), Fonthill (1823), Ashridge (1823), Eaton Hall (1826), Brighton Pavilion (1826), Deepdene (1826), Cassiobury (1837), Toddington (1840) and Windsor (1842); then the series closes abruptly. During the Georgian boom of country house visiting, any house of any pretensions was viewable (especially when the family was away, and frequently when they were at home) by any sufficiently gentlemanly passer-by who wanted to see it. A mass of country house guidebooks was the result. In the Victorian period the number of viewable country houses diminished sharply, and the guidebooks dried up to a trickle. A Regency gentleman was anxious to put his own taste on display and learn from the taste of others; to a Victorian gentleman his house was (or ought to be) a temple not of taste but of the domestic virtues, its privacy only accessible to his family and friends.

It would be absurd to pretend that all Victorian gentlemen were earnest, godly and high principled. There were worldly families, frivolous families, families who took advantage of the fact that the circumstances of their life made work unnecessary and the pursuit of enjoyment easy. And there were hard-working political families who combined a busy career with enjoyments of which Dr Arnold would not have approved. But between 1840 and 1870 the bias of upper-class life was towards seriousness; the facade at least had to be sober, and mistresses, if kept at all, were kept discreetly in St John's Wood.

7. *The Victorian Gentleman's House*

By 1850 there was a more or less generally accepted view of the kind of house suitable for an English gentleman. With a shift in emphasis here and there it was to remain current for the rest of the century. Not surprisingly, it was a reflection of the qualities discussed in the previous sections. A gentleman's house should be substantial, serious and preferably in a style associated with the traditions of English country life. It should be dignified, as was suitable for the rank of its owner, but not ostentatious; designed for family life and the entertainment of friends rather than for show. It should provide decent quarters for servants. It should protect the womanliness of women and encourage the manliness of men. It should be comfortable but not luxurious.

The architectural expression of these qualities was not, as in previous centuries, worked out by the upper classes themselves. There was no Victorian Sir Roger Pratt or Lord Burlington. Regency taste had been formed as much by discriminating amateurs as by professionals. William Beckford, Uvedale Price, Payne Knight, Thomas Hope, Lord Sudeley and Sir Charles Monck were important theorists or acknowledged experts, and the last four designed influential and admired country houses for themselves. The Victorian amateurs—Lord Lovelace, Sir Edmund Beckett, Charles Fowell Buxton, the Scawen Blunts[21]—are an entertaining group, but a small one, and of minimal importance in the history of the Victorian country house. Alexander Beresford-Hope, the most considerable of amateur writers on architecture, specialized in church architecture, a significant shift in interest from that of Thomas Hope, his father.

An emphasis on moral and physical well-being, rather than aesthetic sensibility, was typical of the high-Victorian age in general and one reason for the decay of the amateur country house architect: the energies of the time could express themselves more convincingly and attractively in churches, schools and model cottages. But the decay of the amateur was also helped along by the increasing organization of the architectural profession. The Victorians had a genius for analysis and definition; everything was to be divided up into departments. It was both their strength and weakness. One result of this, greatly helped along by the growing status of the middle classes, was the development of professionalism. The Institute of British Architects was founded in 1834 and became Royal in 1866; the Architectural Association was founded in 1847. The *Builder* started up in 1843, the *Building News* in 1855, the *Architect* in 1869, the *British Architect* in 1874. The basic sources of information about Victorian country houses comes not from splendid folios subscribed to by the aristocracy and gentry and available in their libraries, but from the building magazines which they would never have seen: a literature by professionals for professionals.

8. *The Building of a Country House*

THE SAME frame of mind which led Victorian architects to start organizing themselves into a profession also expressed itself in the increasingly organized way in which country houses were planned and built.

Lady Charlotte Guest, on the verge of remodelling a country house in Dorset in July 1848, wrote in her journal, 'Merthyr arranged that Barry should endeavour to get the work at Canford put into the hands of Cubitt, or some great builder, to carry on and complete. This I really believe is the only way to get it done with any certainty, as to time and expense.'[22] General contractors had been a product of the early nineteenth century, under the stimulus of large-scale speculative building, especially in London, and of the growing scale of public works. Their employment spread to the country house world, where the convenience and avoidance of bother that resulted from employing them was very tempting, especially as the new materials and services outlined in the succeeding sections made building a large country house an increasingly complicated process. More and more Victorian country houses were put into the hands of one of the big London builders—in particular William Cubitt and Son, George Myers and, a little later, Trollope and Sons. The Cubitts[23] built, among many other houses, Osborne in the Isle of Wight, Tyntesfield in Somerset, Elveden in Suffolk and Wykehurst in Sussex. An out-of-London builder with a more than local reputation was Estcourt of Gloucester, who worked for Burges at Castell Coch, in South Wales, and for Webb at Clouds, in Wiltshire. Kimberley, of Banbury, crossed the Irish Sea to build Humewood in County Wicklow—an expedition which ended in tears, as related in Chapter 19.

Up till the 1870s, there were still a considerable number of Victorian country houses which were built in the eighteenth-century manner, by a mixture of direct labour and small separate contracts, co-ordinated on the site by the Clerk of the Works. The examples include not only modest buildings like Milton Ernest, or big extensions as at Shadwell, but enormous mansions like Westonbirt and Bear Wood, elaborately equipped with gas, central heating, ventilating plant and fireproof construction. Very complete documentation survives for Westonbirt,[24] including the correspondence between the Clerk of the Works and the architect. When building was at its height nearly 300 men were on the payroll. At Bear Wood, in June 1868, no less than 380 workmen sat down for a banquet given by the owner, John Walter of *The Times*, to celebrate the roofing-in of the house.[25] One tends to forget what a formidable project building a country house was in terms of man-power, before the advent of cranes, diggers and other mechanical plant.

By the 1880s it was considered eccentric to do otherwise than give out the contract to a builder. Swaylands, in Kent, was remodelled without employing one in 1879–82, with the result that the house cost £20,000 instead of £6,000; the client, George Drummond, refused to pay the architect's fees and the architect, George Devey, went to law with him. He won the case, and Drummond was severely snubbed by the judge (and the newspapers), on the lines that gentlemen who tried to be their own builders deserved to get their fingers burnt.[26]

9. *The Choice of an Architect*

ON 18 May 1848 W. S. Dugdale recorded in his diary[27] that his friend Frederick West had asked him for advice about an architect, and that he had recommended Henry Clutton, who had worked for him on his own property at Merevale. Ruthin Castle in Denbighshire was the result. In June 1868 John Walter of *The Times*, in the course of the speech to his workmen at the Bear Wood banquet, revealed that he had selected Robert Kerr as architect because he had read his book, *The Gentleman's House*.

Personal knowledge or recommendation, and advertisement, whether by publishing a book, exhibiting at the Royal Academy, or being featured in the architectural press, were the two main ways by which an architect found country house clients in Victorian times. Some of them kept entirely to the first way. Throughout the period there was a succession of architects who kept mainly or entirely to country house work, deliberately avoided every kind of advertisement, but nevertheless built up a large practice. They make up a small but powerful group, composed of William Burn, Edward Blore and Anthony Salvin in the first half of the period, and George Devey, Philip Webb and W. E. Nesfield in the second. Sir Charles Barry could be added to their number, in the sense that he did little to publicize his country house work; but unlike the others he was as much a public as a private architect and the Houses of Parliament put him more in the public eye than any form of self-advertisement. In contrast were the architects who exhibited and were illustrated, men such as T. H. Wyatt, David Brandon, S. S. Teulon, P. C. Hardwick, E. M. Barry, John Norton, Norman Shaw and Ernest George, who all had large country house practices. G. G. Scott did not exhibit his country house designs, but as in the case of Kerr his book *Secular and Domestic Architecture* was followed by a clutch of country house commissions.

One would expect that the new rich, venturing into an unfamiliar field, would tend to be ignorant or apprehensive of the first group, and would choose either a local man or a self-advertising Londoner. In the first half of the Victorian period this was to a large extent true and as a result Burn, Blore and Salvin had predominantly upper-class practices. It may be that they were deliberately exclusive. In 1858 George Moore, the self-made lace manufacturer who hunted his way into friendship with the landed gentry, 'persuaded' Salvin to remodel Whitehall, his house in Cumberland, through the good offices of his social sponsor, Henry Howard of Greystoke Castle.[28] The phrase comes from Samuel Smiles's biography of Moore, and suggests that, in accepting a self-made man as a client, the patronage was on Salvin's side.

Upper-class society in early Victorian times was highly political, and it was not surprising that architects who worked through personal recommendations should have not only a cohesive body of clients, but one with a particular political flavour. Blore's and Salvin's clients were predominantly Tory; Burn's were more mixed though with a Tory bias; Barry was the favourite of the Whigs.

In the first years of Victoria's reign, when the new men were very much in a minority as commissioners of country houses, architects could afford to be snobbish. As they increased both in numbers and in wealth these blue-blooded practices disappeared. This was perhaps partly because architects could not resist adventuring into so rewarding a field, partly because in any case society itself was becoming less exclusive. In fact both background and politics were becoming less of an obstacle to social relationships, and as a result the practices of even the non-advertising architects Devey, Webb and Nesfield were more variegated than those of their predecessors Burn, Blore and Salvin. Webb's practice advanced on an 'artistic' front; his clients varied widely in background but were frequently friends or patrons of Rossetti and Burne-Jones. Nesfield worked partly through family connections and partly through contacts made in artistic circles; Devey had an impressive selection of aristocratic clients, but the hard core of his clientele were the grander banking families. But his practice, though more socially variegated than it would have been forty years previously, was politically remarkably consistent, being firmly and profitably founded on the friends and political supporters of Gladstone.* Curiously enough the most exclusively aristocratic of mid-Victorian practices was that of S. S. Teulon, although he was far from shy of publicity; E. M. Barry and Norman Shaw specialized in the new rich; the other self-advertisers collected a mixed bag. To a greater or lesser degree their buildings have an element of flashiness, designed to catch and hold the passing eye at the Academy; the other group, secure in their personal clientele, could afford to be less demonstrative, indeed on occasions a greater sense of showmanship would have done their buildings no harm.

10. Materials Old and New

THE SOLIDITY of Victorian houses has always been remarked on, especially by those who have had to demolish them. It was a by-product of Victorian seriousness; everything had to be what it seemed to be, and made to last. Stucco, and above all stucco pretending to be stone, was the final abomination; Queen Victoria and Prince Albert were much criticized when they built Osborne with stucco facades in 1844–8 (and employed a builder instead of a professional architect to design it).

The banishment of stucco meant that exposed brick came back into fashion for country houses, especially since it could be used to produce the polychromatic effects that mid-Victorians admired. But other and less traditional materials were also to be found. Iron had been used structurally since at least the early nineteenth century, when the development of technology perfected beams made of wrought rather than cast iron, and therefore strong in tension as well as compression. Sir Robert Smirke was a pioneer in the use of iron beams for country houses; his pupil William Burn learnt from him and employed them widely, as, for instance, at Prestwold in 1843 and Fonthill in 1856.[29] At Merevale (1839–43) Blore used iron beams and iron strengthening to wooden joists to get larger openings and ceiling spans. At Mentmore (1850–5) Paxton bridged the forty-foot span of the central hall with wrought iron riveted girders supporting one of his ridge-and-furrow roofs. The conservatories attached to most Victorian houses of any size were usually built of iron and glass. Iron also became popular for its non-combustibility as well as its

* His sponsor was Sir Walter James, a close personal friend of the Gladstone family. Devey also worked for the Duke of Argyll, the Duke of Sutherland, Lord Granville, Lord Rosebery, Lord Wolverton and Lord Carlingford, all ministers in one or other of Gladstone's governments; for Samuel Morley, M.P., the hosiery millionaire, described (D.N.B.) as 'an unswerving and almost unquestioning follower of Gladstone'; and for bankers such as the Glyns, Smiths, Barings, Curries and Rothschilds, who supported and entertained Gladstone. At Coombe Warren, the house designed by Devey for Bertrand Currie, a temple was built in the garden to contain the bust of Gladstone, who once held a cabinet meeting in the house 'when temporarily indisposed'.

strength. What was called 'fireproof construction', with ceilings made up of iron girders supporting shallow brick or concrete vaults, was extensively used in mid-nineteenth-century houses. This method had been invented for factories and warehouses in the late eighteenth century. An early example is at the Heath House, Staffordshire, built in 1836–40 for the Philips family, whose fortune came from textiles. There are numerous later examples, such as Victoria and Albert's Osborne, and the massive high-Victorian mansions of Grittleton (1848–56), Thoresby (1864–75), Westonbirt (1864–71) and Kelham (1858–62).

At the Heath House the girders were plastered in the bedrooms and totally concealed in the reception rooms. At Mentmore a more conventional ceiling, of wood ribs filled with glass panels, was slung from the girders. At Kelham the main rooms were rib-vaulted and exposed iron girders are only to be found in the bedrooms and (suitably decorated) supporting the staircase landing and the roof of the *porte-cochère*. At Rousdon the Gothic cloister, round which the houses is planned, is vaulted with exposed fireproof construction of brick and iron. Such exposed construction was a consequence of Ruskinian doctrines of truthfulness. Unfortunately iron, if exposed, ceases to be fireproof; it will quickly fail under heat, unless protected. The resulting dilemma, and the failure of exposed fireproof construction to resist fire, probably helped to make the use of iron unfashionable in later Victorian country houses.[30] Some architects continued to use iron joists, however, none more so than Norman Shaw and W. E. Nesfield (both of whom had been in Burn's office). Shaw used concealed joists and stanchions of rolled iron (and, from the 1880s, of Bessemer steel) with increasing frequency and ingenuity from the late 1860s onwards, especially when he wished to plan an upper floor in independence of the floor plan below it.[31]

Iron had been the material of the moment in the 1840s and 1850s, but was less talked about in mid-Victorian days, when the delicacy of structure it could produce was rejected for chunkier effects. It was concrete that was interminably discussed in the architectural press of the 1860s and 1870s. Concrete for foundations had been

10. Fireproof construction in a bedroom ceiling at the Heath House, Staffordshire, 1836–40.

pioneered in England by Smirke, and was used at Corsham (1845–9) and Bear Wood (1865). Rendcomb (1863–5) has concrete floors supported on iron girders, and concrete was quite often used as an alternative to brick in fireproof construction. The Highlands (c. 1874) was built of exposed half-timbering, with a concrete infill. But the most daring use of concrete in a country house was at Down Hall, near Harlow (1871–3), where the main structure and external facades are of poured and shuttered concrete, with rudimentary iron reinforcement and a few ornamental trimmings of stone. The architect at Down Hall was F. P. Cockerell, but the consultant was Charles Drake, one of the pioneers of concrete construction.[32]

The change in size of window panes brought about one of the most obvious changes in the appearance of Victorian country houses. Blown glass, such as was used up till the end of the eighteenth century, cannot be made into panes of large size. The techniques of manufacturing sheet and plate glass were developed in the 1830s, and by 1840 very large pieces of glass were available. But in early Victorian days sheet and plate glass were extremely expensive, owing to excise duty and window tax. Glass was taxed by weight and large panes of sheet or plate glass were much heavier than a combination of smaller panes of blown glass. When the excise duty was removed in 1845, the price of glass was cut by half. Window tax was abolished in 1851. Not surprisingly, the size of window panes became increasingly large in the 1850s. Scott considered 'plate glass, as undivided as possible . . . one of the most useful and beautiful inventions of our day, and eminently calculated to give cheerfulness to our house'.[33] He used glass panes of very large size for the big casement windows at Kelham, although the weight of the glass caused problems in the hanging of the casements. Sash windows were much more suited for plate glass, and plate-glass sashes, with huge single sheets in the upper and lower frames, were very popular by the late 1850s. Scott thought sash windows were un-Gothic; but P. C. Hardwick introduced plate-glass sashes into a Gothic house at Addington Manor about 1856, and his example was followed by Waterhouse at Hinderton in 1859, and by many architects in the 1860s. Plate-glass sash windows were installed in

11. Down Hall, Essex, built of concrete in 1871–3.

innumerable houses, both new and old, in the 1860s and 1870s, although by the 1870s they were competing against a revived fashion for leaded lights and small panes—a blow against technology by those who considered themselves 'artistic'.

11. Technology and the Country House: Plumbing, Heating and Ventilation

THE TECHNOLOGY of lighting, heating and plumbing was advancing rapidly throughout the nineteenth century and country houses were inevitably affected by it, though to varying extents according to the degree of conservatism of the patron.

Plumbing, with all its refinement of hot and cold water, baths, and water closets, was available from the beginning of the Victorian period, even if in cumbrous form. Water closets were liberally provided from an early date; in 1839 William Burn's Stoke Rochford had fifteen of them. Wash basins were less in evidence, although from the 1860s it became common (but far from invariable) to have both wash basins and w.c.'s convenient to the entrance hall, and to the billiard and smoking rooms. Baths were a luxury, but not a rare one, though very seldom provided in large quantities; the staple method of washing was by hand-filled basins and hip baths, set up in the bedrooms. Stoke Rochford had two bathrooms in 1839, and as late as 1873 Carlton Towers had none; yet a year or more earlier Wykehurst was divided up into separate bedroom suites each with its own bathroom, a rare refinement for what was clearly intended to be one of the most luxurious houses of its age. But Carlton was built for a Catholic nobleman, Wykehurst for a city banker. Hot water, if piped, probably needed a central boiler room to heat it,

22

12. Queen Victoria's bath and shower at Osborne, 1844–8.

though sometimes there were individual boilers in the bathrooms. In any case piped water, whether hot or cold, made a water tank necessary, and provided a nice excuse for building a tower to contain it; an early example of a water tower was at Somerleyton (1844–51), supplied by a steam pump with its own engine house next to the boiler room in the back yard.

Central heating, forgotten since the Romans, was reintroduced in late Georgian times, when three rival systems, by steam, hot air and hot water, were developed. In the country house world the library at Bowood was heated with steam pipes (not very successfully) in the 1790s, and Sir Walter Scott installed steam heating in the hall at Abbotsford in 1823.[34] By 1807 Richard Lovell Edgeworth was heating the hall at Pakenham Hall, County Westmeath with hot air,★ and ducted hot-air systems involving more than one room were installed at Abercairny, Perthshire, in 1829[35] and Coleshill, Berkshire, in 1814, the latter designed by J. C. Loudon. Hot-water systems came a little later, but several hundred feet of hot-water piping were installed for the Duke of Wellington at Stratfield Saye in 1833.[36]

Steam heating, which was expensive and technically difficult, was not developed in Victorian times. Initially, hot air seems to have been the favourite, but the problem of providing air of sufficiently good quality for breathing was seldom solved and, as radiators became more efficient, hot-water systems became more popular, though they were always cumbrous. Central heating of one form or another was on the increase all through the period. Comparatively early examples were at Osmaston (1846–9, hot air), Flixton (1847, hot air), Tortworth (1849–52, hot air) and Mentmore (1850–5, hot water).† But it never became invariable, and seldom extended beyond the entrance hall, corridors and possibly the main downstairs rooms. As late as 1880 J. J. Stevenson, in a full discussion on heating in his *House Architecture* could say, 'for heating English houses the best system, on the whole, is the old one of open fires'.[37]

From well before Victorian times it was realized that heating and ventilation were complementary problems, and as windows and doors became increasingly better fitted, houses warmer, and gas lighting more common, the problems were aggravated. They were never properly solved, which was one reason why central heating and gas lighting did not spread more quickly, while open fires, which provided a rudimentary ventilation system up the chimney, retained their popularity. A good many houses had ventilation shafts fitted to the rooms (e.g. Kelham, Mentmore, Dobroyd, Wykehurst) but it was complained that they more frequently let cold air in than foul air out.[38] More comprehensive heating and ventilation systems (of which there were several urban examples)[39] were much more rare. The most elaborate was at Osmaston in Derbyshire, designed by H. J.

★ 'The immense hall so well-warmed by hot air that the children play in it from morning to night. Lord L[ongford] seemed to take great pleasure in repeating 20 times that he was to thank Mr. Edgeworth for this.' Letter from Maria Edgeworth quoted in Elizabeth Inglis-Jones, *The Great Maria* (London, 1959), p. 92. Pakenham Hall is now known as Tullynally Castle.
† Disraeli's Lord Marney comments on the 'lazy pampered menials' in his local workhouse, which 'is heated with hot air, and has every comfort. Even Marney Abbey is not heated with hot air. I have often thought of it . . . but I am afraid of the flues.' (*Sybil; or the Two Nations* (1st edn, 1845), Book III, Ch. II.)

Stevens of Derby for Francis Wright, a rich ironmaster, in 1846–9.[40] Cold air was drawn into the house through a shaft by the kitchen, heated in the basement, and distributed through ducts all over the house. This hot-air system was supplemented by coal fires in the individual rooms, through which the used air was drawn into chimney flues which went *downwards* into a horizontal main flue and was finally ejected up a giant communal chimney in the kitchen garden. The horizontal flue was heated and the chimney was 150 feet high, to provide the draught necessary to make the down flues work. As a result the house had no stacks, which allowed for flat uninterrupted roofs; and the great chimney was fitted with a staircase, and a belvedere gallery for the view from the top. The system was described with enthusiasm by the architect in 1851 but does not seem to have lasted many years.[41]

12. *Gas and Electricity*

IN 1787 Lord Dundonald used gas to light the hall of Dundonald Abbey in Scotland.[42] Sir Walter Scott, who was fond of gadgets, installed gas lighting at Abbotsford in 1823, but it proved expensive and malodorous.* John Claudius Loudon, in his *Cottage, Farm and Villa Architecture* (1835 edn) remarks that 'lighting rooms by gas has hitherto been chiefly employed in towns and suburban villas; we have no doubt that, with the progress of improvements, it will be found worth while to adopt it in all country villas'.[43] But in early days very considerable quantities of gas were needed to provide very moderate amounts of light; as a result it was expensive, and problems of smell and heat made it unsuitable except for open air thoroughfares and large rooms. Improved techniques (including the regenerative burners invented in 1853–4) of enabling gas to be burnt at much greater heats, and therefore to produce light more economically, made it a feasible proposition for domestic use. It could still be both hot and smelly, unless adequately ventilated: hence the ventilation grills often concealed in the central ornaments and cornices of Victorian ceilings. In the 1880s the incandescent gas mantle was developed; this was much more economic and less heat producing than earlier systems, and made gas a competitive alternative to electric light in its early days.

Tortworth and Abney Hall (both of *c.* 1849–50) are the first Victorian country houses that I have come across which were equipped with gas, though I would not be surprised to hear of earlier examples. Paxton supplied gas lighting to the castle and town of Lismore for the sixth Duke of Devonshire in 1852; similarly at Kelham (1858–62) the gasworks lit the house and village. There were gasworks and gas lighting at Hemsted (*c.* 1862), Tyntesfield (1863–6), Bayham Abbey (1869–71) and Nutfield (1870–4). At Stanmore (*c.* 1870) the house drew piped gas and water from the public works at Bridgnorth, two miles away. But for most country houses installing gas involved building a gasworks and taking some kind of technician on the payroll; this and other drawbacks meant that many houses continued to rely on

*J. G. Lockhart, *Life of Scott* (1869 edn), pp. 500–1. 'The blaze and glow and occasional odour of gas, when spread over every part of a private house, will ever constitute an annoyance for the majority of men.'

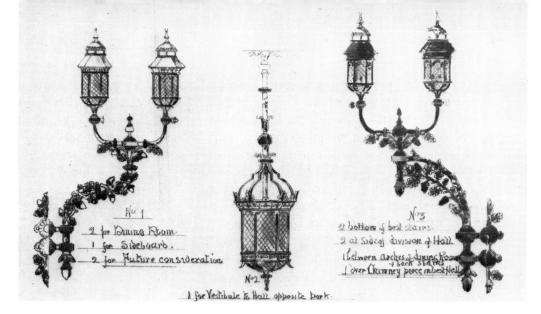

candles or colza lamps. From 1860 American kerosene, cheaper and less smelly than the oils previously available, provided another alternative.

The first English country house (and one of the first houses in the world) to be lit by electricity was Cragside, where Sir William Armstrong, the inventor and armaments manufacturer, installed Swan lamps at the end of 1880. He was run a close second by Lord Salisbury at Hatfield.★ Octavius Coope, the brewer, who had installed gas at Berechurch Hall about 1860, remodelled it and replaced gas by electricity in 1882. Smallwood Manor, Staffordshire, completed in 1886 for G. A. Hodgson, is the first documented example I know of a house built, rather than converted, for electricity, with light fittings designed by its architect, R. W. Edis. Stokesay Court in Shropshire (1889) is another early example, and some of its rooms still preserve the original arrangement of the lights.

13. Other Services

MANY large Victorian houses had lifts for goods and luggage (e.g. Kelham, Overstone, Bayham, Wykehurst). These were usually manually operated. At the pioneering Osmaston Manor a hydraulic lift went from the basement up to the bedroom floor as early as 1846–9. At Alnwick in the 1850s a hydraulic lift carried food up from the kitchen to the dining-room level; and in the 1870s Cragside, as the residence of a hydraulic engineer, was rich in hydraulic devices. Passenger lifts come right outside the period, as far as country houses are concerned. The wire-operated bells, which are still a prominent feature of many country house corridors, were improved on by pneumatic bells (Rousdon, 1874) and ultimately by electric bells (Hewell, c. 1890).

★ For Cragside, see p. 306. The electric light system at Hatfield was installed by Lord Salisbury in the winter of 1880–1 and was working (on and off) by the summer. 'When the lights collapsed his voice could be heard through the darkness amidst the general outcry of laughter and dismay, commenting meditatively upon the answer this supplied to some as yet undetermined problem of current and resistance.' Earlier on he had experimented unsatisfactorily with Jablokhoff arc-lights inside and outside the house. Gwendolen Cecil, *Life of Lord Salisbury*, III, pp. 3–9.

13. Designs for gas lamps at Flixton Hall, Suffolk, by Anthony Salvin, c. 1869.

Attempts to prevent fire sometimes led to fire hydrants on every floor, supplied from the water tower (Tyntesfield), supplemented by internal iron rolling shutters (Wadhurst). At Normanhurst, fireproof construction and a liberal supply of water hydrants did not prevent the house being gutted by fire in the 1920s.

At Stancliffe there was an iron billiard table. At Enbrook in Kent (c. 1854) the carriage porch was paved with india-rubber; at Tettenhall in Staffordshire the music-room floor was on india-rubber springs and iron rollers. Cavity walls[44] appeared in the early 1860s at Overstone Hall; Godwin used them at Dromore Castle, County Limerick (1868–70), but failed disastrously to keep the damp out.★ Cranfield Court, Bedfordshire (before 1874), had double glazing with sunblinds fitted between the two panes of glass. Lord Salisbury put internal telephones into Hatfield in the 1870s.† Before 1882 Tettenhall had telegraphic communication between the dining room on the ground floor and the smoking room in a tower; at the top of the tower was a 'flashing apparatus like the one used in Zululand'.‡ At Batchwood, the house outside St Albans, designed for himself by Sir Edmund Beckett (later Lord Grimthorpe) in 1874–6, the w.c. doors would not open until the w.c. had been flushed.[45]

14. Technology, Comfort, Snobbery and Aesthetics

IT IS HARD to say, on the evidence available, whether the upper classes were slower than the new families to fit up their houses with new technical appliances. Technologically minded middle-class owners (e.g. Wright at Osmaston, Thorneycroft at Tettenhall, Walter at Bear Wood, Salomons at Broomhill and Armstrong at Cragside) were no doubt commoner than upper-class ones (e.g. Lord Salisbury at Hatfield), as one would expect from their background. Owners of inherited houses were under no great pressure to modernize them as long as labour to carry coals, water and candles remained cheap, and no doubt there were conservative landowners who were suspicious of new gadgets when rebuilding. But many new upper-class country houses, especially the larger ones (such as Tortworth, Westonbirt, Kelham, Bayham and Eaton Hall) were as fully fitted up as the equivalent new middle-class ones (such as Osmaston, Bear Wood, Tyntesfield, Overstone and Wykehurst). Certainly in the early Victorian

★ 'When offered a commission in Ireland, refuse it.' E. W. Godwin speaking at the Architectural Association, Manchester, reported British Architect, 10 (1878), p. 211.
† He tested the system himself, 'Visitors were startled by hearing Lord Salisbury's voice resounding oratorically from selected spots within and without the house, as he reiterated with varying emphasis and expression "Hey diddle diddle, the cat and the fiddle".' Cecil, Salisbury, III, pp. 3–9.
‡ Lt.-Col. Thorneycroft of Tettenhall must have been one of the most indefatigable of Victorian amateur technologists, and communicated a long description of his ventilating and other innovations to the Builder of 24 Jan. 1880 (pp. 7–8 with illustrations). 'There are two billiard rooms opening into the music room, a Roman or Turkish bath, a conservatory, a dinner service room with gas plate warmer, and American dinner-heating or cooking range, a lift to upper rooms, two cascades, one falling 45 feet, and a sort of small running brook; and when the stage, which is fixed on trestles, is removed, you can play at lawn-tennis, badminton, skate with rink skates bound with india-rubber tires, and use the india-rubber bicycle.' The visual results of all this were distressing.

period the middle classes expected the aristocracy to live luxuriously, and at times castigated them for it. Only towards the end of the century does one sense a growing attitude that comfort (and the new techniques that went with it) is *nouveau-riche*, unhealthy, or, even worse, American.★ Lord Ernest Hamilton says that electric light was considered insufferably vulgar in its early days, and that the bathrooms of his country house boyhood were 'never used for the purposes for which they were no doubt originally designed'.[46] Augustus Hare, in his interminable country house peregrinations, uses the word 'luxurious' almost exclusively for the houses of the new rich. Hutton Hall (home of the Middlesbrough Peases) is 'this intensely luxurious house'; the Guinness Elveden is 'almost appallingly luxurious'. Worst of all were the Montefiores at Worth Park, who had the presumption to make their servants comfortable as well as themselves: 'I went to Worth, the ultra-luxurious house of the Montefiores, where the servants have their own billiard tables, ballroom, theatre and pianofortes, and are arrogant and presumptuous in proportion.'[47]

It is always intriguing to speculate on the interactions between technology and style. Just as small panes, sash bars and mullions and transoms fitted in conveniently with the small-scale networks of early Victorian facades, the black voids of plate-glass windows accentuated the deliberate heaviness of the mid-Victorians. Structural polychromy was made easy by the possibility of transporting different materials by railway. The heat and smell of gas lighting encouraged high rooms in mid-Victorian times; in the 1880s low ceilings and cosiness were made much more feasible by electric lighting and the incandescent gas-mantle. The inglenook had originally been designed to trap heat in at least a corner of an inefficiently insulated room; it disappeared when better fitting joinery and windows encouraged an attempt at warming the whole room. But Victorians could afford to keep the heat of a fire in an inglenook, and warm the rest of the room by central heating.

 ## 15. *The Country House Plan*

IT IS THE organization of the plan of Victorian country houses which remain perhaps their most fascinating aspect.[48] They were enormous, complicated and highly articulated machines for a way of life which seems as remote as the stone age, served by a technology as elaborate as it is now obsolete. The houses have now become, too often, stranded monsters, with abandoned gasworks, abandoned billiard tables, gigantic boilers and miles of pipes rusting in the basement, long rows of bells rusting in the back corridors, the butler's pantry, brushing rooms and laundries empty, or occupied in this new society by typists, nurses, schoolgirls or delinquents.

Victorian country houses were complicated partly because they had to contain so many people, to a lesser extent because of the new mechanical services that were

★ Conversely, Americans were horrified by the discomfort in which the English lived. For example, Stephen Fiske, *English Photographs* (London, 1869), pp. 196–7: 'If there be a bathroom in an English house, it must answer for the whole household . . . Heated air is considerably unhealthy . . . The English wrap themselves up to cross the hall as though they were going out of doors', with much else in the same vein.

incorporated in them, but mainly because the activities and interrelationships of their occupants were so minutely organized and subdivided. In an age when government was organized into departments, the middle classes into professions, science into different disciplines and convicts into separate cells, country house life was neatly divided up into separate parcels. Even nature, much though it was admired, was kept in its place. Conservatories were almost automatic appendages to any large Victorian country house; but Regency experiments in breaking down the barrier between inside and outside, by means of loggias, french windows and dispersed plans, were little developed in Victorian times.

The largest houses (such as Eaton or Thoresby Halls) had forty or more indoor staff; anything eligible for the title of a country house was unlikely to have less than eight.[49] In the period between the reduction of infant mortality and the introduction of birth control, families of twelve or more children were by no means uncommon, and children had their own retinue of governesses, tutors, nannies and nursery maids. The new railways made it easy for friends and relatives to come to stay in large quantities, each bringing a valet or lady's maid. A great country house at its busiest might contain 150 people, and a population of forty or fifty would not be out of the ordinary.

These large numbers of people were carefully stratified and subdivided; there were territories reserved for each stratum and territories common to one or more; each territory was subdivided according to the activities that went on in it; this analysis of activities became more and more exact, and more and more activities were given a separate room. The household was divided into family, guests and servants; the servants were divided into upper and lower servants; the family into children and grown-ups; the children into schoolroom and nursery. It was considered undesirable for children, servants and parents to see, smell or hear each other except at certain recognized times and places. Guests and family met on common ground, but each had private areas to retire to.

Owing to these subdivisions the activity of eating became complicated. The main meals were often served in at least five different places, the dining room, the schoolroom, the nursery, the steward's room (for the upper servants) and the servants' hall (for the lower servants).★ If the household was not big enough to run to a steward's room, the upper servants ate everything but their main course in the housekeeper's room. Tea, for the grown-ups and guests, was invariably served in a different room from lunch and dinner; large houses often had a separate breakfast room. Outside eating hours the sex division was important. The mistress of the house had her boudoir to work in; the master, his study or business room. The drawing room (or rooms) was considered the ladies' territory, but the gentlemen

★ The serving of afternoon tea could be even more complex. At Pakenham Hall (now Tullynally Castle) in Ireland, just before the 1914–18 war, a full tea was regularly served in eleven places: drawing room (gentry); nursery (younger children, nannies and nursery maids); schoolroom (older children and governesses); housekeeper's room (upper servants); laundry (laundry maids); kitchen (kitchen maids); housemaids' sitting room (housemaids); still room (charwomen); servants' hall (footmen); harness room (grooms); and to the visiting riding master in a separate room, as being too grand for the servants but not grand enough for the gentry. (Recollections of Miss Reason, lady's maid, preserved at Tullynally.) The system probably dated back to the nineteenth century.

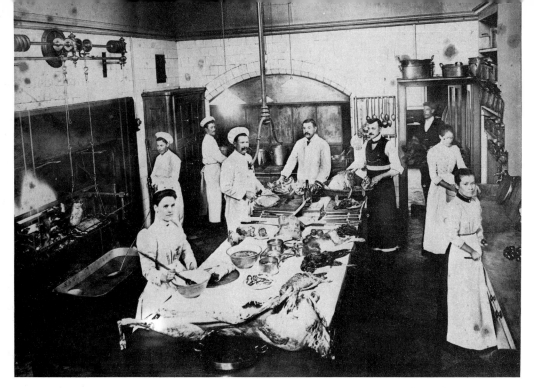

were allowed in; the opposite was the case with the library. The billiard room tended to become exclusively male territory. Among guests, the bachelors were kept in a separate corridor from the unmarried ladies. Above all, the menservants slept separately from the maids, and often did not even have the pleasure of passing them on the stairs, separate men's and women's staircases being provided.

Among, so to speak, optional extras for a Victorian country house were a conservatory and chapel and, less frequently, a ballroom, picture gallery or music room. A refinement quite frequently found was a separate family wing, containing a sitting room, master-bedroom suite, and nurseries. In a few very large houses, such as Trentham and Eaton Hall, the family wing became a virtually self-contained house, to which the family retired when they were not entertaining.

16. The Servants' Wing

VICTORIAN analysis of activities and their containment in separate spaces reached its most frenzied elaboration in the domestic offices. Robert Kerr, in his classic exposition of high-Victorian planning, *The Gentleman's House* (1864),[50] divides them into nine divisions, made up of Kitchen Offices, Upper Servants' Offices, Lower Servants' Offices, Laundry Offices, Bakery and Brewery Offices, Cellars Storage and Outhouses, Servants' Private Rooms, Supplementaries, and Thoroughfares. This was a division based on what was usual, as a quick look through Victorian house plans makes clear. Within the divisions were a multiplicity of subdivisions. Among the upper servants the housekeeper had her housekeeper's room, with still room (where cakes were made), store room and china closet attached. The butler had his pantry, with plate safe and plate scullery leading off it, and usually his own or a footman's bedroom

29

14. The kitchen at Keele Hall, Staffordshire, in the late nineteenth century.

adjoining, to protect the safe from burglars. The lower servants' rooms could include a separate brushing room, knife room, shoe room and lamp room, with housemaids' closets scattered at strategic positions over the house. A highly organized laundry department would have its wash house, drying room, mangling room, ironing room, folding room and laundry-maids' room arranged in a functional sequence so that dirty clothes went in at one end and clean clothes came out at the other. As for the kitchen, it had acquired, as Kerr wrote, 'the character of a complicated laboratory, surrounded by numerous accessories specially contrived in respect of disposition, arrangement and fittings, for the administration of the culinary art in all its professional details'. The accessories might include scullery, pantry, meat larder, game larder, fish larder, dairy and dairy scullery. The game larder was sometimes a detached building, and could be made a picturesque feature in the middle of the kitchen court, as at Shadwell.

All Victorian architects were obsessed by the need to keep kitchen smells out of the rest of the house. One must remember that Victorian country house kitchens catered for far larger numbers than their modern counterparts, that much Victorian cooking consisted of roasting in front of an open flame, and that there were no mechanical extractors. Although closed kitchen ranges were pioneered by Count Rumford in the early nineteenth century, they were remarkably slow in catching on. Accordingly, almost all Victorian kitchens in big country houses had their own roofs, with lanterns or top lighting to let the light in and the smells out. In connecting the kitchen to the dining room the architects had to steer between placing them too far apart, so that the food arrived cold, or too near, so that the kitchen smells penetrated to the dining room. On the whole Victorians chose distance rather than smells, with a hot plate in the serving room next to the dining room to warm the food up. Skilful use of kinks or cross-draughts in the connecting links were always appreciatively noted in the building journals.

30

15. Pull-out racks in the drying room at Tullynally Castle, Co. Westmeath, c. 1860.

17. Nuances and Drawbacks of Victorian Planning

To MARSHAL the immensely complicated accommodation of a Victorian country house in such a way that all the elements were conveniently placed and adequately lighted, that the important rooms had the right prospect and aspect, that no one saw what he shouldn't see or met those whom he shouldn't meet, was a formidable task for an architect. Half the skill lay in the correct analysis and disposition of lines of communication. Basement offices became increasingly unfashionable for reasons of privacy, freedom of planning and regard for the comfort of the servants. The usual arrangement was to have a main block with a (usually lower) service block to one side; and the two most common dispositions for the main block were round a central top-lit hall or staircase, or to either side of wide corridors or galleries running through the house, one above the other on each floor. But within these main lines much ingenuity was shown in ensuring, for instance, that the food got to the dining room or the butler to the front door without disturbing the privacy of the family, or even meeting them in the corridors. A sizeable country house could easily have six staircases; men's and women's staircases in the servants' wing; the main staircase; the back staircase (it was, of course, inconceivable that servants could go up the main staircase, except to clean it); a family staircase leading from outside the boudoir up to the master-bedroom suite and on up to the nurseries; and a bachelors' staircase. Entrances could be equally complicated: not only a front and back entrance but a garden entrance; a men's entrance, coming in by the smoking and gunrooms; a business entrance, for the business room; and a luggage entrance, to which carriages could move on after dropping guests at the front door.

The Victorian country house at its best was a remarkable achievement of analysis and synthesis, a vast machine running smoothly and with clockwork precision, a hieratic structure as complex and delicately graduated as the British Constitution. But it had its dangers. Unless arranged with skill it could become a warren of small rooms, confused corridors, dark corners and innumerable staircases. Even when well planned, Victorian country houses were inflexible, and the lines of communication were inevitably very long. The disadvantage of dividing a house up into a great number of highly specialized spaces, instead of fewer and less-defined areas, is that not only does the total size tend to increase but as soon as techniques and habits change the spaces become useless or at any rate awkward. That is why Georgian houses, though from the point of view of practical planning much less sophisticated than Victorian ones, tend to be more adaptable.

18. The Historical Development of the Plan: William Burn

LOOKED at historically the Victorian country house plan (before, at any rate, the domestic renaissance of the 1870s) was a matter of

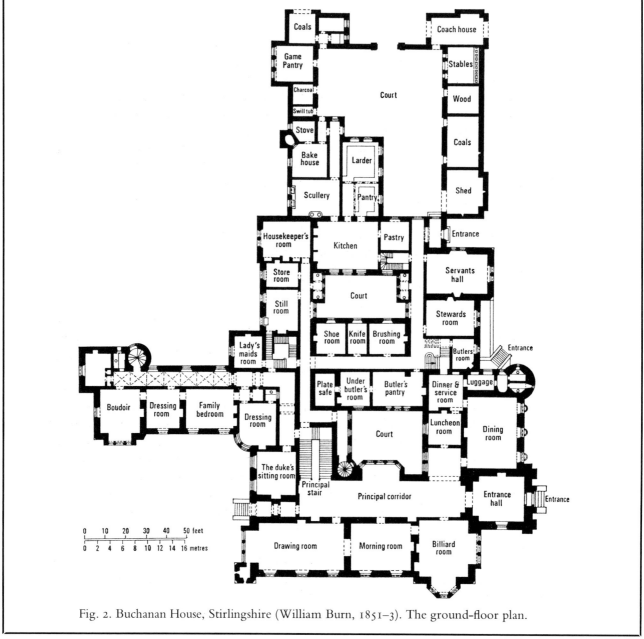

Fig. 2. Buchanan House, Stirlingshire (William Burn, 1851–3). The ground-floor plan.

organization rather than innovation. The 1820s and 1830s were a far more sybaritic period for country house owners than the 1840s, 1850s and 1860s. The late Georgians explored the possibilities of a luxurious, easy and enjoyable existence; the Victorians organized (possibly over-organized) their explorations, and introduced a new concern for the moral and social welfare of the country house community, especially servants and children. Perhaps the most typical element of a Victorian plan was the owner's business room, with its separate entrance and often its little waiting room for visitors, suggesting a serious attitude to running an estate, looking after one's dependants and taking a part in local life; it symbolized a change in emphasis even if in fact the owner did no more in it than smoke a cigar and read *The Times* after breakfast.

32

Almost all the living rooms which feature in Victorian houses feature in late Georgian ones: breakfast room, morning room, drawing room, boudoir, study, business room, library, billiard room, conservatory. The only novelties—one of them just pre-Victorian—were the (revival of the) Great Hall and the smoking room. Houses divided into a main block with service wing attached to the back, corner or side were a late Georgian commonplace. So were houses planned round a central hall or staircase; corridor houses were less common, but there is no shortage of examples (e.g. Abercairny, 1804, Southill, 1796–1803, Fowler's designs for Mamhead, 1822). The offices had already begun to proliferate, at any rate in the more ambitious houses (e.g. Toddington, 1819) although they were often very haphazardly arranged. Self-contained family wings had been pioneered in the eighteenth century at houses such as Holkham, Kedleston and Wardour, and were common enough in the early nineteenth-century; there were lavish examples at, for instance, Ashridge (1815–18) and Eaton Hall (1823–5).

The credit for organizing this rich late Georgian vocabulary was generally allowed to belong to William Burn. In the 1830s, if one wanted to find a sensible hard-working head gardener or agent with no nonsense about him, one looked for him in Scotland. If one wanted an architect to design a sensible hard-wearing country house with no nonsense about it, one went to Scotland too—in particular to William Burn. His success was so great that in 1844 he moved from Edinburgh to London. Thereafter, until his death in 1870, he had the biggest country house practice in the British Isles. Of Scottish architects in general and Burn in particular, Kerr wrote, in his book *The Gentleman's House*: 'It is well known that the most convenient houses in the kingdom have for many years back come from the hands of certain Scotch architects.' Burn's obituary in the *Builder* backs up Kerr's judgement. His reputation had grown by word of mouth alone. He never exhibited at the Royal Academy, never published anything himself, and never, if he could prevent it, allowed others to publish his plans. The *Builder* said that this was 'on the acknowledged ground that he saw no reason why he should enable others to derive advantage from them'.[51]

Burn was the perfecter of the family suite or wing, and of the business room, with its private entrance and waiting room. His larger houses always had a separate wing for the family, often with the relationship between parents' rooms on the lower floor and the children's rooms on the floor above carefully worked out. Business rooms had been an occasional feature of late Georgian houses, as for instance at Humphry Repton's Sheringham (1813–20); but Burn made them one of the stock essentials of the country house repertory. He did the same for the serving room, as an adjunct to the dining room—again an occasional late Georgian feature (Willey, 1812), but certainly not a usual one. It was Burn who first systematized the offices, dividing them up into zones under butler, housekeeper and cook, each with its own corridor, and providing separate male and female staircases, and the servants' hall and steward's room at the meeting of the zones. He organized bedrooms, nurseries and schoolrooms with the same care; he invented the luggage entrance; he worked out the lines of communication. It was not so much that he was an innovator, as that in a Burn house the client could be certain that every possible aspect of privacy, convenience and comfort had been considered. It was only in the next generation,

when the Burn mystique was on the wane, that the debit side of his method, in the shape of interminable passages and excessive numbers of minute rooms, began to be realized.

A Victorian innovation for which Burn was not responsible, but which later became a usual though not invariable feature of Victorian country houses, was the men's cloakroom, complete with wash basins and w.c.'s off or close to the entrance hall. ('The reason for having these conveniences connected with the Entrance', wrote Kerr, 'is that they are provided for the use chiefly of gentlemen visitors who can always find their way to the Entrance Hall without trouble, if nowhere else.')[52] A cloakroom without toilets appears at Somerleyton (1844–51); the complete arrangement is found in Salvin's Peckforton (1847–50) and from then on becomes increasingly common.

19. *The Male Domain*

ONE curious feature of Victorian houses is the increasingly large and sacrosanct male domain, an expansion in size and time of the after-dinner aspect of the Georgian dining room. It was one result of Victorian chivalry: at perhaps no other period in English history has there been so much which it was considered unsuitable for a nicely brought up woman to read, talk about, or listen to. Male preserves were the natural result of this 'remember-there-are-ladies-present-sir' attitude. In the first half of the period under review they were kept in check because of the religious bias of the time and the idealization of the family and the domestic virtues. The second half was increasingly secular in tone, and they proliferated. They were sustained, too, by the great tribes of Victorian bachelors, younger sons of large Victorian families, unable to marry outside their class for snobbish reasons, and inside it for financial ones.

34

16. Billiards in the hall at Lismore Castle, Co. Waterford, *c.* 1830, by an unknown artist.

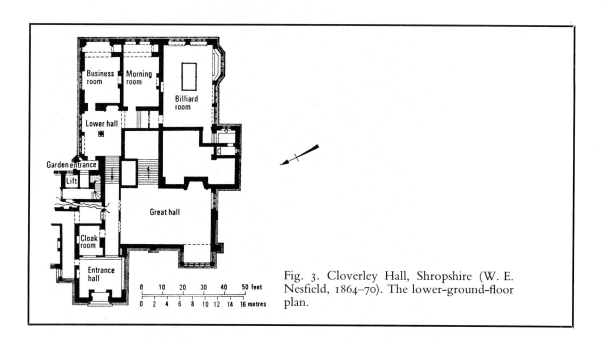

Fig. 3. Cloverley Hall, Shropshire (W. E. Nesfield, 1864–70). The lower-ground-floor plan.

The nucleus of the male preserve was the billiard room. Billiards as a game dates from the sixteenth century, but it had to wait for several hundred years before special rooms began to be built for it, as at Southill (1796–1803), Sezincote (c. 1805) and Toddington (1819–40). In the late Georgian period, however, many country houses were built without a billiard room, or had one combined with another room. At Lismore, a billiard table was set up in the hall in about 1812; a drawing of the 1830s shows a billiard table in the gallery at Capesthorne. In Burn's Lauriston (c. 1825) the billiard room is through an open archway off the drawing room, and there is a similar arrangement as late as 1844 at Osborne (Pl. 122). In Barry's Trentham (1834) the billiard room is a passage-room between the staircase and the drawing room. But self-contained facilities for billiards became an increasing necessity in a country house of any size, and a separate and private room was provided for it. Ostensibly this was because the noise of billiards was a bore to the rest of the house; but one suspects it was as much because the men liked a sanctum to retire to. Billiards, over which Byron and Lady Frances Webster had started an affair in 1813,[53] became more and more of a man's game. If the billiard room was placed next to the owner's study or business room with a w.c. and wash basin adjacent, one had the makings of a comfortable little male territory. At Banks and Barry's Bylaugh Hall (1852) one half of the ground floor was given up to a sequence of billiard room, w.c., dressing room, gentleman's room and library—the latter described by Kerr in a cruelly revealing phrase, as 'rather a sort of morning room for gentlemen than anything else'.[54] A similar combination was given the lower ground floor in W. E. Nesfield's Cloverley (1864–70).

Kerr also writes that 'the pitiable resources to which some gentlemen are driven, even in their own houses, in order to be able to enjoy the pestiferous luxury of a cigar, have given rise to the occasional introduction of an apartment specially dedicated to the use of Tobacco'.[55] This was in 1864, and the smoking room was to become steadily less occasional.

35

In 1839 Lord Melbourne had dismissed smoking as a dirty German habit: 'I always make a great row about it; if I smell any tobacco I swear perhaps for half an hour.'[56] But the Prince Consort introduced this regrettable practice into court circles, and installed a smoking room at Osborne in 1845; it was the only room with a solitary 'A' instead of an intwined 'V & A' over the door—smoking was for men only.[*] The Prince of Wales, with his passion for interminable big cigars, probably did even more than his father to make smoking a fashionable upper-class vice. An early country house smoking room at Mentmore (1850–5) is a tiny room, safely on its own at the end of the conservatory. This was one way to keep the fumes of cigar smoke away from the ladies; another was to isolate it in a tower.[†] There were tower smoking rooms at Breadsall Priory (1861), Winscott (1865), Tyntesfield (1866), Humewood (1867–70, a combined billiard and smoking room) and Hope End (1873); at Cardiff Castle (1868–71) there were two smoking rooms, for summer and winter, in a tower 130 feet high.

An alternative was to put the smoking room next to the billiard room. This was to

[*]Elizabeth Longford, *Victoria R.I.* (London, 1964), p. 212. In 1858 Constance de Rothschild, then aged fifteen, was writing in her journal: 'We talked about ladies smoking in general and about Julia's in particular. We all agreed that we did not like to see a lady smoke regularly day after day but that at times a chance cigar is very pleasant.' But Rothschild young ladies were not typical. (Lucy Cohen, *Lady de Rothschild and her Daughters* (London, 1935), p. 93.)
[†] 'Nobody will even have an Italian villa now without a tower, which I believe is generally devoted to the combustion of tobacco.' Sir Edmund Beckett, *A Book on Building* (London, 1876), p. 98.

36

17. The Moorish smoking room at Rhinefield, Hampshire, 1888–90.

become the standard arrangement, and in many houses the two were combined into one. They were found separate but adjacent at, for instance, Rendcomb (1865), Wykehurst (1872) and Milner Field (1873). At Kinmel (1868–74) there were two smoking rooms in close proximity, a small one leading through an arch off the billiard room and a large one across the passage next to the business room. The culmination of the man's domain was reached at the end of the period; at Bryanston (1890), for instance, the men could retire in stages into their own private wing, from the drawing room to the library, on to the billiard room, through spacious lavatories and a smoking room and sitting room to a cluster of bachelor bedrooms.

By the 1870s the gun room begins to make an occasional appearance in the men's suite. Its appearance marks the progress from the relatively haphazard shooting of the early nineteenth century to the great organized beats of the 1890s, and the development of shooting from a recreation to a mystique. In the anonymous article on the 'Beau Ideal of an English Villa' contributed to Loudon's *Cottage, Farm and Villa Architecture*, 'the hall is the proper place for all sporting instrument, as guns, bows and arrows, fishing tackle, etc.';[57] by Kerr's time the proper place is the gun room, 'indispensable in a country house of any pretensions', but classified among the 'upper servants' offices'.[58] The next step was to make it a snug gentleman's sitting room, with the guns in racks round the walls, between cases of stuffed game and fish. There are good examples next to the billiard room in Norman Shaw's houses at Greenham Lodge (1878) and Cragside (after 1884).

37

18. The winter garden at Somerleyton Hall, Suffolk, erected *c.* 1855 and demolished in 1912.

The billiard room at Brodsworth (1861–3) is an untouched example of a standard Victorian billiard room, with horse portraits round the walls, comfortable padded leather benches raised as a platform for the spectators, and a high leather stool on which some bright little nipper would be given the privilege of sitting and marking up the scores (Pl. 228). Sometimes billiard rooms were given more lavish treatment. At Breadsall Priory the billiard room was Moorish, at Cragside lavishly Jacobean, at Halton House splendidly *Louis Seize*, at Wortley Hall decorated in the Renaissance style to the designs of Sir Edward Poynter. The billiard room which Thomas Vaughan, son of the Middlesbrough iron tycoon, installed at Gunnersgate around 1874, was rumoured to have cost £50,000, and was fitted out with large and horrible paintings of the four seasons, the spirit of billiards, etc. by Stacy Marks.★ Smoking rooms, on the other hand, were usually comfortable rather than elaborate, though the smoking room at Rhinefield (1888) was richly Moorish, and the summer smoking room at Cardiff is perhaps the most splendidly decorated Victorian room in Britain. But this was the whim of a young bachelor millionaire (Col. Pl. XXI).

20. *The Conservatory*

A CONSERVATORY, either attached to the house or freestanding in the garden, had been a prominent and popular late Georgian feature. It was equally popular under Victoria, and advances in glass and iron techniques enabled it to be more spectacular in its design, though not necessarily more imaginative. Norman May's description of the conservatory at Abbotstoke Grange, in C. M. Yonge's *The Daisy Chain* (1856), is a nice example of a romantic Victorian enthusiasm: 'It is a real bower for a maiden of romance, with its rich green fragrance in the midst of winter. It is like a picture in a dream. One could imagine it a fairy land, where no care, or grief, or weariness could come.' In it Meta Rivers, the graceful daughter of the house 'cut sprays of beautiful geraniums, delicious heliotrope, fragrant calyanthus, deep blue tree-violet and exquisite hothouse ferns'.[59]

The Abbotstoke conservatory opened into the drawing room and made 'the whole air fragrant with flowers'. Victorian conservatories usually connected up with one of the living rooms; at Capesthorne it was the library that opened into one of the first and grandest of Victorian conservatories, designed by Paxton about 1837. It was 150 feet long and 50 feet wide, and led from the library to the chapel. At Mentmore the conservatory connected the morning room with the smoking room, at Nutfield (1870–4) the dining room with the billiard room. At Somerleyton a monster conservatory 125 feet by 90 feet, so large as to be called not a conservatory but a winter garden, was added on to one side of the house about 1855. Another sumptuous winter garden at Halton House, Buckinghamshire (1882), was a notable *tour de force* of Rothschild extravagance, roofed with two large and nine small domes and with a skating rink adjoining (Pl. 401).

★ The underwater glass-ceilinged billiard room which Whitaker Wright, the crooked company promoter, built at the bottom of his lake at Witley Park, Surrey, in the 1890s comes just outside the period covered by this book. The room is still there, though no longer furnished or in use.

I. Flintham Hall, Nottinghamshire (Thomas Hine, 1851). The conservatory.

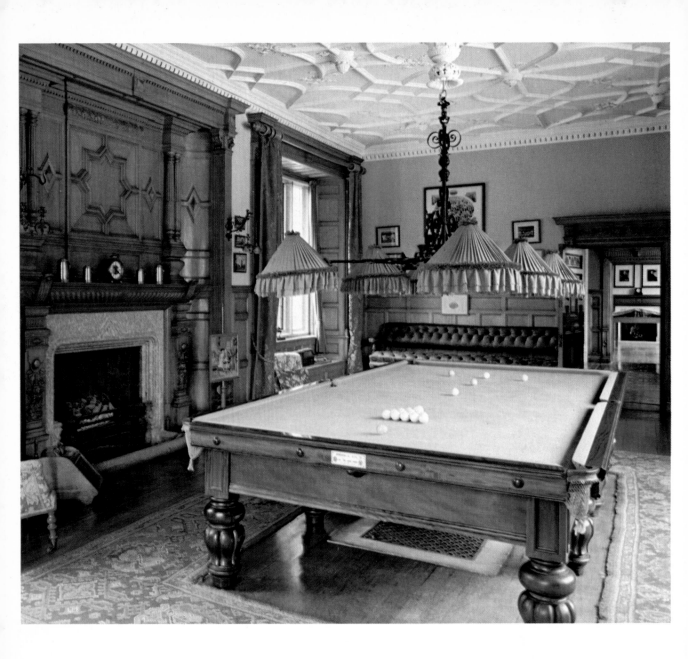

II. (above) Lanhydrock, Cornwall (Richard Coad, 1881). The billiard room.

III. (right) Elvetham Hall, Hampshire (S.S. Teulon, 1859–62). The entrance front, from the architect's drawing.

IV. Ettington Park, Warwickshire (John Prichard, 1858-63). A detail of the *porte-cochère*.

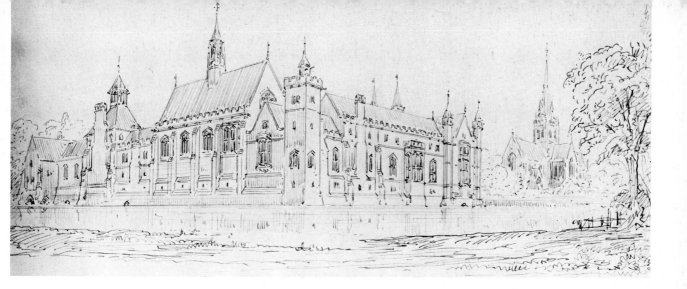

Conservatories are expensive to heat and maintain and the odds against their survival are high, especially if they are large. Those at Capesthorne, Somerleyton and Halton have all been demolished. Of Victorian conservatories attached to the house, the most spectacular still in existence is at Flintham in Nottinghamshire (1851–4; Col. Pl. I) complete with fountain, plants and elaborate vegetable wall lights (the latter trophies from the 1851 Exhibition). One can look into the conservatory through an expanse of great plate-glass windows at the end of the adjacent saloon, or down from a first-floor oriel letting off the saloon gallery. The glazing at Flintham was given a vaguely Tudor look, to go with the glazing of the house; but neither here nor elsewhere did efforts to harmonize these delicate glass monsters with the far from delicate houses to which they were attached meet with notable success.★

21. The Great Hall

IT WAS NOT surprising that the late Georgians, both in their romantic and archaeological moments, were attracted by the idea of reviving the medieval or Elizabethan Great Hall. About 1830 a complete Elizabethan hall was reinstated at Charlcote in Warwickshire; it was two storeys high, with oriel window, screens passage and arched (but not open) timber roof. In 1833 the anonymous author of the 'Beau Ideal of an English Villa' gave an enthusiastic description of a two-storey 'hall in the old English style', rich with panelling, stained glass and coats of arms, and equipped with family portraits, armour, antlers, sporting gear, massive furniture and a letterbox. Such a room, he thought, 'might still be the banqueting room on great festive occasions'.[60]

★ Once the initial enthusiasm had worn off very large conservatories or winter gardens attached to the house seem to have been especially patronized by *nouveaux-riches*, e.g. Somerleyton (*c.* 1855, for the contractor Peto), Normanhurst (1867, for a son of the contractor Brassey), Halton (1882, for a banking Rothschild), Cliffe Castle (*c.* 1880, for the wool-manufacturer Butterfield) and Avery Hill (*c.* 1885, for the nitrate-king North). In Robert Hichens's *The Londoners* (London, 1898), Ribton Marches, the house built by Mr Lite the Bun Emperor, was 'full of winter gardens, and in all these winter gardens there were talking parrots'.

43

19. Merry England Revived. A. W. Pugin's unexecuted design for Garendon Hall, Leicestershire, 1841.

The architect Anthony Salvin was keen on great halls, from the time, perhaps, when as a young man in 1829 he worked on the restoration of the medieval hall at Brancepeth Castle in his native Durham.[61] He installed a superb two-storey Jacobean hall at Harlaxton (1831–8) and by 1835 had equipped the more intimate single-storey entrance hall at Mamhead with a Perpendicular fireplace and screen. At Mamhead the problem of what to do with this archaic apartment was solved by putting the billiard table in it. The modest though roomy hall at Scotney (1835) was a sensible compromise between archaeology and comfort, with the entrance porch at one end, no screens, and the billiard table in the bay window at the other.

In 1836 the two first full-blown revived medieval great halls began to rise up, at different ends of the country, and probably quite independently. One, designed by Augustus Welby Pugin, was at Alton Towers in Staffordshire; the other, with which Salvin may have been connected, was at Bayons Manor in Lincolnshire. 'As regards the hall', Pugin wrote to his patron Lord Shrewsbury, 'I have nailed my colours to the mast—a bay window, high open roof, two good fireplaces, a great sideboard, screen, minstrel gallery—*all or none*. I will not sell myself to do a wretched thing.'[62] He got what he wanted. The hall at Bayons was just as complete and almost as splendid (Pl. 83). Each, unlike any previous nineteenth-century halls, had its own roof, projecting prominently above the skyline of the house. So did the hall (Pl. 77) which Pugin designed for Scarisbrick in Lancashire in 1837 (and this, unlike the other two, is still in existence).

44

20. Eustace Tennyson D'Eyncourt proposes a toast in the new great hall at Bayons Manor, Lincolnshire, 1842.

Pugin was anxious to restore the medieval hall for social as well as romantic reasons. He explained himself in his *True Principles of Pointed or Christian Architecture* (1841):

The almost constant residence of the ancient gentry on their estates rendered it indispensable for them to have mansions where they might exercise the rights of hospitality to their fullest extent. They did not confine their guests, as at present, to a few fashionables who condescended to pass away a few days occasionally in a country house; but under the oaken rafters of their capacious halls the lords of the manor used to assemble all their friends and tenants at those successive periods when the church bids all her children rejoice, while humbler guests partook of their share of bounty dealt to them by the almoner beneath the ground entrance of the gate house. Catholic England was merry England, at least for the humbler classes.[63]

As a formula for dealing with discontent among the lower classes, and yet retaining the upper classes in a gratifyingly condescending role, Pugin's brand of Christian paternalism met with a responsive audience. The Young Englanders swallowed it whole and in *Coningsby* (1844) Disraeli transferred the setting sketched out by Pugin into early Victorian England, almoner and all. At Christmas in the great hall at St Genevieve, the home of Eustace Lyle (a pseudonym for Pugin's friend Ambrose Phillipps de Lisle) 'all classes are mingled in the joyous equality that becomes the season', and the Young Englanders, thinly disguised under psuedonyms, wassailed and mummed to their hearts' content.[*] A delightful lithograph shows the tenantry being entertained in the hall of Bayons Manor in 1842.[64] And indeed, relieved of its most extravagant absurdities, the formula was found to work remarkably well; with the squire and his tenant farmers in the hall, the rest of the gentry in the dining room and the labourers in a marquee in the park, the Victorian countryside sailed out of agrarian discontent into the calm waters of mid-Victorian deference. Surtees gave a cynical picture of a Puginesque squire in his description of Squire Jawleyford:

His communications with his tenantry were chiefly confined to dining with them twice a year in the great entrance hall, after Mr. Screwemtight had eased them of their cash in the steward's room. Then Mr. Jawleyford would shine forth the very impersonation of what a landlord ought to be. Dressed in the height of fashion, as if by his clothes to give the lie to his words, he would expatiate on the delights of such meetings of equality; declare that next to those spent with his own family, the only really happy moments of his life were when he was surrounded by his Tenantry; he doated on the manly character of the English farmer.[65]

Alton, Bayons and Scarisbrick were followed by other great halls such as Peckforton (1844, by Salvin; Pl. 138), Hall (1844, by Philip Hardwick), Lismore (1849, by Crace and Pugin; Pl. 423) and Canford (1850, by Barry). The halls at Lismore and Hall were neither entry nor thoroughfare rooms, but detached banqueting halls—and as such rather better suited for Victorian entertaining.

*Disraeli, *op. cit.* Pt. IX, Ch. I. One wonders whether Disraeli had seen A. W. Pugin's exquisite little book of unexecuted designs for remodelling the de Lisle home at Garendon (Pl. 19).

Beneath the gilded timbers and glowing stained glass of the Lismore banqueting hall the sixth Duke of Devonshire, on his annual visit to Ireland, used to give two great entertainments, one for the local gentry and one for the local tradespeople and farmers. It was a shrewd and immensely popular move on his part, and a good example of the use to which such a room could be put. But in the 1850s the popularity of the great hall, especially in its more full blown form, was on the decline. Its possible function as a depository for coats, guns or billiard tables had been taken over by other rooms; the feeling of the time was against large rooms for show alone; and in the secure mid-Victorian years it may have seemed less necessary to feed up the tenant farmers. Scott in his *Secular and Domestic Architecture* (1857) gives a good Puginesque puff to the great hall as a vehicle for 'that broader hospitality which belongs especially to the great landlord'. But he also perceptively suggests its possibilities as 'a delightful sitting room, particularly in summer'.[66] It was this potentiality of the great hall that was to be taken up by Nesfield and Shaw, and led to a great revival of its popularity in the 1870s.

22. *The Picturesque versus the Functional: Pugin*

IN the early Victorian years there were two opposing approaches to the design of country houses, one on the wane and the other developing. The theory and practice of the picturesque had been established in England since the early years of the century. An architect who was designing in the picturesque idiom was principally concerned with how a building looked—whether it fitted into a landscape, whether its horizontals and verticals mixed in an irregular but balanced composition, whether its light and shade were nicely contrasted. His attitude to style was an eclectic one; he chose whatever seemed most suited to the site, the associations of the property, and the tastes of the client. But the picturesque approach influenced the way styles were used; total symmetry went out of fashion, and the usual treatment even for a classical house was to combine a symmetrical main block with a lower and more irregular office wing attached to one side. At the Deepdene in 1818–23 Thomas Hope developed a more adventurous form of the classical picturesque, with numerous symmetrical units loosely and asymmetrically grouped together, and a skyline enlivened by Italianate towers with shallow deep-eaved roofs. As for material, effect was all that mattered; if an architect wanted the effect of marble, stone or wood, and lacked the money or the means to use the genuine material, he had no qualms about imitating it in painted and modelled plaster. No good architect would have denied the importance of a convenient plan; but visual effect came first, and convenience was often made to suffer in order to obtain it.

Pugin wrote in direct reaction to the picturesque movement, and pronounced two iconoclastic doctrines: that plan came before appearance, and that buildings should be what they seemed. Because he contended that Gothic architecture fulfilled these provisos, and that it was English and Christian, as opposed to classical architecture, which was foreign and pagan, he argued that all buildings should be

46

Gothic. In short he was against eclecticism, and replaced a visual approach by a moral one. Plaster imitating stone was a sham and therefore bad; so were houses pretending to be castles. Nothing was worse than, 'when a building is *designed to be picturesque* by sticking as many in and outs, ups and downs, about it as possible'. Instead, 'an architect should exhibit his skill by turning the difficulties which occur in raising an elevation from *a convenient plan* into so many *picturesque beauties*'.[67] Inconvenient symmetry was as bad as inconvenient asymmetry; both were distorting the convenient arrangement of a building for reasons of appearance.

When Bayons Manor was nearing completion in 1836 its composition was felt to be unsatisfactory; a tower was suggested, as the required central accent; a flag was hoisted where the tower would go, to give some idea of its effect; the effect was approved and the tower was built. Later, the entire house was surrounded by sham fortifications. Bayons is a perfect example of the picturesque approach that Pugin so hated; and yet, ironically, its detail is as authentic and convincing as anything that Pugin ever designed. What Pugin provided was not so much new knowledge as a new point of view. At Scarisbrick—an exact contemporary of Bayons—the hall, chapel, kitchen and clock tower, four principal functional elements, were each given a separate and distinct articulation, but no effort was made to combine them into a conventional picturesque composition. Even what survives at Scarisbrick is notably disconnected in comparison with the deft mixes of picturesque buildings; at Alton Castle the three elements of main block, chapel and wing appear from some views like three independent buildings, loosely yoked together. This jerky or staccato quality is characteristic of Pugin.

47

21. Alton Castle, Staffordshire (A. W. Pugin, 1847–51).

Pugin's contention that the outside of a house should express what was going on inside provided a design philosophy that affected almost all Victorian country houses to a greater or lesser extent; at the expense, often, of a roof plan of appalling complexity, it enabled architects to give visual emphasis to their pride in their elaborate and elaborately worked-out plans. But the Pugin approach was swallowed in its entirety comparatively seldom. Eclecticism continued to flourish; in 1864 Kerr was offering his readers nine different styles to choose from.[68] Stucco went out of fashion as an external treatment; so, rather more slowly, did marbling and graining as internal ones. Fewer and fewer castles were built. Puginesque ideas of functional expression led to prominent staircase projections or windows, and eye-catching kitchens (or, at Scott's Hafodunos, billiard rooms) inspired by the Abbot's kitchen at Glastonbury. A functional excuse, however thin, was required for a tower; it had to contain a clock, water tank or smoking room. A great deal of attention was given to planning; a certain amount of upping and downing, of grouping of tower and gables, paid at least lip service to picturesque principles. But the asymmetry of many Victorian houses looks confused rather than picturesque; it is sometimes hard to decide whether this is just incompetence, or the result of a moral 'I put the windows where they are needed and damn the consequences' approach.

23. *Barry, Blore, Burn and Salvin*

AMONG early Victorian country house architects apart from Pugin, Barry was the most flamboyant, Blore, Burn and Salvin the most successful. All four were considerably older than Pugin, and all four survived him. All four were prepared to design in a number of different styles, but each had his preferences.

Barry was a brilliant showman in the picturesque tradition. Thomas Hope's experiments at the Deepdene had been too adventurous and unfamiliar for English tastes; Barry developed them into something more conventional, more grandiloquent, less original, but much more palatable to upper-class taste. His work at Trentham (1834–42) is an example of the skill with which he could add to and remodel an older house to produce an irregular but balanced composition made out

48

22. Trentham Hall, Staffordshire (Sir Charles Barry, 1834–40).

23. (right) Walton House, Surrey (Sir Charles Barry, 1835–9).

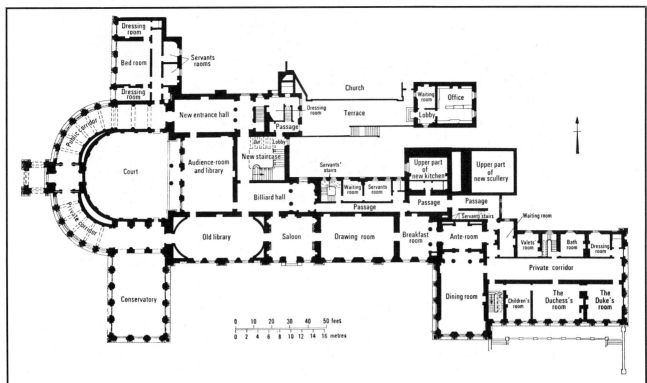

Fig. 4. Trentham Hall, Staffordshire (Sir Charles Barry, 1834–40). The ground-floor plan (this plan is to 88% scale of the other plans).

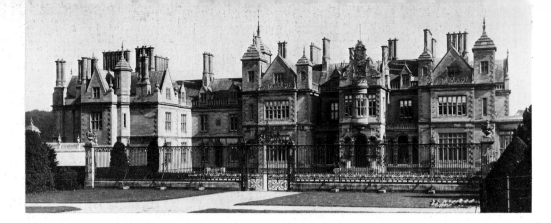

of classical elements. At Walton House (1835) he did the same kind of job on a less than ducal scale, with very pleasing results. The Italianate tower (derived from the Deepdene) was a favourite Barry feature, and one that was to be much imitated. Internally he was a skilful deviser of long and richly formal routes from the entrance to the drawing room.

In his time there was a shifting of values inside the picturesque movement; the sublime was out of fashion (ever since the symbolic collapse of Fonthill in 1807) and the quality most admired was intricacy. Barry was a master at producing intricacy, by means of a small-scale applied order, elaborate quoins, rich cornices, and an even spread of ornament. For his classical buildings he found the Italian Renaissance a new and rich source of inspiration; at Highclere he played the same game with a different vocabulary, inspired by the non-gabled variety of Elizabethan architecture. The result (which he called Anglo-Italian) was imitated with panache by his son at Bylaugh and with rather less skill by John Thomas, his collaborator on the Houses of Parliament, at Somerleyton. Among Victorian classical country houses obviously derived from his work one of the earliest is Osborne (1844–8) and one of the latest Rendcomb (1863–5). Barry's shares started high but were on a falling market; even though he did without porticoes, his buildings were too obviously designed for show to accord with the growing Victorian preference for what Kerr called 'elegance and importance without ostentation'.

50

24. (top) Stoke Rochford, Lincolnshire (William Burn, 1839).

25. One of William Burn's first designs for Fonthill Abbey, Wiltshire, 1852.

In 1833 Edward Blore was scornfully dismissed by the Duchess of Sutherland as 'the *cheap* architect'.[69] In the event the Duke of Sutherland chose Barry for Trentham, Stafford House and Dunrobin; his brother, Lord Ellesmere, chose Blore for Worsley (1840–6). The Duke was a Whig, his brother a Tory; the hard core of Barry's clientele were Whig peers and of Blore's Tory gentry. Tory gentry were perhaps suspicious of Barry's smooth Italian grandeur—and of the bill that came in afterwards. Blore was never flashy; his buildings were gently picturesque and gently Elizabethan—in the good Old English style. He gave them just enough intricacy to suit the taste of the times but not enough to push the bill up unreasonably. His drawings are remarkably attractive, his buildings often remarkably feeble. His planning was competent, but, by the 1840s, a little old fashioned. The Duchess's gibe suggested that his houses were not expensive, and that he kept to his estimates. Barry's estimate for Trentham was £40,000, the actual cost was £72,000; the millionaire Sutherlands could take this kind of thing in their stride.

26. The approach to the keep, Alnwick Castle, Northumberland (Anthony Salvin, 1854–65).

Blore retired from general practice in 1849, though he still had thirty years to live. For some years his reputation had been over-shadowed by two younger men, William Burn and Anthony Salvin. Burn was brought up in the picturesque and eclectic tradition; he could do you something classical or Elizabethan or Scottish Baronial. He introduced the latter style to England at Fonthill Abbey, built for the Marquess of Westminster in the late 1850s, as a dour Victorian exorcism of Beckford's extravagant fantasies. Burn would perhaps have agreed with Kerr's dictum that 'the merits of this school make no pretensions to be of the artistic order, but turn entirely upon practical usefulness'.[70] His reputation, as already described, rested upon his skill as a planner, and the feeling that his buildings were gentlemanly—that is, not too showy. The quality of his work declined with the visual sensitiveness of his patrons; but some of his earlier houses, such as the House of Falkland in Scotland and Muckross House in Ireland (Pl. 422), have a workmanlike crispness that is very agreeable.

Of all the architects of his generation Salvin was best able to combine sensible planning, skilful composition and scholarly detail. His earlier works at Harlaxton and Scotney Castle (the latter described by Christopher Hussey in *English Country Houses, Late Georgian* (1958)) are both, in their different ways, amazing buildings, securely based on the picturesque tradition but full of forecasts of the future. Peckforton Castle is a remarkable *tour de force*, a scholarly and yet free re-creation of a medieval castle combined, against all the odds, with a clever and up-to-date plan. But at Peckforton one can already sense a hardening of the arteries. It became increasingly evident in his later country houses, even though he was still capable of splendid things, like the vaulted approach at Alnwick Castle (1854–65). His practice was a huge one, he built numerous new houses and added to even more old ones. His speciality was castle architecture, but he designed many Elizabethan houses, a few classical ones, and could add to classical houses—such as Petworth and Encombe—with notable restraint. He was always conscientious—but there is a coldness, even grittiness, about his later houses that is a disappointment after his early brilliance.

24. *The Battle of the Styles*

ALTHOUGH all but the most exotic styles remained open to choice for country houses throughout the Victorian age, their degree of popularity was shifting. The different varieties of classical styles were losing ground all the time. My sample of Victorian country houses shows that 41 per cent were classical in 1840–4, 32 per cent in 1850–4 and only 16 per cent in 1860–4. As early as 1833 Loudon was attacking the Greek style (by which he meant the whole English classical tradition since Inigo Jones) as unsuitable for country houses; it had no associations with the English countryside, indeed, 'a villa in the Grecian style generally reminds us more of the town than the country'.[71] To the charge that classical architecture was urban and un-English Pugin added that it was pagan. Comparatively few country house architects and even fewer patrons would have been as overwhelmingly bigoted as Pugin, but even so there was a growing feeling that it was a style either for the town or for the proud and the worldly. R. S. Holford commissioned the palatially Italian Dorchester House in Park Lane but his equally palatial country house at Westonbirt (Pl. 415) was Elizabethan. In Charlotte M. Yonge's *Heartsease* the worldly and ambitious Nightingales rebuild their country house as a 'great pile of building' with 'innumerable windows, the long ascent of stone steps, their balustrade guarded by sculptured sphinxes . . . a great hall, where a vista of marble pillars, orange trees, and statues opened before her'.[72] Here is Scott on classical houses in 1857: 'Their cold and proud Palladianism, so far from inviting, seems to forbid approach . . . the only rural thoughts they suggest are of gamekeepers and park rangers.[73] With classical Victorian country houses one always suspects either new city money or worldly owners, bringing a touch of smart London drawing rooms down to the country—even though porticoes (considered especially haughty) are almost invariably absent, and the house is suitably countrified by having a Barryesque tower, in his Italian-villa style, tacked on to one side.

On the other hand, both Elizabethan and Gothic were, for the mass of country house owners, entirely acceptable, as the two varieties of the 'Old English' style. The choice depended on the tastes of the person building; if he saw himself as an English gentleman he would tend to build Elizabethan, if as a Christian English Gentleman, Gothic—a 'pile of modern building in the finest style of Christian architecture' such as delighted Coningsby when he visited Eustace Lyle at St Genevieve.[74] Up till about 1870 the religious tone in country house life was on the increase, and Gothic was easily leading Elizabethan; after 1870 the situation was reversed, owing to the change in atmosphere described in a later section.

 ## 25. *The High-Victorian Years*

MID-VICTORIAN country houses can be presented in terms of a calm but tedious background, and a confused foreground; a mixed bag of neurotic, pedantic, perverse, adventurous or amazing buildings. In the background Salvin and Burn pursued their unruffled and prosperous course, leaving in their wake a formidable string of Elizabethan or baronial mansions. In the same convoy were a number of younger and lesser men, of whom the former partners T. H. Wyatt and David Brandon were the most successful—indefatigable purveyors of Elizabethan houses designed, to judge from the results, when they had more important matters on their mind. A little apart from these were what one might call the unadventurous Goths, rolling out Puginesque houses every year or two with all Pugin's facility and little of his conviction. In this group one can put Pugin's biographer Benjamin Ferrey, whose many country houses never have the freshness of his early churches, and John Norton and P. C. Hardwick, though the last two have their lively moments.

It is hard to believe that Elizabethan houses of this date will ever be very much admired.★ They are not without their virtues; their lack of flashiness, their large,

★ 'Elizabethan-revived country houses are mostly gentle looking things, without much character either bad or good.' E. W. Godwin, 'Modern Architects and their Work', Pt. II, *Building News*, 12 July 1872, with much more in the same vein.

high-ceilinged and well-lit rooms, can be agreeable enough to live in; David Brandon's first and freshest independent commission, Falconhurst Lodge (1851), was a case in point. But as a group they are a dim and mechanical lot. The most palatial of them, Salvin's Thoresby (1864), in spite of its grand plan, and grandly lit, grandly proportioned rooms (Pl. 414), is a depressing decline from Harlaxton, its equivalent in size and splendour designed by the same architect thirty years earlier. It is a cold house, dead in its handling and dead in its detail. Yet Salvin, particularly in his less ambitious works, such as his additions to Fawsley (1867) could still produce sensible, straightforward building of high quality.

These are the typical country houses of their period, and express what the average mid-Victorian gentleman thought a gentleman's house should be. There remain the houses designed by architects whose main interests lay in other fields, for patrons whom piety, snobbery, romanticism or new money set a little apart from their neighbours. It is among the architects in this group that one looks for entertainment and for new ideas, even if brutally presented; they are the hards as opposed to the heavies. There was a certain amount of interaction between the two groups; the output of the heavies changed slowly if slightly in character under the influence of the hards; the hards tended to rely on the experience of the heavies for the mechanics of country house planning.

26. Muscularity

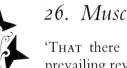

'THAT there is a spirited and substantial vigour in the presently prevailing revival of medieval architecture is not to be questioned—far less explained away. People may not sympathize with the demands of pre-raphaelite enthusiasm, or the affectations of sentimental romance; they may smile with more or less disdain, or laugh with more or less amusement, when they see common-sense unreservedly and even angrily cast overboard; they may very fairly be permitted to express a doubt whether so singular

54

27. Thoresby Hall, Nottinghamshire (Anthony Salvin, 1864–75).

an enthusiasm as this "Gothic mania" ever seized upon Art before, or ever will seize upon it again: they may reasonably speculate upon the questions how long it is to endure, and what amount of ridicule is to be visited by posterity upon its borrowed plumage; but all this does not deprive muscularity of its muscularity.'[75]

This is Kerr, writing about the Gothic of his day. 'Muscular' and 'vigorous' were adjectives commonly applied to it by critics of the time; Sir Edmund Beckett gives a characteristic dig at 'that modification of French and Italian Gothic to which its patrons have dexterously affixed the epithet "vigorous", though it would have been just as appropriate to call it "feeble".'[76] But in spite of Sir Edmund, one can see why the adjectives were used. There is an obvious movement, between early and high-Victorian Gothic, away from the intricate, delicate and pretty, towards the chunky, massive and what critics at any rate called ugly—'an incredible worship of the Ugly', as Kerr put it. Buildings became at first wiry and then heavy. Abundance of mouldings and clustered columns were given up for plain chamfers and squat massive columns. Outlines became simpler, and roofs prominent and less cut about. The delicate patterns, naturalistic ornament and soft tints of the 1840s gave way to larger patterns, simple geometric shapes and strong primary colours. It was a shift of taste that led naturally to earlier and earlier brands of Gothic—especially across the channel to early French Gothic.

At the time 'muscularity' was a slang architectural term applied specifically to the early Gothic school, of which G. E. Street and William Burges were the leaders. It is tempting to apply it to the whole high-Victorian period. Some of the older Gothic architects of the Pugin generation made their buildings do very savage things in the 1860s, without adopting the mannerisms of the younger men. Among the eclectics, it is interesting to compare Kerr's staircase tower at Bear Wood (Col. Pl. XX) with

28. The great hall and entry hall at Crewe Hall, Cheshire (E. M. Barry, 1866–71).

Barry's staircase tower at Highclere (Pl. 108) on which it is unmistakably modelled.★ At Bear Wood the cornice, pilasters and skyline have become heavier and more crowded; the glazing is set back more deeply and below the pilasters come rumbustious scrolls, concatenations of chamfers and violent diagonals. E. M. Barry's Crewe Hall (1866–71) was a somewhat similar attempt, by an outsider to the style, to liven up Victorian Elizabethan. In classical buildings, too, there is a shift towards detail that can be called either vigorous or coarse, depending on the quality of the work and the attitude of the onlooker.

The 'vigorous' school in architecture goes with the Victorian cult of manliness, of which Carlyle was the prophet, Kingsley the high priest, and Thomas Hughes (of *Tom Brown's Schooldays*) the acolyte. Manliness meant both physical and moral fibre; or as Carlyle put it in *Past and Present* (1843) 'sheer obstinate toughness of muscle; but much more what we call toughness of heart'.[77] The qualities of Tennyson's 'great broad-shouldered genial Englishman' were on the up; sensitivity, gentleness, a sense of beauty, were on the down. 'We are of a different race from the Greeks, to whom beauty was everything', said John Thornton, the northern manufacturer in *North and South*; 'our glory and our beauty arise out of our inward strength'. Kingsley, who described himself as 'a strong, daring, sporting, wild man-of-the-woods', preached 'a healthful and manly Christianity, one which does not exalt the feminine virtues to the exclusion of the masculine'.[78] Hughes wrote that 'from the cradle to the grave, fighting, rightly understood, is the business, the real highest, honestest business of every son of man'. A contemporary critic, W. R. Greg, sarcastically commented on this kind of attitude: 'What unspeakable joy and relief for a Christian to discover that he is not called upon to control his aggressive instincts, but only to direct them.'[79] This could just as well be a brief for a Christian architect as a Christian gentleman; for S. S. Teulon, for instance. The apparent failure of the strong, daring, sporting Victorian age to produce a style of its own was causing a good deal of disquiet in the 1860s. At worst, by ignoring all the conventions, and indulging in deliberate extremes of eccentricity, an architect could both work off his inhibitions and persuade himself that he was helping to create a genuine Victorian style. At best, he could use a discipline of strong geometric shapes and vividly formalized ornament as an escape from historicism, often with highly exciting results.[80]

Kingsley's muscular christianity and worship of masculinity and the mid-Victorian architects' pursuit of vigour can both have a hysterical quality. Some of Teulon's more extreme efforts, such as the entrance porch of Bestwood, and practically the whole of Elvetham, are unbelievably perverse; but they also contain fascinating experiments in architectural form and colouring. The porch at Bestwood looks as though a surgeon had been at work, cutting away the flesh in layers to reveal the bone and muscle. The result is a startling piece of architectural sculpture: whether it is an agreeable way to enter a country house is another matter. At least it could never be described as a lifeless copy of genuine medieval work.

★ In the issue of 6 May 1864 the *Building News* described Barry's Palace of Westminster as 'effeminate in its detail to the last degree'. Compare with this, for instance, the same journal's commendation of William Burges for 'his very masculine designs' (1868, p. 287).

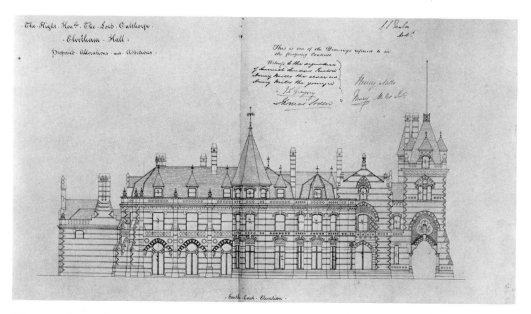

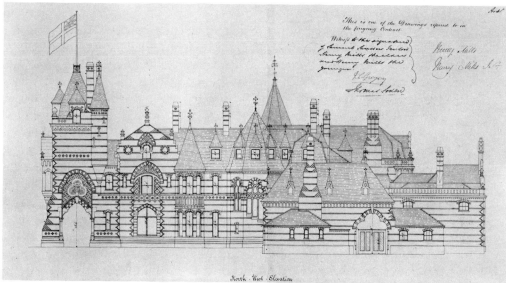

Muscularity, for better or worse, encouraged a buccaneering spirit towards both Gothic and classical architecture, which on occasions became only a starting-off point for the architect's private fantasies.

27. *Texture, Colour and Ruskin*

THE VICTORIAN hatred of stucco and shams led to a growing interest in building materials and from there to a feeling for texture. In late Georgian times the ideal was smooth ashlar stonework; if this was not available or could not be afforded, the builder did the best he could with stucco or precise smooth-faced brickwork. Once 'shams' were disallowed architects began to think about the potentialities of other materials; and the 'vigorous' school, in their reaction against smoothness, found that rough stone,

57

29. High-Victorian polychromy. Two elevations of Elvetham Hall, Hampshire (S. S. Teulon, 1859).

flint and cut brick gave them the effects they wanted, besides being conveniently cheaper than ashlar. This feeling for materials took some time to develop; it is not to be found in Burn, Salvin or even Pugin, whose buildings are often depressingly dead in texture. But it is pleasingly evident in J. L. Pearson's Treberfydd, impressively vigorous in the work of William Burges and William White, startling in E. B. Lamb's notched brickwork at Nun Appleton, and reaches heights of daring and sophistication in Teulon's Shadwell, where, for instance, flint and smooth stone are beautifully combined to set each other off.

Different materials could be combined not only to obtain contrasts of texture but also contrasts of colour. Structural polychromy became very popular in high-Victorian times, especially with Gothic architects; it went with asymmetry and variety of skyline as a protest against the monotony thought to be a result of the Renaissance. Ruskin and Street popularized its use as found in Italian Gothic architecture; and the railways made it easy to bring together different materials. Polychromy could be used to obtain the violent contrasts popular with the vigorous school, as with Teulon's lively diaperings at Elvetham (Col. Pl. III), the most extreme country house example of what was known as the 'streaky bacon style'. William Butterfield, one of the high-priests of structural polychromy, employed it with considerable subtlety at Milton Ernest, his only complete country house (Col. Pl. XV). There is a sensitive example of Ruskin's influence at Ettington Park where John Prichard combined four different varieties and colours of stone in a polychromatic display of captivating delicacy and prettiness (Col. Pl. IV).

Ettington also shows the influence of Ruskin in its abundance of carving. In the preface to the second edition of the *Seven Lamps of Architecture* Ruskin wrote: 'There are only two fine arts possible to the human race, sculpture and painting . . . What we call architecture is only the association of these in noble masses, or the placing them in fit places; all architecture other than this is, in fact, mere building.' The idea that architecture could only be made high class by slapping on plenty of carving appealed to a generation that had a great deal of money to spend, and was always ready to point a moral or adorn a tale. If structural polychromy could be involved as well, so much the better.

58

30. High-Victorian Polychromy. Ettington Park, Warwickshire (John Prichard, 1858–63).

Yet while it was generally agreed that, for instance, churches and town halls were suitable vehicles for rich sculpture, its use tended to be avoided in country houses, because of the feeling, to quote Kerr, 'that English taste among the superior orders is averse to rich or sumptuous effects. Excessive ornament is almost invariably vulgar.'[81] The group of highly carved country houses is a relatively small one, and mostly confined to a few years: Ettington (1858), Teulon's Shadwell (1856), Elvetham (1859) and Bestwood (1862), T. H. Wyatt's Capel Manor (1859, with plenty of structural polychromy) and Scott's Kelham (1858). Considerably later came Burges's amazing and wonderful interiors, but these were a world on their own, and even further removed from the general taste of the time.

Ettington and Bestwood are plentifully adorned externally with sculptured scenes from the history of Sherwood Forest and the interminable genealogy of the Shirley family (there was plenty of scope, for they had owned Ettington since before the Conquest). Shadwell and Kelham are richer in foliage carving. The great series of Kelham capitals, unfinished though they are, are amongst the finest examples of their type and period in England (Col. Pl. XVIII). For the Victorians the study of nature had a moral value, as the study of God's handiwork; and a deliberate attempt was made to go direct to Nature as a source for artistic inspiration and a means of escape from what was considered the artificiality of the Georgian tradition. The conservatory, the foliage capital and the young ladies' albums of pressed flowers, were different aspects of the same taste. Similarly, structural polychromy could be seen as an exhibition of the variety of God's creation, in stone externally, in marble and wood—and showcases of minerals—internally. An extreme example was the house designed by James Gowan for himself outside Edinburgh, where the stones were 'arranged in regular geological stratifications, beginning with red and grey granites and ending with the sandstone which belong to the coal and iron measures'.[82]

28. High-Victorian Attitudes: the Pugin Tradition

THE SYMMETRICAL square-built house of the eighteenth century had failed to survive two waves of attack; first from the picturesque brigade, on the grounds that it was uninteresting, and secondly from Pugin and his friends on the grounds that (as sacrificing function to form) it was immoral. Its reputation was at rock-bottom in mid-Victorian years. Among country-house architects the dominant philosophy was Pugin's: that elevation should be subservient to plan, and that the different elements of a house should be expressed externally as 'distinct and beautiful features'.[83] But the Victorian emphasis on convenient planning, and the increasing complication of the country house machine made it tempting to use Pugin as an easy way out; instead of 'raising an elevation from a convenient plan into so many picturesque beauties' (True Principles),[84] to raise an elevation from a convenient plan and leave it at that, to make the elements of a house 'distinct' and not to bother whether the result was 'beautiful'. Beckett, always a skilful needler of professional architects, attacked 'the modern notion that

cutting out a lot of rooms in cards and throwing them together anyhow is the way to plan a Gothic house'.[85] (Cutting out rooms in cards was a method recommended by Kerr in the *Gentleman's House*.)[86] Scott was worried that Pugin was being abused; an architect 'must neither make his plan independently of his elevation, nor his elevation of his plan, but, in making his arrangements, must ever keep a side look at the architectural part of the question. Pugin would do this so instinctively as to be almost unconscious of it; but his words, taken without their guard, might lead young architects to think no such double exercise of skill needful.'[87]

Moreover, how many elements of a house needed a distinct expression? The hall, the kitchen, the entrance, of course; but did each staircase need a separate turret? and every bedroom a different type of window? The opportunities for exaggeration were endless; and the Victorian hatred of monotony added to the fun. This also had a moral slant, much reinforced by Ruskin: uniformity was the result of the classical strait-jacket, variety showed the unfettered joyfulness of the medieval craftsman. And so developed, to quote the irrepressible Beckett, 'the modern Gothic practice of breaking up the roofs of even small houses, and a *portion* of large ones, into as many bits and gables of unequal heights and widths as possible, though the architects know very well that that increases the expense both of building and of keeping in repair.'★ A quick look at Minley Manor will show what he was getting at.

★ Sir Edmund Beckett, *A Book on Building* (London, 1876), p. 105. Burges put it more concisely: 'Modern buildings look very much as if they had been shaken about in a hat.' (*Builder*, 18 June 1864, p. 448.)

31. (top) Muscular Gothic. Knightshayes Court, Devon (William Burges, 1869–71).
32. High-Victorian Anarchy. Minley Manor, Hampshire (Henry Clutton, 1858–62); the wing to the left by Arthur Castings, *c.* 1887.

The aggressive anarchy of Minley (what would Blore have thought of his favourite pupil?) had no shortage of counterparts, but not all mid-Victorian country houses were so extreme. Symmetry, however, became rarer and rarer. Even the neo-Elizabethans who (like the Elizabethans themselves) usually made their main fronts symmetrical in the 1840s very seldom did so in the 1860s. A popular game to play was that of approximate symmetry. Architects designed houses with features that more or less balanced each other but made them just a little different, to show their independence and distrust of facility. Even Salvin was playing this game by the time he designed Thoresby. Burges plays it in the grandly muscular front of Knightshayes, though one has to look for some time before one sees how. It was not a game that would have made any sense to late Georgian architects; it needed the background of Victorian architectural morality to become enjoyable.

29. High-Victorian Attitudes: the Picturesque Tradition

THE LAST section was concerned with the Pugin anti-picturesque tradition, and the excesses into which it strayed on occasions. But the picturesque tradition was far from dead, though it was changing.

33. (top) Late Georgian composition. Tregothnan, Cornwall (William Wilkins, 1816–18).

34. The arrival of the diagonal. Scotney Castle, Kent (Anthony Salvin, 1835–43).

The most interesting high-Victorian houses are those which experiment with new ways of visual organization, but keep a sensible dialogue going between practical and visual standards.

The standard late Georgian picturesque composition is based on a combination of horizontals and verticals, mixed asymmetrically but with an approximate balance, and building up to a dominating central feature. Diagonals—and therefore roofs and gables—play a minor part, often no part at all. Even in neo-Tudor buildings, where gables could not easily be avoided, the usual practice was to carry a strong horizontal line, in the form of a battlemented bay or a string-course, across the base of the gable.

Salvin gave this treatment to Mamhead (1827–33) but a few years later he was experimenting with new arrangements. The entrance front of Scotney is, in a deliberately unostentatious way, a highly original composition. The tower to the left of the porch has three storeys of windows, arranged on a rhythm of 3:1:2. The single window in the middle storey has a blank space to either side of it, and beneath it. As a result the windows form a pattern like a St Andrew's cross, with two strong diagonal lines crossing each other. The parapet is emphatically lopsided, with three steps of battlements leading up to a raised platform (for the flagstaff): the result is another diagonal. The upper portion of the middle section of the facade is all on one plane, but in silhouette is irregular; horizontal eaves, then a small gable, then a larger gable. The right-hand portion of the facade is mostly composed of blank wall, with a central chimneystack and only one window, in the top right-hand corner. The irregular mixing of window and blank wall, so that the blank wall plays a positive part in the composition, and the subtle interplay of diagonals, sets this Scotney front apart from late Georgian picturesque facades. One finds the same kind of composition in the garden front of Harlaxton, where the blank wall is provided by the enormous chimneystack and the diagonals by its offset outline, etched against the smooth ashlar adjoining it.

It is interesting to move on twenty years and look at Quar Wood, designed in 1857 by Salvin's pupil Pearson (and alas, emasculated some years ago into neo-Cotswold of the most banal variety). The rather overpowering churchiness of this house (it was built for a prosperous squarson) should not blind one to its great virtuosity. Blank wall and diagonals play a prominent part, as at Scotney, but twenty years have made a difference, and not only to the detail. A consciousness of the potentialities of the diagonal has led, naturally enough, to an exploitation of roofs. Quar Wood can be analysed either as a skilful combination of roofs of different shapes—plain gable, hipped gable, pyramid, spirelet and wedge—or as a dramatic essay in rising and falling skyline. The pyramid outline of the little summer house sinks to a horizontal, rises sharply in a mixture of verticals and diagonals to the tip of the spirelet, sinks again, rises to a long horizontal, rises again to the culminating bold outline of the tower, and then drops to the ground—for the tower is at the corner, not as at Scotney or in most late Georgian picturesque compositions in the centre. Blank wall is skilfully used, on the right to emphasize the diagonal climb of the skyline, on the left to bring the whole composition to a halt: the lower half of the tower is completely without windows.

The Victorians were increasingly conscious of skyline: not that the late Georgians

ignored it, but they saw it as an offshoot of the composition as a whole, whereas Victorian skylines acquired a vivid individual existence. Godwin's romantic little silhouette of Dromore Castle is an example of this Victorian characteristic.★ A late Georgian architect would never have drawn a building of his in this way. The

★ 'He had seen it by moonlight, seen it from the lake, from the road, and at a distance, at every angle, and the silhouette was about as charming a thing as ever he saw in his life, notwithstanding that it was his own work.' Report on talk by E. W. Godwin to the Architectural Association, Manchester, *British Architect* (1878), X, p. 211.

35. (top) The silhouette of Dromore Castle, Co. Limerick, from a sketch by the architect, E. W. Godwin, 1868.

36. Pyramidal grouping. Quar Wood, Gloucestershire (J. L. Pearson, 1857).

skyline potentiality of Gothic was one of its great strengths; the Classicists had to introduce the French mansard roof as their answer to the Goths. French mansard roof Classicism had such a notable success, and is so nostalgically high-Victorian, that it is given separate treatment in Chapter 22.

The roots of Victorian picturesque can be found in the late Georgian *cottage-orné*; in Nash's Blaise Hamlet and Wyattville's Endsleigh Cottage (1810–11) the conventional picturesque apparatus of horizontals and verticals is supplemented by a riotous conglomeration of diagonals. But the inspiration of these buildings was so clearly vernacular cottage architecture that it was considered inappropriate to apply this style to conventional country houses which needed at least a touch of the grand manner. The Victorians, with their genuine feeling (however unlikely the expression of it may sometimes have been) that what they were after was 'quiet comfort without ostentation',[88] were not so circumscribed. Even that feature so beloved by mid-Victorians, the hipped gable, is to be found at Endsleigh and Blaise Hamlet. It has made the country house proper (discreetly, in the stable wing) by S. S. Teulon's Tortworth (1849–52), and afterwards it was to proliferate.

Tortworth is an interesting example of a house which combines strong Puginesque influence with picturesque showmanship. The different parts of the building are given separate expression with frantic enthusiasm, not only 'all speaking their respective purposes' as the *Builder* put it at the time, but shouting them. But the innumerable parts are combined together in a skilful picturesque composition, building up to the huge pyramidal tower which contains a sensational staircase clearly inspired by Wyattville's Ashridge. The same architect's Shadwell is an example of his skill in piling up triangles and diagonals—a skill also to be found in the highest degree at White's Humewood, and Butterfield's Milton Ernest. Muscular enthusiasm for the spiky or knobbly often resulted in the basic pyramids or cones of roofs being broken by dormers and chimneys, or outlined by little fences of cast iron, or sticklebacks of tiles. Burges's—as always highly individual—essays in this direction can be seen at their most elaborate in his service wing at Gayhurst

64

37. Nun Appleton, Yorkshire (E. B. Lamb, 1864).

(1859), at their simplest and most effective in the funnel-shaped chimneys that sprout out of the roofs at Castell Coch (Pl. 324). If one turns from general composition to detail one can see the influence of the diagonal and triangle at work, for instance, in White's and Teulon's extraordinary notched and chamfered woodwork, or a *tour de force* like the brickwork of E. B. Lamb's additions to Nun Appleton (1864). In these the diagonal has been put to the service of muscularity; another nice example of this is the staircase expressed externally by a diagonal run of windows, with deliberately shocking effect, as at Shadwell, Hemsted, Bear Wood and Carlton Towers.

Quar Wood is much higher and tighter than Scotney, with less spread, and steeper pitched roofs. This is a general characteristic of high-Victorian buildings. A roof pitch of 60° was favoured by Goths of the day; William White maintained that the best Gothic buildings were based on the equilateral triangle.★ Beckett characteristically pointed out that 60° roofs were impractical and J. J. Stevenson that they were dangerous to the workmen who repaired them.[89] In spite of this they proliferated; a typical high-Victorian composition builds up different sized equilateral triangles into a tight mass, approximately pyramidic in outline.

There is a tension about these high tight compositions that is typical of the period. High-Victorian buildings are not relaxing. By the 1860s the later pre-Raphaelites had created an escape route into a secret enclosed Gothic world, heavy with hopeless passion and swooning ecstasy. In architecture the interiors of William Burges had something of the same atmosphere. Most of their contemporaries thought it very unhealthy. But Low Church muscular Gothic, and mansard roofed pseudo-chateaux, although firmly seated in the world of hunting squires and prosperous bankers, can be just as highly charged. One is reminded of a phrase used by George MacBeth when discussing the same period but a different medium; they have a 'hallucinatory vividness'.[90]

★ *Ecclesiologist* (1853), XIV, pp. 313–30. White was a member of the Alpine Club; the high-Victorian preference for high-pitched roofs and pyramidal composition was often accompanied by a taste for Alpine scenery.

38. Tortworth Court, Gloucestershire (S. S. Teulon, 1849–51).

30. *The Revolt of the Goths*

IN THE 1860s a number of the younger and abler Gothic revival architects, who had started life as enthusiasts for the Gothic style, found themselves having doubts about the sense of reviving Gothic for nineteenth-century people to live in. In one way or another they kicked over the traces; by the 1870s they were in full revolt and the older Gothic men discovered to their horror that almost all their cleverest pupils had deserted the cause. The anti-Goths may have been amused at first at their rivals' comical dismay and confusion; they found it less funny when the young men burst into their own preserves, and began to perform there with a mixture of new and old tricks, a joyful contempt of the rules, and far more dash and brilliance than they themselves had ever been capable of.

The Gothic revival had been preached by its first advocates with dedicated missionary enthusiasm. To take to Gothic was like taking the pledge: one never touched another style again. Gothic architecture was truthful, Christian and English; and if transplanted into nineteenth-century soil it would become once more a living and developing style. By the late 1860s, when the first enthusiasm had gone, the arguments began to sound less convincing. A system based on stone-arch construction, however truthful, was usually irrelevant to modern needs; the pointed arch, divorced from masonry vaults, was awkward and light-consuming; the Gothic virtues of avoiding counterfeit materials, structural deceit or unnecessary symmetry could be exercised without using Gothic detail. It no longer seemed so important (or even true) that Gothic was Christian architecture. In the 1860s the great Victorian religious revival was losing its force, and in the 1870s it was definitely on the wane. Looked at from a cynical point of view, religion was no longer an obvious route for social advancement, as it had been when Charles Kingsley described Alton Locke's uncle in 1850: 'He was the owner of a first-rate grocery establishment in the City and a pleasant villa near Herne Hill, and had a son . . . at King's College, preparing for Cambridge and the Church—that being now-a-days the approved method of converting a tradesman's son into a gentleman.'[91] In the later 1860s the number of school-leavers from Rugby and Harrow destined to go into business exceeded those destined to go into the church for the first time; and from then on the gap steadily widened.[92]

The revival had started with a dominantly religious bias; its protagonists had been in the first place architects of churches or religious buildings. Although the country houses designed by the best Gothic architects had been amongst the most interesting of their period, they were only a sideline (if in some cases a considerable one) in their designers' practices, and only a small group compared to those designed by Salvin, Burn and other professional country house architects. The architects who specialized in Gothic country houses tended to be the dimmer or less dedicated Gothicists, men like Ferrey, Norton and P. C. Hardwick. The situation changed as religious enthusiasm cooled. Webb, Nesfield, Shaw and Godwin, the cream of their generation among the Gothicists, were all concentrating on domestic work in the 1860s. They became increasingly aware how many agreeable and livable-in houses

66

had been built in England after the Middle Ages; even if their taste was still unable to go beyond the early eighteenth century the claim that Gothic was the only national English way of building began to seem ridiculous.

31. *The Architect as Artist*

THE WAY that Gothic architects lived was changing too. The older men were very conscious of leading the architectural wing of a religious revival; they were high minded, earnest and often a little forbidding. Architects like Scott, White and Teulon came from backgrounds which were heavily encrusted with clerical relatives. The first notable deviant was William Burges, an architect who seems to have had no strong religious feelings, irritated his fellow architects by his irrepressible facetiousness, and had a weakness for Bohemian society. W. E. Nesfield was described by Simeon Solomon as 'a fat, jolly, hearty fellow, genuinely good natured, very fond of smoking and, I deeply grieve to say, of women'.[93] J. J. Stevenson was known to his family as 'Uncle Jaughty', an abbreviation for 'Naughty John'.[94] Edward Godwin cut himself off from conventional society by eloping with Ellen Terry, and ended up working almost entirely for artists and for the theatre. In a rather different category was Philip Webb, serious minded and high principled to the point of prickliness, a latter day Butterfield in fact, but an agnostic Butterfield.

J. M. Brydon, nostalgically describing Nesfield's office many years later, wrote that it resembled 'the studio of an artist rather than the business room of a professional man'.[95] By the 1890s Sir Charles Nicholson could refer to 'the atmosphere savouring of the Latin quarter in some of the architects' offices in those days'.[96] Socially, one can picture the first generation Gothicists as moving from rectory to rectory, their pupils as moving from studio to studio. Burges, Nesfield, Godwin and Webb moved in the same overlapping circles as Rossetti, Morris, Burne-Jones, Whistler and Albert Moore. They thought of themselves as artists not professionals. They were full of scorn for 'practical men'.

These particular groups of architects and artists moved together because they disliked the society into which they had been born. So to some extent, at least, had the earlier generation of Gothicists, but for different reasons. They had been part of a middle-class revolt against upper-class values, against what they considered a frivolous, corrupt, heartless and godless society. Now a part of the middle class were revolting against middle-class values, against an earnest, smug, hypocritical, joyless and above all ugly society. As the great Victorian boom continued, its visual results became increasingly dominant; more and more fields and orchards were swallowed up by new housing estates, more and more factories and slums rose around larger and larger industrial towns. The medieval church mercilessly scraped and made shiny with encaustic tiles seemed as much a product of an age insensitive to visual values as the prosperous merchant in his Bayswater house, with garish colours in the drawing room and family prayers in the dining room.

Reaction against mid-Victorian surroundings impelled people in various directions. First, it sent them back once more to the Middle Ages, but this time they went there for social and aesthetic rather than religious reasons, because they found them the complete antithesis to an industrial and urban society. But once the religious element was removed there was no reason why other pre-industrial societies, whether in Japan, Greece or Florence, should not appear equally attractive. Above all, the whole English rural tradition began to seem increasingly precious and threatened, and it was seen that this tradition included not only medieval churches and barns, but sixteenth- and seventeenth-century farmhouses, red-brick early Georgian houses in the market places and backstreets of country towns, in short the whole English vernacular tradition.

 ## 32. *Artistic Houses and Artistic People*

THE YOUNG artists and artist–architects of the 1860s and the patrons who supported them, knew what to call themselves: they were 'artistic'.[97] The expression, so sadly devalued today, was then the label of the *avant-garde*. Artistic people were not exclusively dedicated to the arts of one period; in an artistic house everything down to the smallest detail was selected with a discrimination that could make a harmonious whole out of new and old, and out of elements derived from all over the world. The idea of an architect enlisting the help of his fellow artists to produce an entire environment had originated with William Morris's Red House. In 1872 Shaw's Grim's Dyke, built for the Academician Frederick Goodall, was described in the *Building News* as 'an artistic house by an artist for an artist'.[98] But, although many of these houses were built for artists, even more were built for those of the rich who enjoyed the company and neighbourhood of artists. Almost all of them were designed by architects trained in the Gothic tradition, and almost none of them were Gothic. The sight of their best pupils abandoning the straight and narrow path for a wide-ranging eclecticism was very painful to the first generation Gothicists, especially since it brought in clients in shoals to the younger men.

For architects and society were changing together, and creating the atmosphere of late Victorian England in which heightened visual awareness was one aspect of a new feeling for the pleasures as well as the duties of life. Moral earnestness began to seem a little absurd, and it was becoming more fashionable to be beautiful, clever or rich than to be good. The increasing and increasingly educated middle class provided the main recruiting ground for that typical phenomenon of the 1870s and 1880s, the lady of artistic tastes. But the change affected all ranks of society, and in the circles that pivoted round Rossetti, Burne-Jones and others of the later pre-Raphaelites the old and the new rich mixed freely with artists in a *camaraderie* of beauty lovers—just as the old and new rich of another type circled round the Prince of Wales in a *camaraderie* of dash and money.

33. Kerr and Stevenson

ONE CAN sense the change of atmosphere very nicely in W. H. Mallock's *New Republic* (1879). The book includes the description of a sophisticated and free-thinking house party collected by Otho Laurence in the house of his uncle, who had been 'possessed of a deep though quiet antipathy to the two things generally most cherished by those of his time and order, the ideas of Christianity and Feudalism'. From a more architectural angle it is amusing to read in succession Robert Kerr's *The Gentleman's House* (1864) and J. J. Stevenson's *House Architecture* (published in 1880, but, according to its author, written at intervals over the previous twelve years). Kerr belongs to the secular wing of high-Victorian architecture and his book is quite without the moral earnestness of Scott's *Secular and Domestic Architecture*; but Stevenson's book is much lighter in touch, more elegantly presented, and with a feeling that houses should be designed to be enjoyable as well as convenient. Typical of Stevenson is his comment on the nurseries: 'a view of scenery is of little importance; children will find a farmyard, where they can see cocks and hens and pigeons, or even the rubbing down of horses, much more interesting'.[99] Or on bedrooms: 'one group may be appropriated to bachelors, a separate group to young ladies, giving facilities for those long talks at night in each other's rooms when, with their back hair down—if we take Mr. Thackeray's word for it—they open their hearts to each other in mutual confidences'.[100] Kerr recommends the same arrangement for a different reason: 'when young ladies are placed altogether under the responsible charge of the governess, she will prefer that their sleeping rooms and her own should adjoin'.[101]

Stevenson criticized Kerr, explicitly or implicitly, for the compartmentalization typical of the high-Victorian age; in Kerr's case compartmentalization of classes and of functions. He attacked Kerr for his treatment of servants as an inferior class, 'whom it is shocking to the refined feelings of their superiors to see or to come in contact with'.[102] He considered that 'the economic development of the servants' offices characteristic of modern planning is not without its disadvantages. All these places, with the interminable passages connecting them, have to be kept in order'.[103] A favourite idea of his was that of replacing a number of separate sitting rooms by 'one great room'.

Stevenson could appreciate what a 'very pleasant and homely sitting room' a kitchen–living room in 'simple old houses' could be;[104] but he would never have conceived the possibility of his readers living in this kind of a room. Even his feeling for servants turns out to be thickly hedged with reservations ('none of their windows should command the lawn or private garden',[105] etc.) and the 'one great room' is only recommended for 'seaside villas or country summer quarters, where the restraints of society are lightened, where formal calls are happily unknown, and neighbours gather familiarly on wet days in each other's houses'.[106]

The (to Victorian eyes) informal way in which 'artistic' people lived was in advance of general standards; in particular, in most country houses the 'restraints of society' were still far from light. The architects under discussion found their most sympathetic clients among artists and the friends of artists, among the livelier middle

classes, among able industrialists who had not yet gone county. Stevenson's book was explicitly slanted towards 'the requirements of the upper middle class'. It was the moderate-sized houses they built which gained English domestic architecture an international reputation in the late nineteenth and early twentieth centuries. Impressive though many late Victorian country houses are, their architects did their best work on a smaller scale and in a more informal manner than the country house tradition would allow.

34. *Five Architects*

WILLIAM BURGES stands apart from other dedicated Gothicists because his relationship with the Middle Ages was almost entirely a romantic and visual rather than a religious one—so that his interests could spread quite naturally outside the bounds of Christianity to Turkey, Greece and Japan. His work, which was almost equally divided between religious and secular architecture, is neither religious nor secular in tone, but consistently Burgean throughout, distinguished by a crowded and individual imagination, a wide range of scholarship, a rich texture of decoration and iconography and a minute attention to detail. At Gayhurst (1859) his additions and decorations to an earlier building provided one of the first foretastes of the artistic house. The combination of painting, carving and sculpture found in its interior flourished amazingly in the later work he did for the Marquess of Bute (1868–81) and for himself in Kensington (1875–81). But Burges always remained a medievalist, and his buildings preserved until the end the bulk and weight of the 1860s. They were too overpowering to be easy to live in for anyone but their creator. They are wonderful buildings, but their influence was waning in the 1870s. The men who counted in the domestic revolution of those years were William Eden Nesfield, Richard Norman Shaw, Philip Webb and, to a lesser extent, John J. Stevenson.

The background of the four men was interesting and varied. Shaw and Stevenson had connections in the business world, which were to be important in their practices. Shaw's brother was the founder of the shipping firm of Shaw, Savill & Co.[107] Stevenson's family were prosperous Durham chemical manufacturers, with a

39. Muscular Gothic. Outbuildings by William Burges at Gayhurst, Buckinghamshire, 1859. The building on the left contained lavatories grouped round a common ventilating shaft.

factory at Jarrow.[108] Nesfield's connections were equally important to him, but of a different kind. He was the nephew of Salvin and the son of W. A. Nesfield, the most successful early Victorian landscape gardener. He had county relations,[109] had been to Eton and was socially a cut above the other three. Webb was the son of a country doctor, and the brother of a clergyman—good Tractarian material. Webb was in Street's office from about 1853 to 1859, Shaw from 1858 to 1862 or 1863. Stevenson was in Scott's office in the late 1850s.

Nesfield did not have this dedicated Gothicist background. He was in the office of Burn from 1851 to 1853 and of his uncle Salvin from 1853 to 1856. Shaw was in Burn's office before he went to Street, and while in it had been the star architectural student at the Royal Academy school. The two young men made friends. They became keen Goths together, travelled in France in 1854 and went to see Viollet-le-Duc. Nesfield set up in practice on his own in 1860, and Shaw joined him in 1862 or 1863. Their training had given them a nice balance: Salvin represented the best of the picturesque tradition, Street the best of the Gothic revival, and Burn the greatest professional competence in country house planning. The combination was to be reflected in their architecture.

Shaw and Nesfield form a couple not unlike Vanbrugh and Hawksmoor. It is hard to disentangle who influenced whom, and Shaw's reputation ultimately completely swallowed up that of Nesfield. The work done during the few years of the partnership is usually attributed in contemporary sources to one or other of them individually, and Brydon, who was in Nesfield's office later on, says that each of them kept to his own work.[110] But there must have been much mutual discussion and enthusiasm in those years, which continued after the partnership was dissolved in 1868, for they shared an office until 1876. Blomfield's dictum that 'Nesfield talked about the work and Shaw did it'[111] is nonsense; Shaw was a great architect but Nesfield was a gifted one, and between them they revolutionized English domestic architecture.

35. *The Old English Style*

THE COURSE the partnership was to steer was set by Nesfield before Shaw joined him. In the long list of 'Selected examples of Gothic buildings' at the end of Eastlake's *History of the Gothic Revival* (1872) buildings are classified (by the architects themselves, on forms which were sent to them by Eastlake) under the date, situation, architect and style. In the 'style' column the line of 'Early English', 'Very Early Decorated', 'Geometrical Decorated', 'Geometrical Second Pointed', 'Early Middle Pointed' or, more loosely, 'Domestic Gothic' is suddenly interrupted by the gloriously vague 'Old English'.[112] The description is applied by Nesfield to his half-timbered and plastered cottages at Hampton-in-Arden in Warwickshire (*c.* 1860–8). Nesfield and Shaw were to use it for many of their domestic buildings, and it came to be applied to the movement in domestic architecture that they inaugurated. 'Old English' had been a term widely used earlier in the century to describe both Tudor–Gothic and Elizabethan houses. By reviving it, Shaw and Nesfield were perhaps affirming their

approval of the picturesque tradition. But they were also underlining their distaste for their age, for Modern French and Modern Gothic, the Gothic of plate-glass sash windows and structural polychromy. Its lack of precision, too, was just what they needed. It expressed a preference for eclecticism rather than scholarship, for ways of building rather than stylistic correctness, for the vernacular rather than high style (which in Gothic tended to mean church style), for plastering, brickwork, half-timbering and tile-hanging rather than plate-tracery and stiff-leafed capitals.

In 1864 Nesfield brought the vernacular into the heart of London in the little tile-hung lodge that he designed in Regent's Park. In 1866 his red-brick lodge in Kew Gardens was a more stylistically ambitious excursion into the seventeenth century. But these were both small buildings. Cloverley Hall in Shropshire, the great house commissioned by the Liverpool banker J. P. Heywood on which he spent most of his energy between 1864 and 1868 was a superb and early example of an artistic house. His friend Albert Moore collaborated on the details which included a great eaves frieze of sunflowers and other flowers made of beaten lead, and numerous sculptured chimneypieces. Its clusters of elongated chimneystacks and profusion of carved texts which would undoubtedly have been called 'quaint' at the time were later, along with sunflowers and lilies, to become clichés in all 'artistic' buildings. But in spite of these enrichments, and a touch of Japanese ornament here and there, the house remained unmistakably Gothic and in the grand manner.

In 1865 Nesfield applied his Old English manner to Farnham Park, a small country house in Buckinghamshire, designed for a successful London solicitor. This was a low comfortable brick building with many tile-hung gables, a small tower, wooden-framed windows and a wooden verandah in his characteristic style of joinery. In the same year Shaw was working in a similar manner at Willesley in Kent for J. C. Horsley, the Royal Academician. His work here consisted of tile-hung and plastered additions to an old Kent farmhouse; besides being one of the first commissions of his private practice, it was the first of many jobs that came to him from the Royal Academy. It was followed by a delightful new house in the same manner, Glen Andred (1866), for E. W. Cooke, the marine painter. This was roomy, but far from large. In 1868 he designed a grander job, Leys Wood, for J. W. Temple, managing director of the Shaw, Savill Line, the shipping line started by his brother in the 1850s. He exhibited a drawing of the house at the Royal Academy in 1870, and it quite rightly caused a sensation.

40. Artistic Gothic. Cloverley Hall, Shropshire (W. E. Nesfield, 1864–70).

41. Old English. Leys Wood, Kent (R. Norman Shaw, 1868).

36. Leys Wood

CONTEMPORARIES had no hesitation about choosing an adjective to describe Leys Wood. It was 'quaint'; and it suddenly became clear both to City businessmen looking for a quiet corner to commute from, and to prosperous artists anxious to invest their Academy winnings, that quaintness was what they wanted. Moreover, its quaintness was served up with dash and brilliance and, as Eastlake put it, 'for all its quaintness there is nothing in the interior of the house incompatible with modern ideas of comfort and convenience'—as long, at any rate, as labour to dust the quaint corners and mend the innumerable roofs still remained cheap. Its effect had been obtained by a radical revision of the image of a country house, from a picturesque rather than a practical point of view. In the 1860s the standard country house consisted of a basic formula, however much notched, faceted and tricked out with gables and towers, of a high main block adjoining a lower servants' block. It stood on a levelled site, with formal gardens and terraces round it. Its rooms were high and its windows large and filled with plate glass. Its architect could pinpoint its style with confidence, if not accuracy, as Early Middle Pointed, Scotch Baronial, Palatial Italian, or one of a dozen others. But Leys Wood had no garden to speak of and followed the contours in the middle of a wood on the edge of a rocky drop. It was designed as a cluster of different elements and roofs of different heights around a courtyard. Leaded lights and plate glass, large windows and small ones under the eaves, high rooms and low rooms, were skilfully mixed up together. Under the blanket of 'Old English' it drew on a number of different periods and strata, with Gothic arches, Tudor windows, seventeenth-century chimneystacks, half-timbering and tile-hanging artistically sprinkled with panels of sunflowers and other aesthetic trimmings. Inside, that picturesque feature of yeoman homesteads, the inglenook, had been brought up to date with panelling and Japanese porcelain and made a feature of the dining room. Shaw had already used the inglenook at Willesley and Glen Andred; and Nesfield, at Farnham Park.[113] Nesfield had used rooms of different levels and of different heights at Cloverley. Yet as a whole the recipe was new and took the country, or at least the home counties, by storm. 'Old English' had been put on the map; and 'Old English' meant, not the imitation of a style, but the creation of an atmosphere.

73

42, 43. Old English cosiness and oriental china. Inglenooks at Leys Wood, Kent (R. Norman Shaw, 1868); Farnham Park, Buckinghamshire (W. E. Nesfield, c. 1865).

The Leys Wood formula, especially as greatly enlarged and much publicized at Cragside, suggested an alternative setting for the country house: not the house in the park, but the house in the forest. The later Victorians had no great love for open spaces; a number of other country houses, such as Beauvale, Blackmoor and Minley Manor, were to be closely hemmed in by woodlands. But the formula was to be especially popular for more modest houses, where generous planting of conifers assured privacy on a site of two or three acres. Hence arose the great suburban forests of the Home Counties.

37. 'Queen Anne'

THERE WAS just enough of Gothic detail at Leys Wood, combined with what was considered the Gothic spirit in which the plan and composition had been handled, to make it acceptable to the strict Gothic Revivalists. But in 1873 indignant explosions were to be heard in the architecture room of the Royal Academy as they saw what their golden boy had got up to now. New Zealand Chambers in Leadenhall Street, designed in 1872 as the offices of the Shaw, Savill Line, was a brilliant variation, in bright red brick and clean white painted woodwork, of the mid-seventeenth-century Sparrowe's House in Ipswich. Hanging on the walls around it was further evidence of revolt in the Gothic ranks, in the work of three of G. G. Scott's most promising pupils, Bodley, J. J. Stevenson and E. R. Robson. Bodley's London School Board Offices were inspired by the French Renaissance; Robson and Stevenson exhibited drawings of the first of a long series of London Board Schools, bold and original designs avowedly based on 'the simple brick style . . . of the time of the Jameses, Queen Anne and the early Georges'.

Although the style that came to be christened (for no very good reason) 'Queen Anne'[114] first hit the public notice in 1873, it had been germinating for a number of years, marked at one end by Philip Webb's Red House in Bexley Heath of 1859, at the other by J. J. Stevenson's Red House in Bayswater of 1871. Webb's Red House was in the Butterfield vicarage tradition; a simple red-brick Gothic revival design but with small-paned sash windows of early eighteenth-century type. In his Lincoln's Inn Field's offices (1861), in the house that he designed for the aristocrat artist George Howard on Kensington Palace Green (1868) and in his first large country house, Rounton Grange in Yorkshire (1872–6), the post-medieval elements became steadily stronger (Pl. 411). Nesfield's lodge at Kew had been followed around 1870 by his masterpiece at Kinmel, closely followed by Stevenson's Red House, the prototype of hundreds and probably thousands of terrace houses of the late nineteenth century.

The essence of 'Queen Anne' was the combination of Gothic Revival grouping, free planning and asymmetry with detail drawn from the whole range of English and Dutch red-brick architecture of the seventeenth and early eighteenth centuries (with French and Flemish touches from the sixteenth century). 'Free Classic' and

74

'Anglo-Dutch' were more sensible descriptions suggested for it, but 'Queen Anne' was the one that caught on. It enfuriated both the old Gothicists and the old Classicists, the Gothicists because it was classic and the Classicists because it was Free, and because by those brought up in the Barry Italian palazzo tradition, Anglo-Dutch brick architecture was considered beneath contempt. But its prettiness and liveliness proved irresistible, and it had an enormous success.

Among the cheerful diversity of Queen Anne town and suburban houses, riverside villas, seaside hotels, public houses, town halls, schools, colleges, flats and hospitals there are, perhaps not surprisingly, almost no Queen Anne churches and more curiously, very few Queen Anne country houses. An explanation for this is suggested by a remark in the text of Bruce Talbert's *Examples of Ancient and Modern Furniture* (1876). He, like most of his contemporaries, thought of Queen Anne as essentially a brick style, and brick, he wrote, 'is not adapted to the refinements of which the more noble materials are capable, and though quite suitable to the picturesque or quaint style of building, it is quite unfitted for the development of what is admitted to be the higher order of architectural art. A Queen Anne house in stone or marble! It would be an absurdity.' Absurdity or not, Talbert's old employer J. J. Stevenson designed a stone Queen Anne house at Ken Hill in Norfolk, in 1879, and the *Building News* commented: 'picturesque enough and quaint, but not very like a gentleman's house'.[115] Kerr's qualities of 'elegance and importance without ostentation' were still considered necessary for a country house and Queen Anne was not thought of as an 'important' style. It would do well enough for the seaside, or even the London season, but for a country J.P. to get himself up in this Kate Greenaway rig was a different matter.[116] Yet to present day eyes Ken Hill (Pls. 349–60) and Nesfield's Loughton Hall in Essex may seem amongst the most attractive of Victorian country houses.

38. Shaw: Composition and Planning

IN THE LATE 1860s two small country houses in Kent, Fowler's Park and West Wickham House, were remodelled by Shaw in a pioneering version of the Queen Anne style. The equally modest Banstead Wood (1884–90) was in his tile-hung Old English manner with a flavour of Queen Anne to it—a ponderous description which gives no idea of the freshness and charm of one of his most engaging designs. But he never built a large Queen Anne country house. For the important commissions which

75

44. 'Queen Anne'. Loughton Hall, Essex (W. E. Nesfield, 1878).

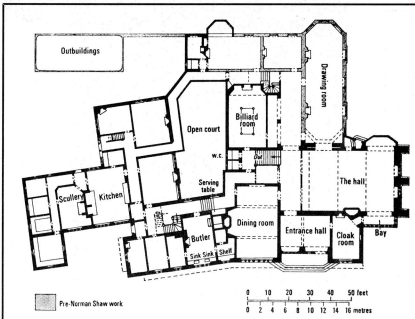

Outbuildings

Drawing room

Open court

Billiard room

w.c.

Out

Serving table

The hall

Scullery | Kitchen

Butler

Dining room

Entrance hall

Cloak room

Bay

Sink Sink Shelf

Pre-Norman Shaw work

| 0 | 10 | 20 | 30 | 40 | 50 feet |
| 0 | 2 4 | 6 8 | 10 12 | 14 | 16 metres |

Fig. 5. Pierrepont, Surrey (R. Norman Shaw, 1876–8). The ground-floor plan.

came his way in the 1870s and 80s he evolved a more 'important' version of Old English, displayed at Adcote (1877), Flete (1878), Greenham Lodge (1879), additions to Cragside (1884) and Dawpool (1882). These more monumental, usually stone-built buildings were thought of by his contemporaries as wonderful re-creations of Old English manor houses; but analysis shows how highly personal was his mixture of medieval, Tudor and Jacobean motifs.

Like Pugin, but for picturesque rather than moral reasons, Shaw split his houses up into numerous different elements. He must have seen and been attracted by the haphazard contrasts and combinations to be found in an old country house which has grown up by accretions over the years. But he replaced the accidental effects of old buildings by deliberate and sophisticated contrasts of roof lines, windows and the slope of gables. The framework of his compositions is usually provided by the long horizontal lines of his roofs contrasted with the drawn-out verticals of his chimneystacks; the total effect is of something much longer and lower than the more hunched up masses of high-Victorian design. Shaw had probably studied to good effect the spread-out combinations of horizontal and vertical to be found in early nineteenth-century castles; but his own buildings produce a quite different effect because of his prominent expanses of steep pitched roof and many gables, always kept subservient to the line of the roof-ridge but playing a variant theme beneath it.

Shaw was also fond of contrasting heavily windowed areas with areas of solid or near solid wall, and of scattering his windows in an apparently random but in fact highly calculated way. He may have got hints in this direction from the work of both Salvin and Pearson, but was probably also influenced by the composition of Japanese prints: Japanese art was much admired by the artistic set in the 1860s and 1870s, and in London Godwin was experimenting with even bolder Japanese-style compositions in his artists' houses in Chelsea.

The separation into elements which is so prominent a feature of Shaw houses externally is also very noticeable internally; one gets the impression of going

76

through a sequence of different units rather than subdivision of one large whole. His plans are additive, made up of pieces put together like a game of dominoes; sometimes they are put together to make up a reasonably solid mass, sometimes, as at Cragside and Flete, they are spread out in a series of limbs. In fact his houses are usually carefully organized around a relatively simple system of corridors; however irregular the external effect, it is much easier to find ones way round a Shaw house than a Burn one.[117] A prominent feature of many of them is a medieval style Great Hall used more as a sitting room than an entrance or dining room; but otherwise, although he loosened up the framework, his houses usually have the same sequence of rooms as high-Victorian ones, and his service wings are almost as large, if slightly less subdivided; but his ceilings tend to be lower, his rooms darker, some windows smaller and others larger so that there is more variety of light and shade than in the houses of the previous generation. Changes of height and level, flight of steps, inglenooks and deep bays of different sizes added to the variety. The results were admired by his contemporaries as piquant, picturesque, old world or quaint. These adjectives, particularly the last two, have been debased since his day so it is perhaps better to describe his special quality as a combination of romanticism and wit, as expressed in the mighty overmantel at Dawpool, with little windows in its upper stages through which people in the upper storeys could peer down into the hall, in the receding timber trellises of his staircase at Flete, or in his inglenooks with their own private windows, making them little rooms within a room.

The irregular and often spread-out plans favoured by Shaw and his imitators, and even more by his independent contemporary George Devey (see p. 83), seem hopelessly impractical in a twentieth-century context. In their own day they made considerable sense. A nation-wide railway network had combined with low taxation and cheap servants to produce the apogee of the country house weekend. Hordes of guests descended suddenly by rail on Friday evenings, and vanished as suddenly on Monday. The additive plan was exactly suited to deal with this violent

45. (above left) Millionaire inglenook-cum-organ at Dawpool, Cheshire (R. Norman Shaw, 1882–4).

46. (above right) The staircase at Flete, Devon (R. Norman Shaw, 1878–80).

fluctuation in a country house population. The sequence of different towers, staircases and wings combined to form a series of different bedroom suites which could be filled up for house parties and conveniently forgotten in the intervals, without the house seeming empty; and the inglenooks, bay windows, galleries and changes in level provided a series of different focuses, of recesses for different groups to retire to, which gave scope for a complex and sophisticated social life.

39. The Hall Revived

ONE SIGN of this diversification of social life was the habit, found in some big houses, of seating the house party at a series of small tables, as though in a restaurant. Mary Gladstone commented on it when she was staying with the Countess Brownlow at Ashridge in December 1875 (with Disraeli as one of the guests): 'To dinner with Mr. Compton. All in small tables.'[118] A late Victorian photograph shows the breakfast room at Eaton Hall arranged in this way.

But the nerve-centre of the later Victorian country house was the hall, in a new role. Sir Gilbert Scott's suggestion that a great hall could make 'a delightful sitting room, particularly in summer', has already been referred to (p. 46). An old photograph shows his music hall at Kelham (1858–61) furnished as a sitting room (Pl. 219). At Cloverley (1864–70) W. E. Nesfield introduced a roomy great hall, separate from the entrance hall and with the main staircase coming down into one end of it. Shaw's Leys Wood (1868) has no more than a staircase hall with a fireplace, but from the mid-1870s onwards nearly all his larger houses have a great hall, usually

78

47. (above left) The breakfast room at Eaton Hall, Cheshire, from a late Victorian photograph.

48. (above right) The hall as living room. Merrist Wood, Surrey (R. Norman Shaw, 1877).

with the main stairs adjacent and the screens passage and gallery combined with the main corridors of the house. George Devey preferred what he tended to call a saloon, a big two-storeyed room, usually with the staircase coming down into it, but with little reminiscent of a great hall in its shape or arrangement. By the 1880s a Nesfield–Shaw hall or a Devey saloon were commonplaces in new country houses of all types and sizes.

These rooms were equipped with a big fireplace (and sometimes an inglenook) and furnished with carpets and at least a few comfortable chairs. Sometimes they were closed off and became living rooms pure and simple, but often, when adjacent or combined with the main corridors and staircases, they acquired a multi-purpose role, part living room, part meeting place, a venue for games and parties, and a setting for afternoon tea, which reached its most flourishing heights in late Victorian days (Margot Tennant's friendship with Benjamin Jowett started when she fell flat at his feet while performing an impromptu dance at tea in the marble hall (Pl. 424) at Gosford). Henry James nicely summarizes the atmosphere of an English late Victorian hall in his novel *The Other House*: 'Bright, large, and high, richly decorated and freely used, full of "corners" and communications, it evidently played equally the part of a place of re-union and a place of transit.'[119]

The flourishing of the hall in this usefully ambiguous role marks the beginning of a movement away from the minutely specialized and sealed-off spaces of high-Victorian houses. But the hall remained only a supplement to the usual living rooms; it was in America, where the idea was eagerly taken up and far more radically developed, that the living hall became increasingly dominant and led the way to the open-plan house.

40. *Philip Webb*

DISCRIMINATING people of the time might have agreed that Norman Shaw and Philip Webb were the leading domestic architects of their day. The inner ring of the discriminating would have put Webb above Shaw. They were born in the same year, they both worked in Street's office as young men, they both broke away from the Gothic discipline, yet they were very different characters, and regarded each other with respect rather than sympathy. Shaw was a natural showman, who used vernacular architecture as material for a new act; Webb saw it as part of a tradition of good building, and himself as playing the role of the honest country builder, who knew his materials and how to get the best out of them. He hated anything fancy, flash or clever. The idea of a pot-pourri of stylistic tit-bits, however cleverly dished up, was repugnant to him; he had no desire to be quaint. He drew ideas from a wide range of sources, but worked and worried over them so thoroughly that the results, both as a whole and in detail, were completely personal. His integrity impressed his contemporaries and remains impressive today. He worked out a body of principles and remained consistent to them. Unlike Shaw, whose buildings always received the maximum publicity both in Royal Academy exhibitions and in the architectural press, he never

exhibited his designs or allowed them to be illustrated. He only employed one assistant, took on comparatively few jobs, and executed them with meticulous thoroughness; as a result his income was never large and he died not far removed from poverty.

Webb was the friend of William Morris, and the favoured architect of a cultivated circle who patronized the later pre-Raphaelites, a circle linked by their artistic interests but ranging over a widish social circuit and including successful professional men, industrialists like the Bells, and aristocrats like the Howards and Wyndhams. Shaw was never an aristocrat's architect; his mainstay were successful academicians and the industrialists who bought their pictures. He bore down on the rich with confidence and charm and took their money off them with gusto. Webb was the acme of rectitude and carefulness about money, but lectured and bullied his clients mercilessly, for the good of their souls—a treatment which they appear to have found enjoyable. Estimation of the relative standing of the two men will always vary from person to person. Shaw was a little lacking in principle and a little too facile; but he had amazing creative abundance and zest for living. Webb was an honourable man; but there are times when one wishes that he could have enjoyed himself a bit more.

 ## 41. *Clouds*

WEBB's *magnum opus* was the very large house he designed for Percy Wyndham, a younger son of Lord Leconfield, at Clouds in Wiltshire. He was given the commission at the end of 1876. It took three years' hard work and several preliminary designs before the design was agreed on in November 1879. Difficulties in finding a builder occupied another two years, but the house was finally started in November 1881 and finished by the end of 1886. Two years later, in January 1889, the greater part was gutted by fire, and another three years were needed to restore it. In recent years the top storey has been removed and the house mutilated inside and out almost beyond recognition.

Balfour was a friend of the Percy Wyndhams and so was Burne-Jones. The two names give the ambience of the house: political entertaining combined with artistic discrimination. The style, sensibility and relative informality with which the two

80

49. Clouds, Wiltshire (Philip Webb, 1879–91).

were pursued made Clouds one of the most famous country houses of its era. The descendants—through blood or friendship—of the Wyndham circle can be traced by way of the Souls and the Clique, through all the ramifications of Wyndhams, Charterises, Asquiths, Manners, Horners, Listers, Grenfells, Tennants, Balfours, Herberts and Lyttons, down to the present day.

Webb's problem was to give architectural expression to this way of life and to produce a 'great house' without being pompous or having to resort to the architectural pastiche or fancy-dress trimmings that he so disliked. Contemporaries thought that he had succeeded: Percy Wyndham told him that it was the 'house of the age'[120] and Scawen Blunt extolled its 'super-excellence as a type of the best Victorian architecture'.[121]

The body of the house was built of green sandstone, but the upper storeys were of brick, or alternating courses of brick and stone, with weather-boarding in the gables. The gables were interrupted by occasional low turrets and there was a big water tower. A service wing, low and inconspicuous in comparison to the high mass of the main block, was attached as a virtually independent building, connected by two long corridors enclosing a courtyard. The windows were mostly sash windows, painted white; there was no carving externally, but a good deal of modelling, in the form of recessed arches, moulded window surrounds, and elaborate corbel tables. The result was a building that could only have been designed by Webb, entirely personal and original. It is hard to judge it today, especially as Webb did not design houses to be photogenic but to be lived in. One gets the impression of a house big-boned in its main lines, rather fussy in its details, and with a complete lack of stylishness—but then did Webb want stylishness? Even so, it is difficult not to feel that too much care and thought went into the detailing, and that through its immensely long gestation the house lost both in cohesion and spontaneity.

The interior is easier to appreciate, and in its day it was revolutionary. It got away from the tradition of all-embracing intricacy which had been the accepted form of decoration since early Victorian days, and which Webb and Shaw had accepted in their earlier interiors. The dominant colour at Clouds was white, with a touch of colour from Morris materials here and there, and a certain amount of simple panelling of unstained wood. Photographs give the impression of big, light, uncluttered rooms and of reticent decoration, the perfect background for large and informal weekend parties. Clouds was one of the houses that set the style for a

50. The library at Clouds, Wiltshire (Philip Webb, 1879–91).

particular way of country house life, perhaps one of the most agreeable ways of living that has ever been devised. It proved itself adaptable to the loss of its most unsympathetic feature, the community of servants living apart and literally on a different plane, flitting inconspicuously up and down the back staircases. As Lethaby put it, 'it was the affectation of the time that work was done by magic: it was vulgar to recognize its existence or even to see anybody doing it'.[122]

42. *Shaw's Contemporaries: Ernest George*

NESFIELD and Shaw's Old English style influenced many of their contemporaries, such as Ewan Christian at the Highlands (*c.* 1874) and Waterhouse in his additions and interiors at Blackmoor (1882). Cowdray Park in Sussex (1875, architect unknown) is one of innumerable minor examples to be found of an Old English house in the Shaw manner. In the north John Douglas and E. A. L. Ould, both of Cheshire, specialized in half-timbered houses derived from their close study of local examples, but were noticeably influenced by Shaw's mannerisms, as at Broxton and Wightwick. Among the younger contemporaries of Shaw much the most successful was Ernest George. Rousdon (1874), his first country house (Pl. 9), and his earlier buildings in London have many Shaw touches about them, though the plan of Rousdon is more regular than anything Shaw would have done at that date. In Harrington Gardens and Cadogan Square he went on to develop his own overpoweringly quaint Flemish-Renaissance manner, a kind of *paté de foie* architecture which in small sharp doses can be highly enjoyable. Either he or his patrons must have considered the style too exotic for country house use, and he only employed it out of London at the ebullient Buchan Hill (1882), the ostrich feather merchant's house in Sussex (Pl. 389). One could have done with more Buchan Hills; but as George's practice grew more aristocratic his buildings became better behaved. Stoodleigh (1883), Batsford (1889) and Motcombe (1893–5) are large, competent and tasteful houses that inspire little affection.

82

51. The hall at Buchan Hill, Sussex (George and Peto, 1882–3).

43. *George Devey: a Postscript*

THE MOST interesting country houses designed outside the immediate Shaw–Nesfield–Webb circle were by George Devey.[123] Devey ought, chronologically, to have had an earlier mention. He was ten years older than Shaw and his earlier buildings anticipated the way Shaw, Nesfield and Webb were to go well before they had achieved their first independent commissions. He was the first Victorian architect to work out a way of building derived from the local vernacular, at a time when other architects tended to see their buildings as existing in a vacuum, independent of any local traditions. In the early 1850s he was designing cottages in the Kent vernacular manner at Penshurst, and in 1856 went on to use his local knowledge on a country house scale at Betteshanger (described on pp. 215–19). Its rambling plan, low-ceilinged rooms, and mixture of details drawn from different periods, are suggestive of what Shaw and Nesfield were going to do ten years later; it incorporates the pedimented Flemish gables which were to become a favourite motif of the 'Queen Anne' style. In between these two extremes his many-gabled Hammerfield (1856–9) at Penshurst was a modest but comfortable gentleman's house which became a prototype of what contemporaries called his 'cottages'—a label which at the best known of them, Ascott (1874–86), was attached to a house of some thirty bedrooms. Devey developed the Betteshanger and Hammerfield formulas as the basis of a steadily increasing country house practice, which reached its peak in the 1870s. The device of adding on a wing at an apparently haphazard obtuse angle to the main body of the house, which Shaw used at Grim's Dyke (1872) and Pierrepont (1876) had already been used by Devey at Coombe Warren (c. 1865) and was developed to excess in the zig-zag plan of his later houses. By the time of his death in 1886 he had designed more country house work than Shaw, Nesfield and Webb put together.

Devey has not been given precedence of treatment because as an architect he deliberately kept out of the main stream; he practiced in isolation in a secure little world of aristocrats and rich bankers. Like Webb, he never exhibited his designs, and never let his buildings be published; unlike Webb, he was never one of a close circle of architects and artists who knew and admired what he was doing. But although there is no positive evidence it is tempting to surmise some contact between him and the younger men in the 1860s; the fact that Nesfield and Shaw had their office in the next street to his would have made this topographically easy.

52. (above left) Hammerfield, Penshurst, Kent (George Devey, 1856–9).
53. (above right) Coombe Warren, Surrey (George Devey, 1870).

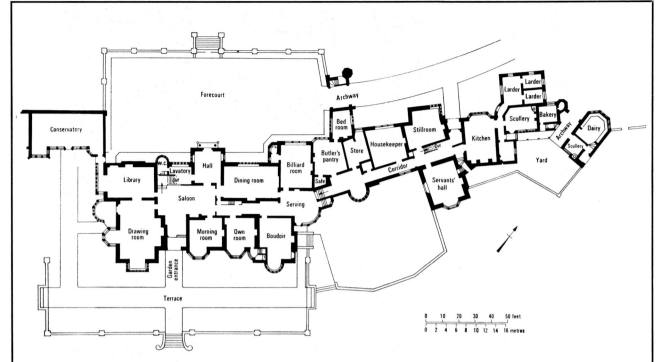

Fig. 6. Goldings, Hertfordshire (George Devey 1871–7). The ground-floor plan (this plan is to 79% scale of the other plans).

Nesfield and Devey had both, at different times, studied under J. D. Harding, the artist and art teacher, who was a prolific depictor of old manor houses and crumbling cottages. Devey had also studied under Cotman; and Nesfield, through his father, was well acquainted since childhood with the whole closely-knit world of water-colour artists working in the picturesque manner. This background was important to Devey, Nesfield and Shaw; but whatever the similarities their approach was basically a different one. All three got ideas from the accidental asymmetries of country houses built and altered over a long period. But Shaw (and to a lesser extent Nesfield) used this kind of building as a starting point from which he developed his own taut and highly calculated compositions. Devey wanted his houses to be as rambling and accidental looking as their prototypes. Although he had an architectural training, his training as a painter under Cotman and Harding was a more formative influence in his life. Harding's ivy-clad rural buildings have an obvious relevance to Devey's country houses, which appear to have been deliberately designed to be heavily festooned in ivy. Devey's own water-colour sketches for his buildings can be enchantingly delicate, but he lacked the ability to project this soft water-colour world into three dimensions.★ His weakness is especially apparent in his larger buildings; and his big country houses are very big

★ 'When asked by his client to join a house-party, Devey would make the most fascinating catch-penny sketches while dressing for dinner and present them during dessert, charming everyone but getting them worked out by his clerks.' Reminiscences of Voysey, quoted by J. Brandon-Jones, 'C. F. A. Voysey, 1857–1941', *Architectural Association Journal*, LXXII (1957), p. 241. Devey was a supporter of Voysey's father and his Theistic Church, and Voysey became one of these clerks in 1880–2. His earliest surviving designs are in the Devey manner.

indeed. However fascinating the plan of a house like Goldings may be as an example of capable planning combined with apparent haphazardness on an enormous scale, the actual house is depressingly shapeless: it seems to dribble on for ever. But Devey's clients saw his buildings through water-colour tinted spectacles, and were clearly delighted with the results. His considerable talents suffered from running in over-gilded channels, and being put to the service of opulent bankers with a staff of thirty servants who liked to convince themselves that they were living unassumingly in a rambling old-world manor house. Webb and Shaw with their overgrown farmhouses for artistic businessmen, were too often in the same world of rich man's makebelieve. It was a situation from which Shaw emerged with the least damage, because, while Devey and Webb would probably have preferred to design genuine farmhouses and manor houses on a modest scale, the element of make-believe appealed to Shaw, and he had a gift for managing large and complicated entities which the others lacked.

44. *The First Steps to Neo-Georgian*

ONE OF THE pleasures of Old English and Queen Anne was that there were no rules; but after twenty years of cheerful free-for-all a substantial number of architects began to find the freedom less exhilarating and to feel yearnings for a style that had some kind of discipline built into it. The way was open for a return to a much closer interpretation of the seventeenth- and eighteenth-century classical tradition.

There had already been foretastes of this. The main block of both Nesfield's gigantic Kinmel (1870; Pls. 308–12) and Webb's small and delightful Smeaton Manor (1877) had been symmetrical designs closely based on country houses of the seventeenth and early eighteenth centuries; but in both cases these had been combined with a much freer arrangement of wings and outbuildings in an asymmetric whole. The new entrance front that Nesfield put onto Bodrhyddan in Flintshire in 1872 had been a captivatingly romantic but completely formal design in high roofed French Pavilion style. But perhaps the most remarkable house of this type to be built in the 1870s was the notably anti-romantic Crabbet Park in Sussex, designed in 1873 by two amateurs, Wilfred Scawen Blunt and his wife.

54. New wing at Walmer Castle, Kent, 1872, from the drawing by Devey.

Scawen Blunt, poet, womanizer and Arab nationalist, was a first cousin of Percy Wyndham of Clouds, and in the 1890s was to become a friend of William Morris and rent to Philip Webb the little house where he lived in his retirement. In August 1894 he was at Kelmscott, and wrote in his diary: 'Made a late start as I dawdled on talking with Morris, and trying to prove to him that he and Ruskin had done more harm than good by their attempt to make English people love beauty and decorate their architecture . . . I maintained that the old-fashioned square cardboard box style was less abominable, as were the days when it was considered bad taste to attempt any kind of prettiness.'[124] He and his wife had indeed designed a house that, but for a few minor eccentricities of detail, might have been a sensible pedimented brick box of late seventeenth-century date.

Crabbet is interesting because it was so completely independent of its age, and in its architecture more reminiscent of 1910 than 1870. But it had little or no influence at the time it was built. Neither did Sir Edmund Beckett's equally sober Batchwood (1874–6), another example of an owner-designed house. When Norman Shaw went dramatically classical at Bryanston (1890) and Chesters (1891), the style of the two houses was still soaked with his own vigorous romanticism. Even so, they were classical rather than 'free classical' buildings. A few years previously Bodley and Garner had designed Hewell Grange in Worcestershire in a style that was neither Old English nor free Elizabethan in the mid-Victorian manner, but a careful combination of elements from Montacute and Charlton Park in Wiltshire to produce what could almost be mistaken for a genuine Elizabethan house.

At Hewell Grange one can see the first freezing of the smile on the face of the country house, regarded as an independent architectural tradition. The reasons were economic and social. Country houses had been growing fat on their own poison. The great Victorian efflorescence of new and enlarged country houses had been a side-result of the growth of industry and the towns, and this same growth gradually toppled the country landowners from their position as leaders of the nation. The shift in power, which had been under way in 1830, had gone a great deal further by 1890. The agricultural depression (the direct result of an industrialized society) dimmed the glory of landed estates. Landowning families made haste to move capital out of land into shares, and to send their younger, and even their elder, sons into business. The House of Lords, the stronghold of the landed interests, received its first large injections of industrial and commercial peers from Gladstone in 1885–6 and from Lord Salisbury in 1886–92. In 1885, for the first time in the history of the House of Commons, the members representing landed families were in a minority. The social prestige of country houses remained very great; many new families still set themselves up as country landowners; but increasing numbers contented themselves with a main house in London and weekend or holiday houses in the country. By 1908, when Asquith became the first English prime minister not to own a country estate, England could no longer be said to be ruled from her country houses. Many new ones were still to be built; Lutyens was still in his prime; but as architectural patrons country house owners were becoming increasingly cautious, conservative and nostalgic for the past, more concerned to preserve their existing heritage than to create new forms.

55. (top left) Crabbet Park, Sussex (W. S. and Lady Anne Blunt, 1872–3).
56. (top right) Bodrhyddan, Flintshire (W. E. Nesfield, 1872–4).
57. (centre right) Smeaton Manor, Yorkshire (Philip Webb, 1877–9).
58. (centre) Bryanston, Dorset (R. Norman Shaw, 1890).
59. (bottom) Hewell Grange, Worcestershire (Thomas Gardner, 1884–9).

2.VICTORIAN COUNTRY HOUSES

1. *Harlaxton Manor, Lincolnshire*

TODAY we went to see the house Mr Gregory is building, five miles from here. He is a gentleman of about £12,000 a year, who has a fancy to build a magnificent house in the Elizabethan style, and he now is in the middle of his work, all the shell being finished except one wing. Nothing can be more perfect than it is, both as to the architecture and the ornaments; but it stands on the slope of a hill on a deep clay soil, with no park around it, very little wood, and scarcely any fine trees. Many years ago, when he first conceived this design, he began to amass money and lived for no other object. He travelled into all parts of Europe collecting objects of curiosity, useful or ornamental, for his projected palace, and he did not begin to build until he had accumulated money enough to complete his design. The grandeur of it is such, and such the tardiness of its progress, that it is about as much as he will do to live till its completion; and as he is not married, has no children, and dislikes the heir on whom his property is entailed, it is the means and not the end to which he looks for gratification. He says that it is his amusement, as hunting or shooting or feasting may be the objects of other people; and as the pursuit leads him into all parts of the world, and to mix with every variety of nation and character, besides engendering tastes pregnant with instruction and curious research, it is not irrational, although he should never inhabit his house, and may be toiling and saving for the benefit of persons he cares nothing about.[1]

The date is 4 January 1838; the house visited is Harlaxton; the writer is Charles Greville. He was staying at Belvoir Castle; among the party who rode over with him were the Duke and Duchess of Sutherland, Lady Salisbury, Lord Aberdeen, and Lord John Manners—the future hero of Young England.

60. (preceding pages) Harlaxton Manor, nr Grantham, Lincolnshire (Anthony Salvin, 1831–7; William Burn, 1838–44). Looking north across the former brewery in the north-east wing.
61. Salvin's elevation of the entrance front, 1834.
V. (right) Looking through the lodge gates to Harlaxton Manor.

Greville's description is intriguing enough, but the reality even more extraordinary. Harlaxton has to be seen to be believed; and even when one has seen it, it is not always easy to believe in it. It floats like a vision at the end of its avenue; it rises mysterious out of the snows or ebullient from the late summer cornfields; it changes from season to season, and light to light. It is a work of genius—but whose genius? All the relevant building accounts and family papers, and all but a handful of designs, have disappeared.

Gregory Gregory (1786–1854) for whom it was built was rich, but not all that rich. Greville's £12,000 may have been an underestimate, but his income, which derived from inherited estates in Lincolnshire, Leicestershire and Nottinghamshire, is unlikely to have been more than £20,000.[2] Yet Harlaxton suggests an income of at least £50,000; Greville rightly called it a palace, for it is ducal and even royal in its pretensions. One is tempted to look for some extra source of wealth, or history of family or political rivalry to explain it; but Greville's sympathetic account suggests that this is unnecessary. Harlaxton was a personal fantasy, to which Gregory devoted all his energies and most of his life; the £200,000, spread over twenty years, which tradition says he spent on the house, is a perfectly possible sum for a bachelor with no other commitments, whose house appears to have been his only extravagance.

There is, in fact, little doubt that Gregory himself, rather than his architects, is the key figure. J. C. Loudon, who visited Harlaxton in May 1840, wrote that 'from entering so completely into both the design and the practical details of execution he may be said to have embodied himself in the edifice, and to live in every feature of it'.[3] Although the house was not started until 1832, he began to collect ideas, money and fittings for it ten years earlier. Ultimately he travelled all over Europe, as far as Constantinople and the Crimea. But to begin with he confined himself to England, for his first plans were limited to building a house in the Jacobean or Elizabethan style. He told Loudon that ('there being, at the time he commenced, few or no books on the subject'), he visited and studied, among other buildings, Bramshill, Hardwick, Hatfield, Knole, Burghley, Wollaton, Kirby, Longleat, Temple Newsam, and the Oxford and Cambridge colleges.

In turning his attention to Elizabethan architecture in the 1820s, Gregory was a pioneer, but by no means alone. The publication of Scott's *Kenilworth* in 1821 no doubt helped to popularize the Elizabethan age, but it would have come into fashion anyway. Alarmed by industrial and social unrest, the English upper classes were already beginning to look for the kind of benevolent and paternalistic image which Young England was to preach in the 1840s. Elizabethan manor houses suggested what was called at the time 'Old English hospitality' just as visibly as mediaeval ones, and without the undertones of violence, superstition and discomfort which put many people off the Middle Ages. Visually, Elizabethan architecture could produce the kind of picturesque skyline and varied modelling that was admired by practitioners of the picturesque. Moreover, it appealed to patriotic sentiment; it was uniquely English.[4]

On the other hand, the cavalier way in which the Elizabethans distorted or misunderstood the language of classical architecture was bound to be a stumbling block to those brought up in the classical tradition. Architects, in particular, found it

VI. Harlaxton Manor. The staircase.

hard to stomach what Horace Walpole had described as its 'mongrel character'. The revived 'Old English' manor houses of the 1820s tended to be more Tudor–Gothic than Elizabethan—or, if they were more or less Elizabethan, 'mongrel' classical detail was left out. Only in the 1830s, when reaction against the purity of neoclassicism was rampant, did Elizabethan ornament begin to become acceptable.

Country gentlemen may have been less worried by Elizabethan stylistic improprieties than architects. In 1835 it was a committee of landowners, not architects, who coupled Elizabethan with Gothic as one of the two acceptable styles for entries to the competition for the new Houses of Parliament. Gregory's own interests may have been turned to Elizabethan by the fact that he owned an Elizabethan house himself. The old manor house at Harlaxton had not been lived in by the Gregory family for many years, and was falling into ruin; but it was a remarkably picturesque example of the style.[5] Sixty years later Gregory would have devoted his energies to a loving and careful restoration of the old house; instead he built himself a superb neo-Elizabethan mansion and kept the old one as a picturesquely decaying feature at the edge of his new park.

It was probably in 1831 that the architect Anthony Salvin was called in to, as Loudon put it, 'embody Mr Gregory's ideas in such detail as to fit them for the practical builder'. Salvin was not a surprising choice. Although only at the beginning of his career, he had already established a reputation as a rising country house architect. At Mamhead (1826–37) and Moreby (1827–33) he had already designed two extremely capable Tudor-Gothic houses, and by the 1830s he was probably quite ready to be pushed further along the Elizabethan road. Moreover he was an adept at picturesque composition; a house designed by him would be sure to fit into its setting.

94

62. Harlaxton Manor. The south-east front.

The house that he designed (no doubt primed by Gregory with innumerable suggestions and possibly even sketch designs) was a masterly combination of ingenious planning and picturesque composition. It was literally dug into a hillside, with the ground sloping up behind it and to one side, and down on the other two sides. This means that the main room could be put on the first floor, and yet open straight onto the garden on the two sides where the house hit the hill; and the service rooms could be in a basement which became a well-lit ground floor on the sides facing the entrance court and the service yard.

On the basis of this clever plan (which Salvin was later to adapt for Keele and Thoresby) the vocabulary derived from Gregory's extensive tours was used to achieve modelling, intricacy and skyline according to picturesque principles. Salvin's beautiful elevations are the only drawings to survive,[6] and show how he thought in terms of light and shade, producing the broader modelling by turrets, chimney-breasts and bay windows, the intricacy by applied decoration, and the skyline by turrets, gables, and chimneystacks. The entrance front was splendidly symmetrical, and clearly inspired by the entrance front at Burghley; the rear facade, facing the hill, was made picturesquely asymmetrical by the irregular fenestration, bold bay window and prominent chimneystack of the great hall.

Building work started in 1832, the central tower was up by 1836, and the house was substantially completed by 1844.[7] But in mid-course two new elements were introduced; Gregory discovered the Baroque, and changed his architect.

Had Harlaxton been completed as it was originally planned, it would have been a neo-Elizabethan house on the grand scale, remarkable enough, but not all that unlike a number of its contemporaries. Behind its uniqueness lies a brilliant new idea: the idea that Elizabethan and Jacobean could be fused with Baroque. The

95

63. The south-west front.

64. Harlaxton Manor. Looking through the forecourt gates to the entrance front.

results are epitomized on the entrance front. The Elizabethan centre-piece of the house is framed by gigantic gate-piers and pavilions in which Baroque outlines are combined with Jacobean ornament. The resulting impression of power, exuberance and abundance is sensational.

The mixture is continued in varying proportions all through the house. The gargantuan scrolls in the entrance hall are, if anything Baroque, but there are Jacobean touches in the detailing of the arches. The stairs that lead up from it to the main floor have Baroque balustrading under a ceiling studded with Elizabethan pendentives. The great hall and dining room to which it gives access both suggest Old English hospitality; but the roof trusses of the hall are supported by groaning Baroque Atlantides. Through the hall is the main staircase, and beyond it the drawing room, ante-room, and gallery. The decoration of these three rooms is almost entirely Baroque; but the enormous conservatory into which they both look is an extraordinary mixture of Baroque and Elizabethan shapes and ornament. The staircase itself is the glory and surprise of Harlaxton's interior. It is entirely and unbelievably Baroque; through struggling Atlantides, swarming cherubs, and tasselled festoons of drapery it soars up to an illusionist Baroque heaven, under which more cherubs climb and a figure of Time unrolls a plan of Harlaxton.

The decoration is far more robust and boldly modelled than in most equivalent work of the same date; in particular, the Elizabethan ceilings make any similar ceilings of the 1830s and 1840s seem feeble.[8] Some of the detail, such as the trophies attached to the arches in the lower hall, is grotesquely exaggerated in scale, and the

96

65. (upper right) A detail of the staircase.
66. (lower right) One of the many door fittings made by Gibbons of Wolverhampton.

67. Harlaxton Manor. The dining room.

general effect is of a bursting and pullulating abundance that has an almost dreamlike quality. The result is like a series of stage sets, linked together with theatrical genius to provide continuous contrasts in shape, size, character and lighting, as one moves from floor to floor, or room to room.

Who designed all this? Was it Salvin, or William Burn, who superseded him, or David Bryce, who was Burn's chief assistant? Salvin is known to have been in Munich and Nuremberg in 1835.[9] It is hard to believe that this visit had nothing to do with Harlaxton. The illusionism and some of the detailing of the staircase appear to be directly inspired by the Asamkirche in Munich—although, typically, the illusionism which the Baroque used for symbolic and religious purposes is transferred at Harlaxton into a purely secular and picturesque context. On the other hand the interior decoration at Harlaxton is unlikely to have been started before 1837, and probably went on well into the 1840s; and the conservatory, stables, garden terraces and forecourt gate, all of which have Baroque elements, date from 1840 at the earliest. In 1838, and possibly even in 1837, Salvin ceased to have

68. Harlaxton Manor. The great hall.

69. The drawing room.

anything to do with Harlaxton. After an interim period, during which Gregory consulted Blore, Burn took over; he was in charge by at least December 1838.[10]

Burn was well established in Scotland but Harlaxton was his first English commission; indeed, it was the foundation of his great English practice. Its service wings and courtyards may be due to him; certainly nothing like them is shown on the surviving Salvin elevations. On the other hand he was always a dry and at times a dull designer; it is hard to believe that he was responsible for something as ebullient as the detail at Harlaxton. But Burn's chief clerk (and from 1841 his partner) David Bryce was a different matter.[11] Not only was he a much more spirited designer than Burn; unlike Salvin he liked the Baroque. He designed buildings in the Baroque manner, or with Baroque details, on and off from 1835. Did Gregory send or take Salvin to Munich to study Baroque buildings, but replace him because Salvin either could not or would not produce the new mixture that Gregory wanted? Was Burn brought in because he had a clever designer in his office who knew about the Baroque?

Even less is known about the craftsmanship at Harlaxton than about the architecture.[12] Apart from Gibbons of Wolverhampton, who signed lavish Rococo-style door furniture throughout the house, its decorators are all anonymous. The plasterwork has, almost inevitably, been attributed to foreigners. Gregory's constant travels through Europe certainly put him in a good position to pick up foreign craftsmen. But on the other hand Harlaxton's Baroque relates as much or more to what was going on in England. From the late 1820s onward England experienced a revived fashion for decoration in the Baroque or Rococo manner, sheltering under the blanket title of 'Louis Quatorze'. The stylistic distance between George IV's staterooms at Windsor (1826–30) or Earl de Grey's entire house at Wrest Park (1833–9) and the drawing room and ante-room at Harlaxton is not so very great; the final leap to the staircase is much greater, but not impossible. The long-established firm of Francis Bernasconi and Son, who modelled the plasterwork at Windsor and probably also at Wrest, would have had the technical competence to produce that at Harlaxton—even the staircase. In general, many of the English firms who were to flood the 1851 Exhibition with 'Louis Quatorze' (and in some cases even Louis Quatorze combined with Elizabethan) were already flourishing by 1840.[13]

Although Harlaxton was described as 'mostly completed' by 1842, it continued to be embellished right up to Gregory's death in 1854. Gregory's buildings spread further and further over the surrounding landscape, by way of stables, gatehouse,

100

70. (above) The lower hall.
71. (right) Harlaxton from the air.

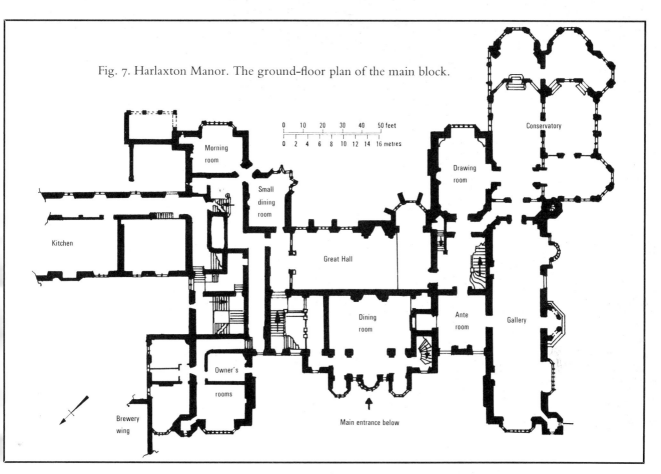

Fig. 7. Harlaxton Manor. The ground-floor plan of the main block.

Morning room

Small dining room

Kitchen

Great Hall

Drawing room

Conservatory

Dining room

Ante room

Gallery

Owner's rooms

Brewery wing

Main entrance below

0 10 20 30 40 50 feet
0 2 4 6 8 10 12 14 16 metres

kitchen garden and lodge gates to one side, and terraces, pavilions and grottoes to the other. Everything was in the grand manner, of the best possible quality, and richly ornamented in the style of the house. Indoors, Gregory's decorators continued to work until even the attic bedrooms had ornamented ceilings and good fireplaces. The planning and practical aspects were as exhaustively considered as the decoration. Although Gregory never married, had (by Victorian standards) a modest staff[14] and seems never to have entertained, everything was prepared for a swarm of servants, children and guests. An elegant family staircase served a family suite at the north end of the house. In addition to the main back stairs, service stairs rose discreetly from the basement to the underneath of the main stairs and to a serving lobby by the dining room. Ponderous brass levers under the main stairs opened hot air grates strategically placed in the main rooms. Coal or wood was brought in at high level from the hill top and fed by railway through a curving and covered-in viaduct to the top storey; from there it was dropped or lowered to collection points in other parts of the house.[15]

Gregory had moved in by the time the 1851 census was made, but died in 1854. He had hoped that all his property would ultimately go to his friend, cousin and neighbour Sir William Welby of Denton. But the major part of it was entailed in another direction; the Welbys inherited the contents of Harlaxton, but not Harlaxton itself.[16] After passing through several different hands, and narrowly escaping demolition it was first leased, and finally bought, by the University of Evansville, the present owner.

102

72. Harlaxton Manor. The railway viaduct leading into the service wing.

2. Bayons Manor, Lincolnshire

THE ENCHANTED palace of the Sleeping Beauty, hidden and asleep behind its impenetrable hedge, is one of the more haunting of fairy-tale inventions; yet something not so very far removed from it survived until a few years ago, lost in the beautiful landscape of the Lincolnshire Wolds. Here was a huge castle of honey-coloured stone, a cluster of gables and towers surrounded by battlements and a moat; empty and deserted except for the pigeons that wheeled and fluttered endlessly through its ruined halls; and with the undergrowth closing in, the weeds and reeds thick and high in the moat, the long grass rippling on what were once smooth lawns, the garden wall smothered by saplings, so that from outside little could be seen except a wall of greenery, with towers rising here and there mysteriously behind it.

The house was called Bayons Manor and was built by Charles Tennyson d'Eyncourt, the uncle of Alfred Tennyson. It was sold by his descendants after the Second World War, stood derelict for many years and was demolished in 1965. It was not only built for romantic reasons; it was to be a demonstration of the social status of the Tennyson family, concealing behind its haze of battlements and turrets the truth of their comparatively recent rise to fortune. George Clayton Tennyson, the poet's grandfather, came of an old line of yeoman farmers and professional men, who originally lived in south Yorkshire, but moved to Lincolnshire in the eighteenth century.[1] George's father, Michael, was a surgeon in Market Rasen, and married an

73. Bayons Manor, Tealby, Lincolnshire (W. A. Nicholson and Charles d'Eyncourt, 1836–7). The west front.

heiress, Mary Clayton, whose family owned much of Grimsby. The Claytons were proud of their position as co-heirs of the Earls of Scarsdale and descendants of the medieval family of d'Eyncourt. George became the most successful solicitor in Lincolnshire and South Yorkshire. The profits of his business, combined with shrewd purchase of farm land at slump prices, made him a rich man.

At the end of the eighteenth century he set up as a country gentleman, bought Bayons Manor, at Tealby in Lincolnshire, and built up a property round it. The house was little larger than a cottage when he bought it, but it was in a singularly beautiful position on the west slope of the Wolds. Moreover, in the Middle Ages it had been the property of his ancestor, Francis Lord Lovel and d'Eyncourt, and there were traces of a medieval castle by the house. He enlarged the existing buildings, planted trees and formed a park. Having acquired wealth, property, and what, by a slight stretch of the word, might be called an ancestral home, he decided that his eldest son George, the poet's father, was unfit to succeed him. He disinherited him, supplied him with a family living at Somersby, and concentrated his energies and money on his second son, Charles.

Young George Tennyson was warped for life by this act of his father. His increasing bitterness and gloom and ultimate drunkenness; the unhappiness and uneasiness of life at Somersby; the brood of Tennyson children, four daughters and seven huge and swarthy sons, packed uncomfortably into the vicarage, wandering across the Wolds in dirty clothes singing poetry as they went, or sunk at times into a melancholy as deep as their father's; the ultimate glory of the rejected branch when Alfred Tennyson became one of the most famous Englishmen of the century—all this has become part of literary history. The story of the younger branch of the family is less well known.

Old George Tennyson died in 1835, leaving Bayons and the bulk of his property to his younger son. Almost immediately Charles added d'Eyncourt to his name. The adoption of this name (on rather tenuous grounds) was both a romantic gesture and a demonstration of the antiquity of his lineage. Its corollary in stone came soon after, when Charles began to convert the unassuming Regency house at Bayons into a romantic castellated pile.

He employed a Lincolnshire architect with antiquarian interests, William Adams Nicholson. But the design of Bayons was due as much to Charles d'Eyncourt himself as to Nicholson, whose other known work is rather dull. Charles was an interesting man. Most builders of nineteenth-century castles were Tories; but Charles (like his friend Bulwer Lytton) was a Radical politician and M.P., and also an antiquary, a bibliophile, a man of principle and honour, endowed with the dark Tennyson good looks. At the same time his mind, as Sir Charles Tennyson puts it in his biography of the poet, was 'remarkable for a restless and almost feverish subtlety'. He had an infinite capacity for worrying about trifles; perhaps this explains why he never quite gained the worldly success for which his father had hoped.

When he was up in London, he would write several times a week, sometimes daily, to his stewards or sons (George, Louis, Edwin and Eustace) at Bayons. His letters are immensely long, illustrated with little plans and sketches, and they circle

interminably round the same points: where the drains are to go, how the library is to be arranged, whether to have a door in the stable wall, and so on. These letters must have driven their recipients mad at the time: but they are invaluable today, for together with the replies to them they are the most important surviving evidence for the building of the house. An interesting collection of plans and drawings also survive, but Nicholson's own letters and most of the accounts have disappeared.

The letters make it quite clear that Charles d'Eyncourt had a large share in the design of Bayons. It was not his first excursion into architecture. Between 1818 and 1825 he had been busily engaged in advising and helping his brother-in-law, the millionaire Durham coal owner Matthew Russell, in the task of resurrecting one of the most magnificent modern castles in England from the scanty ruins of medieval Brancepeth Castle. With this experience behind him and with considerably increased antiquarian knowledge, he embarked on a similar task at Bayons.

The house, when Charles d'Eyncourt started on it, was a long thin block with two bow windows side by side at the west of its narrow ends.[3] He sandwiched it between two large additions; a wing to the south, of which the main feature was a big free-standing great hall; and a wing to the north, containing a magnificent library (about the design of which Salvin made suggestions).[4] Projecting in the middle of the west front were the two bows of the original house, which were given a suitable Gothic disguise. The foundations of the new work were laid early in 1836, and the shell was nearing completion by the end of the year.

The family immediately began to feel misgivings. 'It masses admirably, instead of appearing to creep along the ground, as some expected it would', wrote Charles's eldest son, George, but he did not convince the rest; the building, they thought, was too straggling, and the massiveness of the hall outbalanced everything else. Early in 1837 someone (probably Charles) conceived the idea of adding a tower as a vertical accent to pull the composition together. Edwin d'Eyncourt hoisted a flag as high as the tower would rise, to give some idea of its effect, and wrote that it would be a 'monstrous improvement'. The tower was accordingly started on, and finished by the end of the summer.

It was judged a huge success, and the d'Eyncourts were now delighted with their

74. Bayons Manor. The fortifications, seen above the encroaching undergrowth.

new house. 'It will be fit for the highest nobleman in the land', wrote Eustace. His mother Fanny, thought it 'a beautiful building and much observed and talked of'. His daughter Clara sent a drawing of it out to George in Corfu. 'People from all parts go to see it', she said. Louis admired the view from the papermill most: 'It looks so very gentlemanlike from there.' Over the hall was carved the motto, 'en avant': Fanny thought this signified the family's ambition to get on in the world and was afraid of 'animadversions from the envious and jealous, against whose darts there are no shields'. Clara, however, interpreted the motto as designed to 'reassure the intruder should he venture so far', undeterred by the frowning battlements and overhanging walls.

The house was by this date more of a Gothic manor house than a castle; but in the spring of 1839 Charles conceived the idea of defending it with elaborate and massive fortifications. He made a sketch of these in a letter to George written on 27 April.[5] West of the house an immense castellated wall, pierced north and south by two formidable gateways and fortified with numerous bastions and towers, was to surround the stable and kitchen court; and a second outer wall, much lower, was to extend from this and run right round the house. The second wall would be negotiable only by a gatehouse on the north side (the barbican gate), defended by a moat and drawbridge.

His daughter greeted his sketch with charming romantic-young-lady enthusiasm. It 'would make a magnificent thing were it completed I think. I should like the water for the sake of its *reflecting* the buildings—Reflection is always so *excessively* pretty— but unless you have a *real-looking* drawbridge, I would just as soon have a simple, heavy, ponderous, massive and mysterious-looking entrance. But perhaps you don't want my opinion so I will bid you Adieu.'

The scheme did not remain on paper. The walls, tower and gateways were built, the moat was formed, and, as an added improvement, in 1842 a huge ruined keep was built on a mound inside the inner wall. Visitors arriving along the main drive from the south no longer went straight up to the hall, as they had previously done.

106

75. (above) Bayons Manor. The barbican gateway, with the house to the right.

76. (right) Another view of the barbican gateway.

77. Bayons Manor. The great hall.

Instead they went right round the outer wall to the moated barbican gateway on the north; through this to the inner wall; through the north gate into the stable; past the east or kitchen front of the house which was Gothicized in 1841 to make it more suitable for visitors; through two more gates below the keep and so out at last on to the south front of the great hall, having completely circled the house and passed through a succession of baronial splendours.[6]

To judge from contemporary descriptions,[7] the interior of Bayons was an antiquarian chiaroscuro very much in the style of Scarisbrick, though Pugin would probably have been loath to admit it. The main framework was Gothic, with open timber roofs and elaborate Gothic chimneypieces[8] in the hall and others of the main rooms. Crace installed painted decorations and wallpapers by Pugin.[9] Armour, weapons, heraldry and stained glass abounded. But there were also busts of Napoleon and Byron, classical tapestries, Etruscan vases and pictures by Van der Neer and Guardi. The literary equivalents of Bayons are the novels of Walter Scott and still more of Charles d'Eyncourt's friend Bulwer Lytton, who wrote *Harold the*

78. Inside the great hall.

79. Under the final gateway.

Last of the Saxon Kings (1848) during a stay there.★ Charles was himself a bad poet in the manner of Scott.[10] He considered his nephew's poetry 'horrid rubbish' and was disgusted when he was made Poet Laureate. He looked backwards to the late Georgian tradition; sham fortifications and a purely picturesque attitude to design were being viciously attacked by Pugin and other young men as Bayons was going up. But as a piece of scenery Bayons was superb. Charles d'Eyncourt built it up like a picture or series of pictures, adding a tower here and a wall there, taking down or altering a turret or gable, and mixing his light and shade and his horizontals and verticals like a painter playing with his paint. The decay and destruction of the house was a sad end to his dynastic ambitions; but at least it meant that for a few years Bayons became far more picturesque than he could ever have dreamed of, indeed more beautiful and more romantic than many a genuine ruined castle.

★ He dedicated it to his host: 'With all those disburied spectres rampant in thy chamber, all the armour rusting in thy galleries, all those mutilated statues of early English kings niched into thy grey ivied walls—say, in thy conscience, O Host, shall I ever return to the nineteenth century again?'

3. *Scarisbrick Hall, Lancashire*

IN 1837 A. W. Pugin received what for an architect aged twenty-four was a very enviable commission. Charles Scarisbrick, an exceedingly rich Lancashire landowner, wanted his house redone in the Gothic style, and was prepared to pay handsomely for it. Pugin prepared a sketch design in the form of one of the most attractive drawings he ever made. It exactly illustrated the analysis he was later to make of an 'old English Catholic mansion', with the various kinds of accommodation 'not masked or concealed under one monotonous front, but by their variety in form and outline increasing the effect of the building, and presenting a standing illustration of good old English hospitality'. The great hall with its oriel window and separate roof, the lofty chapel and loftier clock tower were all prominent external features. Few clients could have resisted the design. Between 1837 and 1845 the house was remodelled very much as Pugin had originally suggested.

The landscape round Scarisbrick is a curious one, and it is a considerable experience to drive out to it from Southport. Once out of the town one comes on to the immense flatness of Martin Mere, drained in the eighteenth century by Charles Scarisbrick's grandfather, but still with much of the space and loneliness of a marsh—huge fields where the geese feed in winter and stunted trees bent permanently east by the gales that drive in from the sea. The emptiness is suddenly ended by the long wall of the Scarisbrick woods, above which rises the distant and solitary finger of a great spire. Then follows a narrow avenue of pines piercing through flat tree-enclosed fields, and a long curve and twist of drive; and one comes out before the main front of the house to be staggered by the fantasy of the sight that meets one's eyes. On the left is Pugin's wing, in the centre is his great hall—but in

110

80. Scarisbrick Hall, nr Southport, Lancashire (A. W. Pugin, 1837–45; E. W. Pugin, 1862–8). The entrance front, with E. W. Pugin's tower to the right.

place of his clock tower a monstrous spire rises above ornate and caparisoned gables and a turret surmounted by the fluttering wings of eagles.

This end of the house was designed by Edward Pugin to replace his father's tower and wing, and shout down the quieter proportions of his design. But even discounting what Edward Pugin did, Scarisbrick as built came out rather differently from Scarisbrick as drawn. The drawings suggest a re-creation of a medieval manor house, carried out with tremendous competence and impressive unity of conception. But the building is in many ways uneven and immature; and the more one looks into it the less medieval and also the more interesting it becomes.

The old, and probably half-timbered, house at Scarisbrick had been refaced with stone Gothic facades in 1815. Pugin's work was largely confined to remodelling and altering the existing house. Even the bay windows of the hall had been there in some form before. A large collection of Pugin's drawings have survived and are now in the R.I.B.A. drawings collection. Minor designs in 1836 are followed by designs for the complete remodelling in 1837. In the same year detailed drawings for remodelling the west wing were made. This was a straightforward revamping of the 1815 work, leaving the shapes of the rooms and main lines of the facades unaltered. Pugin added buttresses, pinnacles and chimneystacks, and redid the windows, but the results were not very inspiring. Drawings for the north front were made in 1838, with results that were not much better, apart from the agreeably original porch,

81. Drawing by A. W. Pugin for the great hall.

82. The exterior of the hall.

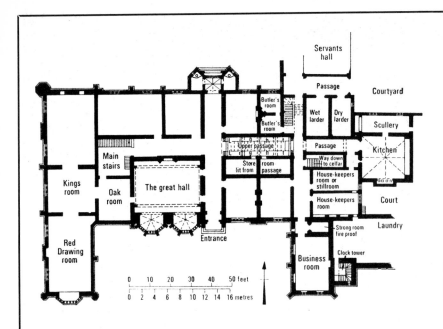

Fig. 8. Scarisbrick Hall. The ground-floor plan, based on a drawing by Pugin.

with its canted turrets and bay window. The now-demolished west wing and tower followed in 1839. A carving on the staircase probably shows their final form. The device of an oriel window supported on a buttress between two smaller windows was to reappear at Pearson's Treberfydd in 1848 and Daukes's Horsted in 1850. The clock tower with its clock-stage slightly projecting beyond the body of the tower, almost certainly suggested the shape of the clock tower of the Houses of Parliament, which Barry designed in the mid-1840s.[1]

The final stage of Pugin's work at Scarisbrick was the building of the great hall. There are designs for its upper portions dated 1840, and for the porch, which was an afterthought, dated 1841; round the arch is the inscription, 'This hall was built by me, Charles Scarisbrick, MDCCCXLII. Laus Deo.'★ The lantern was not designed until 1845. The hall as it was built was considerably more elaborate than as shown in 1837 drawings, largely because of the richer treatment of the parapet, lantern and bay windows. The latter, in both design and execution, were probably the most assured and splendid pieces of work to be produced to date by the Gothic revival in England. When one looks at the house as a whole, the richer treatment and separate roof of the hall produces a noticeably disjointed effect; but, as discussed in the introduction, Pugin may have aimed at this deliberately, in reaction against the carefully worked out compositions of the picturesque tradition.

One sees the interior of the house without Charles Scarisbrick and without any

★ Scarisbrick is liberally covered with texts of a pious nature, most of which (and certainly those carved in stone along the front of the hall) are probably due to A. W. Pugin rather than his son. They are an early example of what was to become an obsessive Victorian habit. 'Except the Lord buildeth the house, they labour in vain that build it' (painted around the hall) became a special favourite in English or Latin: e.g. around the entrances of Ferrey's Clyffe House and Teulon's Shadwell. Whistler satirized the habit when, on leaving his house in Chelsea subsequent to his bankruptcy in 1879, he inscribed above the door: 'Except the Lord buildeth the house, they labour in vain that build it: Edward Godwin, F.S.A., built this house.'

112

but the rump of Charles Scarisbrick's collections. He was a mystery to his contemporaries, and remains a mystery today.[2] Although he came of an ancient Catholic family, there is nothing to suggest that Pugin found him the same kind of militantly Catholic and medievalist patron as Lord Shrewsbury and Ambrose Phillips de Lisle. It is not surprising that the great chapel shown in Pugin's drawing was never built. To the Jesuits at Stonyhurst, where he was educated, he was 'a source of puzzlement'.[3] Shortly after work started at Scarisbrick, he formed a liaison in Germany where he produced a brood of illegitimate children. At Scarisbrick he lived a life of increasing seclusion, refusing to see even his own steward, and becoming a fertile source of gossip to the neighbourhood. It was said that 'he was the victim of some abiding fear' and that 'he kept a gambling house in Paris before succeeding to the estate'.[4] One fact above the uncertainty of gossip was that he was a shrewd and sharp business man, who bought up the land on which Southport was to develop, and died worth about £3,000,000. He lived alone, and spent his wealth on his collections. After his death these were put up to auction at Christie's over fourteen days of sales in 1860 and 1861. The pictures were sold in 750 lots, and the drawings in 526. There was little that was medieval about them; the main part of the collection consisted of Dutch works of the seventeenth century—landscapes and conversation pieces innumerable, and, according to the catalogue, four Rembrandt

113

83. Scarisbrick Hall. The interior of the great hall.

oils, eleven Rembrandt drawings and a very large collection of Rembrandt etchings. Among contemporary painters Charles Scarisbrick had a fondness for Benjamin West and was the principal patron of John Martin, whose *Joshua Commanding the Sun to Stand Still, The Deluge* and *The Fall of Nineveh* hung at Scarisbrick along with twenty-one more of his oil paintings.

The sale included a valuable library, bronzes, ivories, silver, gems, cameos, missals, a large collection of armour and arms, 'beautiful ancient carved ebony furniture' and 171 lots of woodcarvings including doors, panels, screens, friezes, stalls, canopies, frames, cabinets, bookcases, tables, overmantels and altarpieces dating from the fifteenth to the eighteenth century.

A residue of the woodcarvings was left at Scarisbrick—presumably anything that was considered a fitting rather than a furnishing—and apart from a few casualties is there still. The carvings are fixed to walls, built into doors or fireplaces, fitted into alcoves and on staircases, and in the extraordinary little oak room are used like wallpaper. In date they are as varied as the carvings that were sold. The *chef-d'oeuvre*, at any rate in size, is the enormous early seventeenth-century *Christ Crowned with Thorns*, said to come from Antwerp Cathedral, on the west wall of the hall. It is framed by twisted Baroque pillars and surmounted by a late Flemish Gothic canopy with figures of the same date thickly crowded above it. It is often difficult to distinguish what is Pugin's framework, and what is made-up old work. In devising a setting for Charles Scarisbrick's collection he made his own work play some curious tricks. The pullulating chimneypiece in the Red drawing room is late Flemish Gothic in inspiration, but is surmounted by urns of Renaissance type. The big doorcase in the same room is a mongrel mixture of classical and Gothic. In the spandrels of the hall roof are dragons which look more like trophies from the

114

84. Scarisbrick Hall. The oak room.

Brighton Pavilion than from the Middle Ages. The oak room chimneypiece starts off with pieces of medieval choir-stalls and ends up with a canopy (eighteenth century or Pugin?) of pure Rococo design.

When one tries to visualize the surviving Pugin work at Scarisbrick as the setting of the vanished collection, one ends up with something not in the least bit medieval in feeling, but more like the sumptuous *bric-à-brac* backgrounds of some of Rembrandt's paintings, or the variegated chiaroscuro and multitude of incident in Charles Scarisbrick's favourite Martins. It was in fact an antiquary's hide out, a glorified junk box put together with jackdaw rather than connoisseur enthusiasm— to be compared with other late Georgian or Victorian antiquarys' houses, such as L. N. Cottingham's house in Waterloo Bridge Road, Tennyson D'Eyncourt's Bayons or the armour-filled and relic-studded rooms of Scott's Abbotsford. Its colour-schemes must have been Rembrandt or Martin rather than pre-raphaelite; sombre and dusky, with dark varnished woodwork everywhere. Pugin's adventures as a colourist did not really start until the mid-1840s, with his interiors at the Houses of Parliament and gorgeous decoration for the church at Cheadle. What colour there was at Scarisbrick would have come mainly from the pictures, of which only those *in situ* remain, built into the red drawing room overmantel and the panelling of the next door King's room. The former are especially charming and show Charles Scarisbrick and (presumably) his mistress and illegitimate children in medieval dress before Scarisbrick Hall; the latter feature Kings and Queens, many of them based on original portraits but still looking like early Victorian ladies and gentlemen in fancy dress posing before stage-set backgrounds.[5] Their soft dappled colouring contrasts notably with the expanses of primary reds and blues applied to the ceiling when Crace decorated it for Anne Scarisbrick in the 1860s; but the combination of the two

85. (above left) The chimneypiece in the red drawing room.

86. (above right) Charles Scarisbrick, his mistress, and children in Tudor dress before Scarisbrick Hall, Lancashire, *c.* 1840, by an unknown artist.

with Pugin's rich panelling and joinery, here entirely Gothic, make this little room the richest, least bizarre and most successful of all the interiors at Scarisbrick.

In the three reception rooms in the west wing—the red drawing room, the King's room and another drawing room damaged by fire in this century and with no original decoration—Pugin was confined to the simple rectangular shapes of existing rooms. Elsewhere he had a little more latitude, and his treatment of space is curious and individual. He seems to have thought of it not as enclosed in well-defined units between walls, but as something continuous in which he erected a series of frameworks. He avoided rooms with hard edges and was fascinated by the idea of a scaffolding of timber hanging or rising in a vacuum. The walls of the hall are like pierced curtains, with the space running out into the bay windows. There is a curious aerial framework up at the top of the roof, and an even more delicate and elaborate one supporting the roof of the kitchen (patterned after the Abbot's Kitchen, Glastonbury). The spindly scaffolding of the main staircase is a highly personal version of the continuous-newel staircases of the early seventeenth century. The upper corridor is top-lit and half the width of the lower, allowing light to come down to it through an elaborate pierced wooden framework of openings, beams and balusters.

In 1860 the corpse of Charles Scarisbrick was carried, as he had directed in his will, in a straight line from the house to the church, across three ditches, a meadow, a

116

87. (above left) Scarisbrick Hall. The staircase.

88. (above right) The kitchen roof.

wheat-field and a field of cabbages, and through a gap in the presbytery wall which he had ordered to be left open, to the mystification of the workmen, when the wall was built twelve years earlier. In the next year his sister Anne, Lady Hunloke (soon to call herself Lady Scarisbrick) made a triumphant entry into her inheritance, driving out from Ormskirk through cheering crowds of tenantry. The latter, however, were considerably reduced, for Charles Scarisbrick had left everything he could to his illegitimate children. Anne Scarisbrick inherited a house stripped of its contents, and it was probably with no friendly feelings toward her brother that, at the age of seventy-two, she started on a building programme that seemed deliberately designed to outshine and overpower his work. As her architect she employed Edward Welby Pugin, who was not the man to be averse to beating a big drum, even when it involved destroying the balance of his father's design. The date 1862 is carved at the end of his new east wing, and the house was described and

89. The King's room.

illustrated in the *Building News* of 24 April 1868, when it was said that the new work had cost £85,000.

The younger Pugin was a wildly uneven architect, but in his defence it needs to be said that his work at Scarisbrick is perhaps the best he ever did. Moreover, as the eye travels along the house, the move from early Victorian richness to mid-Victorian fantasy gives a feeling of growth and change which his father might not have been averse to. For art-historical reasons it would have been amusing to have had the precursor of Big Ben's tower still in existence, but one would not wish Edward Pugin's amazing 170-foot-high landmark away. The influence of French Gothic is apparent, and the chunkiness and muscularity of the 1860s is displayed in the stable block, and in the fireplaces and joinery internally. The stables are based, in their main outline but not at all in their detail, on the elder Pugin's unexecuted designs; he would not have liked the suggestion of fortifications for horses, and apertures for boiling oil over the entrance arch.

According to the *Building News* the 'whole of the interior has been executed since Lady Scarisbrick came into possession', Hardman, Crace, Farmer and others being employed. This is an exaggeration, but Crace was certainly at work painting, and probably papering, Charles Scarisbrick's reception rooms, for Anne Scarisbrick's

90. Scarisbrick Hall. The main corridor.

initials are painted on the ceiling of the King's room. Most of the colour in the house, including the Minton tiles in the long corridor, probably dates from this period. A for Anne Scarisbrick and P for Pugin are frequently incorporated in the decoration, and the two are shown side by side in a stained-glass window by Hardman on the staircase in the new wing. Rightly or wrongly this suggests that the widow in her seventies had become a bit sweet on her young architect, for it was unusual for a Victorian architect to be commemorated in this way.

Anne Scarisbrick died in 1872 and after a complicated passage between various descendants and branches of the Scarisbricks, and a few unfortunate years of crisis during which the house lost some of its fittings and carvings, it was bought for use as a school in 1963.

91. E. W. Pugin's stable block.

4. Merevale Hall, Warwickshire

MEREVALE is typical of Blore both in its architecture and its builder. William Stratford Dugdale, like most of Blore's clients, was a substantial Tory landowner, M.P. for his county and member of an old and well-established family. He was a descendant of Sir William Dugdale, the great herald and antiquary. Merevale had come into his family through the marriage of his father to Penelope Stratford, whose ancestor had bought the property about 1650. On the site of the present building was an old house remodelled in the eighteenth century and a fine eighteenth-century stable block. According to W. S. Dugdale's diary,[1] he originally brought Blore in to add some bedrooms on top of the old dining room, which was where the drawing room is today. The old house was built of stone quarried at Merevale, of poor quality and in bad condition. The walls of the dining room turned out to be too weak to build on, and it was pulled down. Demolition revealed that the walls in the centre of the house were rotten, so the centre was demolished as well. In the end, probably the only parts of the old house to be incorporated in the new were in the servants' wing. In 1841 it was decided to rebuild the Georgian stables, which by then must have looked very old fashioned in comparison with the new house. What had been intended as a quick £5,000 job ended up by taking six years to build and costing £35,000.

The history of the Blore building is fully documented. Blore's sketches are in the British Museum; over three hundred working drawings are in the Print Room of the Victoria and Albert Museum; there are account books in the Cambridge University Library and at Merevale.[2] Blore paid his first visit on 23 April 1838. Work started in June and Blore visited the site regularly five or six times a year until his final visit on 3 April 1844. Day to day supervision was provided by 'Mr Jennings', probably Robert Jennings, who later designed the Corn Exchange at

120

92. Merevale Hall, Atherstone, Warwickshire (Edward Blore, 1838–44). The south-east front from below the terraces.

Atherstone in a style obviously influenced by that of Merevale. The first set of workmen were union men and went on strike in June 1839. Dugdale sacked the lot, and 'by September I collected another set of workmen who conformed to my rules and not to those of the Union—we had no more trouble with them during all the time the house was building'. The outside facades were built of brick faced with Hollington stone from Derbyshire; the brick was left exposed on the internal courtyards. Cast iron beams were used to span all the larger openings and cast iron ties to strengthen the longer timber beams. There was no central heating and only one bathroom.

Blore had made his reputation as a Gothic architect, but Merevale is one of a group of houses by him in the Elizabethan style, a style that he helped to make respectable. In the early 1830s he had failed to persuade the future Lord Wenlock to transform Escrick in Yorkshire into a nineteenth-century version of Burghley. He had more success at Pull Court, Worcestershire (1834–9), which was followed by Ramsey Abbey, Huntingdonshire (1837–9), Worsley Hall outside Manchester (1837–43) and Merevale (1838–44).

Merevale has a dramatic position on the end of a narrow peninsular of hill above Atherstone. To the south-west the hill rises above the house but on the other three sides the ground drops precipitously, and there are long views in all directions. The opportunities to enrich the skyline were too great for any Victorian architect to

121

93. (top) A distant view.

94. The north-west front today.

resist; the old house had been long and low with rooms only nine feet high but the
new one had much higher rooms, as well as one large and one small tower, besides
numerous turrets, so that it is a prominent landmark for miles around. But the
treatment of the towers show Blore's weakness as an architect; they are too skimpy
for the mass of the house, and the north-west front, in spite of its sensational hilltop
position, looks better in Blore's drawing of it than in reality. The south-east front,
which is a more conventional composition directly inspired by Elizabethan country
houses, is more successful and forms an impressive enough conclusion to the long
walk and flights of terraces laid out, almost inevitably at that date, by W. A.
Nesfield. The main wall surface, of the smoothest of smooth ashlar, forms a
backcloth for the various frills and prettinesses in the way of window and cornice
enrichment which the early Victorians delighted in; the result, particularly when the
front is seen in steep perspective, has the same kind of flicker and laciness as Barry's
facades at Highclere. It is interesting to compare this front with the lodge gateway
designed in 1848–9 by Henry Clutton, Blore's ex-pupil and a more interesting
architect. Blore's smooth regular stonework and small-scale detail and Clutton's
bold shapes and irregular courses of less finely jointed masonry, epitomise the
differences between early and mid-Victorian architecture, and show how great a
difference ten years and one generation could make.★

The main entrance was originally planned to have been in the conventional

★ 'Joseph Floyd, who is to inhabit the gate-house, is in a fuss about the winding stairs. He says, "How
is my coffin to be got down it. I suppose you intend me to die downstairs." ' (W. S. Dugdale's diary,
12 Mar. 1848). Clutton had worked under Blore at Merevale and succeeded him as the Dugdales'
architect.

122

95. Merevale Hall. Blore's drawing for the north-west front.

position, in the centre of the main south-east front. But most of the living rooms were strung along this front, and Mrs Dugdale is said to have complained that callers would pass her at the window as they drove up to the door, and make it embarrassing for her to say she was not at home. In the summer of 1842, as Blore's drawings and accounts make clear, it was decided to give convenience priority over symmetry and to move the entrance round the corner to the end of the house. A similar arrangement had already been adopted at Sheringham (1812–19) and Mamhead (1827–33), and it was to become a common one for Victorian houses, as, for example, at Bilton Grange, Horsted, Kelham and Brodsworth.

One of the best views of the house is as one approaches it from the south and sees the main bulk of the house rising in a picturesque confusion of battlements, chimneys and turrets above the stables. The effect is not accidental, for it is shown in a nice sketch by Blore in the British Museum. The stables and kitchen wing are of rusticated stone instead of ashlar, and mildly Gothic instead of Elizabethan. The approach runs along them into a forecourt in front of the new entrance. A wide corridor (remodelled by Clutton in 1853) leads from this into the staircase hall, linked by a screen of three arches to what was originally intended to be the entrance hall. The staircase is the pivot of the house. On the first floor, the arches of the screen are repeated in the form of an arcade, opening on two sides into the bedroom corridors and on the other two sides filled with windows looking on to small internal courtyards. It is an attractive arrangement, classical and late Georgian in its main lines but given an agreeable early Victorian flavour by a gentle infilling of Elizabethan ornament, and by the heraldic stained glass which fills the windows.

The ground floor rooms are very high, as was the fashion at the time; the dining

123

96. (above left) Looking along the south-east front.

97. (above right) The gatehouse, designed by Henry Clutton, 1848.

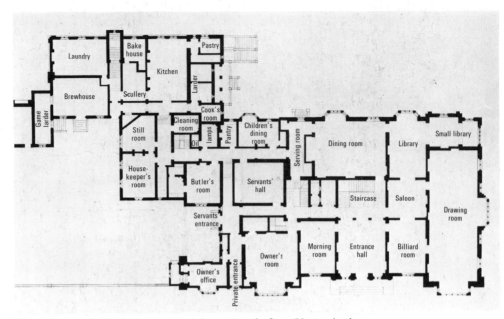

Fig. 9. Merevale Hall. The ground-floor plan, before Clutton's alterations.

98. (above) Merevale Hall. The entrance court on the south-west.

VII. (right) Scarisbrick Hall, Lancashire. A. W. Pugin's design for the hall fireplace.

VIII. (top) Scarisbrick Hall, Lancashire. Drawing of the exterior by A. W. Pugin.

IX. Scarisbrick Hall, Lancashire. Two roundels by A. W. Pugin.

room is 19 feet high and the other rooms 17 feet 3 inches. They are arranged conveniently and easily around the staircase hall and a top-lit vestibule that leads off it. The dining room has a two-tier Jacobean chimneypiece and a formidable sideboard recess lined with velvet and looking-glass. The room was furnished and curtained in 1844 by W. & E. Snell, of 27 Albemarle Street. They supplied the Jacobean sideboard and side tables with their bulbous legs, the ornately bulging wine cooler, the Jacobean plate warmer and the twenty-four elegant Victorian rococo chairs, which still retain their 'seats and backs stuffed and covered in Claret Morocco Leather'. Snell's bill came to about £1,000 and the firm took the Georgian dining room furniture from the old house in part payment for £146. The dining room lights (of Argand type, and originally made for oil) came from Perry and Co. of New Bond Street.[3]

The most attractive of the living rooms is the L-shaped library between the dining room and the huge drawing room. Most of the rooms have Elizabethan chimneypieces, but others have chimneypieces of more classical design, probably put in by Clutton in the 1850s.[4] Inside and out Blore's plastering and stonework are of mechanical precision and smoothness, qualities which readily distinguish it from genuine Elizabethan work, but were no doubt thought of by the early Victorians as an improvement on the original—as was the use of large sheets of glass instead of leaded lights in the windows.[5] Blore's Elizabethan detail is derivative and

127

99. Merevale Hall. The dining room.

100. Merevale Hall. The entrance hall.

101. The head of the staircase.

uninteresting, but it is also agreeably unobtrusive; the rooms are spacious, well lit and sensibly planned, and when one is in them one can understand why Blore was so successful a country house architect. William Stratford Dugdale described Merevale in his diary as 'handsome and very comfortable'.

The diary is a full one covering most of his life, and gives an interesting picture of a Victorian country gentleman who followed the trend of his age toward the serious. By 1848 he was regretting that he had not restored the church before he rebuilt the house—'I didn't at that time consider these duties as I ought.' There was coal on his estate, which he exploited on a considerable scale. With Clutton as his architect he built a church for his colliers at Baddesley in 1845–6 and a new rectory and gateway by the church at Merevale in 1848–9. Both his son and grandson were at Balliol under Jowett, who became a family friend.★ One still gets a feeling of Jowett at Merevale—a sense of a hard-working and conscientious upper-class Victorian family, not especially sensitive to visual niceties, as the cases of stuffed birds and comfortable miscellany of contents make clear.

★ E. Abbott and Lewis Campbell, *Benjamin Jowett* (London, 1897), I, pp. 126–7; II, p. 195. It is nice to think of Jowett reciting Homer's account of the death of Hector to the eight-year-old son of his host in the nursery at Merevale.

102. (upper right) A corner of the library.

103. (right) Balliol mementoes in the owner's dressing room.

5. Highclere Castle, Hampshire

HIGHCLERE is a good example of how an eighteenth-century house and park were worked over to make them palatable to early Victorian taste. The property was inherited in 1833 by Henry John George Herbert, third Earl of Carnarvon, whose family was a younger branch of the Herberts of Wilton. It consisted of a house remodelled in 1774–7 and a park of great natural beauty which had been plentifully sprinkled with temples and arches in the eighteenth century, and given its final form by Capability Brown in 1770–1.

The third Earl had been a traveller and author and both his travellings and writings were typical of his age. He toured extensively in North Africa, Spain, Portugal and Greece; he wrote several travel books, a poem in six cantos, *The Moor*, and a tragedy, *Don Pedro: King of Castile*, which was produced at the Drury Lane Theatre in 1828. Neither the correct but somewhat frigid classicism of the house nor the smooth Capability Brown vistas of the park were to his taste. The park could be dealt with easily enough by lavish planting of conifers and rhododendrons, and by adding a few frills to the principal temple. But for the house (as for the temple) he called on the services of Charles Barry.

The Georgian house was of reticent design; Alfred Barry in his biography of his father called it an example of the 'comparative flatness and insipidity of bare

130

104. Highclere Castle, nr Newbury, Hampshire (Sir Charles Barry, 1840–50). The south front, from a Victorian photograph.

classicism'.[1] It had an engaged central portico and groups of pilasters at the corners, separated from each other by plain, undecorated facades. Barry set out to replace these differentiations in emphasis by a rich overall intricacy, and to liven up the skyline. He made three separate sets of designs, in 1838, 1840 and 1842, before he satisfied his client. The designs are still preserved at Highclere but all letters and accounts have disappeared.[2]

The first scheme is dated 22 May 1838 on the plans and elevations, but is best illustrated by a water-colour perspective. It shows the house transformed into something resembling Barry's Italianate work at Trentham Park, though without the tower. The groups of Doric pilasters are still there; but they have lost their isolation and are linked together by rows of pilaster strips which run all the way round the house. Both wall-surfaces and skyline have been enriched, the former by the provision of elaborate rustication and of pediments to the first-floor windows, the latter by the addition of little Italianate turrets to the main block, and of a turreted conservatory at one corner.

Lord Carnarvon clearly wanted something richer still: and perhaps as a Tory he also wanted something distinguishable from the Italianate mansions Barry had built for his Whig patrons. Barry's second and third designs were what he called 'Anglo-Italian', by which he meant the kind of architecture produced by the Elizabethans and Jacobeans when most under classical influence. The change of style enabled him

131

105. (top) The Georgian house.

106. Barry's 1838 design for remodelling.

107. Highclere Castle. A detail of the east front.

to apply ornament and incident, in the form of turrets, towers, obelisks, strapwork, enriched pilasters and carved panels under the windows, so as to give a far richer effect than anything he had so far done in the Italian line. The two sets of designs (the second one similar to but slightly more elaborate than the first) are dated May 1840 and February 1842; the final form of the great tower was decided on later still, and its foundation stone was laid by Lord Carnarvon's son, Lord Porchester (later Colonial Secretary and Viceroy of Ireland) on 24 June 1842, his eleventh birthday. The remodelling was only skin deep; the old Highclere (which was of brick) is still all there behind the new stone outer crust, and according to Alfred Barry, not only were the main walls preserved, with scarcely any extensions of the building or plan other than the building of the tower, but even the secondary features were not altered; 'in no case was the level of any floor or the opening of a window changed'.

Alfred Barry goes on to say of his father that 'the building thus transformed was one of his favourite works'. Although it is possible to trace many of its features back to Elizabethan and Jacobean sources, the final effect is unlike that of any house of that date. In its main outlines it is reminiscent of the Elizabethan Wollaton Hall, near Nottingham; both houses have four corner turrets, a great central tower and a recessed front, and are decorated with alcoves and ornamented pilasters. But the proportions at Highclere are quite different; the corner towers, like the skimpy turrets at Merevale, are much slenderer than anything the Elizabethans would have used in a similar position; and above all the facades are modelled in a peculiarly early Victorian way. The windows are joined to each other horizontally and vertically by mouldings and panels; the facades are thickly scattered, and at skyline level encrusted with ornament; and as a result the house has a net-like and almost lacy quality which is accentuated by the shallow bowls of light and shade provided by the alcoves on the tower and east front. This fondness for intricate and all-over ornament was typical of the period, as is clearly shown by the type of building that

132

108. The house from the north-east.

was then admired, such as the more elaborate late Gothic buildings of northern France or Belgium and the intricate honeycomb decoration of the Alhambra in Spain.★ On his travels as a young man Barry had been much struck by Egyptian architecture for similar reasons. 'The impressions made on him', says his son, 'by the mixture of general grandeur of outline and dimensions with profuse richness of detail was never effected.' In fact the facades of the Houses of Parliament, on which he was working at the same time as he designed Highclere, have a system of grid-like and encrusted decoration, leaving no plain wall spaces, which is exactly similar to that employed at Highclere, though carried out in Gothic rather than 'Anglo-Italian' idiom; and at Bridgewater House Barry managed to transmute Italian Renaissance architecture into something as similarly and elaborately early Victorian.†

There is little of Barry's inside the house; the interior (with the exception of one room) is of a notably lower standard than the exterior. Barry had prepared designs for an overpoweringly rich Italianate central hall to go with the 1840–2 scheme, and a rather soberer hall, in his Reform Club manner, for the scheme of 1838. But—either because the money ran out, or because Barry and Carnarvon quarrelled, or because operations were cut short by Carnarvon's death in 1849—nothing was done. It was left to Lord Carnarvon's son, the fourth Earl, after his marriage in 1861, to take on where his father left off.

★ 'The minute carving, the delicacy yet richness of detail, produce an indescribable fascination on the traveller who beholds it for the first time; with little variety of surface or bold projection all is graceful and harmonious, and like the regular features of perfect beauty, for a few minutes rivet his attention.' (Lord Carnarvon on the Alhambra, in the introduction to Canto V of his poem *The Moor* (2nd edn, 1827).)
† 'Well do I remember Lord Beaconsfield walking with some of us in front of the house, suddenly coming to a halt, and in impressive tones ejaculating: "How scenical! how scenical!"' (Lady Dorothy Nevill on Highclere, in her *Reminiscences* (London, 1906), p. 141.)

133

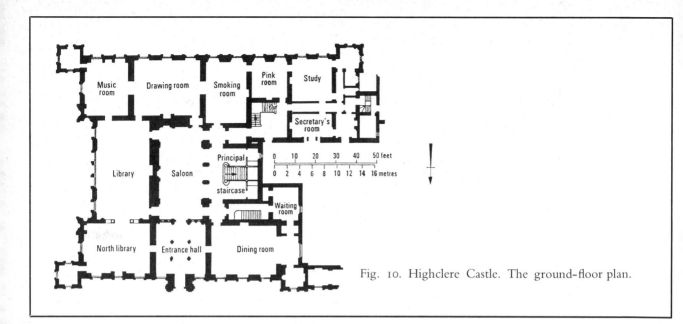

Fig. 10. Highclere Castle. The ground-floor plan.

Barry had died the previous year; and the fourth Earl went instead to Thomas Allom, a man who was better known as an illustrator and architectural draughtsman than as an architect. He had produced a series of topographical picture-books, covering subjects ranging from the counties of England to Constantinople; and he was much in demand by other architects when they wanted attractive water-colour drawings made of their designs. He had worked in this way for Barry, producing a series of water-colours of the Houses of Parliament which had been much admired; and it was no doubt his connection with Barry which got him the Highclere commission. In 1862 he exhibited at the Royal Academy an *Interior of the Hall at Highclere Castle*, on which the *Civil Engineer and Architect's Journal* commented: 'An artistic composition, if we regard only the general effect. A close scrutiny betrays questionable details.' Their critic spoke with some justice; for the design was an illiterate and curiously old-fashioned one in the Gothic of the 1820s, rather than the 1860s, and furthermore was executed in stucco, a material by then regarded with the deepest distaste. The main staircase with rather eccentric Gothic–Elizabethan detailing is probably the only interior carried out to Barry's designs;[3] on the first landing is a charming childhood group of Lord Porchester (later the fourth Earl) and his sister, Lady Evelyn Herbert, carved in Rome by Tenerani in 1839.

In contrast to the saloon and staircase the great chocolate-and-gold library at Highclere is in the best tradition of Victorian club room architecture and has the rich plumminess and masculine opulence which the Victorians could produce better than any other age. But it is not clear who was responsible for its decoration. There are various designs by Allom for redecorating the two rooms of which it consists, but they all envisage using them as a drawing room and billiard room; the only feature in common with what is there today is the screen of columns between the north and south sections of the library.

The music room, drawing room and entrance hall are quite different not only from the saloon and library but also from each other. The music room is an odd example of eighteenth-century fragments made up in Victorian times: long strips of

134

109. (right) The main hall (Thomas Allom, 1862).

embroidery alternate with painted panels, said to have been brought from Italy; the oval canvas set in the ceiling looks more like English early eighteenth-century work, and might come from the pre-Victorian Highclere. The adjoining drawing room was redecorated about 1900 by the fifth Earl, the great Egyptologist and discoverer of Tutankhamen's tomb, and is a lavish example of late Victorian rococo. In complete contrast is the serious and solid Gothic revival work of the entrance hall. With its gleaming encaustic-tiled floor (designed by no less an architect than Butterfield[4]) and its scholarly stone rib-vaulting it is very different from the stucco Gothic of the adjoining saloon and adds the final touch of variety to the curious miscellany of Highclere's interiors.

136

110. (above) Highclere Castle. The staircase.
111. (upper right) The library, possibly decorated by Allom.
112. (right) The entrance hall.

6. *Prestwold Hall, Leicestershire*

WHEN Charles William Packe inherited Prestwold Hall in 1837 it cannot have given him much pleasure. It was an extremely plain mid-eighteenth-century house to which William Wilkins had made minor alterations about 1805.[1] In 1842 he called in William Burn to remodel and enlarge it. He probably went to Burn on the strength of his work at Harlaxton (1838) and Stoke Rochford (1839), both about twenty miles from Prestwold. These two houses were Elizabethan, like most of Burn's English houses; at Prestwold he kept to the classical style of the building that he remodelled. His client was a Leicestershire squire with a comfortable income (£11,807 from 6,234 acres) descended from a Lord Mayor of London who had bought the estate in the mid-seventeenth century. The alterations to Prestwold suggest that he had conservative taste and was cautious with his money. But the cautiousness and the conservatism are equally typical of Burn, whose houses were never as opulent as those of his contemporary Barry. Indeed they are often rather dull; but Prestwold is one of his more successful designs, and it is a pleasure to see how neatly, and with what comparatively modest means, he brought the house sufficiently into line with the taste of the 1840s.

Barry would almost certainly have added a tower, to give picturesque variety to the skyline. Burn contented himself with additions that obtained a similar effect but also usefully increased the accommodation of the house. He lengthened the south front by four bays and brought it forward at either end, in the form of shallow projecting wings, each three bays wide. There were already two similar wings on the west (entrance) front; Burn gave the house greater variety of modelling by increasing them to four, inserting a *porte-cochère* between the wings on the west front, and building a columned conservatory in a similar position on the south front. He combined this increase of variety in the major masses with richer modelling of

113. (above) Prestwold Hall, nr Loughborough, Leicestershire (William Burn, 1842–4). The entrance front.
114. (upper right) The garden front.
115. (right) The house in the late eighteenth century.

the individual facades; he refaced them with Ancaster stone and added mouldings to the windows, quoins at the corners, a balustrade above the cornice and arched heads to the ground-floor windows on the south front. The enrichment was extended to the surroundings. The plain turf that in the eighteenth century had come right up to the house was replaced by a formal garden separated from the park by a balustrade. Rather surprisingly the new east front was built of rendered brick, on one plane only, and with no parapet. A new service wing was added, sufficiently elaborate, although not approaching the complexity found in Burn's grander commissions. A separate staircase served a family suite, including a ground-floor sitting room for Mr Packe and a boudoir for his wife immediately above it.

Except, possibly, for the round-headed windows there is no sign of the current Italianate fashion in the external detail; the most apparent influence is that of the plainer houses of the early eighteenth century, Talman's Dyrham in particular. But inside, Italian influence is much in evidence in the hall and corridors. Burn put a large new dining room and drawing room into his eastern extension and ran three old rooms on the south front together to make an agreeable and unusual library, in enfilade with the drawing room. He made generous use of iron beams, which bridge the wide spans of drawing room and dining room, carry the billiard room lantern, and support brick partition walls (and at least one chimney-breast) on the second floor, above the recess off the drawing room and the openings between the three sections of the library.[2] Drawing room and library have views into the conservatory; the drawing room is flooded with light and sun coming through low-silled windows facing south and east. But its decoration and that of the dining room have been somewhat altered, while the library was refitted by Gillows in 1875. The elaborately decorated circulation spaces have remained untouched.

The original Georgian entrance had been on the south front. Wilkins moved it round to the west, made a new hall and formed a long narrow corridor leading past the staircase to a domed vestibule next to the dining room. Burn widened the corridor and linked it by screens of arches to the entrance hall and to a top-lit billiard room formed in an open space between the old house and Burn's new dining and drawing rooms. The corridor also opened out into the staircase and a surviving portion of Wilkins's vestibule.

The effect of these alterations was to open up the whole spine of the house into a series of linked spaces, each space being treated individually as a formal and symmetrical design, but all the spaces adding up to an irregular and asymmetrical whole. To go from the *porte-cochère* to the drawing room involves a long and variegated walk, first crossing the hall diagonally to pass through the screen into the corridor, and then walking along the corridor with a series of different vistas opening out to one side. It is a synthesis of classical and picturesque principles of planning that was to be frequently used by the Victorians when they wanted to produce an impressive effect both in classical and in Gothic houses—as, for example, at Brodsworth and Kelham. But both the two latter houses are extravagant in their use of space; it was typical of Burn that he achieved his effect with Scottish economy, using functional counters—a hall, staircase and billiard room, all of moderate size.

This internal planning is the counterpart of his three-dimensional alterations

116. (upper left) Prestwold Hall. The entrance hall.

117. (upper right) The former billiard room.

118. (lower left) A lobby at the end of the corridor.

119. (lower right) The main corridor.

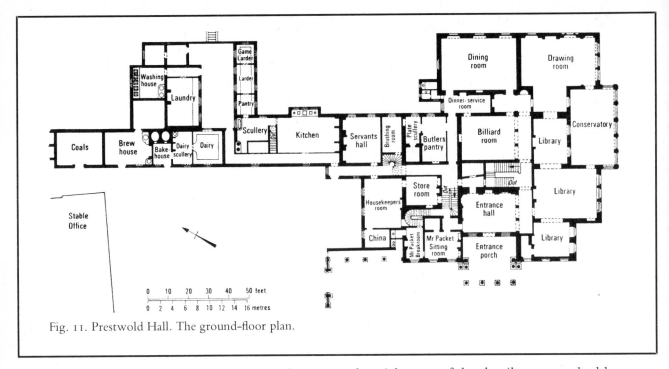

Fig. 11. Prestwold Hall. The ground-floor plan.

externally; in the same way his external enrichment of the detail was matched by internal enrichment of the decoration. The unifying motif is a series of arches and vaults which spring from square piers and half-piers, instead of from columns and pilasters. The motif had been used a few years previously, and on a far larger scale, for the new entrance hall added by Henry Thomas Hope to the Deepdene, possibly to his own designs.[3] This hall was marbled like that at Prestwold and had similar circular medallions in the spandrels. The source may well have been Alberti's external arcade at the Tempio Malatestiano at Rimini. Renaissance influence is also apparent in the painted coved ceiling of the hall at Prestwold, inspired by Raphael's grotesques in the Vatican. On the cove are little framed landscapes, showing Prestwold before and after alteration; in the lunettes between them are portraits of British poets from Chaucer to Scott. The artist is not known, but the decorations are strongly reminiscent of those which the German artists Frederick Sang and Naundorff painted in 1844 or 1845 on the similarly coved ceilings of the hall and staircase at the new Conservative Club in St James's Street.[4]

The walls throughout are very skilfully painted in oil colours to simulate marble. The hall is marbled in green, brown and red; the lunettes above the doors have a porphyry background; the ceiling is richly polychromatic. The corridor has ribbed vaults with pendentives, making a network of light and shade that combines with the patterning of walls and ceiling to produce the rich overall play of decoration and chiaroscuro that the Victorians delighted in.

Charles Packe had no children; the estate was entailed on his brother. In later life he quarrelled with his heir about the felling of some timber, abandoned and partly dismantled Prestwold, and bought the Branksome Park estate outside Bournemouth, where Burn designed him another house in 1852. He and his wife were buried on their Bournemouth property; their mausoleum still survives, marooned among later villas.[5]

142

X. (right) Prestwold Hall, Leicestershire. The hall ceiling

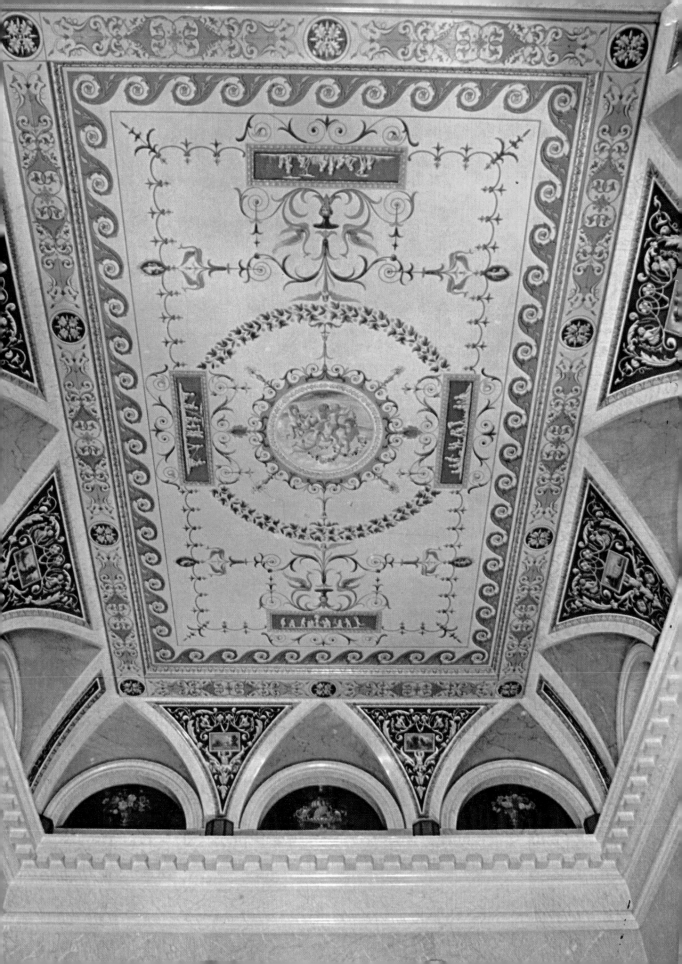

XI. Highclere Castle, Hampshire (Sir Charles Barry, 1840–50). Barry's 1840 design for remodelling the house.

XII. (right) Osborne House, Isle of Wight. The ground-floor corridor, which links the Royal Pavilion to the main block.

XIII. Osborne House, Isle of Wight (Thomas Cubitt and the Prince Consort, 1844-8). The garden front, with the Royal Pavilion to the right.

7. Osborne, Isle of Wight

EARLY in her reign Victoria began to consider the possibility of using her private fortune to buy a house where she could retire in the summer, in order to obtain a certain amount of seclusion. She had visited the Isle of Wight as a girl and stayed at Norris Castle outside Cowes; in 1839 and 1843 there was a possibility that she might have bought it. In the end she bought the adjacent Osborne House estate from Lady Isabella Blachford. The sale took place in March 1844. It was decided to rebuild the existing house, and the foundation-stone of the new building was laid in June 1845.[1] It was to be divided into two main parts, a pavilion for the royal family and a big adjoining block for visitors and courtiers. The Royal Pavilion was ready for use in 1846. The old house was left untouched until the Pavilion, which was built next door to it, was ready; it was then demolished and replaced by the main block which was finished in 1848. The house (it was deliberately a house, not a palace) became one of the best known, most illustrated and most imitated in the world. Its popularity extended to America and the colonies, as well as within England. It inspired town halls, station buildings, suburban villas and seaside hotels as well as country houses. In the country house field a sudden rush of mini-Osbornes in the late 1840s was followed by a decreasing number of offspring until as late as the 1870s.[2]

Osborne was influential because of its royal occupants and prominent position above the Solent, more than through any originality or high quality in its architecture. It was a variant on the theme which Barry had worked out at

147

120. The entrance front.

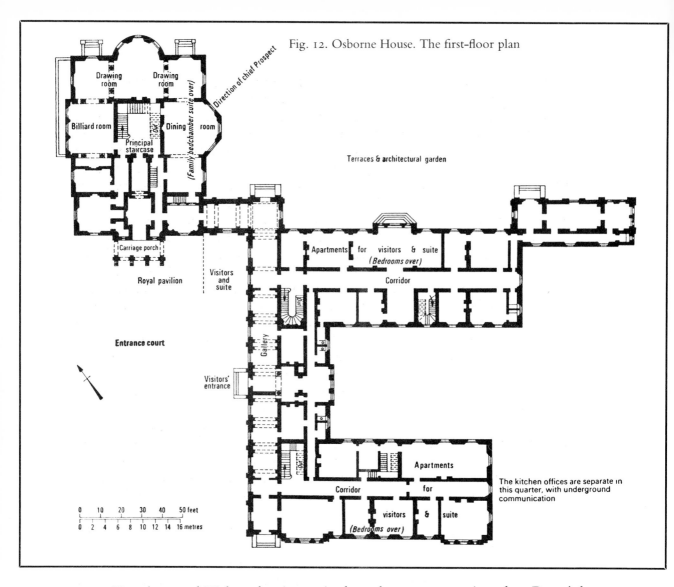

Fig. 12. Osborne House. The first-floor plan

Trentham and Walton, but it acquired much greater notoriety than Barry's houses because the latter were only known to a small, if select, circle. Barry would have been the obvious architect but he was not chosen. Albert may already have taken against him; by 1853 he was saying that 'every step Sir Charles takes requires careful watching'.[3] In any case he probably did not want to employ someone with a big name, and Victoria deferred to him in artistic matters. The Victorian royal family had an undistinguished record as patrons of architects; but, whereas Victoria and the Prince of Wales probably chose dim architects owing to ignorance or lack of interest, Albert chose them because he liked to have the ideas himself and employ a professional to work them out.

At Balmoral he employed William Smith, an obscure architect from Aberdeen. At Osborne he employed Thomas Cubitt, who was an able and distinguished man, but distinguished as a builder and property developer rather than as an architect. He had developed much of Bloomsbury and almost all of Belgravia; in middle life he started to design the terraces which he built. Albert probably selected him on the

148

strength of his Belgravia development which was literally at the bottom of the Buckingham Palace garden. In the eighteenth century he would have been accepted as an architect; in the professionally conscious Victorian age Robert Kerr called him 'perhaps as near an approach to an architect as any man not an architect could be'.[4] As a designer he was a product of the Georgian terrace tradition; although by the 1840s he was facing his buildings with fashionable Italianate detail in the Barry manner, the kind of complicated composition which Albert wanted at Osborne was more than he and Albert between them could manage.[5]

The basic division into a main block with a family pavilion attached to one side was almost certainly derived from Barry's Trentham, for Victoria was a friend of the Sutherlands and knew the house well. But the professional ease with which Barry would combine symmetrical parts into an irregular whole is noticeably lacking at Osborne. The main block is like a vastly overgrown Belgravia mansion, to which the Royal Pavilion is uncomfortably attached by an umbilical cord of open arcading. At one corner of the Pavilion is a Barryesque belvedere tower; a slightly different tower is attached by more arcading to the opposite side of the main block. To incorporate two prominent towers of the same size into a picturesque composition would have presented difficulties to the most skilful of architects; at Osborne they are placed so as to give the impression of a design that was intended to be symmetrical, but which at some stage has gone astray.

The most agreeable aspect of Osborne is the feeling it gives of being a holiday residence by the sea. Whether the sea is to be thought of as the Mediterranean or the English Channel remains uncertain, probably due to the separate ambitions of Cubitt and Prince Albert. The stucco facades, and the striped Trafalgar balcony of the Royal Pavilion, suggest that Hove is not so far away; the open loggia along the south-west front of the main block and the terraced gardens stretching down through ilexes and cedars towards the waters of the Solent give something of the illusion of a Mediterranean villa.★ The main axis of the house is set slightly askew to the axis of the vista down to the sea, probably in order to give two fronts of the Pavilion the benefit of the sea view. It means, however, that the building is on a diagonal slope; the attempts to ignore this in the formal planning of the gardens and terraces led to some curious though quite ingenious makeshifts.

Once inside the Royal Pavilion, Albert's and Cubitt's work appears in a more agreeable light. There is a family feeling about it. This was what Victoria and Albert were after and it makes the idea of a separate Pavilion seem a very sensible one. The rooms are not too large, but spacious, light and well proportioned. Cubitt's Belgravia drawing room plasterwork, resembling Regency decoration gone to seed, is not very discriminating, but it is undemanding and pleasingly coloured in a gentle harlequinade of soft blues, pinks, greens and golds. The bay windows diversify the shape of the rooms and the views across the terrace and down to the sea are always a pleasure, for the situation is a beautiful one and the garden design more competent than the architecture. The rooms are grouped round a central staircase, at

★ 'A Sicilian palazzo with gardens, terraces, statues and vases shining in the sun, than which nothing can be conceived more captivating.' (Disraeli on Osborne, quoted Robert Blake, *Disraeli* (London, 1966), p. 418.)

the head of which is a great fresco by Dyce of *Neptune Entrusting the Command of the Sea to Britannia* with many frolicking mermaids in attendance. All around this is decoration in the manner of Raphael's Vatican loggias, probably by Ludwig Gruner.

The feature which was most at variance with accepted Victorian standards of planning, and which Kerr inevitably picked out to condemn, strikes one today as especially agreeable and sensible. The billiard room, the drawing room in three sections and the dining room in two, all open into each other round three sides of the staircase, with screens of scagliola columns to mark the divisions. The advantage of this open plan was that all the necessary equerries and ladies-in-waiting could be in attendance without the rooms seeming too large, and that they could be conveniently on call round the corner without having to stand because they were in the royal presence. The idea of linked saloons probably derived from the Riesensaal at Schloss Ehrenburg in Albert's Coburg, but there the sequence is in a straight line. By bending it round three sides of a square the arrangement was made much less formal.

New furniture was designed for the reception rooms by Henry Whitaker and made by Hollands. Mary Thorneycroft's pretty if sentimental sculptures of the Queen's four eldest children as the Seasons were installed in the drawing room in 1846; the baby princess Beatrice seated in a shell was added in 1858. The elaborately inlaid billiard table, with cues and score-board to match, was made by Messrs Thurston and is another original fitting. When trying to visualize the rooms as they were in the 1840s one has to think away a mass of later accretions; originally they would not have been at all crowded. In particular, Victoria's private rooms are full of the fascinating junk of a lifetime's hoarding. These private rooms—Victoria's and

121. (above) Osborne House. *Neptune entrusting the Command of the Sea to Britannia* at the head of the main staircase. Fresco by William Dyce.
122. (upper right) The billiard room, from a Victorian photograph.
123. (right) The drawing room, from a Victorian photograph.

Albert's on the first floor and the nurseries above—were pleasantly and unassumingly furnished by Dowbiggin, and are agreeably domestic. Albert's dressing and writing rooms were originally lined with paintings by Giorgione, Mantegna, Bellini and other early Italians—all long ago removed to the National Gallery, or to Buckingham Palace and other royal residences.

Victoria and Albert each had a separate dressing room complete with bath and shower; in Victoria's dressing room they were nicely concealed in cupboards (Pl. 12). This was very progressive for the date. Cubitt buildings were always technologically in the van of contemporary developments. Osborne is an early example of fireproof construction applied to domestic design; its use enables the buildings to have flat promenade roofs, with a double skin for insulation. There was no central heating, perhaps because the house was intended as a summer residence. The Pavilion tower contained a water tank, the other tower a clock. Albert stood at the top of the towers and directed the planting of the garden by semaphore flags. The kitchens are on the far side of the main block, with amazingly inconvenient connection by underground passage to the Pavilion. Much more agreeable is the connection between the two buildings on the ground floor, by a large and spacious corridor, lined with statues in alcoves and gay with Minton tiles. This corridor is underneath the open loggia, which performs a similar function on the floor above.

Osborne was enlarged and embellished by Queen Victoria in her later years. In 1853 a Swiss chalet was shipped over in pieces and erected in the grounds for the royal children. Its beautifully functional little kitchen is much the most capable piece of design at Osborne. About the Durbar wing added in 1890 the less said the better. The design of the huge Durbar Room was the responsibility of Rudyard Kipling's father, in collaboration with Bhai Rham Singh, an expert on Indian decoration.

When Queen Victoria died in 1901 the main block became a Naval College, and later a convalescent home for civil servants; the Pavilion was shut up and the contents left largely as they were. The Pavilion is now administered by the Department of the Environment and open to the public.

124. (above) The kitchen for the royal children in the Swiss Chalet.

125. (right) Osborne House. Queen Victoria's writing desk.

8. Peckforton Castle, Cheshire

TRAVELLERS on the line between Chester and Crewe must frequently have been jerked from their somnolence by the abrupt eruption of a group of steep and jagged hills from the flat Cheshire plain. The shape and suddenness of these hills is not the only strange thing about them. On the crest of the one nearest to the railway crouches the squat but powerful silhouette of Beeston Castle. Along the top of the lower hill beyond it rides the extended silhouette of another castle, bigger and, as far as can be judged through the enveloping trees, better than Beeston. The combination of two such ambitious fortifications gazing at each other across a space of a few hundred yards is not the result of some forgotten feud of the Middle Ages. Beeston is a genuine castle of the thirteenth century; Peckforton Castle, its rival, was built between 1844 and 1850 by John (later the first Lord) Tollemache to the designs of Anthony Salvin. To build in such open competition with the genuine article was a typical example of Victorian self-confidence. Peckforton emerges at least with honour; whether the contest should have been entered on in the first place is, of course, another matter.

Many did not think so at the time. A few years after it had been completed, Sir George Gilbert Scott made an anonymous but easily identifiable attack on it in his *Remarks on Secular and Domestic Architecture* (1858). 'The monstrous practice of castle-building', he wrote,

> is, unhappily, not yet extinct . . . The largest and most carefully and learnedly executed Gothic mansion of the present day is not only a castle in name—it is not a sham fortress, such as those of twenty years back, whose frowning gateway is perhaps flanked on either side with a three-foot clipped hedge—but it is a real and carefully constructed medieval fortress, capable of standing a siege from an Edwardian army . . . Now this is the very height of masquerading. The learning

154

126. Peckforton Castle, Tarporley, Cheshire (Anthony Salvin, 1844–50). The castle from the distance.

and skill with which the pageant has been carried out reflect the highest credit upon the architect; yet I cannot but feel it to have been a serious injury to our case, that so unreal a task should have been imposed on him.[1]

This kind of criticism was not confined to Scott. The great age of the sham castle was already over when Peckforton was started. In the 1830s and 1840s, Pugin and others began to make fun of the whole idea of modern castles, with formidably fortified gateways on one front and rows of plate-glass windows and a conservatory on the other. The satire had its effect, and it became increasingly hard to build a sham castle with an easy conscience. There remained two alternatives; either not to build a castle at all, or to build one with such overpowering scholarship as to flatten criticism. Most people took the former course, and the stream of sham castles grew thinner as the century went on. A few took the latter—like Lord Tollemache himself, or Lord Bute in Wales, or Lord Limerick in Ireland. The disadvantage of these serious-minded Victorian castles was that they were inevitably harder to live in than the more easy-going Regency ones. Small windows and bare stone walls tended to freeze the owner out in the end. Lord Bute's Castell Coch was never seriously lived in at all. Lord Limerick's Dromore Castle was sold by the Limericks in the 1920s, and finally dismantled some years ago. Peckforton has not been lived in since the war.

The character of Peckforton must owe a good deal to the character of the man

155

127. John, Baron Tollemache (1805–90), the builder of the castle, by Duff Tollemache.

who built it. Lord Tollemache[2] had inherited the Cheshire estate, along with Helmingham Hall in Suffolk, from his mother, who was a sister of the last Earl of Dysart, and whose husband had taken the Dysart family name of Tollemache. The original family house in Cheshire had been pulled down in the eighteenth century and his parents' house, Tilstone Lodge, was large but undistinguished. He built Peckforton to replace it, sat for Cheshire in Parliament from 1841 to 1872, and was created Lord Tollemache in 1876. He was one of those tremendous rock-hewn Victorians who seem built on a larger scale than ordinary men. He was a champion athlete when young, had twenty-four children, drove a four-in-hand in his eighties, and died, still vigorous, at the age of eighty-five. His convictions were as strong and unyielding as his body. He was a fervent evangelical, Bible-reader and Sabbatarian, and his family went in awe of him. He was of the generation of the Young Englanders, an upholder of the rights and powers of the landowning class, but with equally strong feelings about their duties to their dependants. 'The only real and lasting pleasure to be derived from the possession of a landed estate', he wrote, 'is to witness the improvement in the social condition of those residing on it.' Each labourer on his Cheshire estate—a big one of 26,000 acres—was supplied with a substantial cottage and three acres, which he could use to supplement his farm wages. There were 250 such holdings on the Peckforton estate, and the phrase 'three acres and a cow' has some claims to have originated from them. He liked his farms to be of 200 acres, no less and no more; he broke the estate up into 200 acre units, and built between fifty and sixty new farmhouses at a cost of £148,000. In all he had expended £280,000 on farm homesteads and new cottages up to 1881. Peckforton (which cost £68,000) was a modern feudal castle from which he could rule his great estate with the benevolent autocracy of a modern feudal overlord.[3]

Whatever reservations contemporaries may have had about Peckforton there was

156

128. Peckforton Castle. Looking along the outer wall to the great tower, as drawn by Salvin.

a general agreement that no one could have executed the commission better than Salvin. As the architect Alfred Waterhouse wrote to Lord Tollemache in 1878: 'Mr. Salvin is, of course, celebrated for the way in which he can combine the exterior and plan of an Edwardian Castle with nineteenth-century elegance and comfort.' In 1868 Sir Charles Barry's son Edward, in spite of doubts about 'castles built now-a-days as residences for nineteenth-century Englishmen', found its execution admirable and its architecture 'just what I should have expected from Salvin, good, simple and free from extravagance'.[4]

On the basis of Peckforton, Salvin was commissioned to restore or add to numerous castles, including the Tower of London in 1853–78, and Alnwick Castle, on which he expended a quarter of a million of his client's money in 1854–65. He deserved his reputation. Peckforton is a convincing re-creation of a medieval castle because Salvin had a feeling for the grouping of a castle as well as for its detail, indeed more feeling for the former than the latter. The plan of Peckforton and Salvin's own beautiful drawings for it[5] bring this out particularly clearly—more so, in some respects, than the buildings themselves, for the growth of the trees since the castle was built makes it hard to appreciate many of the features of the original design. Salvin realized that the distinguishing feature of most medieval castles is the way they are based on a defensive wall surrounding one or more irregularly shaped courts, with towers spaced along the outside of the wall and the domestic buildings built along the inside of the wall looking into the courts. By reproducing this arrangement in its main outlines he was able to fit in far more, and more complicated, accommodation than would ever have been found in a genuine castle, and, for the sake of convenience, make a number of deviations from strict archaeological correctness yet still keep a convincingly genuine general effect.

Salvin also realized that genuine castles were intended primarily for use, not effect,

157

129. The great tower, seen over the outer wall.

130. A detail by the coach house, in the entrance court.

had little elaborate ornament, and were built no higher than considerations of defence made necessary. The great tower at Peckforton is perhaps higher than it would have been in the Middle Ages, but the general effect of the whole building is long, low, sober and business-like, very unlike the earlier more flashy sham castles such as Belvoir and Penrhyn. Indeed, the way Salvin plays it quiet at Peckforton can be a little disappointing on a first visit; the idea of building a nineteenth-century castle on such a scale and in such a position is so extravagant that one expects the architecture to be equally extravagant; but it is not.

Salvin's feeling for the Middle Ages was perhaps a Victorian characteristic, but it was subtly combined at Peckforton with a quality which derived from his early training. Like Nash, whose pupil he had been, but in a much more sober way, he worked in the tradition of late Georgian picturesque. If one looks at his beautiful water-colours of Peckforton one can see how he composed it pictorially, subtly adjusting the angles of his walls and roofs so as to get different gradations of light and shade and contrasts between horizontal battlements and sloping gables. The apparently haphazard relationship of the various buildings is the result of a far from haphazard artistry. But the detail and texture of Peckforton are frequently not up to the level of its composition; superbly cut and laid though it is, the exterior stonework has as a result a mechanical quality that is slightly repellent—this is perhaps its least attractive feature, and the one that distinguishes it most clearly from a genuine medieval building.

The asymmetry of the courtyard allowed Salvin to adopt a remarkably functional plan—considering the limitations which the whole castle idea imposed on him and accepting, as the Victorians were prepared to, the possibility of having the kitchen sixty yards away from the dining room. Going in clockwise order round the courtyard; first, to the right of the entrance gateway, came the free-standing chapel;

131. (upper right) Peckforton Castle. One of Salvin's water-colours of the castle, with Beeston Castle in the distance.
132. (middle right) A Salvin sketch for the courtyard.
133. (right) A photograph from the same viewpoint today.

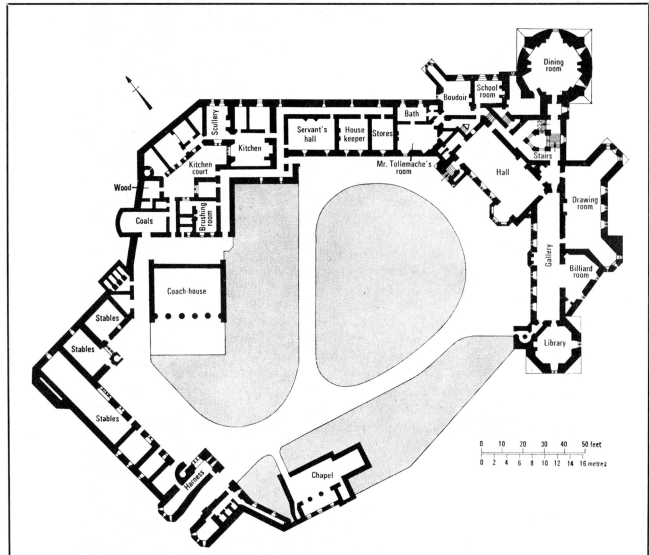

Fig. 13. Peckforton Castle. The ground-floor plan. The service wing is on a lower level than the main block, with access from kitchen to dining room under the family rooms.

then, to the left of the entrance, the stables and coach house; then the kitchen and servants' wing, grouped round its own small internal courtyard; and finally the main rooms of the house. These were arranged on a V-shaped plan, with two sloping wings leading up to a grand central mass composed of the great hall, with its porch and oriel, and the great round tower rising up slightly to one side behind it. A rather similar arrangement, though on a much smaller scale and with one wing instead of two, is found at Luscombe Castle in Devonshire, designed by Salvin's old master Nash, and so probably familiar to him.[6]

When one examines the plan of the principal rooms in detail, one realizes that it is remarkably ingenious and original, a piece of formal dexterity such as one does not usually associate with the nineteenth century. It is based on the interaction of two different axes, one at 45° to the other. The main axis is that of the gallery, drawing

160

134. (upper right) Peckforton Castle. The entrance front of the main building.
135. (right) The main staircase.

room, schoolroom and boudoir. Working against this is the diagonal axis of the great hall, which is echoed in the slanting recesses that lead off the angles of the drawing room and boudoir. The intersection of the two axes produces the octagonal library and dining room, the pentagonal staircase and the billiard room, which is an irregular hexagon leading off the gallery. Like all good formal plans the result is visually very successful; the shapes of the drawing room and staircase, for instance, are novel and effective, as is the way one corner of the hall butts into the end of the long gallery. Hall and gallery look inwards onto the courtyard; the other rooms, before the trees grew up, had superb views outwards to north, south and east, to Beeston Castle and the Cheshire plain.

The hall, staircase and dining room are the dividing zone between the big living

162

136. Peckforton Castle. The cellar, at the base of the great tower.

rooms and the family suite of boudoir, schoolroom and study. They form a sequence which although a little grim is none the less exceedingly impressive. The rusticated stone of the exterior gives way here to vaults and walls of smooth-cut ashlar. The general effect is one of immense strength and solidity. The staircase rises in broad and easy flights round a pentagonal central wall into which it looks by means of internal windows; the well was originally top-lit by a lantern. As a dramatic essay in massive stonework, with the minimum of ornament, it is strongly reminiscent of Salvin's superb vaulted approach to the courtyard of the keep at Alnwick (Pl. 26). As always with Salvin, the simpler the detail the better; the great hooded stone chimneypiece in the hall is more effective than the wooden screen, with its rather mechanical Gothic tracery; best of all is the huge cave-like wine cellar, under the dining room at the base of the great tower.

In the other rooms more concessions were made to nineteenth-century ideas of comfort. Windows, doorways, chimneypieces and arches are of exposed stone, but the walls are plastered and panelled and the ceilings are not vaulted but composed of massive timber beams enclosing plastered panels. One could not say that the rooms are light; but they are remarkably light considering the small size of the windows. The immense top room in the tower, above the dining room, was used as a racquets court. When built the castle had no central heating; later on a system was installed, the huge rusting pipes of which now crawl all over the flat roofs of the castle.

137. (above left) The dining room.
138. (above right) The hall.

9. *Treberfydd, Breconshire*

TREBERFYDD is a house that still evokes, in a convincing and attractive way, the serious mindedness and genuine piety of the people who built it. There can be few places in which it is so easy to capture the feeling of life as lived by a Tractarian family. It was built by a young, rich, religious and, one suspects, romantic Yorkshireman named Robert Raikes. He had been at Oxford in the 1830s, felt the magic of Keble, Newman and Pusey and become a convinced Tractarian. He married into the Tauntons, an equally religious Oxford family; and he, his wife, her two unmarried sisters Emma and Caroline and her widowed mother Lady Taunton were caught up by the idea of starting a centre of Tractarian worship in a lonely part of Wales where the energy and influence of the church had sunk to a low ebb. He bought a small modern house called Treberfydd, near the Llangorse lake. Half a mile from the house, on the edge of the lake, was the little church of Llangasty Tal y Llyn. It was in a poor state of repair; there was no vicarage and few services; the rector lived the life of a country gentleman on his own estate ten miles away. In 1848–50 Robert Raikes rebuilt the old church, all but the base of the tower, and built a schoolhouse next to it. The rector provided a resident curate, and some years later built a rectory. Mrs Raikes trained a choir, and put them into surplices; she was the organist and her sisters sang in the choir. Services were held, not only in English and Welsh on Sundays, but on holy days and week days. In the words of a local historian, 'It is true to say that Mr and Mrs Raikes were pioneers in Breconshire of the great revival in the work and life of the Church which marked the second half of the Nineteenth Century.'[1]

The Raikeses were an old merchant and banking family originally from Hull[2] but with many ramifications. They produced Thomas Raikes the diarist, Robert Raikes the founder of the Sunday school movement and two governors of the Bank of

164

139. The church and school of Llangasty Tal y Llyn, nr Treberfydd. They were built by the Raikes family to Pearson's designs.

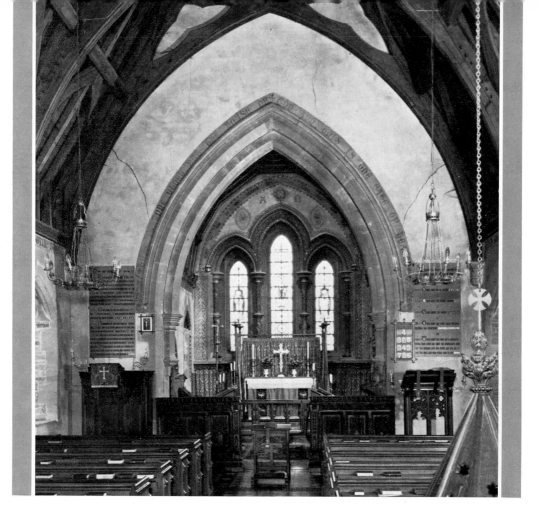

England. The father of Robert Raikes of Treberfydd was a banker in Hull, and lived at Welton House in the Yorkshire Wolds. In 1844 his mother built a little church at Wauldby near Welton to the designs of J. L. Pearson. It was one of his first commissions, and was the beginning of a long connection and friendship with the Raikes family.★ He designed the church, school and house at Treberfydd for Robert Raikes; another church, parsonage and school at Freeland near Oxford for the Raikes and Taunton families;† and Quar Wood in Gloucestershire for Robert Raikes's brother-in-law, the Revd Robert W. Hippisley.

The deed of sale for Treberfydd survives, and is dated 3 October 1848. Jones and Bailey in their *History of Brecknock* date the rebuilding of the house to 1850–2. In the list at the back of Eastlake's *History of the Gothic Revival* (1872), which is based on questionnaires filled in by the architects themselves, it is dated 1848–50. The same source says that Pearson was 'first employed to make a small addition to a square-built modern house, but from time to time further alterations were required until at

★ A letter from Pearson to Mrs Raikes, dated 8 Feb. 1892, asks her to accept a 'little old loving cup' as a golden-wedding present. 'I am in hopes that the friend you so freely made of me some 48 or 49 years ago may have the privilege on an occasion so unusual of asking you to do so.' The loving cup and letter are still at Treberfydd.
† The Tauntons lived at Freeland Lodge nearby. Their donations to the church included the Taunton chalice, set with Lady Taunton's jewels, presented in 1894.

165

140. Inside the church.

least nearly the whole of the original house was pulled down. Unfortunately, however, some of the old arrangement of rooms, etc. had to be retained, which to some extent interfered with the architect's intention in design.' The date 1852 is carved on the top of the tower. Probably the 'small addition' was made in 1848, and more extensive rebuilding was started in 1850, after the church and school had been finished.

The church and school are small, solidly built, unpretentious and full of charm. The interior of the church is an almost untouched Tractarian survival, with stencilled chancel, glazed tiles, brass candelabra and stained-glass windows. The house is also completely without pretensions, and this makes it one of the most attractive and successful of Victorian country houses. The most obvious influence in it is that of Pearson's slightly older contemporary Pugin; but Pearson, like his master Salvin, had the art of making his building look convincing, something that Pugin, for all his great talents and infectious enthusiasm, never really acquired.

The masonry, for instance, is handled much more sensitively than in most of Pugin's buildings. The main stone used is local old red sandstone, laid in irregular courses of small roughly dressed stones, with an occasional larger stone and with big ashlar blocks for the quoins; the whole completely escapes the mechanical effect of typical Pugin masonry. The dressings, apart from the quoins, are of Bath stone. The sandstone has weathered to a pinkish-grey, with much very pretty grey and orange lichen. Most of the Bath stone has gone a yellowish grey that contrasts agreeably but not too violently with the rest of the masonry; occasionally in the more sheltered places, it retains its original rather raw yellow and provides the only discordant note in the colouring of the house. The red tiles have weathered very dark and are pleasingly variegated at intervals by a row of tiles with rounded edges.

166

141. (above left) Treberfydd, nr Brecon (J. L. Pearson, 1848–52). The north front.
142. (above right) Looking past the entrance front to the stables.

The entrance front faces approximately north, and is given incident by the tower over the porch, the bedroom oriel and the bay window of the dining room. On the east the facade is continued by the long line of the wall behind the conservatory, ending in an archway into the garden. On the west is the stable yard, entered by an archway with its own smaller tower. The entrance to the house, with the Raikes arms carved above it, is very much in the Pugin manner; so is the way that the windows are glazed (as at Pugin's Scarisbrick) with leaded lights in a variety of different and highly decorative patterns, many of which survive, although there has been a certain amount of re-glazing with plate glass. There is another small tower on the garden side of the house, from which the south and east fronts run back in two long irregular lines of gables and chimneys. The garden rises up in terraces; from the highest of these there is a view down on the house looking low, solid and friendly, with the noble curve of Myndd Llangorse behind it to the right. The terraces and the original garden layout were designed by W. A. Nesfield; his juniper trees and elaborate beds laid out on the Raikes monogram have disappeared, though there are old photographs in the house that show them.

Pearson's original elevation survives in the house, and shows it without the garden tower; but this has been roughly sketched in pencil on one of the drawings and must have been an afterthought. Otherwise the drawings correspond, with only minor deviations, to the house as it was built—suggesting a more straightforward rebuilding or remodelling than that described by Eastlake. Even so, if Pearson had had a virgin site, the result would probably have been less rambling and irregular. But one cannot help agreeing with Eastlake's comment, that, in spite of the architect's dissatisfaction at not being given a free hand, 'this accident led to a picturesque treatment of the design, which no one would regret'. The medley of

167

143. The house from the south.

roofs and chimneystacks, as seen for instance from the back of the stable yard, is full of charm; and the stable yard itself is a real little masterpiece, using Gothic forms and details in a natural and unforced way that is completely satisfying.

The plan of Treberfydd is a straightforward one. The entrance porch leads into a hall and staircase. To the left and beyond these, running along the east side of the house, are the two intercommunicating drawing rooms (with a conservatory leading out of them), the library and the billiard room. To the right are the dining room, kitchen and offices. Almost all the rooms have Gothic stone chimneypieces of varying degrees of elaboration; the ones in the dining room and drawing rooms are especially handsome. The joinery throughout is of pitch-pine.[3] The drawing rooms must have been redecorated about 1900 when the existing plaster frieze and chimneypiece tiles were put in. The staircase hall has been widened; the chimneypiece was originally flush with the overhang above it. The library is one of the least altered rooms in the house, its shelves still lined with Robert Raikes's Tractarian and other religious books, and edged with scalloped and stamped leather flaps to keep the dust out.

One cannot help feeling that in fitting out the house Pearson must have been influenced by what he saw in the Medieval Court at the Great Exhibition of 1851, the contents of which were almost all designed by or under the influence of Pugin. Certainly the chimneypieces, staircase balustrade and other fittings are very much in the same manner, and the original drawing room wallpaper, shown in an old photograph, was actually a Pugin one. But unfortunately all the original accounts have disappeared (except for a few fragments), so that it is impossible to document who for instance (probably Minton) made the tiles in the hall, or supplied the armorial glass on the staircase landing.

It would be particularly interesting to know more about the Gothic revival furniture, of which a number of pieces are scattered about the house. They include beds, massive cupboards, a dressing table, washstand, chairs and tables. The beds

169

144. (upper far left) Treberfydd. In the stable yard.
145. (upper left) The staircase.
146. (left) The study.

147. (above) Furniture in the house, possibly designed by Pearson.

originally had higher backs, which have been cut down; and some of the pieces (all of which are of oak) have been stripped of their original varnish. All this furniture was probably made for the house; the detail of the beds, for instance, is very close to that of the staircase. Pearson may well have been the designer; one suspects that the actual makers were the firm of John G. Crace and Son, who were the leading makers of Gothic furniture at that period, and were supplying similar pieces (some of them made to Pugin's designs) to, for instance, Lismore Castle in the 1850s.[4]

Robert Raikes played an active part in county business, was High Sheriff in 1851, became an enthusiastic officer of the Volunteers when they were enrolled in 1859, and was a great lover of horses. His later life was not without difficulties, for the failure of the family bank in the 1860s (although he had long given up any active connection with it) brought him financial liabilities which he shouldered with courage. Treberfydd was let from 1873 to 1894, and from 1873 to 1890 he acted as agent for the nearby Glanusk estates. He retired in 1890 and died in 1901. In 1895 his son, Robert Taunton Raikes, came back to Treberfydd, which is still lived in by the family.[5]

170

148. (above) Treberfydd. The drawing room in Victorian days.
149 (upper right) Croquet on the lawn.
150 (right) The female staff.

10. Horsted Place, Sussex

THERE had been a house of some kind at Horsted long before the present one was built, though it was on a different site, on the edge of the existing gardens where they are skirted by the Uckfield–Lewes road. But in April 1849 the property was sold to Mr Francis Barchard, who had been taken into partnership by his uncle and godfather, a prosperous London dyer, and been left a comfortable fortune when the latter died in 1845. He pulled down the old house and built a new one a little further from the road, on a ridge which commands agreeable views to the south over to the Downs, and to the west across the gently rolling fields and woods of central Sussex.

The original building contract still exists, dated 2 October 1850. George Myers, builder, contracts to build a house at Horsted, 'under the direction and fully to the satisfaction of the Architect . . . Francis Barchard Esq., having determined upon building a mansion at Horsted aforesaid from designs and specifications prepared by

151. Horsted Place, nr Uckfield, Sussex (Samuel Daukes, 1850–4). A corner of the entrance front.

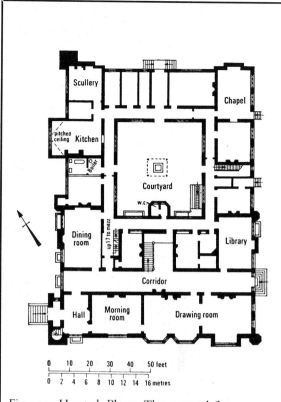

Fig. 14. Horsted Place. The ground-floor plan.

Samuel Whitefield Daukes, architect, of 14 Whitehall Place, London.' A very full specification of the house, room by room, follows. It was to be completed by 31 August 1851; the original estimate was for £14,390, though in the end the house, exclusive of furniture and decoration, cost £16,816.[1]

The house is built of red brick with black-brick diapers and dressings of Bath stone. Its plan is similar to that of Salvin's Mamhead (1827–33) and Pugin's Bilton Grange (1841–46). The main block is arranged around a central corridor, running from end to end of the house; at the back is a lower servants' wing, grouped round an open courtyard. In a plan of this type symmetry would have suggested making the main entrance in the centre of the long south front; at Mamhead, Bilton and Horsted convenience placed it round the corner, leading into one end of the corridor. At Horsted the entrance hall was placed off-axis to the corridor, enabling draughts to be avoided and the corridor to be better lit. As a result the entrance is at the corner of the house, with its position emphasized, because the corner is carried up into a tower, rising a storey above the rest of the house, with a staircase turret at the outside corner rising higher still. The strong accent on one corner makes even an approximation to symmetry impossible. This was no disadvantage in Victorian eyes; even more emphatic corner towers were to reappear at, for instance, Pearson's Quar Wood and White's Humewood.

173

152. The entrance

The entrance tower at Horsted is a skilful exercise in the asymmetrical combination of windows, doorway and unpierced wall-surfaces of diapered brickwork; the line running from the turret across the first-floor parapet to the buttress by the entrance archway produces a diagonal thrust reminiscent of the entrance front at Scotney. In general the house is in the Scotney tradition; its irregular gabled facades are agreeable and friendly, with little elaborate ornament; its irregularities are based on good sense, but disposed with an eye to visual effect. Inside, the broad corridors are spacious and straightforward, and the big rooms are simply decorated. Although the white paint of the photographs is post-Victorian and all the rooms probably had wallpapers such as that illustrated in the dining room, the big windows must always have made it a light house.

But Horsted is distinguished from Scotney by a strong infusion of Puginesque detail. This is particularly noticeable inside the house, where at least one feature is Pugin rather than Puginesque. The staircase was designed by Pugin, and made by Myers, the builder of Horsted. A portion of it was exhibited in the Medieval Court of the Great Exhibition in 1851. It was intended for Horsted, as the *Illustrated London News* made clear at the time.[2] The heraldic birds carved on the newel posts and in the panels were the Barchard crest. A water-colour of the Medieval Court, formerly at Horsted, shows the staircase and a large and elaborate Gothic fireplace, also by Pugin and Myers and also intended for Horsted. It was rejected (because it was too elaborate, according to family tradition) and ended up, with the Barchard emblems removed or altered, in the Duke of Devonshire's banqueting hall at Lismore Castle in Ireland. But the many other Gothic fireplaces at Horsted, though simpler, are completely in the Pugin manner; so are the linenfold panelling, the doorcases and much of the furniture. It is scarcely surprising that according to family tradition both house and furniture were designed by Pugin.

Where does Samuel Daukes[3] come into all this? Although in 1845 he had designed the church of St Andrew's, Wells Street, London, which later became a famous Tractarian stronghold under Benjamin Webb, he was not a Tractarian himself. Unlike Pearson, whose Treberfydd is in many ways similar to Horsted, he could never be considered a disciple either of Pugin or of the *Ecclesiologist*. He was an eclectic; he designed a curious Norman Revival church, St Peter's, Cheltenham;[4]

174

153. (above) Horsted Place. The house from the south-east.
154. (upper right) The dining room.
155. (right) The staircase, designed by A. W. Pugin and shown in the Great Exhibition.

he designed Colney Hatch lunatic asylum, an enormous and by no means unpleasing Italianate building of which Myers was also the builder; and his most important country house job was the remodelling of Witley Court, Worcestershire (1855), on a gigantic scale and in a sumptuous classical style. But in 1845–6 he also designed the Agricultural College, Cirencester, an agreeable design in the Pugin manner which anticipated Horsted. Myers (who was Pugin's favourite builder) may possibly have supplied some chimneypieces based on Pugin designs to Horsted,[5] but there is no reason to suppose that the house was not substantially designed by Daukes; Pugin's diaries for this period survive, and make no mention of Barchard, Daukes or Horsted.

The Pugin-style furniture[6] at Horsted was supplied, along with much else, by John Webb, of 13 George Street, Hanover Square; his elaborate and detailed bill survives. Pugin had been dealing with Webb since the mid-1830s, chiefly as a source from which to obtain antique furniture and carvings for patrons such as Charles Scarisbrick and the Earl of Shrewsbury; in the late 1840s Webb made much splendid furniture to Pugin's designs for the House of Lords and adjacent rooms.[7] But Webb only started delivery at Horsted in July 1852; Pugin had gone mad six months previously and died in September. Perhaps, like the firm of Crace, Webb had Pugin designs in stock, or could produce designs in the Pugin manner. He decorated the house from top to bottom, and the miscellany of articles he supplied makes it unlikely that they all came from his own workshops. By no means everything was Gothic. He supplied a great deal of other furniture, in carved and inlaid walnut, and

176

156. Horsted Place. One end of the drawing room, with furniture possibly designed by Pugin.

159. (top) The chimneypiece originally designed by Pugin for Horsted. It was shown at the Great Exhibition, and ended up at Lismore Castle in Ireland.

160. The chimneypiece in the Justice Room.

57, 158. (above) Pugin-style furniture from Horsted.

in the Elizabethan, Carolean or Georgian styles. He supplied water cans, hip-baths, bell-pulls, carpets and wallpapers, complete with the paperers to hang them, and Tudor portraits and Dutch landscapes (very good ones[8]) to hang on the wallpapers.

In the entrance hall, paved with Minton encaustic tiles, the umbrella-stand and letter-box were provided by Webb, and the javelins of Francis Barchard's bodyguard as High Sheriff of Sussex, a post he held in 1854, used to hang on the walls. The scales on the charming little fireplace in the business or justice room, next to the dining room, commemorate his position as a Justice of the Peace. Javelins and fireplace underline his pride in these two posts, which were recognized landmarks on the route of new families anxious to establish themselves among the country gentry. Francis Barchard first came to Sussex in 1846; he rented a house near Lewes before he bought Horsted. The fact that he was High Sheriff eight years later shows how quickly a new man could be accepted by the local gentry in Victorian times. No doubt his path was eased if he supported local activities, as Francis Barchard's account books show that he did, and was sensible and likeable, as the house he built suggests that he was.

178

161. Horsted Place. The entrance hall.

11. *Milton Ernest Hall, Bedfordshire*

WILLIAM BUTTERFIELD's serious-minded religious temperament led him to design churches, rectories, schools, colleges, convents and hospitals. He never showed any inclination to enter on the profitable Victorian market for country houses. What little work of this kind that he did was done for friends or as a side product of other projects. Milton Ernest was the only complete new country house that he ever designed,[1] and the client, Benjamin Helps Starey, was his brother-in-law.[2]

The Starey family came to London from Tenbury in Worcestershire in the eighteenth century. They separated into a number of different branches, all merchants of one kind or another. B. H. Starey, in partnership with a Mr Oswald, appear as 'Starey and Oswald, linen bleachers' in London directories from 1835, first sharing the premises in Bow Lane of B. H. Starey's cousin Thomas, who was a coal merchants of one kind or another. B. H. Starey, in partnership with a Mr Oswald, Street, off Fetter Lane. B. H. Starey is also said to have invented a plaited wick that did not need snuffing, and had some connection with Price's Patent Candle Co. Ltd, of which he later became a director. He made a small fortune, and was already living in a substantial house at Reigate before he moved to Milton Ernest. By 1853

162. Milton Ernest Hall, nr Bedford (William Butterfield, 1853–8). The entrance front.

the Californian and Australian gold rushes of 1849 and 1850 had enormously increased world supplies of gold. B. H. Starey (as he reveals in his diary) decided to invest in land as a precaution against inflation, and bought the Milton Ernest estate in 1853. It is interesting to know why he made the purchase, for one normally thinks of Victorian manufacturers and merchants as setting up as country landowners for social rather than business reasons.

There was a house on the property but it was not in good repair. He wrote in his diary for 28 September 1853: 'I took Mr. Butterfield to see the house and garden which was desolate. The house thoroughly bad irreparable: and it was decided to build a good family residence which the plans for were then put in hand and in February 1854 we began to take down the old house and stack away the materials.'

Although by the 1850s it was becoming common to make the building of a country house the responsibility of one firm of builders, Milton Ernest was built in the old way with labour engaged piecemeal under different contracts, and co-ordinated by the architect and the clerk of the works. The stonework was laid by London masons; the stone was quarried two miles away at Pavenham, and a boat was bought to carry it down the Ouse, which flowed immediately below the house. Sand and gravel were dug in the park. The joinery was contracted for by Reynolds, a Bedford builder. The house was started in the summer of 1854; the shell was completed in 1856 and the family moved in in July 1858. Butterfield also designed farm buildings and a boat house near the house, a mill and mill-house (1857) and a

163. A Butterfield cottage in the village.

number of cottages (1857 and 1867), besides restoring Milton Ernest Church at the Stareys' expense.[3]

Butterfield built his life round the Church of England and Gothic architecture. He did not keep them in separate compartments; building was his way of serving the church, and Gothic architecture an expression of the traditions and values he found in Christianity. He was not fanatical or pedantic in his devotion to it. He could appreciate good building and craftsmanship wherever he found it, and lived and worked in contentment in a Georgian house in Bedford Square. He recognized that medieval houses were draughty and that medieval furniture was ponderous and uncomfortable; the design of his domestic furniture is based on Georgian traditions and in his domestic buildings he commonly employed small-paned sash windows of early eighteenth-century type because he found them sensible and pleasing. In this way he tried to treat Gothic as a living language, and to develop it so that it would make sense for all aspects of nineteenth-century life. He worked out a vocabulary delicately graded to shade from the simplest to the grandest kinds of buildings. His simple buildings have prominent and generous roofs, sturdy joinery and almost no ornament or obviously 'period' detailing. The cottages, farm and boat house at

181

164. Milton Ernest Hall. The boat house.

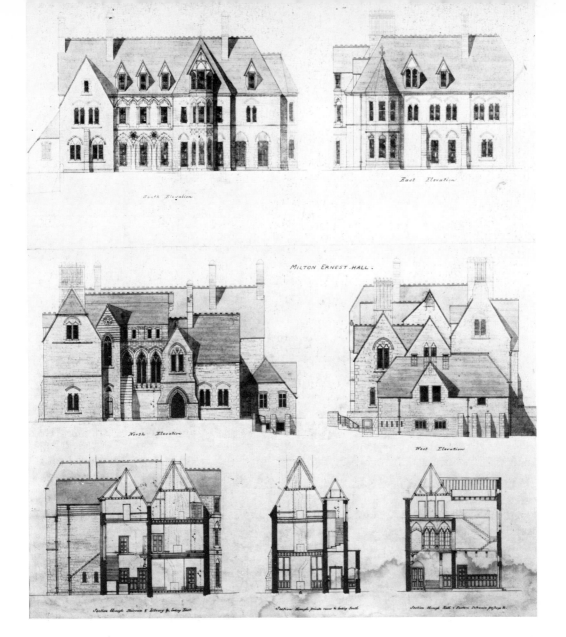

Milton Ernest are beautiful examples of his work at this level. As his buildings rise in the scale of importance specifically Gothic detail becomes increasingly prominent, and so does the use of structural colouring, the feature for which he is best remembered. At Keble College in particular his stripes, chequers and diapers in black, red and yellow bricks worried his contemporaries and in the post-Victorian reaction were thought to epitomize all that was crudest about Victorian architecture. In those lean years even the small group of Butterfield admirers analysed with fascination what John Summerson called his 'sadistic hatred of beauty'. But Butterfield described his Keble facades as 'gay'.[4] The scanty evidence of his few surviving writings suggest that he set out to please rather than to shock. If one looks at his buildings, especially those dating from the first half of his career, without preconceptions, 'gaiety' begins to make sense.

Approval of gaiety did not mean that he was easy going. Unswerving adherence to his principles, deep but narrow piety and rigid self-discipline made him an

165. Milton Ernest Hall. Butterfield's designs for the house.

impressive but not a comfortable character; and his character was expressed in his buildings. In old age, when both the Gothic and the religious revivals were on the wane, he became a lonely and formidable old bachelor, living guarded by a butler in Bedfore Square, 'tall, dignified, remote, but very courteous'.[5]

One of Butterfield's exquisite and delicately coloured drawings summarizes what he was aiming at at Milton Ernest in one sheet of elevations and sections. He always loved a generous, conspicuous and simple main roof; but he liked to use it as a dominating background against which to play out a sequence of minor themes. At Milton Ernest the unifying element is the L-shaped main block, with its steep and high roof and level ridge unbroken except by occasional tall and monumentally simple chimneystacks. On the south front, facing the garden and corresponding to the long stroke of the L, the facade is diversified by two projections below the level of the ridge: a stone gable, and a three-storey projection with a tall, narrow, bay window culminating in an elaborate timber gable. The north front is more complicated. Within the angle of the L is an elaborate sequence of roofs and gables running down the hill towards the river in three main descending divisions. The highest of these contains the main staircase, the position of which is distinguished by large traceried windows; the lowest is built below the terrace on which the rest of the house stands, and contains the kitchen, scullery and pantry, with cellars and a water tank below them. The sequence of squat powerful buttresses at the angle of the kitchen block is not decorative, but built to contain the pressure of the water tank. Seen from the lower level by the river the house builds up in one of those pyramidal compositions of roofs and gables which the best high-Victorian architects were adept at contriving.

183

166. The house from down by the river.

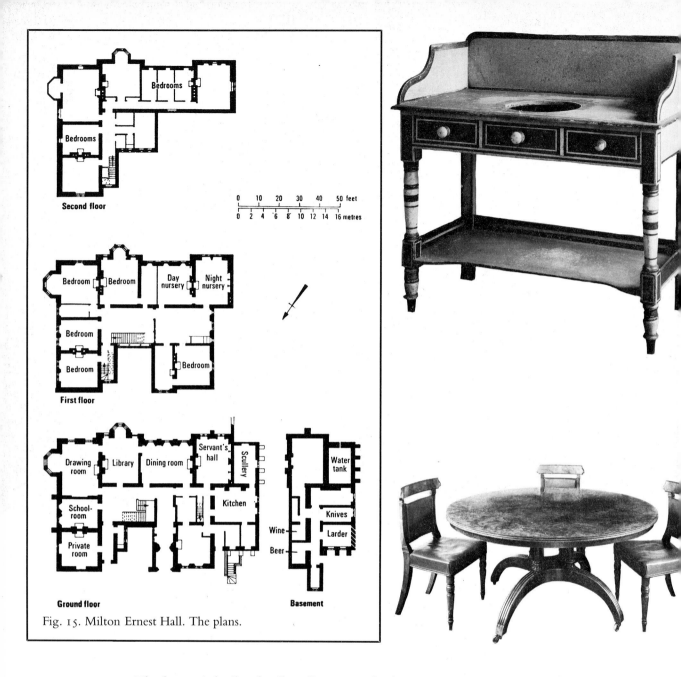

Fig. 15. Milton Ernest Hall. The plans.

The house is built of yellow limestone laid in irregular courses of smallish stones with raked joints. The dressings are of smooth ashlar, very precisely jointed. There are brick relieving arches over all the windows, and the contrast in colour and texture between the yellow of the rougher stonework, the lighter yellow of the ashlar and the lacings of red brick is very pleasing. The staircase division is treated with a more elaborate chequering of brick and stone. The main entrance is in a big gabled projection to the right of the staircase; under the taller and narrower gable to the left is the business entrance, with what was originally B. H. Starey's business room or study immediately to the left on entering it.

In colour, texture and design the entrance front is a piece of architectural

184

167, 168. (above right) Butterfield furniture from Milton Ernest.

pyrotechnics, difficult to capture in a photograph, but executed by Butterfield with consummate skill and obvious enjoyment. It develops the Pugin tradition of giving separate expression to the separate parts well beyond all practical limits. It results in an immensely elaborate roof system, the complications deriving from which have put the future of the house in jeopardy. But it remains an exciting experience to come down the long approach to Milton Ernest, with the high hunched roofs at the end of the garden wall, and drive into the courtyard to find Butterfield's simple and elegant farm buildings to one side and the virtuosity of the entrance front to the other.

The dominant memory of Milton Ernest is of the contrast between the complications of this front and the relative simplicity of the garden side, with its high roof and little dormers lined with lead and fitted with candle-extinguisher caps. But although the main outlines of this front are simple, the modelling and design of the windows is very complicated. There are two kinds of surface arcading, a great variety of window frames, and much chequering and striping of brick and stone. The alternate stone and brick voussoirs of the ground-floor windows are especially effective. But in spite of the unifying factor of the roof there is a little too much going on on this front for comfort. Butterfield had to work in with the standards of

169. (above left) The staircase to the second floor.
170. (above right) The library.

his time (and there is no reason to suppose he did not accept them). They decreed that Milton Ernest, as the seat of a local landowner, had to be given sufficient ornament to mark it off from buildings of a lower social grade. It is interesting to compare Milton Ernest with Philip Webb's Red House, designed for William Morris in 1859–60. Webb admired Butterfield more than any other living English architect; his contribution at the Red House was not to work out a new style, for it was entirely in the Butterfield manner, but to apply the simple treatment of Butterfield's smaller rectories to a gentry house not very much smaller than Milton Ernest. Even Webb, however, in his biggest houses felt constrained to work out a manner or ornament that would give them sufficient importance. Although he discarded Butterfield's Gothicism in his later buildings, one wonders whether he knew Milton Ernest and had its arcaded and multi-coloured facade at the back of his mind when he was designing Clouds.

Although Milton Ernest was unmistakably a house of some pretensions, there are elements about it which suggest that both Butterfield and Starey were not prepared to swallow what George Borrow called 'gentry nonsense' whole. It ran against Victorian standards of propriety to put the farm buildings next to the house; it was equally unconventional to give the servants' hall a view of the garden. The interiors are hard to judge today, for they have been somewhat altered. But by Victorian standards they were simple and straightforward. The chimneypieces are all of wood with simple Gothic detailing and a little effective patterned inlay in the marble surrounds to the fireplace openings. Otherwise, apart from the Gothic tracery of the staircase, there is little ornament in the rooms, which are well and sensibly lit by sash windows, and have occasional deep and generous bay window recesses. A certain amount of furniture designed by Butterfield for the house survives in the possession of members of the family. There is nothing Gothic about it; it is simply and sensibly designed in the Regency tradition, but given an unmistakably Butterfield twist; a set of bedroom chairs and washstand, for instance, are gaily painted with Butterfield stripes.[6]

The house had originally no gas, no central heating and no bathrooms. There was no running water laid on to the ground-floor sinks; water had to be pumped up from the tank in the basement. All this suggests an element of austerity which was probably deliberate. There is no denying that the ecclesiastical detailing and slightly stiff-necked disposition of Milton Ernest gives it the feeling of a lay rectory. In effect, this is what it was. The Stareys were a deeply religious family, kindly but strict.[*] The life of the family centred around religious devotion and religious reading and the ladies framed and embroidered texts to Butterfield's design.

As an investment Milton Ernest did not turn out a success. It was sold by B. H. Starey early in the 1870s. Between about 1906 and 1919 it became the home of the second Lord Ampthill, who added to the kitchen wing with the greatest tact. It was bought back by B. H. Starey's son, sold again in 1968, and is now a hotel.

[*] Butterfield himself thought that 'it is *quite* unsafe to allow children any greater licence than speaking when they are spoken to. Above all they ought not to ask questions.' (Quoted Paul Thompson, *William Butterfield* (London, 1971), p. 21.)

171, 172. Milton Ernest Hall. Victorian photographs of the staircase hall and drawing room.

12. Woodchester Park, Gloucestershire

WOODCHESTER PARK is concealed at the bottom of a tree-enclosed valley, unknown except to local people and a few Victorian enthusiasts. It was never finished; it is unlikely to have been visited by other Victorian architects or to have had any influence on contemporary architecture. But it is one of the most remarkable country houses of its time.[1]

The 1,000-acre Woodchester property was bought from the Earl of Ducie by William Leigh (1802–73) in November 1845. Leigh had been living in Staffordshire, but his money came from Liverpool; he was the son of a Liverpool merchant with property interests at Adelaide in Australia.[2] He joined the Oxford movement and became a Catholic in 1844. His conversion was not well received by his Staffordshire neighbours and he moved to Gloucestershire. There was a Georgian house on the site of the present one at Woodchester; on Pugin's advice it was pulled down and Pugin made designs for a new house in much the same manner as his designs for Bilton Grange. But plans for rebuilding were delayed by Leigh's religious enthusiasms. In 1846 he gave land and endowments for a Catholic cathedral in Adelaide, and in the same year he got in touch with Father Dominic Barberi, the Passionist priest who had received Newman into the Catholic Church in the previous year, and invited him to found a community at Woodchester. Pugin made designs for a monastery which Leigh thought too expensive; he switched architects and gave the commission to Charles Hansom. The monastery was built in 1846–53 (it was demolished in 1970) and Leigh then turned his attention back to the house. But instead of Hansom he employed a completely unknown local boy called Benjamin Bucknall.

The tower at Woodchester is dated 1858. All the designs are now in Gloucestershire County Record Office and are signed by Bucknall but not dated.

188

173. Woodchester Park, nr Stroud, Gloucestershire (Benjamin Bucknall, *c.* 1854–68). The house in its hidden valley.

According to a contemporary newspaper, 'building went on in a very leisurely "day-work" manner for over fourteen years till toward the end of the 1860s all work ceased'. If work started in 1854, it would have started when Bucknall was only twenty-one. He had been born at Rodborough, two miles from Woodchester, in 1833. He was baptized in the Church of England; as his work in England was done for Catholic patrons he was presumably one of Barberi and Leigh's local converts. No details of his training have come to light.[3]

Bucknall is remarkably interesting because he is the only English architect who could be described as a disciple of Viollet-le-Duc. He first visited him in France in or before 1861; among Viollet-le-Duc's papers are seven letters from him, all written in French, the first dated 27 December 1862 and the last written in 1875, when he was at the beginning of a seven-year period devoted to translating his 'dear Master's' works.[4]

Much the most interesting of Bucknall's letters is the first one. In it he thanks Viollet for helping a young English architect whom he had introduced to him and goes on with a great deal of praise of Viollet. He refers to Pugin as a true artist and distinguished architect, the first to make people see their barbarism and to indicate the true principles so well known in the past but till now forgotten. Unfortunately his death has largely stopped this progressive trend and the only true way now is through Viollet-le-Duc's books. Bucknall significantly says he has been studying architecture for ten years. Viollet's books are an inestimable source of pleasure and knowledge. He is pleased to consider himself his most devoted and informed student. He dreams of translations which will permit greater acquaintance with his books. He asks advice on the use of cast iron for construction, alone or in conjunction with stone. He then refers to a house he is doing outside Stroud for a Mr Leigh who much admires Viollet. The chapel is finished and he would like to know of a good glass maker, for they are very expensive in England. He also discusses gargoyles.

189

174. A. W. Pugin's design for the house, 1844.

The letter makes clear that the main design of the house had been made before Bucknall had met Viollet-le-Duc, but suggests that it was made under the influence of his books and an admiration for Pugin. The starting point was probably Pugin's design but little is left of it except the relative positions of the tower and chapel. Bucknall accepted Pugin's doctrine that construction should not be hidden, but he also benefited from Viollet-le-Duc's much deeper knowledge and analysis of Gothic as a rational system of building in stone. At Woodchester he set out to achieve what Pugin had never attempted, a country house built of stone throughout—walled with stone, roofed with stone and vaulted with stone, with stone staircases, stone gutters, stone downpipes and even a stone bath. Wooden rafters support the stone-tiled roofs and in the upper rooms the floors and ceilings were to have been of wood, though supported on stone arches; but all the main rooms, the staircases and corridors are vaulted, or were intended to be; in some rooms only the springing of the vaults was constructed before work stopped and much of the upper half of the

190

175. Woodchester Park. A ruined bedroom.

house is an enormous pigeon-inhabited void. The vaults vary in elaboration from carved lierne vaults in the chapel and drawing room to plain sexpartite or quadripartite vaults in the corridors. Most of the windows were never glazed (although at Bucknall's request Viollet-le-Duc sent over French glaziers to glaze the chapel) and the drawing room is the only living room that came near completion.

Woodchester is one of the first Victorian buildings in which the architect showed an interest in local traditions. The detail of the chapel is based on a study of the early fourteenth-century transept at nearby Minchinhampton church. The main outline of the house, with its generous gables, square-headed windows and roofs covered in local stone tiles is unmistakably Cotswold. The stone is superb oolitic limestone, probably quarried at Minchinhampton. In spite of the big square-headed windows and lierne vaults there are touches of early French Gothic here and there; the gargoyles—genuine water-spouting gargoyles—may have been inspired by the ones which Viollet-le-Duc put on Notre Dame at Paris. This eclecticism is kept subservient to the unity of the whole design. The south front is a real Gothic wall of glass supported on a stone framework; on the ground floor the glazing is continuous from end to end, except where it is divided by the buttresses; these are put there to hold the building up, in contrast to the decorative buttresses which too many Victorian architects were fond of attaching to their buildings for no functional reason, in spite of their lip-service to Pugin's principles. Inside, the square-headed windows are carried up above the arches of the vault, and the continuation gives an

176. (above left) The chapel vault.

177. (above right) A staircase in the unfinished house.

effective feeling of an inner framework of construction and an outer skin of glazing.

It is interesting to compare this south front with the facades of Kelham, contemporary to Woodchester and perhaps the only equivalent of a vaulted Victorian country house. The simplicity of Bucknall's design—glass, buttresses, three gables and a big roof—runs dead against the current of Victorian architecture, and makes the learned variety, elaborate carving and self-conscious asymmetries of Scott's windows and skyline seem pretentiously tedious. On the east front the fenestration is much more irregular, but the irregularity looks sensible rather than wilful, and the composition is held together by the three big gables and the great traceried window of the chapel.

During all these years William Leigh had been living at the top of the hill in a house which Bucknall had enlarged to a very comfortable size. From his windows he could look down on the shell of his great mansion, but either his money or his enthusiasm ran out before it was completed. To Bucknall the point of Gothic was that it was a system of construction; to revive the detail without the construction was to play at fancy-dress architecture. At Woodchester he made no compromises, and the result was a building that, by nineteenth-century standards, was uneconomic and probably uninhabitable. Others of his generation felt the dilemma, and their answer was 'Queen Anne'. Bucknall's answer was to emigrate to Algiers, where he spent twenty years successfully designing villas for French and Arab clients before his death in 1895. But his masterpiece, however uneconomic and uninhabitable, was also virtually indestructible. Unloved, unlived in, unglazed and unmaintained, it has lasted for over a hundred years and is still in mint condition.[5]

193

178. (upper left) Woodchester Park. The chapel front.
179. (left) Effigy of William Leigh, the builder of the house, in the abbey church at Woodchester.
180. (above) The domestic front.

13. Shadwell Park, Norfolk

If ONE WANTS to savour the difference between early and mid-Victorian architecture there is no better place to do so than at Shadwell, where the two periods exist side by side. One end of the house was remodelled and enlarged in 1840–2, to the designs of Edward Blore. Its competent but mechanical Jacobean detail, its gently picturesque grouping, its smooth surfaces of honey-coloured stone are typical of the architect and of the years in which it was built. So, in an entirely different way, are the additions designed by S. S. Teulon in 1855–60. They are prickly, rocky, dramatic, assertive; they bristle with individuality; they have one of those wonderfully evocative skylines, which the high-Victorians produced with such unfailing resourcefulness. If the Blore end is a little tame, the Teulon end is more than a little wild.

Shadwell was originally built in 1727–9 as a summer retreat from the Buxton's main house at Channonz Hall in the same county.[1] It proved so much more pleasant to live in that Channonz was abandoned. Shadwell then became too small, and after several abortive schemes Sir John Jacob Buxton (his grandfather had been created a baronet in 1800) called in Blore in 1839.[2] Blore enlarged the service wing and built out a large extension on the garden side with two storeys of high rooms to

194

181. Shadwell Park, nr Thetford, Norfolk. The eighteenth-century house.

XIV. (right) Shadwell Park, Norfolk. Looking from the tower down to the stable yard.

XV. Shadwell Park, Norfolk (Edward Blore, 1840–2; S.S. Teulon, c.1856–60). Looking through the clock tower arch to the game larder.

correspond to the three lower storeys of the Georgian house. This was given a new Elizabethan-style surface inside and out, with much strapwork detailing, rather more agreeable in the low and intimate rooms of the old building than in the big high-ceilinged reception rooms of the new block.

Sir John Jacob, who had waited for his inheritance until the death of his father, aged eighty-six, in 1839, died two years later. His heir, Sir Robert Jacob Buxton, was still a minor, and it was left to his widow to complete Blore's plans. Lady Buxton was a character who might have come out of a Trollope novel: a Dowager both formidable and slightly absurd, moving through life in an aureole of good works and admiring clergymen.★ She managed Shadwell in her son's minority, and perhaps in his majority as well, for she continued to live in the house not only after he came of age, but after he married. It was at Shadwell that she died, in 1884, at the age of eighty-one, only four years before her son, having, according to a local paper, 'allowed no pressure of advancing age to withdraw her from any of the work of active benevolence in which her whole life had been spent'.

In the four years that followed her husband's death she supervised the completion of the house, and a certain amount of planting and construction of terraces in its surroundings. In 1850 her son came of age, and there were three days of banquets, balls, speeches and fireworks at Shadwell.† To accommodate these festivities two

★ Her passionate flirtation with the septuagenarian Bishop of Ely is richly documented in the Buxton MSS.: 'Oh my Love, how happy you were when we were recently together. How you let your head repose upon my breast. What exquisite sensations we had!', and much more in the same vein.
† His uncle Sir Montagu Cholmeley proposed his health. The *Norfolk Chronicle* commented: 'The heart and soul of an English gentleman spoke out there, in vivid contrast to the debasing sophistries of the Manchester school.' The Buxtons were die-hard Tories.

197

182. Blore's garden front.

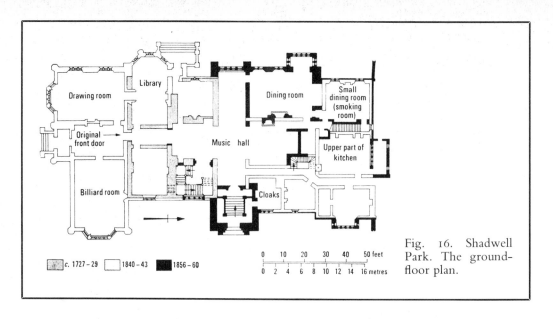

Fig. 16. Shadwell Park. The ground-floor plan.

temporary rooms had to be built out from the house, for Shadwell as Blore had left it was still of only moderate size. Perhaps these temporary rooms gave Sir Robert Buxton the idea of building something permanent to accommodate large-scale entertaining. In the first five years of his majority, however, he confined himself to the estate and the surroundings of the house. In 1855 the Dowager wrote that 'the axe is changing the features of the park tho' many a consultation takes place before an old favourite is condemned'. About the same time the eighteenth-century lake was greatly enlarged. In 1852 Sir Robert and his mother together rebuilt the nearby parish church of Brettenham; in 1855 the remains of the old college of Rushford were restored and largely rebuilt as a rectory, and a bridge was built across the adjoining ford. The architect for all three buildings was Samuel Sanders Teulon. As soon as they were finished the same architect set about making sensational additions to Shadwell itself. Work seems to have been started about 1856 (the date on the drainpipes in the stable courtyard) and finished about 1860, in which year (as the one surviving bill shows) the organ was set up in the music hall. The *Builder* described and illustrated the house on 21 August 1858, when the work was described as 'in progress'. Unfortunately, the building accounts and almost all the original drawings have disappeared, nor are there any letters from or to Teulon amongst the Buxton papers. Although Teulon's additions give the impression of having been built regardless of expense, in fact they were based on the walls of the existing house, presumably to keep down the cost. Blore's office wing, for instance, was left largely untouched, but was refaced and had an extra storey added; an enormous cruciform music hall was created, utilizing the walls of the old main staircase and the kitchen courtyard; Blore's small tower on the east front, similar to the one that survives on the west, was replaced by a very much larger one; a new dining room was built, to the north-west, and a new stable courtyard to the north.

'You will, I think,' wrote the Dowager to a cousin in America, 'be astonished when you see poor dear Shadwell again.' By the 1850s Samuel Sanders Teulon, after a slow start, had developed into one of the *enfants terribles* of Victorian architecture, about as far removed as possible from Georgian standards of reticence and good

behaviour. Indeed his reputation had been partly gained by his drastic remodelling of Georgian churches, and one can imagine him advancing on them with a kind of terrible glee, sharpening his knives; the frightening but impressive results can still be seen at St Mary, Ealing, and Holy Trinity, Leicester. Although nominally a Gothicist, he was capable, like many of his contemporaries, of ruthlessly altering, selecting or transfiguring Gothic detail to produce the effects he wanted. Anything striped, spiky, knobbly, notched, fungoid or wiry fascinated him. His buildings can be brutally crude, but his work at and around Shadwell shows him at his best. It is earlier than the belligerent chaos of Elvetham (1859) and Bestwood (1862–4); his brashness is still kept under control and his creative originality is at its peak. The church at Brettenham, the college at Rushford, and a number of smaller buildings on the estate are, in fact, remarkably pleasant and unassertive examples of local materials sensitively handled. His work at Shadwell itself could never be described as unassertive; but it is a dazzling display of Victorian fireworks, in its way a work of genius.

A number of qualities make it so. One is the amazing virtuosity in the use of materials. Teulon (employing local craftsmen, according to the *Builder*) used Norfolk Carstone, local brick and above all flint, combined with other materials in

183. Shadwell Park. An old photograph of the music hall.

184. The entrance front. Blore to the left, Teulon to the right.

the traditional East Anglian way and with superb craftsmanship. The variety is endless; flint is laced with stone or brick, bricks of different colour are mixed together, rough surfaces are contrasted with smooth and one colour with another, like a series of architectural cocktails, and with equally exhilarating effect.

Shapes are contrasted too. It would be hard to find a view which has more of the quintessence of Victorian romanticism than from the top of the great tower at Shadwell. The different gables of the stables and the brewhouse, the wonderful fantasy of the clock tower, with the echoing spire of the game larder beyond it, combine in an inspired chorus before the luxurious East Anglian background of rich parkland, huge fields and long belts of trees. Teulon, like most Victorians, loathed symmetry, but he was an adept at building up skilfully irregular compositions, usually a series of roughly pyramidal shapes based on a combination of triangles and diagonal lines. The east front of Shadwell is an impressive example of his skill in solving the problem of how to add onto Blore's existing building, yet produce a coherent result. Teulon achieved this by building a central tower, then a lower wing and smaller gable that only half-balance the Blore wing and finally, to remedy the balance, a clock tower set in front of, and at right angles to, the main block of the house.

Apart from the straight approach from the east, Teulon designed an approach from the west which gave full scope to his sense of the dramatic. The drive comes through the spacious vistas of the park, with the lake to the left, and a distant view of the house to the right and sweeps round a bend straight down onto the bold spikiness of the stable arch. Just before one goes under this there is a view to the left up to Brettenham church, and to the right down an avenue to the silhouette of an urn. Then one comes through the archway and sees the amazing mass of the clock tower ('the tower of Babel, we call it', wrote Lady Buxton) in front, and all the variety of the stable courtyard around one. The approach continues under the clock tower and one draws up at the steps of the main entrance, which lead up into the great tower through a Gothic doorway of magnificently vigorous design and carving, beautifully set off and contrasted by the flint walling into which it is set.

The steps lead straight into the great cruciform music hall, a Victorian cathedral in miniature, rich in carving and (originally) in stained glass. Its shape was to a considerable extent conditioned by existing walls, and as a result each of the four

185. (upper left) Shadwell Park. The entrance.
186. (upper right) The arch into the stable yard.
187 (lower left) The music hall in Victorian days.
188. (lower right) Looking along the entrance front to the stable block.

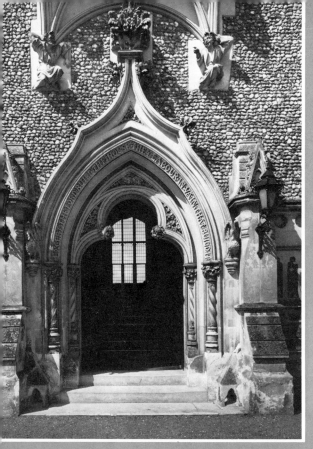

189. Shadwell Park. The stable yard.

arms is of a different size and shape. This asymmetry does not seem to have bothered Teulon; indeed he accentuated it by giving each arm timber roofs of different type and heights. Although the resulting proportions are not entirely satisfactory, the room remains one of the most impressive of surviving Victorian domestic interiors, impressive in its scale, in the inspired eccentricity of its woodwork and in the abundance and quality of its stone carving.

The woodwork culminates in the extraordinary notched timbers over the crossing, which swoop down in the centre to support a wrought iron chandelier. The stone carving—much in evidence here and elsewhere at Shadwell—is probably by Thomas Earp, who worked for Teulon at Elvetham and Bestwood. Particularly attractive are the Victorian sporting scenes, neatly infiltrated into two of the capitals in the hall, and the bundles of pheasants over the arch of the clock tower. Birds stuffed, rather than carved, lurk in immense numbers in the hall, in show-cases which can be revealed by removing the panels of the panelling. There are, or were, similar cases of minerals on the staircase; this was moved to its present position by Teulon, re-employing the balustrading designed by Blore.

'A great painted glass window', wrote Lady Buxton, in describing the hall, 'glowing with the west sun takes the eye as soon as you have ascended from the basement storey . . . you will know your Cousin Robert's fertile imaginative brain to which he flatters himself that this window and Hall effect will do full justice being unlike anything else in England.' There was more stained glass in a rose window in the north arm of the hall above an organ encased in elaborately notched and chamfered woodwork, with wrought iron trimmings by Skidmore.[5] Just as eighteenth-century churches, with their fireplaces in comfortably padded pews, often seem a Sunday extension of the house, so some Victorian country houses have more than a little atmosphere of the church; 'Except the Lord build the house they labour in vain that build it' is carved in great Gothic letters over the entrance to Shadwell, and there is no lack of evidence of the strongly Church of England atmosphere (Middle to Low, I suspect, rather than High) in which the Buxtons moved. Teulon himself, although he built a number of large country houses, was primarily an ecclesiastical architect; his sister, who died young after a long illness,

190. The music hall roof.

wrote two volumes of religious poems, *Blossoms in the Shade* and *Fruits of the Valley*;
one of his sons became a Prebendary of Chichester and Vice-Principal of the
Theological College there. The architecture of Shadwell should be seen against this
background. It is perhaps not surprising that, in a more secular age, the stained glass
and organ should have been removed, as have more stained glass and Teulon's
panelling in the adjacent dining room.

The music hall and dining room were the only Teulon interiors of importance at
Shadwell. As Lady Buxton remarked, in a typically double-edged way, 'The House

will have a very imposing effect—& yet after all a few Batchelor Rooms is all the addition that we gain to our accommodation.' The new work was more for show than use, and must have been expensive. Although the Buxtons had inherited Wiltshire property from the Jacob family in the early nineteenth century (hence their use of Jacob as a Christian name) their income was only about £8,000 a year—a substantial country gentleman's estate but not more than that. They were country gentry pure and simple, and had no connection with the brewing Buxtons, of anti-slavery fame. Perhaps Sir Robert Buxton's building hurt his estate; at any rate Shadwell failed to weather the agricultural depression and in 1898, a few years after his death, it was sold to Mr John Musker,★ the grandfather of the present owner.

★ He and his partner Julius Drewe were the founders of the Home and Colonial Stores. Both men retired from the business in 1883, having made large fortunes very rapidly; in 1910–11 Drewe employed Lutyens to design him Castle Drogo in Devon.

204

191. Shadwell Park. Carving in the hall.

14. *The Crossleys of Halifax and their Buildings*

As so MANY Victorian country houses were built by the new rich, it seemed worth while to trace one family in its progress from mill to mansion, and to illustrate the architectural by-products of the journey.

A good few people would react to 'Crossley' by saying 'carpets', but one has to go to Halifax to see what Crossley carpets meant in the terms of a Victorian manufacturing town. One narrow valley choked with the Crossley mills paid for the Crossley orphanage, the Crossley almshouses, the Crossley chapel, Crossley Street, the Crossley hotel, the Crossley baths, the Crossley park, Crossley model housing and a ring of the Crossleys' own houses. Crossleys were Mayors and M.P.s; Crossleys contributed to every conceivable charity and headed all the subscription lists; Crossleys were in the thick of every local activity during their lives, and at intervals the whole town closed up the shutters and turned out for an enormous Crossley funeral.

The Crossley business was started by John Crossley (1772–1837), a self-made man who worked his way up from weaver to foreman and from foreman to mill owner.[1] In 1802 he took a lease of the Dean Clough mill on the edge of Halifax and set up in a small way as a carpet manufacturer. By his death in 1837 the business was flourishing. It was continued by his three younger sons, John (1812–79), Joseph (1813–68) and Francis, generally known as Frank (1817–72). In the decade after their father's death the three brothers started to investigate the possibilities of harnessing steam power for carpet manufacture. This had already been successfully achieved for linen, cotton and cloth, but the heavier and more complex carpet looms were less adaptable. The Crossleys took a clever inventor, John Collier, on their pay roll, and he did the trick for them. In 1851 they took out a patent for a new steam-driven

192. The Crossley Mills, Halifax.

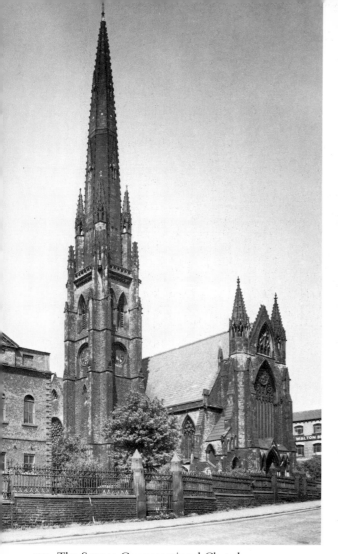

193. The Square Congregational Chapel.

194. The White Swan Hotel, and the Town Hall in Crossley Street.

loom for weaving velvets and carpets. It enabled them to produce carpets in enormous quantities and at much lower prices. Carpets ceased to be a rich man's luxury. Other carpet manufacturers either had to pay the Crossleys for the right to install their looms, or go out of business. Crossley carpets inundated the markets not only of England but of Europe and America.

The result was a great deal of money for the Crossleys and, indirectly, a great deal of money for Halifax. By 1869 the Dean Clough valley contained eight huge Crossley mill buildings, the biggest 120 feet high. The works employed 4,400 workmen and covered twenty-seven acres. In the early days of one solitary small mill building old John Crossley's wife, coming to the mill to start work at four o'clock one morning, had made a vow: 'If the Lord does bless us at this place, the poor shall taste of it.' The poor did taste of it; though admittedly the rich tasted more.

All three brothers were insatiable workers; every morning at six they rode down to the mills on their little cobs. Joseph was completely absorbed in running the

206

195. The Crossley Orphanage.

business; his superintendence left the other two time for public life—John mostly at local level and Frank at national level. John was prominent on the Halifax council and was Mayor in 1849–51 and 1861–3. Francis was M.P. for Halifax in 1852–9, and for the West Riding from 1859 until his death in 1872. Among the three brothers Frank had the ideas, Joseph the perseverance and John the softest heart and the worst head for business; his two brothers each died worth about a million pounds, but John developed an appetite for speculation in his old age and lost all his money. All three were ardent Non-Conformists, Sabbatarians and Radicals.★

The brothers contributed to provide most of the cost of building the Square Congregational Church, built in 1855–7 to the design of Joseph James, with a delicate decorated spire shooting up at the valley bottom, beside the river and the railway. In 1857–64 they were the builders of the Crossley Orphanage, accommodating 170 boys and 100 girls in an enormous and early example of the full-blown mansard-roof style, designed by John Hogg.

Apart from these joint enterprises the brothers had their individual projects. During the 1850s, when the money started to pile in, they each built sizeable houses on the edge of the town. John chose his architect by setting a competition with a short list of six competitors. The prize went to the London firm, Parnell and Smith, who in 1852–3 built him a large prickly Gothic villa called Manor Heath on the edge

★ One suspects that there was a certain rivalry between the Non-Conformist Crossleys and the Church of England and socially better-established Colonel Edward Akroyd (of James Akroyd & Sons, worsted manufacturers). Akroyd's buildings, all close to each other on the northern edge of Halifax, included his own house, Bankfield, G. G. Scott's sumptuous All Souls, Haley Hill (1856–9), and the model estate of working men's dwellings at Akroydon. Akroyd tried to get Scott the commission to design a Gothic town hall on a different site to that finally chosen; the Crossleys prevailed, with Crossley Street and Barry. Both families were staunch Liberals, and the rivalry would seem to have been a friendly one.

196. Manor Heath (Parnell and Smith, 1852–3).

of the town.[2] But John's most interesting venture was the buying up of old property in the centre of the town and its redevelopment on a T-plan of two spacious streets, Crossley Street and Prince's Street. At the junction of the two, closing the vista down Prince's Street, he sold a site to the Town Council on which to build the Town Hall, designed by Sir Charles Barry in 1859, and completed after his death by his son. In 1863, the year in which it was finished, John Crossley was Mayor; the Prince of Wales came up to open it, and stayed at Manor Heath. Round the nucleus of the Town Hall the streets filled up with handsome stone-faced Italianate buildings, soon to turn black with northern soot. John Crossley built the grandest of these himself, and decorated it with his coat of arms and monogram as though it was his own palazzo, although it was in fact built as the White Swan Hotel. It was opened in 1858; the architect of its superbly opulent facade is not recorded, but one suspects the firm of Parnell and Smith, whose talents were better adapted to this kind of classical grandeur than to the Gothicism of Manor Heath. No doubt in all this development John Crossley had an eye to his own pocket, but the result was a piece of town planning and street scenery for which Halifax had every reason to be grateful, and which the post-war generation of planners have done their best to make meaningless.

John also built an Italianate model lodging house in Smith Street, and in 1863–8 laid out the West Hill Park estate of model dwellings, a non-profit making development designed to provide freehold houses for working men. His brother Joseph, the least assertive of the three, built his own house, Broomfield, and a large group of almshouses very agreeably grouped around three sides of a big private garden in Arden Road. These were Gothic, designed by Roger Ives and Son of Halifax, who also built the earlier Crossley mills. The Arden Road almshouses form one end and the West Hill Park estate the other of a great swathe of Crossley territory. The middle is filled with the projects of the third brother, Frank: the People's Park, the Margaret Street almshouses and his own house, Belle Vue.

197. (upper right) The Crossley Almshouses.
198. (middle right) The Crossleys' People's Park.
199. (right) Belle Vue from the People's Park.

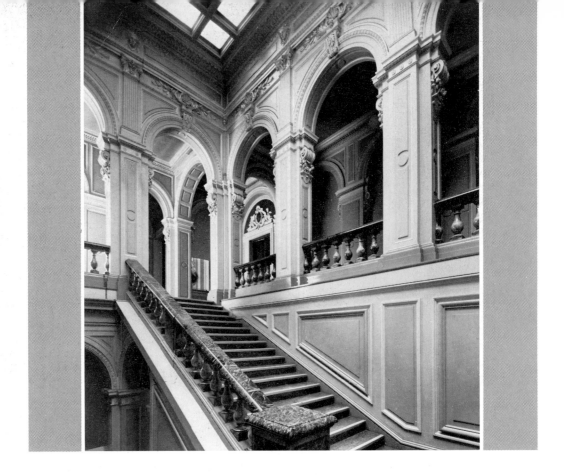

Frank Crossley had bought a small house at Belle Vue in 1845 and in 1855 built the Margaret Street almshouses next to it. Like his brother's almshouses they were designed by Roger Ives. In the same year he went on a trip to America and Canada. He was so impressed by the panoramic view from the White Mountains that on the spot he decided to see what he could do for his own home town. The result was the People's Park of 12½ acres—a little absurd in comparison to the White Mountains but with considerable charm when considered on its own merits. It was laid out by Sir Joseph Paxton; Frank Crossley may have come across him in connection with the Crystal Palace, for Crossley's supplied the carpets for the opening ceremony. The park was equipped with a little lake and a fountain, and a brass band playing every day except Sunday, and a raised terrace lined with urns and statues. In the middle of the terrace Paxton's son-in-law G. H. Stokes designed an arcaded pavilion in which grateful fellow-citizens later placed a statue of Frank Crossley by Joseph Durham. The inscription on the pavilion, 'Blessed be the Lord, who daily loadeth us with benefits', suggests a backward glance at the Crossley carpet profits. The park was opened in August 1857 with a procession, several brass bands, detachments of local Friendly and Temperance societies, and 3,000 Crossley workmen each carrying a little banner made of Crossley carpeting.

Frank Crossley's own house, Belle Vue,[3] looked across a public road onto the park, and was remodelled and enlarged by G. H. Stokes in 1856–7. The result was an agreeable Louis XIV chateau, with high roofs and discreet classical facades. Inside there was a good deal of moderately lavish plasterwork, and a spacious sequence of

210

200. The staircase at Belle Vue (G. H. Stokes, 1856–7).

halls and corridors leading to a very swagger grand staircase. But the house was of comparatively modest size, and the garden was far from large: a big square of lawn and flower beds and then trees, a high wall, a Gothic tower to hide a neighbour who refused to be bought out, and a view of the spire of the Congregational Church.

The Crossley brothers were hard-working, open-handed, chapel-going Yorkshiremen without much education but with plenty of sense and no pretensions. Like many self-made men they were proud of their origins. A good proportion of Frank Crossley's speech at the opening of the People's Park was given over to praise of his mother, who had been cook–housemaid to a local farmer and in addition to her normal duties had milked the cows and done all the spinning. Halifax was the Crossleys' territory, with almshouses and orphanages to close the vistas instead of temples and obelisks. They showed no inclination to leave it; John had a big house on Lake Windermere, but it was a manufacturer's house for the holidays, not a country seat.

Frank Crossley was a Radical and, in his young days at any rate, a staunch opponent of privilege, primogeniture, the Established Church and the House of Lords. He bought T. H. Maguire's big picture *Cromwell Refusing the Crown of England* to hang at Belle Vue. The West Riding had been solidly Cromwellian in the Civil Wars and Cromwell—breaker of kings and scorner of privilege—had become a hero among West Riding manufacturers, a kind of honorary Yorkshireman.

But in 1862 Frank Crossley was created a baronet, and in 1863 he bought the Somerleyton estate of 3,224 acres in Suffolk.[4] The house at Somerleyton had been remodelled, regardless of expense, by Sir Morton Peto, the great contractor, in 1844–51; its most famous feature was its huge winter garden, 100 feet square (Pl. 18). The designer was John Thomas, a sculptor and ornamental mason who had worked on the Houses of Parliament (for which Peto had been the contractor) and had

201. Statue of Sir Savile Crossley in the entrance hall, Somerleyton Hall, Suffolk.

turned his hand to architecture. It came on the market because Peto was running into financial difficulties, which ended in bankruptcy in 1866. The discriminating might make disparaging comments on its quality and Robert Kerr called it 'a design characterized by a good deal of pretentiousness, and that of an unsuccessful kind'[5] but to most people it would have seemed that Sir Francis had got hold of a plum.

It is always interesting to speculate on the reasons that make someone strike out on a new line. It was not especially surprising that Sir Francis, millionaire as he was, should buy a country estate, but it *was* surprising that he bought it in East Anglia, considering how deeply bound up he was with Yorkshire, by inheritance, interests and tastes. The explanation (as, one suspects, with many other new rich who took to the country) lay in his wife. He had married into the business; his wife was a carpet manufacturer's daughter, but her father was a Kidderminster carpet manufacturer, not a Yorkshire one. She disliked Yorkshire and had social ambitions that extended beyond a big villa in the suburbs of Halifax, sandwiched between a cemetery and a public park. In 1857, after twelve years of marriage they had an only child, Savile Crossley. In 1872 when her husband died at the age of fifty-five (of overwork, like several of the Crossleys) she shut up Belle Vue and moved all the best contents to Somerleyton.[6] Perhaps it was significant that the only picture of importance left behind was *Cromwell Refusing the Crown of England*. Sir Savile was brought up as a country gentleman, educated at Eton and sent into the army. He was M.P. for North Suffolk in 1885–92 and for Halifax in 1900–6, following in the steps of his father, but as a Conservative, not a Liberal. In 1902–5 he was Paymaster-General, in 1916 he was created Lord Somerleyton and in 1918–24 he served as Lord-in-Waiting. Belle Vue was bought by Halifax Corporation in 1890, and became the Public Library.★

★ Other branches of the Crossleys remained in Halifax, and continued to build large villas and play a prominent part in the life of the town. Joseph's son Edward Crossley (Mayor of Halifax, 1874–6) built the Elizabethan Bermerside on Skircoat Moor about 1872 and equipped it with an observatory. John's son Louis John Crossley of Moorside was a musician and a pioneer electrical scientist, and fitted out his house with electrical clocks, a telegraph transmitter, an electrical laboratory, an electric tramway, a lighthouse on top and an enormous organ, before dying of overwork at the age of forty-nine. Both houses are illustrated in *Picturesque Views of Castles and Country Houses in Yorkshire* (Bradford, 1885).

202. Somerleyton Hall (John Thomas, 1844–51). Sir Francis Crossley bought the house and estate in 1863.

15. *George Devey in Kent*

DEVEY made his first recorded appearance in Kent at Penshurst in 1850, as a young and unknown architect working for Lord De L'Isle and Dudley. Round the nucleus of a group of fifteenth-century half-timbered houses next to the church he designed an open square of plastered, half-timbered and tile-hung buildings, which, for better or worse, were a milestone in nineteenth-century building. There was nothing fancy-dress, and only a hint of exaggeration about them: they were built with the same techniques and of the same materials as the old cottages in the neighbourhood, of which Devey had made a careful study. At more than a passing glance one would take them for fifteenth-century work.

Over the next ten years he built numerous cottages and other estate buildings in Penshurst and its vicinity, including a saddler's and butcher's shops and a rustic well

213

203. One of George Devey's cottages at Betteshanger, nr Deal Kent.

in the village.★ They all resolutely turned their back on the nineteenth century and went for inspiration to old traditions of country craftsmanship.† He also worked at Penshurst Place itself, and built a largish house, Hammerfield, in its immediate neighbourhood. This was as determinedly old world as the cottages, if considerably less convincing.

At Redleaf, on the edge of the village, lived Sir Walter James,[1] a young baronet whose father had died when he was two and who had been brought up by his step-father, Lord Hardinge, at South Park just outside Penshurst. He married a northern heiress, Sarah Caroline Ellison, in 1841. He sold his inherited property in Berkshire when still a young man, and settled in the county in which he had been brought up. He lived at Redleaf for a few years, but it was only rented and had little land attached to it. In 1850 he bought the Betteshanger estate of several thousand acres, a few miles from Deal in East Kent.

The house at Betteshanger was a comfortable late Georgian villa with bay windows and barge-boarded gables, designed by Robert Lugar and illustrated in 1828 in his *Villa Architecture*. In 1854 Salvin, who had worked at South Park, made unexecuted designs for adding a wing and tower. In 1856 he was replaced by George Devey, whom Sir Walter James must have got to know of through his Penshurst connections. Devey became a friend of the family and worked at Betteshanger at intervals until his death in 1886. Through the Jameses he came to know the circle of friends and supporters of Gladstone who were to be the backbone of his practice for the rest of his life.

Sir Walter James (1816–93) had been a political follower of Peel, and became an admirer and friend of Gladstone,‡ who made him a peer, as Lord Northbourne, in 1885. He was as serious and religious as Gladstone, taught every Sunday in the village Sunday school, and as a devout Puseyite rebuilt the church (to Salvin's design) before he remodelled the house. He was an amateur artist, studied, as did George Devey, under J. D. Harding and carved part of the pulpit in the church. He bought Arthur Hughes's *Ophelia*, Watts' cartoon for his huge *Caractacus*, paintings by Frederick Goodall and E. W. Cooke, and sculpture by the pre-raphaelite Alexander Munro. He combined religious and artistic tastes with an enthusiasm for farming, and as an improving landlord built numerous cottages on the estate, to Devey's designs.

★ *Country Life* of 23 December 1899 reports two villagers discussing the well at Penshurst: 'Might so well have gied us a pump, mightn't he?' 'Lord love ye, that wouldn't have been quaint fashioned enough.'
† Devey's knowledge of country traditions was not confined to building. 'His knowledge of whips, harness and all the requirements and specialities of the stable was little short of that of an expert, and he could have made without hesitation working drawings of carriages and coaches, so perfectly did he know their "build" and how to judge them.' Walter Godfrey on Devey, *R.I.B.A. Journal*, 3rd series, XII (1906), pp. 506–7. Devey's maternal grandfather was Durs Egg, a well-known maker of sporting guns (and father of Augustus Egg, the painter).
‡ The James town house was in Whitehall Gardens, next door to that of Disraeli, who was fond of pacing up and down in his garden. 'My little pupil, Walter John James (later the 3rd Lord Northbourne) used to watch him, shake his fist at him, and ejaculate "serpent".' (Letter from his governess, preserved at Northbourne Court.) For the effect of the family's Liberal connections on Devey's practice, see introduction, p. 19n.

Devey must have fitted very comfortably into the serious-minded, gently artistic and country-loving James family, who seem to have travelled with their sketchbooks at the ready, quick to make a record of a litter of pigs or a picturesque cottage, or to turn out one of those mildly facetious drawings which the Victorians produced with such distressing ease. The artistically inclined among the guests at Betteshanger used to leave little drawings behind them in the visitors' book; Devey was a regular contributor, along with the numerous members of the Hardinge family, the artists Warwick Brookes and E. W. Cooke, and James Nasmyth, the inventor of the steam hammer, for whom Devey had designed Hammerfield at Penshurst in 1856–9.[2] Another friend and visitor was William Oxenden Hammond, a neighbouring landowner and an enthusiastic and accomplished water-colourist. He and Devey became friends (they were both bachelors and the victims of unhappy love affairs★) and Devey did much work for him from at least 1867 onwards, culminating in the rebuilding of his house, St Alban's Court, in 1875.

The design of Betteshanger was worked out over twenty-six years, no doubt as the result of many sketchbook discussions, with constant second thoughts leading to minor alterations or touching-up of effects on work that had been done several years previously. Sketches, photographs,[3] and dates on the building enable the progress of

★Devey, as a young man, had been in love with Flora Hoskins, the daughter of the vicar of Chiddingstone, near Penshurst. He left her £5,000 in his will 'on account of the engagement so cruelly broken off between us'. In 1857 she married another clergyman, the Revd H. W. Streatfield, of the Chiddingstone Castle family. He died in 1866 and Devey then proposed to her again (W. H. Godfrey in *R.I.B.A. Journal*, 3rd series, XII (1906), p. 505). Owing to 'certain divergences he was preferred as a friend'. The divergences were probably religious. Devey later supported the Theistic Church of the Revd Charles Voysey (father of the architect), who was expelled from the Church of England in 1871 for denying the doctrines of everlasting Hell, the inspiration of the Bible, the divinity of Christ, etc.

215

204. A sketch by Devey in the visitors' book at Betteshanger.

the work to be charted with approximate accuracy, and show that by 1861 Devey had evolved almost all the characteristics of the more ambitious country houses that he designed in the 1870s and 1880s.

The complete reshaping of the house may have been envisaged from the start, but the first work to be done was the building of a new wing and tower and a new entrance porch in 1856–8. The main block of the house was then remodelled inside and out; the date 1861 is carved on a window on the garden front. Salvin had suggested a tower immediately adjoining the main block; Devey built his tower (now known as the James tower) as an outrider joined to the main block by a considerably lower wing. This combination of main block, wing and tower became a favourite motif of his and was re-employed in several of his larger houses. The main block at Betteshanger originally had exposed eaves and an attached wing of the same height; Devey hid the eaves behind a parapet so as to raise the walls by about a foot, and by lowering the height of the wing made the adjacent facades seem taller still. As a result the main block, which looks very insignificant in old photographs and drawings, showing it before alteration, was given considerable presence without any actual increase in the size of the rooms.

A walk round Betteshanger makes clear, not only that Devey had studied East Kent buildings very closely, but that certain kinds of building especially attracted him. He liked houses that had grown up over the years and had become a patchwork of different dates and styles, and of different materials all jumbled up together, with wings at odd angles to each other. At Betteshanger he made the dangerous decision to try and create similar effects in a design conceived within a comparatively short time. Dubious though the ultimate results were to be, even in his own buildings, at Betteshanger he worked with a freshness and enthusiasm which produced a building of considerable charm—although the haphazard way in which it was enlarged and altered over the years gives it a somewhat makeshift and even amateurish character. He provided the house with a complete and entirely bogus pedigree which ran somewhat as follows. All that remained of the medieval house was a curious old tower, which had been re-windowed and repaired with different materials over the centuries. A low rambling wing had been added in Elizabethan times, entered by a quaint Renaissance porch with a carved oriel window over its archway. A grander rebuilding or additions of about 1630 produced a bay-windowed block of higher

216

205. Betteshanger, nr Deal, Kent (George Devey, 1856–82). The garden front.
206. (upper right) The entrance front.
207. (right) Fake antique in the tower.

rooms with the shaped Flemish gables typical of the neighbourhood; it was built of brick, with panels and diapers of flint here and there; a new window in the side of the porch, with a gable above it, introduced a patch of brickwork into the stone and flint of the original structure. Early in the eighteenth century a wrought iron balustrade had been placed across the arch of the porch, and a Georgian wooden staircase inserted in the middle of the Jacobean state rooms.

All this was not worked out exactly or to be taken too seriously, but it provided a framework on which to construct an irregular rambling country house with frequent changes in levels, eclectic in its detailing and with touches of deliberate quaintness—little peep-hole windows of no possible practical use, or features like the garden oriel with its engaging lantern-window top. In the low wing the rooms were only about 8 feet 6 inches high; these included family living rooms and bedrooms as well as servants' rooms, with what must have been deliberate cottage effect. The entrance was moved from its previous symmetrical position adjoining the main block to a vestibule on one side; an archway was opened out to link it up with the staircase, an organ put in and the combined space became part hall, part living room. Some windows were blocked up altogether, others reduced in size and the mullions changed from wood to stone and thickened throughout, making the rooms considerably darker than in pre-Devey times. All these features anticipated 'Old English' and 'Queen Anne' developments by about ten years, and the shaped gables, besides reappearing in numerous Devey buildings, were to become one of the favourite motifs of the 'Queen Anne' movement.

Some time in the 1870s the round bay on the entrance front, which had been planned from the start, was finally built, and the little gable on the garden side filled

218

208. Betteshanger. A musical evening in the hall.

with decorative plasterwork. The barge-boards on this gable came later still, as did the replacing of overhanging eaves on the porch gable by a brick coping. In 1882 what is now known as the Ellison tower was added at the end of the entrance front, crowned by a wooden cupola that appears very prettily over the roofs in the view from the garden. There were numerous other minor alterations, and the history of the servants' wing is past unravelling, as a result of further additions and alterations made in 1893 and 1899, after Devey's death.* Devey also re-planned the gardens, placing urns at strategic points and making a symmetrical array of steps, balustrades and terraces to lead down from the house to the church (once described by a guest as 'fastened like a dinghy at the bottom of the garden').

As a country house architect Devey developed remarkably little; he spent twenty-five years producing bigger, but not necessarily better, variations on the formula he had worked out for Betteshanger. He seldom remedied its worst qualities—a lack of distinction in the interior detailing and a rather unpleasing heaviness in the glazing, with plate-glass lights squeezed between thick mullions and transoms. In houses three or four times the size of Betteshanger his loose and rambling plans could become depressingly formless. On the credit side the complete lack of tension, or any desire to show off, can be agreeably relaxing as a contrast to some of the cleverer productions of the Norman Shaw school.

St Alban's Court is the best of later Devey houses, perhaps because W. O. Hammond was a friend, and he and Devey had had ten years or so of working together before they came round to rebuilding the house. Moreover Hammond was a man of strong character and decided views; it was probably his influence that made Devey give the house a touch of formality that distinguishes it to its advantage from other big houses which he was designing at the same time.†

Devey's earlier work for Hammond had probably consisted of cottages, and of alterations and additions to the old house at St Alban's Court. This was on low ground at the bottom of a hill; Devey built the new house on a fine levelled site higher up the hill, and demolished the old house, all but a fragment of early work, to which he added much convincing half-timbering so as to make it a picturesque feature (rather like the church at Betteshanger) at the bottom of the new garden.

The contract drawings[4] for the new house are dated July 1875; 1875 is carved in two places on the fabric; the chimneypiece in the first-floor corridor is dated 1878. The fact that the house is planned round three sides of a hollow square, with a service wing to one side, and that it is only one room thick, combine with its dominating

---

* These included the addition of an enormous and unlovely dining hall, with an equally large studio adjoining. The studio has a special entry for horses and cattle, which the second Lord Northbourne (an amateur artist like his father) was addicted to painting.

† In social life Hammond's old-fashioned formality of manner could be alarming, especially as it started at breakfast. 'At 9 o'clock the whole party was expected to assemble in the library. Until the last guest came down no move was made, however late that unfortunate proved to be; when he or she made a shame-faced appearance, then, and not till then, did Mr. Hammond approach what Beatrix and I called the "top-lady" and arm her into the breakfast room . . . Smoking was not allowed in any part of the house except the kitchen, after the servants had gone to bed.' (Typescript reminiscences of Mrs Curtis Green, widow of the third Lord Northbourne, now at Northbourne Court.)

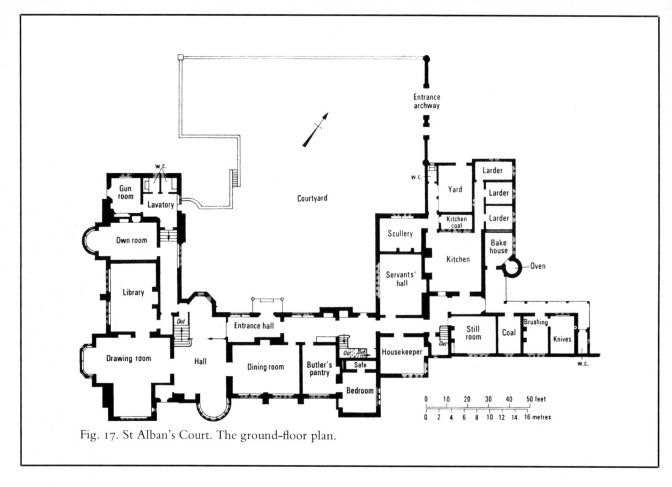

Fig. 17. St Alban's Court. The ground-floor plan.

site to make it seem bigger than it really is. The design combines regularity and approximate symmetry in the main masses with complete irregularity in fenestration and subsidiary features. Its plan is more compact and much more straightforward than other Devey houses of its date; its detail is more cohesive than at Betteshanger, predominantly Elizabethan, though with early sixteenth-century excursions.

The lower storey of St Alban's Court is of stone, the upper brick. There is a ragged edge between the two with little outriders of stone floating among the brick. The device is in direct descent from the patched walls at Betteshanger and was probably the ancestor of similar tricks that became clichés among suburban architects in the twentieth century. At St Alban's Court the stone is dressed so as to give it a rough and rather mealy texture, and the brick is a hot and unattractive red, two qualities which rule out any possibility of mistaking it for a sixteenth-century house. This is rather surprising when one considers the immense care Devey took in the texturing of his cottages.

Inside and out the most impressive feature of the house is the hall. It is a development of the combined hall and staircase at Betteshanger, with the hall separated by another room from the entrance, increased in size, raised to two storeys in height and given galleries at first-floor level. Similar rooms, called either halls or saloons, but in either case distinct from the entrance hall, were incorporated by

220

209. (upper right) St Alban's Court, Nonington, Kent (George Devey, 1875–8). The house from the garden.
210. (right) The entrance front.

211. St Alban's Court. The hall.

Devey into Goldings (1871) and Killarney (1877). Killarney like St Albans had an enormous two-storey bow window adjacent to a chimneypiece. Externally the St Alban's Court bow window makes a prominent and splendid feature on the garden facade. Internally, the semi-circle of glazing, rising to a great height out of the circumscribed ground space of the hall, combines with the vanishing flight of stairs and the trellis work of balusters and columns to produce what is probably the most effective of Devey's interiors. It is both spatially exciting and, because of the warm, honey-brown of the oak panelling, extremely agreeable in its colouring. Otherwise there is little of interest inside the house; the drawing rooms have Devey's routine Jacobean ornament, the library is early eighteenth century in manner, with a coarseness in the detail which reveals its date. It is remarkable that Devey was producing Georgian interiors in the 1870s, but their date is the only interesting thing about them.[5]

222

212. (upper right) The hall bay window, on the garden front.

213. (right) The hall bay window from inside.

16. Kelham Hall, Nottinghamshire

KELHAM originally belonged to the Sutton family. In 1717 Bridget, the heiress of
Sutton, second Lord Lexington, married John Manners, third Duke of Rutland. She
rebuilt the house in 1728–31 and left it to a younger son, who changed his name to
Manners-Sutton. In 1844–6 his descendant, John Henry Manners-Sutton, employed
Salvin to add a big Jacobean-style servants' wing to the house,[1] and in 1857
commissioned George Gilbert Scott to make minor alterations. On the night of 26
November 1857 all the house except the new wing was gutted by fire. The fire was a
piece of luck for Scott. He had been inserting plate-glass windows, adding a
conservatory and otherwise tinkering around with a house that he cannot have
found sympathetic; he was now presented with an empty site, a compliant patron
and what seemed a long purse. The resulting phoenix of hard red brick that emerged
from the ashes still surprises travellers who cross the River Trent at Kelham; and its
amazing silhouette enriches the view for miles around.

The main part of Scott's enormous practice consisted of churches, cathedral
restorations and public buildings. His country houses make up a small but decidedly
heavyweight episode in his career. The most important of them were designed in a
five-year period, between 1856 and 1861. In these years he diverted a portion of his
tremendous energy away from ecclesiastical pastures, and in 1857 published his
Remarks on Secular and Domestic Architecture Present and Future. It was an eloquent and
detailed plea for building Gothic houses and public buildings, as well as Gothic

224

214. Kelham Hall, nr Newark, Nottinghamshire (Sir George Gilbert Scott, 1858–61). The west
front.

churches. Its first two chapters were based on a lecture given at Newark, which may have been what first brought him to Manners-Sutton's notice.

The resulting commission gave Scott a wonderful opportunity to prove his point and confound the opponents of modern Gothic houses who dismissed the style as dark, archaic and only suitable for churches. He succeeded to the extent that he produced a spacious, well-lit house equipped with numerous up-to-date devices. Moreover any building so huge, so solid, so elaborately, learnedly and expensively Gothic, so redolently, earnestly and undilutedly Victorian is bound to exert a fascination that will increase over the years. But as a design, in spite of its memorable silhouette, Kelham does not bear too much looking into; and as a private house it was an absurdity because Scott was unable, architecturally speaking, to stop preaching a sermon or addressing a public meeting. Kelham is not noticeably different in tone or treatment from his Town Hall at Preston, or his hotel and booking office at St Pancras. It is scarcely secular, and not at all domestic.

There is a crassness about this which is typical of Scott. 'Amongst Anglican architects', he wrote, 'Carpenter and Butterfield were the apostles of the high church school—I, of the multitude.'[2] There is nothing wrong in addressing the multitude, but like many popularizers, Scott owed his success to a combination of hard work, self-advertisement and a kind of sincere banality. All his many talents, his real knowledge of the Gothic style and enthusiasm for reviving it, his thousand buildings and fortune of £180,000, do not make him more than a second-rate architect—as his fellow Gothicists were well aware.

But his office was a formidable organization. Not only was it very large, by Victorian standards, but it had a permanent staff that was technically of the highest competence, and a steady through traffic of brilliant young men. In his *Recollections* he refers, with rather engaging candour, to 'the extent of my business, which has always been too much for my capacity of attending to it'.[3] Sir Thomas Jackson, who was his pupil, describes how 'he was up to his eyes in engagement and it was hard to get him to look at our work ... The door flew open and out he came: "No time today!"; the cab was at the door and he was whirled away.'[4] With Scott's best work one always has to wonder how much is due to Scott, how much to Street, or Bodley, or J. J. Stevenson, or E. R. Robson, or Thomas Jackson or his own son George Gilbert, Junior.

The plans for the house were worked out during 1858, and the foundations laid in April 1859. The 1844–6 servants' wing was left untouched. Work was approaching completion when the house was described in the *Building News* of 28 June 1861. In view of the disaster of 1856, the house was designed to be fireproof. All the rooms on the ground floor were rib vaulted in stone and brick, as was the first-floor corridor. Elsewhere the rooms and corridors were either brick vaulted or had fireproof ceilings of iron and concrete (put in by C. C. and A. Dennett of Nottingham).[5] The stairs were of stone and iron, the only wood employed being for the handrail of the north staircase. The corridor and staircase floors were of marble, tiles or cement. The roofs were of wood, but subdivided by brick party walls.

The house was built by William Cubitt & Co. of bricks from near Retford, and of Ancaster stone. It was gas-lit. A gasworks was built for this purpose near the hall,

which also lit the village street, and supplied gas 'at a nominal cost' to any of the villagers who wanted to be connected to it. There was an elaborate heating system; hot air came in through grills in the floor and was taken away by ventilators near the ceiling; many of these, with their pierced cast iron grilles, still survive. The rooms were mostly lit by casement windows, filled with great sheets of plate glass, sometimes as much as ten feet high; in the music hall the windows (since replaced) were of plate glass three-quarters of an inch thick, fixed into the masonry. A luggage lift went up the hollow stone newel of the clock tower staircase. There was a plentiful supply of water closets, though still only one bathroom to a floor. The many appendages to the house included the gasworks and the new farm buildings; the little tower of the latter builds up nicely, in some views, to the great mass of the main house.

All this is rather impressive; the facades are less so. Although Victorian Gothicists attacked classical architecture because it sacrificed convenience for symmetry, one often gets the impression that they made their own designs asymmetrical as much to show they were on the right side as for any practical purposes. Kelham is doggedly asymmetrical all the way through; but it is hard to think of any reason of convenience which made, for instance, one end of the west front gabled and the other horizontal or introduced a piece of cathedral arcading in front of the dining

226

215. Kelham Hall. The east front.

room windows. Visually, it is a major criticism of Scott that he failed to organize his irregular assemblage of gables and towers into a convincing whole. Both of the main fronts suffer from an uncomfortable tug-of-war between the two ends; the clock tower, for instance, is too skimpy for the mass of the house, but prevents the south-east tower from being a dominating feature. Yet the latter is by itself a grand design, with that 'certain squareness and horizontality of outline'[6] which Scott says he derived from Italian Gothic, and first worked out in 1856 for his unexecuted Gothic design for the Foreign Office. He considered it an effective feature to combine with 'gables, high-pitched roofs and dormers'. He must have been pleased with the clock tower, for he re-used it, with variations, at Hafodunos and the St Pancras Hotel.

Scott dealt the death blow to the cohesion of his design by his determination to show how 'the number of changes that may be rung on this one feature, the window, are as inexhaustible as they are charming'.[7] There are some nine different window designs on the east front, nine on the south front and fourteen on the west front. Each living room and staircase (and many of the bedrooms) has its own variation. Scott's knowledge of the cathedrals of England and France, and the palaces of Venice, is made abundantly evident, but the result, although sumptuous enough when looked at in detail, combines to produce an effect both fussy and forbidding.

227

216. Inside the former carriage-court.

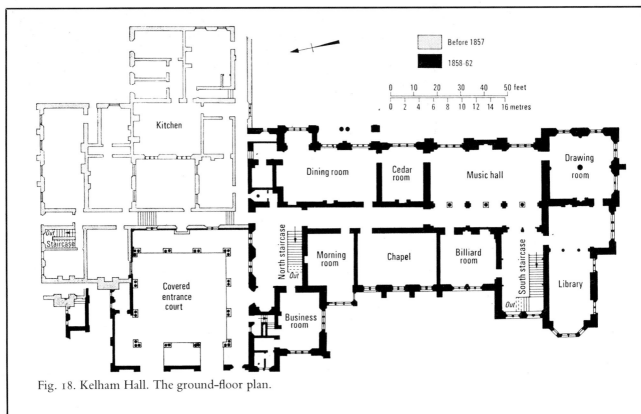

Fig. 18. Kelham Hall. The ground-floor plan.

217. (top) Kelham Hall. The first floor corridor.
XVI. (right) Milton Ernest Hall, Bedfordshire (William Butterfield, 1853–8). The garden front.

218. Kelham Hall. Looking from the first-floor corridor into the music hall.

The accommodation at Kelham is strung along either side of central corridors that run from end to end of the house, including the service wing. The top-floor corridor is mainly top-lit; those on the ground and first floors borrow light from the north and south staircases and the two-storey music hall, which is separated from them by arcades. As at Merevale the main entrance is at the end of the main block, where it joins the service wing. It leads into the north staircase by way of a gigantic covered carriage court. Separate entrances lead off the court to the service wing and the inevitable business room.

Certain weaknesses reveal that Scott was not a professional architect of country houses. The morning room faces west; the chapel is next to the billiard room; worst of all, everything is on the grand scale, there is no family end to the house and no rooms that can be described as intimate. But the interior is certainly impressive. The wide and roomy corridors tunnelling through the house give a feeling of great spaciousness, besides making it easy to find one's way around. The route to the drawing room by way of covered court, corridor and music hall is magnificently ostentatious, in the Barry manner; was this Scott's idea of how a landowner should 'quietly and gravely' express the fact that 'he has been blessed with wealth, and he need not shirk from using it in its proper degree'?[8] The corridors are treated with decreasing richness as they go up; the detailing of the first-floor one is an impressive

XVII, XVIII. (preceding pages) Brodsworth Hall, Yorkshire. Two details in the ground-floor corridor.

XIX. (left) Kelham Hall. A capital in the music hall.

219. Kelham Hall. The music hall in Victorian days.

example of Scott (or his office) in a more sober mood. In the drawing room a central marble pier, with its capitals gilded on a chocolate background, supports an elaborately decorated vault; stencilled decoration covered the walls except where interrupted by panels of dark green velvet (now replaced with wallpaper). There are huge trefoiled mirrors between the windows, a chimneypiece of inlaid marble and much carving and gilding everywhere.

There are more painted vaults in the library and dining room. But the grandest room in the house is the music hall. This has a cathedral arcade and triforium gallery down one side, and an immense hooded chimneypiece on the other; originally, as old photographs show, it had painted decoration from floor to ceiling, and what survives is splendid enough with the capitals gilded and the mouldings gilded on their projections and painted red in the hollows. The capitals here and elsewhere are superb examples of the way the Victorians went direct to natural forms for inspiration. They are based on a great variety of flowers and foliage, carved with great botanical accuracy and a strong touch of formalism. Scott, unlike G. E. Street,

234

220. The drawing room.

221. The entrance and former carriage court.

did not design his capitals himself: 'he gives drawings, while I do my work by influence; but the results in both cases are of a high order'.[9] The carving at Kelham, as in many of Scott's buildings, is by Brindley of the firm of Farmer and Brindley; and Scott had good reason to be pleased with the results.

A particularly splendid archway under the arcade of the music hall should have opened onto a magnificent south staircase. In fact, it leads to a cramped wooden stairs with rooms beyond it, for the staircase designed by Scott was never installed. The intended conservatory was never carried above foundation level; the clock tower was left without a clock; throughout the house there are empty sockets and hanging capitals still waiting for their marble columns. The Manners-Sutton property of 5,500 acres, bringing in £11,500 a year,[10] did not justify the building of a house so very much grander than the one it replaced. Although an immense collection of Scott's drawings for Kelham survive, all private family papers have disappeared, and one can only guess at the reasons for J. H. Manners-Sutton's extravagance. But the agricultural depression was too much for the estate. When he died in 1898, the mortgage on his property was foreclosed and it came into Chancery. The Society of the Sacred Mission rented the house in 1903, and ultimately bought it. A new quadrangle was added in the 1920s, including a chapel, and the silhouette of C. C. Thompson's huge Byzantine dome now adds a calmer note to Scott's jagged skyline.[11] The Society left Kelham some years ago, and it is now the headquarters of Newark District Council.

17. *Brodsworth Hall, Yorkshire*

THE GREAT HOUSE at Brodsworth was one of the direct consequences of the famous Thellusson will—a will that achieved national fame at intervals over a period of sixty-three years, and that blighted or warped the lives of a large number of people during that period.[1] It is an odd and intriguing story with more than a touch of *Bleak House* about it.

Peter Thellusson, a rich city banker of Swiss origin, died in 1797. He left a portion of his property worth about £100,000 to his wife and six children. The remainder, estimated at roughly £700,000, he assigned to trustees to accumulate at compound interest during the lives of his sons and his sons' sons. On the death of the last survivor, the estate was to be divided equally among 'the eldest male lineal descendants of his three sons then living'.

The will caused a sensation. It was calculated that by the time of its division the estate might have accumulated to £35,000,000. A law was passed, by which it became impossible to make a similar will again. For sixty-three years of law suits and appeals, until the last of the intervening generation had died and for several years after, the members of the family contested the will, contested the way it was being administered, litigated against each other, and disputed the meaning of the phrase, 'eldest male lineal descendant'. Finally, in 1859, the House of Lords delivered the final judgement. The estate was to go to Peter Thellusson's great-grandsons, Lord Rendlesham and Charles Sabine Thellusson. But litigation and mismanagement had left it little if any larger than the original capital. Charles Sabine Thellusson's share consisted of Brodsworth Hall, which his great-grandfather had bought not long before his death, landed property bringing in about £17,000 a year, and a valuable coal mine on the Brodsworth estate.

On the strength of his inheritance he demolished the big Georgian house at Brodsworth and built a new one on a new site. The original specification survives

236

222. Brodsworth Hall, nr Doncaster, Yorkshire (Chevalier Casentini and Philip Wilkinson, 1861–70). The exterior.

and is dated February 1861.[2] The house was more or less completed by the end of 1863, but the work on the gardens and fittings was carried on for several more years. It was built of stone quarried at Brodsworth which has not worn well, and has left a mounting problem for Thellusson's successors. The architect was an unknown Italian, described on his one surviving design as 'Chevalier Casentini, Arch. & Sculp., Lucca, Toscana, Italia'. It remains obscure why Charles Sabine Thellusson employed an Italian architect; he presumably met him in Italy and the reason may have been connected with his enthusiasm for modern Italian sculpture, to which the house bears abundant witness. Casentini probably never visited Yorkshire, or even England, and the execution of his design was entrusted to an equally obscure English architect, Philip Wilkinson, of 74 Connaught Terrace.[3]

At first sight, one might not guess that Brodsworth was by an Italian architect, perhaps because most high-Victorian classical architecture in England was in any case derived from Italian Renaissance examples. But a closer look reveals differences. There is no reflection in the design either of the picturesque tradition, or of the specifically Victorian feeling that regularity was deceitful and therefore morally wrong. Not only are all the main facades symmetrical, which would not have been uncommon in country houses designed by English classicists of the time, but there is no tower and the service wing is discreetly concealed behind shrubbery. As a result the main block stands visually on its own, instead of being part of an irregular composition with a variegated skyline. This main block is endowed with considerable bravura by the raised and urn-crowned panels along the parapet, by the great *porte-cochère* with its rusticated columns, and the long line of the garden front behind it. The detail is rather better than most English architects could have provided at the time, for Victorian Classicism was going to seed by the 1860s; it has a typical nineteenth-century richness, but is never coarse or overabundant. Moreover, the house has the feeling of being all of a piece; the whole building, together with its setting, was designed and built within a few years; the statues that dot the grounds, the long terraces with their steps flanked by greyhounds of Italian marble, the temple to the west of the house, the formal garden with its fountain, are all in keeping.

A design by Casentini of the exterior survives and indeed is the only evidence that he was the architect, but there are no designs for the interior to show how much was due to him and how much to Wilkinson. Certain peculiarities of the plan suggest a foreign hand. Basically it is similar to the plan of Horsted, a rectangle with a long central corridor and a service wing at the back; to give the main rooms a private and garden view the main entrance is at the end of the rectangle, instead of at the centre of the main front. But the kitchen is much nearer to the dining room than most English Victorian architects would have allowed it to be, and is next door to the billiard room. This was an unconventional combination, but not without logic. In both rooms, though for different reasons, it was convenient to have top-lighting which was obtained by placing them side by side at the bottom of an internal courtyard.

A weakness, by Victorian standards, is that food can only get from the kitchen to the dining room by crossing the grand central corridor. Victorian ideas of propriety would have been outraged by the idea of servants carrying steaming dishes across its

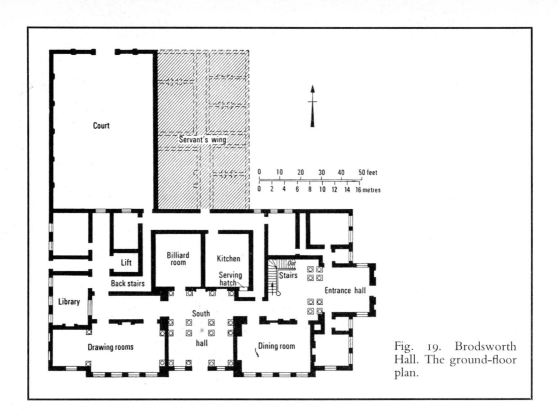

Fig. 19. Brodsworth Hall. The ground-floor plan.

marbled splendours; but Italians, like Englishmen in the eighteenth century, were probably more easy going. In any case, the superb wastefulness of space and skilfulness of arrangement of this central line of communications suggests the mysterious Chevalier Casentini at work.

The house is divided up internally into a sequence of spaces, the combined size of which is out of all proportion to their utility; a large entrance hall, an even larger staircase hall, a short stretch of corridor, a grand pillared south or garden hall and finally a broad arcaded and mirrored corridor leading to the drawing rooms and library. A similar, though simpler corridor leads off the staircase landing on the floor above.

The walls of these halls and corridors are for the most part marbled in various shades of yellow, grey, green and red. There are terra-cotta scagliola columns in the entrance hall, and yellow scagliola and yellow damask in the south hall. Underfoot are Minton tiles and crimson Axminster carpets. Space flows freely into space, organized on two offset but overlapping axes that produce two main vistas; from the entrance hall into the staircase hall and slantwise into a corner of the south hall; and from the staircase hall through the south hall and down to the glowing stained-glass window that divides the corridor from the library.

In the rich gloom of the library end of the corridor a white marble figure reclines on a marble couch beneath the stained glass. There are statues lining the corridor and reflected in its mirrors, statues in the staircase hall, statues framed between the columns. 'Marble Works, Statues, etc' worth £2,750, including the greyhounds and steps of the garden terraces, were sent over from Italy by Casentini in 1866. His design for the house shows an enormous and elaborate conservatory attached to the

238

223. (upper right) Brodsworth Hall. The garden hall.

224. (right) The entrance hall.

west end; it was probably also intended to be a sculpture gallery, but was never built. Some of the statues are unsigned, others are by sculptors well known in their time but largely forgotten today, such as Professor G. Lazzerini, Pietro Franchi and Giosue Argenti. They differ a good deal in quality; almost all share a vein of sentimentality that varies from the charming to the cloying. Taken as a whole their silent marble assembly enormously enriches the character of the house.

The chimneypieces in the south hall and some of the bedrooms, and a number of mahogany doors, come from the old house. To incorporate Georgian details in this way shows an appreciation of the eighteenth century rare in the 1860s. Generally speaking, the whole house expresses an attitude of mind sympathetic to the eighteenth-century tradition, though, with typical Victorian self-confidence, its architects were prepared to set out to do everything just a bit better. The two drawing rooms are essentially Victorian versions of late Georgian drawing rooms, but slightly more flamboyant, coarser and heavier in all their details. The total effect is very splendid. Both rooms are hung with rich red damask framed by gilded and festooned panels. There is a continual glitter of huge gilt-framed mirrors reflecting enormous crystal chandeliers, of gilding, marble, knick-knacks and looped and draped pelmets. The curtains and chairs are gold and crimson like the walls. White Corinthian columns, with grey and gold capitals, screen off the two rooms from each other, and frame the alcove at the end of the bigger room. The ceilings are

240

225, 226. (above) Brodsworth Hall. Two views in the halls and corridor.
227. (right) The drawing room.

228. Brodsworth Hall. The billiard room.

painted with flat arabesque designs, predominantly pink and green in colour. The surviving accounts make no mention of these ceilings. There are similar ones at Grimston Park in Yorkshire and Locko Park in Derbyshire, the latter painted by an Italian artist, Romoli, about 1861–4.[4]

Other rooms of interest are the library with its splendiferous Victorian paper of blue, pink and gold in which hangs Largillière's portrait, signed and dated 1725, of Peter Thellusson's mother, depicted with gay rococo flourishes in a yellow dress and pink draperies; and the billiard room with its leather-padded raised benches for the spectators. This, besides being an untouched Victorian period piece, is remarkable for its horse portraits, including four by James Ward.

The handsome patterned carpets, of Savonnerie type, were supplied by Lapworth Brothers of 22 Old Bond Street, 'carpet manufacturers to Her Majesty and the Royal Family', according to their bill head. The two carpets are described as 'Extra Superfine Real Axminster Carpets to Special Design, Italian Scrolls ornament and flowers to plan of rooms' and cost £367 10s. They were no doubt made at the firm's factory at Wilton. Lapworths not only carpeted but also curtained and furnished the entire house (perhaps in the latter case acting as middle men).

The house and grounds were completed by 1870, by which time about £60,000 had been spent on house, park, gardens and furniture. Charles Sabine Thellusson died in 1885, leaving four sons, each of whom inherited Brodsworth in turn, and none of whom had children. On the death of the fourth son, in 1931, the property went to his nephew, Charles Grant-Dalton, whose mother was the younger of Charles Sabine Thellusson's daughters.

242

18. Tyntesfield, Somerset

LOOKING back over the distance of a hundred years or so the great merchant and industrial dynasties of the nineteenth century tend to seem all of a piece. It is easy to forget from what a wide variety of backgrounds they emerged. At one end of the spectrum were families like the Crossleys, who worked their way from mill-hands to millionaires in two generations. Families of this kind were likely to be chapel rather than church, and Radical rather than Tory; however much money they made, the psychological break involved in setting up as members of the landowning classes was a considerable one. In complete contrast were families like the west-country Gibbses who came from a background of small squires, country bankers, merchants and professional men. Such people were likely to be Church of England and conservative by inheritance; and even if they made their million on the basis of little or no inherited money, to own their own country house and estate was the natural goal of their ambitions.

For thirty-three years, up till his death in 1875, William Gibbs of Tyntesfield (b. 1790) was head of the firm of Antony Gibbs and Sons. The firm had been founded by his father.[1] Antony Gibbs was the son of an Exeter surgeon who also owned a small property called Pytte at Clyst St George, near Exeter; his family had been living there since the sixteenth century.

Antony Gibbs's elder brother Vicary became an eminent lawyer and judge; another brother was a merchant in Bristol. Antony himself started life as a wool merchant in Exeter. His business failed in 1789, but he re-established himself in Madrid (and later Malaga and Cadiz) selling English cloth in Spain and exporting Spanish wine and fruit to England. He was driven out of Spain as a result of the

243

229. Tyntesfield, nr Bristol (John Norton, 1863–6). The house and conservatory from the west, in 1878.

Napoleonic Wars, and moved to London, where he founded the firm of Antony Gibbs and Sons in 1809.

At first the firm dealt with Spain and Spanish America; but the Spanish trade gradually dwindled away, while the South American trade increased, and became the basis of the firm's great prosperity in the mid-nineteenth century. This was largely based on guano and nitrate. The guano came from the sea-bird droppings which accumulated on rainless and uninhabited islands along the Pacific coast of America; it was the main fertilizer in use in the mid-nineteenth century, and the firm was largely responsible for introducing it to England. Nitrate of soda was mined in desert territories, and gradually replaced guano as the principal fertilizer as supplies of the latter were worked out. Antony Gibbs and Sons leased or bought deserts and islands, had offices in Peru, Ecuador, Chile and Bolivia, and extracted, treated, exported or acted as agents for the two products.

Antony died in 1815, leaving two sons, Henry Hucks and William. William's elder brother died in 1842, and William became head of the firm. From then till his death in 1875 the partners' profits were averaging between £80,000 and £100,000 a year. William was sole partner in 1843–7, had a share varying from 50% to $69\frac{3}{4}$% in 1848–64, and was still drawing $30\frac{1}{4}$% as he began to pull out in the last ten years of his life. In the 1860s he had £1,500,000 of his own capital in the business.

The growth of this great fortune (in terms of Victorian money values) led to its almost inevitable Victorian conclusion. In 1843 William Gibbs bought an estate and small country house called Tyntes Place, a few miles west of Bristol. In the 1840s he made minor additions to it; in the 1860s he remodelled it entirely, and renamed it Tyntesfield. Meanwhile he had been increasing the size of the estate, until by his death it amounted to nearly three thousand acres.[2]

But he put his fortune to another use, equally typical of his era. He was a deeply religious man, and an ardent supporter of the High Church movement.[3] Much of his wealth went on building and endowing churches and other religious foundations. Butterfield's great chapel at Keble College was built entirely at his expense; after his death his two sons paid for its hall and library. He built the new churches of St Michael's Paddington, St Michael's, Exeter, and St Mary's, Flaxley, in Gloucestershire. He contributed munificently to the restoration of Exeter and Bristol Cathedrals. His remodelling of Tyntesfield included an oratory; in 1873–5 this was replaced by a free-standing chapel, splendid enough for an Oxford or Cambridge college. He had two successive chaplains at Tyntesfield, both bachelors, living in High Church celibacy in a chaplain's cottage by the rose garden. His wife, Matilda Blanche, who was a remarkable and attractive woman, was as religious as he was. She was the sister of Sir Thomas Crawley-Boevey, of Flaxley Abbey; she and William married in 1839, and had seven children and eighteen grandchildren.

The marriage was one of a complex series, starting in the late eighteenth century, which interlinked the Gibbses with the Crawleys and Crawley-Boeveys of Flaxley, and the Yonges of Puslinch in Devon—to whom Charlotte M. Yonge, the novelist, belonged. Besides her family connection, C. M. Yonge was a close friend of Mrs Gibbs. She often stayed at Tyntesfield with her and 'good old Mr Gibbs', as she called him.

'That beautiful house', she wrote, 'was like a church in spirit, I used to think so

when going up and down the great staircase like a Y. At the bottom, after prayers, Mr Gibbs in his wheeled chair used to wish everybody good night, always keeping the last kiss for "his little maid", Albinia, with her brown eyes and rich shining hair.'[4] The atmosphere of her novels, in which earnestness and piety are combined with a considerable sense of fun, and the schoolrooms and nurseries are crowded with romping good-hearted boys and little girls in brown-holland pinafores is probably not very different from the atmosphere of Tyntesfield in Victorian days.

The architectural setting for life there was largely provided by John Norton (1823–1904), the architect responsible for remodelling and enlarging the house in the 1860s. Norton was a pupil of Benjamin Ferrey (himself a pupil of A. W. Pugin). He was born and educated in Bristol, and although his main office was in London kept a strong local connection. He designed many churches in and around Bristol from the 1850s onwards, and in the 1860s was responsible for three big country houses in the Bristol neighbourhood, Chew Manor, Brent Knoll and Tyntesfield. These marked the beginning of a sizeable country house practice.

Norton worked out his designs for remodelling Tyntesfield during the spring and summer of 1863; building work seems to have started by October.[5] In February 1866 the *Builder* described the house as 'just completed', and having cost nearly £70,000. The earlier house was incorporated in Norton's new building. Its shape can still be recognized in the central block on the south front of Tyntesfield. Norton added an extra storey, and built single-storey wings to either side, containing a drawing room and library. The result is a handsomely balanced composition; but

245

230. Tyntesfield. The south front, before the demolition of the tower.

for someone working in the Pugin tradition, like Norton, it was unthinkable to make it completely symmetrical. The drawing room wing is higher than the library wing, and has different windows; the two sides of the central block have different detailing. Moreover, the south front merged into the irregular and elaborately picturesque composition created by Norton's other additions. Behind the library a prominent turreted and steep-roofed tower rose over the main entrance porch; beyond it a long east wing ended in a corbelled-out turret with a candle-snuffer spire; on the west front of the house was one of the largest and most elaborate of country house conservatories. Although most of the detailing of the house was inspired by English perpendicular, the mid-Victorian taste for more exotic varieties of Gothic was also in evidence. The great tower and the east-wing turret derive from the tower over the bridge and the Old Town Hall chapel at Prague; the gilded copper dome of the conservatory was designed (according to the *Builder*) 'after the model of S. Marco at Venice'; the roofs are diapered with slates of a different colour, in the French or German manner.

The medley of roofs at Tyntesfield was enriched still further when the chapel was added to the north-east corner of the west wing in 1873–5. Its architect was Arthur (later Sir Arthur) Blomfield, son of the Bishop of London and a prolific designer of churches. It was built up on the first floor above an undercroft, in order to fit more comfortably into the hill that rises behind the house; its design was clearly inspired by that of the Sainte Chapelle in Paris. Old photographs show how its high French roof merged with Norton's extravagant skyline. But Tyntesfield's complex roofs and elaborate ironwork trimmings were built with typical Victorian disregard for future maintenance; the conservatory was demolished in 1919 and the tower in 1935.[6]

Inside, Norton grouped the rooms of the enlarged house round a very big top-lit staircase hall. Here and elsewhere in the house he showed considerable ingenuity in the design of exposed timber roofs. Indeed, although Tyntesfield, like other houses of the date, is rich in carved stonework, tiles, stained glass and marble inlay, it is the woodwork of its panelling, fittings, furniture and roofs which is especially memorable. Norton's great library is entirely lined with oak—oak shelving, boarded oak walls and an open oak roof. The warm brown of books and woodwork sets off the richer colouring of the Chinese and Japanese porcelain on the gable wall and above the bookcases; at one end an archway opens onto a huge bay window looking east along the drive; and the result is one of the most liveable-in and sympathetic of Victorian libraries.

The drawing room also rises into the roof, and originally had walls and ceiling covered with elaborate stencilled and painted decoration; but unlike the library it has been considerably altered since Bedford Lemere photographed it in 1878. The billiard room, on the other hand, remains evocatively Victorian. The need to produce satisfactory top-lighting inspired Norton to produce the most imaginative of his Tyntesfield roofs. It is boarded and curved like the hull of a ship, but cut into on either side by clerestoreys of triangular-headed windows. Yet more light is produced by a great bay window to the west.

The billiard table at the heart of this splendid room is rich with Gothic detailing and elaborate carving. It was made by Plucknett of Warwick for William Gibbs's

246

231. (upper right) Tyntesfield. The library.

232. (right) The drawing room, photographed in 1878.

233, 234. (top) The family chaplain and Mrs William Gibbs.
235. A cricket week at Tyntesfield in late Victorian days.
236. (right) The billiard-room ceiling.

son Antony, who succeeded his father in 1875. The inglenook recess also dates from Antony's time, and was inserted in 1885 to the designs of Henry Woodyer. At this date the billiard room became the smoking room; previously (according to the *Builder*) the smoking room had been at the top of the tower on the south front.

In about 1885–9 Woodyer made a number of other alterations.[7] He added the verandah outside the drawing room, and replaced the Y-shaped main staircase by a single flight going round the outside walls of the staircase hall. He enlarged Norton's narrow entrance hall at the expense of the dining room, and knocked what remained of the latter into the former housekeeper's room to make a very large new dining room, lit by three new bay windows. He installed new panelling and floors throughout the house. Tyntesfield is still rich in Victorian panelling and furniture of all dates, from the 1860s to the 1880s. The later furniture tends to be chunkily Gothic in the high-Victorian manner and much of it is probably by Plucknett. The earlier was almost certainly supplied by Crace and is in the Pugin tradition; the great sideboard in the dining room is an especially lavish variant of a design first made by Pugin in the 1840s.[8]

Not surprisingly, the pictures and furnishings brought in by later generations have diluted the Victorian Gothic and semi-ecclesiastical atmosphere which the house had when it was first built. But the spirit of William and Matilda Blanche Gibbs is still strong in the hall and passages, and some of the less-used rooms. Above all, the vaulted chapel remains very much as they left it, an epitome of High Church piety, complete with glass by Powell and Wooldridge[9], ironwork by Hart, Son, Peard and Co., and mosaics by Salviati (designed by Wooldridge).

250

237. Tyntesfield. The smoking room in the tower, photographed in 1878.

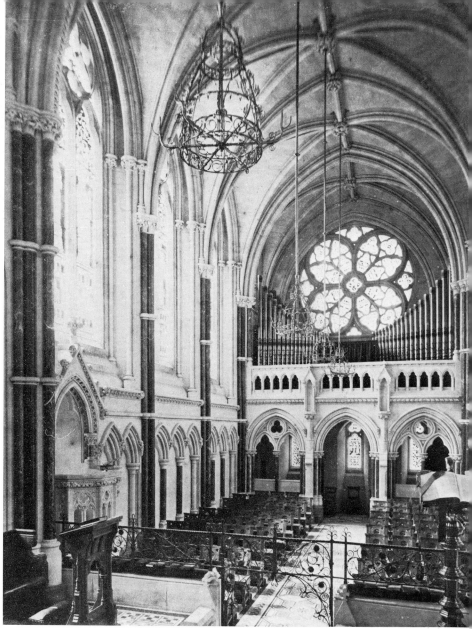

Technologically, Tyntesfield was elaborately up to date. It was heated by hot air; gasometers near the kitchen garden supplied gas to light house, stables and lodges, and illuminated the clock-face in the great tower. Two water-wheels pumped (and still pump) water to reservoirs on the hill above the house. Much concern was shown about fire precaution; the kitchen was roofed with fireproof construction and fire hydrants were (and are) distributed on all floors. A massive bath-tub on the first floor, complete with shower, must date at least from the 1880s, and possibly from the 1860s. William's son Antony installed electricity in the 1880s, and was probably responsible for the hydraulic lift by the kitchen.[10] He was interested in new techniques and had a lathe room in the house, on which he turned ivory with remarkable skill. His son was created Lord Wraxall in 1928, and was the father of the present owner.

238. (top left) A desk, probably by Collier and Plucknett, *c.* 1880.
239. (bottom left) A cupboard of *c.* 1880, formerly at Tyntesfield, now at Temple Newsam.
240. (above right) Looking west in the chapel (Sir A. W. Blomfield, 1873–5).

19. Humewood Castle, County Wicklow

IN THE HOLIDAY months of the 1860s a striking but curious figure might have been met striding over the slopes of the Alps. He wore a flannel suit, brown canvas gaiters and boots with porpoise-hide laces. A puggaree of Indian cotton hung from the back of his hat, to protect his neck from the sun; a brown veil shielded his eyes from the snow; a whistle hung from his buttonhole. On his back was slung his own invention, the Patent Alpine Porte-Knapsack, 'said to place no pressure on the back or arm'. Its few and carefully selected contents paid attention to cleanliness and godliness; a prayer book with hymns was only to be expected in the luggage of the son of a clergyman, the brother of the Archdeacon of Grahamstown and the brother-in-law of the Bishop of Madagascar; into the P.K.S. bath frame (invented

252

241. Humewood Castle, Kiltegan, Co. Wicklow (William White, 1866–70; James Brooks, 1873). A detail of the tower.

by Mr J. Edward White) the P.K.S. waterproof neatly fitted to make a bath, or could conveniently be transformed into a cape in wet weather. But in conversation with travelling acquaintances he would maintain, with clumsily expressed but infectious enthusiasm, that 'shaving brush, razor and strop are of course superfluities, being not merely cumbrous, but injurious to the health in their use, by a constant and needless irritation of the skin'. The generous beard obscuring his lower face and chest showed that he stuck to his principles; and through this undergrowth issued, on propitious occasions, a curious sound, the *Alpine Queen or Mountaineer's Song*, 'written by himself, dedicated to the Alpine Club and set to music by "Lalla" '.

This Alpine traveller was William White, F.S.A., a man of many enthusiasms; advocate of Swedish gymnastics, loose clothing, brighter workhouses and prisons, subsidized housing and legislation against bad landlords; enthusiast for mountaineering, concrete and Gothic architecture; investigator into the psychology of colour and the trigonometric basis of proportion; author of *The Tourist's Knapsack and its Contents, Domestic Plumbing* and innumerable articles and lectures; inventor of a valveless closet, a wasteless lavatory, a springless lock and a door handle which could not come off; an architect whose buildings were as muscular as his mountaineering, and designer of churches, schools, rectories and a small group of country houses amongst which the great granite mass of Humewood takes the pride of place.[1]

White spent much of his life balanced on the boundary between crankiness and brilliance; in the end he fell off on the wrong side, and a large proportion of his last years were wasted in trying to prove that Shakespeare was Bacon. The crankiness should not be allowed to obscure the brilliance. As an architect he is one of the most interesting and least known of Victorian Gothic Revivalists. But as Eastlake commented in his *History of the Gothic Revival*, 'ingenuity and vigour in design' existed side by side with 'those eccentricities of form either structural or decorative which distinguish nearly every building that he has erected'.[2] 'Mr. White's work . . . occasionally seems to want repose,' the same author gently remarks a paragraph further on; and his work reflected his mind. A certain lack of ballast prevented him from reaching the top of his profession. The slender campanile of his All Saints', Talbot Road, presides over the shoppers in the Portobello Market, his soaring spire rises abruptly on a hill top out of the High Street of Lyndhurst; but he never designed a major public building.

His designs for Humewood made him famous in architectural circles, but not for the happiest of reasons. *Kimberley* v. *Dick and White* was, unfortunately, a landmark in architectural case law.[3] In the summer of 1866 White heard from Mr Fenton, the agent of Mr W. Wentworth Fitzwilliam Hume Dick, a rich Irish landowner and Conservative M.P. for County Wicklow. Mr Dick wanted a new house on the Wicklow property where his ancestor, Thomas Hume, had settled in 1704. He spent most of the year in England or France; the Irish house was intended as 'an occasional resort in the summer recess or shooting season' and was not to cost more than £15,000.

White went over to Ireland in August and examined the site. In March 1867 he showed Albert Kimberley, a Banbury builder, some very sketchy designs, on the

242. Humewood Castle. The entrance front.

basis of which Kimberley, who was keen to get the commission, made a tender for £13,560. Work started at once and the foundations had been completed before, on 10 June, a clerk hurried down to Banbury and Kimberley signed the seventy-page contract, without (as he later maintained) having time to read it. The house had already grown from the one originally contemplated and its size and expense mounted as the work went on. Kimberley thought that White and Hume Dick had settled the increased cost between themselves. Hume Dick was basking innocently in White's original guarantee of a ceiling of £15,000; in June 1870 he was presented with a bill for £25,000 and refused to pay the difference. Kimberley sued Dick and White; the case, with appeals, dragged on for five years, and in May 1876 Kimberley won it on all counts with costs, said to amount to £10,000.★ The architectural papers had reported the proceedings at length; and when everything was over the *Architect* commented: 'Perhaps the most striking feature in the case is the rashness and lack of caution displayed by all parties concerned.'

It was a stupid story, and White deserved to get into trouble. He was never given another country house commission and his whole career suffered. But the loss was architecture's, for this odd, original, gifted, cranky, over-sanguine and unconventional architect had designed one of the most remarkable of Victorian country houses.

Most Victorian architects were at their best working under constraints. Cheap Victorian brick churches in the slums tend to be better than slap-up churches built for rich patrons. Rectories, schools and cottages put up on a limited budget are often more interesting than country houses where money was no object. White's smaller

★ In the course of the dispute some of the stonework supplied by Kimberley to Humewood was rejected and returned to England. He said that it would be good enough for his tombstone, and it can still be seen, in the form of a rugged monolith, in Banbury churchyard. (Information from his descendant Mr J. M. Kimberley.)

buildings are often his best. Humewood is far from small but it was built under two constraints, of money and material. However disastrously White exceeded his price ceiling the fact that it existed steered him away from too much elaboration. Moreover, all the external walling was of granite, a stone calculated to discourage an architect from being too flashy or fanciful; a stone, in fact, that seemed designed for a muscular architect. White had started his practice at Truro, in a granite country; he knew his material and it brought out the best in him. 'In the treatment of granite', he wrote, 'especial care is required to make the mouldings of a broad, bold and massive, rather than a small or delicately undercut character, and to avoid as far as possible anything like minuteness and pettiness in the finish.'[4] The massive walls of Humewood are built of blocks of granite which are not squared and laid in level courses but fitted together in an irregular jigsaw. The windows are simple rectangular holes punched through the thick walls with the minimum of mouldings. The many gables mounting upwards in flights of steps, the chimneystacks and buttresses reducing in a series of batters produce an intricate mixture of diagonal lines, counteracted by long horizontals of massive corbelling and thin strips of granite binding the irregular courses together. Out of these elements White built up a wonderfully skilful composition, of different pyramids and triangles rising and falling but gradually mounting upwards to combine in one great irregular pyramidal mass that culminates in the corner turret of the central tower.

White thought that the equilateral triangle was the basis of good proportions.[5]

255

243. The stable archway.

247. A portion of the garden front.

The main house at Humewood is a brilliant example of his skill in juggling with triangular forms; and so, on a smaller scale, are the stables. The long line of arches, of splendidly simple granite detailing, is echoed by the line of gables above; the big clock tower gable slides down into a smaller gable and the big entrance arch into the smaller cloister arch; everything builds up to the apex of the main triangle above the clock. From the stable yard one can look across to the roofs of the main house, and admire its strange granite landscape of chimneystacks, sprouting in high, slightly inward-sloping pinnacles from the apexes of the gables. All the best Victorian Gothicists hoped that the architecture of their day would develop on the basis of Gothic Revivalism into an independent style. In principle they would have agreed that form, plan and materials were more important than ornament; in practice their sketchbooks were too well-filled and Gothic ornament kept flooding in, especially when they had money to spend. White got further away from his Gothic starting point than many of his contemporaries, partly because of his unconventional mind, partly because his early training had not been with an architect of the Gothic school,

257

244. (upper left) Humewood Castle. The double silhouette.
245. (middle left) Granite in the rain.
246. (left) The view from the stable yard.

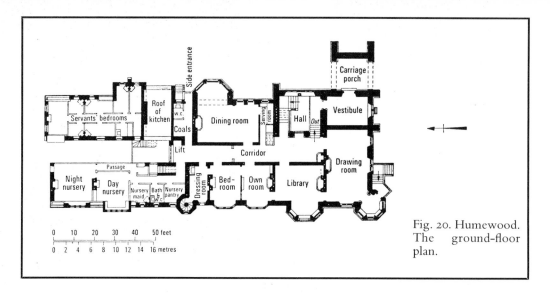

Fig. 20. Humewood. The ground-floor plan.

but with a builder at Leamington. He was always fascinated by materials. His church of St Saviour's, Aberdeen Park, hidden away in a leafy north London cul-de-sac, and completed the year after Humewood was started, is built almost entirely of brick, inside and out; and the modelling of its brick buttresses, pinnacles and corbelling gives it an abstract sculptural quality reminiscent of that provided by the chimneystacks at Humewood. At Humewood granite is more important than Gothic; the whiffs of Scottish baronial, and the more conventional historic detailing, such as the Gothic plate tracery of the hall windows, seem out of keeping with the severity of the building as a whole. The house is not very reminiscent of anything else built in England at the time; but one cannot help being reminded of the granite masterpieces that H. H. Richardson was to put up in America in the 1870s and 1880s.

'For exterior effect', wrote White, 'our attention must be directed to the sky outline before expending it upon minutiae; and this is of the greatest consequence in an undulating and picturesque country.' Humewood lies on the edge of the Wicklow mountains. White obviously considered with some care the juxtaposition of the mountain silhouette with his own richly romantic Victorian skyline of towers, gables and spirelets. But however extravagant this skyline might seem today, it grew out of a plan carefully worked out by White with regard to Victorian standards of convenience and comfort.

The ground drops six feet from north-east to south-west and White used the fall to provide the house with a basement. Basements were not usual in Victorian country houses, but White hotly defended his decision in a paper on the house that he delivered to the R.I.B.A. in 1869. It made use of the ground; it was convenient for service; it lifted up the main rooms and gave them a better view. Moreover, 'it was of the greatest consequence to elevate the "living" part of the house above the colds and damps of the country'. In a typically Victorian way it was taken for granted that the servants in the basement would survive these 'colds and damps', and that brick vaults and frosted glass were necessary to prevent any possibility of their overlooking or overhearing their employers. In White's defence, however, it must be remarked that the basement today strikes one as remarkably dry, light and cheerful, even though it is to a large extent disused.

258

A basement with small strongly barred windows was also considered necessary because 'it was desirable to build a house capable of defence in case of attack'. This reads oddly today, but the old house had been garrisoned in the 1798 rebellion and 1867 was the year of the Fenian troubles in Ireland. The vaulted carriage porch with a room above it designed to command the entrance through holes in the vaulting was intended as another discouragement to rebels.[6]

The main rooms face west, south and east. The stables are to the north-east, in order that the damp south-west wind should carry the stable fumes away from the house. The need to deal with cigar fumes and to provide water tanks gave at least some practical pretext for building what every Victorian landowner loved to have, a tower; the vaulted room at the top of this was intended to be a billiard and smoking room, though in fact it proved too remote to be used for smoking or, as far as I know, anything else. The high louvred pyramid at the north end is the ventilated roof of the drying room; a carefully worked-out sequence, north of the main house, of wash-house, drying room, mangling room, ironing room, folding room and maids' room conveyed the washing on a functional conveyor belt into the house.

The sequence of arriving at and walking through the house was obviously worked out with the greatest skill and care. From the *porte-cochère* one goes into a little low dark vaulted hall, lit by two small stained-glass windows. A discreet doorway in this

248. (above left) Humewood Castle. The upper staircase.

249. (above right) Looking from the staircase hall to the upper staircase.

leads conveniently down into the basement, but the main route goes up to the principal floor and White obviously delighted in the contrast of coming out from a relatively small dark space into the higher and lighter one of the staircase hall. This is the *pièce de résistance* of the interiors; its windows are rich with stained glass and heraldry; at the top of the stairs two elephantine columns of black Irish marble stand guard over a discreetly nude Victorian nymph.[7] Through the columns is the corridor that serves the principal rooms; it is vaulted like the two halls, and preserves its original brass light-fittings. A tempting vista from the top of the main stairs leads through an arch into the staircase up to the second floor; and half way up this staircase one gets a tangled peep, past the extraordinary notched woodwork of the staircase newels, to the nymph between her columns. Above the main corridor is a bedroom corridor, of equivalent size but not vaulted.

In the main living rooms, high ceilings and generous proportions, chunky marble chimneypieces, thick walls, ceiling beams and tremendously solid doors, shutters

260

250. Humewood Castle. The view into the library.

and bookshelves, give a superb feeling of Victorian security. The detail throughout
would have been described at the time as 'muscular'. The joinery in particular is
unique, eccentric and extraordinary. Even his contemporaries were startled by it.
Robert Kerr attended the talk given by White when he exhibited his drawings of
Humewood to the R.I.B.A. in 1869. 'The mouldings', he commented in the
discussion afterwards, 'are such as I never saw before', and he was obviously half
repelled, half fascinated by what he called White's 'firm and muscular resolve to
make a thing crooked . . . One cannot ask him to explain the principles on which he
chooses to design; but there is a unity running through the whole.' This is a fair
comment; one has the feeling throughout the house that White knew exactly what
he wanted, and achieved it. But his methods were certainly curious. The strange
totem poles up the staircase have already been referred to; the angular arches over
the turret recess in the drawing room are another typical detail; and the doors and
the shutters in the main rooms are strange and fascinating pieces of construction, in a

251. Looking up in the staircase hall.

252. Humewood Castle. The staircase hall.

subtle polychromy of deal, oak, sycamore and black bog-oak. White seems to have designed comparatively little furniture for the house, though the bookcases, of course, are his, and so, to judge from their appearance, are the chairs in the library.[8]

The bedroom and 'own room' marked on the original plan beyond the library are now one room, the present dining room. The end occupied by the nurseries was raised a storey in 1873, and remodelled to contain an enormous two-storey banqueting hall. Hume Dick must have had his fill of White but he sensibly employed an architect who was sympathetic to his work, in the person of James Brooks, one of the best of Victorian church architects.[9] The additions were tactfully made, but inevitably detracted from the proportions of the house and darkened the internal corridors. A final, very Victorian afterthought was the extraordinary tower at the end of the stable block. It was ostensibly built, unlikely as it may seem, to provide extra rooms for men servants.[10]

20. Bear Wood, Berkshire

ROBERT KERR's *The Gentleman's House* is frequently referred to in this book; in its time it was an influential and much-read publication. But in fact Kerr had little experience to build on, and his book was essentially a capable analysis of the plans of others. He was a clever, self-assertive and fluent Aberdonian who had been to America as a young man and came back full of American bounce. In 1845, at the age of twenty-one, he published a noisy and irreverent book of architectural essays, *The Newleafe Discourses*. In 1847 he was one of the founders of the Architectural Association, and in 1861 became Professor of the Arts of Construction at King's College in the Strand. Whenever a discussion was held, a deputation mounted, or a correspondence embarked on he was certain to be in the foreground.★ But his career had brought him more publicity than jobs. His book went out on the waters as tempting bait to rich clients.

He immediately caught one very large fish, in the person of John Walter, the chief proprietor of *The Times*.[1] *The Times* was then at the height of its reputation, with its Crimean War triumphs fresh in people's memory and government scalps still hanging from its windows. It was the voice of the professional and middle classes, rampant against privilege and nepotism and only prepared to accept an aristocracy if it behaved itself. Unlike other Victorian new rich, and in spite of his great wealth, Eton education and estate of 7,000 acres, neither John Walter nor his family ever seems to have shown much ambition to mix with or marry into the aristocracy.[2] As a young man he had flirted briefly with the Young England movement; but there is little trace of Young England romanticism in the house he built at Bear Wood. He

★ 'We mention him, not because of his works, but because his loquaciousness makes him prominent', E. W. Godwin, 'Modern Architects and their Work' I, *Building News*, 5 July 1872. The younger generation had little use for Kerr, although curiously enough he was sympathetic towards the 'Queen Anne' movement.

253. Bear Wood, nr Wokingham, Berkshire (Robert Kerr, 1865–74). The entrance front.

twice refused a peerage; he was a reserved and formal little man,[3] who ruled with a kind of jealous integrity over his independent kingdom at Bear Wood and Printing House Square. It is interesting that he went in the first place to William Burn, an aristocrat's architect if ever there was one, but in the end rejected him for Kerr, who typified the new type of Victorian professional man (though at the same time he was a fervent admirer of Burn's abilities as a planner).★

★ Burn's (Elizabethan) designs are now in the R.I.B.A. drawings collection. The loss of the commission to Kerr must have been especially galling to him, because they were not on speaking terms. In 1864 Kerr had asked if he could reproduce a plan of one of Burn's houses in the *Gentleman's House*. Burn gave permission but indignantly rescinded it when he discovered that Kerr had already acquired copies of his plans without his knowledge from one of the assistants in his office. Kerr accordingly had to publish a 'design on the modern Scotch model' of his own, professedly in Burn's manner, although Burn said that it was an incompetent travesty. An angry correspondence is preserved at the R.I.B.A.

264

254. (above) John Walter of Bear Wood, chief proprietor of *The Times*.

XX. (right) Bear Wood, Berkshire. Looking up the main staircase.

The Bear Wood property had been undeveloped wood and heath belonging to the Crown until John Walter's father bought it in 1816, built a classical villa, and made a park and lake. The ostensible reason for rebuilding was to accommodate a large and growing family (eight children and five more to come) but it was probably as much to accommodate a large and growing income, which by 1865 was around £50,000 a year.

Like many serious-minded Victorians when they were about to spend a great deal of money on themselves, John Walter eased his conscience by building a church

XXI. (left) Bear Wood, Berkshire. A detail of the entrance front.

255. (above) The *porte-cochère*.

first.★ The sumptuous St Paul's, Wokingham, designed by Henry Woodyer, went up in 1861–4; Bear Wood followed in 1865–74. John Walter was technically minded and had been personally responsible for giving *The Times* the most up-to-date printing works in the world. On a crossing to America in 1866 he spent most of his time in the engine room. At Bear Wood he was his own builder; the bricks were made up in his own brick-kilns (4,477,000 were used in the house), the joinery and carpentry done in his own workshops. The house was heavy with Victorian technology. It was raised up on cellars, brick-vaulted with beautiful precision. The upper floors were of 'fireproof' construction, with up to a foot of concrete between iron girders. A ponderous heating apparatus was installed, at a cost of over £3,000. The house was lit by gas, from a gasworks built next to the sawmills and workshops, down by the lake. It had twenty-two w.c.'s and five bathrooms, the latter a very

---

★ As a young man Walter had a Tractarian period, but in middle age he become uncontroversially Broad. The piety of the Victorian middle classes can be exaggerated. In 1872 three of the boys at Wellington College, of which John Walter was a governor, were accused of sleeping with a fourteen year old maid. 'Some of the governors dealt with the offence as a light matter, and when Benson pointed out the general purity of the school, John Walter scoffed at him and indulged in distasteful reminiscences of his Eton days.' D. Newsome, *A History of Wellington College* (London, 1959), pp. 168–9.

256. Bear Wood. The garden front.

generous supply for a Victorian house. An engine house in the kitchen court pumped water to the top of the water tower at the end of the garden front.

The design was as heavyweight as the technology. Kerr's references in his book, and his comments on William White's Humewood (see p. 119) show that he was fascinated by the 'muscularity' of high-Victorian Gothicists. Bear Wood was an attempt to make Elizabethan equally muscular. The entrance front is like a sock on the jaw. The influence of Barry's Highclere is apparent, but it is as if Highclere had been sent on a weightlifting course. The great tower, with the two violent slopes of its staircase windows, and with its proliferation of pinnacles and pilasters in the upper stage, looks as though it is about to explode with energy. The pillars of the *porte-cochère* are strapped and banded, and support brackets that are like rolls of muscle. The favourite Victorian game of near-symmetry is played with abandon. If one starts from the right-hand gable the design is a straightforward symmetrical one, until the left-hand gable crashes head-on into the great tower; one is half-buried in the other, and a little staircase turret has got involved in the collision.

The square outline of the big tower is echoed by the smaller tower at the end of the servants' wing, and the sloping windows of the main staircase by the miniature slope of the little staircase where the wing joins the main building. The front, as a result, has a basic unity in spite of its multitude of elements. There is little unity about

269

257. (above left) A panel from the sliding doors between the drawing rooms.
258. (above right) The hall screen.

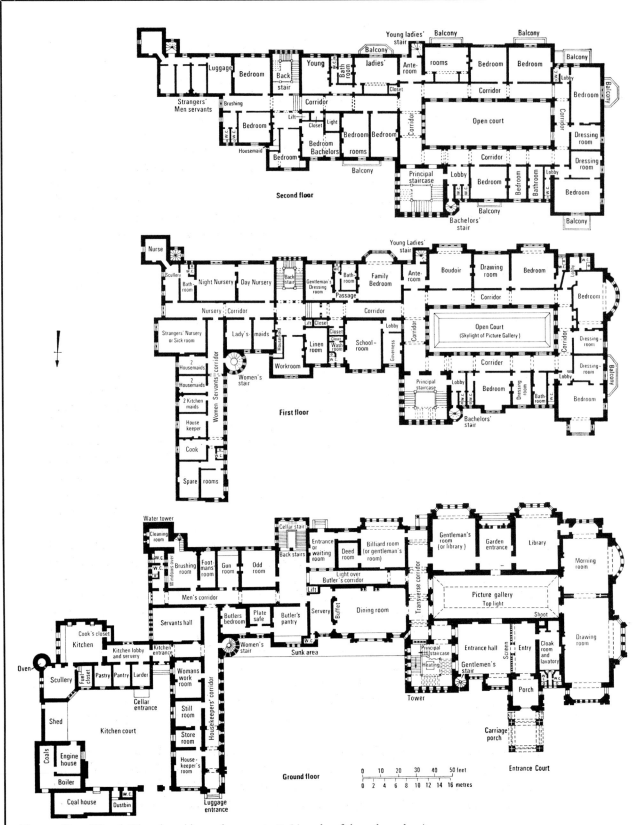

Second floor

First floor

Ground floor

Fig. 21. Bear Wood. The plans (these plans are to 87% scale of the other plans).

the garden front. Perhaps Kerr wanted the entrance front to be vigorous and masculine, the garden front to be gracious and feminine—a difference symbolized by the high-born Victorian ladies (disguised as angels) carved to either side of the garden entrance. But the result is merely confused; after a little near-symmetry by-play it dissolves into a mix-up of towers, turrets, roofs and gables that rambles on for nearly a hundred yards, until brought to an end by the inevitable water tower.

Looking at the plan of Bear Wood is like reading a synopsis of the contents of Kerr's book. There are the interminable offices, the housekeeper's corridor, the men's corridor, the butler's corridor, the bachelor apartments and, at the opposite side of the house, the young ladies' rooms. There are the principal staircase, the back stairs, the women's stairs, the men's stairs, the bachelors' stairs and the young ladies' stairs, all, with Victorian honesty, easily distinguishable from the outside by their fenestration. There are the main entrance, the luggage entrance, the garden entrance, the business entrance, the kitchen entrance and the cellar entrance. The young ladies are safely placed above Mrs Walter's bedroom and boudoir, and handy for the governess and schoolroom. The bachelors' stair is described in Kerr's book as 'one by which single men can reach their own rooms, from perhaps dirty weather outside, without using the chief thoroughfares'.

John Walter had inherited a large collection of Flemish pictures from his father and needed a picture gallery. Kerr, instead of building one shut off on its own, sensibly made it a top-lit thoroughfare, into which all the main living rooms opened. 'To attach such a Gallery to the house as a mere showplace', he wrote, 'is an idea wanting in that domesticity of motive that ought to pervade everything connected with a private building.' In spite of its scale 'domesticity of motive' is apparent at Bear Wood. It is not a palace; it is a villa complete with Italianate tower, set in spacious coniferous grounds, made muscular and blown up to enormous size. Inside, with the exception of the main staircase, the rooms are large rather than grand. The gallery, now that the pictures have gone, is a little sad. The main feature of the rooms today is the elaborate and massive joinery, made in the Bear Wood workshops. Its craftsmanship reaches its peak in the richly inlaid double doors which, at the touch of a finger, slide into the walls between the drawing room and the morning room. The hall retains its elaborate screen and walls of stamped and gilded leather; it is on the great hall model but reduced in size from the elaborate examples of the 1840s. Inside and out the most sensational feature at Bear Wood is the main staircase. It runs up to the second floor, and is of the usual substantial craftsmanship. But the surprise (and it is a startling one) comes when one raises one's eyes and finds oneself looking up past the stairs and through a remote flood of golden light to the roof of the tower, 88 feet above, painted dark blue and sprinkled with gold stars. It is a brilliant piece of showmanship, brought about by filling the upper windows with tinted glass, and half separating the upper space from the rest of the stairs by a coved gallery and a gilded cast iron balustrade.

Bear Wood was proudly illustrated and described in the second and third editions of Kerr's book.[4] It led to a commission for a smaller house at Ascot for Walter's editor, John Delane; and the book attracted another rich client, Mr Spender-Clay, for whom Kerr designed the appalling Ford Manor at Lingfield in Surrey in 1868.

But in the 1870s his country house practice fizzled out. He was possibly more noisy than efficient, and too brash for the taste of his clients. In 1868, Delane wrote, 'I shall certainly set up as an architect since it is clear that I possess the only qualification necessary—perfect ignorance of the business. My architect has no notion of aspect or prospect, and not much of respect.'[5] By the time Bear Wood was finished in 1874 it had cost £120,000—more than twice Kerr's original estimate. In 1875 Kerr wrote to Walter suggesting that he be paid an extra two per cent on his commission because of 'special services, exceptional trouble and alteration of the design and drawings'. Later on he changed tack and asked for 'kind and confidential consideration' on the ground that Bear Wood had taken up so much of his time that he had been running his practice at a loss. Walter remained icily unforthcoming and an uncomfortable correspondence petered out with Kerr making empty threats to go to law.[6]

Walter had no reason to be pleased with the bill, especially as the relationship of Bear Wood to *The Times* turned out to be rather like that of the Viceroy's Palace at New Delhi to British India; even before this massive monument was finished, *The Times* started to go into a slow decline. It was unable to stand up to the challenge of the cheap press; its circulation was wavering from 1865 until 1875, and sank steadily from then on. In 1908 control of *The Times* passed to Lord Northcliffe. In 1911 considerable portions of the Bear Wood estate were sold; in 1919 the house and 500 acres became the new home of the Merchant Seamen's Orphanage. The school is now re-established as a public school that includes Merchant Navy children and has taken the name Bearwood College.

272

259. Bear Wood. A late Victorian view of the drawing room.

21. Cardiff Castle, Glamorganshire

In 1800 Cardiff had a population of 1,000. It was part of the Welsh property of the Marchioness of Bute, to whom it had descended by the marriage of her grandfather Thomas, Viscount Windsor, to the daughter and heiress of the seventh Earl of Pembroke. Her son, the second Marquess, had the intelligence to see that the growing iron and coal industry of South Wales needed an outlet, and the daring to provide it by sinking his fortune into the construction of docks at Cardiff. He died suddenly in 1848; his work was carried on by the trustees of his son, and finished in 1859. The sensational result was the creation of modern Cardiff, one of the main commercial ports of the world. The population figures speak for themselves: 1,018 in 1801, 85,378 in 1881 and 243,627 in 1951.

About 1855 a firm of marine engineers, Walker, Burges and Cooper, took over the completion of the East Bute Docks at Cardiff.[1] The dock-building Lord Bute and the marine engineer Alfred Burges both had sons whose attitude to life was in striking contrast to that of their fathers. They were fascinated by the past; they used the money which their fathers had made from industry to finance an escape from industrialism into a dream medieval world. The young Lord Bute's voracious reading since his preparatory school days culminated in his becoming a Roman Catholic in December 1868. In the sensitive religious climate of the time the

273

conversion of this young millionaire nobleman caused a sensation and provided the inspiration for Disraeli's novel *Lothair*. William Burges's medieval interests had taken him into architecture, and he became one of the most Gothic of the Gothicists. Their paths joined in 1865 when the medievalist peer was aged only eighteen and the medievalist architect was thirty-eight. The man who brought them together was probably John M'Connochie, who had worked for Walker, Burges and Cooper on their Cardiff job, and stayed on to become chief engineer of the Bute Docks.[2] Lord Bute remained the main support of Burges's practice until the latter's death in 1881. He was a patron for architects to dream of, for his wealth was enormous. It derived from the docks and growing town at Cardiff and from estates in England, Wales and Scotland; by 1868 their combined income was approaching £300,000 a year.

Lord Bute and Burges were both instinctive antiquarians, and learned and erudite men, but in other respects they must have made a curious pair.[3] Bute was tall, handsome, strong-willed and capable, but shy and very reserved; there was something of a medieval monk or mystic about him. As for Burges, as Lethaby put it, 'the idea of being a medieval jester must have occurred to his quick mind'.[4] He was small and facetious (his friends called him Billy Burges; one cannot believe that Butterfield was known to anyone as Billy Butterfield), very short sighted, with an eye-glass that kept dropping out; he talked at great speed with his head on one side; he owned a couple of medieval outfits which he wore on occasions in his rooms in Buckingham Street. His enemies and even his friends said that he had never completely grown up.*

In spite of his oddities and his escapism, in spite of the fact that he did comparatively little work, and that much of it consisted of remote commissions for private patrons, in the 1860s Burges was one of the heroes of the young architects. He was a leader and pioneer of the muscular Gothic school. His unexecuted but published designs, as much and probably more than his buildings, suggested a new vision of overpoweringly massive forms irradiated by medieval fantasy. He had a feeling (perhaps acquired from his engineer father) for the way buildings worked and were put together, for the jointing of timber and the weight and strength of stone. But in all his designs strong and simple basic shapes are set off by the lesser shapes that crawl over, sprout out of, or are threaded through them. His conical roofs break out into tubular shafts, his hooded chimneypieces into crockets or canopies. His surfaces, as a result, tend to be knobbly or chunky. His compositions are often top heavy and his detail ponderous. This formidable heaviness was transformed by an imagination grotesque, exuberant, overflowing with jokes and puns, haunted by the glitter of crystal and the ripple of long flowing hair, an imagination that seized upon anything and everything, mermaids and knights in armour, the signs of the Zodiac, the Labours of Hercules, fishes, parrots, crocodiles

*There's a babyish party named Burges
Who from infancy hardly emerges
  If you had not been told
  He's disgracefully old
You would offer a bull's eye to Burges.
(Limerick by D. G. Rossetti, *Rossetti Papers*, ed. W. M. Rossetti (1903) p. 494.)

and monkeys, and turned them into decoration for a chimneypiece or a ceiling, a washstand or a bell-push.

The religious background to Gothic architecture was of no especial importance to Burges. His enthusiasms were visual and romantic, not moral. He was in reaction against the ugliness of an industrial age; his friends were architects and artists in similar reaction, men like Rossetti, Godwin, Swinburne and Simeon Solomon. Like Rossetti in his water-colours he created an escape route from everyday life into a richly coloured medieval world, with an atmosphere of 'secret enclosure in palace chambers far apart' as James Smetham described Rossetti's *Wedding of St George*.[5] To create such an atmosphere in three dimensions needed a long purse and an inch-by-inch attention to detail. Burges had the enthusiasm and the readiness to supply the time, for he received a comfortable private income from his father and could do without a large practice. It was harder to find clients prepared to commission such expensive and overpowering surroundings. But Lord Bute was more interested in atmosphere than a convenient house to live in, and his restless mind and bottomless fortune led him on to new schemes well before the first ones were finished.

In 1865 Burges wrote a report on the possibility of restoring Cardiff Castle. It was a huge walled enclosure on the edge of the town, around the remains of a shell keep; along one side was a range of medieval lodgings which had been remodelled and given a veneer of Georgian Gothic detail by Henry Holland about 1776. Burges's work at Cardiff[6] mainly consisted of the reshaping and enlargement of these lodgings. In 1866–7 he had been one of the unsuccessful competitors for the Law Courts competition; and in a brilliant and brilliantly drawn design he had presented one of the most sensational pieces of scenic architecture ever devised.[7] Between 1868 and his death he was occupied, on a smaller but far from small scale, in turning the park facade of Cardiff Castle into a compensation for his failure, a similarly extended range of massive stone facades breaking into an amazing skyline of contrasted towers. Work started in 1868, the year Lord Bute came of age, with a clock tower 150 feet high at one angle of the castle enclosure. Lord Bute did not marry until 1872; the tower was designed as a bachelor suite, with a winter and summer smoking room, a bedroom and bathroom and servants' rooms.

Externally the top-heaviness of the design, the long shaft sprouting out into the complex pyramidal top, is typical of Burges (though with debts to Barry's clock tower at Westminster). The tower is approached by way of a dark arrow-slitted gallery (originally open) leading from the main castle lodgings along the top of the reconstructed castle wall. At the end is a heavy door with an iron grille. This opens onto a small space before another door, the latter of formidable weight and richness, red and gold, with splendidly curving gilded ironwork and a handle delicately wrought in the form of a gilded bird. On the floor between the two doors are representations in mosaic of Cerberus and other mythical dogs; on the ceiling is a monstrous face of ebony and ivory, with huge hooked fangs and claws. The doors lead into the winter smoking room. Both this and the bedroom above are richly painted and decorated, with carved and painted chimneypieces. In an alcove off the bedroom is a magnificent Roman marble bath, converted for Victorian plumbing and inlaid with metal figures of fishes, newts and an octopus. Stairs lead further up,

261. Cardiff Castle,
Glamorganshire
(William Burges,
1866–85). The towers
from the park.

262. Looking along
the east front.

263. Burges's design
for the Law Courts,
1866.

264. The fiend guarding
the clock tower
entrance.

265. Sections of the
clock tower.

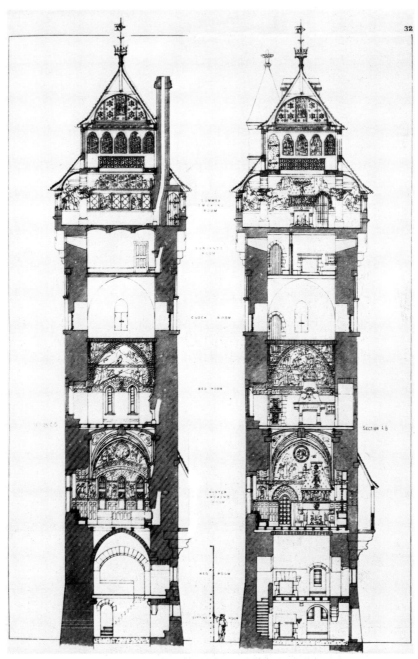

past a servant's room and the door that guards the works of the clock, to the summer smoking room, perhaps the strangest and most wonderful of all Victorian rooms.

It was an inspired freak of fantasy to set this room up 101 winding steps at the top of its high tower, and enrich it with all the wealth of colour, light and allegory that architect and patron could devise. Dark red and gold are the predominant colours among many; there are no plain surfaces, but pattern, modelling and decoration everywhere. The room fills two floors, curving boldly inwards to a balcony at first-floor level and then rising up to the second curve of the roof. The lower half has small windows, shuttered with gilded lattice-work; behind the gilded ironwork of the balcony a gallery walk surveys, through a continuous band of windows, the panorama of Cardiff and the docks, the Bristol Channel, the Somerset coast and the hills and mountains of South Wales. Down from the roof hangs a huge gold chandelier, in the shape of the rays of the sun, with a gold Apollo standing triumphant at the centre. When the candles are lit they glitter in the crystal outer band of the chandelier, in the crystal centre of the roof, and in the crystal stars, surrounded by gilded aureoles, with which the rest of the roof is spangled.

The great frieze of glazed tiles depicts mythological scenes seen through Victorian medievalizing eyes; it is based on Burges's own cartoons, and its pale colours contrast strangely, but not unpleasantly, with the richer tones of the rest of the room. The glorious tiled floor has a map of the world in the centre, surrounded by the spheres of the medieval universe, and circles of spouting whales, ships, huntsmen and horses. The tiles were provided by W. B. Simpson and Sons, and have a texture much closer to that of genuine medieval tiles than the flat shiny patterns manufactured by Minton. Figures of the winds sprout out of columns and support heavy brackets beneath the balcony at the four corners of the room; on the hood of

278

266. Cardiff Castle. The summer smoking room.

the fireplace a winged God of Love, with parrots on his wrists, sits above a carved frieze depicting the summer amusements of lovers; the winter amusements are on the fireplace of the winter smoking room downstairs. The sculpture, here and throughout the castle, is by Thomas Nicholls, who did all his best work for Burges, and had a genius for transforming the latter's sketches into gently romantic figures and grotesquely delightful animals, all richly coloured and patterned by the firm of Campbell and Smith.

In the summer smoking room the floor is dated 1871, the gallery door 1873, and a cartoon for one of the scenes on the tiles 1874. By then Lord Bute and Burges had already turned their attention to the main castle buildings. By 1885 these had been transformed inside and out. On the east front to the court much of Henry Holland's work was allowed to remain; his work was in any case based on a series of projecting bays or turrets which dated from the fifteenth century. Between these bays and the new clock tower a new wing was inserted, complete with tower. On the west front

279

267. *Summer Amusements of Lovers* in the summer smoking room.

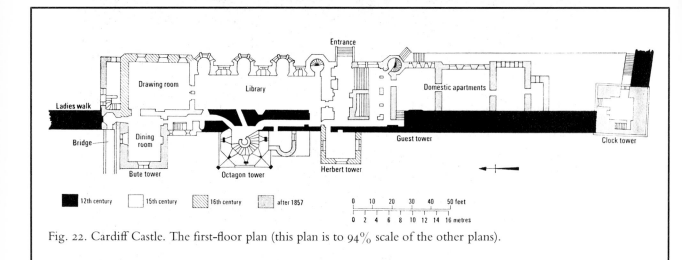

Fig. 22. Cardiff Castle. The first-floor plan (this plan is to 94% scale of the other plans).

to the park a tower known as the Bute Tower was added at the opposite end to the clock tower. In between the square sixteenth-century Herbert tower was raised and given a high pitched roof, and an octagon tower of the fifteenth century was finished off with an elaborate timber flèche. From the park all five towers, each with its different silhouette, appear in enfilade, to produce a wonderfully crowded, variegated and romantic Victorian skyline. But fantasy in the skyline is combined with extreme solidity and even sobriety in the masonry; the stonework is massive and beautifully laid, the windows small and there is little ornament; only the prickly richness of the octagon flèche is carefully contrived to contrast with the military strength around it.

Taking the main castle building from north to south the first portion to be described is the Bute Tower, the foundations of which were laid on 24 April 1873. This tower contained (in order of ascent) a dining room, Lady Bute's boudoir, Lord Bute's bedroom and an open peristyle roof garden. The dining room ceiling is a typical and fascinating example of Burges's joinery, with huge elephant-leg members and little inset coffers and domes, like those in the summer smoking room, derived from the roof of the cathedral at Messina. The fireplace (first sketched out by Burges in the summer of 1873) is surmounted by statues of Sarah and the three angels, the latter under Gothic canopies; but its best feature is its frieze, a vigorous mixture of foliage, animals and human figures. The stained glass, of very good quality, was probably made by Saunders and Co., like most of Burges's glass. The firegrate, with its winged dragons, was almost certainly supplied by Hart, Son, Peard and Co., who did most of Burges's metalwork. The wooden bell-push is a typical and entertaining Burges–Nicholls product, in which the bell (presumably pneumatic) takes the form of a nut in the mouth of a monkey.

A considerable amount of decoration still survives in the room above the dining room, but Lord Bute's bedroom a storey higher is more complete. It is a rich, sombre and at the same time glittering room, with red–brown woodwork on walls and the ceiling gilded, painted and inset with mirrors. As in all the bedrooms that Lord Bute constructed for himself there is a magnificent bathroom adjoining, in this case lined with panels of sixty different polished marbles, with windows (originally)

280

268. (upper right) Cardiff Castle. The dining-room ceiling.

269. (right) The dining room.

of transparent alabaster. Above is the roof garden with elaborate tile decorations of animals and scripture scenes on the walls, and an arcade supported on cast iron columns looking onto an open courtyard.

South of the Bute tower is the fifteenth-century octagon tower, restored, added to and redecorated by Burges. Work started on it at the end of 1872, when Burges made the first sketch for the timber flèche, and went on intermittently over the next seventeen years. The lower part of the tower is filled with an octagon staircase, elaborately and ingeniously vaulted all the way up. At the top of the baluster is a typical Burges touch, a crocodile which as one goes down the stairs is seen to be contemplating a plump baby on the rail beneath him. At the bottom of the rail is a

282

270. (top) Cardiff Castle. A monkey bell-push in the dining room.
271. Lord Bute's bedroom and bathroom.
XXII. (right) The summer smoking room.

XXIII. (preceding page left) Cardiff Castle, Glamorganshire. A tile panel in the summer smoking room.

XXIV. (preceding page right) Waddesdon Manor, Buckinghamshire (G. H. Destailleur, 1874-89). A detail of the entrance front.

XXV. (above) Chateau Impney, Worcestershire (A. Tronquois, 1869-75). The garden front.

helmeted or muzzled lion, the lion signifying the Bute family's royal Stuart descent, the muzzle the bar (through illegitimacy) to the throne. Burges designed the crocodile in the spring of 1874 and the lion at the beginning of 1876. Nicholls did not estimate for the lion until February 1879 and the painted decorations (by Messrs Campbell, Smith and Campbell) were not carried out until 1884, three years after Burges's death. The staircase leads past the little oratory (fitted out in 1876) to the Chaucer room. This is a small room but one of the most richly decorated in the castle, presided over by the figure of Chaucer above the fireplace. The lantern is a superb (and unusually delicate) example of Burges's genius in the construction of roofs. The panelling, with its exquisite inlay, dates from 1884, well after Burges's death; the attractive wall decoration is later still, carried out by Campbell, Smith and Campbell in 1889. Behind the bay windows on the west front are the library, with the banqueting hall above it. The banqueting hall is the biggest and most ambitious room in the castle, but not the most successful. The upper part of the walls is covered with frescoes by H. N. Lonsdale, who, here and elsewhere, was required by Burges and Lord Bute to cover areas rather greater than his talents deserved.[8] The chimneypiece, in the form of a little castle with figures waving and blowing

272. Cardiff Castle. The octagon staircase.

273. Sketches by Burges for the octagon staircase and a set of plates for Lord Bute.

trumpets from the battlements, is a typical Burges creation and is in fact another version of the fireplace he designed for the library of his own house in Kensington. It shows Robert, Earl of Gloucester, the second owner of Cardiff Castle, riding out to the wars while his wife waves him farewell and Robert, Duke of Normandy (imprisoned in the castle from 1126 to 1134), looks out through a little barred window. The chimneypiece was possibly carved in 1875, and estimates for painting it were made in February 1877.

The elaborate carving of the doors in the banqueting hall (enriched with, among other animals, an owl, an eagle, a fish, a goggle-eyed frog and a huge bristly boar) reappears in even lusher form in the doors of the library where tree trunks are carved in the hollow of the arches and little monkeys climb and grimace up them. The library as a whole, long and low, with glowing red and gold wallpaper and inlaid bookcases projecting to form alcoves all the way along, must have been a sympathetic room when it was still in use and filled with books. The bookcases and library tables were supplied by Gillows, with marquetry designs by Lonsdale; the doorways were being carved in 1880, the last year of Burges's life; but the chimneypiece, with five figures holding tablets of five different alphabets, was designed and carved in 1875. In the same year Burges designed a magnificent vaulted staircase hall, which was to be built at the south end of the library leading up to the banqueting hall. It was never completed, and there is a simpler and smaller staircase in its place today.

The last room to be described is the Arab room on the first floor of the Herbert tower. Its intricate and amazing roof must have particularly engaged Burges, for the construction of roofs always brought out the best in him. It should be compared with the Arab room designed at almost exactly the same time by his friend George

288

274. (top left) Cardiff Castle. The Chaucer Room.
275. (top right) Doors in the library.
276. (right) The banqueting hall.

Aitchison for Lord Leighton's house in Kensington in 1877–9. On the fireplace appear the initials of Burges and Lord Bute and the date 1881. This was the year of Burges's death; the Arab room appears to have been the last room he worked on at Cardiff and Lord Bute probably had the two sets of initials carved as a memorial of their sixteen years' partnership. At the base of the roof are carved eight magnificent parrots, Burges's favourite bird; he loved the parrot, according to his brother-in-law, because of 'its grotesque motions, its fine colouring and its great intelligence', a phrase that tells one a considerable amount about Burges.

At his death much of the decoration of the castle was still incomplete. It is remarkable how long drawn out the work at Cardiff was; the decorating of one comparatively small room often lingered on over seven or eight years. 'Why should I hurry over what is my chief pleasure', Lord Bute once said. 'I have comparatively little interest in a thing after it is finished.' The remark helps to explain the endless suites of rooms that he decorated at his many houses;[9] they are more intellectual exercises than rooms in which to live. His character is an enigmatic one. Was there a certain lack of warmth about him? Or was he, behind the outer shell of diffidence and reserve, a man of strong feelings? An obituary notice talked of his 'yearning for communion with the invisible'. The sympathetic biography by his friend Abbot Hunter Blair leaves one with the feeling that one has not penetrated to the private world in which he lived, imprisoned there, perhaps, as a result of his own temperament, his solitary childhood and his great wealth.

He died in 1900, at the comparatively early age of fifty-three. After his death his son built the existing great walls round the castle courtyard, on the basis of the walls of a Roman castrum which excavations had uncovered underneath medieval earthworks in 1889. In 1947 the castle was given to the City Corporation of Cardiff by his grandson.

290

277. Cardiff Castle. The Arab room ceiling.

22. *The Nouveau-Riche style*

AMONG early and mid-Victorian country houses it is impossible to distinguish anything that could be called a *nouveau-riche* style. The new rich who bought country estates were usually anxious to be accepted by their neighbours, and built their houses in the same manner, even if sometimes distinguishable by a touch of ineptness or ostentation in their design. But the 1870s saw a shift in the social balance that was much commented on at the time, usually unfavourably.* The previously exclusive preserves of London society became more quickly and easily accessible to self-made millionaires. The change was partly due to steady changes in the economic structure, although it was well under way before the traumatic experiences of the agricultural depression. It was encouraged by the Prince of Wales, who enjoyed the company of the new rich and found them useful in keeping him financially afloat while his mother was alive.

The resulting growth in prestige and self-confidence led to a specifically *nouveau-riche* style. It flourished in defiance of the Victorian doctine that a gentleman's house should be marked by 'elegance and importance without ostentation'.[1] It was imported from France, from the Second-Empire world of new families and new and sometimes shady fortunes. It was, in short, the revived French Renaissance style as

---

* 'Certainly *money* is a vulgar thing, and money is what rules us now. I quite agree with Weigall who, talking of Barons Grant, Sturrs, Oppenheim, Boutil and Co. said, "What right have such people to force themselves into our society?".' Dowager Countess Cowper to Earl Cowper, October 1874, quoted *Memoir of Earl Cowper*, by his wife (privately printed, 1913). In 1877 W. P. Frith painted a series of five pictures, *The Race for Wealth*, showing the rise, social success and ultimate crash of a fraudulent financier. Trollope's *The Way we Live Now*, which dealt with a similar subject, was published in 1875.

278. Normanhurst, Sussex (Habershon, Brock and Webb, 1867).

opulently expressed in Visconti and Lefuel's new block at the Louvre, built in 1852–70.[2]

In its early days the style was far from *nouveau-riche* in its associations. Although it reached its culmination in the England of the 1860s and 1870s, there are a number of earlier examples of French houses in England, built, on the whole, for a very different clientele. French influence hit England in two waves. A fashion for the *dix-huitième*, which produced the opulent interiors of Crockford's Club, London (1827), and Belvoir Castle (*c.* 1825) culminated in a complete Louis XV chateau at Wrest Park, Bedfordshire, designed for himself in 1834–9 by the second Earl de Grey, the first president of the Institute of British Architects. The Louis IX French roofs which Salvin put on Oxonhoath in Kent for Sir W. R. P. Geary, in 1846–7 probably represented the backwash of this revival. It was given fresh impetus (with a tendency to the sixteenth rather than the eighteenth century) by the new Louvre and related buildings erected in France in the 1850s. In 1854–5 R. C. Carpenter transformed an early nineteenth-century house at Bedgebury in Kent into a French Renaissance chateau. His patron was Alexander Beresford-Hope, the champion of the Ecclesiologists; it is curious to find him building so notably un-Gothic a house. Salvin effected a similar transformation at Marbury Hall, Cheshire, for J. H. Smith-Barry in 1856–8. Ferrey built a large gloomy François I chateau with *pavillons* and high mansard roofs at Wynnstay in Denbighshire for Sir Watkin Williams-Wynn, after the old house had been burnt in 1858. Paxton and Stokes designed a Louis XIII mansion on the outskirts of Halifax for Sir Frank Crossley in about 1857 (Pl. 199) These houses derived, in one way or another, from French classical examples. But Paxton and Stokes also exploited the possibilities of French Gothic chateaux at Battlesden in Bedfordshire for Sir Edward Page-Turner in 1860–4. Similar essays had already been made by Pearson at Quar Wood in 1857, for the Revd R. W. Hippisley and by Clutton at Minley in 1858–62, for Raikes Currie (Pls. 32, 36).

A high proportion of these houses were built for well-established landowners, lordly or otherwise. Up till 1860 the French Renaissance was primarily a style for country houses and for gentlemen. Very few of the houses were illustrated in the press, and at first the style made little impact on London. The only exception was essentially an invasion of the town by the country. In 1853–9 Montagu House, a very large and very competent French chateau, complete with *pavillons* and high roofs, slowly arose in a superb position between Whitehall and the Thames. William Burn, the doyen of country house architects, was the designer, and the Duke of Buccleuch, one of the grandest and richest of British dukes, was the client.[3]

The appeal of these French houses was an obvious one. The Victorians had become increasingly conscious of skyline, and attracted by buildings with a lively silhouette. The Gothic Revival was well adapted to cater for this taste; the Classicists, with their undemonstrative Italian parapets, found themselves at a disadvantage. By the 1850s the rich cornices, low tiled roofs and Italianate towers popularized by Barry were thought not to have gone far enough. French roofs provided the answer.

The situation was described by Beresford-Hope, when he spoke to the supporters of the Architectural Museum on 24 March 1863.[4] Hope, calmly ignoring his own house, was speaking as a Goth, and celebrating the 'confessions of victory we have won from the other side'. By this he meant the way in which the Classicists had been forced to modify their buildings in order to compete with the Goths. 'I recapitulate our gain as follows', he said: 'The reality of the materials, the carefulness of the carving and above all, the attention which has been paid to the skyline. You know how we have insisted on the pre-eminent necessity of the skyline, and how we have denounced the scowling cornice, unrelieved beyond the street line . . . The principle of playing with the skyline has been recognized and adopted.'

As examples to illustrate his point he listed a number of new London buildings. 'Look at the Renaissance house in Upper Brook Street, erected for Mr Emanuel, with its high roof and varied skyline. Look at the house in the course of construction for Messrs Longman in Paternoster Row, with its high French roofs and carved stone work; look at the Grosvenor Hotel, the Westminster Palace, and the London Bridge Hotel, and at the gigantic structure of a similar class about to be erected in Langham Place, and look at Montague House and many others I could mention.'

Hope could refer to the French origin of these skyline developments but among other contemporary sources there was a curious reticence about doing so. The *Building News*, commenting on the Charing Cross Hotel on 9 December 1864, said that 'Its style may be called broadly Italian'; but although the facades, as in other hotels of that decade, were only distinguished from stucco Itanianate of the 1850s by an extra lushness in the details, its roofs were noticeably French. In the next year the much more thoroughly French Inns of Court Hotel in Holborn was described as 'modified Italian', and the entirely Second-Empire design in Kerr's *The Gentleman's House* (1864) is unashamedly labelled 'English Renaissance'.[5] One explanation for this curious phenomenon might be that in the early 1860s anti-French feeling in England was strong, especially among the more prosperous classes. And admittedly some of the buildings—notably those designed by James Knowles—were remote enough from French or any other prototypes, even in the shape of their roofs, for their architects to describe them as in 'the Modern style'.

Hope's list of examples is interesting. Apart from Montagu House they were all in course of building, or had been built in the last four years. They consisted of a shop in Mayfair, a city office block and four hotels. By 1863 the French style was pre-eminently that of the great hotels which formed the most notable new eruption on the London skyline. An earlier forerunner of these French hotels was P. C. Hardwick's Great Western Hotel by Paddington Station, designed in 1852. In 1860 the immense mass of Knowles's Grosvenor Hotel by Victoria Station, layer upon layer of rumbustious cornices and ornate windows surmounted by bulbous roofs, introduced a flood of new hotels, all in the French manner—or at least with high roofs: the London Bridge Hotel (Henry Currey, 1861), the Westminster Palace Hotel (before 1863), the Langham Hotel (John Giles, 1864–6), the Charing Cross Hotel (E. M. Barry, 1863–4), the City Terminus Hotel in Cannon Street (E. M. Barry, 1865–6) and the Inns of Court Hotel in Holborn (Lockwood and Mawson, 1865). The fashion spread to the provinces. Henry Currey, for instance, designed the Palace Hotel in Buxton in 1868; the most overpowering of the many provincial mansard-roof hotels was Cuthbert Broderick's Grand Hotel at Scarborough

(1863–7), as ebullient as the Grosvenor Hotel, and in a far more sensational position.

These hotels were in complete contrast to the converted private houses, with their select upper-class clientele and old retainer discomforts, which had previously done duty for hotels. Their hundreds of bedrooms, fireproof construction, gas light flaring on marble columns, huge gilded coffee rooms, central heating, lifts, speaking tubes, relative abundance of bathrooms and running hot and cold water, offered the latest refinements of luxury and technology to a predominantly middle-class clientele, and underlined the fact that London was now the commercial centre of the world.

Not surprisingly the more self-confident of the new commercial and industrial rich, when they invested in country estates, began to build houses that reflected the luxury, opulence and stylistic peculiarities of the new hotels. These country houses tarred the French Renaissance style with such a *nouveau-riche* brush that the older families gradually dropped it. They dropped it first and fastest in the countryside, as the feeling grew stronger that a country gentleman should build something 'English'. After James Knowles's Hedsor House (1865–8, for Lord Boston) in his own ebullient version of the high-roof style, and the splendidly spiky outburst of French Gothic roofs an Waterhouse's Eaton Hall (1870–2, for the Duke of Westminster), upper-class high-roof houses peter out with Banks and Barry's feeble Stevenstone (1869–74, for the Hon. Mark Rolle) and the deflated French roofs of T. H. Wyatt's Nuneham Paddox (1875, for the Earl of Denbigh). Full blown French Renaissance was left to the enjoyment of parvenus. And enjoy it they did.

Among the first of these brassy French chateaux was Normanhurst[6] in Sussex, built in 1867 for Thomas Brassey, one of the three sons of the great railway contractor. Habershon, Brock and Webb, the architects, in fact owed much to

294

279. Hedsor House, Buckinghamshire (J. T. Knowles, 1865–8).

Pippingford Park, Sussex, designed in 1857 by the French architect Henry Horeau.[7] 'The outlay has, of course, been large', said the *Builder*, and the house set the tone for its successors, announcing as loudly as it could that its builder had a great deal of money and was determined to show it. The house was of fireproof construction with piped water supplying hydrants at frequent intervals. There were French roofs with little cast iron palisades round the top, a clock tower fitted with musical bells, a huge water tower, a conservatory forty feet square, stables with a covered drive 'to exercise the horses in inclement weather' and a great deal of François I detail.

In 1869 two more chateaux, this time certainly by Frenchmen, began to rise up in Worcestershire and Durham. Impney Hall—soon to be renamed Chateau Impney—was built in 1869–75 for John Corbett (1817–1901), one of the liveliest of self-made Victorian industrialists. He had started work at the age of ten working for his father in a small business running carrier boats on the canals. He built up a large fleet of boats but sensibly sold the business in 1852, before the railways killed it. He invested the money in buying up the derelict Stoke Prior Salt Works near Droitwich, and turned them into 'the most perfect system of salt manufacture in the world' with an annual output of 200,000 tons.

At Impney he employed Auguste Tonquois (1829–85), an architect with a considerable practice in and around Paris.[8] One wonders how he came to know of him, and whether he had business connections with France. The executive architect was the English-born R. Phené Spiers, one of the very few English architects with a Beaux-Arts training. It is surprising that Spiers did not cash in on the French fashion and design French chateaux himself; perhaps others made use of his experience, for he was just the kind of hesitant and self-effacing personality who would have ghosted for more pushing architects.

295

280. The Bowes Museum, Barnard Castle, Durham (Jules Pellechet, 1869).

It is a curious experience to find the exotic skyline, hard red brick and fancy trimmings of Chateau Impney at the end of a coniferous park drive on the edge of Droitwich; one would take less notice of it if one came across it where spiritually it belongs, built to house an industrialist or Second-Empire baron on the outskirts of a manufacturing town in France. Similar reactions are inspired by the enormous bulk of the Bowes Museum, on the outskirts of Barnard Castle; it looks like a French *hôtel de ville*, and that, indeed, is near enough what it is, for it is closely modelled on Brunet-Debaines's Hôtel de Ville at Le Havre (1855). The architect was Jules Pellechet (1829–1903), with J. E. Watson of Newcastle-on-Tyne as the executant. It was built by John Bowes of Streatlam Castle for his wife, and was originally intended to be part house, part private art gallery and museum.[9] John Bowes was far from being a self-made man, but his career and social position were somewhat ambivalent. He was the illegitimate son of the tenth Earl of Strathmore, who left

296

him estates and coal mines in the north; he lived much of his life in Paris, where he married his mistress, the actress Josephine Benoite, bought and managed a theatre for her benefit, and bought her an Italian title to conceal her ambivalent origins.

In Victorian times when the prestige of English country house life was at its height, and English architects were exporting their expertise throughout Europe, it was rare to find the architectural current flowing in the other direction; it is a measure of the attraction of the French roof manner that it should have produced two English houses by French architects in the same year. The next few years showed (or at least appeared to show) that there was no need to go abroad to buy this kind of merchandise. In 1870 Thomas Cundy, who had built the first important row of terrace houses with French roofs in Grosvenor Place in 1868, designed a country house in the same manner at Park Place, Henley-on-Thames, for J. Noble, of Noble's Paints and Varnishes. In 1872 E. M. Barry underlined the attraction of the style for those embarking from the City into country life by exhibiting three big country houses in a row at the Royal Academy: Cobham Park, Surrey (1870–3), for the City brewer C. J. F. Combe; Shabden, near Chipstead in Surrey (1871–5), for a city merchant, John Cattley; and Wykehurst in Sussex (1871–4), for Henry Huth, the son of a City banker, and a famous bibliophile. Of these Wykehurst is the grandest and much the most impressive. An earlier design by Barry at the R.I.B.A.,

297

282. Wykehurst, Sussex. The entrance front.

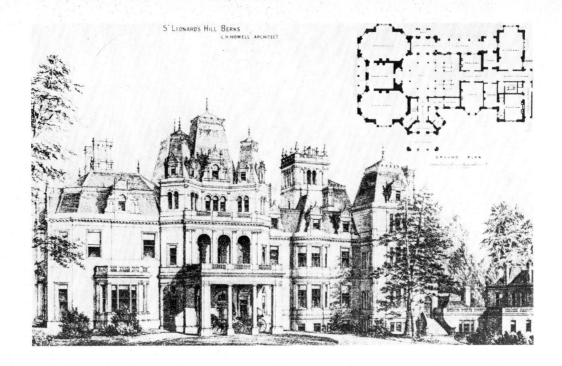

dated June 1871, shows a remarkably feeble Jacobean country house with vaguely French roofs and cornices; the finished result was so much more competent that one wonders whether Barry had brought in expert assistance in the interval.

At any rate, at Wykehurst the cosmopolitan comforts and rich orchestration that Barry had provided for his two London hotels at Charing Cross and Cannon Street were transferred to the countryside. The house was built by William Cubitt and Co. and incorporated everything that high-Victorian technology had to offer. It was an early example of cavity wall construction, and had double framed fireproof floors of concrete and iron. It was heated by warm air; water pipes ran internally and were kept from freezing by being run through one of the hot air flues. Hot water was supplied to all floors from the kitchen range; the bedroom floors were divided up into self-contained suites, each with its own bathroom. There were ventilation flues, folding external shutters built into the thickness of the walls for all windows and lifts for luggage and coal. Less impressively, the house was raised on a basement in which the servants had to live, looking out onto an area as narrow and dark as anything built in the eighteenth century.

The outside of Wykehurst is much more consistently French than Barry's hotels, though with an unmistakably high-Victorian twist. The detail is far from reticent, and there are some jarring passages of top-heaviness, as in the entrance porch and the way the massive cornice is carried round the smaller corner turrets, with which it is completely out of scale. But as a whole the exterior has an infectious brio and consistency. The lush detail, the fat balusters and chunky modillions, the deep reveals, opulent curves, tangled skylines and facades crowded with movement and incident are all of a piece. Two of the rooms were lined with sixteenth- and eighteenth-century boiseries imported from France, a feature that was soon to become almost obligatory for millionaire financiers' houses.

283. St Leonard's Hill, Berkshire (C. H. Howell, 1875).

Cobham is the least impressive of E. M. Barry's three French houses. Shabden is quiet going after Wykehurst; its reticent facades have a certain leathery and rather unpleasing individuality. Like Wykehurst it had cavity walls, internal pipes, and elaborate ventilation and hot-air heating systems. Unlike Wykehurst it is planned in an attempted French manner, with interlocking rooms with the corners cut away to make octagons and half-octagons. The architect has made a considerable mess of what was obviously an unfamiliar form. A more professional piece of planning in the same manner was at the now demolished St Leonard's Hill, near Windsor. The design was exhibited at the Royal Academy in 1875; the architect was C. H. Howell and the client Francis Tress Barry, of the firm of Mason and Barry, who made a fortune out of copper mining in Portugal. The exterior was full of *nouveau-riche* ebullience, and cheerfully got the best of both worlds by combining steep and fancy French roofs with an Italianate tower in the Barry manner.

It was in 1875 that Trollope's *The Way we Live Now* satirized the growing Victorian worship of money, and the adulteration of society by financiers both shady and flashy. In 1876 the flashiest and shadiest of Victorian financiers, Baron Albert Grant, started to build an enormous house in Kensington; the architect was

284. St Leonard's Hill. The hall.

J. T. Knowles, Junior, and the house was almost inevitably in the French mansard-roof style, Knowles no doubt being chosen because of his father's Grosvenor Hotel. In 1879, after £270,000 had been spent on it, Grant was overtaken by bankruptcy; the house, still unfinished and unoccupied, was demolished in 1883 (it was replaced by the houses in Kensington Court) and its gilded rooms were soon forgotten though the staircase survived for another fifty years at Madame Tussaud's.

The spectacular rise and fall of both Baron Grant and his brassy mansion must have helped to bring the French style into disrepute, and encourage both the old and new rich to go off in their various directions, to Devey, Webb or Norman Shaw.[10] But it did not prevent the Rothschilds from giving the style its last fling, as far as country houses were concerned, with as much glitter as Grant and on a firmer social and financial basis.

In 1874 Baron Ferdinand de Rothschild (of the Austrian branch of the Rothschilds, but settled in England since he was twenty-one) bought the Waddesdon and Winchenden estates in Buckinghamshire from the Duke of Marlborough. By 1889 with the help of a specially constructed steam tramway, teams of Percheron mares imported from Normandy, and an immense expenditure of money, a bare and windswept hill on the estate had been planted with hundreds of fully grown trees and surmounted with formal gardens, a menagerie, an aviary, and an enormous chateau of bright yellow Bath stone. ('Chambord has 450 rooms', the Baron modestly remarked. 'Waddesdon is a pygmy beside it.') The house was designed by a French architect, Gabriel-Hippolyte Destailleur, and the gardens laid out by the French landscape gardener Lainé. Among English houses of the period it is closest to Wykehurst, although considerably larger. Architecturally Wykehurst wins in the comparison, for it is more of an entity than Waddesdon, which is a patchwork of elements from Blois, Chambord, Anet, Maintenon and other historic chateaux, pieced together with no particular sensitivity. Inside, Waddesdon also resembles Wykehurst in that its main rooms are lined with re-erected French boiseries. But Waddesdon went much farther than Wykehurst or any other house of the period in its employment of (mainly) French boiseries, furniture and *objets d'art* of superb quality, combined with such abundance as to produce an entirely Rothschild rather than *dix-huitième* impression.

The luxury and splendour of Waddesdon made a big impact on those who visited it. Their reactions varied, however. The Baron's cousin, Constance de Rothschild, commented rather naively: 'The Christy Minstrels and a Hungarian Band performed alternately, and gave great satisfaction, particularly the latter. But the house itself with all its wonders, pictures, *objets d'art* and magnificent couches and satin cushions and palms and photos of crowned heads with autograph signatures, was a never ending source of pleasure.'[11] Gladstone's daughter Mary, who came there with her father in August 1885, was less enthusiastic. 'Felt much oppressed with the extreme gorgeousness and luxury', she wrote in her diary. 'Pottered about looking at calves, hothouses, everything laid out with immense care, some rather cockney things, rockeries and such like, a large aviary with gaudy plumaged birds . . . The pictures in his [the Baron's] sitting room are too beautiful, but there is not a book in the house save 20 improper French novels.'[12]

300

285. (right) Waddesdon Manor, Buckinghamshire. The morning room.

286. Halton House, Buckinghamshire (1882–8).

In 1882–8 Baron Ferdinand's cousin, Alfred Charles de Rothschild, built another French chateau on similar scale a few miles away from Waddesdon at Halton. It was in the Waddesdon manner, but with a much stronger admixture of the *dix-huitième*, and with the individual speciality of an enormous winter garden attached to the house. Its architect would seem to have been William R. Rogers, the design partner of William Cubitt and Co.[13] At Halton Alfred de Rothschild lived a bachelor life of magnificence in much the same style as his cousin at Waddesdon but with an extra touch of millionaire eccentricity. He used to conduct his own band in the winter garden, or, fitted out with a white overcoat, whip and gloves, to direct his troupe of circus ponies and dogs; he had his private team of firemen, with a special uniform, and a team of zebras to pull his pony cart.

Halton was the last of the big French country houses. This is not the place to describe the style's development in civic and urban architecture, or its adventures in America, where it had its greatest success and was most fully absorbed into the vernacular. In London it went out in a blaze of glory, with Jabez Balfour's Hyde Park Mansions (now the Hyde Park Hotel), and Whitehall Court on the new Victoria Embankment. Suitably enough, in view of the style's slightly raffish associations, Balfour was in gaol for fraud before either of these two spectacularly skylined buildings had been completed.

302

XXVI. (right) Cragside, Northumberland. Lord Armstrong and the Prince of Wales smoking on the terrace, from the water-colour by H. H. Emmerson.

23. Cragside, Northumberland

SINCE the trees grew up the distant view of Cragside exists no longer. One can be grateful that it is preserved in old photographs, but dearly wish that one were able to lift one's own eyes and see that amazing improbable vision floating above the barren hillside. Passers-by must have wondered what on earth it was. What modern warlord or robber–baron had retired to this rock fastness? Norman Shaw may have had some such thought at the back of his mind when he designed it, for it was built for Sir William Armstrong (1810–1900), the greatest of Victorian armaments manufacturers. But Armstrong cannot be written off in such crude terms; he was an inventor and scientist, and armaments were only one facet of his activities.[1]

He was the son of William Armstrong (1778–1857), a prosperous Newcastle merchant and amateur mathematician who became Mayor in 1850. He spent the first decade of his working life as a solicitor. In these years he had two enthusiasms outside his work, fishing and scientific experiment. While fishing one day on the River Coquet he noticed how inefficiently a waterwheel on the river made use of water power. He turned his attention to hydraulics, with such success that in 1846 he was elected a Fellow of the Royal Society as a result of his researches and inventions. In the next year he gave up his solicitor's business and launched an engineering works, specializing in hydraulic cranes and lifts. The works were at Elswick on the Tyne above Newcastle; and after a slow start they made him a rich man.

In 1854, when indignation at the inefficient management of the Crimean War was at its height, he began to experiment with the possibilities of a new type of gun. The

XXVII. (left) Cragside, Northumberland (R. Norman Shaw, 1869–84). The inglenook in the drawing room.

287. (above) The house before the trees grew up.

result was the Armstrong gun, breech instead of muzzle loaded, firing a shell instead of a ball, with a rifled barrel instead of a smooth one, and made of coiled and welded steel instead of cast iron. His Armstrong guns sold all round the world and brought him a second and much greater fortune than his hydraulic machines. By the 1880s he was making the antidote as well as the disease; more efficient guns stimulated a demand for armour plating, and huge ironclads were slipping out of the Armstrong yards to supply it. By the time of his death in 1900, three years after he had been ennobled as Lord Armstrong, the Elswick works competed with Krupps for the doubtful distinction of being the biggest armaments factory in the world.

For fifteen years he deserted his old fishing haunts and companions and never took a holiday. In 1863, after an exhausting session presiding over a meeting of the British Association at Newcastle, he went up the Coquet to recuperate. A chance remark from a friend, that the hillside along the river near Rothbury would make a pretty park if cleared, led to his buying twenty acres of land and building a small shooting or fishing lodge. Cragside escalated from that. He brought more land and spent six years clearing, planting and making roads. Between 1869 and 1884 the house grew enormously in all directions, with Norman Shaw as the architect. By the time of Lord Armstrong's death in 1900 he owned Cragside, Bamburgh Castle and 16,000 acres of land in Northumberland. The Cragside pleasure grounds covered 1,729 acres on which 7,000,000 trees and innumerable rhododendrons had been planted, a string of lakes formed and many miles of paths and roads built through the woods.

Lord Armstrong had the reticence and precision of a scientist, and none of the panache that one expects of a tycoon. He seems never to have put on the airs of a great man; he remained on the best of terms with his old fishing cronies along the Coquet. Contemporary newspapers describing him as 'destitute of pride and unaffectedly simple in manner'. 'To judge from the outside, he is the mildest mannered and most gentle of Northumbria's sons.' The mild manner concealed a mind and will that never let go. When other boys were throwing stones through windows the young Armstrong systematically smashed every window of the house opposite his own with a crossbow loaded with broken clay pipes.[2] His fame and enthusiasm as a fisherman are not surprising, for it was a sport that called for his pre-eminent qualities of patience, skill and tenacity. Problems were there to be solved, and he seems to have had little interest in the larger issues that solving them led to. Cragside presented a problem, like guns and water power, how to break windows and how to break strikes; in this case how to conjure a forest out of a wilderness and balance a mansion on a crag. He spent thirty years happily overcoming the obstacles that stood in the way and applying his scientific knowledge to the embellishment of his new domain.

He was a friend of Joseph Swan, the pioneer of electricity, who was a fellow Newcastle man. Cragside was the first private house in England and perhaps the world to be properly fitted with electric light. Swan lamps were installed throughout the house and were working by December 1880; previously there had been an arc light in the picture gallery.[3] Power for the lamps came from a water turbine, fed from the string of lakes which had been formed at the top of the hill. The house had a hydraulically operated passenger lift; the kitchen was equipped with a

hydraulically turned spit, the central heating was worked by a hydraulic engine, and the heavy pots in the conservatories could be moved by hydraulic machinery. There was telephone communication from room to room and from the house to a shooting lodge on the moors, an electric sewing machine, a system of electric gongs, and a laboratory and telescope under a glass dome at the top of the south-east tower. A cast iron footbridge of amazing lightness spanned the gorge beneath the house.

To contemporaries there was something miraculous about the gurgling Armstrong machinery which effortlessly worked great dockside cranes or lifted up the massive leaves of Tower Bridge to let the ships steam through; about the huge ironclads spitting flame and death; and about the palace in the wilderness, the forest sprouting from the rocks, the electric light blazing from the innumerable windows, and the ribbons of iron leaping across the gorge. It was, as a contemporary paper described it, 'truly the palace of a modern magician'.[4] Shaw's triumph was to provide an architectural expression for this, to create, against considerable odds, something that was part magician's palace, part baron's castle, that could house a family in domestic comfort, and at the same time impress the Japanese and Chinese warlords, the King of Siam, the Shah of Persia and the Crown Prince of Afghanistan, who came to Cragside to buy its owner's dangerous wares and leave their strange hieroglyphics on page after page of his visitors' book.

The commission must have appealed both to the romantic and to the bandit in Shaw. It almost certainly came to him through the artist J. C. Horsley. One of

288. Cragside. Looking along the entrance front to the 1883–4 drawing-room wing.

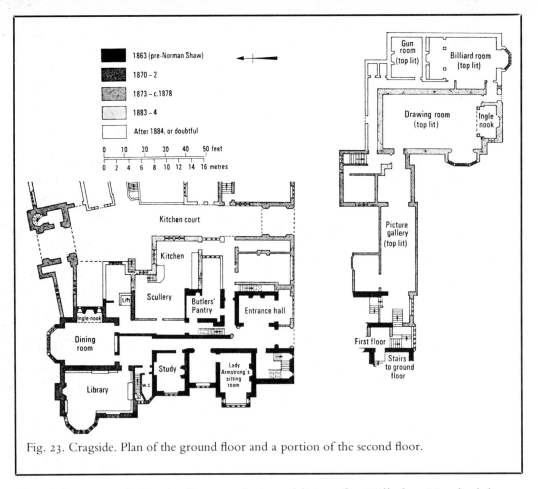

Fig. 23. Cragside. Plan of the ground floor and a portion of the second floor.

Legend in figure:

1863 (pre-Norman Shaw)
1870–2
1873 – c.1878
1883 – 4
After 1884, or doubtful

0 10 20 30 40 50 feet
0 2 4 6 8 10 12 14 16 metres

Labels in figure: Gun room (top lit); Billiard room (top lit); Drawing room (top lit); Ingle nook; Picture gallery (top lit); First floor; Stairs to ground floor; Kitchen court; Kitchen; Scullery; Butlers' Pantry; Entrance hall; Lift; Ingle-nook; Dining room; Study; Lady Armstrong's sitting room; Library; w.c.

Shaw's first commissions had been to design additions for Willesley, Horsley's house in Kent, in 1864–5. Horsley had sold pictures to Armstrong, and become a friend; Lady Armstrong had stayed at Willesley.[5] The Armstrongs may also have seen Shaw's designs for Leys Wood, a house in a heathy and rocky landscape similar to that of Cragside (Pl. 41). At the end of 1869 Shaw was invited up to the north and made his first Cragside designs. According to Blomfield they were made in a day; 'the house party had gone out shooting and when his host returned Shaw was ready for him with his drawings, and his design was accepted.'[6] These preliminary drawings have disappeared, and it is not clear how much of what was subsequently built was envisaged from the start. The first surviving drawings,[7] dated 1870, are only for adding a new library and dining room, with bedrooms above, to the north of the original shooting lodge. This was built in 1871; by May 1872 the central tower was being built and designs had been made for remodelling the old lodge and adding a new entrance front on the south. Drawings for extending the north front over an archway are dated 1873. The existing south front was different from that envisaged in 1872; it had been built, complete with a gallery over a second archway, and a second tower, by 1879 and probably several years earlier. The gabled top to the tower was designed from the start, but for several years the tower was surmounted by the glass roof of the observatory;[8] this was replaced by gables between 1884 and 1891. The prominent south-east wing, containing the drawing room, was added about 1882–3, and enlarged in 1895.

308

Cragside was a crazy site on which to build a large house. There may have been a natural ledge in the steep slope at this point, but if so it was a narrow one, and more space could only be obtained by digging out at the back and building up in front. When the house was extended to the back, in 1873 and later, the extension butted straight into the hillside, and had to be carried over archways to keep the back route to the kitchen open. What is the ground floor at the entrance on the south front is a storey up by the north-west corner, leaving Shaw room to fit the heating plant and bathrooms underneath the library. Conversely the drawing room, like the picture gallery which leads to it, is between the first and second floors of the main house, and at ground level at the back; and space for the billiard room behind it could be obtained by sawing out a hole in the hillside.

All this was meat and drink both for Lord Armstrong, directing his men as they dug and built and blasted, and for Shaw, who turned all the difficulties of the site to dramatic use, making the best of the great blank walls of abutting stonework, the archways pierced through the back of the house, the necessarily rambling plan, the changes in level and the view from higher up the hill, where one looks down on the many roofs, and the house seems like a fortified village, with two towers and the forest behind it.

The nature of the site and the building history of the house combined to produce a sprawling and additive plan of just the kind to which Shaw's development was already tending. Perhaps no other English architect could have lived from hand to

289. Cragside. The house from the valley today.

290. Shaw's drawing of the tower.

mouth as Shaw virtually did at Cragside, and emerged at the end with a house that was—not quite a cohesive design, but not a muddle either. Inevitably there are weaknesses. The west front is sensational through its position, but confused as a composition.★ In Shaw's defence it has to be said that more of the original lodge was preserved than he had wanted; its facades are there untouched up to the roof line and can be picked out by their distinctive rusticated quoins. Shaw's particular quality as a designer comes out most clearly in the south front with its spectacular build-up to the tangled skyline of the tower. The contrast between the long uninterrupted horizontal of the picture gallery and the drawn-out verticals of the chimneystacks is typical of him; so is the contrast between the blank stone walling, below the gallery and to the left of the entrance, and the many-lighted projecting window that lights the upper staircase.

Shaw's earlier work is full of romantic twists and the distinctive vocabulary of the

★ 'The house at Harrow Weald and the castellated mansion at Cragside are also picturesque, and contain many exquisite bits, but both these works seem to me disjointed; each looks as if two or three houses had been brought together and shuffled up somehow into one.' E. W. Godwin in the *Building News*, 24 Oct. 1873.

310

291. (top) Cragside. Looking down on the house.

293. (above right) The entrance front.

292. (above left) The north archway.

London artistic set. Into the tower in particular he put everything he had and perhaps more than he ought: panels of sunflowers and suns, twisted and moulded chimneystacks, Notre Dame gargoyles, an elaborate wrought iron wind vane and the crowning device (developed from the gatehouse at Leys Wood) of a half-timbered hutch behind battlements. Shaw needed half-timbering for the particular romantic effects he wanted; he reached out for it like an artist reaching out for a tube of colour, and in his earlier days it did not worry him (though it has worried his critics since) that he used it with complete disregard of the vernacular traditions of the neighbourhood.

After the high spirits of the tower Shaw sobered up. His later extensions at Cragside, starting with the nobly robust north archway, follow the development of his later country houses towards simpler and more massive effects. There is a similar contrast within the house, in atmosphere if not in elaboration. The dining room and library are full of pre-Raphaelite enthusiasms, with a hint of the current taste among artists for the Orient. In the dining room the Leys Wood inglenook has been transformed into a formidable erection of stone. The heavy stone apron beneath the arch—too heavy for the comfort of the occupants—is derived from the similar features above the fireplace in the kitchen at Fountains Abbey; Shaw had sketched it when he went to Yorkshire with Nesfield in 1861.[9] Inside is a romantic hide-out, with hooded chimneypiece, patterned tiles and pre-Raphaelite ladies in Morris-style stained glass. The suitably quaint and domestic inscription over the fireplace, 'East or West, Hame's best', had appeared in a similar position at Cloverley. The built-in sideboard with curved top (derived from Pugin's free-standing sideboards of a generation earlier) was to be much imitated in later Victorian houses. The panelling is delicately carved by James Forsyth with flowers, animals and birds.[10] Forsyth was probably also responsible for the superb stone frieze above the inglenook, with dogs hunting among the foliage.

The library, next door to the dining room, is one of the most sympathetic Victorian rooms in England. By high-Victorian standards it is a low room for its size; there is a deep bay window at the fireplace end, and the lower half of the walls are lined with books and panelling. The windows look west down to the ravine, the bridge and the enormous stillness of the conifers; the evening sun streams into the room and lights up the warm brown of the oak panelling and woodwork, and the soft red of the capacious leather chairs and sofas. The panelled frieze is painted with delicate sprays of flowers on a gold background; flowers and other devices were carved by Forsyth on the row of alternately square and circular 'pies'[11] which runs along the top of the panelling.

There can be little doubt that in both the dining room and the library Shaw kept a close hand over the contents as well as the fittings and that he certainly selected and possibly designed most of the furniture.[12] The decorative scheme was nicely balanced between his two poles of interest in the 1870s, the Middle Ages as seen through pre-Raphaelite eyes and the Orient as it was becoming fashionable in Chelsea studios. The upper lights in the library are filled with Morris glass showing scenes from the life of St George, from cartoons by Rossetti.[13] The elegant upright chairs, of black ebonized wood, have flower designs of aesthetic Oriental flavour stamped on their

312

294. (upper right) Cragside. The library.

295. (right) The dining room in 1890 with the original 1880 electric light fittings.

leather backs or inlaid in the wood. Along the shelves above the bookcases were jars and dishes of Oriental and Hispano-Moresque pottery.[14] These were an integral part of the decoration from the start, and are shown in similar positions in one of Shaw's detailed designs. Shaw shows some of the jars converted into oil-lamps, with glass burners protected by glass globes; in 1880 the lamps were reconverted for electricity but with similar globes. At this time the ceiling lights had clusters of exposed bulbs; the existing elegant shades were installed some time between 1891 and 1895.

Many of the pictures originally in the room were sold in the Armstrong picture sale of 1910;[15] the showpiece used to be Albert Moore's great picture *Follow My Leader* (1872). This, like two important pre-Raphaelite drawings formerly at Cragside, Rossetti's *Marguerite* (1868) and Burne-Jones's *Sleeping Beauty* (1871), probably represented Shaw's choice rather than that of Lord Armstrong, who inclined more towards landscapes and the sentimental, animal or anecdotal vein. The chimneypiece is of remarkably simple design for the date: huge slabs of Egyptian onyx set in a narrow moulded surround. The panels to either side of the fireplace opening are decorated with scroll and figure designs by Alfred Stevens,[16] and were originally flanked by splendid Renaissance fire irons, also by Stevens.

The corridor of the original shooting lodge, rather narrow now for a house of the size of Cragside, joins the library and dining room to the entrance hall and the staircase that leads to the bedrooms and the reception rooms on the upper level. The main body of the staircase is panelled, and carved lions on the newel posts hold alternate electric light standards and banners inscribed 'A' for Armstrong. An upper flight, lined, like the corridor, with patterned tiles, leads to the long top-lit picture gallery. This was originally a cul-de-sac, but the addition of a new wing in 1883-4 made it the introduction to the great new drawing room.

By the mid-1880s Shaw had drifted away from his earlier associates; he had become the favoured architect of very rich industrialists, shipowners and businessmen, and had grown to distrust William Morris and his associates, and to abandon the more fanciful or romantic elements of his earlier style. His development is symbolized by the enormous chimneypiece in the new drawing room, a design as robust as it is ostentatious, twenty feet of carved alabaster framing an inglenook that is a complete little room in itself, lined with elaborately veined marble.[17] Apart from a bay window at one end and a peep hole in the inglenook, the drawing room is top-lit, for it was designed to supplement the gallery as a setting for Lord Armstrong's pictures, including Millais's *Chill October*.

The drawing room was inaugurated in August 1884, when the Prince and Princess of Wales used Cragside as their base for an official visit to Newcastle, and were splendidly entertained by the Armstrongs.[18] An illuminated record of the visit was presented to Lord and Lady Armstrong by the inhabitants of Rothbury. It is full of vivid pictures by two Northumbrian artists, J. T. Dixon and Henry Hetherington Emmerson (who also painted a delightful portrait of Lord Armstrong in the dining room inglenook). A conversation piece, showing the royal party and Lord Armstrong smoking cigars on the terrace outside the front door, underlines the fact

296. Cragside. The drawing room.

297. The picture gallery.

298. The billiard room.

300. Lord Armstrong in the dining-room inglenook, by H. H. Emmerson.

that at this date there was no smoking room at Cragside.★ The need was supplied in 1895 when a combined billiard and smoking room was built out at the back of the drawing room. The architect was Frederick J. Waller of Gloucester;[19] the result has none of Shaw's brilliance, but even so, the lushly Jacobean billiard room and the adjoining gunroom[20] lined with cases of stuffed birds, are splendid period pieces.

Since the photographs illustrating the book were taken, Cragside has become the property of the National Trust, and there have been alterations in the contents, arrangement and decoration of the rooms. Pictures on loan from the De Morgan Foundation and elsewhere have helped fill the gap left by the sale of 1910. Sadly, some of the original contents, including the Stevens fire irons and the Hispano-Moresque pottery in the library, have been removed to Bamburgh Castle.

★ 'At one time Lord Armstrong, who was always a most hospitable host, had no smoking room; and it was curious to see a row of Japanese or other foreign naval officers, in charge of some war vessel building at the famous Elswick works, sitting in a row on the low wall outside the front door, puffing away for all they were worth.' *The Onlooker*, 2 Jan. 1901.

299. (left) Cragside. The stairs to the picture gallery.

24. Kinmel Park, Denbighshire

KINMEL seems an unbelievably palatial house for a Victorian commoner, until one knows something both of the history of the house and of the family who built it.[1] Their fortune was found by the Revd Edward Hughes, an obscure curate in an obscure parish in Anglesey. He married his vicar's daughter, who inherited a small and apparently barren property named Llys Dulas on the same island. In 1768 a seam of copper of astonishing richness was discovered in a hill known as Parys mountain, one half of which belonged to Llys Dulas and the other half to the Baylys of Plas Newydd (and later to the Marquesses of Anglesey). In 1774 Edward Hughes together with an Anglesey lawyer and a London banker founded the Parys Mine Company to develop his share of the mountain. By the end of the century the company owned smelting and other works in Lancashire, Buckinghamshire, Flintshire and Swansea, and had joined forces with the Grenfells of Taplow Court, who had copper interests in Cornwall. According to Hughes's grandson: 'Lord Anglesey and the Rev. Edward divided more than once upwards of £300,000 in a year.'

By the time of his death Edward Hughes had invested £500,000 in property in Anglesey and North Wales. He bought the Kinmel estate in 1789. It included an Elizabethan or Jacobean manor house, the ruins of which still stand in the kitchen garden. Hughes abandoned it, and built a small but elegant classical villa a few hundred yards away, to the designs of Samuel Wyatt. It was later enlarged both by

318

301. Kinmel Park, nr Abergele, Denbighshire (William Burn, 1855). The stables.

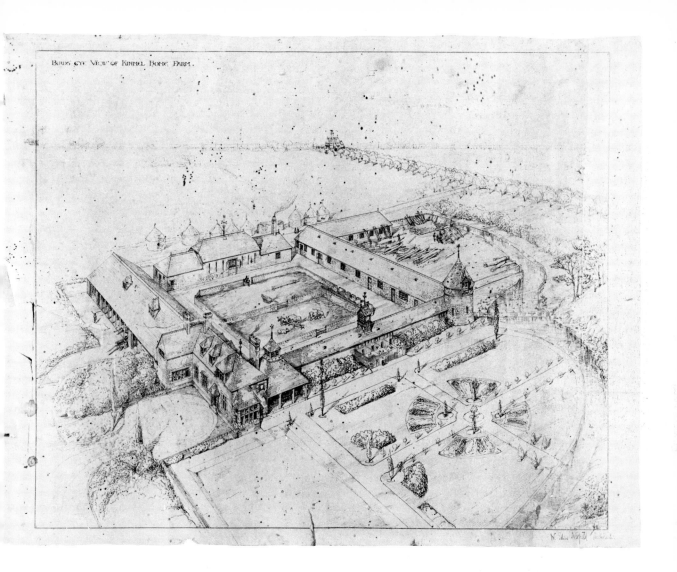

Hughes and by his son, who was created Lord Dinorben in 1831. The house was gutted in September 1841, and rebuilt, probably to the designs of Thomas Hopper. Lord Dinorben died in 1852, and his son only survived him for a few months. The heir was the first Lord Dinorben's nephew, Henry Robert Hughes (1827–1911).

H. R. Hughes inherited a large and not very interesting Greek Revival house, and was engaged in building at intervals for the next twenty-two years. His first venture was a new stable block. The house was built in a fine position on a platform cut into a gradually sloping hillside, with spacious views down to the coast and the Irish sea two miles away. The house followed the line of the slope; the new stables were built at right angles to it, on a higher level looking down across its forecourt. According to T. L. Donaldson's obituary memoir of William Burn, he designed 'additions at Kinmel Park' in 1855. An outline plan now at Plas Kinmel is captioned 'Plan showing Hall and New Stables at Kinmel, 1855'; and a survey isometric drawing, 'Kinmel Hall with new stables about 1856, by J. Crickmay, Archt.' There can be little doubt that the major and only surviving part of Burn's additions were the stables, for he was one of the very few Victorian architects who could have designed

319

302. W. E. Nesfield's drawing for the home farm.

them.[2] They are a capable, attractive and unusual exercise in the early eighteenth-century manner. Not surprisingly they have frequently been described as 'all that remains of the eighteenth-century house'.

H. R. Hughes's next architectural venture was of a different nature. In 1866 he built a new home farm and dairy on the other side of the main road and opposite the end of the main drive. His architect was William Eden Nesfield, at that time in partnership with Norman Shaw. Presumably he chose him because he had already done work of this kind: a farm and dairy at Shipley Hall in Derbyshire in 1860–1 and a dairy at Croxteth Hall in Lancashire in 1861. The energies expended by Georgian landowners on building follies and temples were often canalized by the Victorians in a direction which enabled them to combine usefulness with ornament. The home farm at Kinmel was perfectly designed to provide Victorian ladies with an afternoon's outing. It included a dairy, entered through a picturesque verandah, a series of enclosures for ornamental fowl, and a highly romantic medieval dove-cot. Dairy, fowls and dove-cot looked onto an elaborate garden, laid out by Nesfield's father; and along the boundary of the garden ducks paddled on a little stream. Nesfield drew a charming birds-eye view to show his client what it would all look like.[3] When the big house at Kinmel was sold in 1934 the Hughes family moved into the home farm, and renamed it Plas Kinmel. The garden side of the house was a good deal enlarged and altered; but the dove-cot remains and most of the entrance front is as Nesfield left it, though not as shown in the original drawing. It is a brilliant little design, a translation into stone of his Old English manner, combining with the

303. (above left) The home farm (now Plas Kinmel), 1866.
304. (above right) Kinmel Park. The Lodge (W. E. Nesfield, 1868).

greatest panache the diagonals of gables, roofs and chimney-breast with the horizontals of the porch eaves and the long verticals of the chimneystacks. The carved panels of arms and monograms and the Gothic ironwork of the porch are typical of the sensitive detail which Nesfield and Shaw delighted in designing, at least in their earlier days. Inside, some agreeable stained-glass panels of sunflowers and other plants favoured by the artistic of the day survive from Nesfield's work.

Understandably Nesfield was a success with his patron and in the next few years he worked his way up to the house. In 1868 he designed a small but sumptuous lodge on the main road between the house and the farm. Unlike the farm it is a classical building, but classical in a highly idiosyncratic way. It is reminiscent of Nesfield's 1866 lodge in Kew Gardens, but given a French flavour and a strong infusion of Nesfield's personal style of ornament. It is thickly encrusted with sunflowers: there is a literal flowerbed of them carved over the porch; elsewhere they appear sprouting out of the two-handled pots that Nesfield and Shaw favoured, and they feature in wrought iron on the balconies. Sunflowers and lilies had been put on the artistic map by Rossetti and William Morris in the 1850s, and through Nesfield and Shaw they became (sunflowers in particular) an ornamental cliché by the 1870s and 1880s. Another distinctive Shaw and Nesfield feature of the lodge is the use of the ornamental discs which they called 'pies'. The main source for this motif was probably Japanese porcelain and engravings, in which similar circular features are often incorporated in what seems, to Europeans, a very random way. Rossetti had started collecting Japanese blue china in about 1862 or 1863, and pies appeared

321

305. (above left) 'Pies' in the frieze above the staircase window.
306. (top right) 'Pies' in the hall panelling.
307. (bottom right) 'Pies' on a nineteenth-century Japanese dish.

embossed in the gilt frames of his pictures shortly afterwards. Nesfield also collected blue china;★ he and Shaw were using pies in their buildings from about 1865, but gradually gave them up in the 1870s. As their sketchbooks show, their sources were not only Japanese, for they had noticed the use of similar roundels both in medieval joinery and in Romanesque stone carving. Their pies are filled with motifs both European and Japanese, flowers, whorls and stars being especial favourites. Nesfield incised pies freely in the plasterwork of his lodges and cottages and used flower pies worked in lead by Forsyth along the parapet at Cloverley. In the lodge at Kinmel very large stone pies fill the whole frieze.

★ J. M. Brydon, 'William Eden Nesfield, 1835–88', *Architectural Review*, I (1897), p. 286. See also Simeon Solomon in *The Swinburne Letters* (ed. Cecil Y. Lang, New Haven, 1959–62), II, p. 32, writing *c.* Sept. 1869: 'His rooms are in Argyll Street near mine, and he has a very jolly collection of Persian, Indian, Greek and Japanese things that I should really like you to see.'

308. Kinmel Park. Looking through the forecourt gates to the house (W. E. Nesfield, 1868–74).

The widening of Nesfield's horizons in the later 1860s can conveniently be linked to Kinmel by a drawing in one of his sketchbooks in the R.I.B.A. showing the garden front of Hampton Court Palace. It is accompanied by a note: 'Went to Hampton Court May 25, 1868. Mr. Hughes, Mrs. Hughes and children. Mr. Hughes drove his drag—very pleasant day—hot.' The object of this agreeable summer excursion was presumably to get ideas for the remodelling of the big house at Kinmel. One immediate result was the wrought iron gates to the forecourt, which are dated 1868. They are clearly inspired by Tijou's wrought iron screens at Hampton Court, and contrast curiously with Nesfield's medieval ironwork at the home farm.

309. (top) The entrance front.

310. One end of the entrance front.

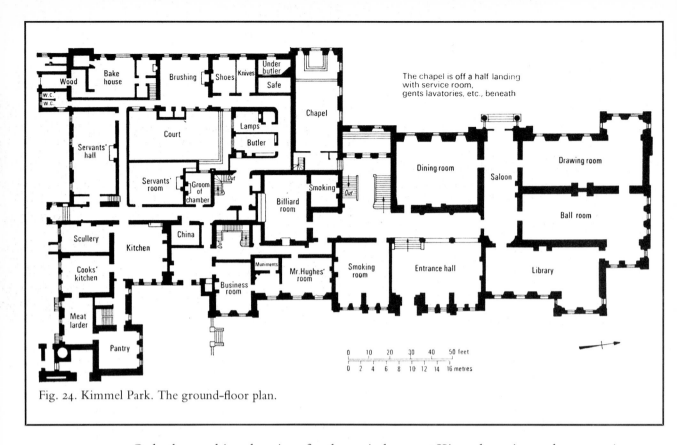

Fig. 24. Kimmel Park. The ground-floor plan.

Only the working drawings for the main house at Kinmel survive and are now in the Victoria and Albert Museum. The earliest is dated February 1871, and the building carries dates from 1871 to 1874. The interval between May 1868 and the beginning of 1871 was probably spent in working out a design. Nesfield's first attempt was not acceptable to his clients. According to his pupil J. M. Brydon, 'Nesfield's enthusiasm for this revived classic, of which he was a pioneer, ran away with him to such an extent that the first design for Kinmel, when it came to be estimated for, proved too costly, so it had to be reduced and done all over again, much to his regret.'[4] What was carried out in the end was not a rebuilding but a remodelling. Most of the old window openings remained undisturbed. A distinctive feature of the old house was that the porticoes on the entrance and garden fronts were not on the same axis. This feature was repeated by Nesfield, who replaced the porticoes with pavilions. His main additions consisted of superimposing high-pitched roofs to contain an extra storey, building out a two-bay extension to the north and a chapel and servants' wing on the garden side, and joining up the stables to the house.

The red-brick facades with their carved stone dressings, the great sash windows with thick glazing bars and many panes, the generosity of scale and element of formality all derive from Hampton Court. Because of these features the house was admired and sketched by neo-Georgian architects in the 1890s. But other features anchored it firmly to its own decade; instead of seeing it as an isolated forerunner of neo-Georgianism, it is more sensible to treat it as one of the pioneers of 'Queen Anne', with an extra touch of grandeur due to the scale on which it was built.

324

The plan makes clear how Nesfield was engaged, as Goodhart-Rendel put it, in 'a Gothic game played with classical counters'. Classical symmetry and axial design played no part in the shape and arrangement of the rooms. The main entrance leads into one corner of the entrance hall; the main rooms are grouped irregularly around an L-shaped corridor; the library, ballroom and drawing room are also L-shaped, with projections at one end in the Elizabethan manner. The entrance front of the main block is very grandly symmetrical, and so is a portion of the garden front; but the side front is not symmetrical at all; and seen as a whole both fronts form rambling, irregular and picturesque compositions diversified by such features as the little tower on the entrance front and the prominent mass of the chapel projecting into the garden. By joining the house onto the stables Nesfield accentuated this irregularity and produced an amazing backcloth of up-and-down and in-and-out buildings that unrolls itself for 500 feet or more. Even in the central entrance pavilion the high roof ends in one of Nesfield's distinctive chimneystacks, defiantly positioned off-centre to make it quite clear that Nesfield was prepared to ignore symmetry whenever it was inconvenient to him.

It is not surprising that Nesfield and the Hugheses were unable to stomach the level parapets of Hampton Court, and gave Kinmel a series of French mansard roofs, such as were being popularized all over England in the 1870s, although by architects with whom Nesfield can have felt no sympathy. These roofs, and the higher central pavilions on the two main fronts, give the house a strong French flavour, although there is nothing French in the detail. Nesfield's pies appear in lead on the parapet over the staircase windows, and are incised in the plaster cove of the servants' wing, and carved in the panelling of the hall where they float across the upper panels at random intervals in the Japanese manner. Their sporadic appearance in the main house suggest the last fling of a Bohemian turning respectable. There are, it is true, potted flowers incorporated everywhere in the decorations, but they merge imperceptibly into the rich sobriety of the detail, such as the flowers and musical

311. Kinmel Park. The house from the garden.

312. (facing page) Kinmel Park. The central pavilion.

313. A lobby off the upper corridor.

314. The staircase hall.

instruments delicately carved by James Forsyth[5] on the keystones of the larger windows.

The main entrance leads into the hall, separated from the central corridor by a parapet and screen of three richly marbled arches. Diagonally across the corridor from the hall is the main staircase, lit by huge, many-paned sash windows over what was originally a conservatory on the half-landing, and with Nesfield's potted flowers prominent in the plaster work of the ceiling. A separate flight of steps leads from the half-landing into the large but simply decorated chapel, and at the top of the main stairs is another broad corridor, with lobbies off it leading to the bedrooms. Hall, corridors and staircase flow into each other, with great spaciousness but no pomposity. Kinmel has not been a private house for many years, and it is difficult to judge how the main living rooms would have looked in the Hughes's time. The Victorians were in difficulties with these kind of rooms, because, with their emphasis on the virtues of domesticity, they had a prejudice against state rooms, and yet a house of the size of Kinmel seemed to demand something on a considerable scale. The big living rooms are very large but not grand, like ordinary living rooms inflated to six times the size; the compromise must have made them a little bleak when the house was still a private one.★

A serious fire at Kinmel in 1977, which gutted the chapel and much of the wing and upper floor, seemed likely to lead to the demolition of the whole house; but at the time of writing there are hopes that it will be restored.

★ 'The rebuilding of Kinmel caused some amusement and ridicule among Mr Hughes's less affluent neighbours. Many of them were amazed, and doubtless made jealous by his fancy antics, such as getting a man down from London to cut his hair, and having his luggage and domestic linen marked H. of K. An acquaintance of about forty years ago once described to me his being shown round Kinmel by H. of K. himself; a proud man and proud of his new creation. A footman accompanied them to open and close the doors. On entering a small room on the ground floor my friend asked Mr Hughes for what purpose it was used. He confessed that he did not know, and enquired of the footman, who, with due gravity, supplied the answer, "It is only used for ironing the newspapers, Sir." ' (Information from Lt-Col Carstairs Jones-Mortimer).

328

315. Kinmel Park. The upper corridor.

25. *Beauvale Lodge, Nottinghamshire*

BEAUVALE is an unusual example of a small Victorian house built for a very rich man. The explanation is that the seventh Earl Cowper, for whom it was built, already had more houses than he needed. In addition to the Cowper family house, Panshanger[1] in Hertfordshire, he had inherited Brocket in Hertfordshire and Melbourne in Derbyshire from his grandmother Lady Palmerston in 1869. His grandmother's estates included valuable coal-mines and several thousand acres in Nottinghamshire, on which there was no house. A conscientious Victorian landowner felt uneasy about being an absentee, and if he owned several properties liked to spend a portion of the year on each of them. For a couple like Lord and Lady Cowper, rich, cultivated and recently married, it must have been nice to be able to produce excellent moral reasons for having a little fun.

So they built a house, a romantic house in a romantic position, but by the standards of a Victorian nobleman so small that they cannot have intended spending more than occasional short visits there. In his letters Lord Cowper referred to it as 'my new cottage'.[2] His architect was Edward Godwin, whom he chose because of the gatehouse and walled garden which he had designed for his father-in-law Lord Northampton at Castle Ashby in 1867–8. The site was fixed at the end of October 1871; according to Lady Cowper the choice was made 'after driving about all over the country, by Francis upsetting the dog-cart in the middle of the wood and our deciding that it had thus been settled for us where it should be'.[3] They stayed in the house for the first time almost exactly two years later, and found it very comfortable and very pretty. A full set of drawings survives in the R.I.B.A., none of them dated. The house was illustrated and briefly described in the *Building News* of 3 and 10 July 1874, where it was stated that 'the cost has been under £6,000'.

Godwin was one of the most interesting and gifted of Victorian architects,[4] but in the early 1870s his fortunes were at a low ebb. His career had started brilliantly when

329

316. Beauvale Lodge, Eastwood, Nottinghamshire (E. W. Godwin, 1871–3). Godwin's drawing for the house.

he won the competition for Northampton Town Hall in 1861, at the age of twenty-eight. The Town Hall at Congleton (1864) was followed by two Irish country houses, Dromore Castle (1866–73) and Glenbegh Towers (1867–70). His connection with Glenbegh ended in row with his client that can have done his practice no good. From 1868 to 1875 he was living with Ellen Terry and rumours of his private life may have kept respectable clients away. Certainly during much of this period little or no new work came in. He supported himself by doing odd jobs for his friend William Burges, and by architectural journalism, especially in the *Building News*. His intelligent and irreverent articles are very readable but he did not suffer fools gladly, and his writing probably made him more enemies than friends. All in all the Beauvale commission must have been very welcome when it came in 1871, for it involved farms and a clergy house in the village as well as Beauvale itself. But it did not stop the bailiffs from clearing out his London house early in 1875.

In the 1860s Godwin and Burges were the Castor and Pollux of architecture, and

330

317. Beauvale Lodge. The house from the south.

there is a strong family likeness between their romantic, richly wrought and highly impracticable Gothic buildings. At Dromore Godwin used the excuse of protection from Fenian revolutionaries to design a heavily fortified castle that proved almost impossible even for an enthusiastic Victorian earl to live in. His enormous kitchen garden at Castle Ashby had crenellated medieval walls designed to enclose sleeping princesses rather than cabbages. At Beauvale he built that favourite of the Victorian romantic imagination, a house in the middle of a forest, with a high tower in which Rapunzel should have been spinning and singing and looking out over the tree tops. But by 1873 the architectural routes of Burges and Godwin were diverging. Burges remained loyal to his mediaeval vision; but Godwin, even though his more daringly adverturous houses for artists were still in the future was coming under the influence of Norman Shaw and the Old English style. Beauvale was designed at a turning point of his career; it has all the romanticism of his Irish castles, but is a house in which it is possible to think of oneself living with pleasure.

331

318. The house from the east.

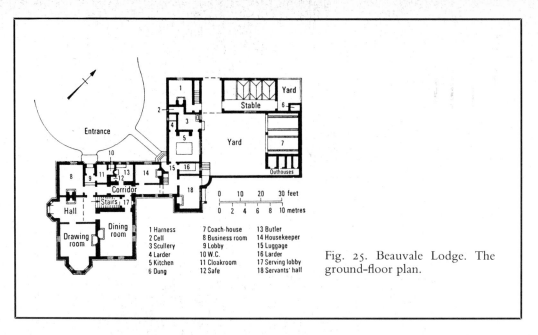

1 Harness
2 Cell
3 Scullery
4 Larder
5 Kitchen
6 Dung

7 Coach-house
8 Business room
9 Lobby
10 W.C.
11 Cloakroom
12 Safe

13 Butler
14 Housekeeper
15 Luggage
16 Larder
17 Serving lobby
18 Servants' hall

Fig. 25. Beauvale Lodge. The ground-floor plan.

The site was a virgin one, towards the top of a hill in a surviving stretch of Sherwood Forest. Rides were cut through the woods from the north, west and east, all trained on the house and its ninety-foot tower. The house mounts up in a spiral:[5] first a comparatively low entrance front, then the high main block of the house with steep climbing roofs, then the tower. The entrance front is extended to include a service wing and as a result the main impression is of the long horizontal line of the roof below the high vertical of the tower. From the garden side only the main block is visible and the effect is quite different: a high tight pyramidal composition in the 1860s manner with 60° roofs and gables and tall, ribbed chimneystacks building up to the pyramid roof of the tower. Perhaps the most attractive view is from the east, from where one sees the main block and the service wing together, with the full height of the tower at their junction. The house is mainly built of brick, but there is a good deal of tile-hanging and the first floor of the main block is half-timbered with brick infilling. The detail of the half-timbering is northern French rather than English. The roofs give the house a strong Gothic flavour, but elsewhere there is little Gothic detail and no elaborate ornament or carving. All the windows are square-headed, with wooden casements and a high proportion of leaded lights.

Inside, the house was grouped round a two-storey entrance hall, the top half of which has since been made into a bedroom. The staircase leads out of the hall. Throughout the house the detail is simple but original and full of thought. The timber barrel roof to the staircase and the bold, coved chimneypiece in the dining room are especially impressive. An upstairs bedroom has a brick chimneypiece so simple that it is hard to believe it dates from the 1870s; but there are said to be similar chimneypieces in Godwin farmhouses on the estate. There is an ingenious spiral wooden staircase in the upper storeys of the tower. The house was originally papered throughout with wallpapers designed by Godwin,[6] but they have long ago disappeared; there are some agreeable panels of stained glass in the upper lights of the hall and staircase windows.

332

319. (right) Beauvale Lodge. The staircase.

The steep roofs of Beauvale were used by Godwin for other buildings on the estate, with picturesque though not always practical results. They include the charming entrance lodge, which is like a Hansel and Gretel cottage, and the parson's house (now known as the Manse) in the adjacent hamlet of Moor Green. The latter has white painted sash windows, and very simple detail; it is moving towards Godwin's individual version of 'Queen Anne' and his strikingly original artists' houses of the late 1870s and 1880s. The design of the parson's house was published in the *Building News* of 6 March 1874. It caught the eye of Jonathan Carr, and the result was a commission for the first two prototype houses at Bedford Park.

When Lord Cowper died in 1905 the estate was sold to the father of the present owner, Sir William Barber, Bart.

334

320. The Lodge.

321. (top) Beauvale Lodge. Stained glass in the hall.

322. (above left) The dining-room fireplace.

323. (above right) An upstairs fireplace.

26. Castell Coch, Glamorganshire

THE FIRST view of Castell Coch leaves one in no doubt that it was the work of someone who knew what architecture (or at any rate the formal side of architecture) was about. 'Study the great broad masses, the strong unchamfered angles', William Burges once told a lecture hall of students;[1] and it is the clean lines, the strength, the directness, the simple yet varied forms of Castell Coch that make it so impressive. What could be better contrived than the contrast in height, roofs and shapes between the three towers on the entrance front? Or more inspired cubic geometry than the way the funnel chimneys melt into the towers, and the towers merge, in great curving loops, into the massive abutment of the lower walls. The whole building exudes a pride in the weight and power of stone: it has something of the precision and strength of a Doric column. With Burges vigour tends to become clumsiness, imagination to run wild into the grotesque; but in the exterior of Castell Coch he made no mistakes.

On 27 December 1872 Burges presented Lord Bute with a lavish folio report on the ruins of the medieval Castell Coch, an outlying portion of his Cardiff property a few miles out of the city up the valley of the River Taff.[2] After a detailed archaeological discussion he ended up: 'There are two courses open with regard to the ruins; one is to leave them as they are and the other to restore them so as to make

324. Castell Coch, nr Cardiff, Glamorganshire (William Burges, 1872–9). The castle from the approach.

XXVIII. Castell Coch, Glamorganshire. Looking through the woods to the castle.

CASTELL COCH

a Country residence for your occasional occupation in the summer.' A series of exquisite drawings illustrated the possibilities of the second alternative. Lord Bute's decision was easily predictable; it was not, however, until August 1875 that Estcourt, a Gloucester builder, contracted for the first part of the restoration work. The main structure was finished by the end of 1879; but the decoration of the interior had only got a little way when Burges died unexpectedly in April 1881.

He was succeeded as architect by his assistant, William Frame, whom he had originally taken on from his friend Prichard of Llandaff to help him at Cardiff Castle.[3] On occasion Frame consulted with J. S. Chapple, who for many years had been the chief assistant in Burges's London office.

Burges's cross-section in his report, showing the castle before and after restoration, make clear how much new work had to be done. The original ground plan could be worked out with accuracy, and Burges followed it exactly in his

339

XXIX. (left) Castell Coch, Glamorganshire. The drawing-room ceiling.

325. (above) Burges's first proposal for the castle, 1872.

rebuilding; but the restoration of the upper portions was almost completely conjectural. The restoration of a thirteenth-century castle and the working out of the minutest details of its defensive system appealed immensely to the archaeologist, the artist and the schoolboy in Burges. None the less, what had stood there in the fourteenth century must have looked very different from what Burges put back in the nineteenth. In the first place the castle was originally built of undressed stone with occasional ashlar dressings, and would not have had the tremendous precision and power of the buildings as re-erected by Burges. Secondly, the proportions would almost certainly have been lower and squatter, with towers of approximately equal height. Finally the existing skyline, with its chimneys and above all its three conical roofs is archaeologically very dubious—the towers probably had roofs of a low pitch rising scarcely, if at all, above the parapet. Burges supported his roofs with a considerable body of examples of doubtful validity; the truth was that he wanted them for their architectural effect.[4]

The southern portion of the castle is built directly on an outcrop of rock, with massive stone abutments to hold up the towers; the lower parts of these abutments are of the red stone of which the whole castle was originally built (Castell Coch means the Red Castle), but above this the grey limestone which Burges used for the restoration work takes over. On this side the ground falls steeply down into the river valley, relatively narrow at this point and effectively dominated by the castle. But to the north the castle faces onto a shelf in the hillside. Here it is defended by a deep ditch; as one comes up the approach road, through beech woods carpeted with wild garlic in the summer, one's first impression is of the three eastern towers, and the long tongue of the wooden bridge crossing the ditch and vanishing into the entrance archway. Above this is a painted statue of the Virgin and Child, carved in 1878 by Fucigna—an Italian who did other work for Burges, and carved the elaborate ornamental stonework of the Royal Holloway College at Egham.

Through the archway (gleefully equipped by Burges with drawbridge, portcullis and holes for boiling oil) one comes into the courtyard, a little claustrophobic and perhaps too self-consciously picturesque after the grandeur of the exterior. To the right is the well tower—still with its medieval well, and dungeon in the basement,

340

326. Castell Coch. The castle from the valley.

but without the chapel that it was planned to build up in the roof. Ahead is the curving gallery and arcade of the curtain wall, ending in the kitchen tower, and to the left are the stairs leading up to the main apartments.

These form a sequence of four, each with a different type of roof and a different character. The roofs were designed by Burges and the idea of a sequence of contrasting rooms was probably his; but most of the decoration was carried out after his death, on the basis of rough sketches, which showed no details. The architect and craftsmen had all worked under him and tried with self-effacing enthusiasm to finish the work in the same spirit; but the exuberance and the overcrowding, the heaviness and the jokes of his Cardiff Castle interiors were considerably toned down. All the rooms are very dark, and the furniture is impressive rather than comfortable; but unlike Cardiff the building was never intended to be seriously lived in.

The hall is the most austere of the four rooms; the dim light enables one to concentrate on the simple and massive outlines of the cedarwood roof and the furniture, and to gloss over the anaemic wall paintings, executed by Campbell and Smith in 1878, and the statue of King David on the fireplace hood, which is one of Thomas Nicholls's less happy works. Through the hall is the drawing room. Here, in contrast to the comparative reticence of the hall, is a rich world of gold and blue, of carved butterflies and painted animals and flowers. The dominant feature is the vault, suspended over the room like an immense glittering starfish, or a fireworks

341

327. The view from the bedroom into the courtyard.

329. Lord Bute's bedroom.

display, with the gilded flickering rays of the sun like a Catherine-wheel in the centre, and the ribs falling down from it in lines of gold; filled with the movement of the wings of butterflies, and of flying birds, and with stars twinkling between them on a background of rich and deep blue. The vault represents the sky; below the gallery one is back on earth, the birds and butterflies are still there but they are now fluttering and settling amongst the branches of trees and gigantic hollyhocks and sunflowers, and have been joined by foxes, monkeys, squirrels and other animals: lower still there is dark green panelling, with panels of flowers painted on a rich gold ground. The whole scene is surveyed by the three Fates, spinning and clipping their thread in the alcove over the fireplace.

Around October 1880 Burges's notebooks record payments to Nicholls for carving in the drawing room, which probably included the butterflies and other details of the vault: the three Fates were probably executed after Burges's death, for they were certainly not hauled into position until October 1886. The panelling and painting of the room was carried out in 1886 and 1887; the painting, as elsewhere in the castle, was executed by the firm of Campbell and Smith. The splendid grate (by Hart, Son, Peard and Co.) and the equally fine tiles (by Simpson and Sons) had been made, but probably not fixed, before Burges died.

Off the drawing room one can inspect the formidable machinery of the drawbridge and portcullis, still in perfect working order, and then go on up the corkscrew stairs to Lord Bute's bedroom, above the entrance gate. This was the last room to be decorated: Campbell and Smith were painting it in 1888 and Nicholls

328. (left) Castell Coch. The hall.

probably carved the chimneypiece, in the same year or a little before. The roof is a massive open timber one; the fireplace is equally massive, as is the furniture, the joinery of the window, and of the balcony outside it; although the window is larger than elsewhere in the castle (it faces into the courtyard, so defensively this makes sense) the room is a dark one. Frame, incidentally, instructed Campbell and Smith to 'treat the roof like the Banqueting Hall somewhat but rather more elaborate'; this is one of the pieces of evidence to show that Burges himself had made no designs for these kinds of details.

More corkscrew stairs lead up to Lady Bute's bedroom at the top of the tower; and here the door shuts behind one and one is transferred to a remote and separate existence; for the roundness of the room and the curved dome of the roof have this quality of creating a little independent world. Subdued light seeps through the windows, and although through them one has a vista of Welsh valley and hill with Cardiff and the sea in the distance, their small size and the great thickness of the walls makes all this seem remote and unreal, a Lady of Shalott prospect; the reality momentarily seems inside; the fragmented dull gold, green and red of the decoration, the extraordinary furniture, the animals and foliage in the roof, the great bed with its glittering crystal balls, have an odd intense life of their own.

But although the shape of the room and probably the conception of the decoration is due to Burges, the execution dates for the most part from well after his death.[5] Hart, Son, Peard and Co. delivered the grate early in 1881 and Nicholls was

344

330. (above left) Castell Coch. Lady Bute's bedroom.

331. (above right) The drawing room.

doing some unspecified carving at the end of 1880; but he did not carve the birds and foliage of the corbels or the angel and shield on the fireplace until 1887; on 18 July Frame wrote to Nicholls asking him whether he thought a heart-shaped shield 'would be correct, or would Mr. Burges have done it? I think a shield similar to what was upon his rough drawing had better be used'. Campbell and Smith carried out the painting in 1887–8.

The Department of the Environment own the designs for the dressing table and washstand, signed John S. Chapple, architect, 7 John Street, Adelphi, November 1891. The two pieces are very much in the Burges tradition, and resemble the castellated fireplaces in the Banqueting Hall at Cardiff Castle and in the library of his own house in Melbury Road, Kensington. The two towers of the washstand contain tanks for water, which is piped to the central tap, made in the shape of a fish; from here it spouts into the china basin, also decorated with fishes. Like the rest of the furniture in the castle these pieces were probably made in the furniture and joinery workshop[6] which Lord Bute set up in Cardiff; this workshop was continued by the next Marquess and did not close down until about 1929.★

★ In 1875 Lord Bute planted a vineyard at Castell Coch, from which wine was produced and sold commercially for the next forty-five years. 'The marquess frequently had his wine served at his table, and used to ask his guests their opinion of it. "Well now, Lord Bute", said Sir Herbert Maxwell on one occasion, "it is what I should call an interesting wine". "I wonder what Sir Herbert exactly meant", remarked Lord Bute thoughtfully some time later' (*Western Mail*, 16 Nov. 1929).

332. Lady Bute's wash stand, designed by John Chapple, 1891.

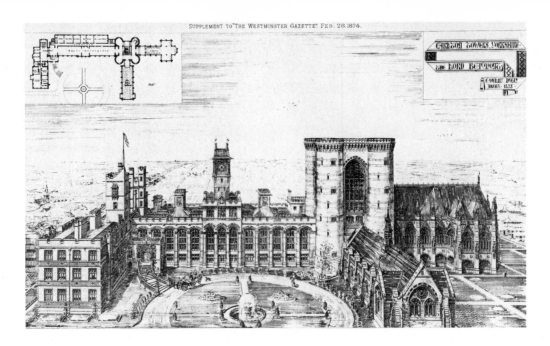

27. Carlton Towers, Yorkshire

IN SPITE of appearances, the Victorianism of Carlton Towers is only skin deep. Almost everything that is there today was there, though without the amazing trimmings, by the end of the eighteenth century, as comparison with a drawing of that date makes clear. The property at Carlton had gone by descent since the Norman Conquest, first to the Bruces and then to the Stapletons, dashing medieval warriors who produced some of the first Knights of the Garter.[1] The three-storey block shown on the left of the drawing was built by Elizabeth Stapleton, granddaughter of Bess of Hardwick, in about 1615. The long wing out to the right was added in the 1770s to contain a chapel, priest's lodgings and stables. The Stapletons had remained devout Catholics, and had suffered for it in the difficult years of the sixteenth and seventeenth centuries.

In 1795 Thomas Stapleton laid claim to the barony of Beaumont, a barony by writ created in 1309 and inheritable through the female line. The claim was allowed in 1840, in favour of his great-nephew Miles Thomas Stapleton. He celebrated his promotion to a Gothic peerage by covering his house with anaemic Gothic trimmings, and by giving up his ancestral religion, dismantling the chapel and bringing up his children in the Church of England.

He died in 1854, when his eldest son Henry was only six. The latter came of age in 1869 and became a Catholic in the same year, the year after the multi-millionaire Lord Bute had gone the same way. Manning had just succeeded Wiseman, and the Victorian Catholic revival was at its height. For the young Lord Beaumont full coffers after a long minority, pride in his ancestors, an enthusiastic return to their religion and contempt for his father's feeble Gothic were all inducements for building; an amazing design by the Catholic architect E. W. Pugin, with a huge Baron's hall, an even huger chapel, and towers, turrets and coats of arms innumerable was the result.

346

333. Carlton Towers, nr Goole, Yorkshire (E. W. Pugin, 1873–5; J. F. Bentley, 1875–7). Pugin's proposals for Carlton Towers, 1873. The right half was never built.

334. The house in the late eighteenth century.

Although the design was far beyond Lord Beaumont's means, this would have been no deterrent either to him or to Pugin. They were both, as their careers showed, fond of flamboyant gestures. Edward Welby Pugin took on his father's practice when he was only seventeen and, like his father, died at the age of forty-one after an equally hectic career.[2] At one time he was one of the most successful architects in England with an income of £8,000 a year. Apart from innumerable works in England, he built a cathedral, churches and convents in Ireland, a church and a big country house in Belgium and an uninvestigated number of buildings in America. He was warm-hearted and generous, but had all the disadvantages of an impulsive temperament: an uncontrollable temper, a passion for rows and litigation and a complete lack of prudence. The money that rolled in from fees rolled out again in lawsuits and speculation. In 1872 his disastrous investment in the Granville Hotel at Ramsgate—which he built and owned—forced him into liquidation with liabilities of nearly £200,000. In the last few years of his life he appeared so often in the courts that he became almost a music-hall figure. He died of heart failure in 1875, worn out by rage and lawsuits, and the poor of Ramsgate followed his coffin in crowds, strewing the hearse with flowers.*

★ 'On my tomb I should like written "Here lies a man of many miseries".' Remark quoted in his obituary in the *Builder*.

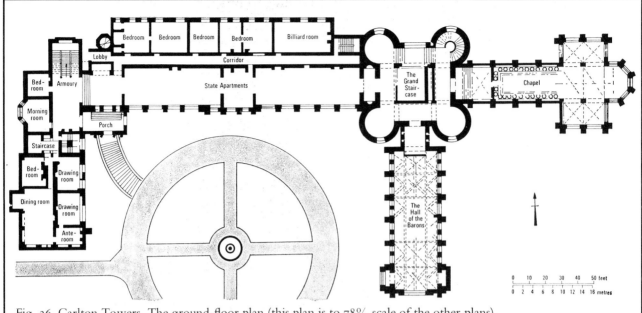

Fig. 26. Carlton Towers. The ground-floor plan (this plan is to 78% scale of the other plans).

Edward Pugin's architecture reflects his character, often in its least attractive aspects. One of his obituaries described his buildings as 'free, bold, vigorous conceptions'.[3] There is some truth in this, but at their worst they can also be ill digested, insensitive and bellicose. In his buildings as in his quarrels he never knew when to stop. Like his father he was an incredibly fast and prolific designer, but the quality both of his and his father's work suffered as a result. There is such a curious similarity between their two lives as to suggest that Edward was deliberately aiming to continue the Pugin legend. The architectural results, however, had little in common, as the juxtaposition of their work at Scarisbrick made clear. Edward Pugin's Gothic moved with the current of taste towards chunkiness, vigour and muscularity; and there was an element of extravagance verging on megalomania in his character that his father was without. Lord Beaumont[4] was a patron more likely to encourage than restrain his excesses. He was an unsatisfactory creature, who left little behind him except Carlton Towers, debts and an atmosphere of ineffective melodrama. In 1873–4, while Pugin was at work, he was fighting in the army of the pretender Don Carlos in Spain; by 1875 he was living in West Kensington, building speculative housing[5] and grandiloquently calling himself 'Chargé d'Affaires, Spéciel et Officieux of H.M. Charles VII'.

Early, comparatively unambitious designs by Pugin survive at Carlton, dated December 1871. They were rejected in favour of a design dated 1873, and published in the *Building News* for 20 February 1874. The extravagant right-hand portion of the design, which was for new buildings, was never carried out. The left-hand half only involved the recasting of the existing house, and was carried out exactly as shown in the drawing. The old facades were of brick, which Pugin covered with a cement facing scored with remorseless horizontal grooving. Some of the new embellishments—notably the corbelled-out arcading on the east wing, the elaborate

348

entrance porch and the upper stage of the clock tower are of stone, but the dominant element in the colouring remains huge expanses of dun-coloured cement.

Even without the staircase tower, Pugin's work more than justified the house's ensuing change of name from Carlton Hall to Carlton Towers. He added three towers, and any number of turrets. The stone staircase attached to the Jacobean building was carried up three storeys and finished off with crazy stepping at one corner to support a flagstaff. Above the centre of the east wing the large plain clock tower added by the eighth Lord Beaumont was replaced by one far more elaborate ending at the skyline with four Stapleton talbots and with the Stapleton motto, *Mieux sera*, carved round the parapet. The turrets to either side of this are disguised chimneystacks. A third tower was built at the north-west corner to contain the front staircase. If one looks at the house from the west one gets all three towers in one gulp. It is a disturbing experience.

Pugin, like many of his contemporaries, was never a copyist and used genuine Gothic examples in rather the same buccaneering spirit as the Elizabethans had used Renaissance ones. The silhouette of the clock tower at Carlton is like nothing from

349

335. Carlton Towers. The clock tower from the roof.

338. The staircase tower and clock tower.   339. The porch.

the Middle Ages, but unmistakably high-Victorian. The detailing of the staircase tower, with its two flights of lancet windows and brutally crinkled corbels, is even more original. Touches like these stop one from dismissing Edward Pugin as merely a loud-mouthed architect, though he is certainly not an attractive one. The lush carving of the front entrance porch is more obviously derivative; like similar detailing at Scarisbrick, it must be the result of Pugin's Belgian commissions, for it is inspired by the late Gothic of the Low Countries and northern France. But this porch, and the great flight of steps leading up to it, have real swagger. Huge S's and the drunken date 1875 are cunningly introduced into the luscious and deeply undercut foliage; and above the windows lively little dragons open their mouths at each other. Inside is an entrance vestibule, with a flight of marble steps leading up to a row of elephantine piers.

Edward Pugin died suddenly on 4 June 1875. Some time at the beginning of 1875 he and Lord Beaumont must have fallen out[6], for the earliest of a series of designs by John Francis Bentley for the interior of Carlton is dated 22 March. Bentley and Pugin were then the rising and falling stars among Catholic architects. One can imagine the former giving a slight frown of distaste as he first looked at Pugin's extraordinary facades. He was a shy and reserved man, quite without Pugin's aggressiveness or showmanship; and stylistically, like many Gothic-revival architects of the time, he was reacting against the heavy-footed originality of the high-Victorians in favour of something more scholarly and more refined.

351

336. (upper left) Carlton Towers. The three towers.

337. (left) The entrance front.

340. Carlton Towers. The entrance hall.

His work at Carlton was mainly carried out in 1875–7 and was confined to decorating and furnishing rooms that were already there. The principal of these were the state apartments in the east wing. They were basically the same as the chapel, sacristy and 'overstables' room into which the wing had been divided when it was built in the 1770s; the chapel had been secularized in 1842 and the rooms now became the Venetian drawing room, card room and picture gallery. Joining them to the old wing of the house was a large galleried space known as the armoury, with a staircase leading off it. Bentley also decorated a hall, chapel and study in the old wing and converted the upstairs drawing room into a library. In the range behind the state apartments (probably originally built in 1844) he furnished the bedrooms and fitted up a large and elaborately decorated billiard room, which has since been subdivided.

Bentley's experience of domestic work had been confined to relatively small jobs—a house in Notting Hill, two in Sydenham and additions and alterations to a house in Sussex for the poet Coventry Patmore. Otherwise most of his work had consisted of chapels, altarpieces and other fittings for Catholic churches. He had done a great deal in this field and gained a reputation for high standards of design and craftsmanship and loving attention to detail. At Carlton he applied the same standards to the decoration of a large country house. The admirable biography by his daughter, Mrs de l'Hôpital,[7] describes the time and trouble he spent on the designs, which included curtains, wallpaper and furniture. Several rolls of beautiful detail drawings are now at Carlton, and many more must have been destroyed. He asked for the same high standards from his craftsman. The woodwork is by J. Erskine Knox, who did much work for Bentley; the paintings in the Venetian drawing room are by N. H. J. Westlake whose firm, Lavers, Barraud and Westlake, made the stained glass; the glittering fenders and grates are by Longden and Co.; many of the fireplace tiles were supplied by William de Morgan. Mrs de L'Hôpital does not record if it was also Longden and Co. who made the sumptuous chandeliers that enfilade through the state rooms. The heraldry was worked out by General de Havilland,★ a Carlist friend of Lord Beaumont and Bentley, who enjoyed a field day amongst the riches of the Stapleton family tree.

The most splendid room is the Venetian drawing room, the first of the three state rooms. Its name is said to have come from a set of Venetian glass, which Bentley found at Carlton and put on display in the drawing room cupboards. The panelling was painted by Westlake in sympathy, with characters from the *Merchant of Venice*. But the dominant features of the room are the walls, which are of plaster, richly stamped and gilded to give the effect of leather, and the monumental heraldic chimneypiece, with a huge coat of arms surmounted by the Stapleton Turk's head. The contours of the chimneypiece are reminiscent of those designed by William Burges; it is worth remembering that Bentley, before he set up on his own, had been in the office of Burges's old partner, Henry Clutton. In their minute attention to detail and elaborate all-over decoration the Carlton state rooms are akin to the even more splendid ones designed by Burges for Lord Bute at Cardiff; the decoration of the two was going on at the same time, and as Lord Bute and Beaumont were exact contemporaries, and were converted to Catholicism in successive years, one suspects that Carlton was decorated in emulation of Cardiff. But Bentley's detailing is less ponderous than Burges's, though also less fanciful and inventive; and his colouring tends to be cooler. The walls of the Venetian drawing room are grey, dun-colour and gold; the ceiling is predominantly green, gold and pink. Bentley designed curtains to match, made of green and terracotta silk velvet. The room's least successful feature is the black panelling, which is too low for the scale of the room and out of key with the rest of the colour scheme.[8] In the other two rooms Bentley followed the trend of the 1870s and used a light brown oak, with more attractive results. The card room, though much smaller, is as richly decorated as the Venetian drawing room; the huge picture gallery is simpler (the money was probably running out), with two massive chimneypieces of Portland stone. These three rooms are joined together by double doors of superb craftsmanship. When they are opened one gets a vista of 147 feet from end to end; if the double doors into the armoury are opened too the vista is extended to 195 feet. Yet conscientious, competent and splendid though these great rooms are, they are rather depressing to be in. It is partly, perhaps, because Bentley was more at home as a church than a country house architect; partly because the kind of life which the rooms were built to cater for only survived their completion by a few decades, and they are now only very occasionally used. The most successful Bentley interior at Carlton is the room known as the armoury. It is in fact a series of different spaces all running into each other, with intriguing vistas up and down flights of steps, through into Pugin's entrance vestibule or up into the gallery. The basic plan is due to Pugin, and is shown

★ 'Huge and hideous, and a general in the Carlist, not the English army.' Information from Mrs de l'Hôpital.

in his design. But the decoration is all Bentley's; by putting stained glass into the windows he filled the whole complex of spaces with a subdued and glowing light in which all the various elements of the decoration merge into a rich and evocatively Victorian whole. Moreover these spaces, unlike the state rooms, have always been in constant use, for the lines of communication to and from the different parts of the house pass through them.[9]

In 1870 Lord Beaumont dashed off to serve on the staff of the Prussian Crown Prince in the Franco–Prussian war. In the Zulu war of 1879 he was briefly attached to the British army and fought at the Battle of Ulundi. These escapades were combined with financial speculation encouraged by a mysterious Mr Campbell. By 1879 the estate was saddled with a debt of nearly £250,000, and Lord Beaumont went to live abroad. The agricultural depression cannot have helped his finances. In 1888 he married a cheerful hunting girl, Violet Wootton Isaacson, with a fortune of £120,000, derived from 'Madame Elise', a fashionable dress shop in Regent Street. The marriage was not a success, and his wife soon ceased to let her fortune be used to stave off her husband's creditors. Most of the estate was sold in 1888–9. Lord Beaumont died childless in 1892, aged forty-three; he was succeeded by a much more sensible brother, whose marriage to an heiress saved the house and what remained of the land from going the same way as the rest of the estate.

354

341. (above) The armoury.

XXX. (right) Carlton Towers, Yorkshire. The Venetian drawing room (J. F. Bentley, c. 1875).

XXXI. (above) Ken Hill, Norfolk (J. J. Stevenson, 1879-80). The house from across the park.

XXXII. (right) Wightwick Manor, Staffordshire (Edward Ould, 1887-93). The bay window in the great parlour.

28. Adcote, Shropshire

SHAW's early houses were not built for very rich patrons. Willesley, Glen Andred and Grim's Dyke were for Academy artists; the Corner House at Shortlands was for a novelist; although Leys Wood was for a successful businessman, it was only a moderately large house with little land attached. Cragside was his first country house proper, and the first house built for a client with a great deal of money. But Cragside seems to have been originally envisaged as a moderate enlargement of a shooting lodge; it started to grow outrageously almost at once, but it remained an exercise in the Leys Wood manner. In the later 1870s Shaw had four more big country house commissions: Pierrepont (1876), Adcote (1876), Flete (1878) and Greenham (1878). In these houses he worked out a weightier and more sober version of his Old English style. The Victorians had a nice sense of hierarchy; these were what the building magazines distinguished as 'mansions' rather than 'residences' or mere 'houses'. Mansions had to have a certain importance; the quaintness and farmhouse tricks of the first Old English houses were not appropriate.

The working drawings for Adcote are dated 1876[1] and the design was exhibited in the Royal Academy in 1879. The client was Mrs Rebecca Darby, who like many of Shaw's richer clients came from an industrialist background, though in her case it was a long-established one. Her husband had been one of the Coalbrookdale Darbys, the pioneers of iron manufacture; she herself was a Miller Christy, of a family who had made a fortune as hatters. She had a young son being educated at Eton, and a clutch of bachelor brothers who lived with her at Adcote.

XXXIII. (left) Standen, Sussex (Philip Webb, 1891–4). The garden front.

342. (above) Adcote, nr Shrewsbury, Shropshire (R. Norman Shaw, 1876–81). The house from the garden.

The seven years between Cragside and Adcote had made a big difference. The exuberance and freshness of Cragside have gone, but so have the clumsiness. At Adcote Shaw is the maestro in complete control, who knows just what he is capable of and never puts a foot wrong. The starting point for the design, as with many of Shaw's houses, is the idea of a country house built at several periods: at Adcote a house where a medieval great hall has been added to in the sixteenth century. Shaw may even have had a particular house in mind, for a similar combination is found at Southwick Hall in Northamptonshire, which he had sketched in the 1850s.[2] But Shaw, unlike Devey, had a long way to go from this initial starting point. He had no desire to deceive the spectator into thinking that Adcote was really an old house. The idea of haphazard growth suggested a method of composition which he then worked up into something much tauter and more controlled, a conscious and carefully calculated work of art.

Adcote stands in the middle of a flat and not very interesting park and seems to have been designed to be seen from the enclosures around it more than from the distance. To get an idea of the structure of the house it is best to go down on the great lawn to the south. From there, rising above a hedge and frieze of hollyhocks, one sees four gables in a row; these correspond at ground-floor level to the entrance block

361

343. (left) Adcote. The hall bay window.

344. (above) The entrance front.

(billiard room, hall and business room), the great hall, the drawing room and the library and dining room. The way the four units overlap and interlock internally, and are combined and contrasted on the exterior, is a wonderful exhibition of Shaw's skill. The facade of the house advances to the hall gable and then retreats again; the stroke of genius is the contrast between the bold 60° gable of the hall and the shallow gable next door to it. The two gables at either end are both surmounted by splendid examples of Shaw's typical long drawn out chimneystacks, but their treatment is different; at the entrance end the gable virtually is the chimneystack which projects boldly to provide space internally for inglenooks on the ground and first floors; the right-hand chimneystack melts gradually into the wall.

The tile-hanging and half-timbering of Shaw's first Old English manner have disappeared, except for one half-timbered gable inconspicuously tucked away on the north front. The chimneystacks are of brick, with the brick drawn down into the stone gables. But Adcote is predominantly a stone house, of superb local limestone superbly used. Shaw's feeling for stone is shown to the greatest advantage, inside and out, in the hall, which is deservedly one of his best-known pieces of design. The device of the three buttresses at the gable end had already been used at Grim's Dyke

362

345. Adcote. The great hall in 1909.

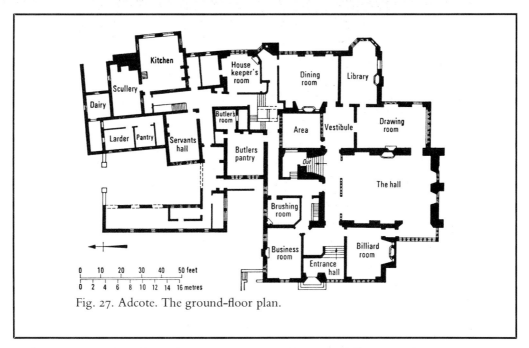

Fig. 27. Adcote. The ground-floor plan.

and Pierrepont; but the scale of the ones at Adcote, and their combination with the high rectangular cage of stone and glass adjoining produces a far more powerful effect than in any of Shaw's previous domestic work.

There was probably no other architect in England at the time who could have changed a rhythm of three to a rhythm of four with such apparently effortless competence as Shaw achieved in the entrance front. He seems to have done it as much for the hell of it as for any functional reason, in a kind of you-think-I-can't-do-it-but-I-can spirit. But there was a certain practical advantage. The three gables corresponded to the bedrooms on the top floor; on the ground floor the need for an entrance and for windows to the hall, business room and billiard room suggested a division into four; the first-floor rhythm of oriel, window, oriel, window, makes the transition between them. A small subtlety is the way the upper floors slightly overhang the lower, and the oriels overhang still further, giving the whole front a slight and almost imperceptible sense of spring.

The front door is set, probably deliberately, off the axis of the central corridor, so that one does not see down it until one has walked diagonally across the entrance hall and climbed a flight of steps. To the right one then looks through a screen into the great hall, with its massive hooded stone fireplace, three great stone arches supporting the roof,[3] and flood of light coming through the great bay window at the far end. A stone staircase leads under a balcony to the gallery; as one climbs it there is a vista in chiaroscuro along the enfilading arches of the hall. Hall, staircase and gallery form a powerful and vigorous combination. But the hall has travelled a long way from Shaw's more informal hall–living rooms. It may have been useful for dances but, even though old Country Life photographs show what appears to be a tea-table in the bay window, one cannot visualize anyone ever sitting in it with pleasure; its presence must have cast a certain chill on the house when it was still a private one. Indeed it is better suited for a school, and its existence was one of the main inducements for the school to buy the house.

At the end of the passage is a lobby leading to the library, drawing room and dining room. The dining room is very much in the Cragside manner, panelled, with a built-in dresser, and a big stone-faced inglenook. The latter has Morris windows and the lower half is lined with delightful de Morgan tiles. It is shallower even than the Cragside one and is for effect rather than for sitting in. In contrast the inglenook in the billiard room, though much less ambitious, is clearly designed for use. In the bedrooms there are a variety of very pleasing chimneypieces in the Queen Anne manner. But there are stretches of the interior where one feels that Shaw's attention was beginning to wander—rather too common a characteristic of his later houses. Even so the house remains a masterpiece. It is a cold masterpiece; there is a slight sense of unreality about it, and one has the uneasy foreknowledge that this kind of brilliance is heading down a dead end, and will lead to the slick and sterile competence of millionaire Elizabethan houses of the 1920s. But it is still a masterpiece.[4]

346. (facing page) Adcote. Looking along the hall roof from the staircase landing.

347. (left) A bedroom chimneypiece.

348. (below) The dining room.

29. Ken Hill, Norfolk

THE GREENS of Ken Hill are an interesting example of an industrialist family who like many similar families bought and built with a perception above the average. Their fortunes were established by Edward Green, father of the Edward Green who bought Ken Hill.★ He was an inventive man, who had the ingenious idea of catching and recirculating the previously wasted heat from steam boilers. He patented his invention and put it on the market as 'Green's Economizer'. The Economizer dramatically cut the costs of the factories that installed it, and increasing numbers did so through the nineteenth and into the twentieth centuries. The business grew, the works in Wakefield grew and the family fortune grew with them. The younger Edward Green (1831–1923) was an inventor and a shrewd and energetic businessman like his father. In the 1850s a sales office was opened in Manchester and he was put in charge of it. While living in Manchester he met and married (in 1858) his wife, Mary Lycett.

The elder Edward Green was a tough and single-minded Yorkshireman who dedicated all his energies to the business and expected his son to do the same. When he died in 1865 Edward Green the younger found himself in sole command of a business that brought him a large and increasing income and the means to adventure into less constricted spheres. In the same year he took a lease of Heath Old Hall, an historic Elizabethan house a mile or two outside Wakefield. According to his wife, 'When we took it, ivy grew inside, and owls made their nests in what are now guest

★ For Edward Green and the firm of E. Green and Son, see *Waste Not* (London, 1956), a history published for the firm, with a foreword by Simon Green. 'Waste not' is the family motto.

349. Ken Hill, Snettisham, Norfolk (J. J. Stevenson, 1879–80). The house from the park.

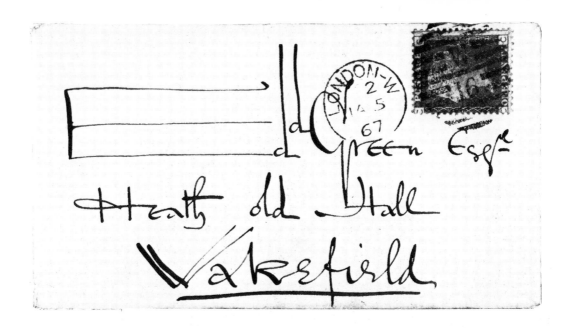

chambers.' During the next few years the house was restored, decorated and furnished. The architect in charge was Thomas Jeckell, a member of the most advanced and interesting coterie of artists then at work in London.

Jeckell★ was at no stage of his life widely known, and it is at first sight mysterious that he should have been employed by the Greens, who at this period had no base in London. The connecting link was almost certainly another artist largely forgotten today, Thomas Armstrong (1832–1911). In his autobiography[1] Armstrong refers to the 'Edward Greens, old North Country Friends'. As Armstrong was a Manchester man it is reasonable to assume that the friendship dated from the Greens' Manchester days. In 1857 Armstrong went to study painting in Paris, where he made friends with George du Maurier and Whistler, and shared in the life later recreated by du Maurier in *Trilby*. In the 1860s the group were back in London, cheerful, struggling young artists with their way to make. Their circle was joined by, amongst others, Tom Jeckell, whom du Maurier had known before he went to Paris, and whom Armstrong describes as 'a very clever architect . . . well known to and much liked by the "Paris Gang" when in London'. Armstrong was the most generous and helpful of men, always ready to put in a good word for anybody, and almost certainly it was he who suggested to the Greens that they employ Jeckell.

Jeckell was an oddity. He was a little bald man who went round in knee-breeches and buckle shoes; he was 'looked upon as peculiar'. He practised as an architect and designer, alternating between Norwich and London. In Norfolk he built churches and chapels which, apart from a few details, are indistinguishable from a thousand other provincial Victorian buildings, and designed ironwork of superb quality for the Norwich firm of Barnard, Bishop and Barnard. His first important work for them was a massive set of gates, exhibited at the International Exhibition of 1862; these were bought by the gentry of Norfolk as a wedding present for the Prince and

★ For Jeckell (or as he liked to improve the spelling, Jeckyll) see Peter Ferriday, 'The Peacock Room', *Architectural Review*, June 1959, pp. 407–14. His handwriting is a nice example of the *zeitgeist*, with exaggerated horizontals and verticals like a Norman Shaw design.

367

350. Jeckell writes to Green.

Princess of Wales and erected at Sandringham. Some years later Jeckell designed a series of cast iron grates which were sold commercially by the same firm and became very fashionable in certain circles: to instal a Jeckell grate in the 1870s showed that one was 'artistic'.[2] But his *chef d'oeuvre* for the firm was the cast iron pavilion sent to the Philadelphia Exhibition of 1876. This amazing creation, surrounded by a railing of sunflowers and enriched with delicate oriental reliefs and an inventive wealth of incised and interweaving patterns, was re-erected by Norwich Corporation in Chapel Fields, but neglected by their successors, and demolished some years ago.

A leather-bound volume at Ken Hill is inscribed in gold letters 'Designs by T. Jeckyll' and contains a complete set of contemporary photographs of the Philadelphia Pavilion. Filed loose in the book is a small collection of sketches, letters and envelopes from Jeckell, all connected with his work for the Green family. In 1889 Lady Green (as she had become) published a monograph on Heath.[3] It has, unfortunately, nothing detailed to say about the work done in furnishing and decorating the house. But an engraving of the 'Oak Parlour' shows the round table and Jacobean dresser now in the dining room at Ken Hill. There is little reason to doubt that all the furniture in the Ken Hill dining room was designed by Jeckell, the remnant of a much larger collection designed for Heath Old Hall, probably between 1866 and 1870.

This furniture is interesting, because it probably pre-dated the Barnard, Bishop and Barnard grates, and certainly pre-dated the Philadelphia Pavilion.[4] It fills the gap between them and the Sandringham gates. In the 1860s the circle in which Jeckell moved was intrigued by Oriental art. The grates and pavilion, unlike the gates, show very strong Japanese or Chinese influence. In the furniture it is already

368

351. Ken Hill. Sideboard in the dining room by Jeckell, under *The Olive Pickers* by Thomas Armstrong.

apparent, although much less strong. In a letter of 26 September 1866 to Edward Green, Jeckell enclosed a series of designs for monograms and commented, 'I like the Chinese looking one.' The designs were probably for either the round table or the chairs now in the Ken Hill dining room; they both have monograms of an Oriental flavour. Japanese or Chinese influence is noticeable in the scrolls on the incised designs on the legs of the main dining room table, and some of the proliferation of incised patterns on the sideboard. Among Jeckell's sketches, on paper watermarked 1868, are ones for a chair with Japanese flower decoration, and a bracketed shelf for Oriental porcelain. Kept in store at Ken Hill is a curious overmantel with a row of genuine Japanese plates inset along the bottom, and pastiche panels in the style of Hiroshige along the top. Between these are a round mirror and round marble plaques carved with reliefs of Edward Green's two sons. Jeckell's sketches show that this was made in 1872, presumably for Heath.

As Heath was only leased it was almost inevitable that Edward Green would want to acquire a country property of his own. In 1877 he bought the Snettisham estate in Norfolk. It had an early eighteenth-century manor house in the village but he built a new house called Ken Hill, in its own park a mile or so away. As he was still running the family business and living most of the year in London or Yorkshire, Ken Hill was essentially a holiday house for the shooting; this is why, by Victorian standards, it is not at all large. Later on, when it became a full time residence, a small wing was added at the back.

352. (above left) Sketch by Jeckell for a chair with oriental motifs.
353. (top right) A table.
354. (bottom right) An overmantel.

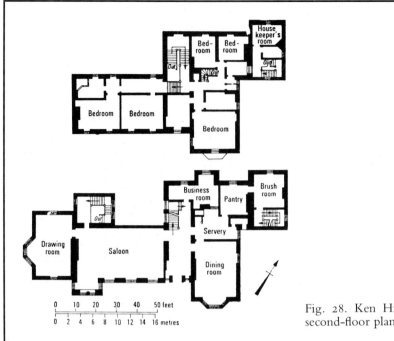

Fig. 28. Ken Hill. The first- and second-floor plan.

The obvious architect for the new house would have been Thomas Jeckell. But although he was conveniently in Norwich he was, less conveniently, in the Norwich Asylum, for he had gone mad in 1877 and died insane in 1881. His earlier connection with the Greens was no doubt responsible for the family legend that 'the house was designed by your great-grandfather and a mad architect'. In fact, the architect was a very sane Scotsman, John J. Stevenson. The choice was an unconventional one, for, although in the 1860s Stevenson had designed at least one country house in Scotland, his reputation was based on his town houses of the 1870s.

As discussed in the introduction, Stevenson was one of the creators of the 'Queen Anne' style, and had made his reputation with his own house, the Red House in Bayswater (1871). He exhibited drawings of Ken Hill at the Royal Academy in 1879 and 1880;[5] it is worth comparing its design with the London Board schools that he designed in partnership with E. R. Robson (c. 1873–5) and his fine house in Lowther Gardens for Colonel W. T. Makins (1878). Like them it is an attractive and original expression of the Queen Anne formula, the combination of Gothic freedom with modern comfort and classical detail. The basic concept of Ken Hill is not that of a typical Georgian house, a single symmetrical block subdivided internally, but of a Gothic house, an irregular assembly of different units. The lack of symmetry, the high roofs on different levels, the great hall rising up in the centre, the huge chimneystacks, the oriel windows, are inspired by a medieval manor house; but inside and out, all the detail derives from the seventeenth or eighteenth century. Stevenson's London buildings were all of brick, but Ken Hill is of deep-brown local carstone, of the greatest beauty.

In his book *House Architecture* (1880) Stevenson wrote that 'the place of great reception rooms might in many cases be supplied by a Hall of the old type, which would have even greater dignity, without their dismal character when out of use.

355. Ken Hill. The view from the front door.

Such a hall forms a charming feature even in a moderately sized country house. It is much better than a drawing room for dancing and games; for the oak floor may be left exposed opposite couches and fireplace, and instead of the quantities of fragile furniture and ornaments with which a drawing room is usually encumbered, a few oak benches and tables are all that is required.'[6] A quick look at the plan shows how closely the Ken Hill saloon is modelled in position and shape on a medieval great hall, but transmuted into a comfortable late-Victorian living room, with curtained windows and a flat ceiling plastered between the beams. At one end, where the solar would have been, is the drawing room; at the other the medieval screens passage, open to the hall, has been closed in, widened and converted to a modern staircase hall. Beyond this is the dining room, taking the place of the kitchen, which is on the floor below.

One of the peculiarities of the plan of Ken Hill is that the main living rooms are all on the first floor. This was perhaps to get an improved view, across the flat parkland to the sea nearby; it is a plan not without its inconveniences, but it gives the house much of its character. On the ground floor were the kitchen and its attachments, the servants' hall and bedrooms, and the smoking room suitably isolated underneath the drawing room and approached by a little private stair off the saloon. The main bedroom is above the dining room; there are more bedrooms, with charming

371

356. (upper left) Ken Hill. The entrance front.

357. (lower left) The saloon.

358. (left) 'Queen Anne' in a bedroom.

359. (below) The drawing room.

Queen Anne fireplaces, up in the roof above the saloon, at a higher level owing to its height; the drawing room is lower than the saloon but higher than the dining room, because it has no bedrooms above it and can extend up into the roof. These differences in heights and levels would have been virtually impossible in a conventional classical plan, but were easily obtainable in a Gothic one. The freedom has its disadvantages as well as advantages for the changes in levels, little runs of steps, and complicated roof plan that result are by no means convenient. But they have a lot of charm.

Queen Anne architects were cheerfully eclectic in their sources. The bold steps and terrace leading to the front door derive (like the similar feature in Lowther Gardens) from the seventeenth-century great hall at Glasgow University, which Stevenson illustrated in his book; the rusticated windows are early eighteenth century; the drawing room plasterwork is inspired by Adam. Inside the house the family friendship with Armstrong is made evident both by his own *Olive Pickers* (1877) in the dining room and his friend Spencer Stanhope's *Love in the Garden* (1877) in the saloon. Opposite the latter, and in striking contrast to its pale pre-raphaelite fantasy is a superb piece of Edwardian bravura, C. W. Furse's *Cubbing with the York and Ainsty* of 1904. It shows the grandchildren of Edward Green, (a baronet since 1886) out with the hunt, of which their father (another Edward) was the master. Like other industrialists the Greens combined aesthetic discrimination with social ambition, and hunted and shot their way into the upper classes. Ken Hill was strategically placed next door to Sandringham; the Prince of Wales came over to shoot; and it may have been young Edward who in 1891 suggested that he stay for the fateful week of Doncaster Races with his father-in-law, Arthur Wilson, at Tranby Croft.

374

360. *Cubbing with the York and Ainsty*, by C. W. Furse. The grandchildren of Sir Edward Green of Ken Hill.

30. *Wightwick Manor, Staffordshire*

WIGHTWICK[1] neatly illustrates three aspects of Victorian taste: the existence towards the end of the century of a large body of cultivated upper middle-class families who read their Ruskin and Morris and expressed their artistic tastes in their houses; the way in which the ideas of Shaw and Nesfield had spread through the country and were imitated by provincial as well as London architects; and the way in which the Shaw Old English style was modified around 1890 into something softer, lusher and much closer to an imitation of genuine old work.

In 1887 Theodore Mander, partner in a firm of varnish and paint manufacturers at Wolverhampton, acquired a property at Wightwick, three miles west of his home town. In the same year he bought a copy of Ruskin's *Seven Lamps of Architecture* and began to build a house.[2] His architect was Edward Ould, of the Liverpool and Chester firm of Grayson and Ould, and an ex-pupil of John Douglas of Chester.

In the late 1850s the Chester architects T. M. Penson and James Harrison had started a revival of half-timbered architecture in Chester—a natural enough development considering the wealth of medieval and Elizabethan half-timbering in their own town and the countryside around it. By 1870 the revival was in full swing and between then and 1900 the main streets of Chester were lined with richly old world facades that greatly outnumbered the genuine article, though few tourists in Chester today realise it.[3] A high proportion of this Victorian half-timbering was designed by John Douglas, the most successful and ablest of the Chester architects, who had a practice that extended to country houses and large villas all over North Wales, Cheshire, Lancashire and the West Midlands. Grayson and Ould's domestic

375

361. Wightwick Manor, Wolverhampton, Staffordshire (Edward Ould, 1887–93). The entrance front.

practice dealt more in villas than country houses; they did work at Port Sunlight, and Ould's half-timbered designs for a villa at Bechry, Flintshire, and at Dee Hills outside Chester (the latter for Judge Thomas Hughes, the author of *Tom Brown's School Days*) were illustrated in the *Building News* for 24 April and 21 August 1885. In 1904 he collaborated with J. Parkinson on a book called *Old Cottages, Farm Houses and other Half-Timber Buildings in Shropshire, Herefordshire and Cheshire*.

Although this school of half-timbered architecture had its own local roots, from at any rate 1870 onwards it was influenced by the buildings of Shaw and Nesfield. The influence is evident in the earlier portions of Wightwick, which are built on an L-shaped plan round a brick tower, and comprise the first three gables of the long south front to the garden. The mixture of brick, tile-hanging and half-timber, the Old English range of sources from late Gothic to Jacobean, the slender chimneystacks fanning out at the top in multiple over-sailing courses, the little window in the chimney-breast, the way the porch is set crooked onto the house, and the inglenooks, screens of turned balusters and use of stained glass internally, all derive from Shaw and Nesfield; so does the determination that although the building is to be quaint, it is to be quaint in a Victorian way, with hard red Ruabon brick and bright red Broseley tiles.

A large extension was added to the east in 1893, apparently because Theodore Mander decided to organize cricket weeks, and wanted accommodation for big house parties. Ould was still the architect, but the new work was built in a different spirit. There is much more and much richer half-timbering; the red-brick walls have been replaced by a low base-course of local sandstone; and at first sight one might reasonably be deluded into thinking that this was a real old manor house of the early

376

362. Wightwick Manor. The 1893 wing.

sixteenth century—until the feeling begins to percolate that it is too good to be true; the carving lusher, the oriels quainter, the window glazing and timber work even more elaborate than the fanciest of sixteenth-century examples. It is in fact an anthology of half-timbering, with extracts from houses as far apart as Little Moreton Hall in Cheshire and Ockwells in Berkshire. In his book Ould recommended modern half-timbered houses because 'no style of building will harmonize so quickly and so completely with its surrounding and so soon pass through the crude and brand-new field'. Judging from the earlier part of Wightwick he was unlikely to have felt the same in 1887; the 1893 wing represents a stage in the half-timber revival between Shaw's early houses, bright, clean and shiny, and the pickled oak and carefully warped beams which become fashionable for those who went old world in the early twentieth century.

Of the two halves of Wightwick, there is no doubt that the later is the winner, because it is so much more competently carried out. There is in fact a possibility of an *éminence grise* at Wightwick, in the person of C. E. Kempe. Kempe is best known as a maker of stained glass, but he was also a decorator who could turn his hand to architecture. His own house, Lindfield Old Hall in Sussex, was a genuine Elizabethan half-timbered house which he enlarged and touched up to make it even more genuine—with results similar to those at Wightwick. Another house in the same vein is the Wood House near Epping in Essex; ostensibly this was designed by Kempe's nephew Walter Tower, but according to tradition in the family for whom it was built Kempe was the dominant personality behind the design.[4] At Wightwick Kempe is known to have designed the stained glass in the hall and drawing room of the first building, was consulted about the plaster frieze and colour scheme for the

363. The house from the garden, with the 1893 extension to the right.

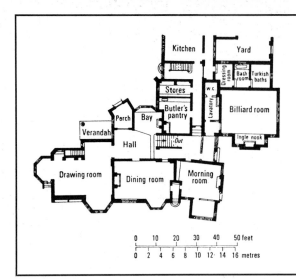

Fig. 29. Wightwick Manor. Ground-floor plan showing the house in 1889, before the 1893 alterations and additions.

Great Parlour in the new wing, and his name appears in the visitors' book for 1893; one cannot help wondering whether his influence extended further.

It may be because of Kempe that there is little contrast between the 1887 and 1893 wings internally. The porch leads into a long corridor opening into a recess complete with inglenook to the north, and with the drawing room, morning room and former dining room (now the library) off it to the south. These are all in the 1887 part; the corridor then takes a right-angled turn to the left and leads to the Great Parlour, with dining room and new billiard room beyond, all in the new wing.

The inglenook recess has glass in its upper lights by Kempe; each light contains a female figure in rich medieval dress carrying a standard bearing the mottoes *Pax huic domui, Pax intrantibus, Pax habitantibus* and so on. These beautiful designs are typical of Kempe, lusher, richer and greener in tone than the equivalent glass produced by the Morris company. But it was all the same artistic world, and Morris's *Earthly Paradise* provided the subjects for more Kempe glass in the drawing room. In comparison to a Blore Elizabethan room, with its high ceilings and mechanical plasterwork, the long low proportions of this room and the rich ceiling, which at first sight could convincingly date from the early seventeenth century, show what a

365. The dining-room sideboard.   366. The Hall.

revolution had taken place in interior design as a result of the artistic movement of the 1870s. There is similar plasterwork, with friezes beautifully modelled by L. A. Shuffrey, in the billiard room and dining room. Like most of the rooms the dining room is panelled and has a built-in recessed sideboard in the Shaw manner. The grandest interior at Wightwick is the Great Parlour, a room on the Great Hall pattern converted into a living room *à la* Nesfield and Shaw. The decoration is an epitome of artistic taste of the 1890s, with blue and white china in cupboards along the walls, a plaster frieze of intertwined roses above the fireplace in the inglenook, a great frieze under the roof of Orpheus and Eurydice (suggested by Kempe, and obviously inspired by the hunting frieze at Hardwick) and a multitude of hangings, embroideries and coverings from the Morris workshops.

Wightwick is typically Old English in that the inspiration of the exterior is mainly early sixteenth century, and of the interior early seventeenth century. Typical also is the wealth of patterns, in Morris designs, Oriental carpets, plasterwork, inlaid furniture and tiles. It all successfully combines to give the feeling of 'artistic' eclecticism that the late Victorians aimed at achieving. But Theodore Mander had bought comparatively few pictures before his early death in 1900. In 1937 Wightwick became the property of the National Trust, although the Mander family stayed on as tenants. In recent years Lady Mander and the Trust between them have enriched the interior with more Morris fabrics and a rich collection of pre-raphaelite and other Victorian pictures.

364. (left) Wightwick Manor. Stained glass by C. E. Kempe in the hall.

31. *Standen, Sussex*

EARLY in 1891 Philip Webb was approached by J. S. Beale with a request to design him a house on the Hollybush Farm estate which he had bought near East Grinstead.[1] The collaboration turned out a happy one. For a convinced Socialist and a man of abstemious and slightly Puritanical tastes like Webb, working for very rich clients such as George Howard, Percy Wyndham and Sir Lowthian Bell must have imposed considerable strains, however much he liked them personally. J. S. Beale was far from poor, but his background was neither opulent nor aristocratic. He was a successful solicitor; his family came from Birmingham, and he ran the London office of the family firm, solicitors in independent practice but with an important retainer from the Midland Railway. In London he lived in Holland Park and his family moved in the cultivated Holland Park circles of the Ionides, and Coronios, the Alexanders of Camden Hill and the Debenhams of Addison Road. It was possibly the Ionides family who put Beale onto Webb, for he had done work for them in their London houses in Holland Park and in the country at Camberley in Surrey.[2]

Beale wanted a house for holidays and weekends. It had to be large, to accommodate guests and a large family, but he did not want anything grand; it was not to be a 'seat', like Clouds and Rounton Grange. Before he commissioned Webb he had already decided where he wanted the house to be, and gone to considerable expense in cutting back rock in preparation. Webb decided that the site must be moved and got Beale to agree, against his judgement at first, although he came round to the change later. This behaviour was typical of Webb, who was never a complaisant employee; but although he and Beale had their disagreements, they liked and respected one another. Webb was an incurable snuff-taker; and when the

381

367. (upper left) Wightwick Manor. The great parlour.
368. (left) Wightwick Manor. The drawing room.
369. (above) Standen, East Grinstead, Surrey (Philip Webb, 1891–4). The farm court.

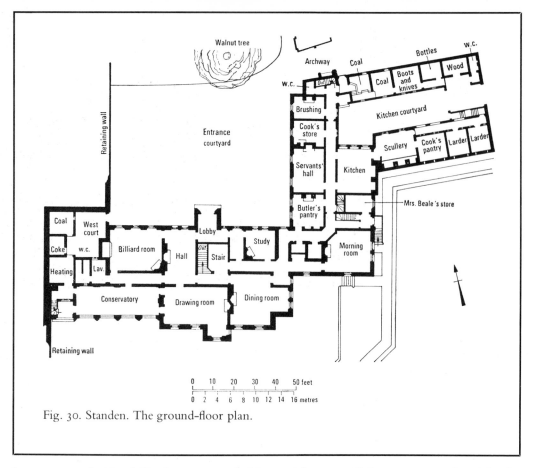

Fig. 30. Standen. The ground-floor plan.

house was finished Beale presented him with a snuff box engraved with the inscription: 'When clients talk irritating nonsense I take a pinch of snuff.'[3]

The first plan, produced in May and June 1891, was judged too large; a reduced version had been made by the end of July and was played around with until in September the house as it is today had been worked out apart from a few minor changes. The specification survives and is dated June 1892; contracts were signed in October, and the family moved in during the summer of 1894.

The surroundings of Standen are not unlike those of Norman Shaw's Leys Wood and Glen Andred, ten miles away. There is a tree-covered shoulder of hill running through the estate, with a good many outcrops of rock, and a small abandoned quarry excavated into its side. It is interesting to see in what different ways Shaw and Webb treated this kind of site. Shaw liked to build up his houses above the rocks; Webb fitted Standen in snugly beneath the hill. His image of perfection was a farm or manor house in fields and orchards, not a castle on a crag. The hill curves down and round past the west end of the house and in front of its north side, in which Webb put the entrance. The public road ran to the north; owing to the slope it was impracticable to bring the drive straight from the road to the house, and Webb made it take a loop round the spur of hill and come in from the east. He turned the detour to advantage. The original Hollybush farm was at the end of the spur; it was a simple tile-hung building with a generous roof, of the kind that Webb loved. He kept it, and built a stable yard at the back. The drive comes down past the stables,

which are on a higher level than the house. It then swings to the right into a large and welcoming grass court—the 'house green', Webb called it on his early plans. The green is open to the east; on the north are the farm buildings, on the west the cottage, and on the south the outbuildings of the kitchen yard. A long line of roof joins the cottage to the main house. The drive takes a right-angled turn and dives through an archway beneath this roof into the entrance court, which is between the stable and the house.

The house is built on an L-shaped plan round two sides of the entrance court, with the hill and a steep rise to the stables on the other sides. The main block, with its high roof and tall chimneystacks, forms the principal stroke of the L; at right angles is a gabled wing containing kitchen, offices and bedrooms; at the junction is a broad squat tower containing the water tank. This basic L shape is complicated by two additions. On the garden front a five gabled projection from the main block contains the drawing room and dining room, with bedrooms above it; a long low conservatory joins it to a little pavilion tucked into the hill. At the end of the kitchen wing, and at an angle to it, there is a low tail of larders and store rooms built round a long narrow kitchen court.

By the 1890s Webb had given up any kind of elaboration of ornament in his houses, and any attempt to derive features from the more ambitious examples of the historic styles. His inspiration came from local building traditions; many of the features of his houses were derived from a close study of cottages, farms, barns and the smaller houses in the neighbourhood in which he was building. He introduced variety by the shape of his roofs and the combination of different materials. At Standen the variety is great and the combinations often very complex. On the entrance front the main block is built of red brick of two different colours, with a red tiled roof. The porch and surround to the window above it are of local yellow limestone; but the porch arch is made of receding bands of brick under the wooden eaves of the deeply projecting roof. The bay window (an insertion made in 1898) is of a grey stone. The tower is covered with a brownish-yellow rough cast. The gables and upper half of the wing are weather-boarded. All the bedrooms and living rooms

383

370. Standen. The entrance front.

have windows with white-painted wood surrounds and white wood bars—sash windows on the lower floors and casements up in the roof. Windows of passages, halls, lofts and store rooms on this front and throughout the house are distinguished by leaded lights.

On the garden front the use of materials is even more complex. The ground floor is of stone, but the windows are set in recessed arches with thin brick surrounds. There are similar brick surrounds to the first-floor windows, but these are projecting not recessed, with panels of tile-hanging between them. Both the first floor and the projecting drawing room bay on the ground floor have boldly projecting plaster coves; above the first-floor cove are five weather-boarded gables. The lower half of the conservatory front is of stone; the upper of brick with elaborately recessed brick arches; the wall above is rough cast.

There are similar combinations on the east front, together with a few idiosyncrasies characteristic of Webb: the two windows of the morning room, recessed under a pair of brick arches with a stone corbel at their junction; the narrow two-storey recessed panel containing the garden entrance; the bold combination of two tall chimneystacks built up at right angles to each other.

Inside the house there is the same apparent simplicity which has had a great deal of painstaking work put into it. The entrance leads into a vestibule with the hall to one side of it—a draught-preventing device which Webb was fond of using. The billiard room is to one side of the hall and the drawing room beyond it, with a long corridor leading through the staircase and past the dining room to the morning room. There is a similar corridor on the bedroom floor. The rooms are either panelled up to within a few feet of the ceiling, or papered with Morris wallpapers. The panelling is painted white in the billiard room and hall but in the dining room it is an attractive and distinctive blue–green, a favourite colour in the 1890s when it was known as 'William and Mary'.[4] There is a deep recess off the dining room fitted with built-in

384

371. (above) Standen. The dining-room alcove.
372. (upper right) The house from the kitchen garden.
373. (right) The house from the garden.

drawers and shelves of a light brown oak that contrasts very agreeably with the panelling. The room has Morris tapestry curtains, and the chair seats were embroidered by the Beale family. Over the fireplace the panelling is in lozenges with a frieze of simple fretwork ornament above it; the panelling is stopped off with an ogee curve that is nicely caught up by the curves of the plaster cove above. This fretwork and shaped panelling is one of two ornamental devices used by Webb inside the house; the other is the use of stone chimneypieces, fashioned in a great variety of chunky shapes and with very simple mouldings. The fireplaces are often combined with panelling, built-in cupboards and alcoves; in the drawing room and one or two other rooms the panelled surround to the fireplace forms an isolated feature in the otherwise unpanelled room. Wherever one looks one starts noticing little bits of Webb's individual fancy, such as the cupboards in a recess in the corridor and the built-in shelves, marking board and seats for spectators in the billiard room. The house had some central heating and electric light from the start; the original wall lights are still used in the drawing room, suspended on brackets attached to

374. Standen. A detail in the ground-floor corridor.

embossed copper panels designed by Webb. There were originally two bathrooms, one on each upper floor. The entrance hall was used for tea and music, and proved too small; in 1898 Webb built out the bay window to give more room.

When thinking back about Standen one finds oneself adding up credits and debits; for although it is one of Webb's happiest houses it is by no means free of his own special brand of awkwardness. The credits are the friendliness and openness of the house green, with long low roofs leading up to the gables, clustered chimneys and turret of the main house; some of the garden views, where the five little gables play against the simple bulk of the big roof;[5] the warm gravel and scent of flowers on the sunny south terrace, looking along the house with its friendly creeper and the gay and neat combination of brick and tile hanging in two shades of red, and white painted woodwork; the house sheltering under the lee of the woods, and the ground dropping away to the kitchen garden and a vista of Sussex fields and woods; and the feeling everywhere of Webb's hatred of pretentiousness, his conscientious thoroughness, and concern for the people who were to live in the house. There are a

375. A bedroom chimneypiece.

number of his courtly and quietly humorous letters preserved at Standen. He discusses the best position for beds and cupboards in the bedrooms; he hopes that the new bay window in the hall 'would allow of a gleam of the setting sun entering the end of the room in summertime'; he pours cold water on a suggestion for decorative tiles in the conservatory; they would clash with the flowers and 'any kind of glazed tile is disagreeable to walk on, and more so from the nails on country shoes'. There is a little room up a flight of stairs in the pavilion at the end of the conservatory; he told Miss Helen Beale, the youngest of the family, that it would be hers if she gave him sixpence; and it has been a delight to children to keep house in it ever since.

The weaknesses of Standen are the result partly of the basic difficulty of treating a house of its size as though it was simply an over-large farm; partly of Webb's dogged determination that his buildings should never show off and never be smooth or pretty, combined with a painstaking conscientiousness that could make him worry away at details long after he should have stopped. There are viewpoints from which the house looks disjointed and the tower clumsy and heavy; on the entrance front, which suffers anyway from the disadvantage of being shut in and facing north, the combination of windows of different types and spacing is very restless. Webb might have argued that it was his business to build a comfortable house, not to make

376. Standen. The hall.

telling compositions; but much of Standen has to stand or fall on visual grounds, for there is little practical reason for its complicated groupings and combinations of materials. This elaboration does not make the house look ornate or fussy, because it is all pitched in such a low key, but a little less of it would have done no harm; many of the fireplace surrounds, for instance, on which Webb spent so much care, seem unlovely, unnecessary and would have been better away. Webb's assistant George Jack spoke of his master's 'very inventive imagination at all times struggling with an austere restraint which feared unnecessary expression'. He seems to have been torn between a desire to enjoy himself and a puritanical compulsion to tone his enjoyment down. He wrote a charming and typical letter to the Beales describing a visit in their absence: 'While having my dinner in the dining room (which should have been in the servants' hall, but your butler insisted on trying to make a gentleman of me) I could not but enjoy looking through a partly open window on the south and seeing the lovely wooded hill on the other side of the valley: and this—perhaps—the more so, that I had to refrain from a lovely fruit pie and strawberries with cream set out to tempt me from the path of wisdom.' One can't help feeling that Webb would have been a happier man and a greater architect if he had helped himself to more strawberries and cream.

377. The drawing room.

3. CATALOGUE

I HAVE tried to make this catalogue cover all the houses mentioned in the text, and in addition have added a number of houses where size, quality of the architecture, importance of the client or familiarity to the public suggested they should be included. Houses given separate chapters in the main body of the book are not included. The Irish and Scottish sections cover only houses partly or wholly designed by English architects. Technical details refer to what the house was equipped with when built, not, unless specifically stated, to what is there today.

At the end of each entry I have given brief details where, if anywhere, illustrations, plans and further information can be found. For these the following abbreviations have been used:

A   Architect
AR   Architectural Review
B   Builder
BA   British Architect
BN   Building News
CL   Country Life
P   Plan
I   Illustration
D   Description

Eastlake: C. L. Eastlake, *History of the Gothic Revival* (London, 1872; ed. with footnotes and additions J. M. Crook, London, 1970) with an appendix of 'selected examples of Gothic buildings erected between 1820 and 1870'.

Muthesius: Hermann Muthesius, *Das Englische Haus* (Berlin, 1904–5). Abridged English translation 1979.

B of E: Means a more detailed description in the relevant volume of the Penguin *Buildings of England* series. If there is an illustration as well, I is added.

Morris: Means that the building is illustrated in F. O. Morris, *Picturesque Views of Seats*, 6 vols. (London, 1877–80?). The accompanying text contains little of value, other than genealogical information.

NMR: Means that there are photographs in the National Monuments Record. If Bedford Lemere added, these are from the superb series of photographs taken by this photographer in the later nineteenth century.

RIBA: Means that there are designs by the architect in the Royal Institute of British Architects.

V & A: Means that there are designs by the architect in the Victoria and Albert Museum.

ENGLAND AND WALES

ABBERLEY HALL, nr Stourport, Worcestershire

By Samuel Daukes for John Lewis Moilliet, a Birmingham banker, 1837. Restored by Daukes after being gutted by fire in 1845. Italianate house with tower in the Osborne manner (but the top stage has been removed). Elegant neoclassical interiors. The enormous free-standing Gothic clock tower in the park is by J. P. St Aubyn, 1883, for the new owner, John Joseph Jones, a cottentot. (*B. of E*; *BN* 5 Oct. 1883, ID of clock tower; *CL* CLIV (1973), 1915, I of hall.)

ABBEY CWMHIR HALL, nr Rhayader, Radnorshire

One of the many branches of the Philips family (Manchester cotton) settled in this remote Welsh valley, and built the little church (1866) and then the house (1868–9) in an approved Victorian sequence. The architects were Poundley and Walker, a Liverpool firm who designed Gothic buildings somewhat in the Bassett Keeling manner. The polychromatic church, with its stumpy bell turret, and the house on the hill above it, with amazing scalloped bargeboards, form a lively and muscular couple. (*CL* CXXV (1959), 94, I.)

ABBEYSTEAD, Wyresdale, Lancashire (Pl. 380)

A stone-built shooting lodge on the grand scale, by John Douglas, 1886–8, for the Earl of Sefton. Elizabethan of the scholarly variety and still lived in by the Sefton family. (*Muthesius* I, Fig. 108; *BN* 9 July 1886, ID.)

ABBOTSFIELD, Wiveliscombe, Somerset

The only country house known to have been designed by Owen Jones, *c.* 1872, for Charles Lukey Collard, of the leading Victorian piano-making firm, Collard and Collard. Wagner stayed here, Adelina Patti sang here. 'Mixed in its elements and put together without much taste or character.' (*B of E*.)

378. (preceeding pages) Witley Court, Worcestershire (remodelled, Samuel Daukes, 1855).

379. Abney Hall, Cheadle, Cheshire. The dining room, from a Victorian photograph.

ABERMAD, nr Aberystwyth, Cardiganshire

By J. D. Seddon for L. Pugh Pugh of Aberystwyth, *c.* 1872. Presumably an off-shoot of his amazing University building in Aberystwyth. Externally rather a grim early Gothic stone house, with a little Ruskinian carving, especially on the arcaded *porte-cochère*. Inside, a splendid Gothic staircase in pitch-pine, and a rose window in the drawing room filled with the Seven Lamps of Architecture in stained glass. Now divided into flats. (*A* 12 Oct. 1872; ID; *BA* 21 July 1882, ID.)

ABNEY HALL, Cheadle Cheshire (Pl. 379)

Remodelled *c.* 1849–51, for James Watts, later Mayor of Manchester, by Travis and Magnall of Manchester, possibly with embellishments by A. W. Pugin. On the borderline between large villa and small country house. Elaborately decorated in the Gothic style by J. G. Crace, with a few contributions from Pugin. Pugin furniture, superb Hardman gasoliers. James Watts, junior, was an amateur photographer and photographed the house in detail in 1912, when it was unaltered. Now Cheadle Town Hall. See pp. 24, 445 n. 41. (*CL CXXXIV* (1963), 1846–9, 1910–13, ID; NMR.)

ADDINGTON MANOR, nr Winslow, Buckinghamshire

By P. C. Hardwick, 1856–7, for J. G. Hubbard, later Lord Addington, a High Church Russia merchant and banker. 'Domestic Pointed'. Demolished. See p. 21.

ALBURY PARK, nr Guildford, Surrey

A. W. Pugin remodelled it for Henry Drummond, of Drummond's Bank, 1846–52. Tudor Gothic, with elaborate brick chimneystacks. A large house, but on the whole one of Pugin's feebler designs. He did little inside. (*CL CVIII*, 598, 674, ID.)

393

380. Abbeystead, Lancashire (John Douglas, 1886).

ALDERMASTON COURT, nr Reading, Berkshire (Pl. 383)

By P. C. Hardwick, 1848–51, for Higford Burr, M.P. Hardwick's first country house (but see Hall, Devon). A large and ambitious building of brick with stone dressings, in an over-elaboration of the Pugin manner, with much diapering and restless chopping-up of roofs. Altered and enlarged, 1894, by Brightwen and Binyon. The grand tower, boldly patterned in brick and stone, is the most memorable feature. (P. Ferriday, *Victorian Architecture* (London, 1963), Fig. XII; *CL* VI, 240–4, ID.)

ALDWORTH HOUSE, Blackdown, Sussex

Built for Alfred Tennyson, 1867–9, from designs by his friend J. T. Knowles, junior. French and English sixteenth-century Gothic. 'Fussy small hotel.' (*B of E*.)

ALLERTON HALL, nr Knaresborough, Yorkshire

A curious Gothic–Elizabethan house built in 1852 for Lord Stourton, with a large central Gothic lantern lighting the staircase. Architect James Firth. At one time known as Stourton Hall. (*Morris* II, 27.)

ALNWICK CASTLE, Northumberland (Pl. 26)

Between 1854 and his death in 1865, the immensely rich fourth Duke of Northumberland (income about £110,000 from land and £25,000 from minerals) spent a quarter of a million pounds on restoring and largely rebuilding the castle. Almost all the delicate Georgian Gothic of Paine and Adam was swept away, and replaced with substantial feudal exteriors by Salvin, and palatial Renaissance interiors designed by a team of distinguished Italian architects and artists. (Architect in charge: Luigi Canina, succeeded by Giovanni Montivoli. Chimneypieces by Strazza and Nucci. Paintings by Mantovani.) Much of Salvin's work, especially the vaulted entrance way and inner court of the keep, is extremely impressive. See p. 25 (*B* 18 Feb. 1865; *CL* LXV (1929), 890, 952; LXVI (1929), 16, 52, PID.)

ALTON CASTLE, nr Cheadle, Staffs. (Pl. 381)

Designed by A. W. Pugin for the sixteenth Earl of Shrewsbury, 1847–51. It stands next to the Hospital of St John (church, schools and almshouses) built by Pugin for the same patron, c. 1840–4. Who, if anyone, Lord Shrewsbury intended to live in the castle remains obscure. Its sensational clifftop position, across the valley from Alton Towers, was put to brilliant effect by Pugin, no doubt with a backwards look at the castles of the Rhine. Now a convent school. (*CL* CXXVIII (1960), 1226–9, ID.)

ALTON TOWERS, nr Cheadle, Staffordshire

The house and fantastic gardens were the creation of the fifteenth Earl of Shrewsbury, c. 1814–27, but A. W. Pugin made numerous alterations and additions for his successor. The most important of these were the building of the chapel (1835) and the Great Hall (1836). The house is now dismantled and largely gutted, but still an extraordinary spectacle. The transformation of the property into a playground for the potteries, with an aerial railway in the gardens, refreshment rooms and roundabouts in and around the house, and a model railway in the chapel, is by no means entirely a disaster. See p. 44 (*C.* CXVIII (1960), 1226, ID.)

ARLEY HALL, nr Northwich, Cheshire (Pl. 382)

By J. Latham, 1833–41, with further work by Salvin, 1853, and T. H. Wyatt, 1860. For R. E. Egerton-Warburton, a hunting squire who wrote successful sporting verses. The main facade is by Latham. A large and typical example of Victorian Elizabethan with much mechanical detailing in the high and spacious rooms. A Gothic private chapel, by Salvin, 1843–5, with aisle added by Street, 1856–7, is attached to one corner. Has been partly demolished. (*CL* XVI, 942, ID.)

ARUNDEL CASTLE, Sussex

Restored and largely rebuilt by C. A. Buckler for the fifteenth Duke of Norfolk, 1879–c. 1890. Enormous, feudal, ducal and in the architectural context of its time entirely out of date. (*B of E*; *BN* 31 Mar. 1882, PID.)

ASCOT HEATH HOUSE, Ascot, Berkshire

By Robert Kerr for John Delane, 1868. See p. 271. The house is now used as offices by the racecourse.

ASCOTT, nr Wing, Buckinghamshire (Pl. 384)

By George Devey for Lionel de Rothschild, 1874–5, 1878–80, etc. Final additions after Devey's death, by his partner Isaac Williams, but to Devey's designs. An immensely overgrown half-timbered cottage, designed from the first to be smothered with creeper. Gladstone's daughter Mary described it in 1880 as 'a palace-like cottage, the most luxurious and lovely thing I ever saw'. Now National Trust. Much redecoration inside. (*CL* II, 210; VIII, 240, ID; *B* 8 Dec. 1888, PID.)

AVERY HILL, Greenwich

By T. W. Cutler, c. 1885–91, for Col. J. T. North, who made a huge fortune from Peruvian nitrate. Enlarging of an older house to enormous size and shapelessness. A curious mixture of Italianate and 'Queen Anne'. Domed winter garden, billiard room lined with marble, Turkish bath, electric light,

381. (upper right) Alton Castle, Staffordshire (A. W. Pugin, 1845–41).
382. (middle right) Arley Hall, Cheshire (J. Latham, 1833–41).
383. (right) Aldermaston Court, Berkshire (P. C. Hardwick, 1848–50).

centrally heated stables. Now a Training College, and has been partly destroyed by fire, but the winter garden remains. (*BA* 3 Jan. 1890, PID.)

BAGSHOT PARK, Surrey

Largish, dimmish Tudor–Gothic house, by Benjamin Ferrey, 1877, for the Duke of Connaught. Like most of Ferrey's later houses, of interest only because, apart from a certain hardening of the detail, it might have been designed thirty years earlier. (*B* 1877, 1198, PID; *Morris* VI, I.)

BALLARDS, nr Croydon, Surrey

By F. P. Cockerell for C. H. Goschen, merchant banker, 1873. The house was in the 'Queen Anne' style, and one of the group of buildings (Shaw's New Zealand Chambers, Bodley's London School Board Offices, schools by Robson and Stevenson) designs for which were exhibited at the Royal Academy in 1873, and announced the arrival of 'Queen Anne' to the general public.

BANK HALL, Chapel-en-le-Frith, Derbyshire

Of interest only because of the room which W. E. Nesfield added in 1875 to an uninteresting earlier Victorian house, for Henry Renshaw of Manchester. The room is a beautiful example of the collaboration between fellow-artists so popular in the 1870s; Nesfield designed the setting, Thomas Armstrong and Randolph Caldecott painted the delightful canvases of birds and classical scenes let into the panelling, and the windows have elaborate stained glass. Nice lodge, also by Nesfield. (*CL Annual* 1970, 29–36, ID.)

BANSTEAD WOOD, nr Epsom, Surrey (Pl. 385)

A lively and delightful house by Norman Shaw for the Hon. Francis Baring, 1884–90. Tile-hung Old English with touches of 'Queen Anne'. Now a hospital and engulfed by later additions. (*B of E*, I.)

396

BATCHWOOD, nr St Albans Hertfordshire

By Sir Edmund Beckett (later Lord Grimthorpe), for himself, 1874–6. See pp. 26, 85. Now partly demolished and much altered. (P. Ferriday, *Lord Grimthorpe* (London, 1957), 146, I.)

BATSFORD PARK, Moreton-in-the-Marsh, Gloucestershire

By Ernest George and Peto, 1888–93, for A. B. Freeman-Mitford (later Lord Redesdale). A clever working up of the Dorset Tudor–Gothic style into a country house on the grand scale which at first sight (in illustrations, at any rate) might be genuine sixteenth-century work. Inside, a Great Hall with staircase going up to an arcaded gallery. The house was designed to 'avoid prettiness and fanciful features', i.e. in reaction against Norman Shaw, and indeed against George and Peto's earlier manner. (*A* 1 June 1888, PID, 28 Apr. 1893, I; *BN* 4 Jan. 1889, I; *CL* XIV (1903), 18–28, ID).

BATTLESDEN HOUSE, nr Woburn, Bedfordshire

By G. H. Stokes, 1860–4, for Sir Edward Page-Turner. French Gothic. Demolished *c.* 1885. (G. F. Chadwick, *Paxton* (London, 1961), 197, 199, 231, ID.)

BAYHAM ABBEY, nr Tunbridge Wells, Kent

By David Brandon for the Marquess Camden, 1869–71, Jacobean. A large and typical example of this depressing architect's work. Technologically well equipped, with fire hydrants, gas, central heating and luggage lift. Family suite with private stairs. Carving by Earp. (*B* 6 Dec. 1871, 985–7, PID.)

BEAUFRONT CASTLE, Hexham, Northumberland

By John Dobson, 1836–42, for William Cuthbert, partner in Cookson and Cuthbert's glassworks, Newcastle. The most ambitious and impressive of Dobson's later houses. Asymmetric Gothic with tall

tower. Rooms grouped round an impressively top-lit hall-cum-billiard room. (*CL* CLIX (1976), 286–9, 342–5, ID.)

BEDGEBURY PARK, nr Lamberhurst, Kent

In 1854–5, Alexander Beresford-Hope added a French mansard roof and made other additions and alterations to the late classical house (*c.* 1836), inherited from his stepfather, Viscount Beresford. R. C. Carpenter was his architect. Chapel in the Louis XIV style. Large and famous Victorian pinetum. (*B of E.*)

BENENDEN see Hemstead

BERECHURCH HALL, Colchester, Essex

Expensive remodelling of 1882, by E. C. Lee for O. E. Coope, the brewer. Described as 'domestic French Gothic', and shows the influence of Burges, whose pupil Lee was—but with Nesfield chimneys-tacks. Of interest because it was one of the earliest houses to be equipped with electric light. See p. 25. Fireproof construction. (*BN* 16 June 1882, ID.)

BESTWOOD LODGE, nr Nottingham (Frontispiece, Pl. 387)

By S. S. Teulon for the Duke of St Albans (an early friend of the Prince of Wales), 1862–4. Fourteenth-century Gothic. As asymmetric and confused as Teulon could make it, with much of his tough and memorable detail (e.g. the extraordinary entrance porch, and the open timber roof of the billiard room). Red brick with stone dressings. Figurative and other carvings by Earp (Robin Hood, etc.). Landscaping by Thomas. Church also by Teulon. Post-Teulon wing replacing the conservatory and added to contain a drill hall for the volunteers. A good deal altered inside. *The Ecclesiologist* complained that the servants' hall looked like a chapel; it is now used as one. (*B* XXI (1863), 639, I; *BN* XVII (1869), 152–3, I; 170, D; *Morris* III, 61.)

BILTON GRANGE, nr Rugby, Warwickshire

Large addition to an older house, by A. W. Pugin for Captain Washington Hibbert (step-father to the seventeenth Earl of Shrewsbury), 1841–6. A likeable red brick Tudor–Gothic house, now a school and engulfed by later additions. Planned round a broad central corridor, with service courtyard to the rear. Typical Pugin chimneypieces and panelling. (*BN* 29 May 1857, 555, I.)

BISHOPSCOURT, Sowton, nr Exeter

Remodelling by William White for John Garratt (son of a wholesale tea-merchant from London), 1860–4. The house was a residence of the medieval Bishops of Exeter, but had been much altered. '1st Pointed', using seven or eight varieties of stone. Architecturally eccentric and not nearly as impressive as Humewood, perhaps because White was inhibited by the existing structure. The best feature is the chapel, virtually rebuilt and a complete Tractarian survival. Interesting Gothic furniture designed by White was in the house in 1970. A pious Victorian house, like Treberfydd, Blackmoor and Milton Ernest; three of John Garratt's brothers became clergymen.

BLACKMOOR, nr Petersfield, Hampshire

By Alfred Waterhouse for Roundell Palmer (later created Lord Selborne), the High Church Lord Chancellor, 1869–72, and 1882–6. Palmer thought the gain in status worth the loss of income resulting from investing in land. A dour Gothic house surrounded by pine woods. The tower shows the influence of Norman Shaw. Church, rectory and almshouses also by Waterhouse. Until recently evocatively unaltered internally, with an inglenook, tiled chimneypieces and much Gothic furniture by Waterhouse. Jeckell grates in the bedrooms. The contents were sold in 1976. (*CL,* CLVI) (1974), 554–7, 614–17, PID.)

397

385. (above left) Banstead Wood, Surrey (R. Norman Shaw 1884–90).
386. (above right) Batsford Park, Gloucestershire (George and Peto, 1888–92).

387. Bestwood Lodge, Nottinghamshire, in about 1865 (S. S. Teulon, 1862–4).

388. (right) Bodrhyddan, Flintshire (W. E. Nesfield, 1872–4). The hall.

BLAKESWARE, Widford, Hertfordshire

By George Devey for Mrs Gosselin, 1876–9. Elizabethan. 'The composition and details both as good as the time could make them.' (B of E.)

BODRHYDDAN, Rhuddlan, Flintshire (Pl. 56)

By W. E. Nesfield for C. G. H. Rowley-Conwy, 1872–4. Large additions and partial remodelling of a seventeenth-century house. Red brick. The tall narrow entrance front, with hipped roof, small-paned sash windows and low wings, is entirely symmetrical. Inside the long low great hall (following the ceiling height of the old house) is a remodelling by Nesfield, with an inglenook and stamped-leather walls. (Nesfield drawings in the house and at the V & A; CL CLXIV (1978), 158–61, 226–9, ID.)

BODNANT, nr Conway, Denbighshire

By W. J. Green for H. D. Pochin (rich from china clay), 1881. Dim and grim Old English. (BN 29 July 1881, PID.)

BOLDRE GRANGE, nr Lymington, Hampshire

By Norman Shaw for J. L. Shrubb (brother of C. P. Shrubb of Merrist Wood), 1873–4. Old English. (B of E.)

BOWES MUSEUM, Barnard Castle, Durham (Pl. 280)

By Jules Pellechet, 1869–71, for John Bowes. See p. 296 (B 14 Jan. 1871, 27–9, PID.)

398

BRANTINGHAM THORPE, nr Hull, Yorkshire, E.R.

Remodelled by George Devey, for Edward VII's unfortunate friend Christopher Sykes, 1868–82. A typical rambling Devey job, with shaped Carolean gables. (CL XVII, 342, ID.)

BREADSALL PRIORY, nr Derby

By Robert Scrivener of Hamley, c. 1861, for Francis Morley of the hosiery firm. A remodelling and enlargement in the ogee Gothic style, expensive but undistingusihed. See p. 36 (BN VII (1861), 857, 881, ID.)

BROOMHILL, Southborough, Kent

A Decimus Burton house of the 1830s much altered and enlarged by the Salomons family, 1854, 1863, etc. Sir D. L. Salomons, second Bart, built a water tower surmounted by a telescope, and an enormous French Renaissance stable block (1870–4) to his own designs. He was an able scientist, and installed electricity in the 1880s. Now a convalescent home.

BROXTON HALL, nr Chester

By John Douglas for Sir Philip Egerton, Bart, c. 1873. Half-timbered Old English with high chimneystacks and a rambling plan, clearly influenced by Norman Shaw. A reconstructed old farmhouse forms the core. (BN XXIV (1873), 558, PID.)

389. (right) Buchan Hill, Sussex (George and Peto, 1882–3).

BRYANSTON, Blandford, Dorset (Pl. 58)

By Norman Shaw, 1890, for the second Viscount
Portman. Built on a colossal scale, out of London
ground rents. Norman Shaw working in the grand
manner, in full reaction against the quaintness of his
Old English and 'Queen Anne' days. The house is
built on an early eighteenth-century plan of central
block and two symmetrical wings: the vast high-
ceilinged reception rooms are in the central block, the
lower-ceilinged family and servants' rooms in the
wings. The picturesque planning of earlier Shaw days
is replaced by two spacious corridors running
through centre and wings on ground and first floors,
and joined together by an enormous circular rotunda,
with spatially sensational effect. There is a kind of
baroque romanticism about the scale and swagger of
the interior, and about the striped and heavily
rusticated exterior, of red brick with stone dressings.
A major criticism must be that the simplicity,
amounting to blankness, of the main block combines
unhappily with the nervous rustications of the wings.
Now a school. (*RIBA*; R. Blomfield, *Richard
Norman Shaw* (London, 1940), 28–9, PID; NMR
(Bedford Lemere).)

BUCHAN HILL, nr Crawley, Sussex (Pls 51, 389)

By Ernest George and Peto, 1882–3, for P. Saillard,
an ostrich-feather merchant. Large and florid, in
George's Harrington Gardens style. Everything that
a Victorian *nouveau-riche* house should be, in a
cheerful combination of hot red brick and yellow
stone, with a big tower, fancy gables, much early

Renaissance ornament and a top-floor loggia (for the nurseries) externally, and baronial fireplaces, minstrels' gallery, carving, embossed walls and rich panelling to the heart's content within. Ostrich feathers discreetly painted on the roof of the hall. Now Cottesmore House School. (*BN* 7 July 1882, PID; *B* 15 May 1886, I.)

BUTLEIGH COURT, nr Glastonbury, Som. (Pl. 390)

House (1845) and extensive restoration of adjoining church by J. C. Buckler for the Hon. and Revd G. Neville Granville, a local squarson. The house, of medium size but richly detailed, is a very competent essay in late manorial Gothic, in beautifully weathered local stone. Had been gutted and was a highly picturesque ruin, until restored and converted into flats in recent years. (*RIBA*; Photographs before dismantling, NMR.)

BYLAUGH HALL, nr Foulsham, Norfolk

By Banks and Barry for Edward Lombe, 1849–51. In the symmetrical 'Anglo-Italian' manner of Highclere. Built, like the Houses of Parliament, of limestone from the Grissell quarries. Originally had painted decorations by Sang, and bas-reliefs of Peace and War by Raynard Smith. Landscaping by W. A. Nesfield. Now a desolate but impressive ruin. See p. 35. (*BX* (1852), 517–19, PID; *BN* XIV (1869), 272, ID.)

BYRKLEY LODGE, nr Burton-on-Trent, Staffordshire

By R. W. Edis for Hamar Bass, the brewer, 1887–91. A large and unlovely Elizabethan house, still in the Highclere–Bylaugh tradition. Main block planned round a central hall, with a service wing attached to one corner, and six bathrooms on the main bedroom floor. (*BN* 14 Oct. 1887, PI.)

CANFORD MANOR, nr Wimborne, Dorset

By Edward Blore, 1826, for Lord de Mauley, greatly enlarged and remodelled by Sir Charles Barry, 1848–52, for Sir John and Lady Charlotte Guest. Further additions, 1887. In an unhappy combination of white brick and stone dressings. The tower, the entrance gallery, the Great Hall and the grand staircase are Barry's. The detail is mostly Gothic, the grouping in the picturesque tradition, the grand sequence of circulation spaces typical of Barry. The extent of Pugin's contribution to the Houses of Parliament is made abundantly clear. Now a school. See pp. 7–8, 16, 45. (A. Barry, *Sir Charles Barry* (1867), PID.)

CAPEL MANOR, Horsmonden, Kent

By T. H. Wyatt, 1859–62, for F. Austin, who, according to Eastlake, exerted considerable influence on the design. Italian Gothic in three colours of stone, with much carving. Now demolished. (NMR.)

CAPERNWRAY HALL, nr Carnforth, Lancashire

By Edmund Sharpe for George Marton (of a well-

390. Butleigh Court, Somerset (J. C. Buckler, 1845).

established gentry family), 1844. A nice picturesque design with rich late Gothic detailing and a castellated central tower. Symmetrical garden front, the rest irregular. (*Morris*, IV, 15; *B of E*, I.)

CAPESTHORNE, nr Macclesfield, Cheshire

A huge charmless building. Blore put a Jacobean entrance front onto the Georgian house for E. D. Davenport, in 1837. Paxton added a big conservatory before 1843. The central block was destroyed by fire in 1861, and rebuilt by Salvin for Bromley Davenport. The enormously long entrance front (central block and wings) is based on Blore's design and is completely symmetrical. The Jacobean detail, inside and out, is depressingly hard and dead, as in too much of Salvin's later work. The conservatory was demolished *c.* 1920. (*Morris* III, 29; Chadwick, *Paxton*, 98–9, ID.)

CASTLE ASHBY HOUSE, Northamptonshire

There were considerable Victorian embellishments to this for the third Marquess of Northampton. In 1861–5 M. D. Wyatt was active in the garden, his *chef d'œuvre* being the symmetrical combination of conservatory, Italian garden and columned screen, the whole making up a piece of fanciful classical design on a grand scale and of the highest quality. In 1868–70 E. W. Godwin built a Gothic lodge and the splendidly romantic kitchen gardens, both still there. In 1875 Burges made elaborate designs for decorating a room; if executed, this does not seem to have survived. Finally, competently, if less memorably, Sir T. G. Jackson and others were busy inside the house in the 1880s and later (e.g. the richly decorated neo-Wren chapel). (*B of E*; *A* 10 June 1871, PID (Godwin's lodge).)

CHANTER'S HOUSE, Ottery St Mary, Devon

Enlarged and remodelled by William Butterfield, 1881–2, for his friend Lord Coleridge, who had been appointed Lord Chief Justice in the previous year. The house faces inwards onto what is virtually the close at Ottery; outwards, to open country. Butterfield enlarged a modest eighteenth-century and earlier house to considerable size, the *pièce de résistance* being the enormous two-storey library, with two distinctive Butterfield chimneypieces, a first-floor gallery and a life-size memorial to Lord Coleridge's first wife in a kind of chantry which opens off the gallery. The exterior is in the hard Gothic of Butterfield's later years, with much diapered brickwork and plenty of character. The interior, in spite of a certain amount of de-Victorianizing by Lord Coleridge's son, is still redolent of a High Church Victorian lawyer's household. Butterfield designed a delightful conservatory with aviary attached, and installed marble and iron cases for radiators, and

much in the way of painted decoration, tomato-red walls and patterned tiles, some of which survives.

CLIFFE CASTLE, Keighley, Yorkshire, W.R.

By George Smith of Bradford, 1875–8, and Wilson Barley of Bradford and Keighley, *c.* 1880, for H. I. Butterfield, a Keighley textile manufacturer with French connections. Elizabethan, with four towers, two of them eighty feet high. Interior decoration by Harland and Son, and Greenard of Paris. Ceiling paintings by Levaux of Paris. Stained glass by Powell brothers, including the Butterfield family in Elizabethan dress. In the later wing a smoking room in the tower, and a winter-garden with sixty-five foot dome. Now a museum, with many of the trimmings removed. (*Castle and Country Houses in Yorkshire*, 1885.)

CLIVEDEN HOUSE, nr Taplow, Buckinghamshire

Rebuilt by Sir Charles Barry, 1850–1, for the Duke

401

391. Cliveden, Buckinghamshire (Sir Charles Barry, 1850). The Clock Tower (H. Clutton, 1861).

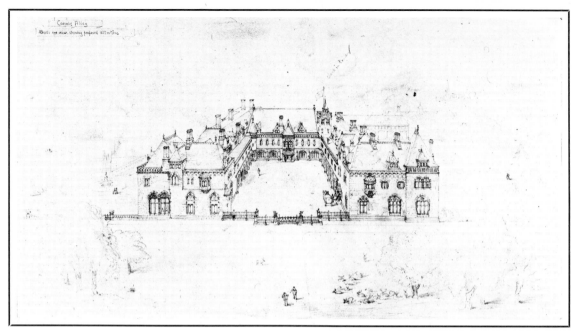

392. Combe Abbey, Warwickshire, 1862. W. E. Nesfield's design.

of Sutherland. A grand symmetrical design, set in a formal layout in a superb position above the Thames. The house consists of a central block and matching wings, with none of Barry's usual picturesque groupings. The detailing is competent but undistinguished, the facades of brick faced with Portland cement—a late example of this treatment for a country house. In complete contrast to the cold splendour of the main house is Clutton's extraordinary clock tower (1862) attached to the stable block. This is a design of inspired extravagance, with a circular staircase in the Vignola manner half exposed on one facade. The house was bought by the American millionaire W. W. Astor in the 1890s, and much redecorated internally by J. L. Pearson and others. Now National Trust. (*B* VIII (1850), 318, ID; *CL* XXXII (1912), 808, 854, LXX (1931), 38, 68, ID.)

CLOUDS, East Knoyle, Wiltshire (Pls 49, 50)

By Philip Webb for the Hon. Percy Wyndham, 1879–91. See pp. 80–82. The servants' wing has been demolished, the top storey of the main block removed and the interior altered, but the house is still worth a visit.

CLOVERLEY HALL, nr Whitchurch, Shropshire (Pl. 40. Fig 3)

By W. E. Nesfield for J. P. Heywood, the Liverpool banker, 1864–70. See pp. 35, 72, 78. The main block was rebuilt in the 1920s; the servants' wing with dove-cote and the big stable block with clock tower survive. Church and cottages by Nesfield, in the village. (H. R. Hitchcock in *The Country Seat*, ed. Colvin and Harris (London, 1970), 252–61, PID; *CL* CLXIII (1978) 679, ID.)

CLYFFE HOUSE, Toncleton, Dorset

By Benjamin Ferrey for Charles Porcher, 1841–3. An inoffensive but rather dim Tudor–Gothic remodelling in the Pugin manner, with rather more of symmetry than Pugin would have given it.

COBHAM PARK, Surrey

By E. M. Barry, 1870–3, for C. J. F. Combe, the brewer. See pp. 297, 299.

COMBE ABBEY, nr Coventry, Warwickshire (Pl. 392)

W. E. Nesfield made elaborate designs for remodelling and enlarging the house in the Gothic style for the Earl of Craven in 1860. Only one large wing was built, and this has been demolished. (*Eastlake*; *CL* XXVI (1900), 794–806, 840–8; designs in the V & A.)

COOMBE WARREN, Norbiton, Surrey (Pl. 53)

By George Devey, c. 1865, for Bertrand Currie (son of Raikes Currie of Minley Manor). Rebuilt after a fire in 1870 on an enlarged scale, and to a somewhat different design. One of Devey's most elaborate and best-known houses, in a mixture of stone, brick, plaster and half-timbering, with numerous shaped brick gables of Betteshanger type. The typical disjointed Devey plan of the 1870 house, with the service wing stretching out in a series of zigzags from the main block, was anticipated in simpler form in the first design. Elaborate Jacobean decoration inside. Large formal gardens with orangery and temple to Gladstone. Has been demolished but the adjacent COOMBE COTTAGE (now Coombe Wood) of c. 1863 with additions of 1870–4 survives. This was built for E. C. Baring (later Lord Revelstoke) of

Barings' Bank, with a low tower and numerous gables of different sizes, some of them weather-boarded. The result, though far from cottagey in size is intimate in scale and dainty and very pretty in effect. Charmingly rural stables, dated 1863, next to the house. (For both houses see W. H. Godfrey, Introduction, note 123, PID.)

COWDRAY PARK, Midhurst, Sussex

For the Earl of Egmont, 1875. Architect unrecorded. Stone-built Old English with a central tower, great hall, bits of half-timbering and fancy timber gables. Alterations for Lord Cowdray, who bought it in 1908. (*Morris* V, 51.)

CRABBET PARK, Worth, Sussex (Pl. 55)

See p. 85. Pioneer neo-Georgian house designed for themselves in 1872–3 by Wilfred Scawen Blunt and his wife Lady Anne, daughter of the first Earl of Lovelace (see Horsley Towers). An elaborate classical pavilion near the house, containing Royal tennis court and swimming bath, was built in 1908, probably to Lady Anne Blunt's designs. (Earl of Lytton, *Wilfred Scawen Blunt* (London, 1901), 245.)

CRAWLEY COURT, nr Winchester, Hampshire

By F. P. Cockerell, 1877, for A. S. Kennard, a London banker. A curious collision between country house demands for dignity, and the 'Queen Anne' style, of which Cockerell was one of the pioneers. A big E-shaped house, symmetrical in the Elizabethan manner with central porch and turrets in the angles of the entrance court. But the gables, window surrounds and much of the wilful detail were in the 'Queen Anne' manner, in rubbed and moulded red brick that contrasted very gaily with the grey flint of the walls. The general effect was cheerful, if eccentric and rather over-busy. Has been demolished.

CREWE HALL, Cheshire (Pl. 28)

Gutsy 'restoration' by E. M. Barry for the third Lord Crewe of a famous Jacobean house after it had been destroyed by fire, 1866–71. 'I will restore what is good, I will discard what is bad or obsolete, and I will add all that I consider necessary in the altered circumstances of my own time.' Inevitably, the result was overpoweringly high-Victorian. Barry filled the central courtyard of the old plan with a two-storey hall, and the best feature of the house is the way space flows between the lush decor of this hall, the entrance hall, the original Great Hall and the staircase. Elsewhere room after room of abundantly lavish decoration, with much use of figurative plasterwork in the Jacobean manner, but suitably refined to suit Victorian taste. (E. M. Barry, *Lectures on Architecture* (1881), 318–31; *CL* XI (1902, 1), 400–9, XXXIII (1913, 1), 634–40. Plans at RIBA.)

DAWPOOL, THURSTASTON, Cheshire (Pl. 45)

By Norman Shaw, 1882–4, for T. H. Ismay, owner of the White Star Line. A very large, stone-built country house in the manner of Adcote and his later wing at Cragside, that is to say much more sober than his earlier Old English work. The plan was irregular but straightforward, with the main rooms loosely grouped to either side of a broad central corridor. The most extravagant feature was the enormous inglenook-cum-organ in the late French Gothic manner which dominated the two-storey picture gallery (a near contemporary of the similar room at Cragside). The panelled timber ceilings of the living rooms were suspended from structural ceilings of fireproof construction and the electric light fittings shown in the *Country Life* photographs look original. Demolished in 1926; the dining-room chimneypiece was reused as the box-office in a Birkenhead cinema. The gallery chimneypiece is at Port Meirion. (V & A; *A* 25 Oct. 1884, PI; *CL* XXIX (1911), 234–41, PID.)

THE DEEPDENE, nr Dorking, Surrey

The remarkable house remodelled by the banker Thomas Hope to his own designs in 1807–23 was again externally remodelled and enlarged about 1836–40 for his son Henry Thomas Hope. The result was much heavier and richer than what preceded it and was one of the pioneer works in the formation of the Victorian Italianate style. Inside most of Thomas Hope's interiors were left untouched, but a monumental new entrance hall of two storeys with galleries and colonnades was an exact contemporary of Barry's similar hall at the Reform Club. The architect has not been established, but may have been Henry Thomas Hope himself. The house has recently been demolished. (D. Watkin, *Thomas Hope* (London, 1968), 182–9, ID; *CL* V, 624, I.)

DENBIES, nr Dorking, Surrey

Designed for himself by Thomas Cubitt, 1850. A sober Italianate house which could well have stood at the corner of Belgrave Square. Demolished.

DENNE HILL, nr Canterbury, Kent (Pl. 393)

An interesting small country house by George Devey for Col. Edward Dyson, 1871–5. Devey used his favourite-shaped gables for a symmetrical red-brick design in the mid-seventeenth-century manner, with none of his usual Elizabethan or Jacobean detail. Roundel busts of Inigo Jones and Rubens to either side of the entrance demonstrate what he considered his sources. What, if any, was the connection with the 'Queen Anne' movement?

DOBROYD CASTLE, Todmorden, Yorkshire, W.R. (Pl 394)

By John Gibson, 1866–9, for John Fielden (son of John Fielden, the radical cotton manufacturer,

393. Denne Hill, Kent (George Devey, 1871–5).

Unitarian and philanthropist). The relationship of the Fieldens to Todmorden was similar to that of the Crossleys to Halifax. With Gibson as their architect they built the sumptuous little Corinthian town hall (1870), the large Unitarian Church (1865) and Todmorden Castle, the silhouette of which rises spectacularly above the town. It is best left as a silhouette, however, for closer inspection reveals little more than a castellated villa with remarkably unappetizing detailing. Inside, however, an imposing staircase ('as in a club or hotel', *B of E*) with stained glass and carvings illustrating the life of John Fielden, senior, and (originally) splendid central gaslight. See also Nutfield Priory. (*B* 1869, 945; 1875, 953, PID.)

DOWN HALL, nr Harlow, Essex (Pl. 11)

By F. P. Cockerell for Sir H. S. Ibbetson, Bart, 1871–3. A symmetrical classical house with loggia and corner pavilions. Main rooms grouped round an entrance hall treated as a Pompeian atrium. Sgraffito decoration by Wormleighton and Wise of South Kensington. But the importance of the house is that it is an early example of concrete construction (though with stone dressings). See p. 21. (*BN* 4 July 1873, PID.)

EASNEYE, nr Ware, Hertfordshire

By Alfred Waterhouse for T. Fowell Buxton, son of the liberal anti-slavery brewer, 1867–9. 'Thirteenth-century Domestic.' (*Eastlake*, App. 298.)

EATON HALL, nr Chester (Pls 1–3, 47)

Remodelling by Alfred Waterhouse for the first Duke of Westminster, 1870–82. See pp. 2–4, 29, 78. All but the chapel, clock tower and stable court were demolished in 1961. (*CL* II, 182; IX, 496; XLVII, 724, NMR.)

ELLEL GRANGE nr Lancaster

For William Preston, a merchant, 1856. Architect

unknown. A nice Osborne Italianate villa with tower. Fine ceilings and impressive main staircase. (*B of E*.)

ELVEDEN HALL, Suffolk

A Georgian house was remodelled *c.* 1870 by John Norton for the Maharajah Duleep Singh (who had been removed from India just before the Mutiny and lived extravagantly in England, alternating between chorus girls and the country). Red-brick classical exteriors, remarkably pretty glass and plaster interiors in the Indian manner. Inlays by Maw and Co., painted decoration by Holzmann, silvered glass by

Powell. In 1893 Lord Iveagh, the Guinness king, bought the estate. He duplicated the Norton building and built up an enormous Indian hall in marble at the junction. The new wing has expensive and depressing neo-Georgian interiors by William Young. (*B* 18 Nov. 1871; PID; *A* 18 Mar. 1871, ID.)

ELVETHAM HALL, Hartley Wintney, Hampshire (Pl. 29, Col. Pl. III)

Remodelled by S. S. Teulon for Lord Calthorpe (landed gentleman, but owned Edgbaston), 1859–62. Polychrome Gothic in hard red brick liberally patterned with black. A picturesque composition in Teulon's later manner, so chopped-up and busy as to appear on the verge of disintegration. The plan is an additive one of bay-windowed rooms that in some ways anticipates Shaw. Plate-glass sash windows and highly curious tracery on the staircase and elsewhere. Lush carving (by Thomas Earp) inside, especially on the chimneypieces. Much stained glass. Ironwork by Skidmore. The house was much added to early this century, still in the Teulon manner. Teulon's contract drawings and water-colour perspectives preserved at the house. (*B* XVIII (1860), 332–333, ID BN VI (1860), 419, I; *CL* CXLVIII (1970), 1282–6, ID.)

ENBROOK, Sandgate, Folkestone

By S. S. Teulon for the Hon. J. D. Bligh, *c*. 1854. Largely demolished but the entrance facade now incorporated in the Police Training Centre at Sandgate. (*B* XII (1854), 486–7 PID.)

ETTINGTON PARK, nr Stratford-on-Avon, Warwickshire (Pl. 30, Col. Pl. IV)

External remodelling by John Prichard of Llandaff for E. P. Shirley, 1858–63. High roofs and near-symmetrical facades. A triumph of Ruskinian polychromy and sculptural adornment. English '1st Pointed' with touches of Italian and French Gothic. Built of five different varieties and colours of stone, arranged in horizontal bands in the Italian manner. Much figurative and foliage sculpture by Earp. Little of Prichard inside. Now a hotel. See pp. 58–9 (*Eastlake*, 304–6, ID; *BN* XVI (1869, 1), 158, ID; 567, I.)

EYNSHAM HALL, nr Witney, Oxfordshire

Of the house designed by Charles Barry for the Earl of Macclesfield in 1843 only the Italianate lodge gates survive. The estate was bought by the Mason family (of Mason and Barry; see St Leonard's Hill) and the house remodelled by Ernest George (*c*. 1880?) as a large hard Elizabethan mansion in bright red brick. Owen Jones laid out garden terraces in 1872 for the Masons. Now a police college.

FALCONHURST LODGE, nr Edenbridge, Kent

By David Brandon, 1851, for the Hon. J. Chetwynd-Talbot. See p. 54. The main block has been demolished.

FARNHAM PARK, Farnham Royal, Buckinghamshire (Pl. 43)

By W. E. Nesfield for Henry Vallance, *c*. 1865 (date on a rain-water head). See p. 72. About 1920 a new entrance front was added, the windows altered, and the interior almost entirely redecorated; the inglenook illustrated by Eastlake was among the features removed. (*Eastlake*, 344–5.)

FINEDON HALL, nr Wellingborough, Northamptonshire

For William Mackworth-Dolben, *c*. 1851–9. The architect of this curious building is unknown. Eccentric chunky Gothic embellishments added to an earlier house, including a large tower and elaborate stable block. (*CL* X, 48.)

FLETE, nr Ivybridge, Devon (Pls 46, 396)

Built out of Barings' Bank money by Norman Shaw for H. B. Mildmay (whose mother was a Baring), 1878–80. The house was in fact a very complicated remodelling. Shaw did over the exterior of the main block, which was castellated Georgian Gothic, retaining the castellation but refacing it and altering the windows; he retained the long low Elizabethan wing at the back, but gutted it to make a gallery, billiard room and music room; and added a long kitchen wing and a dominating tower on the entrance front. The skill with which he co-ordinated the different and potentially disparate elements into a

394. (left) Dobroyd House, Todmorden, Yorkshire (John Gibson, 1866).
395. (above) Elvetham Park. Hampshire (S. S. Teulon, 1859–62). A chimneypiece carved by Earp.

dramatic composition with gables, roofs, chimney-stacks and battlements building up to the main tower, shows him at the height of his powers. Even so there is a coldness about the house which is not only due to the rather unpleasantly tooled stonework of which it is built. Inside changes of level, flights of steps, contrasted shapes of rooms, play of light, inglenooks and all the rest of Shaw's repertory deployed with unfailing skill and resourcefulness. (*A* 18 Jan. 1889, I; *CL* XXXVII (1915, 2), 680–8, PID.)

FLINTHAM HALL, nr Newark, Nottinghamshire (Pl. 397, Col. Pl. I)

External remodelling and enlargement of Georgian house by T. C. Hine of Nottingham, *c.* 1851–4, for T. B. T. Hildyard. Coarsely classical, with curious classical tracery similar to that designed by Hine for warehouses in Nottingham. Big central porch tower added in front, and a conservatory and galleried saloon at the back. In the nostalgically unaltered saloon is a massive chimneypiece-cum-bookcases in the *cinquecento* manner, made by Holland and Sons to the design of T. R. Macquoid and shown in the 1851 Exhibition. Gas was supplied for the village and house at the time of the remodelling. See p. 43.

FONTHILL ABBEY, Wiltshire (Pl. 25)

By William Burn for the Marquess of Westminster,

1856 (first and more elaborate designs, 1846–52), on a portion of the original Beckford estate. This massive importation of the Scottish Baronial style into Wiltshire was demolished in the 1950s. (*CL* X, 840, ID; RIBA.)

FORD MANOR, Lingfield, Surrey

By Robert Kerr, for Joseph Spender-Clay, a banker from Burton-on-Trent, 1868. Reminiscent of the garden front at Bear Wood although somewhat scaled down. A terrible design. Some of the detail has been scraped off and it is now known as Greathed Manor, and leased to the Mutual Householders' Association.

FOXWARREN PARK, nr Cobham, Surrey

Designed for himself, 1855, by Charles Buxton, a brewer and brother of T. F. Buxton of Easneye, with assistance from Frederic Barnes of Ipswich. He was one of the formidable Quaker-philanthropic complex of Gurneys, Buxtons, Hoares and Barclays, with strong East Anglian connections. The house is in the East Anglian sixteenth-century manner, of unpleasantly hot red brick and terracotta, with crow-stepped gables, diapered and moulded brickwork and no stone used, even for doors or windows. In the home farm enormous overlapping scalloped timber

396. (above left) Flete, Devon (R. Norman Shaw, 1878–80).
397. (above right) Flintham Hall, Nottinghamshire (Thomas Hine, 1851–4).

gables superimposed on East Anglian brickwork, with nightmarish effect. (*B of E*, especially App., I.)

GOLDINGS, nr Hertford (Fig. 6)

By George Devey for Robert Abel Smith, banker, 1871–7. One of Devey's largest and most depressing houses. See pp. 84, 222.

GREENHAM LODGE, nr Newbury, Berkshire

By R. Norman Shaw for Lloyd Baxendale, 1878–9. A variant on the theme of the Elizabethan Shaw House, Donnington, a few miles away, with symmetrical main facades and on a compacter plan than was usual with Shaw at that date. Entrance front of brick, garden front half-timbered. The design is no more than competent, and the house leaves little impression. Great Hall and nice de Morgan tiles inside. (RIBA; *A* 4 Jan. 1889, I; Murray's *Berkshire* (1949), p. 104–5, ID. Saint *Norman Shaw* 98–9, 422 Pl.)

GREGYNOG HALL, nr Newtown, Montgomery-shire

Rebuilt 1837, for the second Lord Sudeley. It replaced a half-timbered house, and is in the same black and white manner, on a generous scale. On inspection the 'timbers' appear to be made of flat strips of metal, set into concrete facades. Now part of the University of Wales.

GRINKLE PARK, Eastington, Yorkshire, N.R.

By Alfred Waterhouse, 1882, for Sir Charles Palmer, the Jarrow shipbuilder. A nondescript garden front, but the entrance front a rather impressive essay in semi-castellated Gothic. The first designs (now at the RIBA) were very much grander. Palmer bought the property because he owned an iron mine nearby; iron from the mine was loaded onto his own ships at the little port, which he built at Port Mulgrave, near Grinkle, and was carried to his shipyards. Now a hotel.

GRITTLETON HOUSE, nr Chippenham, Wiltshire

Lavish remodelling and enlargement of an older house by James Thomson (a villa architect who designed terraces around Ladbroke Grove in London) for Joseph Neeld, who had inherited nearly a million pounds from his uncle Philip Rundell of Rundell and Bridge, the leading silversmiths of late Georgian days. Clutton was also somewhat mysteriously involved *c.* 1848–55. Work seems to have started as early as 1832, and was completed after Neeld's death in 1856 by his brother. The house is massively built of stone, the style Romanesque, turning Jacobean on the skyline. In spite of a long and

confused building history and the eccentric crudity of the Romanesque detailing, this is a house in the grand manner, and by no means to be despised. Two-storey galleries radiate on a cruciform plan from the lantern under the central tower, and form a series of linked spaces designed as a setting for Neeld's enormous collection of contemporary sculpture. The sculpture has gone, but its setting remains as sensational and spatially ingenious as anything to be found in Victorian country house design. Gas lighting, fireproof construction, hot-air heating, eleven w.c.'s, no bathroom. (*B* XI (1853), 279–81, PID; *CL* CXL (1960, 2), 708–12, ID; many ill. NMR.)

GUNNERGATE HALL, Marton, nr Middlesbrough

Thomas Vaughan much enlarged the house of his father, John Vaughan, the great Middlesbrough ironmaster, *c.* 1868–74. The original substantial Gothic house was by J. P. Pritchett of Darlington, 1858. For the billiard room, see p. 38. The house was sold up when Vaughan's business failed in 1879, and has been demolished.

407

398. Grittleton House, Wiltshire (James Thomson, 1848–60).

HAFODUNOS HOUSE, nr Llanrwst, Denbighshire (Pl. 399)

By George Gilbert Scott, 1861–6, for H. R. Sandbach (son of a Liverpool West India merchant, married to a Liverpool Roscoe). Kelham reduced to a slightly more domestic scale. Built of red brick and prettily situated above a small terraced and heavily planted valley. Three-storey main block; clock tower *à la* Kelham and billiard room *à la* Abbot's Kitchen, Glastonbury, to one side; lower service wing and Gothic conservatory to the other. Inside, broad spine corridors in the Kelham manner, a staircase and entrance hall with screens of cathedral arcading, and much typical Scott detail. Foliage capitals probably by Farmer and Brindley. The Roscoe family were the chief patrons of John Gibson, and there are (or were) statues and built-in reliefs by him throughout the house. According to Eastlake it cost £30,000. (*Eastlake*, App. 216.)

HALL, nr Barnstaple, N. Devon

Ostensibly by Philip Hardwick, 1847, for Robert Chichester, but drawings at the R.I.B.A. suggest that his son P. C. Hardwick did most of the work. A largish rather tame Elizabethan manor house. Symmetrical entrance front. The best feature is the Gothic Great Hall attached to one corner, with much decoration of stencilling and painted texts.

HALL PLACE, Leigh, Kent

By George Devey, 1872–6, for Samuel Morley, M.P., a hosiery millionaire, non-conformist, Radical and staunch supporter of Gladstone. Devey's biggest, but not his best, house, an enormous red-brick Tudor design that rambled on interminably, but certainly not disagreeably, in a lushly coniferous setting. The main block had been partly gutted by fire, and was recently demolished. Large stables and other outlying buildings in the same manner.

HALTON HOUSE, Buckinghamshire (Pls 286, 401)

By W. R. Rogers 1882–8, for A. C. de Rothschild. See P. 302.

HATHEROP HOUSE, nr Fairford, Gloucestershire

By Henry Clutton, 1856, for second Lord de Mauley. Bought *c.* 1871 by Thomas Sebastian Bazley, a Lancashire cottentot, and son of the Liberal M.P. for Manchester. A large, stodgily asymmetric house in the Elizabethan style, with a big tower. Glastonbury kitchen. Fine expensive church by Clutton, next to the house. (*B* XIV (1856), 502–3, PID.)

THE HEATH HOUSE, Tean, Staffordshire (Pl. 400)

By Thomas Johnson of Lichfield, 1836–40, for John

399. (above left) Hafodunos House, Denbighshire (Sir George Gilbert Scott, 1861–6).
400. (above right) The Heath House, Staffordshire (Thomas Johnson, 1836–40). The staircase.

Burton Philips, of the senior branch of the great Philips textile clan. A rather thin Tudor–Gothic house, with a big *porte-cochère* tower as the central feature of the symmetrical entrance front. Planned round a very spacious central staircase. Fireproof construction. Of considerable interest because it retains its original furniture, picture collection and wallpapers. Free-standing classical orangery with formal garden, also by Thomas Johnson. (*CL* CXXXIII (1963), 18, 62, ID.)

HEDSOR HOUSE, nr Marlow, Buckinghamshire (Pl. 219)

By J. T. Knowles, senior, 1865–8, for Lord Boston. See p. 294. The French roofs were removed, the windows altered and the interiors expensively neo-Georgianized in 1925.

HEMSTED HOUSE, nr Staplehurst, Kent

By David Brandon, 1862, for Gathorne Hardy, M.P. (later Earl of Cranbrook), a Conservative politician with a fortune derived from the family ironworks in Yorkshire. An attempt by Brandon to give his safe Elizabethan a muscular twist. Big tower with French roof, sloping staircase windows. Gas, fireproof corridors, gunroom, landscaping by W. B. Thomas. The house had a certain alarming vitality, which was largely removed when Lord Rothermere took off the

tower and remodelled the windows early in this century. Now Benenden School. (*B* XX (1862), 242–5, 260, PID.)

HEWELL GRANGE, Tardebigge, Worcestershire (Pl. 59)

Built in 1884–91, at enormous expense, to Bodley and Garner's designs for the Earl of Plymouth, who was ground-landlord of a chunk of Cardiff. Thomas Garner was the operative partner. The house is in strong contrast to the free treatment and asymmetric facades of mid-Victorian Elizabethan houses. It is closely based on Montacute, with a grand symmetrical front looking down over terraced gardens. The principal feature of the interior is the enormous two-storey arcaded entrance hall, Renaissance rather than Elizabethan. Splendidly opulent indicator board for the original electric bell system. Now a Borstal. (*CL* XII, 732; XXIV, 240; NMR (Bedford Lemere).)

HEYTHROP HALL, nr Chipping Norton, Oxfordshire

Archer's great Baroque palace was gutted by fire in 1830, and stood derelict until bought by Albert Brassey (son of Thomas Brassey, the contractor) in 1870. The interior was rebuilt with big classical rooms including a two-storey entrance hall. Surprisingly, Alfred Waterhouse was the architect. He

409

401. Halton House, Buckinghamshire, 1882–8. The demolished winter garden.

exhibited his design of the hall at the Academy in 1880, and it was illustrated in the *Building News* of 18 Dec. 1885. The original drawing is preserved in the house. (*CL* XVIII, 270. I)

HOLKER HALL, nr Cartmel, Lancashire

By Paley and Austin, rebuilt after a fire, *c.* 1873, for the seventh Duke of Devonshire. A red sandstone house of scale and panache, with facades of skilful asymmetry. The detail is part Elizabethan, part Gothic, with a big tower to one side; the composition owes something to Salvin and Shaw, but the architecture of this capable northern partnership was by no means derivative. (*B of E*, I.)

HOPE END, nr Malvern, Worcestershire

By Habershon, Pite and Fawckner, *c.* 1873, for C. A. Hewitt. A large stone house showing the influence of Shaw's Old English style. Tower with smoking room and chapel in the upper storeys. Fireproof corridors and stairs, central heating and ventilation (*B* 8 Nov. 1875, 886–7, PID.)

HORNBY CASTLE, nr Lancaster

By Sharpe and Paley, *c.* 1850, for Pudsey Dawson, the son of a Mayor of Liverpool and brother of James Dawson of Wray Castle. A sensational 'restoration' of a medieval castle, on the edge of the village, with one very large tower and numerous smaller ones. (*B of E*; *B* VIII (1850), p. 402, I.)

HORSLEY TOWERS, East Horsley, Surrey (Pl. 402, 403)

Charles Barry designed a Tudor house here for William Currie in 1834. Large additions, in the same style, including a tower and Great Hall with open timber roof, were made by the first Earl of Lovelace (Byron's son-in-law) in 1847–8, working to his own designs. These pale beside the extraordinary embellishments, in flint and polychrome brick, made by the Earl *c.* 1855–60 and later. They include a brick vaulted horseshoe cloister and chapel and a much larger tower. The approach is by way of two arches, a tunnel under the garden, the cloister, two more arches and then round to the main front. Innumerable buildings in the village and on the estate in the same style. (*B of E*.)

HUGHENDEN MANOR, High Wycombe, Buckinghamshire

Remodelling of a Georgian house by E. B. Lamb, 1862, for Benjamin Disraeli. His Conservative supporters lent him the money with which to buy the property, to give him sufficient standing to be a Victorian Prime Minister. Lamb refaced the facades, with elaborately modelled brick of several colours and added his distinctive corbelled-out surrounds to the windows. The result is by no means disagreeable, and gives some idea of the more extreme effects he devised for Nun Appleton. Main interiors redecorated by Lamb in pleasing but, for the date, very old-fashioned pre-Puginesque Gothic (*CL* CXII (1953), 1604, 1698, ID.)

410

402. (above left) Horsley Towers, Surrey (Earl of Lovelace, 1847–60). The cloisters.
403. (above right) Horsley Towers, Surrey. The approach.

HUTTON HALL, nr Guisborough, Yorkshire

By Alfred Waterhouse, 1865–8, for J. W. Pease, M.P. (Bart, 1882), the Liberal Quaker banker who promoted the development of Middlesbrough. Red brick, described by Waterhouse as 'Early Domestic'. Long, low Gothic house with steep roofs and conservatory, like an overgrown vicarage. (*Eastlake*, App. 270, *Morris* III, 16.)

CHATEAU IMPNEY, Droitwich, Worcestershire (Col. Pl. XXIII)

By Auguste Tronquois, 1869–75, for John Corbett. See pp. 295–6 (*CL* IX, 592, ID.)

IWERNE MINSTER HOUSE, nr Blandford, Dorset

By Alfred Waterhouse, 1878, for the second Lord Wolverton, son of G. C. Glyn (of Glyn Mills), City banker and railway promoter. Still in the forbidding blown-up rectory style of Hutton Hall. Later belonged to J. H. Ismay (son of T. H. Ismay of Dawpool) who altered the interior. Now a school.

KEELE HALL, nr Newcastle-under-Lyme, Staffordshire (Pl. 15)

By Salvin, 1855–61, for Ralph Sneyd. A rebuilding of the house originally built by the Sneyds in the early seventeenth century. The eccentric gables are derived from those on the original house, but Salvin's design is on a much larger scale and much more irregular. His gift for calculated asymmetry was already on the wane and the entrance front is confused rather than picturesque. Two-storey Elizabethan Great Hall, big classical drawing rooms. Now the central building of the University of Keele. (J. M. Kolbert, *The Sneyds and Keele Hall* (Keele, 1967), *CL* XXIII, 306.)

KIDDINGTON HALL, nr Oxford

By Sir Charles Barry, *c.* 1850, for Mortimer Ricardo, of the banking family. A medium rich Italianate house of medium size, with no tower.

KNIGHTSHAYES, nr Tiverton, Devon (Pl. 31)

By William Burges, 1869–71, for J. Heathcoat Amory, Liberal M.P. for Tiverton, to which his father-in-law had removed his lace-making business as a consequence of the Luddite riots in Leicestershire. A robustly muscular early Gothic design in two colours of stone, with little of the romantic effervescence of Cardiff and Castell Coch—as was suitable for a prosperous manufacturer, rather than a millionaire marquess. The main front has two symmetrical bay windows with gables above framing a subtly asymmetrical centre. Burges made elaborate designs for the interior, which are preserved in the house. They were executed only in very cut down form. Further decoration by Crace. 'The feature of the interior is a large hall to be used for the reception of the owner's tenantry.' (*Eastlake* 356–7, ID; *A* 2 July 1870, ID.)

LANHYDROCK HOUSE, nr Bodmin, Cornwall (Col. Pl. II)

Reconstruction of a Jacobean house gutted by fire in 1881, except for the gallery wing. The architect was G. G. Scott's ex-pupil Richard Coad. Although the client, Lord Robartes, is said to have asked for 'a simple family house', the result, now lovingly displayed by the National Trust, is evocative of the comfortable lavishness considered suitable for a late-Victorian peer. The main rooms, smoking room and billiard room have elaborate neo-Jacobean decoration; the three courtyards of service rooms survive intact with all their fittings. (*CL* CLXIII (1978) 382–5, 458–61, PID)

LECHLADE MANOR HOUSE, Gloucestershire

By J. L. Pearson, 1872, for George Milward. One of Pearson's few country houses. It is fifteen years later than Quar Wood, and in the interval his devotion to Gothic had become less exclusive. An Elizabethan design, but with the same gift for irregular composition as had been shown at Quar Wood. (*AR* I (1897), 70–3, PID. Quiney *Pearson*, 179, 269, PID.)

LEONARDSLEE, nr Horsham, Sussex

By T. L. Donaldson, 1853, for W. E. Hubbard, of the same family as Lord Addington, builder of P. C. Hardwick's Addington (they were City Russia-merchants). Italianate outside, Greek inside, with two-storey central hall. Admired by Goodhart-Rendel as a good example of the type of 'houses not pretending to be stately but displaying modest sumptuousness'. (Ferriday, *Victorian Architecture*, 65.)

LOUGHTON HALL, Essex (Pl. 44)

By W. E. Nesfield, 1878, for the squarson of Loughton, the Revd J. W. Maitland, whose sister was married to Nesfield's cousin Osbert Salvin. Nesfield's most likeable country house, altogether delightful in its 'Queen Anne' mixture of seventeenth- and eighteenth-century motifs, of sash windows, leaded lights, gables, cupola, *oeils-de-boeuf*, white painted balustrades, plastered gables, deep roof and tall chimneystacks. The garden front almost completely symmetrical, the entrance front with an off-centre porch. To the right of the entrance hall a very large one-storey great hall intended as a living room. Is the church adjoining (1877) also by Nesfield? (*AR* I, (1897), 293–4, PI.)

404. (above) Malwood, Hampshire (Ewan Christian, 1884).
406. (right) Mentmore, Buckinghamshire (Paxton and Stokes, 1850–5). A Victorian photograph of the hall.
407. (lower right) Milner Field, Yorkshire. (Thomas Harris, 1873). The entrance hall.

LLYS DULAS, Anglesey (Pl. 405)

By Deane and Woodward, 1856, for the Irish-born Lady Dinorben, late of Kinmel Park (see p. 319). Presumably designed by Benjamin Woodward, and very much in the manner of his Meadow Buildings, Oxford, with cross-stepped gables. Venetian balcony and windows, and foliage capitals. Of moderate size; an Elizabethan wing is clearly by another architect. Long derelict and used for storage, and recently demolished. (*Eastlake*, App. 139.)

LYNFORD HALL, nr Thetford, Norfolk

By William Burn, 1856–61, for Lyne Stephens, heir to a rich English merchant in Lisbon, and married to Yolande Duvernay, an ex-ballet dancer of international repute. One of Burn's biggest houses. Jacobean red brick with stone dressings. Interior gutted by fire and restored. (RIBA).

MADRESFIELD COURT, nr Malvern, Worcestershire

By P. C. Hardwick, 1863–85, for the sixth Earl

Beauchamp. A moated house of considerable size, with a sixteenth-century brick wing (much restored) kept as the entrance. The rest is bright red brick, with much half-timbering. The most impressive feature is the narrow, high, internal courtyard, surrounded by black and white work and carved timber. Great Hall. Arts and Crafts embellishments for the seventh Earl, including the library and the chapel, with frescoes by H. A. Payne.

MALWOOD, nr Lyndhurst, Hampshire (Pl. 404)

By Ewan Christian, 1883–4, for Sir William Harcourt. An elaborately half-timbered house, in the style of Christian's The Highlands (*c.* 1874) and Mayfield (a big villa at Blackheath for Lord Penzance), which perhaps owed something to his training under Matthew Habershon. Harcourt, as a Liberal cabinet minister, naturally first thought of Devey, but rejected him because he feared he would be too expensive.

MARTON HALL, nr Middlesbrough

Henry Bolckow, the ironmaster (the man who 'stood by the side of the iron cradle in which Middlesbrough was rocked') built a moderate country residence here in 1854–7, next door to the property of his friend and partner John Vaughan. He remodelled and enlarged it in the boom days of the later 1860s (1867–75), possibly to the designs of C. J. Adams of Stockton, in French hotel or town hall style. Middlesbrough later engulfed it and it has been demolished. (NMR).

MENTMORE, nr Leighton Buzzard, Bedfordshire (Pl. 406)

By Paxton and Stokes, 1850–5, for Baron Meyer Amschel de Rothschild. The main block closely

405. (left) Llys Dulas, Anglesey (Deane and Woodward, 1856).

based on Wollaton Hall. Service wing attached to one corner. No hint of asymmetry in any of the facades. Main block axially planned round a top-lit central hall. Interiors fitted with French *boiseries*, seventeenth-century chimneypieces, etc., an early example of what was to become the norm in Rothschild and other plutocrat houses. The amazing contents were sold in 1978. For the Paxton ridge-and-furrow roof to the hall, see p. 19. Hot-water heating. (*B* XV (1857), 738–40 PID; Chadwick, *Paxton*, 188–92, ID.)

MILLICHOPE PARK, nr Ludlow, Shropshire

By Edward Haycock of Shrewsbury, *c.* 1837–40, for the Revd Robert Norgrave Pemberton. A remarkable house. The setting is exquisitely landscaped, with a rocky and pine-surrounded lake, like a Chinese drawing, below the house. The approach is through a romantic cutting dug out of the rock. The house is on a steepish slope above the lake, Greek, with an Ionic portico. But the original entrance (recently altered) was at the low level through a pair of massive Doric columns inset into the base of the portico. A long tunnel of steps led up from the dark entrance hall into the airy and spacious main hall, filling the centre of the house, with two storeys of Ionic galleries round it and the main staircase (now mutilated and closed in) at one end, through the screen of ionic columns and on the axis of the entrance stairs. The lower floor is of fireproof construction with the shape of the vaulting exposed in the entrance hall. (*B of E*, ID; *CL* CLXI (1977) 310–13, 654–6, ID.)

MILNER FIELD, nr Saltaire, Yorkshire, W.R. (Pl. 407)

By Thomas Harris, *c.* 1873, for Titus Salt, junior, son of the creator of Saltaire. This remarkable and richly embellished house has been demolished. Chunky early Gothic, of stone and brick, built to an irregular, additive, Shaw-type plan in four sections dropping down the hill. Hill top skyline with towers and prominent chimneystacks. Glastonbury kitchen. Cavity walls, three bathrooms. Wrought metal by Richardson Slade and Co., chimneypieces and marble by Burke and Co., carving by Thomas Nicholls, stained glass by Saunders and Co., cartoons and painting by Weekes, furniture by Marsh, Jones and Crib, of Leeds. Did Harris have help in the design? Only the lodges, in the style of the house, remain. (*B* 15 Mar. 1873, 204–7, PID; *BN* 25 Dec. 1874, PID, 5 Jan. 1877, I.)

MINLEY MANOR, nr Farnborough, Hampshire (Pl. 32)

Original house, 1858–62, by Henry Clutton for Raikes Currie, a partner in Glyn Mills bank, Brick with stone dressings, of wildly asymmetrical French Gothic with very tall roofs. George Devey (who had designed Coombe Warren, Kingston, for Raikes

Currie's son Bertrand in 1868–75) designed a chapel (French Gothic) and orangery (seventeenth-century brick classical) in 1886, the year of his death. A big stodgy French wing was added in the late 1880s by Devey's former assistant Arthur Castings. The interiors (Jacobean and classical, rather than Gothic) look more like Devey than Clutton. Now belongs to the army. (NMR (Bedford Lemere).)

MUNCASTER CASTLE, Cumberland

Remodelled and largely rebuilt by Salvin for the fourth Lord Muncaster, 1862–6, in a soberly castellated style. (*Morris* III, 17.)

NARFORD HALL, nr Swaffham, Norfolk

William Burn added a large and capable classical wing with tower to the seventeenth-century house of the Fountains, *c.* 1860.

NETLEY ABBEY, nr Southampton

The old castle was remodelled and added to by J. D. Sedding, 1885–9, for the Hon. H. G. L. Crichton. Tudor and Elizabethan with elaborate interiors; to judge from photographs, not as interesting as one would have hoped in view of the architect. (*Muthesius* I, Figs. 110, 111, 112.)

NEW LODGE, Windsor Forest, Berkshire

By T. Talbot-Bury, 1856–9, for S. Van de Weyer, Belgian Ambassador to Britain, friend of Victoria and Albert and a notable book collector. His American father-in-law Josiah Bates, a partner in Barings' Bank, is said to have paid for the house, which is Tudor–Gothic, in the Pugin–Ferrey manner, but going heavy. Stone, with a big castellated flint and stone tower. Now British Railways. (*Eastlake*, App. 143.)

NORMANHURST, Nr Battle, Sussex

By Habershon, Brock and Webb, 1867, for Thomas Brassey. Probably inspired by Hector Horeau's Pippingford Park, Sussex, 1857. See pp. 294–5. The house was badly damaged by fire early in this century (in spite of its fireproof construction) and has been demolished. (*B* 8 June 1867, 410–11, PID; *Morris* VI, 51.)

NUN APPLETON HALL, nr Cawood, Yorkshire, W.R. (Pl. 37)

E. B. Lamb's wondrous wing of *c.* 1864 for Sir William Milner, Bart, with its notched and chamfered brickwork, has been demolished. (*B* XXII (1864), 188–90 PID with long dissertation by Lamb on its style.)

NUTFIELD PRIORY, Red Hill, Surrey

Bought by H. E. Gurney from Sir John Dean Paul,

Bart, after Paul's Bank crashed (and Sir John went to prison) in 1855. Rebuilt to fifteenth-century Gothic designs by John Norton, 1858–9. Bought by Joshua Fielden, M.P. (brother of John Fielden of Todmorden Castle), after Gurney's Bank crashed (and H. E. Gurney nearly went to prison) in 1866. Rebuilt, except for the conservatory, by John Gibson, 1870–4. Big, charmless, Gothic house of stone, with a tower eighty-six feet high at one end. Rooms grouped round a two-storey Great Hall, originally with organ and stained glass commemorating John Fielden, senior, and the passing of the Factory Bill (by Powell and Son to designs of F. R. Pickersgill). Gas, hot-air heating. Landscaping by Edward Kemp. (*B* 1874, 53, PID.)

OAKMERE HALL, nr Northwich, Cheshire

An interesting early house of *c.* 1872, by John Douglas for John Higson. Stone-built Gothic showing German influence. (Information Peter Howell.)

OLD WARDEN HOUSE, nr Shefford, Bedfordshire

By Henry Clutton, 1872, for Joseph Shuttleworth, a Lancashire cottentot. The design is obviously inspired by the Elizabethan Gawthorpe Hall, Lancashire, built in 1600–5 for Laurence Shuttleworth (with whom Joseph Shuttleworth's family had no provable connection).

ORCHARDLEIGH HOUSE, nr Frome, Somerset

By T. H. Wyatt 1855–8, for William Duckworth (from Lancashire). A large Elizabethan house, tedious inside and out. (Eastlake illustrated it; it is hard to understand why.) Stone-built, symmetrical garden front, the rest irregular. (*Eastlake*, 301–2, ID.)

OVERSTONE PARK, nr Northampton

By William Milford Teulon, 1862, for Lord Overstone (Samuel Jones Lloyd), the multi-millionaire Manchester banker, who expended £1,670,000 between 1825 and 1883 in the purchase of estates of over 30,000 acres. W. M. Teulon was S. S. Teulon's brother and had the worst of his brother's crudities with none of his genius. A terrible bastard Renaissance house, described for no obvious reason as 'simplified François I'. Drearily asymmetrical, with two vamped-up Barry towers and much ornament. Stone-built, with stone and brick cavity walls (a very early example), central heating, gas lighting, lift and plate sashes. Planned round a central staircase hall, with separate family and service wings. Landscaping by William Broderick Thomas. Now a school. (*B* XX (1862), 149–51, PID.)

OXONHOATH, nr Tonbridge, Kent

Remodelling by Salvin, 1846–7, for Sir W. R. P. Geary. See p. 292. (*B of E.*)

PARK PLACE, Henley-on-Thames, Oxfordshire

By Thomas Cundy, 1870, for J. Noble. See p. 297.

PENOYRE HOUSE, nr Brecon, Wales (Pl. 408)

By Anthony Salvin, 1846–8, for Colonel Lloyd Vaughan-Watkins. Salvin's most ambitious classical house. Three-storey main block, two-storey service wing at right angles to it, and an entrance tower with open belvedere top at the junction, approached by a formal avenue of Irish yews. A long conservatory wing (the roof has been altered) at the opposite side of the main block to the tower. The main block in the Barry palazzo manner, with a bold cornice and a loggia of alternate arches and columns at ground-floor level: the whole house built of the finest ashlar

415

408. Penoyre, Brecon (Anthony Salvin, 1846–8).

masonry, with rich and elegant Renaissance detailing. Inside, a big central top-lit hall and first-floor arcaded galleries and a staircase dividing into two flights that come up behind the arcades. Painted decoration in the Sang manner. But the proportions of the hall are awkward and the interiors as a whole disappointing. (Burke, *Visitations* II, 175, ID.)

PIERREPONT, nr Farnham, Surrey (Fig. 5)

By R. Norman Shaw, 1876–8, for Richard Combe of the brewing family. Only a few years later than Cobham Park, built for Richard Combe's grandfather in 1872, but a world apart in style. Half-timbered main block, tile-hung offices. Main front given a twist, and the floor levels varied, for quaintness. But Pierrepont is more impressive inside than out: the varied and contrasted sequence of ground-floor rooms, the two-storey great hall, the long low drawing room, the top-lit billiard room, the dining room with its deep inglenook, the corridor and staircase that string them all together, are beautifully contrived. (*BN* 26 May 1876, PID; *CL* XIV (1903, 2), 506–10, ID; RIBA.)

PLAS DINAM, nr Llanidloes, Montgomeryshire

By W. E. Nesfield, 1872–4, for O. M. Crewe-Read. Old English, rather than 'Queen Anne', and a rather confused design, especially since the large additions made by the Davies family, who bought it in the late nineteenth century. Nesfield needed a touch of formality to bring out the best in him. Gabled and slate-hung; the silvery colouring of the slates is its most attractive feature. Parapet of lead rosettes on the entrance front, as at Kinmel and Nesfield's bank at

Saffron Walden. Inside, a two-storey living hall with the other living rooms grouped round it. (*Muthesius* I, 113, ID.)

POSSINGWORTH MANOR, nr Uckfield, Sussex

By Matthew Digby Wyatt, 1868–70, for Louis Huth (brother of Huth of Wykehurst), a merchant banker and art collector, who in the 1870s was to collect blue china and have his wife painted by Whistler. An expensive and elaborate house of diapered red brick with stone dressings, irregularly grouped round three sides of a courtyard entered by a (demolished) gatehouse, in a way reminiscent of Shaw's Leys Wood. But the house is still firmly in the Pugin late Gothic tradition, as developed in mid-Victorian days, with the house chopped up into a confusion of innumerable pieces, each with its own roof. Inside, a Great Hall with stairs coming down into it, a top-lit picture gallery and much rank Puginesque detail. Stained glass by Lavers and Barraud, carving by Phyffers and Halliday brothers, fibrous plaster decoration by Jackson, landscaping by Marnock. Central heating. (*B* 26 Sept. 1868, PID; *A* 9 Jan. and 10 Apr. 1869, ID, 29 Jan. and 19 Feb. 1870, I.)

PRESTON HALL, nr Aylesford, Kent

By John Thomas, 1850, for Edward Ladd Betts, the partner of Sir Samuel Morton Peto. Expensive and unattractive Elizabethan, like its elder brother at Somerleyton. Symmetrical entrance front with central tower. It had interior decoration by Owen Jones, some of which survives. After the Peto crash it was sold to H. A. Brassey, son of the contractor. Now a chest hospital. (*Morris* III, 76.)

416

409. Rhinefield, Hampshire (Romaine-Walker, 1889–90).

PULL COURT, Bushley, Worcestershire

By Edward Blore, 1836–46, for J. E. Dowdeswell, M.P. Blore's first Elizabethan house, with a weedily symmetrical front. Now a school. (*B of E*, I.)

QUANTOCK LODGE, nr Bridgwater, Somerset

By Henry Clutton, 1857, for Lord Taunton, a Liberal banker. A large, boring Elizabethan house, worth visiting because of the Gothic gatehouse on the main road and the splendidly vigorous Gothic farm buildings (reminiscent of Clutton's gatehouse at Merevale). Now a school. (*Eastlake*, App. 148.)

QUAR WOOD, nr Stow-on-the-Wold, Gloucestershire (Pl. 36)

By J. L. Pearson, 1857, for the Revd R. W. Hippisley. Has suffered a fate worse than death at the hands of its former owner Sir Denys Lowson. See P. 62. (*Eastlake*, 303–4, ID, Quiney *Pearson*, 49–50, 275, ID.)

QUY HALL, nr Cambridge

By William White, 1868, for Clement Francis. A modest remodelling of a gabled manor house, long and low, of diapered red brick, with minimum Gothic detail. Inside, agreeably planned along spacious spine corridors. Dining room had original furniture and stencil decoration (said to be by Gambier Parry). The staircase has an ingenious open timber roof, and is spatially remarkably effective. (*Eastlake*, App. 326).

RAMSEY ABBEY, Huntingdonshire

By Edward Blore, 1837–9, for Edward Fellowes, M.P. (created Lord de Ramsey, 1887), for whom he also designed the classical Haverland Hall, Norfolk (1839, demolished). Elizabethan, round a sixteenth-century core, and one of Blore's biggest houses.

REDRICE HOUSE, nr Andover, Hampshire

By William Burn, 1844, for the Revd Thomas Best. A reticent Greek Revival house with minimum external detail. Two storeys high, long and low, the only accents being an entrance porch and bay windows on the garden front. Top-lit central hall.

RENDCOMB HOUSE, nr Cirencester, Gloucestershire (Pl. 6)

By P. C. Hardwick, 1863–5, for Sir Francis H. Goldsmid, Bart, M.P., the Jewish bullion broker, and one of the founders of University College, London. Big, overbearing house in a prominent hillside position. Classical, but English early eighteenth century rather than Italianate, except for the Italianate tower and *porte-cochère* attached to one corner

(an alternative design, without the tower, is at the RIBA). Spacious, coarsely detailed, classical rooms grouped round a central staircase hall and courtyard. The library has false book fronts with jokey titles (*How to Cure Corns* by Bunyan, etc.). Concrete floors on iron joists, one bathroom. A large French Renaissance stable block with high roofs, some way from the house. Now a public school. (*B* 10 June 1865, 412–13 PID. Original designs at house and RIBA.)

REVESBY ABBEY, nr Horncastle, Lincolnshire

By William Burn, 1844, for J. Banks-Stanhope. A large Jacobean house planned round a central hall, with separate service and family wings. One main front symmetrical, the entrance asymmetric. Inside, Viennese-style Baroque plasterwork, and a Flemish chimneypiece of 1659. (RIBA.)

RHINEFIELD, Brockenhurst, Hampshire (Pls 17, 409)

By W. H. Romaine-Walker, 1888–90, for Lt L. Walker-Munro, R.N., who had married Miss Walker of Barber and Walker, the Nottinghamshire colliery owners. Large and expensive Elizabethan house showing the influence of Norman Shaw. The Moorish smoking room survives. (*B* 17 Aug. 1889, PID; NMR (Bedford Lemere).)

RIBER CASTLE, Matlock, Derbyshire

Designed for himself, 1862, by John Smedley, the founder of Smedley's Hydro at Matlock. Eccentric and unbeautiful, with a memorable hilltop silhouette clearly emulating Hardwick. See *AR* Feb. 1940, 'The Unromantic Castle', by John Coolmore (thin disguise for John Summerson, who was at school there).

ROUNDWYCK HOUSE, nr Petworth, Sussex

By J. L. Pearson, 1868, for Captain Penfold. Built as a manor-farm, and still used as such: a gentleman's house but surrounded by peaceful farmland rather than a park. An unassuming but very prettily

417

410. Roundwick House, Sussex (J. L. Pearson, 1868).

composed half-timbered design, with brick chimneystacks, closely based on the vernacular tradition. It is interesting to see that at this early date Pearson was steering a parallel course to Nesfield and Shaw, with their Old English style. But influence, if any, probably came from Devey, who was Pearson's friend. (*AR* I (1897), I; A. Quiney, *John Loughborough Pearson* (New Haven and London, 1979), pp. 91–6), ID.)

ROUNTON GRANGE, nr Northallerton, Yorkshire, N.R.

By Philip Webb, 1872–6, for Sir Isaac Lowthian Bell, the Middlesbrough ironmaster (for whom Webb had done work at Washington Hall). This great house has, alas, been demolished. The south front in particular, five storeys high, with a tall gable between two massive chimneystacks rising above the high roofs of the symmetrical corner pavilions, must have been a splendid sight. On the other facades photographs suggest a certain shapelessness, in spite of the dominating roofs. The mixture of late Gothic and Georgian motifs, kneaded by Webb into Northern sobriety, is in step with the 'Queen Anne' movement of the 1870s, although Webb went his own way. Inside the main feature was the dining room, richly decorated by William Morris, and with a splendid frieze of embroidery above the panelling, made by Lady Bell and her daughter to the designs of Morris and Burne-Jones in 1880. Large addition by George

Jack, Webb's assistant, *c.* 1900 (*CL* XXXVII (1915, I), 906–12, PID.)

ROUSDON, nr Axminster, Devon (Pl. 9)

By George and Vaughan, 1874, for Sir H. W. Peek, Bart, of Peek Frean biscuits. A large and expensive house with which Ernest George made his name. The influence of Nesfield's and Shaw's Old English is apparent in the tile-hung gables and bay windows, the prominent roofs, tall panelled brick chimneystacks, and Leys Wood style tower; but the house has a not disagreeable touch of 1860s muscularity about it as well, suitable to its exposed position above the sea near Lyme Regis. Immensely solidly built, of flint with stone dressings. A simpler plan than Shaw would have employed at this date, with Great Hall and corridors round a central court, and long straight corridors threading the service wing. It is a young man's house, full of enthusiasm, sometimes at the expense of the client. The courtyard, though picturesquely detailed with a cloister at lower ground-floor level, is too small and dark for the English climate; the Great Hall, complete with inglenook, is dark with stained glass; the staircase is lined with marble and the corridors rich with mosaic floors and figurative decoration. Fives court for the gentry, bowling alley for the servants. Central heating and ventilation by Smeaton. Zimdah's pneumatic bells. Exposed fireproof construction in cloister. Contract was for £78,500. Now a public school. (*BN* 26 June 1874, PID; *A* 2 May 1874, ID.)

418

411. Rounton Grange, Yorkshire (Philip Webb, 1872–6).

RUTHIN CASTLE, Denbighshire

In 1826 Frederick and Maria West built a castellated house in the ruins of the medieval Ruthin castle. In 1848–53 it was greatly enlarged and embellished by Henry Clutton for their son Frederick Richard West. Clutton built a very large main block in Henry VII Gothic of red sandstone with a prominent octagonal tower, and a new service wing of white stone with sandstone dressings. A new clock tower was added to the 1826 wing, with a silhouette of the inspired craziness which Clutton sometimes gave way to on the periphery of his main designs. The sum result was a sensational skyline from the distance; on the whole it is better to stay at a distance, for the spaciously pedestrian interiors (great hall, elaborately unlovely carved stone chimneypiece in the dining room) are a disappointment. Now a hotel. See also p. 17. (*B* XI (1853), 579, ID.)

ST AUDRIES, West Quantoxhead, Somerset

By John Norton, *c.* 1870–2, for Sir Alexander Acland Hood, Bart. A big leathery Tudor–Gothic house in the Pugin tradition. Norton also designed the church and parish school. (*A* 21 Sept. 1872, PID.)

ST LEONARD'S HILL, nr Windsor (Pls 283–4)

By C. H. Howell, 1875, for Francis Tress Barry, M.P. See p. 299. Demolished (*BN* 15 Oct. 1875, PID; *CL* IX, 368, ID; NMR (Bedford Lemere).)

ST MICHAEL'S MOUNT, Cornwall

By J. P. St Aubyn, 1874, for his relative Sir John St Aubyn, Bart. Large additions to the old house, rising straight out of the sea, like a Greek monastery, but in gritty, granite Gothic. Deliberately kept lower than the old buildings (with unusual reticence for the date) in order not to interfere with the famous silhouette. (*BN* 20 Nov. 1874, ID.)

SANDRINGHAM HOUSE, Norfolk

Edward VII (then Prince of Wales) bought the property in 1860, and at first made only minor alterations and additions. In 1870 he started to rebuild the house on a scale large enough to seriously embarrass his finances. The style was Elizabethan, the material a harsh red brick with stone dressings, and the architect the obscure A. J. Humbert, for no good reason a favourite of the royal family (e.g. Royal mausoleum, Frogmore and Whippingham church, near Osborne). R. W. Edis added a ballroom in 1883 and in 1891 there were more alterations and additions, after a fire, including an attractive wing by Edis, built of carstone. The house had a bowling alley and both house and drives were lit by gas. Perhaps the most interesting feature are the enormous and elaborate gates of wrought and cast iron, designed by Thomas Jeckell for Barnard, Bishop and Barnard of Norwich, shown at the International Exhibition of 1862, and given by the gentry of Norfolk as a wedding present to Edward and Alexandra in 1863.

SEACOX HEATH, nr Flimwell, Sussex

By William Slater and R. C. Carpenter, 1862–72, for G. J. Goschen (Viscount Goschen, 1900), the Liberal politician, son of a City of London financier of German origin. Big Gothic house of stone with high roofs, axially planned round an arcaded central hall and generally with more of symmetry than one

419

would have expected at that date. Terraced gardens by W. B. Thomas. Now a country club for the Russian Embassy. (*Eastlake*, App. 322; *BN* 22 (1872), 356, PID.)

SHABDEN, nr Reigate, Surrey (Pl. 412)

By E. M. Barry for John Cattley, 1871–3. See p. 299. A technologically ambitious house. Elaborate hot-air heating and ventilation system. Internal pipes. Cavity walls. Concrete foundations. Damp course. Wrought iron beams. Stained glass (showing country pursuits) by Clayton and Bell. Tiles by Simpson. Carving by Mabey. Decoration by Crace. Holland and Hannen were the builders. Now a hospital. (*B* 9 Aug. 1874, 624–7, PID.)

SHIPLAKE COURT, nr Henley, Oxfordshire (Pl. 413)

By Ernest George and Peto, *c.* 1889–90, for R. H. Harrison, of Hichens, Harrison and Co., London stockbrokers (Robert Hichens of the *Green Carnation* came from the same background). A large well-behaved Tudor house of diapered red brick, in a fine position above the Thames. Archaeological Great Hall, with screens, elaborate stone chimneypiece and open timber roof. Electric light from the start. Now a school. (*BN* 31 May 1889, ID; *A* 16 May 1890 I; NMR (Bedford Lemere).)

SILVERTON PARK, nr Exeter, Devon

By J. T. Knowles, senior, 1839–45, for the fourth Earl

of Egremont. An extraordinarily lavish Greek design, with two storeys of Ionic and Corinthian colonnades running the whole length of the main front, and much elaborate enrichment, all in cement. Bought up by W. H. Smith in the 1880s and demolished in 1900. (P. Metcalf in *The Country Seat*, ed. Colvin and Harris (London, 1970) 254–6, ID.)

SMEATON MANOR, nr Northallerton, Yorkshire (Pl. 57)

By Philip Webb, 1877–9, for Maj. A. P. Godman, the son-in-law of Isaac Lowthian Bell, of Rounton Grange and Washington Hall. A moderate red-brick country house, one of Webb's most attractive designs. The main block entirely symmetrical, with white painted sash windows, a deep and generous hipped-roof, dormers, pantiles and three sturdy chimneystacks rising from the rest of the roof. A long service wing to one side, a short smoking-room wing to the other, both gabled. White painted panelling and tiled chimneypieces inside. Needlessly mutilated in recent years. (*Architectural History* I (1958), 31–58, PID.)

SOMERLEYTON HALL, nr Lowestoft, Suffolk (Pls 201–2)

By John Thomas, 1844–51, for Samuel Morton Peto (Bart, 1855), the self-made building and railway contractor, Baptist and Liberal M.P. Remodelling and enlargement of an older house. John Thomas was a sculptor by profession (his assistant Henry Parsons later claimed he did most of the work) and the house

420

413. Shiplake Court, Oxfordshire (George and Peto, 1889–90).

was amateurishly planned and stylistically a watered-down version of Barry's Highclere. But, as might be expected, the enrichment, much of it by Thomas, in the form of statues, chimneypieces, garden furniture and applied ornament, was very luscious. Stained glass by Ballantyne of Edinburgh, carved oak in library by Willcox of Warwick, dining hall with built-in paintings by Landseer, Stanfield, etc., marbling and graining by Moxon. The house was sold in 1863 to Sir Francis Crossley, a few years before Peto went bankrupt. (See pp. 211–12.) The enormous winter garden (see p. 38) has been demolished, and the two-storey dining hall subdivided. Even so the house, with its gardens laid out by W. A. Nesfield, long ranges of Paxton-roofed hothouses, maze, aviary, outbuildings and model village (also by Thomas) retains an evocative feeling of the mansion of a great Victorian plutocrat. (*B* IX (1851), 355, 365, 407, ID; *Morris* IV, 71.)

SOMPTING ABBOTS, Sompting, Sussex

By P. C. Hardwick, 1854–6, for Capt. H. P. Crofts. Medium size, Tudor–Gothic, of brick and flint, with an aggressive tower rather ineffectively positioned on the entrance front. Now a school. (RIBA.)

STANCLIFFE HALL, Darley Dale, Derbyshire

By T. Roger Smith, 1872, for Sir Joseph Whitworth, the armaments manufacturer. Alterations and additions by E. M. Barry, 1879. Winter garden added, 1885. A François I house, enthusiastically noticed in the *Architect* (perhaps because T. Roger Smith was the editor). Had an iron billiard table. (*A* 25 May 1872, 269, D.)

STOKE ROCHFORD HALL, nr Grantham, Lincolnshire (Pl. 24)

By William Burn, 1839–41, for Christopher Turnor. The house seems conclusive proof that Burn had little to do with the more pyrotechnic aspects of Harlaxton, where he had taken over from Salvin in 1838. A competent but not very interesting re-creation of a symmetrical Jacobean house, with a big service wing to one side. Elaborate quoins and much strapwork ornament inside and out. Great Hall, family wing, two bathrooms and fifteen w.c.'s. (*CL* X, 392; RIBA.)

STOKESAY COURT, Craven Arms, Shropshire

By Thomas Harris, 1889, for H. J. Allcroft, a rich glove manufacturer (partner of the Dents, of Sudeley Castle). A very large, unoriginal but handsome Elizabethan house. Little to remind one of Milner Field, still less of Harris's 'Victorian' style. Equipped with electricity from the start. (*CL* IX (1901), 1),

272–7, ID; R. Banham, *The Architecture of the Well-Tempered Environment* (London, 1969), 66, ID.)

STOWELL PARK, nr Northleach, Gloucestershire

By John Belcher, junior, 1885–90, for the Earl of Eldon. The idea of recreating a composite country house of many dates, pioneered by Devey at Betteshanger, was here developed with the greatest sophistication and competence, in an exceptionally beautiful situation in the Cotswolds, and on the basis of an existing Elizabethan house. The result is a rambling building with, apparently, Gothic, Elizabethan and seventeenth-century contributions. No doubt Beresford Pite, who was in Belcher's office at the time, lent rather more than a hand (*B* 18 June 1887, ID; *Academy Architecture*, 1890, I.)

TAPLOW COURT, Buckinghamshire

Remodelled by William Burn, 1855, for Charles Pascoe Grenfell, brother-in-law of Charles Kingsley and J. A. Froude, and rich from Cornish copper mines. A high, overbearing, unlovable house, four storeys high, of red brick with Bath stone dressings. The entrance front, in a mixture of Tudor–Gothic with Jacobean strapwork cresting, is typical of Burn; less usual is the garden front, with a spired French Gothic tower and windows with lush late French Gothic tracery. The main internal feature is the large central hall in the Norman style, a survival from the earlier house (could it be by Hopper?)

THORESBY HALL, Ollerton, Nottinghamshire (Pl. 27, 414)

By Anthony Salvin, 1864–75, for Earl Manvers. Salvin's grandest house, planned on an enormous scale round a central courtyard, with every front carefully asymmetrical. But what Salvin had done with sense and style as a younger man had by now become a formula with little point or pleasure in it. Even so, Thoresby is worth a visit because of its size and because of its completeness; the rooms are still furnished and decorated very much as they were in Victorian days. Entrance court on a lower level than the gardens and main rooms, as at Harlaxton. Stairs up from the entry to the enormous stone-lined great hall, with a suite of enormous and enormously high reception rooms beyond it. Fireproof construction (it can be seen exposed in what are now the refreshment rooms). The house was originally lit by oil lamps. (RIBA.)

THURLAND CASTLE, Burton-in-Lonsdale, Lancashire

Apparently a casualty of the agricultural depression. Extensive remodelling by Paley and Austin, 1879–85, for North North (whose family had lived there for many generations) and again *c.* 1889 for Col. E. B.

Main house remodelled and formal gardens laid out 1834–40. Sculpture gallery, clock-tower, etc. ('rural' rather than 'palatial' Italian) 1840 and later. See pp. 29, 35, 48–51. The main house has been demolished; the grand columned frontispiece to the west front, the formal gardens, the clock-tower and parts of the service wing, etc., survive. (*CL* CXLIII (1968), 228–31, 282–5, PID.)

WADDESDON MANOR, nr Aylesbury, Buckinghamshire (Pl. 285, Col. Pl. XXIII)

By G. H. Destailleur, 1874–89, for Baron Ferdinand de Rothschild. See p. 300 (*CL* IV, 208, XII, 808, CXXVI (1959), 66, ID.)

WADHURST PARK, Sussex

By E. J. Tarver, 1872–5, for Mr C. de Murrieta, a Spanish banker in London, and one of the new rich who were taken up by Edward VII when Prince of Wales. To entertain him and other smart guests Tarver added a big wing in 1881. In the 1890s de Murrieta ran into financial difficulties and disappeared from English society. The house (which has been demolished) was of red brick, in the Shaw–Nesfield Old English manner, and had high roofs, tall chimneys, numerous bay windows and a big tower with a belvedere gallery and steep wedge-shaped roof. Said to be one of the first houses where guests were seated at separate small tables, as in a restaurant. The house later belonged to J. C. Drewe, one of the founders of the Home and Colonial Stores, who left it for Castle Drogo in Devon, designed for him by Lutyens in 1910. Demolished. (*B* 19 May 1877, 502, ID; 12 Apr. 1884, 508, PID; *BN* 9 and 16 Apr. 1875, PID.)

WALTON HALL, nr Warwick

Remodelling by G. G. Scott, 1858–62, for Sir Charles Mordaunt, later to feature in the notorious divorce case. A big graceless Gothic house with characteristic Scott interiors, especially the library. Not up to the standard of Kelham or Hafodunos. Now a school. (*Eastlake*, App. 164; *B* XVIII (1860), PID.)

WALTON HOUSE (later Mount Felix), Walton-on-Thames, Surrey (Pl. 23)

By Sir Charles Barry, 1835, for the fifth Earl of Tankerville. See p. 50. A remodelling designed in the spirit of a villa by the Thames, rather than the country seat of a nobleman. So it was an undress Trentham, on a moderate scale, with generous pan-tiled Italian roofs, and a big entrance tower. Drawing room on the first floor, with a long formal approach, from the entrance to the main staircase, along two legs of an L. Mostly demolished. (Robert Kerr, *The Gentleman's House* (London, 1864), 468–9, PD; NMR.)

Lees (from Oldham). A competent job in the Elizabethan style. (*B of E*.)

TORTWORTH COURT, nr Thornbury, Gloucestershire (Pl. 38)

By S. S. Teulon, 1849–52, for the second Earl of Ducie. Teulon's first big country house, built of stone, with little of the wilfulness in the detailing or use of materials to be found at Shadwell, Elvetham and Bestwood. See p. 64. The dominant feature is the central staircase-hall, which rises up into a big central tower, as at Wyatt's Ashridge. Stained glass by Gibbs, ironwork by Baily. Gas-lit, heated by warm air, luggage lift, railway to bring in coal. Elaborate boat-house. (*Eastlake*, App. 79; *B* XL (1853), 666–7, 702–3, PID.)

TRENTHAM HALL, Stoke-on-Trent Staffordshire (Pl. 22, Fig. 4)

Remodelling, additions and landscaping by Sir Charles Barry for the second Duke of Sutherland.

422

414. Thoresby Hall, Nottinghamshire (Anthony Salvin, 1864–75). The drawing room.

WARTER PRIORY, nr Pocklington, Yorkshire

A big bleak French house for Charles Henry Wilson, M.P., of the Hull shipping family, *c.* 1878 with large later additions. (*Morris*, VI, 67.)

WASHINGTON HALL, Durham

By A. B. Higham, 1854–7, for Isaac Lowthian Bell, the metallurgical chemist and ironworker, who owned a chemical works near Washington before starting the famous Clarence Iron Works near Middlesbrough. A modest but quite elaborate Gothic house with tower, mainly of interest because of the entrance front added by Philip Webb, *c.* 1864.

WELBECK ABBEY, nr Worksop, Nottinghamshire

Great estates, coal mines, and London ground rents enabled the fifth Duke of Portland (1800–79) to indulge his eccentricities at the cost of many hundred thousands of pounds in the 1860s and 1870s. With the exception of the enormous glass and iron riding school (385 × 112 ft) the results are interesting for reasons of psychology rather than architecture. Underground drive in a tunnel $1\frac{1}{4}$ miles long, vast sunken top-lit state rooms, and much else besides. All gas-lit and heated by hot air. From the time of the sixth Duke, the splendid Arts and Crafts chapel and library by J. D. Sedding and Henry Wilson (1889–96) and extensive alterations and redecorations by George and Yeates, *c.* 1900–2. (*B of E.*)

WELCOMBE, nr Stratford-on-Avon

By Clutton, 1867, for Mark Philips, of the Manchester cotton family. Very large unlovable Elizabethan house, now a hotel. (*B* 6 May 1882, PID.)

WESTON MANOR HOUSE, Freshwater, Isle of Wight

By Goldie, Child and Goldie, 1881–2, for Wilfred Ward of Oxford Movement fame, whose grandfather, a City merchant, had bought large properties in the Isle of Wight. French sixteenth-century domestic Gothic, not large, but with a big private chapel attached. Old fashioned for its date, a somewhat grim but competent high-Victorian design, with high roofs and spirelets and walls of 'crazy paving' stonework. (*BN* 20 Jan. 1882, ID.)

WESTONBIRT HOUSE, Tetbury, Gloucestershire (Pl. 415)

By Lewis Vulliamy, 1863–70, for R. S. Holford, for whom he had designed the superb Dorchester House in London in 1854 (with the expert assistance of his nephew George and, according to Goodhart-Rendel, with extensive contributions from Holford's brother-in-law Coutts Lindsay). In 1838, when in his early 20s, Holford had inherited a fortune of a million pounds from his uncle Robert Holford, and his two huge houses and famous art collection were the ultimate result. Westonbirt is on the grandest scale, superbly built of ashlar masonry of superb quality

423

415. Westonbirt House, Gloucestershire (Lewis Vulliamy, 1863–70).

with park, formal garden and arboretum on the scale of the house. It had everything in the way of gas, central heating, fireproof construction, iron roofs, etc. that Victorian technology could devise. Holford, whose knowledge and enthusiasm were all for the Italian Renaissance, was induced, probably by a sense of propriety, to commission an Elizabethan design for his country residence. It is in the Barry picturesque tradition, that is to say with a symmetrical main block and asymmetric wings, one containing a conservatory. The huge central tower presides grandly over the surrounding parkland. The entrance front draws freely on Wollaton; inside there is little or no attempt to be Elizabethan, and the rooms are sumptuously classical with antique panelling and fireplaces incorporated. Now a school. (CL XVII (1905, 1), 378–85, 414–23, ID; designs and rich documentation at RIBA.)

WHITBOURNE HALL, nr Bromyard, Herefordshire

By Elmslie of Elmslie, Franey and Haddon, the leading architects of Malvern, 1860–2, for Edward Bickerton Evans, whose money came from a vinegar and cordial wine manufactory in Worcester. A curiously late but extremely handsome example of the Greek revival, with a six-columned Ionic portico and other details derived from the Erectheum. The general design however was inspired by that of Strensham Court, near Worcester (John Taylor, 1824). Galleried central hall with grand staircase adjoining. Preserves all its original furniture and fittings. The gutted conservatory is probably a slightly later addition by R. L. Roumieu. (CL 20 and 27 March 1975, ID.)

424

WILBURTON MANOR HOUSE, nr Ely, Cambridgeshire

By A. W. Pugin, 1848–50, for O. C. Pell. A small and little-known house by Pugin, red brick, Gothic, with stone dressings.

WINSCOTT, nr Torrington, N. Devon (Pl. 416)

By William White, c. 1865, for J. C. Moore Stevens. A big square main block with big gables, small windows and no projections, except the porch, with its *porte-cochère* massively supported on squat granite columns. All no doubt in deliberate reaction against fussiness by one of the leading 'muscular' Goths. Has been demolished. (B 21 Oct. 1865, PID.)

WITLEY COURT, nr Kidderminster, Worcestershire

Remodelling and extensive additions by Samuel Daukes, c. 1855–9, for Lord Ward (Earl of Dudley, 1860), one of the richest men in England through a combination of landed property and income from iron and coal. The eighteenth-century Baroque church and the portico designed by Nash, c. 1805, were left untouched but the rest of the house was encased in sumptuous Italian Renaissance facades, built on a palatial scale. There seems to be no adequate record of the decoration of the interior. The house is now gutted and acts as an operatic backcloth to the enormous sculptural fountains carved by James Forsyth as the centrepieces of the largely vanished formal gardens laid out by W. A. Nesfield. (CL XCVII (1945), 992–5, 1036–9, ID.)

416. Winscott, Devon (William White, 1865).

WIVENHOE HALL, Essex

By Thomas Hopper, 1846, for John Rebow. Tudor remodelling of an older house in red brick with stone dressings, with much elaborate strapwork ornament. Now University of Essex.

WOODCOTE HALL, nr Newport, Shropshire

By F. P. Cockerell, rebuilt after a fire in 1876, for C. C. Cotes, M.P. Red brick, shaped pedimented gables, white painted sash windows, symmetrical entrance facade. Designed under the influence of the 'Queen Anne' movement, but the constraint of country house dignity produced an imitation of a seventeenth-century classical house rather than an example of the free treatment and informal quality encouraged by Queen Anneites. Cf. George Devey's Denne Hill.

WORSLEY HALL, nr Manchester

By Edward Blore, 1837–43, for Lord Francis Egerton (later created Earl of Ellesmere) who inherited a large share of the Bridgwater estates. One of Blore's biggest houses. Elizabethan. Symmetrical main block, family wing to one side, big tower and service wing to the other, no bathrooms. The house has been demolished, and to judge from illustrations its disappearance is not especially to be regretted. (*Morris* II, 35. Very full set of designs at RIBA.)

WREST PARK, Silsoe, Bedfordshire

Designed for himself, 1834–9, by the second Earl de Grey (1781–1859), an amateur architect and the first President of the Institute of British Architects. Lord Grey had a taste for the *dix-huitième* not uncommon in his generation, and the house is based on designs from Blondel and Mariette, with elaborate *rocaille* interiors, all carried out on the grand scale and with considerable panache. (*CL* CXLVII (1970, 1), 1250–3; CXLVIII (1970), 18–21, ID.)

WYFOLD COURT, nr Henley, Oxfordshire (Pl. 5)

By G. Somers Clarke, 1872–6, for Edward Hermon, Conservative M.P. for Preston, partner in Horrocks, Miller and Co. of Preston, one of the richest of the cottentots, and like his partner Miller a lavish patron of contemporary artists. An ostentatious and accomplished essay in French Flamboyant Gothic. The entrance front builds up from the *porte-cochère* to the great steep-roofed tower and has so much piled into it that it assumes a slightly manic quality—which makes its present use as Borocourt Mental Hospital not inapposite. After this the long, low disjointed garden front is a disappointment, partly because the top storey originally designed for it was never built. Stone-vaulted main corridor and huge, remarkably undomestic rooms with enormously high ceilings and elaborate Gothic chimneypieces. The big picture gallery is empty, and only a few large and repellent pictures by Stacy Marks survive from the once famous picture collection. (*A* 3 Jan. 1874, PID; Peter Howell in *The Country Seat*, ed. Colvin and Harris (London, 1970), 244–51, PID.)

WYKEHURST PARK, nr Slaugham, Sussex (Pls 281–2)

By E. M. Barry, 1871–4, for Henry Huth. See pp. 297–8. (*B* 20 July 1872, 565–7 PID; *BN* 19 Feb. and 5 Mar. 1875, ID.)

417. Wynnstay, Denbighshire (Benjamin Ferrey, 1858).

WYNNSTAY, nr Ruabon, Denbighshire (Pl. 417)

Main block by Benjamin Ferrey, 1858–61, for Sir W. Williams-Wynn, the owner of 150,000 acres, after the partial destruction of the Georgian house by fire. In the Henri III style, with the influence of Ancy-le-Franc much in evidence. Its huge size, bleak position, grey-green stone, dominating French roofs and soberly elegant detail make it a house that remains in the memory. But the inside is a let-down; a *porte-cochère* (now filled in) leads into an enormous, barren, coarsely decorated great hall, and the rest is in keeping, in spite of some extravagantly sculptural chimneypieces. Now a public school. (*Morris* III, 67; NMR; *CLI* CLI (1972, 1) 782–6.)

YATTENDON COURT, nr Newbury, Berkshire (Pl. 418)

By Alfred Waterhouse for himself, 1880–1. Waterhouse was the only Victorian architect who set up as a full-blown country gentleman. The house, which has been demolished, was in his later manner. Tudor–Gothic (with Old English elements) of red brick and buff terracotta, with tower, Great Hall and pitch-pine interiors. (*BN* 4 June 1881, PID; RIBA.)

IRELAND

ADARE MANOR, County Limerick (Pl. 419)

An eighteenth-century house in a lush and historic river-meadow setting, added to, remodelled, enlarged and Gothicized by the second and third Earls of Dunraven, with a long and complicated building history from 1832 to 1862, under three architects and with important design contributions from the Dunraven family. Work was started under James Pain of Cork in 1832–6 and the splendid first-floor gallery, 132 feet long, with Willement stained glass and re-erected woodwork from the Low Countries, dates from this period. The Great Hall seems to have been designed by the Dunravens *c.* 1840 and to have been inspired by medieval hall-churches rather than medieval halls, with remarkably successful and original results. Pugin was called in in 1846 to decorate the hall and other rooms and design the main staircase. Finally, in 1850–62 P. C. Hardwick added a big overbearing wing and tower, in his unsympathetic version of the Pugin manner. (*CL* CXLV (1969, 1), 1274–7, 1302–6, 1366–9, ID.)

CLONGHANODFOY CASTLE (now Castle Oliver), County Limerick

By G. Fowler Jones of York, *c.* 1850, for the Misses Gascoigne of Parlington, Yorkshire. A splendidly robust design in the Baronial manner, of local sandstone, with battered walls, stepped gables and corbelled-out corner turrets. Fortified *porte-cochère*. Interiors on the grand scale, with arabesque decoration and stained glass 'painted by the lady proprietors'. Has been empty for many years. (*B* 23 Nov. 1850, ID.)

418. Yattendon Court, Berkshire (Alfred Waterhouse, 1881).

CROM CASTLE, Newtown Butler, County Fermanagh

By Edward Blore, 1830–9, for the second Earl of Erne. A castellated Tudor–Gothic mansion on the edge of Lough Erne, some of whose many islands were peppered with turrets to go with the castle. Shortly after completion the entire house was burnt down; Lord Erne, on being asked what should be done, merely replied, 'Build it up again.'

DARTREY, County Monaghan

By William Burn, 1844–6, for Lord Dartrey. This large Elizabethan house has been demolished, but Burn's big neo-Georgian stable block remains, no doubt inspired by the smaller (and rather nicer) eighteenth-century stable block alongside it.

DROMORE CASTLE, nr Limerick (Pl. 35, 420)

By E. W. Godwin, 1866–73, for the young third Earl of Limerick, whose family had built the Georgian area of Limerick city. See pp. 26, 63, 155. The Fenian rising gave Godwin a wonderful, if specious, excuse to build a castle with a good conscience; he measured and studied Irish castles with enthusiasm (in company

419. (top) Adare Manor, Co. Limerick. Children playing in the hall.

420. Dromore Castle, Co. Limerick (E. W. Godwin, 1868–74).

A large and extraordinary house, built by the Puxley family, who owned copper mines in the neighbourhood. It was designed in 1866 by J. T. Christopher of London, who had travelled in Italy with Norman Shaw in 1855. The sensational hall derives from medieval Mayfield Palace, by way of Shaw's competition design for Bradford Exchange (1864). The influence of Nesfield's Cloverley is also in evidence. The executive architect was E. H. Carson of Dublin, father of Sir Edward. Mrs Puxley died in childbirth in 1872; her husband abandoned the house, which was never finished, and was burnt out by the I.R.A. in 1921. Now a splendid ruin by the edge of Bantry Bay. (*AR* August 1974, 120–4, PID.)

GLENBEGH TOWERS, County Kerry

By E. W. Godwin, 1867–70, for the Hon. Rowland Winn. His partner Henry Crisp was the executive architect. A smaller, less fortified version of Dromore, in a beautiful situation above Dingle Bay. Of local sandstone, simple and massive with a very slender square tower 100 feet high. 'Though the windows look small, yet in form and size they are sufficient.' The damp came in, and the commission nearly ended in a lawsuit, to the detriment of Godwin's career. Only a fragment of the house remains. (*A* 13 May 1871, PID.)

KILLARNEY HOUSE, County Kerry

By George Devey, 1877–80, for the fourth Earl of Kenmare. One of Devey's largest houses, on high ground looking over the lake, with a strung-out line of mixed straight and pedimented gables, and many prominent bay windows. Separate chapel and big bow-windowed saloon, as at St Alban's Court. Has been demolished. (RIBA.)

KILLYLEAGH CASTLE, County Down

By a freakish law decision of 1697, the house was divided between two families, with the main castle going to the Hamiltons and the gatehouse to the Blackwoods. In 1849–51 the castle was sensationally remodelled, for Archibald Rowan Hamilton, by Lanyon and Lynn, the Belfast architects, with Baronial facades and Elizabethan interiors. In 1860 Lord Dufferin rebuilt the gatehouse and adjacent walls to the designs of Benjamin Ferrey and presented it to the Hamilton family as a romantic gesture to atone for the family feud. In 1862 he married the Hamilton daughter, and in 1869 an indenture of friendship was drawn up between the two families, and the Hamiltons agreed to pay annual rent for the gatehouse of a golden rose and a pair of silver spurs. (*CL* CXLVII (1970, 1), 690–3, 774–7.)

with his friend William Burges) and, on a wooded hilltop near the Shannon estuary, produced a splendidly vigorous, amply defensible and almost uninhabitable building. The detail of the exteriors derived from Irish examples of the fifteenth and sixteenth centuries, with a Romanesque round tower thrown in to enliven the skyline; inside, the massively Gothic interiors were enriched with Japanese-inspired detail, Oriental porcelain and Godwin furniture, though damp prevented the intended wall decorations by Stacy Marks from being completed. The house was dismantled *c.* 1954; the shell and silhouette remain and there are said to be Godwin chimney-pieces remaining in the gutted interiors but these are hard of access owing to the filling in of the windows. Godwin furniture is probably languishing unidentified in local houses. (*BN* XIV (1867), 222, 755, PID; XXIV (1873, 1), 330, 390, 1; *A* IV (1870, 2), 104, 1; *CL* CXXXVI (1964, 2), 1274–7, ID.)

421. Dunboy Castle, Co. Cork (J. T. Christopher, 1866). The hall.

LISMORE CASTLE, County Waterford (Pls. 16, 423)

The medieval castle high above the River Blackwater had been largely rebuilt by the Earl of Cork in the early seventeenth-century and became abandoned and derelict in the eighteenth century. In 1811–12 and 1849–58 it was restored on an increasingly magnificent scale by the sixth Duke of Devonshire. The main living apartments were rebuilt in 1811–12 to the design of William Atkinson. In 1849 J. G. Crace was commissioned to restore the ruined chapel as a banqueting hall and he brought in Pugin as a collaborator on its elaborate decoration (for the purchase of the Horsted chimneypiece, see p. 174). Pugin also designed chimneypieces and furniture for other rooms in the castle; and after his death in 1851 Crace supplied a great deal more furniture in the Pugin manner. Over the next seven years the skyline of the castle was transformed by the elaborately castellated additions and rebuildings made to the designs of Paxton and Stokes; of these the Carlisle tower, which was to have been 170 feet high, and the grandest of the many towers, was never completed owing to the Duke's death in 1858. The interiors, after all the drama of the skyline, are remarkably unassuming, for in the context of the immense Devonshire properties Lismore was basically a glorified lodge for holidays. (*CL* CXXXVI (1964), 336–40, 389–93, ID.)

429

422. (top) Muckross House, Co. Kerry (William Burn, 1838–43).

423. Lismore Castle, Co. Waterford (A. W. Pugin and J. G. Crace, 1850–1). The hall.

MUCKROSS HOUSE, Killarney, County Kerry
(Pls. 422, 427)

By William Burn, 1839–43, for H. A. Herbert, in a beautiful position on Killarney Lake. A clean, unfussy Elizabethan design with big bay windows. Interior open to the public and being refurnished in Victorian style.

Burn also designed Bangor Castle, County Down (1847) for R. E. Ward and Castle Wellan, County Down (1854) for the Earl of Annesley. Blore did work at Castle Upton, Country Antrim (1836–8) for Lord Templetown, and at Mallow Castle (1837–8) for the Jephsons.

SCOTLAND

ARISAIG HOUSE, nr Fort William, Inverness

By Philip Webb, 1863, for P. D. P. Astley (from Lancashire and Cheshire). Webb's first big country house, built of two local varieties of stone, in a simplified Gothic style. Webb later said that the house was 'a product of his ignorance' but approved of the

stable block, in which a single huge roof covered stables, coach house, carts and cow-byres. The house was badly damaged by fire in 1935 and rebuilt in cut-down form; the stable block and a pair of small houses by Webb survive.

DUNECHT HOUSE, Aberdeenshire

Large addition by G. E. Street, c. 1866–71, for the accomplished twenty-fifth Earl of Crawford. This would appear to be Street's only important country house work. It is in a curious, rather forbidding, Romanesque style, and includes a chapel and an enormous top-lit library, built for Lord Crawford's famous book collection. The house was bought by Lord Cowdray in 1908, and somewhat enlarged and altered.

DUNROBIN CASTLE, Sutherland (Pl. 425)

For the second Duke of Sutherland, 1844–50. Sir Charles Barry made designs in 1844, which were adapted and cut down by W. Leslie of Aberdeen, the executant architect. Barry first visited the site in 1848, when he fixed the final form of the great tower and

430

424. Gosford House, East Lothian (William Young, 1880–90). The Marble Hall.

laid out the terraced garden. The result was a very large extravagantly silhouetted building, added onto the modest original castle in a splendid position above Dornoch Firth. Interiors mostly redecorated in this century, after a fire. (*CL* L (1921), 284, 318, ID.)

GOSFORD HOUSE, Longniddry, E. Lothian (Pl. 427)

Robert Adam's great classical house (1792–1803) stood empty until 1880–90, when the tenth Earl of Wemyss employed William Young to add big wings to the north and south and remodel the east front. The style is more reminiscent of Young's War Office and Glasgow Town Hall than of anything domestic. The main interior feature is the enormous marble hall, with columns and facings of alabaster, and an inglenook uncosily fitted in underneath the double staircase to the galleries. (*CL* XXX, 342–9, PID.)

INVERCAULD CASTLE, Braemar, Aberdeenshire.

By J. T. Wimperis, 1870–5, for Miss Farquharson, whose family had owned the Balmoral property. An ambitious Scottish Baronial remodelling of an older house, in chunky granite with elaborate pitch-pine interiors. J. T. Wimperis was a London architect who built up an extensive town practice, especially in the West End; for a Scottish landowner to employ him was rather like ordering a house at Harrod's. (*B* 5 June 1875, ID.)

VICTORIAN COUNTRY HOUSES ABROAD

In spite of the importation of Italian artists and architects for interior decoration in the first half of the Victorian period, and of French architects for Rothschild and other chateaux in the second, Victorian England was more an exporter than an importer of country house expertise. The following list is mainly culled from the architectural publications of the time; in most cases I have no idea whether the houses still exist, or even where exactly they were built (if they were built at all), but the list may encourage others to do further research. I have not attempted to deal with villas on the Riviera built for English patrons.

431

425. Dunrobin Castle, Sutherland, from a Victorian photograph (Sir Charles Barry and W. Leslie, 1844–8).

ALBERT HARTSHORNE and SOMERS CLARKE, JUNIOR

Elizabethan mansion (with double-glazing), Poland. (*A* 28 Oct. 1871, ID.)

J. T. KNOWLES, SENIOR (1806–74)

Palacio Monserrate, Sintra, Portugal, 1858–65. (Information from Priscilla Metcalf.)

E. B. LAMB

Schloss Prugg in Bruck a.d. Leitha, Austria, 1854–8, for Graf Harrach. Elizabethan remodelling of a Baroque house, with shaped gables and two towers. (*Historismus and Schlossbau,* ed. Wagner-Rieger and Krause (Munich, 1975), 76, Pl. 15.)

Schloss Hrádek, Czechoslovakia. Elaborate Elizabethan interiors for Graf Harrach, *c.* 1850–7. (*Historismus,* 143–50, Pls. 313–22.)

JOHN NORTON

Chateau at Keblas in Livonia, 1859. (*Ecclesiologist* XX (1859), 74.)

Additions to chateau at Weltz, Livonia. (*Ecclesiologist* XXII (1862), 225.)

Fickel Castle, Estonia, for Baron D'Uxkull. (RIBA *Journal,* 3rd series, XI (1904–5), 63.)

SIR JOSEPH PAXTON AND G. H. STOKES

Chateau at Ferrières, near Paris, for Baron James de Rothschild, 1853–9. An enormous house, planned like Mentmore round a covered-in courtyard, with four corner towers and elaborate, vaguely French Renaissance, facades. Chateau at Pregny, near Geneva, for Baron Alphonse de Rothschild, *c.* 1860–4.

JOHN PRICHARD

Mansion at Jerez de la Frontera, S. Spain, 1864, for Señor Don Manuel M. Gonzalez. In the Moresque–Gothic style, with much use of marble. Highly praised by *Building News*. (*BN* 6 May 1864, commenting on the design exhibited at the Royal Academy.) But it seems never to have been built.

E. W. PUGIN

Chateau at S. Michel, Belgium. (*B* 12 June 1875, 522.)

C. J. RICHARDSON

Elizabethan villa at Teplitz, 1852, for Count Kinsky. Elizabethan house at Vrams, Gunnarstrop, Sweden, *c.* 1852. Castellated villa on the Sound near Copenhagen, for Count de Bark. (Richardson, *Picturesque*

EDWARD BLORE

House for Prince Woronzow, Aloupka, Crimea, 1837. The client's father had been Russian Ambassador in England, and his sister married the eleventh Earl of Pembroke. The house (with one Gothic and one Indian front) survives in good condition and was used to lodge the British delegation at the Yalta Conference. (*B* 1850, 354–5 ID.)

E. T. HALL

Chateau on the Aegean, *c.* 1881. (*BN* 26 Aug. 1881, ID.)

432

426. Schloss Hradek, Czechoslovakia (E. B. Lamb, *c.* 1850–7). The staircase.

Designs (London, 1870), 368–71, PID. The text does not make it clear whether these designs were ever carried out.)

E. J. TARVER

Hunting lodge in the Ardennes, *c.*1882, for the Duchess of Ossuna. A modest but attractive design under a single dominating French roof. (*B* 11 Mar. 1882, ID.)

GEORGE VULLIAMY

Gothic villa on the Baltic, for a Russian nobleman, *c.* 1841–3. (See Vulliamy's obituary, *B* 20 Nov. 1886.)

WILLIAM H. WHITE

A rather different case of an architect who set up practice in Paris in the 1860s. Château de Bizy (reconstruction) and Château de Martinvast, nr Cherbourg (large addition) for the Barons F. and A. de Schickler. Restoration of 'old chateau near Bourges' for Prince Auguste d'Arenberg. The Franco-Prussian War finished the practice, and White went first to India and then to London, where he was secretary to the R.I.B.A. from 1878 till his death in 1896.

WILLIAM WILKINSON

Schloss Buonas am Zugersee Switzerland, 1873–7. Gothic. Demolished 1970. (*Historismus*, 163, 175, Pls. 335, 345.)

T. H. WYATT

Mansion, Poland, for the Worontzow faimly. Mansion, Cascais, near Lisbon, for the Duke of Palmella. (*B* (1880, 2), 193–4.)

427. Muckross House, Co. Kerry. A Victorian bedroom.

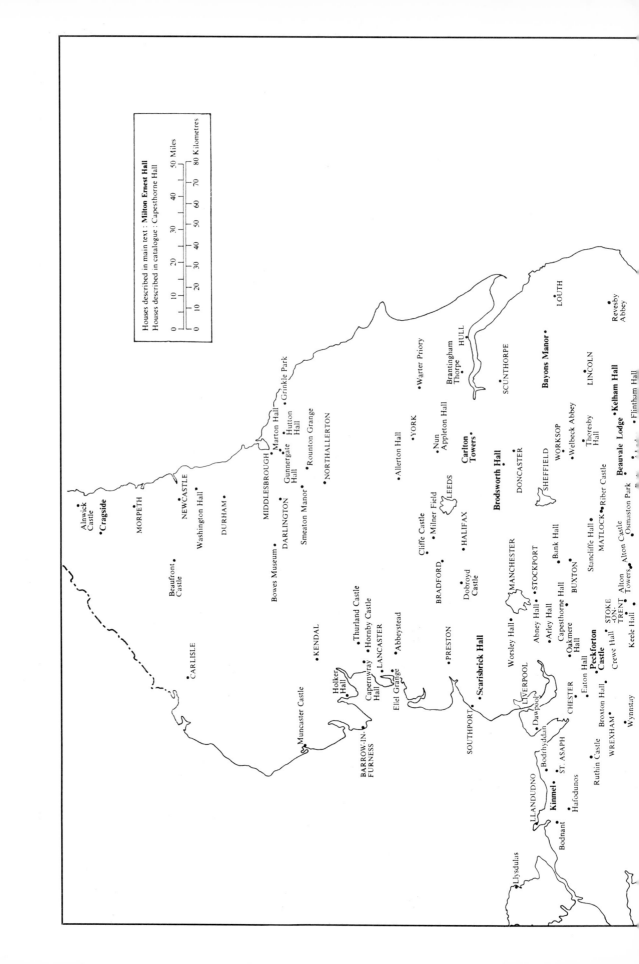

Houses described in main text : **Milton Ernest Hall**
Houses described in catalogue : Capesthorne Hall

0 10 20 30 40 50 Miles
0 10 20 30 40 50 60 70 80 Kilometres

Alnwick Castle
Cragside
MORPETH
NEWCASTLE
Washington Hall
DURHAM
Beaufront Castle
CARLISLE
MIDDLESBROUGH
Bowes Museum
DARLINGTON
Smeaton Manor
Marton Hall
Gunnergate Hall
Hutton Hall
Grinkle Park
Rounton Grange
NORTHALLERTON
KENDAL
Thurland Castle
Hornby Castle
LANCASTER
Abbeystead
Capernwray Hall
Ellel Grange
Holker Hall
Muncaster Castle
PRESTON
Scarisbrick Hall
SOUTHPORT
BARROW-IN-FURNESS
LIVERPOOL
Dawpool
CHESTER
Eaton Hall
Broxton Hall
Peckforton Castle
Crewe Hall
Capesthorne Hall
Oakmere Hall
Worsley Hall
Abney Hall
MANCHESTER
STOCKPORT
Arley Hall
BUXTON
Bank Hall
Stancliffe Hall
MATLOCK
Riber Castle
Alton Castle
Alton Towers
Osmaston Park
STOKE-ON-TRENT
Keele Hall
WREXHAM
Ruthin Castle
Bodrhyddan
ST. ASAPH
Kinmel
Hafodunos
LLANDUDNO
Bodnant
Llysdulas
Wynnstay
Cliffe Castle
Milner Field
HALIFAX
BRADFORD
Dobroyd Castle
LEEDS
Allerton Hall
YORK
Nun Appleton Hall
Carlton Towers
Brodsworth Hall
DONCASTER
SHEFFIELD
WORKSOP
Welbeck Abbey
Thoresby Hall
Beauvale Lodge
Warter Priory
Brantingham Thorpe
HULL
SCUNTHORPE
Bayons Manor
LINCOLN
Kelham Hall
Flintham Hall
LOUTH
Revesby Abbey

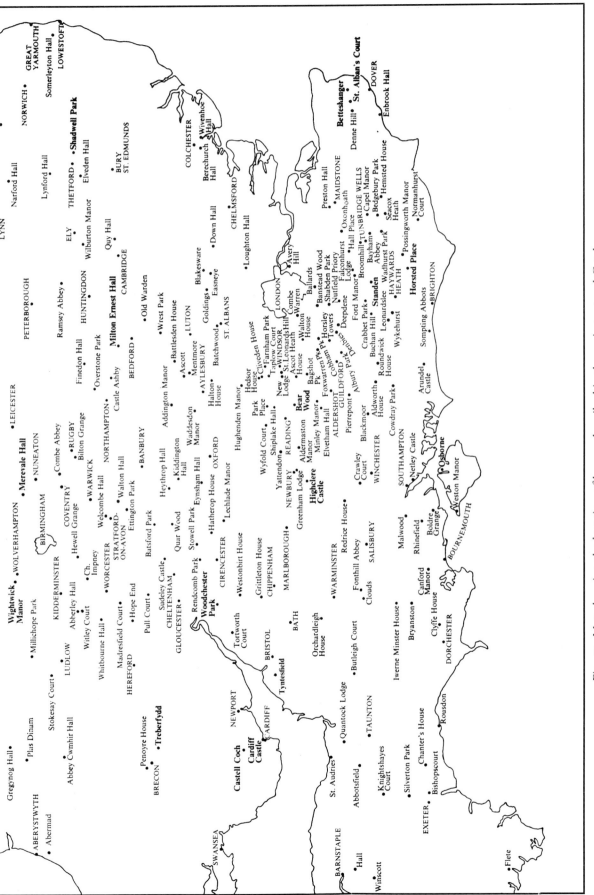

Fig. 31. Map showing the location of houses described in the main text and Catalogue.

BIOGRAPHICAL NOTES ON ARCHITECTS

add. additions
alt. alterations
reb. rebuilt
rem. remodelling
rec. reconstruction
rest. restoration
dem. demolished
gard. gardens.

By a reconstruction is meant something more thorough than a remodelling, resulting in a virtually new house. The description 'dem.' means that I know the house has been demolished, but its absence is no guarantee that the house still exists. Houses in italics are described in the Catalogue or main body of the book.

BARRY, SIR CHARLES (1795–1860; Kt 1852) See pp. 48–51, 130–6.

Horsley Towers, Surrey (W. Currie) 1834; Bowood House, Wilts. (M. of Landsowne; add.; alt.; gard.) 1834–57; *Trentham Hall, Staffs.* (D. of Sutherland; rec.; gard.; largely dem.) 1834–42; *Walton House, Surrey* (E. of Tankerville; rec.; dem.) 1835–39; Kingston Lacy, Dorset (W. J. Bankes; rem.) 1835–9; *Highclere House, Hants* (E. of Carnarvon; rec.) 1838–44; Harewood House, Yorks. (E. of Harewood; alt.) 1843–50; *Eynsham Hall, Oxon.* (E. of Macclesfield) 1843; *Dunrobin Castle, Sutherland* (D. of Sutherland; rec.) 1844–50; *Canford Manor, Dorset* (Sir John Guest; rec.) 1848–52; Shrubland Park, Suffolk (Sir W. Middleton; alt.; add.; gard.); *Kiddington Hall, Oxon.* (Mortimer Ricardo; rec.) c. 1850; *Cliveden House, Bucks.* (D. of Sutherland) 1851.

BARRY, CHARLES, junior (1824–1900)

Eldest son of Sir Charles Barry. In partnership from 1847–72 with Robert Richardson Banks (1813–72) who had been in his father's office.

Bylaugh Hall, Norfolk (Edw. Lombe; gutted) 1849–51; Nawton Towers, Yorks., N.R. (Hon. W. E. Duncombe; alt. 1930) 1855; Bramling House, Kent (S. M. Hilton) 1865; Stevenstone, Devon (Hon. Mark Rolle; largely dem.) 1869–74; Clumber House, Notts. (D. of Newcastle; rec. after fire; dem.) 1880.

BARRY, EDWARD MIDDLETON (1830–80)

Third son of Sir Charles Barry. Professor of Architecture at the Royal Academy, 1874–80. Much more than his elder brother he assumed the mantle of his father, and became a public figure and a successful, if not always a discriminating, architect. Carried on his father's classical tradition, with the addition of French influence in his later buildings. Died at a Royal Academy Council meeting, asking, 'Who is it?'

Henham Hall, Suffolk (E. of Stradbroke; rec.; dem.) 1858–68; Duxbury Hall, Lancs., 1859; Pyrgo Park, Essex (alt.; add.; dem.) 1862; Barbon Park Lodge, Westmorland (Sir J. P. Kay-Shuttleworth; alt.) 1862–3; *Crewe Hall, Ches.* (Lord Crewe) 1866–71; Thorpe Abbots, Norfolk (Sir E. Kay; rem.) 1869–71; *Cobham Park, Surrey* (C. J. F. Combe) 1870–3; *Shabden, Surrey* (J. Cattley) 1871–3; *Wykehurst, Sussex* (Henry Huth) 1871–4; *Stancliffe Hall, Derbys.* (Sir J. Whitworth; add.; alt.) 1879.

BLORE, EDWARD (1787–1879)

See pp. 51–2, 120–9.

The following list is based on his account books in Cambridge University Library (Add. 3954–6) and leaves out a good deal in the ways of alterations and additions, some of them substantial.

Combermere Abbey, Ches. (Lord Combermere) 1830–2, 1837–8; *Crom Castle, Co. Fermanagh* (E. of Erne) 1830–7, 1839; Latimers, Bucks. (Lord Chesham) 1834–8, 1840–2; *Aloupka, Crimea* (Prince Woronzow) 1837; Penge Place, Surrey (John Scott) 1836–7; *Pull Court, Worcs.* (J. E. Dowdeswell) 1836–46; *Capesthorne, Ches.* (E. D. Davenport; alt.; add.) 1837–40; Lodsworth, Sussex (Hasler Hollist) 1837–9; *Ramsey Abbey, Hants* (E. Fellowes) 1837–9; *Merevale Abbey, Warwicks.* (W. S. Dugdale) 1838–44; *Worsley Hall, Lancs.* (Lord F. Egerton; dem.) 1837–43; Haverland Hall, Norfolk (E. Fellowes; dem.) 1838–42; *Shadwell House, Norfolk* (Sir E. B. Buxton; rec.) 1839–44; Moreton Hall, Ches. (G. Holland Ackers) 1840–6; Coolhurst, Sussex (C. S. Dickens) 1841–4; Kingston Hall, Notts. (Edw. Strutt) 1842–6; Thicket Priory, Yorks. (Revd J. D. Jefferson) 1843–6; Fryth House, Herts. (Wm Wilshere; add.; alt.) 1844–6.

BRANDON, DAVID (1813–97)

See pp. 53–4.

From 1838 in partnership with T. H. Wyatt. Set up independently in 1851. Predominantly a country house architect, and kept undeviatingly to the Jacobean style, which he and Wyatt made only too much their own.

Falconhurst Lodge, Kent (Hon. J. Chetwynd-Talbot; largely dem.) 1851; Colesborne House, Glos. (J. H. Elwes) 1853–6; Taverham Hall, Norwich (Revd J. N. Micklethwaite) 1860–1; *Hemsted House, Kent* (Gathorne Hardy) 1860–2; Blackmore Park, Worcs. (J. V. Hornyold) 1861, 1883; Grafton Manor House, Worcs. (E. of Shrewsbury; large add.) 1861; Chilham Castle, Kent (Chas Hardy; large add.) 1863; *Bayham Abbey, Kent* (M. Camden) 1869–71; Stow Hall, Norfolk (Sir T. Hare, Bart) c. 1870; Lytchett Heath, Dorset (Lord E. Cecil) 1874–9; Binnegar Hall, Dorset (O. W. Farrer) 1874; Sidbury Manor House, Devon (Stephen Cave) 1878; Foxbury, Kent (H. Tiarks) 1881.

BURGES, WILLIAM (1827–81)

See pp. 70, 273–90, 336–45.

Gayhurst, Bucks. (Lord Carrington; alt.; add.) 1859–60; *Cardiff Castle, Glamorgan* (M. of Bute) 1866–81; *Knights-hayes, Devon* (J. H. Amory) 1869–71; *Castell Coch, Glamorgan* (M. of Bute) 1872–81. Also made apparently unexecuted designs for *Castle Ashby, Northants.* (M. of Northampton) 1874. In 1862 he exhibited a design for a chimneypiece in the 'Manorial Hall of Colonel Cocks, Cornwall', for Treverbyn Vean, Dobwalls (Lt-Col. C. L. Cocks).

BURN, WILLIAM (1789–1870)

See pp. 31–4, 52.

The long obituary by Prof. T. L. Donaldson in the R.I.B.A. *Journal*, 28 March 1870, pp. 121–9, lists work at 200 houses, including sixty completely new houses, forty in Scotland, sixteen in England and four in Ireland. The following list does not attempt to deal with Scotland, but gives the new houses in England and Ireland, and a selection of the more important alterations and remodellings. At the very end of his life Burn went into partnership with his nephew MacVicar Anderson, who carried on the practice after his death.

New houses: *Stoke Rochford, Lincs.* (Chris. Turner) 1839–41; *Muckross House, Co. Kerry* (H. A. Herbert) 1839–43; South Rauceby Hall, Lincs. (Anthony Willson) 1842; *Revesby Abbey, Lincs.* (J. Banks-Stanhope) 1844; *Dartrey, Co. Monaghan* (Lord Dartrey; dem.) 1844–6; Calwich Abbey, Staffs. (Hon. A. Duncombe) 1846; Bangor Castle, Co. Down (R. E. Ward) 1847; Idsworth House, Hants (Sir J. Clarke-Jervoise) 1848; Sandon Hall, Staffs. (E. of Harrowby) 1851; Castle Wellan, Co. Down (E. of Annesley) 1854; Amport House, Hants (M. of Winchester) 1855; *Fonthill Abbey, Wilts.* (M. of Westminster; dem.) 1856; *Lynford Hall, Norfolk* (S. Lyne-Stephens) 1856–61; Montagu House, London (D. of Buccleuch; dem.) 1857; Ganton Hall, Yorks. (Sir F. D. Legard) 1863; Spye Park, Wilts. (J. W. G. Spicer) 1863–8; Swanbourne, Bucks. (Sir T. F. Fremantle, Bart) 1864; Whittlebury, Hants (Lord Southampton) 1865; Lockerley Hall (formerly Oaklands), Hants (F. G. Dalgety) 1868–71; Rendlesham Hall, Suffolk (Lord Rendlesham; dem.) 1868.

Remodellings, additions or alterations: *Harlaxton, Lincs.* (G. de L. Gregory) 1838–55; *Prestwold Hall, Leics.* (C. W. Packe) 1842–3; *Redrice House, Hants* (Revd T. Best) 1844; Orwell Park, Suffolk (George Tomline) 1851–3, *1871*; *Taplow Court, Bucks.* (C. P. Grenfell) 1855; *Kinmel Park, Denbighs* (H. R. Hughes) 1855; *Narford Hall, Norfolk* (A. Fountaine) *c.* 1860; The Leys, Herefordshire (John Bannerman) 1861; Somerley, Hants (E. of Normanton) 1869.

BUTTERFIELD, WILLIAM (1814–1900)

See pp. 179–86.

Milton Ernest Hall, Beds. (B. H. Starey) 1854–8; *Chanter's House, Ottery St Mary, Devon* (Lord Coleridge; rec.) 1881–2.

CARPENTER, R. HERBERT (*c.* 1842–93)

His father Richard Cromwell Carpenter (1812–55), the darling of the Ecclesiologists, made large additions to Campden House, Glos. (E. of Gainsborough) in 1846 and remodelled *Bedgebury Park, Kent*, for A. Beresford-Hope, 1854–5. Carpenter's practice (including the completion of Bedgebury) was taken on by his former assistant William Slater (1819–72). R. H. Carpenter went into Slater's office

and became his partner in 1863. After Slater's death in 1872 he was in partnership with Benjamin Ingelow.

Seacox Heath, Sussex (G. J. Goschen) 1868–72; Holdenby House, Northants. (Lord Clifden) *c.* 1872–5, 1887–8; Stoughton Grange, Leics. (H. L. Powys Keck) 1879–80; Knoyle House, Wilts. (Alfred Seymour) *c.* 1880; Simonstone Hall, Yorks., N.R. (E. of Wharncliffe) *c.* 1887.

CHRISTIAN, EWAN (1814–95)

Pupil of Matthew Habershon and William Railton. Primarily a church architect, but also had a sizeable, though not very interesting, country house practice. Trod a familiar path; a Pugin man in the 1850s, muscular in the 1860s and Tudor–Old English in the 1870s.

Abnalls, Staffs. (Revd W. Gresley) 1850; East Lavington Manor, Wilts. (Hon. E. Pleydell-Bouverie) 1865–70; Viney Hill, Glos. (Revd W. H. Bathurst) 1865–7; Hinton Daubnay, Hants (Mr Whalley-Tooker) 1868; The Highlands, Glos. (John Griffith Frith) *c.* 1874; Welbeck (W. L. Christie) 1876; Lillingstone Dayrell, Bucks. (Mr Robartes) 1881; Holbrook Hall, Suffolk (Jas Mitchell) 1882; *Malwood, Hants* (Sir W. V. Harcourt) 1883–4; Woodbastwick Hall, Norfolk (A. Cator) 1889; Bodsahan, Cornwall (Mr Vivian).

CLARKE, GEORGE SOMERS, senior (1825–82)

Not to be confused with his nephew George Somers Clarke, junior (1841–1926), who was in partnership with J. T. Micklethwaite. A pupil of Sir Charles Barry, and had a varied and eclectic practice. His country house patrons all from new families.

Cowley Manor, Glos. (James Hutchinson; alt.) 1855; Foxbush, Kent (C. F. Kemp) 1866; *Wyfold Court, Oxon.* (Edward Hermon) 1872–5; Milton Hall, Kent (G. N. Arnold) *c.* 1874; Broadway Manor House, Sidmouth, Devon (G. Balfour) *c.* 1876.

CLUTTON, HENRY (1819–93)

A pupil of Blore, along with William Burges, with whom he was briefly in partnership. Patronized by the Duke of Bedford, for whom he designed churches, redeveloped Covent Garden, etc. His country houses, in a variety of styles, are disappointing, but the smaller appendages to them are sometimes remarkable.

Merevale Hall, Warwicks. (W. S. Dugdale; alt.; gatehouse) 1848–53; *Ruthin Castle, Denbighs.* (F. B. West) 1848–53; *Hatherop House, Glos.* (T. S. Bazley) *c.* 1856; *Quantock Lodge, Somerset* (Lord Taunton) 1857; Battle Abbey, Sussex (Lord H. G. Vane; large add.) 1857; *Minley Manor, Hants* (Raikes Currie) 1858–62; *Cliveden, Bucks.* (D. of Sutherland; add.) 1861; Hoar Cross Hall, Staffs (H. F. Meynell-Ingram) 1862–76; Melchet Park, Hants (E. of Ashburton; rem. 1912–14) 1863–8; Welcombe Manor, Warwicks. (Mark Philips) 1867; *Old Warden, Beds.* (Joseph Shuttleworth) 1872.

COCKERELL, FREDERICK PEPYS (1833–79)

Son of Charles Robert Cockerell and a social and popular figure whose early death seems to have been much mourned. Moved for a time on the edge of the 'Queen Anne' set.

Coleorton Hall, Leics. (Sir G. H. Beaumont, Bart; rem.) 1862; *Down Hall, Essex* (Sir H. S. Ibbetson, Bart) 1871–3;

Ballards, Surrey (C. H. Goschen) 1873; *Woodcote Hall, Salop.* (C. C. Cotes) 1876; *Crawley Court, Hants* (A. S. Kennard) 1877.

DAUKES, SAMUEL WHITFIELD (1811–80)

See pp. 173–6. Sometimes wrongly spelt Dawkes.

Abberley Hall, Worcs. (James Moilliet) *c.* 1846; *Horsted Place, Sussex* (Francis Barchard) 1850–2; *Witley Court, Worcs.* (Lord Ward; rem.) 1855.

DEVEY, GEORGE (1820–86)

See pp. 83–4, 213–22.

This formidable list is largely based on information supplied by Dr Jill Allibone. Works listed are all new or substantially new houses, unless otherwise stated. Numerous less important alterations, etc., are omitted.
Devey died from a chill caught in Ireland, on a journey to Adare Manor to consult with Lord Dunraven about the remodelling of Dunraven Castle; the work was carried out after his death by his assistant Isaac Williams (later of Williams, West and Slade) on the basis of Devey's sketches.

Betteshanger, Kent (Sir Walter James, Bart) 1856–82; *Coombe Cottage, Surrey* (E. C. Baring) *c.* 1863, 1870–4; *Coombe Warren, Surrey* (Bertrand Currie) *c.* 1865–8, reb. 1870–5; Calverley Grange, Kent (Neville Ward; dem.) 1867–75; Wilcote Manor, Oxon. (C. Sartoris; add.) 1867–77; Akeley Wood, Bucks. (Chas Pilgrim) 1867–8; *Brantingham Thorpe, Yorks.* (Chris. Sykes) 1868–83; Lillies, Bucks. (H. Cazenove) 1869–71; *Ascott, Bucks.* (Leopold de Rothschild) 1870–84; Swaylands, Kent (E. Cropper; G. Drummond) 1870–4, 1881–2; Stydd House, Kent (Lady Surtees) 1871–7; Wendover Manor, Bucks. (Lt-Gen. P. Smith) 1871–3; Walmer Castle, Kent (Lord Granville; add.; alt.) 1871–2; Goldings, Herts. (Robt Smith) 1871–7; Send Holme, Surrey (W. Hargreaves) 1871–2; *Denne Hill, Kent* (Edw. Dyson) 1871–5; Bishop Burton, Yorks. (W. F. Watt) 1871–5; *Hall Place, Kent* (Sam. Morley; dem.) 1871–4; Macharioch House, Kintyre (M. of Lorne; dem.) 1872–7; *St Alban's Court, Kent* (W. O. Hammond) 1874–8; Ashfold, Sussex (Eric C. Smith; dem.) 1875–86; Eythrope, Bucks (Miss A. de Rothschild) 1876–9; *Blakesware, Herts.* (Mrs Gosselin) 1876–9; *Killarney House, Kerry* (E. of Kenmare; dem.) 1877–9; Adderley Hall, Salop. (H. R. Corbet; dem.) 1877–81; Membland, Devon (E. C. Baring; dem.) 1877–9; Longwood, Hants (E. of Northesk; dem.) 1897–83; Durdans, Surrey (E. of Rosebery; add; mostly dem.) 1880–4; Melbury House, Dorset (E. of Ilchester; large add.) 1884–6; Monkshatch, Surrey (A. K. Hichens; dem.) 1885–6; Dunraven Castle, Glam. (E. of Dunraven; rem.; add.) 1886–8.

DOBSON, JOHN (1787–1865)

With due regard for capable and successful provincial architects like Douglas of Chester, Haycock of Shrewsbury, Hine of Nottingham, Paley and Austen of Lancaster and Prichard of Llandaff, Dobson's Newcastle practice can reasonably be described as the last of the great provincial practices. The list covers only a selection of houses designed after 1835.

Beaufront Castle, Northumberland (Wm Cuthbert) 1835–41; Holme Eden, nr Carlisle (Peter Dixon) 1837; Sandhoe House, Northumberland (Sir R. Errington, Bart) 1850; Oatlands House, Surrey (W. C. Hewitson) 1851; The

Leazes, Northumberland (Wm Kinsett) 1853; Inglethorp Hall, Norfolk (Chas Metcalfe) 1854–7.

DONALDSON, THOMAS LEVERTON (1795–1885)

Professor of Architecture at University College, London, a powerful figure in architectural politics and scholarship, with a relatively small practice.

Dalby Hall, Leics. (E. B. Hartopp) 1837; Lambourne Place, Berks. (H. Hippisley) 1846; Shobrook House, Devon (J. H. Hippisley; rem.) *c.* 1850; *Leonardslee, Sussex* (W. E. Hubbard) 1853.

DOUGLAS, JOHN (1829–1911)

See pp. 82, 375.

A pupil of Sharpe and Paley. Practised from Chester, first on his own, then in partnership with D. P. Fordham (d. 1899). A successful and very able architect.

Oakmere Hall, Ches. (John Higson) *c.* 1872; *Broxton Hall, Ches.* (Sir P. de M. G. Egerton, Bart) 1873; Shotwick Park, Ches. (H. Trelawny) *c.* 1879; Barrow Court, Ches. (H. Lyle Smith) 1881; Wygfair, Flints., 1884; *Abbeystead, Lancs.* (E. of Seifton) 1886–8; The Wern, Caernarvonshire (R. M. Greaves) 1892; Glangwna, Caerns. 1893.

EDIS, SIR ROBERT W. (1839–1927; Kt 1919)

Colonel of the Artists' Rifles, hence usually referred to as Colonel Edis in contemporary sources. One of the first supporters of the 'Queen Anne' movement; his country houses show little sign of it. Buckden Palace, Hunts. (Maj. A. W. Marshall) 1871–3; Shepherd's Springs, Hants, *c.* 1877; *Sandringham House, Norfolk* (P. of Wales; add.) 1883, 1891; Smallwood Manor, Staffs. (G. A. Hodgson) 1886–7; *Byrkley Lodge, Staffs.* (Hamar Bass) 1887–91.

FERREY, BENJAMIN (1810–80)

See p. 53.

The biographer and fellow pupil of A. W. Pugin, primarily a church architect, but with a comfortable (mainly Tudor–Gothic) country house practice.

Baynards Park, Surrey (Revd Thos Thurlow) 1835–45; *Clyffe House, Dorset* (Chas Porcher) 1841–43; Chase Cliffe, Derbys. (Messrs Hurt; dem.) 1859–61; *Wynnstay, Denbighs.* (Sir W. Watkyns-Wynn) *c.* 1859; Bulstrode, Bucks. (D. of Somerset) 1861–70; Huntsham Court, Devon (C. A. W. Troyte) 1868–70; *Bagshot Park, Surrey* (D. of Connaught) 1877.

FOWLER, JAMES (1828–92)

Practised from Louth. An authority on Gothic architecture, he restored or built many churches in Lincolnshire and surrounding districts. But his country houses are in all styles.

Dalby Hall, Lincs. (Maj. J. W. Preston) 1856; Langton Hall, Lincs. (B. R. Langton) 1866–7; Morton Hall, Notts. (G. W. Mason) 1869.

GEORGE, SIR ERNEST (1839–1922; Kt 1911)

See p. 82.

From 1861 to *c.* 1875 in partnership with Thomas Vaughan and afterwards, first with H. E. Peto (1828–97)

and then with Alfred B. Yeates. Only a selection of his big country house practice after 1890 is given.

Rousdon, Devon (Sir H. W. Peek) 1874; Rawdon House, Herts. (Henry Ricardo; add.) 1881; *Buchan Hill, Sussex* (P. Saillard) 1882–5; Stoodleigh Court, Devon (T. Carew Daniel) 1883; Glencot, Somerset (W. S. Hodgkinson) 1885–7; Dunley House, Surrey (Adm. Maxse) 1887; *Batsford Park, Glos.* (A. B. Freeman-Mitford) 1888–93; *Shiplake Court, Oxon.* (R. H. C. Harrison) 1889–90; Motcomb, Dorset (Lord Stalbridge) 1893–5; North Mimms, Herts. (W. H. Burns; large add.) 1893–4; Crathorne Hall, Yorks. (J. L. Dugdale) 1903–6.

GIBSON, JOHN (1817–92)

A pupil and assistant of Sir Charles Barry. Best known for his National Provincial Banks; his country houses are unfortunately not in their ripe classical style. A volume of photographs of his works, presented by the architect in 1892, is in the R.I.B.A.

Charlecote House, Warwicks. (Mary Lucy; alt.) 1852–3; Myton Grange, nr Warwick, 1857; Plas Power, Denbighs. (T. L. Fitzhugh) 1858; Wroxton Abbey, Oxon. (Lady North; rest.; add.) 1858; Woodcote, Warwicks. (H. C. Wise) 1861; *Dobroyd Castle, Yorks., W.R.* (John Fielden) 1866–9; *Nutfield Priory, Surrey* (Joshua Fielden) 1870–4; Guy's Cliffe, Warwicks. (Lord Charles Bertie-Percy; dem.) 1871; Centre Vale, Yorks., W. R. (Samuel Fielden); Imberhouse, Sussex, 1873.

GODWIN, EDWARD WILLIAM (1833–86)

See pp. 329–34.

Dromore Castle, Limerick (E. of Limerick) 1866–73; *Glenbegh Towers, Kerry* (Hon. Rowland Winn) 1867–70; *Castle Ashby, Northants.* (M. of Northampton; lodges; gard.) 1868; *Beauvale, Notts.* (E. Cowper) 1871–4.

GOLDIE, GEORGE (1828–87)

A Catholic, in partnership as a young man with the Sheffield firm Hadfield and Weightman, and later with Child and his son Edward Goldie. Hadfield, Weightman and Goldie: Westwood Hall, Staffs. (John Davenport) 1850–3. Goldie and Child: Upsall Castle, Yorks., N.R. (Capt. E. Turton; largely dem.) 1873; Goldie, Child and Goldie: *Weston Manor House, Isle of Wight* (G. W. Ward) 1881–2.

HABERSHON, WILLIAM GILBEE (1818–91)

Started work at 5 a.m. every day and had a large and varied general practice. In partnership with A. R. Pite, 1863–78, and J. F. Fawckner, 1870–91. Son and pupil of Matthew Habershon, the author of *Ancient Half-Timbered Houses of England* (1836); his own Bewsey Hall was an early example of the revival of this style for country houses.

Bewsey Hall, Warrington (Lord Lilford; dem.) 1860; Apley Castle, Salop. (St J. C. Charlton; add.; dem.) 1860; Bedwell Park, Herts. (Sir C. E. Eardley, Bart) *c.* 1860; Duncrub Castle, nr Perth (Lord Rollo) 1861; Roydon Hall, Kent (E. A. Cook; rem.) 1871; Hope End, Malvern, Worcs. (C. A. Hewitt) 1873; Castle Irwell, Lancs. (Lord Lilford).

His brother Edward Habershon (d. 1901) designed *Normanhurst, Sussex*, 1867, for Thomas Brassey, in partnership with Brock and Webb, probably adapting a design by Hector Horeau.

HANSOM, JOSEPH ALOYSIUS (1803–82)

The inventor of the Hansom cab (1836) and founder of the *Builder* (1842). A Catholic, with a very large church practice.

Cheeseburn Grange, Northumberland (F. H. Riddell; add.; chapel) *c.* 1860; Lartington Park, Yorks. (Revd Thomas Witham; large add.) *c.* 1862–3; Derwent Hall, Derbys. (D. of Norfolk; rem.; chapel; dem.) *c.* 1881. Also additions and alterations to a large number of other country houses, mostly for Catholic patrons.

HARDWICK, PHILIP CHARLES (1822–92)

See p. 53

Hall, Devon (Robt Chichester) 1847 (with Philip Hardwick); *Aldermaston Manor, Berks.* (Higford Burr) 1848–51; *Adare Manor, Co. Limerick* (E. of Dunraven; large add.) 1850–62; Gilston Park, Herts. (Wm Hodgson) 1852; *Sompting Abbots, Sussex* (Capt. H. P. Crofts) 1854–6; *Addington Manor, Bucks.* (Lord Addington) 1856–7; Adhurst St Mary, Hants (J. Bonham Carter) 1858; *Rendcomb, Glos.* (Sir F. H. Goldsmid, Bart) 1863–5; *Madresfield, Worcs.* (E. Beauchamp) 1863–85; Hassobury, Essex (Robt Gosling) 1869.

HARRIS, THOMAS (1830–1900)

A 'proposed country house' exhibited at the Architectural Exhibition Society, 1868, sounds as though it was in his 'Victorian' style; his known country houses are less eccentric.

Milner Field, Yorks., W.R. (Sir Titus Salt, Bart; dem.) *c.* 1873–7; Bedstone Court, Salop. (Sir H. W. Ripley, Bart) 1884; *Stokesay Court, Salop.* (H. J. Alcroft) 1889.

HAYCOCK, EDWARD (*c.* 1792–?)

A pupil of Sir Jeffry Wyatville, he practised from Shrewsbury, where he designed Lord Hill's Column, 1814–16. But Netley is possibly by his son Edward Haycock, junior.

Millichope Park, Salop. (Revd R. N. Pemberton) 1835–40; Netley Hall, Salop., 1854–8.

HINE, THOMAS C. (1813–99)

A pupil of Matthew Habershon. Worked from Nottingham, where he had a big local practice, including many warehouses in the Lace Market, and the layout of the Nottingham Park estate.

Flintham Hall, Notts. (T. B. T. Hildyard; rem.; add.) *c.* 1851–4; Cranfield Court, Beds. (Revd G. G. Harter) *c.* 1862–4.

HOPPER, THOMAS (1776–1856)

Only houses designed after 1835 are included.

Llanover Court, Monmouths. (Sir B. Hall, Bart) *c.* 1840; Birch Hall, Essex (Charles Grey) *c.* 1845; *Wivenhoe Hall, Essex* (John Rebow; rem.) 1846; Easton Lodge, Essex (Vis. Maynard; dem.) 1847.

KERR, ROBERT (1823–1904)

See pp. 263–72, etc.

Dunsdale, Kent (Joseph Kitchin) 1858; Great Blake Hall, Essex (Chas Skipper; rem.; add.) 1860; *Bear Wood, Berks.* (John Walter) 1865–74; *Ford Manor, Surrey* (Jos. Spender-Clay) 1868; *Ascot Heath House* (J. Delane) 1868.

KNOWLES, JAMES THOMAS, senior (1806–84)

Dangstein, Sussex (Capt. Lyons; dem.) before 1839; *Silverton Park, Devon* (E. of Egremont; dem.) 1839–45; Palacio Monserrate, Portugal, 1858–65; *Hedsor House, Bucks.* (Lord Boston; much alt.) 1865–8.

His son J. T. Knowles, junior (1831–1908), designed *Aldworth, Surrey,* 1867–9, for Tennyson. (List kindly supplied by Priscilla Metcalf, from her work on J. T. Knowles, senior.)

LAMB, EDWARD BUCKTON (1806–69)

'He constantly endeavoured, even at the expense sometimes of beauty, to exhibit originality' (*Builder* obit.). The large country house practice of this individual and independent architect remains unexplored.

Elkington Hall, Lincs. (Revd W. Smyth) 1841; Allenheads, Northumberland (T. J. Beaumont) 1846; Newton Hall, Essex (Sir Brydges Henniker, Bart) 1858; *Hughenden, Bucks.* (B. Disraeli) 1862; Aldwark Manor, nr York (Hon. F. L. Astley) 1862; *Nun Appleton, Yorks.* (Sir Wm Milner, Bart; large add.; dem.) *c.* 1864. Also addition and alterations at Great Brickhill Manor, Bucks. (dem.); Wakefield Lodge, Northants.; Holt Hall, Norfolk; Thornham Hall, Suffolk; Mapleton, Yorks.; Montreal, Kent. Many of the designs in Loudon's *Encyclopedia of Cottage, Farm and Villa Architecture* are by Lamb.

NESFIELD, WILLIAM EDEN (1835–88)

See pp. 70–2, 320–8.

Combe Abbey, Warwicks. (E. of Craven; large add.; dem.) 1862–5; Sproughton Manor, nr Ipswich Suffolk, 1863; *Cloverley Hall, Salop.* (J. P. Heywood; largely dem.) 1854–70; *Farnham Park Bucks.* (H. Vallance) 1865; Hampton-in-Arden Manor, Warwicks. (Sir F. Peel; alt.) *c.* 1868–72; *Kinmel Hall, Denbighs.* (H. R. Hughes) 1870–4; *Plas Dinam, Montgomerys.* (O. M. Crew-Read) 1872–4; *Bank Hall, Derbys.* (H. Renshaw; add.) 1873; *Bodrhyddan, Flints.* (C. G. H. Rowley-Conwy; rem.) 1872–4; *Loughton Hall, Essex* (Revd J. W. Maitland) 1878; Gloddaeth, Denbighs. (Hon. T. E. Mostyn; add.); Kiplin Hall, Yorks. (Hon. W. C. Carpenter; add. 1875).

NORTON, JOHN (1823–1904)

A pupil of Benjamin Ferrey, with a flourishing and varied general practice. See pp. 243–51.

Ferney Hall, Salop. (W. H. Sitwell) 1856–60; *Nutfield, Surrey* (H. E. Gurney) 1858–9; Brent Knoll, Somerset (G. S. Poole) 1862–4; Chew Magna Manor, Somerset (W. Adlam) 1862–4; Framingham Hall, Norfolk (G. H. Christie) 1862–4; *Tyntesfield, Somerset* (Wm Gibbs) 1863–6; *Elveden Hall, Suffolk* (Mah. Duleep Singh) *c.* 1870–1; *St Audries, Somerset* (Sir A. A. Hood) *c.* 1870–2; Summers Place, Sussex (Robt Goff) *c.* 1881. Also Horsted Hall, Norfolk (Sir E. Birkbeck); Mickleham Manor,

Surrey; Badgemore, Oxon.; Monkhams, Essex; and country houses in Estonia and Livonia.

PALEY, EDWARD GRAHAM: *see under* SHARPE, EDMUND

PAXTON, SIR JOSEPH (1801–65; Kt 1851)

His country houses were designed in collaboration with G. H. Stokes (1827(8)–1874) with contributions from Pugin at Burton Closes and Lismore. Stokes entered his office about 1847 and married his daughter in 1852.

Burton Closes, Derbys. (John Allcard) 1846–7; *Mentmore, Bucks.* (Baron M. A. de Rothschild) 1850–5; *Lismore Castle, Co. Waterford* (D. of Devonshire; rem.) 1851–8; *Ferrières, nr Paris* (Baron J. de Rothschild) 1853–9; *Battlesden House, Beds.* (Sir E. Page-Turner, Bart) 1860–4; Pregny, Geneva (Baron A. de Rothschild) *c.* 1860–4.

PEARSON, JOHN LOUGHBOROUGH (1817–98)

See pp. 164–70.

Worked in the offices of I. Bonomi, Salvin and Philip Hardwick, before setting up independently in 1843. His country houses were very much a sideline in his long and busy career as a church architect, and in style and treatment form a curiously varied mixture.

Treberfydd House, Brecon (Robt Raikes; rec.) 1848–50; *Quar Wood, Glos.* (Revd R. W. Hippisley; much alt.) 1857; *Roundwyck House, Sussex* (Capt. Penfold) 1868; *Lechlade Manor House, Glos.* (George Milward) 1872; *Cliveden House, Bucks.* (J. J. Astor; int. dec.) *c.* 1895.

PRICHARD, JOHN (1818–86)

A pupil of A. W. Pugin, he practised from Llandaff, where he restored the cathedral. In partnership with J. P. Seddon, 1852–62.

Beckford Hall, Worcs. (Revd J. Timbrill; add.; alt.) *c.* 1857; *Ettington Park, Warwicks.* (E. P. Shirley; rem.) 1858–63.

After the partnership was dissolved, J. P. Seddon designed *Abermad, Cardigans.* (L. Pugh Pugh) *c.* 1872, and Rosdohan, Co. Kerry.

PUGIN, AUGUSTUS WELBY NORTHMORE (1818–52)

See pp. 46–8, 59–60, 110–16, etc.

Alton Towers, Staffs. (E. of Shrewsbury; add.; alt.) 1836, etc.; *Scarisbrick Hall, Lancs.* (Chas Scarisbrick; rec.) 1837–45; *Bilton Grange, Warwicks.* (Capt. W. Hibbert) 1841–6; Chirk Castle, Denbighs. (Col. R. Myddleton Biddulph; add.; alt) *c.* 1844; *Albury, Surrey* (Henry Drummond; rem.) 1846–52; *Alton Castle, Staffs.* (E. of Shrewsbury) 1847–51; Burton Closes, Derbys. (with Joseph Paxton, for J. Allcard) 1847; *Wilburton Manor House, Cambs.* (O. C. Pell) 1848–50; unexecuted designs for Garendon Hall, Leics., 1841; *Woodchester Park, Glos.,* 1844.

See also under Horsted Place, Sussex (pp. 172–8) and Abney Hall, Ches., Adare Manor, Co. Limerick, and Lismore Castle, Co Waterford, in the Catalogue.

PUGIN, EDWARD WELBY (1834-75)

See pp. 117-9.

Croston Hall, Lancs. (J. R. de Trafford; dem.) 1857; *Scarisbrick Hall, Lancs.* (Lady Scarisbrick; large add.) 1860-6; Garendon Hall, Leics. (A. P. de l'Isle; add.; alt.; dem.) 1866; *Carlton Towers, Yorks.* (Lord Beaumont; rem.) 1873-5; Chateau at St Michel, Belgium.

ST AUBYN, JAMES PIERS (1815-95)

Presumably a connection of the St Aubyns of St Michael's Mount. He was primarily a church architect, but designed a good few country houses, mostly in a rather dour early Gothic style.

Delamore House, Devon (Adm. Geo. Parker) 1860 and 1876; Midelney Place, Somerset (E. B. Cely-Trevilian) *c.* 1868; Greenhurst, Surrey (Thos Lambert) 1871-4; *St Michael's Mount, Cornwall* (Sir J. St Aubyn, Bart; large add.) 1874; Muntham, Sussex (M. of Bath) *c.* 1883. Also Anstie House and Pencallmick House, Cornwall, 1881.

SALVIN, ANTHONY (1799-1881)

See pp. 52, 94-5, 157-63.

This list is based on information supplied by Dr Jill Allibone. Completely new houses, or houses subtantially remodelled, include: Mamhead, Devon (Sir Robt Newman, Bart) 1826-37; Moreby Hall, Yorks. (Henry Preston) 1828-33; *Harlaxton Manor, Lincs.* (G. Gregory) 1831-8; Burwarton House, Salop. (Vis. Boyne; partly dem.) 1835-9, 1876-7; Scotney Castle, Kent (E. Hussey) 1835-43; Cowesby Hall, Yorks. (G. Lloyd; dem.) 1836; Skutterskelf Hall (now Levengrove), Yorks. (Vis. Falkland) 1832-8; *Peckforton Castle, Cheshire* (J. Tollemache) 1844-50; Patterdale Hall, Westmoreland (W. Marshall) 1845-50; *Penoyre House, Brecon* (Lt-Col. L. V. Watkins) 1846-8; Bangor Castle, Co. Down (R. E. Ward) 1852; *Alnwick Castle, Northumberland* (D. of Northumberland) 1854-65; *Keele Hall, Staffs.* (R. Sneyd) 1855-61; Congham High House, Norfolk (R. Elwes; dem.) 1859; Whitehall, Cumberland (Geo. Moore; dem.) 1858-61; *Thoresby Hall, Notts.* (E. Manvers) 1863-75; Crossrigg Hall, Westmoreland (Col. Rigg) 1864; Paddockhurst (now Worth Priory), Sussex (Geo. Smith) 1869-72; Hodnet Hall, Salop. (Ly. E. Heber-Percy; dem.) *c.* 1869.

Among important restorations, additions and alterations are: Brancepeth Castle, Durham (M. Russell; Vis. Boyne) 1829, 1864-73; Kildale Hall, Yorks. (R. B. Livesey) 1827-31; Methley Hall, Yorks. (E. of Mexborough) 1830-6; Pyrgo Park, Essex (dem.) *c.* 1836; *Bayons Manor, Lincs.*, 1836; Danesfield, Bucks. (C. Scott Murray; dem.) 1836-41; Rockingham Castle, Northants. (R. Watson) 1836-52; Greystoke Castle, Cumb. (Mr Howard) 1837-42, 1875-8; Worden Hall, Lancs. (J. N. Ffarrington; dem.) 1840-5; Naworth Castle, Cumb. (E. of Carlisle) 1844-53; *Oxon Hoath, Kent* (Sir W. Geary) 1846-8; Flixton Hall, Suffolk (Sir R. Adair, Bart; dem.) 1846; Hafod, Cardigans. (H. Hoghton) 1846-51; South Park, Kent (Sir H. Hardinge; dem.) 1848; Marbury Hall, Ches. (J. H. Smith Barry; dem.) 1856-8; Warwick Castle (E. of Warwick) 1856-9, 1863-6, 1871-8; Hutton-in-the-Forest, Camb. (Sir H. Vane) 1862-9; Capesthorne House, Ches. (A. H. Davenport) 1865-8; Fawsley Hall, Northants. (Sir R. Knightly; dem.) 1867-8; Dunster Castle, Somerset (G. F. Luttrell) 1868-72; Petworth House, Sussex (Lord Leconfield) 1869-72; Longford Castle, Wilts. (E. of Radnor) 1870-5; Melbury House, Dorset (E. of Ilchester) 1872; Birdsall House, Yorks. (Lord Middleton) 1871-5.

SCOTT, SIR GEORGE GILBERT (1811-78; Kt, 1872)

See pp. 224-35.

Pippbrook House, Surrey (J. Forman) 1856; *Kelham Hall, Notts.* (J. H. Manners-Sutton) 1858-62; *Sudeley Castle, Glos.* (J. C. Dent; rest.; add.) *c.* 1858-63; *Walton Hall, Warwicks.* (Sir Chas Mordaunt, Bart) 1858-62; *Hafodunos House, Denbighs.* (H. R. Sandbach) 1861-6; Lee Priory, Kent (Francis Philips; rem.; dem.) 1861; Brownsover Hall, Warwicks. (E. A. B. W. Boughton-Leigh) *c.* 1877.

SEDDON, JOHN POLLARD (1827-1906)

An unlikely pupil of T. L. Donaldson. *See under* PRICHARD, JOHN.

SHARPE, EDMUND (1809-77)

A pupil of Thomas Rickman, settled in Lancaster and became a writer and recognized authority on Gothic architecture. In 1845 he went into partnership with Edward Graham Paley (1823-95), who had become his pupil in 1838. Sharpe retired from architecture in 1851 and devoted himself to engineering and railway promotion. E. G. Paley took over his practice and in 1868 took H. J. Austin into what proved to be a highly successful partnership.

Capernwray Hall, Lancs. (George Marton) 1844; *Hornby Castle, Lancs.* (Pudsey Dawson; rec.) *c.* 1850. Winmarleigh Hall, Lancs. (Lord Winmarleigh) 1871; *Holker Hall, Lancs.* (D. of Devonshire) *c.* 1873; *Thurland Castle, Lancs.* (N. North and E. D. Lees; rem.) 1879-89. Walton Hall, Warrington, Lancs. (Sir Gilbert Greenall, Bart).

SHAW, RICHARD NORMAN (1831-1912)

See pp. 70-78.

Only country houses are covered.

Fowlers Park, Hawkhurst Kent (J. G. Stewart; dem.) 1864-6; West Wickham House, Kent (W. M. Steuart; rem.; altered) 1869-71; *Cragside, Northumberland* (Sir W. Armstrong) 1869-84; Preen Salop. (Arthur Sparrow; rem.; add.; dem.) 1870-2; Boldre Grange, Hants (J. L. Shrubb) 1873-4; Bourton Manor, Salop. (J. H. A. Whitley) 1874; *Pierrepont, Surrey* (Richard Combe; rec.) 1876-8; *Adcote, Salop.* (Mrs Rebecca Darby) 1876-81; *Flete, Devon* (H. B. Mildmay; rec.) 1878-80; *Greenham Lodge, Berks.* (Arthur Southby) 1878-79; Didlington Hall, Norfolk (W. A. Amherst; alt.; add.; dem.) *c.* 1880; *Dawpool, Ches.* (T. H. Ismay; dem.) 1882-4; *Banstead Wood, Surrey* (Hon. Francis Baring) 1884-90; *Bryanston, Dorset* (Vis. Portman) 1890; Chesters, Northumberland (N. G. Clayton; rec.) 1891; Haggerston Castle, Northumberland (C. J. Leyland; dem.) 1892-7; Overbury Court, Worcs. (R. B. Martin; large add.) 1897-1900 (and 1887).

SLATER, WILLIAM: *see under* CARPENTER, R. HERBERT

SMITH, T. ROGER

Founder and editor of the *Architect*, and Professor of Construction at University College, London. A Goth, until he went François I at Stancliffe.

Stratton Audley Park, Oxon. (Geo. Glen) 1860; Shephall-bury, Herts. (U. Unwin-Heathcote) c. 1866; Blythwood, Bucks. (Geo. Hanbury; dem.) 1869; *Stancliffe Hall, Derbys.* (Sir J. Whitworth) 1872.

STOKES, GEORGE HENRY: *see under*
PAXTON, SIR JOSEPH

TEULON, SAMUEL SANDERS (1812–73)
See pp. 64·5, 198–204.

Totworth Court, Glos. (E. of Ducie) 1849–52; *Enbrook, Kent* (Hon. J. D. Bligh) c. 1854; *Shadwell Park, Norfolk* (Sir R. J. Buxton, Bart; rem.) 1856–60; Gisborough Hall, Yorks., N.R. (Adm. Chaloner) 1857; *Elvetham Hall, Hants* (4th Lord Calthorpe; rec.) 1859–62; Hawkleyhurst, Hants (J. J. Maberly) 1860–1; *Bestwood Lodge, Notts.* (D. of St Albans) 1862–4; Knepp Castle, Sussex (Sir Percy Burrell, Bart) 1863; Woodlands Vale, Isle of Wight (5th Lord Calthorpe) 1870–1; Warlies Park, Essex (Sir Thos Fowell Buxton; add.; alt.); Perry Hall, Staffs. (4th Lord Calthorpe).

THOMAS, JOHN (1813–62)

A sculptor who was taken up by Barry and put in charge of the sculptural work at the Houses of Parliament. He became enormously successful and prolific and it remains mysterious how and why he also fitted a small architectural practice into his short career. He had no architectural training and his assistant Henry Parsons (a pupil of Thomas Cubitt) later claimed to have done most of the work.

Somerleyton Hall, Suffolk (S. M. Peto; rec.) 1844–51; *Preston Hall, Kent* (E. L. Betts) 1850; Headington House, Oxon.

VULLIAMY, LEWIS (1791–1871)

For his early houses and his many additions and alterations see Howard Colvin, *Dictionary of English Architects, 1660–1840.*

Dingestow Court, Monmouths. (S. Bosanquet) 1845; Chestal House, Glos. (James Phelps) 1848; St Margaret's, Isleworth, Middx (E. of Kilmorey) 1852–3; Bramshott Grange, Hants (Sir W. Erle) 1855; Alderley House, Glos. (R. B. Hale) 1859–61; *Westonbirt House, Glos.* (R. S. Holford) 1863–70.

WATERHOUSE, ALFRED (1830–1905)

A Manchester architect who came to London and built up perhaps the biggest practice of his day in England. Its size is indicated by the list of his country houses, which were relatively a sideline. His early houses were unswervingly Gothic, but in the 1870s they tended to acquire an Old English flavour.

Hinderton, Ches. (Chris. Bushell) 1858; *Hutton Hall, Yorks.* (J. W. Pease) 1865–8; *Easneye, Herts.* (T. Fowell Buxton) 1867–9; Allerton Priory, Lancs. (J. Grant Morris) 1867–70; *Blackmoor, Hants* (Roundell Palmer) 1869–73, 1882; *Eaton Hall, Ches.* (D. of Westminster; rec.; largely dem.) 1870–82; Crookhey Hall, Lancs. (Col. Bird) 1874; *Heythrop Hall, Oxon.* (Albert Brassey; rec.) c. 1875–80; Silwood Park, Bucks. (Thos Cordes) 1876; *Iwerne Minster, Dorset* (Lord Wolverton) 1878; *Yattendon, Berks.* (A. Waterhouse; dem.) 1880–1; *Grinkle Park, Yorks.* (Sir Chas Palmer, Bart) 1882; Buckhold House, Berks. (H. Watney?) 1884–5.

WEBB, PHILIP (1831–1915)
See pp. 79–82, 381–9.

Arisaig, Inverness (F. D. P. Astley; partly dem.) 1863; *Washington Hall, Durham* (I. L. Bell; add.) c. 1864; *Rounton Grange, Yorks., N.R.* (I. L. Bell; dem.) 1872–6; *Smeaton Manor, Yorks., NR* (Maj. Godman) 1877–9; *Clouds, Wilts.* (Hon. P. Wyndham; partly dem.) 1879–91; Rushmore, Wilts. (Gen. Pitt-Rivers; alt.; add.) 1883; Tangley Manor, Surrey (Wickham Flower; add.; alt.) 1885; *Standen, Sussex* (J. M. Beale) 1891–4; Forthampton Court, Glos. (J. R. Yorke; rest.; add.) 1891; Exning House, Newmarket (Col. E. W. D. Baird; large add.) 1896.

WHITE WILLIAM (1825–1900)
See pp. 253–62.

Bishopscourt, Devon (John Garratt; rec.) 1860–4; *Winscott, Devon* (J. C. Moore-Stevens; dem.) c. 1865; *Humewood, Co. Wicklow* (W. W. F. Dick) 1867–70; *Quy Hall, Cambs.* (Clement Francis) 1868.

WOODYER, HENRY (1816–96)

Said to have been a pupil of Butterfield, but this is highly unlikely; for a short time he shared an office with him. Mainly thought of as a church architect, but also had a sizeable country house practice. The following list is based on information supplied by Gordon Barnes.

Cosford House, Thursley, Surrey, c. 1848; Muntham, Court, Surrey (Marchioness of Bath; dem.) c. 1850–1; Twyford Moors, nr Winchester (Mr Conway Shipley) 1861–2; Wotton House, Surrey (Mr Evelyn; large add.) 1864; Brandfold, nr Goudhurst, Kent (Jos. Ridgeway; dem.) 1872; Holme Park, Sonning, Berks. (Revd S. Golding-Palmer; large add.) c. 1881; Barrow Court, Somerset (Martin Gibbs; large add.) 1882–91; Tyntesfield, Somerset (Anthony Gibbs: add.; alt.) 1885–9.

WYATT, SIR MATTHEW DIGBY (1820–77; Kt 1855)

A member of the Wyatt clan and the young and abler brother of T. H. Wyatt.

Castle Ashby, Northants. (M. of Northampton; gard.) 1861–5; The Ham, Glam. (Iltyd Nicholl; dem.) 1865; *Possingworth Manor, Sussex* (H. Huth) 1868–70; Oldlands Hall, Sussex (A. Nesbitt) 1874.

WYATT, THOMAS HENRY (1807–80)
See p. 53.

A pupil of Philip Hardwick, and a tireless and tedious architect, who died in harness at the age of seventy-three. In partnership with David Brandon, 1838–51. There is a long (undated) list of his formidable output in his obituary in the *Builder*; the following is a selection omitting, in particular, many of his country houses in Wales, where he was extensively employed.

Llantarnam Abbey, Monmouths. (R. S. Blewitt) 1835; Malpas Court, Monmouths. (Thos Prothero) 1838; Llandogo Priory, Monmouths. (John Gough) 1838; Craigynos, Brecons. (Rhys D. Powell) 1842; Fonthill House, Wilts. (Jas Morrison; dem.) 1848; Hensall Castle, Glam. (Rowland Fothergill) 1848); *Orchardleigh House, Somerset* (Wm Duckworth) 1855–8; Carlett Park, Ches. (John Torr) 1859–60; *Capel Manor, Kent* (F. Austen; dem.)

1859–62; *Arley Hall, Ches.* (R. E. Egerton-Warburton; large add.) 1860; Cranmore, Somerset (Sir R. H. Paget, Bart; rec.) *c.* 1866; Nuneham Paddox, Warwicks. (E. of Denbigh) 1875; Barcote, Berks. (Marchioness of Westminster) 1876; North Perrott Manor, Somerset (H. W. Hoskyns) 1878. Also mansions in Poland, for the Woronzows, and at Cascaes, nr Lisbon, for the Duke of Palmella.

YOUNG, WILLIAM (1843–1900)

Like Norman Shaw and J. J. Stevenson, but with far less talent, he was an ambitious young Scot who came to London and established a successful practice. In true Robert Adam style he published a handsome volume of his own designs, *Town and Country Mansions*, in 1878. But Adam would not have liked what Young did to his own Gosford Hall.

Holmewood House, Hunts. (Wm Wells) 1874; Haseley Manor, Warwicks. (Mr Hewlett) 1875; Oxhey Grange, Herts. (W. T. Eley) 1876; Duncombe Park, Yorks., N.R. (E. of Feversham; rest. after fire) 1879; *Gosford House, E. Lothian.* (E. of Wemyss; rem.) 1880–90; *Elveden Hall, Suffolk* (Lord Iveagh; large add.) 1893.

NOTES TO THE TEXT

INTRODUCTION

1. Quoted by Gervas Huxley, *Victorian Duke* (London, 1967), which I have used throughout this section.
2. See *Dictionary of National Biography* (1st supplement) under Hugh Lupus Grosvenor, first Duke of Westminster (1825–99).
3. Ernestine Mills, *Life and Letters of Frederic Shields* (London, 1912), p. 225.
4. Henry Stacy Marks, *Pen and Pencil Sketches* (London, 1894), I, p. 214.
5. For the reaction of guests see Lord Ernest Hamilton, *Old Days and New* (London, 1924), p. 142; and *Life and Letters of George Wyndham*, ed. J. W. Mackail and Guy Wyndham (London, 1925), I, p. 141.
6. Hamilton, *Old Days*, p. 133.
7. *George Wyndham*, I, pp. 383, 385.
8. Sir George Gilbert Scott, pp. 140–2.
9. Hippolyte Taine, *Notes on England*, tr. Edward Hyams (London, 1957), p. 155. Taine was in England in 1859 and 1862.
10. Sir George Gilbert Scott, *Personal and Professional Recollections* (London, 1879), p. 3.
11. *Lady Charlotte Guest: Extracts from her journal, 1833–52*, ed. Earl of Bessborough (London, 1950), p. 225.
12. The main landmarks in the curtailment of upper-class power may be of interest:

    1832   First Reform Act.
    c. 1845–55   County police forces established.
    1846   Repeal of the Corn Laws removes protection from agricultural interest.
    1867   Second Reform Act.
    1870   Competitive exams for the Civil Service introduced. Board Schools established.
    1871   Purchase of commissions abolished.
    1872   Ballot Act allows secret voting.
    1881   Ground Game Act; tenants allowed to destroy rabbits and hares on their land.
    1883   Agricultural Holdings Act: regulation of bargains between landlords and tenants, to the benefit of the latter.
    1888   Establishment of county councils.
    The establishment of police forces, board schools and county councils had little immediate result, but the intrusion of an increasingly independent civil service into what had been (in the country) a completely gentry-dominated preserve was bound to reduce their power in the long run.
13. F. L. Thompson's invaluable *English Landed Society in the Nineteenth Century* (London, 1963), pp. 121–2. 'Thirty years' purchase' meant that the purchase price was 30 times the annual income from the rents. By 1890 the price was down to 20 or 25 years' purchase, *ibid*, pp. 317–8.
14. It was difficult to decide where to draw the borderline between an old and a new family. For the purpose of my analysis I defined a new family as one that had not owned a substantial country estate for more than two generations. See also Fig. 1.
15. Normanhurst, Sussex (1867); Preston Hall, Kent (bought from E. L. Betts, 1866); Heythrop, Oxfordshire (gutted eighteenth-century house restored *c.* 1870); Apethorpe, Northants (bought 1904).
16. See Henrietta Maria Stanely, 8 Sept. 1845, *The Ladies of Alderley*, ed. Nancy Mitford (2nd edn, London, 1967), p. 84.
    Abbey Cwmhir, Radnorshire (1868–9); Lee Priory, Kent (remodelled 1861); Welcombe, Warwickshire
17. (1867); Heath House, Staffordshire (1836–40).
18. See *Post Office London Directory 1890*, Pt I, p. 1294; Pt II, p. 2405.
19. First published in 1822 but reissued in greatly enlarged form, 1826. Further editions 1828, 1844–8 (revised) and 1877. The 1877 edition did not sell.
20. See E. Wingfield-Stratford, *The Squire and his Relations* (London, 1856), p. 294.
21. For Lovelace, see p. 410; for Beckett, pp. 85, 396, et al; for Buxton, p. 406; for Scawen Blunt, p. 85.
22. *Lady Charlotte Guest*, p. 216.
23. The brothers Thomas (1788–1855) and William (1791–1863) Cubitt split up their joint business in 1827. Thomas's business did not survive him, William's has continued until the present day. In the 1830s he worked with his other brother as William and Lewis Cubitt, in the 1840s on his own and from 1844, with various partners, as William Cubitt and Co. He retired in 1851, when the firm was continued under the same name by this partner until taken over in 1883 by Holland and Hannen. (Information from Hermione Hobhouse.)
24. At the R.I.B.A.
25. *Builder*, XXVI, p. 406.
26. *Builder*, 24 Apr. 1886, p. 601; *Architect*, 25 June 1886, p. 396.
27. Preserved in many volumes at Merevale Hall. See also p. 120.
28. Samuel Smiles, *George Moore, Merchant and Philanthropist* (London, 1878), p. 242.
29. For Smirke's use of iron, see J. M Crook, *The British Museum* (London, 1972), pp. 171–2. For Prestwold, see Chapter 6, and for Fonthill, see *Catalogue of the R.I.B.A. Drawings Collection*, B (1972), p. 124.
30. See J. J. Stevenson, *House Architecture* (London, 1880), II, pp. 189–9.
31. The use of iron and steel by Shaw and Nesfield is discussed in Andrew Saint, *Richard Norman Shaw* (New Haven and London, 1976), pp. 113–15.
32. *Building News*, 4 July, 1873, p. 8; and Peter Collins, *Concrete: The Vision of a New Architecture* (London, 1959), p. 42. The *Building News* of 25 June 1875, refers to a 'Concrete Mansion for Lord Portman' erected by the 'late' James Baker Green.
33. Sir George Gilbert Scott, *Remarks on Secular and Domestic Architecture Present and Future* (London, 1857), p. 35.
34. For Bowood, see Walter Bernan, *On the History and Art of Warming and Ventilating Rooms and Buildings* (London, 1845), essay XIV. For Abbotsford, see J. G. Lockhart, *Life of Sir Walter Scott* (Edinburgh, 1896,

edn), pp. 500–1.

35. Registrar House, Edinburgh, Drummond–Moray Papers, 624.

36. For Coleshill and Stratfield Saye, see C. J. Richardson, *A Popular Treatise on the Warming and Ventilating of Buildings* (London, 1837), pp. 45–6, 48–9. Loudon's plans for Coleshill are now in the Berkshire County Record office.

37. Stevenson, *House Architecture*, II, p. 212.

38. *Ibid*, II, p. 237.

39. Some are described by Reyner Banham, *The Architecture of the Well-Tempered Environment* (London, 1969), secs. 4 and 6.

40. It was described at length by the architect in R.I.B.A. *Transactions* (1st series, III), April 1851, in a paper which also deals with other features of this remarkable house.

41. In 1902, when Osmaston was featured in *Country Life*, XII, pp. 48–55, the roof was liberally equipped with conventional chimneystacks. The house has now been demolished, but the chimney tower survives. There is a smaller gothic ventilating tower, possibly designed by Pugin, at Abney Hall, Cheshire, but its exact relationship to the house appears uncertain.

42. *Encyclopaedia Brittanica* (11th edn, London, 1910), p. 483.

43. J. C. Loudon, *Encyclopaedia of Cottage, Farm and Villa Architecture* (London, 1835, edn), sec. 2055.

44. 'Hollow walls are now at last generally admitted to be expedient though architects are still wonderfully slow to propose them' (Sir Edmund Beckett, *A Book on Building* (London, 1876), p. 155).

45. Information from Peter Ferriday.

46. Hamilton, *Old Days*, pp. 88, 91. Twelve country houses, to my knowledge had electric light in the 1880s: Cragside (1880), Hatfield (1881), Berechurch (1882), Dawpool (1882–4), Broomhill (early 1880s), Smallwood (1886), Woodlands Park, Surrey (*Builder*, 20 Nov. 1886), Wightwick (1887), Eaton Hall (1887), Coombe, Dorset (*Builder*, 28 Apr. 1888), Stokesay Court (1889), Avery Hill (*c*. 1889). Of these only two (Hatfield and Eaton) belonged to old families, though further research might well alter the balance. Tyntesfield is also said to have had electricity installed in the 1880s, but I have not found documentation.

47. Augustus Hare, *The Story of My Life* (2nd series, London, 1890), III, pp. 227, 280, 400.

48. A detailed study of the Victorian country house plan by Jill Franklin is in course of preparation for publication.

49. For a discussion of the size and expense of Victorian country house households, see Thompson, *English Landed Society*. See also Huxley, *Victorian Duke*, for a table showing the size and designation of the enormous estate and house staff at Eaton Hall in the late nineteenth century.

50. Robert Kerr F.R.I.B.A., *The Gentleman's House: or how to plan English residences from the parsonage to the palace* (London, 1864). There were further, enlarged, editions in 1865 and 1871.

51. *Ibid*, p. 476; in the notes to a plan on the 'modern Scotch model'. 'The merits of this school make no pretension to be of the artistic order, but turn entirely upon practical usefulness.' See also *Builder*, 5 March 1870, p. 189; and the long obituary memoir by J. L. Donaldson in R.I.B.A. *Transactions*, 1870, pp. 121–9. For a contemporary study, see David Walker, 'William Burn as Country-House Architect, 1817–50', in *Seven Victorian Architects*, ed. Jane Fawcett (London, 1972). Among much highly interesting material it raises the question of how much Burn's style and planning owed to Sir Robert Smirke, as revealed by the researches of Dr J. M. Crook. Burn was in Smirke's office in 1808–10.

52. Kerr, *Gentleman's House*, p. 167.

53. Peter Quennell, *Byron: The Years of Fame* (London, 1935), p. 216.

54. Kerr, *Gentleman's House*, p. 129.

55. *Ibid*, p. 143.

56. Quoted Elizabeth Longford, *Victoria R. I.* (London, 1964), p. 126.

57. Loudon, *Cottage, Farm and Villa*, sec. 1681.

58. Kerr, *Gentleman's House*, p. 254.

59. C. M. Yonge, Ch. XV.

60. Loudon, *Cottage, Farm and Villa*, sec. 1681.

61. For Salvin, see Christopher Hussey, *English Country Houses, Late Georgian* (London, 1958), pp. 193–205, 220–48; and for his work at Brancepeth, see W. E. Nesfield's obituary notice of him, *Building News*, XLI (1881), p. 893. Dr Jill Allibone is working on a full-length study of Salvin, developed out of her unpublished thesis on him (University of London, 1975). Salvin's uncle, the Revd William Nesfield, was vicar of Brancepeth, and W. E. Nesfield suggests that it may have been as a result of seeing Matthew Russell's 'restoration' work at Brancepeth Castle as a boy (work started there in 1818) that his interests were turned to medieval architecture.

62. Quoted in Dr Phoebe Stanton's unpublished thesis on Pugin (University of London, 1950).

63. A. W. Pugin, p. 61.

64. Charles Tennyson D'Eyncourt, *Eustace: An Elegy* (2nd edn, London, 1851), p. 29. The banquet was to celebrate the birth of the Prince of Wales, and Eustace Tennyson D'Eyncourt's departure to join his regiment in the Barbadoes. He died there of yellow fever six weeks later; hence the elegy by his father.

65. R. S. Surtees, *Mr. Sponge's Sporting Tour* (London, 1852), CH. XIV.

66. Sir George Gilbert Scott, p. 151.

67. A. W. Pugin, *True Principles of Pointed or Christian Architecture* (London, 1841), pp. 62–3.

68. Palladian ('In England it is now little used'), Elizabethan revived, Rural Italian, Palatial Italian, French–Italian, English Renaissance, Medieval or Gothic, Cottage, Scotch Baronial (*Gentleman's House*, pp. 356–97). 'English Renaissance' turns out to be French Second Empire (see p. 293).

69. John Cornford, 'Trentham, Staffordshire, II', *Country Life*, CXLIII (1968), p. 230.

70. Kerr, *Gentleman's House*, p. 230.

71. *Loudon, Cottage, Farm and Villa*, sec. 1653.

72. C. M. Yonge, *Heartsease or the Brother's Wife* (London, 3rd edn, 1855), Pt I, Ch. III.

73. Scott, *Secular and Domestic*, p. 147.

74. B. D. Disraeli, *Coningsby* (London, 1844), Pt III, Ch. IV.

75. Kerr, *Gentleman's House*, p. 382.

76. Beckett, *Book on Building*, p. 96.

77. Thomas Carlyle, *Past and Present* (London, 1843), Book III. Ch. V.

78. Elizabeth Gaskell, *North and South* (London, 1855), Ch. 40; Charles Kingsley, *His Letters and Memories of his Life* (London, 1877), I, p. 180.

79. William Rathbone Greg, *Literary and Social Judge-*

ments (London, 1860), I, pp. 145–6.

80. A fascinating discussion of this is in Charles Handley-Read's illustrated commentary 'High Victorian Design', published in *Design 1860–1960*, the sixth conference report of the Victorian Society. For a discussion of the influence of Ruskin's revised concept of the sublime in producing simplified forms and strong outlines, see Stephan Muflusius, *The High Victorian Movement in Architecture* (London, 1972), pp. 29, 32–4.

81. Kerr, *Gentleman's House*, p. 99.

82. *Builder*, 17 March 1860. For this extraordinary and fascinating house, demolished in 1966, see also Nicholas Taylor, 'Modular rockery', *Architectural Review*, Feb. 1967, p. 147.

83. Pugin, *True Principles*, p. 61.

84. *Ibid*, p. 63.

85. Beckett, *Book on Building*, p. 83.

86. Kerr, *Gentleman's House*, p. 84.

87. Scott, *Secular and Domestic*, p. 120.

88. Kerr, *Gentleman's House*, p. 73.

89. Beckett, *Book on Building*, pp. 178–9; Stevenson, *House Architecture*, II, p. 204.

90. *The Penguin Book of Victorian Verse*, ed. George MacBeth (London, 1969), p. 65 (used as a description of *The Idylls of the King*).

91. Charles Kingsley, *Alton Locke* (London, 1850), Ch. II.

92. See T. W. Bamford, *Rise of the Public Schools* (London, 1967), p. 214, *passim*.

93. In a letter to Swinburne written *c.* Sept. 1869, *The Swinburne Letters*, ed. C. Y. Lang (New Haven, 1959–62), II, pp. 32–3.

94. Information from his great-nephew Sir Steven Runciman.

95. J. M. Brydon, 'William Eden Nesfield, 1835–88', *Architectural Review*, I (1897), p. 238.

96. Preface to B. F. L. Clarke, *Church Builders of the Nineteenth Century* (London, 1938), p. viii.

97. By the 1880s they would also have called themselves 'aesthetic'.

98. *Building News*, 6 Sept. 1872, p. 182.

99. Stevenson, *House Architecture*, II, p. 72.

100. *Ibid*, II, p. 69.

101. Kerr, *Gentleman's House*, p. 165.

102. Stevenson, House Architecture, II, pp. 78–9.

103. *Ibid*, II, p. 80.

104. *Ibid*, II, p. 90.

105. *Ibid*, II, p. 80.

106. *Ibid*, II, p. 60.

107. Sir Reginald Blomfield, *Richard Norman Shaw, R.A.* (London, 1940), p. 1. For the Shaw–Savill line, see Basil Lubbock, *The Colonial Clippers* (Glasgow, 1921), pp. 348–54. It ran a service from London to New Zealand—hence New Zealand Chambers, the name of its London office, which Shaw designed in 1872.

108. See Burke's *Landed Gentry* (1898 edn), 'Stevenson of Westoe'; and Who's Who entries for J. J. Stevenson's brother, James Cochran Stevenson (1825–1905).

109. He designed Loughton Hall in Essex for the Revd John Whitaker Maitland, the brother-in-law of his first cousin Osbert Salvin (see Burke's *Landed Gentry*, 'Maitland of Loughton').

110. Brydon, 'Nesfield', p. 235.

111. Blomfield, *Norman Shaw*, p. 17.

112. C. L. Eastlake, *A History of the Gothic Revival in England* (1872), p. 343.

113. Illustrated by Eastlake, *ibid*, p. 345.

114. For a full-length study of 'Queen Anne', see Mark Girouard, *Sweetness and Light: the 'Queen Anne' Movement, 1860–1900* (Oxford, 1977).

115. *Building News*, 2 May 1879.

116. This was no doubt the reason why most of the few country houses that can be associated with the 'Queen Anne' movement are very much less quaint and more symmetrical than the town or suburban examples, e.g. F. P. Cockerell's Crawley Court and Woodcote Hall (see Catalogue) and George Gilbert Scott, Junior's, demolished Garboldisham Manor in Norfolk (1873).

117. For a discussion of Shaw's country house planning, see Saint, *Norman Shaw*, pp. 110–13.

118. *Mary Gladstone: Her Diaries and Letters*, ed. Masterman (London, 1940), p. 100.

119. Henry James (London, 1893), Ch. II.

120. W. R. Lethaby, *Philip Webb and his Work* (London, 1935), p. 121.

121. *Country Life*, XVI (1904), pp. 255–60.

122. Lethaby, *Philip Webb*, p. 99.

123. A contemporary monograph on Devey is a desideratum. Articles on him by W. H. Godfrey were published in *R.I.B.A. Journal*, 3rd series, XIII (1906), pp. 501–25 and *Architectural Review* XXI (1907), pp. 28–30, 83–8, 293–306. The latter were reprinted separately as *The Works of George Devey*.

124. Wilfred Scawen Blunt, *My Diaries* (London, 1919), I, p. 183.

1. HARLAXTON MANOR

1. C. C. F. Greville *A Journal of the Reign of Queen Victoria* (London, 1885) I, pp. 42–3.

2. Gregory Gregory (known as Gregory Williams until 1822) owned property at Harlaxton and Denton in Lincolnshire, Renton in Nottinghamshire, and Rempstone in Leicestershire. Renton was the original Gregory property; the rest had come through marriages to the heiresses of the de Ligne (Harlaxton) and Williams (Rempstone and Denton) families. In the 1870s (according to Bateman's *Great Landowners of Britain*) the Harlaxton and Renton properties were bringing in £14,657 a year, and the Rempstone property £2,532; the value of the Denton property is uncertain, as by then it had been merged with the much larger Denton estate of the Welbys. Renton increased considerably in value in the 19th century owing to the growth of Nottingham, which now engulfs it. The complex Gregory family history is unravelled in Sir C. G. E. Welby *A note on the manor of Harlaxton and its history* (Denton, 1937), available in typescript at Harlaxton.

3. In a long account of Harlaxton published in *The Gardener's Magazine*, July 1840, pp. 329–42. It includes a description of the village, where Gregory embellished existing cottages with picturesque trimmings in a wide variety of styles.

4. For some account of the revival of appreciation of Elizabethen architecture, see M. Girouard, 'Attitudes to Elizabethan Architecture, 1600–1900' in *Concerning Architecture* (ed. John Summerson, London, 1968) pp. 13–27.

5. Illustrations of the old manor are reproduced in Russell Read, *Harlaxton* (Grantham, 1978) pp. 2–3, and Christopher Hussey's account of Harlaxton in *Country*

Houses: Late Georgian (London, 1900) pp. 1239–48. Although Gregory Gregory is often said to have demolished it, it was still standing after his death, according to the 1856 edition of William White *History, Gazetter and Directory of Lincolnshire* pp. 386–7.

6. In the R.I.B.A. drawings collection. One of a set of three elevations of the north-west, north-east and south-east facades (W8/3B (1–3)) is dated June 25, 1834.

7. In the absence of accounts or other reliable documentation much of the dating at Harlaxton must be imprecise. Salvin sent his assistant James Deeson to draw the old manor in 1831 (drawings now in the R.I.B.A.) and 'the building was commenced in 1832', according to the *Civil Engineer and Architect's Journal*; but Salvin's obituary (Builder, December 1831, p. 810) gives the commencing date of his work at Harlaxton as 1827. The tower was said to be erected (and 'two-thirds of the structure was raised') in 1836, when its completion was celebrated by elaborate festivities at Harlaxton, described in the *Lincolnshire Chronicle*, March 4; but the tower actually carries the date 1837. According to White, op. cit., the house was 'erected chiefly 1831–44' and 'though it was mostly completed in 1842, additions and improvements have continued to be made at intervals to the present year' (1856).

8. Dr Allibone suggests that much of the detail is influenced by a study of Wendel Dietterlin's *Architectura* (1598).

9. Letter from Salvin to Prebendary Wodehouse of Norwich, discovered by Dr Allibone.

10. T. E. Dibden, who visited Harlaxton in the summer of 1837 reported that 'Mr. Gregory has the *rare* merit of being chiefly his own architect . . . Now and then, however, it is said that Mr. Blore whispers in his ear.' (*A Bibliographical, Antiquarian and Picturesque Tour in the North Countries of England and Scotland* (London, 1838) I, pp. 61–2). *The Civil Engineers' and Architects' Journal*, reviewing Dibden in December, 1838 (Vol. I, p. 392), stated that 'Mr. Burn, of Edinburgh' was the architect 'now engaged'. In Vol. II (1839) p. 39, the same journal amplifies on this, probably as a result of complaints by Salvin: Salvin was the original architect, Blore was only consulted, and Burn was 'afterwards engaged to complete the edifice', but to Salvin's designs. Dibden's account suggests that he was at Harlaxton in the interval between Salvin and Burn. The three main fronts as executed correspond fairly closely to Salvin's elevations, but the service front is very different, and the conservatory and the north-east (brewery) wing are not shown on Salvin's drawings at all. The wing carries the date 1844 on its tower; the conservatory appears only to have been a project when Loudon visited Harlaxton in 1840, but is described as existing in the 1842 edition of White's *Directory*. Loudon also describes the forecourt entrance gates, stables, kitchen garden and most of the main garden as projected but not yet executed.

11. For Bryce see *David Bryce: 1803–76* (Catalogue of Exhibition at Edinburgh, ed. Valerie Fiddes and Alistair Rowan, 1976). He introduced baroque details into St Mark's Unitarian Church, Edinburgh (1835) and many of his later buildings, although none have the panache of the Harlaxton baroque. Perhaps closest to the work at Harlaxton is the neo-baroque McGavin monument in the Necropolis at Glasgow, designed in

1834 by his brother, John Bryce.

12. The evidence for dating the Harlaxton interiors is minimal. Neither Loudon (1840) nor the 1842 edition of White's *Directory* do more than give the names and measurements of the rooms; the impression given, but never precisely stated, by Loudon is that the decorations were still far from complete. On the other hand his reference to 'a great deal of handsome scenic effect produced' on the ground floor is perhaps suggestive of the staircase. The bay window of the hall has armorial stained glass by Willement, dated 1838.

13. 'Louis Quatorze' and Rococo were also re-appearing on the Continent in the 1830s and '40s. See, for instance, Marianne Zweig *Zweites Rokoko—Innenräume und Hausgerät in Wien von 1830–1860* (Vienna, 1924) and the many continental exhibits in the style shown in the 1851 Exhibition. Dr Allibone's discovery in Salvin's bank account of a payment of £2,764 made on 5 October to an unidentified J. G. Graef may or may not be relevant to the mysteries of Harlaxton.

14. At the census of 1851 he was living at Harlaxton with fourteen servants.

15. The system is referred to by Loudon, and a tunnel similar to that erected is shown in section on Salvin's 1834 elevation of the north-east front.

16. For Gregory's efforts to escape the entail, and the house's subsequent history see Welby, op.cit., and Read, op.cit. (the latter with many illustrations, old and new).

2. BAYONS MANOR

1. The family background of the Tennysons, and the relationship between the two branches, is dealt with in considerable detail in Sir Charles Tennyson, *Alfred Tennyson* (London, 1950).

2. The letters are now in the Lincolnshire County Record Office, part of the large collection of Tennyson d'Eyncourt papers (H 118–29).

3. There is a plan among the Tennyson d'Eyncourt papers (H 164).

4. 'It is a combination of Mr. Salvin's and Mr. Nicholson's plans, and I prefer it to any yet made.' Charles Tennyson d'Eyncourt to George, 18 July 1836 (H 119/68). Salvin had worked on the restoration of the great hall at Brancepeth Castle in 1829 (see p. 44).

5. H 123/29.

6. Among the adornments of the exterior were two charred medieval statues of considerable interest from the north front of Westminster Hall. They were possibly acquired after the fire of 1834 (*The History of the King's Works*, I, p. 528).

7. There is a long account of the house, with two lithographs of the exterior, in J. B. Burke, *Visitation of Seats and Arms* (London, 1852), I, pp. 236–41.

8. Charles to George, 17 Feb. 1841. 'Show Mr. Nicholson the drawing of the Chimney-piece for Newstead amongst Wildman's plans. It may suggest something to him' (H 125/14). Charles Tennyson d'Eyncourt was a friend of Colonel Wildman, who altered and embellished Newstead Abbey *c.* 1820–30 to the designs of John Shaw and James Trubshaw.

9. 'Crace's men' were painting the library in the summer of 1841 (H 125/38, 41, 44).

10. For his poem *Eustace: An Elegy* see Introduction, note

64. The illustrations, in addition to that of the banquet in the hall, include a delightful distant prospect of Bayons, and a detail of the battlements.

3. SCARISBRICK HALL

1. 'To make the clock-story (at Westminster) duly prominent all sorts of devices were thought of, till at last an example was remembered in which the whole clock-story was made to project beyond the body of the tower. The suggestion was eagerly caught at; the example quoted differed in almost every respect from the character of the tower to be designed and endless modifications were needed; but the general principle was preserved' (A. Barry, *The Life and Works of Sir Charles Barry* (London, 1867), pp. 255–6). The 'example' was almost certainly Scarisbrick; Alfred Barry's failure to particularize Pugin was probably the result of his vitriolic quarrels with E. W. Pugin as to their fathers' respective shares in the design of the Houses of Parliament.
2. For Charles Scarisbrick, see *Gentleman's Magazine*, July 1860, p. 100; J. Wans, *Short History of Scarisbrick Hall* (Liverpool, 1949).
3. M. Trappes-Lomax, *Pugin* (London, 1932), p. 89 (drawing on Stonyhurst MS.).
4. Nathanial Hawthorne, *The English Notebooks*, ed. Randall Stewart (New York, 1941), p. 442 (quoting gossip in a local railway-carriage).
5. An album of thirty-five copies by G. P. Harding of portraits of celebrated people was sold in the Scarisbrick sale, and suggests the possibility that the paintings in the King's room and in the red drawing room overmantel were also by Harding. But Mr Croft-Murray attributes the paintings to Edmund Thomas Parris (1793–1873), and points out that they are based on scenes from the *Roman de la Rose* as depicted in a Franco-Flemish MS. of *c.* 1500 in the British Museum (*Decorative Painting in England* (London, 1971), II, p. 252).

4. MEREVALE HALL

1. Preserved in numerous volumes at Merevale.
2. British Museum Additional MS. 42027; Victoria and Albert Museum 8714 A–B; University Library, Cambridge, Add. 3956 f. 58.
3. Bills at Merevale.
4. These appear to be of marble, but may come from the Magnus Slate Manufactory, of Upper Eaton Place, London. W. S. Dugdale visited it in the summer of 1848 and saw the process by which slate chimneypieces were made 'to represent marble of any colour or pattern'. He was intrigued by the results, and sent Clutton along to have a look at them.
5. The bedrooms have sash windows with small panes divided by glazing bars in the Georgian manner; there are bigger sheets of glass on the first floor, and the biggest of all on the ground floor. If this was the original arrangement the explanation was certainly economy; Merevale was just too early to benefit from the removal of excise duty on glass in 1845.

5. HIGHCLERE CASTLE

1. Alfred Barry, *The Life and Works of Sir Charles Barry* (London, 1867), pp. 109–10.
2. Apart from the drawings at Highclere a fine perspective of the 1840 scheme (OSI/3) and numerous tracings of other Barry drawings for Highclere by his pupils James Murray and Moulton Barrett are in the R.I.B.A. drawings collection.
3. It is shown in a section in the Moulton Barrett collection in the R.I.B.A.
4. Paul Thompson, *William Butterfield* (London, 1971) pp. 101, 413; he also installed central heating, and the fireplace and doorcases in the Music Room.

6. PRESTWOLD HALL

1. For this section I have drawn largely on Christopher Hussey's three articles on Prestwold, *Country Life*, CXXV (1959), pp. 828–31, 890–3, 948–51.
2. The 'iron beams' and the joists they supported are shown in a drawing by Burn at Prestwold. Drawing room and dining room are spanned by three beams each, the billiard room by two. 'Coupled beams' span the drawing room bay and the library opening. The conservatory is roofed by iron trusses. Other building papers at Prestwold include plans, elevations and specifications, all dated 1843.
3. Discussed and illustrated by David Watkin, *Thomas Hope and the Neo-Classical Idea* (London, 1968), p. 185 and Fig. 81.
4. See *Survey of London*, Vol. XXX (St James, Westminster, I), p. 480 and Pls. 109–10.
5. Information from the family; *Buildings of England: Dorset*, under Poole. Packe was largely instrumental in founding the Bournemouth Public Dispensary in 1859. In 1869 Prestwold was in Chancery between his widow and his brother G. H. Packe.

7. PECKFORTON CASTLE

1. Scott, Sir George Gilbert, pp. 14–15.
2. For Lord Tollemache, see his obituary in *The Times*, 11 Dec. 1890; and *Old and Odd Memories* (London, 1908), by his son Lionel Tollemache.
3. 'Though Salvin was the architect, yet the neo-feudal conception and several of the characteristic details were, in great part, my father's own' (Lionel Tollemache, *Memories*).
4. From a collection of letters from visitors to Peckforton preserved at Helmingham Hall, Suffolk, along with a schedule of building costs. These included £341 12s. 10d. to the British Plate Glass Co.; £1,409 4s. 4d. to the Seyfsal Asphalt Co.; £9,836 12s. to Dowbiggin, for furniture and upholstery; and £96 14s. 10d. to Willement for painted glass. The asphalt was presumably for the roofs, as Peckforton is an early example of an extensive use of flat roofing.
5. There is a large collection of Salvin's designs for Peckforton in the R.I.B.A. drawings collection.
6. Jill Allibone suggests that the plan was inspired by that of John Paterson's remodelling of Brancepeth Castle, *c.* 1818–20.

8. OSBORNE

1. I have done no documentary research into the history of Osborne. My main sources have been the official *Guide* (by John Charlton) and *Catalogue* published by the Ministry of Public Buildings and Works, and the chapter on Osborne in Winslow Ames, *Prince Albert and Victorian Taste* (London, 1967).

2. e.g. Abberley Hall, Worcestershire (Samuel Daukes, 1845); Penoyre, Brecknockshire (A. Salvin, 1848); Bricklehampton, Worcestershire (1848); Pantglas, Carmarthenshire (*c.* 1850); Oatlands, Surrey (John Dobson, 1851); Greenlands, Buckinghamshire (*c.* 1853); Ellel Grange, Lancashire (1856); Carpenders Park, Hertfordshire (*c.* 1863); Rendcomb, Gloucestershire (P. C. Hardwick, 1863); Highfield, Gloucester (John Giles, *c.* 1869). E. M. Barry's Pyrgo Park, Essex (1862), and Thorpe Abbotts, Norfolk (1869), derive more directly from his father's work, but no doubt the existence of Osborne encouraged his clients to commission them.

3. Ames, *Prince Albert*, p. 62, n. 3.

4. *The Gentleman's House* (London, 1864), pp. 454–6, with a critical analysis of the plan. The house was also published in the *Builder*, VI (1848), pp. 70–1, 565, with illustrations and plan.

5. The house which Thomas Cubitt built for himself at Denbies, near Dorking, in 1850, was a big detached Belgravia house with no tower.

9. TREBERFYDD

1. Theophilus Jones and J. R. Bailey (later Lord Glanusk), *History of the County of Brecknock* (Brecknock, 1911), III, pp. 216–19.

2. For the Raikeses in Hull see Burke's *Landed Gentry*; and J. J. Sheahan, *History of Kingston-upon-Hull* (London, 1866).

3. The family tradition is that pitch-pine was used instead of oak so that there should be more money to spend on the church and school.

4. See my article on Lismore, *Country Life*, CXXXVI (1964), pp. 389–93.

5. For Treberfydd and Robert Raikes, see also Anthony Quiney, *John Loughborough Pearson* (New Haven and London, 1979), Ch. IV.

10. HORSTED PLACE

1. The contract and numerous accounts, but no drawings, were at Horsted when I wrote the articles published in *Country Life*, CXXIV (1958), pp. 276–9, 320–3.

2. *Illustrated London News*, 20 Sept. 1851.

3. For Daukes, see especially two articles on him by David Verey, *Country Life*, CLIV (1973), pp. 1914–16, 2016–18.

4. St Peter's, Cheltenham, was designed for the Revd Francis Close, the bellicose Low Church clergyman who had battled successfully against the Ecclesiological Society concerning the restoration of St Sepulchre's Church, Cambridge. In his will Daukes left £1,000 each of the British and Foreign Bible Society, the Religious Tract Society, the S.P.C.K. and the S.P.G.—a pointedly Low Church selection (*Builder*, 20 Mar. 1880).

5. In March 1850, six months before the main contract for the house, Myers had contracted to supply chimneypieces for the drawing room, dining room and corridor. In the same month he was paid £250 'extra upon staircase being in oak'. In the previous five months he had been paid for demolishing the old house. It is possible that all this had been done before Daukes supplied his designs.

6. The contents of Horsted were dispersed in the 1960s after the death of Mrs Barchard. The photographs show the house before the sale.

7. Clive Wainwright 'Furniture', in *The Houses of Parliament* (ed. M. H. Port, New Haven and London, 1976) pp. 283–9.

8. Seven of Francis Barchard's Dutch paintings are now in the National Gallery.

11. MILTON ERNEST HALL

1. The only other country house work of any importance by Butterfield was the remodelling and enlargement of Chanter's House, Ottery St Mary, in 1880–3.

2. He met Butterfield's sister while she was working as a governess in the house of his friends Mr and Mrs William Peek (Paul Thompson, *William Butterfield* (London, 1971), pp. 12–13).

3. For Butterfield's relations with the Stareys, and his work for them at Milton Ernest, see Thompson, *ibid*, *passim*.

4. See the letter from Butterfield to Philip Webb, *Architectural History*, X (1967), p. 55.

5. W. R. Lethaby, *Philip Webb and his Work* (London, 1935), p. 69.

6. Thompson, *Butterfield*, pp. 489–91.

12. WOODCHESTER PARK

1. The main source for this section is the article on Woodchester Park by David Verey in *Country Life*, CLXV (1969), pp. 284–8.

2. There is a full account of Leigh in J. Gillow's *Bibliographical Dictionary of the English Catholics* (London, 1885–94), IV, pp. 196–8.

3. The daughter of his brother John later married Sir Ninian Comper.

4. He published translations of the *Histoire d'une maison* in 1874, of the *Histoire d'une Forteresse* in 1875, of the *Histoire de l'Habitation Humaine* in 1876, and of the *Entretiens* in 1877–81.

5. Alas, recent reports suggest that Woodchester is at last beginning to deteriorate.

13. SHADWELL PARK

1. The main sources for the history of Shadwell are the copious Buxton papers, now in the Cambridge University Library.

2. There are drawings by Blore for Shadwell in the British Museum, Add. MS. 42027, ff. 86–7.

3. The organ was illustrated in the *Builder*, XVIII (1860), p. 449.

14. THE CROSSLEYS OF HALIFAX AND THEIR BUILDINGS

1. The history of the Crossley family is very fully treated by R. Bretton in his articles 'The Crossleys of Dean Clough', *Proceedings of the Halifax Antiquarian Society*, especially 1950, pp. 1–9; 1951, pp. 71–83; 1953, pp. 1–20, 87–102; 1954, pp. 11–28. There is a useful collection of newspaper cuttings to do with the Crossleys and their buildings in Halifax Public Library.

2. Manor Heath was illustrated and fully described in the *Builder*, XXI (1863), pp. 206–7. It was demolished shortly after the last war.

3. For Belle Vue see *Building News*, III (1857), pp. 1200–1. It was centrally heated and ventilated, and built by Beanland, of Bradford.

4. The estate had been on the market since 1861, in which year a sumptuously produced and illustrated book of sales particulars was printed. Extracts from this evocative publication have been used as end papers for this book.

5. *The Gentleman's House* (London, 1864), p. 473.

6. See the description of Belle Vue in *Picturesque Views of Castles and Country Houses in Yorkshire* (Bradford, 1885) (reprinted from the *Bradford Illustrated Weekly Telegraph*). 'Both Lady Crossley and her son Sir Saville having by their prolonged absence indicated that they have no liking for the residence'.

15. GEORGE DEVEY IN KENT

1. The best source for his life is a short *In Memoriam* volume, privately printed after his death in 1893.

2. Before Redleaf was occupied by Walter James it had been the home of William Wells, the friend and patron of Landseer and of numerous other Victorian artists. As a young man Walter James almost certainly got to know Wells and his circle; Landseer stayed with him at Redleaf in December 1848, and the names in the Betteshanger visitors' book include E. W. Cooke and Frederick Goodall, who were old friends of Wells. The sketches in the visitors' book were possibly inspired by Wells's famous 'Scribbler's Book' to which all his artist friends contributed sketches (J. A. Manson, *Sir Edwin Landseer, R.A.* (London, 1902), pp. 730s). Devey probably had his own connections with artistic circles through his uncle Augustus Egg.

3. Preserved among the papers at Northbourne Court, near Deal. There is a plan, probably dating from the 1860s, at the R.I.B.A., together with elevations showing the 1856–8 additions.

4. Among the Devey drawings at the R.I.B.A. Walter Godfrey quotes an inscription over the archway into the entrance court (since worn away) as dating the house 1864 (*Architectural Review*, 1907, p. 301). But the evidence of the drawings and surviving dates on the fabric seem to be conclusive. The date in the inscription was in Roman letters and, if it had already begun to deteriorate, Godfrey may have mis-read MDCCCLXXV as MDCCCLXIV.

5. Much research is still needed before Devey's work and importance can be properly assessed. The great collection of Devey drawings at the R.I.B.A. are in course of being catalogued by Dr Jill Allibone. Devey's account books from 1868 till his death are in existence and have been indexed by Nicholas and Hazel Taylor, but payments are entered under clients only, with no indication of what buildings are involved.

16. KELHAM HALL

1. According to Salvin's obituary in the *Builder* of 31 December 1881 he did work at Kelham at these dates and it seems reasonable to suppose that it involved the building of the wing and possible alterations to the old house.

2. Sir George Gilbert, Scott, *Personal and Professional Recollections* (London, 1879), p. 112.

3. *Ibid*, p. 214.

4. *Recollections of Thomas Graham Jackson* (London, 1950), pp. 58–9.

5. *Builder*, 30 June 1866, pp. 482–3.

6. Scott, *Recollections*, p. 178.

7. *Remarks on Secular and Domestic Architecture Present and Future* (London, 1857), p. 41.

8. *Ibid*, p. 142.

9. Scott, *Recollections*, p. 216.

10. In the 1872–3 Return of Owners of Land (Parliamentary Papers, 1874, LXXII) his name is wrongly given as 'J. H. M. Lutton' which is no doubt why he gets no mention in John Bateman, *Great Landowners of Great Britain and Ireland* (1st edn, London, 1876).

11. I have derived much information for this article from the unpublished 'Notes on Kelham and Averham' by Antony Snell, S.S.M., and T. Jones.

17. BRODSWORTH HALL

1. There are articles on the Thellusson will in *Annual Register*, 1859; *Chronicle*, p. 333; and *Notes and Queries*, 8th series, XII, p. 183. See also *Gentleman's Magazine*, 1797, 1798 and 1832. No doubt it suggested to Galsworthy the will of Timothy Forsyte, in *The Forsyte Saga*.

2. The specification and numerous accounts are preserved at Brodsworth, as was Casentini's design until stolen some years ago. No other drawings appear to survive.

3. Philip Wilkinson, of 68 Lincoln's Inn Fields and 2 Greville Place, St John's Wood, died on 30 June 1906, aged eighty according to a brief and uninformative obituary note in the *Builder*. He became F.R.I.B.A. in 1890. The house was to be built 'agreeably to the accompanying drawings prepared by Philip Wilkinson, Architect', according to the specification, in which Casentini is not mentioned.

4. Article on Locko Park by John Cornforth, *Country Life*, CXLV (1969), pp. 1506–10.

18. TYNTESFIELD

1. For the history of the firm of Antony Gibbs and Son, see the introduction to H. H. Gibbs, *Pedigree of the Family of Gibbs* (privately printed, 1904) and J. A. Gibbs, *History of Antony and Dorothy Gibbs* (London, 1922) especially pp. 380–421.

2. John Bateman, *Great Landowners of Great Britain and Ireland* (London, 1876).

3. There seems no adequate memoire or obituary of William Gibbs, and I have had to rely on information from the sources given in note 1. His diary, preserved in many volumes at Tyntesfield provides a brief daily record of most of his life.

4. Christabel Coleridge, *Charlotte Mary Yonge* (London, 1903), pp. 309–10.

5. William Gibbs's diary records visits by Norton in March, April, September and October, 1866, and a first payment to Wm Cubitt and Co., the builders, on 7 October. Designs by Norton, dating from 1863 to 1866, are preserved in the house, along with designs for earlier alterations and additions by other architects. There may be further material among unsorted papers in the house.

6. The iron finials embedded in the turrets had rusted and split the stonework.

7. There appear to be no drawings by Woodyer at Tyntesfield; his presence there is documented in *Country Life*, XI, p. 624.

8. William Gibbs's diary records unspecified payments to Crace in August 1866 (£1,000) and February 1867. Crace's sideboard and the Plucknett billiard table are

illustrated in Elizabeth Aslin, *Nineteenth Century English Furniture* (London, 1962), Pls. 36 and 91.

9. Entries in the Powell archives (kindly sent to me by Martin Harrison) document the attractively aesthetic windows in the nave as being designed by H. Ellis Wooldridge (a friend of Walter Crane) in 1874. The choir windows, which are in a different style, are listed as made in 1875, but no designer is given.

10. Information from the present Lord Wraxall.

19. HUMEWOOD CASTLE

1. Paul Thompson's 'The Writings of William White' (in *Concerning Architecture*, Essays presented to Nikolaus Pevsner, ed. John Summerson (1968), pp. 226–37) is a valuable account of William White as a writer and theorist. The article on White in the series 'Our Architects and their Works', *British Architect*, 16 Sept. 1881, p. 465, provides a portrait and much curious information.

2. C. L. Eastlake (1872), pp. 292–3.

3. See *The Architect*, 10, 17 June and 11 Nov. 1871; 23 Mar. 1872; 20 May 1876. M. D. Wyatt gave evidence against White; T. H. Lewis and Ewan Christian, in his favour.

4. White described Humewood in detail at a meeting of the R.I.B.A. in 1869. His talk was published in the R.I.B.A. *Transactions* of 1868–9, pp. 78–88, and is quoted throughout this article. He had originally wanted to incorporate occasional courses of red brick into the walls 'to take off the coldness of the granite'. A bound volume of his designs is preserved at Humewood.

5. *Ecclesiologist*, XIV (1853), pp. 313–30.

6. The Fenian troubles also gave E. W. Godwin a wonderful excuse to design a modern castle at Dromore for the Earl of Limerick in 1866–73.

7. These columns were the trade mark of the muscular school, just as sunflowers were the trade mark of the artistic school of the next generation. White had used them in 1865 to support the *porte-cochère* at Winscott (Plate 416).

8. A treasure trove of White's furniture—as individual as his architecture—is (or was) to be found at Bishop's Court, near Exeter, remodelled by White for John Garratt in 1860–4.

9. See the list of Brooks's works in the memoir by J. S. Adkins, *R.I.B.A. Journal*, 3rd series, XVII (1910), pp. 84–7.

10. Information from Mrs Hume Weygand.

20. BEAR WOOD

1. Walter revealed that he had given Kerr the commission on the strength of the *Gentleman's House* in a speech to his workmen during the covering-in celebrations in 1868 (*Builder*, XXVI (1868), p. 406).

2. The fullest treatment of John Walter is to be found in Stanley Morison, *History of the Times* (London, 1935–52), II, *passim*. See also his obituary in *The Times* of 5 Nov. 1894.

3. 'A difficult person to know well—very shy, very proud, very independent' (Lady St Helier, *Memories of Fifty Years* (London, 1909), p. 213).

4. It was also illustrated and described in the *Architect* of 1870 and 1871.

5. A. I. Dasent, *John Delane* (London, 1908), II, p. 205 (with photograph of the house on adjacent page).

6. Copies of the correspondence were kindly shown to me by Mrs John Walter of Hove.

21. CARDIFF CASTLE

1. Obituary of Alderman John M'Connochie, *Western Mail*, 29 Mar. 1889.

2. The house in Cardiff which Burges designed before 1874 for M'Connochie survives; it is illustrated in R. P. Pullan, *Architectural Designs of William Burges* (London, 1883), Pl. 38.

3. A good life of Lord Bute by his friend Abbot Hunter Blair (Oscar Wilde's intimate in their undergraduate days) was published in 1921. For his finances, see J. Davis *Glamorgan and the Bute Estate* (Ph.D. thesis, Swansea, 1969). For William Burges, see Charles Handley-Read's essay in *Victorian Architecture*, ed. Peter Ferriday (London, 1963). J. Mordaunt Crook' major monograph is due for publication in 1980. Among contemporary descriptions and references are W. M. Rossetti's *Some Reminiscences* (1906), p. 154; the *Builder* of 10 May 1884 (by George Aitchison); *The Diaries of G. P. Boyce* (Old Water Colour Society's Club, XIX, 1941); R.I.B.A. *Transactions*, 1881–2, p. 183 (by his brother-in-law R. P. Pullan); and the *Art Journal*, 1886 (a full-length appreciation by his friend E. W. Godwin). The character of Master Georgius Oldhousen in Robert Kerr's novel *The Ambassador Extraordinary* (London, 1879) is said to have been inspired by Burges.

4. W. R. Lethaby, *Philip Webb and his Work* (London, 1935), p. 73.

5. *Letters of James Smetham*, ed. Sarah Smetham and William Davies (London, 1892), p. 102.

6. There are eight illustrations (including a section of the tower) and short description of Burges's work at Cardiff Castle in R. P. Pullan, *Architectural Designs of William Burges* (London, 1883). The main manuscript sources are:
   1. A large collection of Burges's cartoons for the internal decorations now in the Cardiff City Archives.
   2. The letter book of William Frame, commencing December 1883, belonging to the Marquess of Bute and now at Mountstuart. Frame was Burges's assistant and was in charge of finishing the work after his death.
   3. Burges's contract book, running from 24 Aug. 1875 until shortly before his death. On loan to the library of the Victoria and Albert Museum.
   4. Burges's notebooks, covering the whole of his working life, now in the R.I.B.A. drawings collection. These contain sketch designs, notes of payment to craftsmen and short diary entries.

7. For Burges and the Law Courts competition, see Sir John Summerson, *Victorian Architecture: Four studies in Evaluation* (New York and London, 1970), pp. 110–11.

8. The paintings were illustrated in the *Architect*, 10 April 1880.

9. His building work included the restoration and rebuilding of Castell Coch, to Burges's designs, 1875–90; the rebuilding on an extravagant scale of Mountstuart, Isle of Bute, after 1877 (designed by Rowand Anderson and Weir Schultz); the restoration, rebuilding and re-decoration at Falkland Palace, Fife, c. 1887–1900 (designed by William Frame and John Kinross); elaborate internal decorations at House of Falkland, Fife; restorations at Old Place of Mochrum,

Wigtownshire; and alterations and elaborate decorations at St John's Lodge, Regent's Park, 1892 onwards (designed by Weir Schultz). The latter were illustrated and described by J. Mordaunt Crook, *Country Life*, CXLIV (1968), pp. 84–7.

22. THE *NOUVEAU-RICHE* STYLE

1. Robert Kerr, *The Gentleman's House* (London, 1864), p. 73.
2. A sketch of such a house, captioned 'The turrets of the *nouveau-riche*' is in Heathcote Statham, *Modern Architecture* (London, 1897), p. 201.
3. In 1857 the first premiums for the competition for the new War Office and Foreign Office were won (little good it did them) by H. E. Coe and H. B. Garling respectively, both with French designs. Burn had been one of the architectural assessors.
4. *The Conditions and Prospects of Architectural Art* (inaugural Lecture of the 1863 session of the Architectural Museum, London, 1863), pp. 17–18.
5. *Builder*, 4 Mar. 1864; and Kerr, *Gentleman's House*, p. 379.
6. For references in the architectural magazines and other sources to the houses described in this chapter, see the relevant entries in the Catalogue.
7. Pippingford was built for John Mortimer—it has been demolished, but the foundation stone survives, dated 1857. In 1859 Horeau exhibited in London a drawing of it entitled 'Castle, recently erected in Sussex' (reproduced *Country Life* CLXV (26 April 1979) p. 1284). Horeau settled in London in the 1850s, and his obituary note in the *Building News* (6 Sept. 1879) stated that 'plans of which he was the author . . . brought fame and fortune to other men of his profession'. I am most grateful to David Le Lay for sending me these references.
8. E. Delaire, *Les Architects éleves de l'Ecole des Beaux-Arts, 1793–1907* (Paris, 1907).
9. For Bowes, see C. E. Hardy, *John Bowes and the Bowes Museum* (Newcastle, 1970). The story that Bowes intended to build in France, but was prevented by the Franco-Prussian War, appears to be apocryphal.
10. For other examples of *nouveau-riche* French country houses, see Marton, Stancliffe and Warter in the Catalogue. A lively suburban example was J. L. Pearson's Westwood House, Sydenham, designed for Henry Littleton, proprietor of Novello's, the music publishers, *c.* 1875 (*Architectural Review*, I (1879), p. 80; A. Quiney *John Loughborough Pearson* (New Haven and London, 1979), pp. 179, 182–3).
11. Lucy Cohen, *Lady de Rothschild and her Daughters* (London, 1935), pp. 173–4.
12. *Mary Gladstone: Her Diaries and Letters*, ed. Lucy Masterman (London, 1930), p. 361.
13. A book of photographs of Halton preserved at the house is inscribed 'To William R. Rogers with sincere gratitude from Alfred de Rothschild, May 1888.' A letter from Mrs E. F. Travers concerning the book says that Rogers 'did the building' (information Jill Franklin). In the last independent days of William Cubitt and Co., Mr Plucknett was the social partner and W. R. Rogers (formerly Rodriguez) the one with architectural pretensions (information Hermione Hobhouse). For William Cubitt and Co., see introduction, note 23. The *Building News* of 12 May 1882 illustrates Rogers's design for 5 Hamilton Place,

designed for Leo de Rothschild, with a very sophisticated plan in the Rococo manner.

23. CRAGSIDE

1. There is no full-scale biography of Lord Armstrong. The long entry in the *Dictionary of National Biography* can be supplemented by many obituary notices, especially 'Reminiscences of the Late Lord Armstrong', by John Worsnop of Rothbury, *Newcastle Journal*, 28 Dec. 1900. See also D. Dougan, *The Great Gunmaker* (1971).
2. The story comes from J. D. Bean, *Armstrong's Men* (1969), an interesting and critical account of Lord Armstrong's relations with his workmen.
3. See Armstrong's letter to the *Engineer*, Jan. 1881.
4. An article in the *World*, 1879, quoted *Newcastle Journal* 28 Dec. 1900.
5. For the Horsley link between Shaw and the Armstrongs, see Andrew Saint, *Richard Norman Shaw* (New Haven and London, 1976), p. 67.
6. Reginald Blomfield, *Richard Norman Shaw* (London, 1940), p. 20.
7. The surviving drawings are in the R.I.B.A. drawings collection (V10/111–20).
8. It is shown in the engraving of Cragside published in the *Newcastle Daily Journal* (Royal supplement), 21 Aug. 1884.
9. Uncatalogued 1860–4 sketchbook (R.I.B.A.).
10. *Building News*, 10 May 1872, p. 376. Forsyth exhibited an elaborate Gothic bookshelf, made to Shaw's designs for his personal use, at the International Exhibition of 1862. After this he did much work for Shaw and Nesfield, in both stone and wood.
11. Shaw describes them as such on his design for the decorative scheme of the library (R.I.B.A.).
12. Shaw was associated with the London joinery firm of W. H. Lascelles from about 1875, and from 1877 was a partner in the firm of Aldam Heaton, suppliers of embroidery, stained glass, carpets, wallpaper, embossed leatherwork and furniture (Elizabeth Aslin, *The Aesthetic Movement* (London, 1969), pp. 76–7). Designs by Shaw exist for the charming owl-finialled bed in one of the main bedrooms. Other furniture at Cragside that may have been designed by Shaw ranges from Old English to 'Queen Anne' and includes the built-in sideboard and bookcases and the massive tables and sofas in the library and dining room, the ebonized chairs in the library and elsewhere, and the inlaid cabinets and sofas in the drawing room. The ebonized chairs have the Gillow mark.
13. The original version of this set was made in 1862, and is probably the one now on loan to the William Morris Gallery, Walthamstow, from the Victoria and Albert Museum. The Cragside set was made in 1873, in which year another set (of 5 panels only) was made for a member of the Pease family (A. C. Sewter in the *Journal of the British Society of Master Glass Painters*, 1961).
14. According to the *Newcastle Daily Journal*, 19 Aug. 1884, a pair of Hawthorn pots in the drawing room were 'from the Rossetti collection'. Perhaps the pot shown in Emmerson's portrait of Lord Armstrong is one of these. Rossetti sold the mass of his collection of blue-and-white and other Oriental china to Murray Marks, the dealer, in about Sept. 1872 (H. Rossetti Angeli, *Pre-Raphaelite Twilight* (London, 1954), Pt II,

p. 67). It would be interesting to know if more of Rossetti's collection went to Cragside, which was being furnished in the years immediately following his sale. In any case it was almost certainly bought through Marks, who was a friend of Norman Shaw, and employed him to design the 'Queen Anne' shopfront of his new premises in Oxford Street in 1875 (G. C. Williamson, *Murray Marks and his Friends* (London, 1919)). Most of the very large collection of oriental porcelain at Cragside was sold at Christie's in June 1910, but a good deal remains in the house.

15. Christie's, 20 and 24 June 1910.
16. *Building News*, 10 May 1872, p. 376.
17. Drawings for the inglenook were made by Shaw's assistant Lethaby, who may have actually designed it.
18. See Mark Girouard, 'Entertaining Victorian Royalty', *Country Life*, CXLVI (1969), pp. 1446–50.
19. For the houses in Tite Street, Chelsea, designed by Waller in 1881, see M. Girouard, *Sweetness and Light* (Oxford, 1977), pp. 178, 229. At Cragside he also altered and enlarged the picture gallery, replacing Shaw's windows by top lighting. His designs for the billiard room are preserved at the house. A number of Armstrong portraits at Cragside were painted by his daughter-in-law, Mary Lemon Waller. My information about Waller at Cragside was kindly provided, along with other material, by Mrs G. F. Pettit.
20. The gun-room was originally used by Lord Armstrong for electrical experiments; it became a gun-room after his death (information Mrs Pettit).

24. KINMEL PARK

1. My information about the Hughes family comes mainly from E. Gwynne Jones's introduction to the catalogue of the Kinmel papers, now in the library of the University College of North Wales at Bangor. There is more about the early history of the family in the first of my two articles on Kinmel, *Country Life*, CXLVI (1969), pp. 542–5.
2. Burn designed stables in a similar but simpler eighteenth-century manner at Dartrey, County Monaghan, Ireland, *c.* 1845.
3. Now at Plas Kinmel, along with Nesfield's specification.
4. J. M. Brydon, 'William Eden Nesfield, 1835–88', *Architectural Review*, I (1897), p. 245.
5. As notes on the working drawings show. For Forsyth, see also p. 312, note 10.

25. BEAUVALE LODGE

1. Under the Cowpers, Panshanger became a noted social centre, somewhat similar to Clouds in the scale and character of its weekend parties (the Percy Wyndhams were friends). Though a generation older, they became associated with the Souls through their niece Mrs Grenfell (later Lady Desborough) of Taplow Court, who inherited Panshanger on Lord Cowper's death in 1905.
2. *Earl Cowper, K. G., A Memoir*, by his wife (privately printed, 1913), p. 204.
3. *Ibid*, p. 204.
4. Dudley Harbron's life of Godwin, *The Conscious Stone*, (London, 1949), though far from satisfactory or comprehensive, gives a good deal of biographical information.

5. Godwin had designed a similar composition, on a much grander scale, in his unexpected competition design for Winchester Town Hall, illustrated in the *Building News* of 25 Aug. 1871.
6. Information from Miss Elizabeth Aslin.

26. CASTELL COCH

1. 'The modern Development of Medieval Art' (Lecture given to the Architectural Association, reported *Builder*, 18 June 1864, pp. 448–50).
2. The report is now in the library of the Historic Buildings Section of the Department of the Environment, who own the castle. The contract drawings for the gate tower, and designs for the hall and kitchen tower, are in the R.I.B.A. drawings collection. The building history is lavishly documented by Burges's contract book and notebooks, and William Frame's letter book, for which, see p. 451.
3. See his obituary in the *Builder*, 21 Apr. 1906. He later superintended the restoration of Falkland Palace and designed the Cardiff Railway Company's offices at the Bute docks.
4. The roofs probably owe more to Viollet-le-Duc's restorations at Carcassonne than to archaeological evidence.
5. On 19 May 1887 Frame was asking them to hurry up with 'the model of Lady Bute's bedroom'. This was probably the exquisitely painted wooden model of the room which was illustrated in W. G. Howell's article on Castell Coch (*Architectural Review*, Jan. 1951, pp. 39–46), but the present whereabouts of which I cannot trace.
6. Information from the late Lord Robert Crichton-Stuart.

27. CARLTON TOWERS

1. The long and complicated earlier history of the house is dealt with in some detail in the first of my three articles on Carlton Towers, *Country Life*, CXLI (1967), pp. 176–80.
2. For E. W. Pugin, see the *Dictionary of National Biography*; *Builder*, 12 June 1875, p. 522; *Illustrated London News*, LXVI (1975), p. 571; C. J. Richardson, *Fragments of History Pertaining to Ramsgate* (London. 1885); and numerous references to his lawsuits and other escapades in the relevant numbers of *The Times* and *Kent Coast Times*.
3. *Kent Coast Times*, 10 June 1875.
4. My information about Lord Beaumont comes mainly from his obituary in the *Goole Advertiser*, 29 Jan. 1892, and family papers at Carlton Towers.
5. Beaumont Crescent and Beaumont Road, on the Kensington Hall estate adjoining North End Road. Houses were tendered for in May 1877 by T. Dudley, architect (*Builder*, 26 May 1877). A faint tinge of the eccentricities of Carlton Towers enliven what is otherwise conventional speculative housing.
6. W. de l'Hôpital, *Westminster Cathedral and its Architect*, 2 vols. (London, 1919).
7. This is probably a rather unfortunate reflection of the current fashion for ebonized furniture.
8. Bentley designed a certain amount of furniture for Carlton, some in the Gothic and some in the 'Queen Anne' manner. He also put in two bathrooms, there having been none before.

28. ADCOTE

1. They are in the R.I.B.A. (V10/32–8) and there are further designs in the Victoria and Albert Museum (D 1690–1704). The superb perspective view of Adcote exhibited at the Royal Academy was presented to the Academy as Shaw's Diploma work.
2. In a sketchbook of *c.* 1855–9 (R.I.B.A. uncatalogued).
3. On the working drawings the roofs timbers between the stone arches are directed to be 'stained and varnished in imitation of oak'. This is a typical example of Shaw's cavalier attitude to Victorian ideals of 'truthfulness'. Elsewhere in the house the floors are supported on concealed rolled iron joists, as was the usual practice in Shaw's buildings.
4. The builders were Messrs Hale and Sons, and the builders' work cost £29,792. Numerous fittings, including the 'dining-room bureau' were supplied by J. Aldam Heaton, who sent in a bill for £1,785 in September 1881. The house was lit by gas. (Bills in the possession of Mrs Darby's descendant Lady Labouchere.)

29. KEN HILL

1. *Thomas Armstrong, C.B., A Memoir*, ed. L. M. Lamont (London, 1912).
2. There are Jeckell grates at Waterhouse's Blackmoor and Devey's Betteshanger.
3. Lady (Mary) Green, *The Old Hall at Heath* (Wakefield, 1889).
4. The room decorated by Jeckell for Alexander Ionides at 1 Holland Park in 1870 had furniture very similar to that now at Ken Hill. See Elizabeth Aslin, *The Aesthetic Movement* (London, 1969), p. 93 and Fig. 51.
5. The 1879 drawing was of the exterior, the 1880 one of the saloon; the latter was reproduced in *Building News*, 25 June 1880. For the *Building News* comment on the 1879 drawing, see see p. 75.
6. J. J. Stevenson, II, p. 65.

30. WIGHTWICK MANOR

1. This chapter is based on articles by John Cornforth, *Country Life*, CXXXIII (1963), pp. 1242–5, 1316–19.
2. The house was illustrated, with a plan, in the *Building News* of 24 May 1889. It was lit by electric light from the start (information from Lady Mander).
3. See David Lloyd's articles on Chester, *Country Life*, CXXXIII (1963), pp. 6–9, 68–71.
4. For Lindfield Old Hall, see *Country Life*, XXII (1907) pp. 414–22; for the Wood House, see *Country Life*, CXXVI (1959), pp. 1300–3.

31. STANDEN

1. There is a certain amount about Standen in Lethaby, *Philip Webb and his Work* (London, 1935), pp. 109, 112. It was described by Laurence Weaver in *Country Life*, XXVII (1910), p. 666, and by Halsey Ricardo in the *Magazine of Art*, *c.* 1900. The specification, a number of plans, and letters from Webb to the Beales are at Standen. I have learnt much of interest from the late Miss Helen Beale, J. S. Beale's daughter, who had lived at Standen since it was built and had many memories of Webb. Standen now belongs to the National Trust, and the contents have been much altered since the photographs illustrating this book were taken.
2. But Miss Beale thought it was Mr Alexander.
3. Information from Miss Beale and John Brandon-Jones.
4. Information from Miss Beale.
5. 'A series of gables like so many waves always appealed to Webb.' Lethaby, *op. cit.*, p. 109.

GENERAL INDEX

Abberley Hall, Worcestershire, 392, 449
Abbey Cwmhir Hall, Radnorshire, 392, 444
Abbeystead, Lancashire, 392, Pl. 380
Abbotsfield, Somerset, 13, 392
Abercairny Perthshire, 23, 33
Abermad, Cardiganshire, 393
Abnalls, Staffordshire, 437
Abney Hall, Cheshire, 24, 393, 445, Pl. 379
Ackers, G. Holland, 436
Adair, Sir R., Bart., 441
Adams, C. J., 412
Adare Manor, Co. Limerick, 197, 426, Pl. 419
Adcote, Shropshire, 76, 359–64, Fig. 27, Pls. 34–8
Adderley Hall, Shropshire, 438
Addington, Lord, see J. G. Hubbard
Addington Manor, Buckinghamshire, 21, 393
Adelaide, Australia, 188
Adhurst, Hampshire, 439
Adlam, W., 440
Aegean, Chateau in the, 432
Aitchison, George, 290
Akeley Wood, Buckinghamshire, 438
Akroyd, Colonel Edward, 207n.
Albert, Prince, 19, 36, 147–52, 445
Albury Park, Surrey, 393
Alderley House, Gloucestershire, 442
Aldermaston Court, Berkshire, 394, Pl. 383
Aldwark Manor, Yorkshire, 440
Aldworth House, Sussex, 394
Alexander family, 381
Alhambra, Spain, 133
Allcard, John, 440
Allcroft, H. J., 421
Allenheads, Northumberland, 440
Allerton Hall, Yorkshire, 174
Allerton Priory, Lancashire, 201
Allom, Thomas, 134
Alnwick Castle, Northumberland, 52, 157, 163, 394, Pl. 26
Aloupka, Crimea, 432
Alpine Club, The, 40n.
Alton Castle, Staffordshire, 47, 394, Pls. 21, 381
Alton Towers, Staffordshire, 44, 394
Amherst, W. A. T., 1st Lord Amherst of Hackney, 441
Amory, John Heathcoat, (Bart., 1874), 411
Amport Ho., Hants., 437
Ampthill, A. O. V. Russell, 2nd Lord, 186
Anderson, John MacVicar, 437
Anderson, Sir Rowand, 451
Annesley, W. R. Annesley, 2nd Earl, 437
Anstie House, Cornwall, 441
Apley Castle, Shropshire, 439
Architectural Association, 16
Argenti, Giosue, 240
Argyll, J. D. S. Campbell, 9th Duke of, 19n., 438
Arisaig House, Inverness, 430
Arley Hall, Cheshire, 394, Pl. 382
Armstrong, Thomas, 367, 374, 396
Armstrong, Sir William, 1st Lord Armstrong, 11, 25, 26, 305–9, 314–7, Pl. 300
Arnold, G. N., 437
Arnold, Matthew, 15
Arundel Castle, Sussex, 394
Ascot Heath House, Berkshire, 271, 394
Ascott, Buckinghamshire, 83, 394, Pl. 384
Ashburton, Francis Baring, 3rd Lord, 437
Ashfold, Sussex, 438
Ashridge, Hertfordshire, 15, 33, 64, 78
Asquith family, 81
Asquith, Herbert Henry, 1st Earl of Oxford and Asquith, 86
Astley, Hon. Francis L'Estrange, 440
Astley, P. D. P., 430
Astor, W. W., 402

Atkinson, William, 429
Austin, F., 400
Austin, H. J., 441
Avery Hill, Kent, 43n., 394, 445

Baddesley, Warwickshire, 128
Badgemore, Oxfordshire, 440
Bagshot Park, Surrey, 396
Baily, ironwork by, 422
Baird, Col. E. W. D. 442
Balfour family, 81
Balfour, Arthur J., 1st Earl Balfour, 80
Balfour, G., 437
Balfour, Jabez, 302
Ballantyne, of Edinburgh, 421
Ballards, Surrey, 396
Balmoral Castle, Aberdeenshire, 148
Baltic, Gothic villa on the, 433
Bamburgh Castle, Northumberland, 306
Bangor Castle, Co. Down, 437, 441
Bank Hall, Derbyshire, 396
Bankes, W. J., 436
Bankfield, Halifax, 212n.
Banks and Barry, 35, 294, 400 and see under Barry, Charles, junior
Banks, Robert Richardson, 436
Banks-Stanhope, J., 417
Bannerman, John, 437
Banstead Wood, Surrey, 75, 396, Pl. 385
Barber and Walker, colliers, 417
Barberi, Father Dominic, 188, 189
Barbon Park Lodge, Westmorland, 436
Barchard, Francis, 172, 178
Barcote, Berks., 443
Baring family, 11, 19n., 396, 405 and see under Ashburton, Lord and Revelstoke, Lord
Barings' Bank, 405, 414
Barley, Wilson, 401
Barnard, Bishop and Barnard, 367, 368, 419
Barnard Castle, Durham, The Bowes Museum, 296, Pl. 280
Barnes, Frederick, 406
Barrett, Moulton, 448
Barrow Court, Cheshire, 438
Barrow Court, Somerset, 442
Barry family, of St. Leonard's Hill, 13, 299
Barry, Sir Charles, 18, 29, 35, 45, 48–51, 55, 56n., 112, 122, 130–3, 138, 147–8, 149, 208, 269, 436, 437
Barry, Charles, junior, 50, 436
Barry, E. M., 18, 19, 56, 157, 293, 297–9, 436
Bass, Hamar, 400
Batchwood, Hertfordshire, 26, 86, 396
Bates, Josiah, 414
Bath, Marchioness of, 442
Bathurst, Rev. W. H., 437
Batsford Park, Gloucestershire, 82, 396, Pl. 386
Battle Abbey, Sussex, 437
Battlesden House, Bedfordshire, 292, 396
Baxendale, Lloyd, 407
Bayham Abbey, Kent, 24, 25, 26, 396
Baynards Park, Surrey, 438
Bayons Manor, Lincolnshire, 44, 45, 47, 103–9, 115, Pls. 20, 73–9
Bazley, Thomas Sebastian, 408
Beaconsfield, Benjamin Disraeli, Earl of, 78, 214n., 274, 410
Quoted, 6, 23n., 45, 53, 133n. 149n.
Beale family, of Standen, 381–2, 386, 388, 389
Bear Wood, Berkshire, 17, 18, 21, 26, 55–6, 65, 263–72, Fig. 21, Pls. 253–9, Col. Pls. XX,XXI
Beau Ideal of an English Villa, 37, 43
Beauchamp, Frederick Lygon, 6th Earl, 412
Beaufront Castle, Northumberland, 396
Beaumont, Henry Stapleton, 9th Lord, 346–8, 351, 353–4
Beaumont, Sir G. H., Bart., 437

Beaumont, T. J., 440
Beauvale Lodge, Nottinghamshire, 74, 329–34, Fig. 25, Pls 316–23
Bechry, Flintshire, 376
Beckett, Sir Edmund, 1st Lord Grimthorpe, 16, 26, 65, 86, 396
Quoted, 36n., 55, 59, 60, 445
Beckford Hall, Worcestershire, 440
Bedgebury Park, Kent, 292, 397
Bedstone Court, Shropshire, 439
Bedwell Park, Hertfordshire, 439
Beeston Castle, Cheshire, 154
Belcher, John, 421
Bell family, 11
Bell, Sir Isaac Lowthian, Bart., 381, 418, 420, 423
Belle Vue, Halifax, 208, 210–11, 212, 292, Pls. 199–200
Belper, Lord, see under Strutt, Edward
Belvoir Castle, Rutlandshire, 90, 157, 292
Benenden, see under Hemsted
Benoite, Josephine, wife of John Bowes, 297
Bentley, John Francis, 351–4
Berechurch Hall, Essex, 25, 397, 445
Beresford-Hope, Alexander James, 16, 292, 293, 397
Bermerside, Halifax, 212n.
Bernasconi and Son, Francis, 99
Bertie-Percy, Lord Charles, 439
Best, Rev. Thomas, 417
Bestwood Lodge, Nottinghamshire, 56–7, 59, 199, 202, 397, Frontispiece, Pl. 387
Betteshanger, Kent, 83, 214–9, 454, Pls. 203–8
Betts, Edward Ladd, 10, 416
Bewsey Hall, Lancashire, 439
Bexley Heath, Kent, the Red House, 68, 74, 186
Bilton Grange, Warwickshire, 123, 173, 188, 397
Binnegar Hall, Dorset, 436
Birch Hall, Essex, 439
Bird, Colonel, 442
Birdsall House, Yorkshire, 441
Birkbeck, Sir E., 440
Birmingham, 11, 381, 392
Bishop Burton, Yorkshire, 438
Bishopscourt, Devon, 13, 397, 451
Bizy, Chateau de, France, 433
Blachford, Lady Isabella, 147
Blackmoor, Hampshire, 74, 82, 397, 454
Blackmore Park, Worcestershire, 436
Blair, Right Rev. Sir David Oswald Hunter, Bart., 290, 451
Blaise Hamlet, Bristol, 64
Blakesware, Hertfordshire, 398
Blewitt, R. S., 442
Bligh, J. D., 405
Blomfield, Sir A. W., 246
Blomfield, Sir Reginald, 71
Blore, Edward, 18, 19, 48, 51–2, 61, 99, 120–8, 194, 196, 202, 436
Blunt, Lady Anne, 16, 85, 403
Blunt, Wilfrid Scawen, 16, 81, 85–6, 403
Blythewood, Buckinghamshire, 442
Bodley, George Frederick, 74, 86, 225, 409
Bodnant, Denbighshire, 13, 398
Bodrhyddan, Flintshire, 85, 398, Pls. 56, 388
Bodsahan, Cornwall, 437
Bolckow, Henry, 11, 412
Boldre Grange, Hampshire, 398, 441
Bonham Carter, J., 439
Bonomi, Ignatius, 440
Borocourt Mental Hospital, see Wyfold Court
Borrow, George, 186
Bosanquet, S., 442
Boston, George Ives Irby, 4th Lord, 294
Boughton-Leigh, E. A. B. W., 441
Bourges, France, Chateau near, 433

Bourton Manor, Shropshire, 441
Bowes, John, 296–7
Bowood House, Wiltshire, 23, 436
Boyne, Viscounts, 441
Bramling House, Kent, 436
Bramshott Grange, Hampshire, 442
Brancepeth Castle, Durham, 44, 105, 441, 445, 448
Brandfold, Kent, 442
Brandon, David, 18, 53, 54, 436
Branksome Park, Bournemouth, 147
Brantingham Thorpe, Yorkshire, 398
Brassey family, 10, 294, 409, 414, 416
Breadsall Priory, Derbyshire, 13, 36, 38, 398
Brent Knoll, Somerset, 245, 440
Brettenham, Norfolk, 198, 199, 200
Bricklehampton, Worcestershire, 449
Brightwen and Binyon, 394
Brindley, architectural sculptor, 235, see also Farmer and Brindley
British Plate Glass Co., 448
Broadstone of Honour, 13
Broadway Manor House, Devon, 437
Brodsworth Hall, Yorkshire, 38, 123, 140, 236–42, Fig. 19, Pls. 222–8, Col. Pls. XVII, XVIII
Brooks, James, 262
Brooks, Warwick, 215
Broomfield, Halifax, 208
Broomhill, Kent, 398
Brown, Lancelot, 130
Brownlow, Countess Adelaide Talbot, wife of 3rd Earl, 78
Brownsover Hall, Warwickshire, 441
Broxton Hall, Cheshire, 82, 398
Brunet-Debaines, C. L. F., 296
Bryanston, Dorset, 37, 86, 399, Pl. 58
Bryce, David, 98, 99
Bryce, John, 446
Brydon, John McKean, 67, 71, 324
Buccleuch, Walter Francis Scott, 5th Duke of, 292
Buchan Hill, Sussex, 18, 82, 399, Pls. 51, 389
Buchanan House, Stirlingshire, Fig. 2
Buckden Palace, Lincolnshire, 438
Buckhold House, Berkshire, 442
Buckler, Charles Alban, 394
Buckler, John Chessell, 400
Bucknall, Benjamin, 188–93
Bulstrode, Buckinghamshire, 438
Buonas, Schloss, Switzerland, 433
Burges, Alfred, 273
Burges, William, 17, 55, 56n., 59, 60n., 61, 64, 65, 67, 70, 273–90, 330, 331, 336–45, 353, 436–7, 437
Burke and Co., 414
Burn, William, 18, 19, 20, 22, 33–4, 35, 48, 52, 53, 58, 71, 77, 96, 98–9, 138–42, 147, 264, 292, 319, 437, 451
Burne-Jones, Sir Edward, Bart., 13, 19, 67, 68, 80, 314, 418
Burns, W. H., 438
Burr, Higford, 394
Burrell, Sir Percy, Bart., 442
Burton Closes, Derbyshire, 440
Burwarton House, Shropshire, 441
Bushell, Christopher, 442
Bute, John Crichton-Stuart, 2nd Marquess of, 273
Bute, John Crichton-Stuart, 4th Marquess of, 290, 345
Bute, John Patrick Crichton-Stuart, 3rd Marquess of, 8, 70, 155, 273–4, 275, 279–80, 287, 290, 336, 339, 345, 346, 353, Pl. 260
Butleigh Court, Somerset, 400, Pl. 390
Butterfield, H. I., 43n., 401
Butterfield, William, 58, 64, 136, 179–86, 225, 244, 401
Buxton family, of Shadwell, 194, 204
Buxton, Charles Fowell, 16, 406
Buxton, Lady, Elizabeth Cholmeley, wife of Sir John Jacob Buxton, Bart., 197–8, 202, 203–4
Buxton, Sir Robert, Bart., 197, 448
Buxton, Sir (Thomas) Fowell Buxton, 3rd Bart., 442
Buxton, Thomas Fowell, 404

Bylaugh Hall, Norfolk, 35, 50, 400
Byrkley Lodge, Staffordshire, 400
Byron, George Gordon, 6th Lord, 35, 108

Caldecott, Randolph, 396
Calthorpe, Frederick, 4th Lord, 405
Calthorpe, Frederick Henry William, 5th Lord, 442
Calverley Grange, Kent, 438
Calwich Abbey, Staffordshire, 437
Camden, John Charles, 3rd Marquess, 396
Campbell and Smith, later Campbell, Smith and Campbell, 279, 287, 341, 343–5
Campden House, Gloucestershire, 437
Canford Manor, Dorset, 7–8, 10, 16, 45, 400
Canina, Luigi, 394
Capel Manor, Kent, 59, 400
Capernwray Hall, Lancashire, 400
Capesthorne, Cheshire, 35, 38, 43, 401
Cardiff Castle, Glamorganshire, 36, 38, 273–90, 339, 353, Fig. 22, Pls. 261–2, 264–77, Col. Pls. XXII, XXIII
Carlett Park, Cheshire, 442
Carlingford, Chichester Fortescue, Lord, 19n.
Carlisle, 7th Earl of, 441
Carlisle, 9th Earl of, see under Howard, Hon. George James
Carlist movement, 348, 353n.
Carlton Towers, Yorkshire, 22, 65, 346–54, Fig. 26, Pls. 333–41, Col. Pl. XXX
Carlyle, Thomas, 5, 56
Carnarvon, G. E. S. M. Herbert, 5th Earl of, 134
Carnarvon, Henry Howard Molyneux Herbert, 4th Earl of, 132, 133, 134
Carnarvon, Henry John Geroge Herbert, 3rd Earl of, 130–3
Carpenders Park, Hertfordshire, 449
Carpenter, Hon. Walter Cecil, 440
Carpenter, Richard Cromwell, 225, 292, 437
Carpenter, R. Herbert, 437
Carr, Jonathan, 334
Carrington, Robert John, 2nd Lord, 437
Carson, E. H., 428
Cascaes, nr. Lisbon, 443
Casentini, 'Chevalier', 237–8
Castell Coch, Glamorganshire, 17, 65, 155, 336–45, Pls 324–32, Col. Pls. XXVIII, XXIX
Castings, Arthur, 414
Castle Ashby House, Northamptonshire, 329, 331, 401
Castle Drogo, Devon, 204n.
Castle Irwell, Lancashire, 439
Castle Oliver, Co. Limerick, see under Clonghanodfoy Castle
Castle Upton, Co. Antrim, 430
Castle Wellan, Co. Down, 437
Cator, A., 437
Cattley, John, 297, 420
Cave, Stephen, 436
Cavendish family, see under Devonshire, Dukes of, and Chesham, Lord
Cazenove, H., 438
Cecil, Lord Eustace, 436
Cely-Trevilian, E. B., 441
Centre Vale, Yorkshire, 439
Chaloner, Admiral Thomas, 442
Channonz Hall, Norfolk, 194
Chanter's House, Ottery St. Mary, Devon, 401
Chapple, J. S., 339, 345
Charlecote, Warwickshire, 43, 439
Charlton, St. J. C., 439
Charteris family, 81, see also Wemyss, Earl of
Chase Cliffe, Derbyshire, 438
Cheeseburn Grange, Northumberland, 439
Cheltenham, Gloucestershire, St. Peter's Church, 174
Chesham, Charles Compton Caverndish, 1st Lord, 436
Chestal House, Gloucestershire, 442
Chesters, Northumberland, 86, 441
Chetwynd-Talbot, Hon. John, 405
Chew Magna Manor, Somerset, 245, 440
Chichester, Robert, 408
Chilham Castle, Kent, 436
Chirk Castle, Denbighshire, 440

Cholmeley, Sir Montague, Bart., 197n.
Christian, Ewan, 83, 437, 451
Christie, George H., 440
Christie, W. L., 437
Christopher, J. T., 428
Cirencester, Gloucestershire, Agricultural College, 176
Clarke, George Somers, Senior, 10, 437
Clarke, George Somers, Junior, 437
Clarke-Jervoise, Sir J., 437
Clayton and Bell, 420
Clayton, N. G., 441
Cleveland, 4th Duke of, see under Vane, Lord Harry George
Clifden, Henry George Agar-Robartes, 4th Viscount, 437
Cliffe Castle, Yorkshire, 43n., 401
Cliveden House, Bucks., 401–2, Pl. 391
Clonghanodfoy Castle (now Castle Oliver) Co. Limerick, 426
Close, The Rev. Francis, 86n.
Clouds, Wiltshire, 17, 80–2, 186, 381, 402, Pls. 49, 50
Cloverley Hall, Shropshire, 11, 35, 72, 73, 78, 312, 322, 402, 428, Fig. 3, Pl. 40
Clumber House, Nottinghamshire, 436
Clutton, Henry, 17, 122–3, 127–8, 292, 353, 437
Clyffe House, Dorset, 112n., 402
Coad, Richard, 411
Cobham Park, Surrey, 297, 299
Cockerell, Charles Robert, 197
Cockerell, Frederick Pepys, 21, 437, 446
Cocks, Lt.-Col. C. L., 437
Coe, Henry Edward, 451
Coleorton Hall, Leicestershire, 437
Coleridge, John Duke, 1st Lord, 401
Colesborne House, Gloucestershire, 436
Coleshill House, Berkshire, 23
Collard and Collard, 13, 392
Collard, Lukey, 13, 392
Colney Hatch Asylum, 176
Combe Abbey, Warwickshire, 402, Pl 392
Combe, C. J. F., 297, 416
Combe, Richard, 404
Combermere Abbey, Shropshire, 436
Combermere, Stapleton Cotton, 1st Viscount, 436
Comper, Sir Ninian, 449
Congham High House, Norfolk, 441
Connaught, H.R.H. Prince Arthur, 1st Duke of, 396
Cook, E. A., 439
Cooke, Edward William, 72, 214, 215, 450
Cookson and Cuthbert, 396
Coolhurst, Sussex, 436
Coombe Cottage, Surrey, 402–3
Coombe, Dorset, 445
Coombe Warren, Surrey, 19n. 83, 402, Pl. 53
Coope, Octavius, 25, 397
Copenhagen, Castellated villa near, 432
Corbet, H. Reginald, 438
Corbett, John, 13, 295
Cordes, Thomas, 442
Coronio, family, 381
Corsham Court, Wiltshire, 21
Cosford House, Surrey, 442
Cotes, C. C., 425
Cottesloe, Lord, see under Fremantle, Sir Thomas Francis, Bart.
Cotman, John, 84
Cottingham, Lewis Nockalls, 115
Cowdray Park, Sussex, 82, 403
Cowdray, Weetman Dickinson Pearson, 1st Viscount, 403, 430
Cowesby Hall, Yorkshire, 441
Cowley Manor, Gloucestershire, 437
Cowper, Countess, Anne Florence, wife of the 6th Earl, 291n.
Cowper, Francis Thomas de Grey, 7th Earl, 329
Crabbet Park, Sussex, 85, 403, Pl. 55
Crace, John Gregory, 45, 108, 115, 118, 170, 176, 393, 411, 420, 429
Cragside, Northumberland, 11, 25, 26, 37, 38, 74, 76, 77, 305–17, 359, 361, 445, Fig. 23, Pls. 287–300, Col. Pls. XXVI, XXVII
Craigynos, Breconshire, 442

Cranbrook, Earl of, *see under* Gathorne-Hardy, Gathorne
Cranfield Court, Bedfordshire, 26, 439
Cranmore Hall, Somerset, 443
Crathorne Hall, Yorkshire, 438
Craven, Earl of, 402
Crawford, Alexander William Crawford Lindsay, 25th Earl of, 430
Crawley Court, Hampshire, 403, 446
Crawley-Boevey family, 244
Crewe-Read, Captain Offley Malcolm, 416
Crewe Hall, Cheshire, 56, 403, Pl. 28
Crewe, Hungerford Crewe, 3rd Lord, 403
Crichton, Hon. H. G. L., 414
Crickmay, J., 319
Crisp, Henry, 428
Crofts, Captain H. P., 421
Crom Castle, Co. Fermanagh, 427
Crookhey Hall, Lancashire, 442
Cropper, E., 438
Crossley family, of Halifax, 205–12, 243
Crossley, Sir Francis, Bart., 205–12, 292
Crossrigg Hall, Westmoreland, 441
Croston Hall, Lancashire, 441
Croxteth Hall, Lancashire, 320
Cubitt family, 10, 17, 152, 444
Cubitt, Thomas, 10, 148–9, 403, 442
Cubitt, William Cubitt and Co., 16–17, 225, 298, 302, 444, 450
Cundy, Thomas, 297,
Currie family, 11, 19n.
Currie, Bertrand, 19n. 402
Currie, Raikes, 292, 414
Currie, William, 410
Cuthbert, William, 396
Cutler, T. W., 394

Dalby Hall, Leicestershire, 438
Dalby Hall, Lincolnshire, 438
Dalgety, F. G., 437
Danesfield Buckinghamshire, 441
Dangstein, Sussex, 440
Daniel, T. Carew, 439
Darby, Rebecca, 10, 359
d'Arenberg, Prince Auguste, 433
Dartrey, Co. Monaghan, 427, 452
Dartrey, Richard Dawson, 1st Earl of, 427
Daukes, Samuel, 112, 173–6, 392
Davenport, Bromley, 401
Davenport, E. D., 401
Davenport, John, 439
Davies family, 416
Dawpool, Cheshire, 10, 76, 77, 403, 445, Pl. 45
Dawson, Pudsey, 410
Dean & Woodward, 412
de Bark, Count, 432
Debenham family, 381
Dee Hills, Chester, 376
Deepdene, Surrey, The, 15, 46, 48, 50, 142, 403
de Grey, Thomas Philip de Grey, 2nd Earl, 100, 292, 425
de Havilland, General, 353
Delamore House, Devon, 441
Delane, John, 271, 272
de l'Isle, Ambrose Phillipps, *see under* Phillipps
de l'Isle and Dudley, Philip Sidney, 2nd Lord, 213
de Mauley, Lords, 400, 408
de Morgan tiles, 364, 407
de Morgan, William, 353
de Murrieta, Charles, 422
Denbies, Surrey, 10, 403, 449
Denbigh, R. W. B. Feilding, 8th Earl of, 294, 443
Denne Hill, Kent, 403, Pl. 393
Dennett, A. of Nottingham, 225
Dent family, of Sudeley Castle, 421
Denton Hall, Lincolnshire, 102
de Ramsey, Lord, *see under* Fellowes, Edward
de Rothschild, *see under* Rothschild
Derwent Hall, Derbyshire, 439
de Schickler, Barons, 433
Destailleur, Gabriel Hippolyte, 300
de Trafford, J. R., 441
Devey, George, 17, 18, 19, 77, 79, 83–5, 213–22, 438

Devonshire, William Spencer Cavendish, 6th Duke of, 24, 45, 174, 429
Devonshire, William Cavendish, 7th Duke of, 410
D'Eyncourt, Tennyson, *see under* Tennyson D'Eyncourt
Dick, W. Wentworth Fitzwilliam Hume, 253–4, 262
Dickens, C. S., 436
Didlington Hall, Norfolk, 441
Digby, Kenelm, 13
Dingestow, Monmouthshire, 442
Dinorben, Lady, Gertrude Smyth, 2nd wife of 1st Lord, 412
Dinorben, William Lewis Hughes, 1st Lord, 319
Disraeli, Benjamin, *see* Beaconsfield, Earl of
Dixon, J. T., 314
Dixon, Peter, 438
Dobroyd Castle, Yorkshire, 23, 403, Pl. 394
Dobson, John, 396, 438
Dolben, William Mackworth, 405
Donaldson, Thomas Leverton, 438, 441
Douglas, John, 82, 375, 415
Dowbiggin, Thomas and Co., 152, 448
Dowdeswell, J. E., 417
Down Hall, Essex, 21, 404, Pl.11
Drake, Charles, 21
Drewe, Julius, 204n.
Droitwich, 13, 295
Dromore Castle, Co.Limerick, 26, 63, 155, 330, 331, 427, 451, Pls. 35, 420
Drummond, George James, 17, 438
Drummond, Henry, 393
Ducie, Henry George Francis Moreton, 2nd Earl of, 188, 422
Duckworth, William, 415
Dudley, William Ward, 1st Earl of, 424
Dufferin and Ava, Frederick Temple Blackwood, 1st Marquess of, 428
Dugdale, James Lionel, 438
Dugdale, William Stratford, 6n., 17, 120–1, 128
du Maurier, George, 367
Dunroy Castle, County Cork, 428, Pl. 421
Duncombe, Hon. Augustus, 437
Duncombe, Hon. William Ernest, *see under* Feversham, 1st Earl of
Duncombe Park, Yorkshire, 437, 443
Duncrub Castle, Perthshire, 439
Dundonald Abbey, Ayrshire, 24
Dundonald, Archibald Cochrane, 9th Earl of, 24
Dunecht House, Aberdeenshire, 430
Dunley House, Surrey, 439
Dunraven Castle, Glamorganshire, 438
Dunraven, Earls of, 426, 438
Dunrobin Castle, Sunderland, 51, 430–1, Pl. 425
Dunsdale, Kent, 440
Dunster Castle, Somerset, 441
Durdans, The, Surrey, 438
Durham, Joseph, 210
Duvernay, Yolande, wife of Lyne Stephens, 412
Duxbury Hall, Lancashire, 436
D'Uxcull, Baron, 432
Dyce, William, 150, Pl. 121
Dyrham House, Gloucestershire, 140
Dyson, Edward, 403

Ealing, Middlesex, St. Mary's Church, 199
Eardley, Sir Culling Eardley, Bart. 439
Earp, Thomas, 202, 396 (Bayham, Bestwood) 397, 405
Easneye, Hertfordshire, 404
East Lavington Manor, Wiltshire, 437
Eastlake, Charles Lock, *History of the Gothic Revival*, 71, 73, 165, 253, 400, 415
Easton Lodge, Essex, 439
Eaton Hall, Cheshire, 2–4, 15, 26, 28, 29, 78, 294, 404, 445, Pls. 1, 3, 47
Edgeworth, Richard Lovell, 23
Edinburgh, James Gowan's House at, 59
Edis, Sir Robert W., 25, 438
Edward VII, *see under* Prince of Wales
Egerton, Sir Philip, Bart., 398
Egerton-Warburton, R. E., 394
Egg, Augustus, 214n. 450
Egham, Surrey, Royal Holloway College, 340

Eglinton tournament, The, 13
Egmont, Charles George Percival, 7th Earl of, 403
Egremont, George Francis Wyndham, 4th Earl of, 420
Ehrenbara, Schloss, Coburg, 150
Eldon, John Scott, 3rd Earl of, 421
Eley, W. T., 443
Ellington Hall, Lincolnshire, 440
Ellel Grange, Lancashire, 4, 404, 449
Ellesmere, Francis Egerton, 1st Earl of, 51, 424
Ellison, Sarah Caroline, wife of Sir Walter James, 1st Lord Northbourne, 214
Elmslie, Franey & Haddon, 424
Elveden Hall, Suffolk, 17, 27, 404–5
Elvetham Hall, Hampshire, 57, 58, 59, 199, 202, 405, Pls. 29, 395, Col. Pl. III
Elwes, J. H., 436
Elwes, R., 441
Ely, Bishop of, Thomas Turton, 197n.
Emmerson, Henry Hetherington, 314
Encombe Hall, Dorset, 52
Enbrook, Kent, 26, 405
Encyclopaedia of Cottage, Farm and Villa Architecture, *see under* Loudon, John Claudius
Endsleigh Cottage, Devon, 64
Erne, Abraham Crichton, 2nd Earl of, 427
Errington, Sir R. Bart. 438
Escrick, Yorkshire, 121
Estcourt, of Gloucester, builder, 17, 339
Ettington Park, Warwickshire, 58, 59, 405, Pl. 30, Col. Pl. IV
Evans, Edward Bickerton, 424
Evelyn, Mr., 442
Exeter, St Michael's, 244
Exning House, Newmarket, 442
Eynsham Hall, Oxfordshire, 405
Eythrope, Buckinghamshire, 438

Falconhurst Lodge, Kent, 54, 405
Falkland, House of, Fife, 52, 451
Falkland Palace, 451
Falkland, Lucius Bentinck Cary, 10th Viscount, 441
Farmer and Brindley, 118, 235, 408
Farnham Park, Buckinghamshire, 72, 73, 405, Pl. 43
Farquharson, Miss, 431
Farrer, O. W., 436
Fawckner, J. F. 439
Fawsley Park, Northamptonshire, 54, 441
Fellowes, Edward, 1st Lord de Ramsey, 417
Fenian movement, the, 259
Ferney Hall, Shropshire, 440
Ferrey, Benjamin, 53, 66, 112n., 245, 292, 396, 402, 438
Ferrières, Chateau de, France, 432
Feversham, William Ernest Duncombe, 1st Earl of, 436, 443
Ffarington J. N., 441
Fickel Castle, Estonia, 432
Fielden, John, 403, 415
Fielden, Joshua, 415
Fielden, Samuel, 439
Finedon Hall, Northamptonshire, 405
Firth, James, 394
Fiske, Stephen, 27
Fitzhugh, T. L., 439
Flaxley, St Mary's, 244
Flete, Devon, 76, 77, 361, 405–6, Pls. 46, 396
Flintham Hall, Nottinghamshire, 43, 406, Pl. 397, Col. Pl. I
Flixton Hall, Suffolk, 23, 441, Pl. 13
Flower, Wickham, 442
Fonthill Abbey, Wiltshire (Beckford house), 15, 50; (Grosvenor house), 19, 52, 406, Pl. 25
Fonthill House, Wiltshire, 442
Ford Manor, Surrey, 271, 406
Forman, J., 441
Forsyth, James, 312, 322, 328, 424
Forthampton Court, Gloucestershire, 442
Fothergill, William, 442
Fountaine family, 414
Fountains Abbey, Yorkshire, 312
Fowler, James, 33, 438
Fowler's Park, Kent, 75, 441

Foxbury, Kent, 436
Foxbush, Kent, 437
Foxwarren Park, Surrey, 406
Frame, William, 339, 344, 345, 451
Framingham Hall, Norfolk, 440
Franchi, Pietro, 240
Francis, Clement, 417
Freeland village and church, Oxfordshire, 165
Freeman-Mitford, Algernon Bertrand, *see under* Redesdale, Lord
Fremantle, Sir Thomas Francis, Bart. (later 1st Lord Cottesloe), 437
Frith, John Griffith, 437
Frith, William Powell, 291n.
Froude, James Anthony, 421
Fryth House, Hertfordshire, 436
Fucigna (C. E. ?) 340
Fuller-Acland-Hood, Sir Alexander Bateman Periam, Bart., 419
Furse, Charles Wellington, 374

Gainsborough, Charles Noel, 1st Earl of, 437
Ganton Hall, Yorkshire, 437
Garboldisham Manor, Norfolk, 446
Garendon Hall, Leicestershire, 441, Pl. 19
Garling, Henry Bayly, 451
Garner, Thomas, 86, 409
Garratt, John, 13, 397
Gascoigne, Misses, 426
Gathorne-Hardy, Gathorne, 1st Earl of Cranbrook, 409
Gayhurst House, Buckinghamshire, 64, 70, 437, Pl. 39
Geary, Sir W. P. R., Bart., 292
Gentleman's House, The, see under Kerr, Robert
George, and Peto, *see under* George, Sir Ernest
George, Sir Ernest, 13, 18, 82, 438–9
Gibbs, stained glass maker, 422
Gibbs, Antony and Sons, 243–4
Gibbs, Martin, 442
Gibbs, William, 13, 243–5
Gibbs family, 243–51
Gibbons of Wolverhampton, 100
Gibson, John, architect, 403, 415, 439
Gibson, John, sculptor, 408
Gillows, furniture makers, 140, 288
Gilston Park, Hertfordshire, 439
Gisborough Hall, Yorkshire, 442
Gladstone, Mary, 78, 300, 394
Gladstone, William Ewart, 6, 19, 86, 214, 402
Glangwna, Caernarvonshire, 438
Glasgow University, 374
Glastonbury, the Abbot's Kitchen, 48, 116, 407
Glen Andred, Sussex, 72, 73, 359, 382
Glen, George, 442
Glenbegh Towers, Co. Kerry, 330, 428
Glencot, Somerset, 439
Gloddaeth, Denbighshire, 440
Glyn family, 19n.
Glyn, George Grenfell, *see under* Wolverton, 2nd Lord
Glyn Mills bank, 411, 414
Glyndebourne, Sussex, 437
Godman, Major A. P., 420
Godwin, Edward William, 26, 63, 66, 67, 76, 112n., 275, 329–34, 451
   Quoted 53n., 263n., 310n.
Goff, Robert, 440
Goldie & Child, 439
Goldie, George, 439
Golding-Palmer, Rev. S., 442
Goldings, Hertfordshire, 85, 222, 407, Fig. 6
Goldsmid, Sir Francis H., Bart., 11, 417
Gonzalez, Senor Don Manuel M., 432
Goodall, Frederick, 68, 214, 450
Goschen, Charles Hermann, 396
Goschen, George Joachim, 1st Viscount, 419
Gosford House, East Lothian, 79, 431, Pl. 424
Gosling, Robert, 439
Gosselin, Mrs. Frances Orris, 398
Gough, John, 442
Gowan, James, 59
Grafton Manor House, Worcestershire, 436
Grant, Baron Albert, 291n., 299–300
Granville, Granville George Leveson Gower, 2nd Earl, 19n., 438

Granville, Neville, 400
Grayson & Ould, 375
Great Blake Hall, Essex, 440
Great Brickhill Manor, Buckinghamshire, 440
Great Exhibition, The, 169, 210
   Exhibits from, in country houses, 174, 406
Greathed Manor, Surrey, *see under* Ford Manor
Greaves, R. M., 438
Green family, of Ken Hill, 11, 366–70, 374
Green, Sir Edward, Bart., 366, 369
Green, James Baker, 444
Green, W. J., 398
Greenall, Sir Gilbert, Bart., 441
Greenard of Paris, 401
Greenham Lodge, Berkshire, 37, 76, 361, 407
Greenhurst, Surrey, 441
Greenlands, Oxfordshire, 449
Greg, W. R., 56
Gregory, Gregory, 90–102
Gregynog Hall, Montgomeryshire, 407
Grenfell family, 81, 318
Grenfell, Charles Pascoe, 421
Gresley, Rev. Sir William Nigel, Bart., 437
Greville, Charles, quoted, 90
Grey, Charles, 439
Greystoke Castle, Cumberland, 441
Grims Dyke, Middlesex, 68, 83, 359, 362
Grimston Park, Yorkshire, 242
Grimthorpe, Lord, *see under* Sir Edmund Beckett, Bart.
Grinkle Park, Yorkshire, 407
Grittleton House, Wiltshire, 20, 407, Pl. 398
Grosvenor family, *see under* Westminster, Duke and Marquess of, and Stalbridge, Lord
Gruner, Ludwig, 150
Guest, Lady Charlotte, 7–8, 16, 400
Guest, Sir John Josiah, Bart., 7–8, 10, 16, 400
Guinness family, 27, 405
Gunnergate Hall, Yorkshire, 38, 407
Gurney, H. E., 414
Guy's Cliffe, Warwickshire, 439

Habershon, Brock & Webb, 294, 414, 439
Habershon, Edward, 439
Habershon, Matthew, 437, 439
Habershon, Pite, and Fawckner, 410
Habershon, William Gilbee, 439
Hadfield, Weightman & Goldie, 439
Hafod, Cardiganshire, 441
Hafodunos House, Denbighshire, 11, 48, 225, 408, Pl. 399
Haggerston Castle, Northumberland, 441
Hale and Son, Messrs., 454
Hale, R. B. 442
Halifax, Yorkshire, 205–12, 404, Pls. 192–200
   Town Hall, 208, Pl. 194 *and see under* Bankfield, Belle Vue, Bermerside, Broomfield, Manor Heath, and Moorside
Hall, N. Devon, 45, 408
Hall Place, Kent, 13, 408
Hall, Sir Benjamin, Bart., 439
Hall, Edwin Thomas, 432
Halliday Brothers, 416
Halton, House, Buckinghamshire, 38, 43, 302, Pls. 286, 401
Ham, The Glamorganshire, 442
Hamilton, Archibald Rowan, 428
Hamilton, Lord Ernest, quoted, 3n., 27
Hammerfield, Kent, 83, 214, 215, Pl. 52
Hammond, William Oxenden, 215, 219
Hampton Court Palace, Middlesex, 323, 324, 325
Hampton-in-Arden, Warwickshire, 71, 440
Hanbury, George, 442
Hansom, Charles, 188
Hansom, Joseph Aloysius, 439
Harcourt, Sir William Vernon, 412
Harding, George Perfect, 448
Harding, James Duffield, 84, 214
Hardinge, Henry Hardinge, 1st Viscount, 214, 441
Hardman, John, 118, 393
Hardwick, Philip, 408, 442
Hardwick, Philip Charles, 18, 21, 45, 53, 66, 293, 439
Hardy, Charles, 436
Hare, Augustus, 27

Hare, Sir Thomas, Bart., 436
Harewood, Henry Lascelles, 3rd Earl of, 436
Harewood House, Yorkshire, 436
Hargreaves, William, 438
Harland and Son, 401
Harlaxton Manor, Lincolnshire, 44, 52, 54, 62, 90–102, 138, 421, Fig. 7, Pls. 60–72, Col. Pls. V, VI
Harrach, Graf, 432
Harris, Thomas, 439
Harrison, James 375
Harrison, R. H. 420
Harrowby, Dudley Ryder, 2nd Earl of, 437
Hart, Son, Peard and Co., 280, 343, 344
Harter, Rev. G. G., 439
Hartopp, E. B., 438
Hartshorne, Albert, 432
Haseley Manor, Warwickshire, 443
Hassobury, Essex, 439
Hatfield House, Hertfordshire, 25, 26, 445
Hatherop House, Gloucestershire, 408
Haverland Hall, Norfolk, 417
Hawkleyhurst, Hampshire, 442
Haycock, Edward, 414, 439
Headington House, Oxfordshire, 442
Heath House, The, Staffordshire, 20, 408, 444, Pls. 10, 400
Heath Old Hall, Yorkshire, 366, 368, 369
Heaton, J. Aldam, 452, 454
Heber-Percy, Lady E., 441
Hedsor House, Buckinghamshire, 294, 409, Pl. 279
Hemsted House, Kent, 24, 65, 409
Henham Hall, Suffolk, 439
Henniker, Sir Brydges, Bart., 440
Hensall Castle, Glamorganshire, 442
Herbert family, 81
Herbert, H. A., 430
Hermon, Edward, 10, 425
Hewell Grange, Worcestershire, 25, 86, 409, Pl. 59
Hewitson, W. C., 438
Hewitt, C. A., 410
Hewlett, Mr., 443
Heythrop Hall, Oxfordshire, 409, 444
Heywood, J. Pemberton, 11, 72
Hibbert, Captain Washington, 397
Hichens, A. K., 438
Hichens, Harrison & Co., 420
Hichens, Robert, 43n., 420
Higham, A. B., 423
Highclere Castle, Hampshire, 50, 122, 130–6, 269, 421, Fig. 10, Pls. 104–112, Col. Pl. XI
Highfield, Gloucester, 449
Highlands, The, Gloucestershire, 21, 82, 437
Higson, John, 415
Hildyard, T. B. T., 406
Hilton, S. M., 436
Hinderton, Cheshire, 21, 442
Hine, Thomas, 406, 439
Hinton Daubnay, Hampshire, 437
Hippisley, H., 438
Hippisley, J. H., 438
Hippisley, Rev. Robert W., 165, 292
Hoar Cross Hall, Staffordshire, 437
Hodgkinson, W. S., 439
Hodgson, G. A., 25, 438
Hodgson, William, 439
Hodnet Hall, Shropshire, 441
Hogg, John, 207
Hoghton, Sir Henry, Bart. (later de Hoghton), 441 ·
Holbrook Hall, Suffolk, 437
Holdenby House, Northamptonshire, 437
Holford, Robert Stayner, 52, 423
Holker Hall, Lancashire, 410
Holland and Hannen, building contractors, 420, 444
Holland & Sons, furniture makers, 150, 406
Holland, Henry, 275, 279
Hollist, Hasler, 436
Holme Eden, nr. Carlisle, 438
Holme Park, Berkshire, 442
Holmewood Ho., Huntingdonshire, 443
Holt Hall, Norfolk, 440
Holzmann, decorative painter, 404

Home and Colonial Stores, 204n.
Hood, Sir Alexander Bateman Periam Fuller-Acland, Bart., 419
Hope End, Worcestershire, 36, 410
Hope, Henry Thomas, 142, 403
Hope Thomas, 16, 46, 48, 403
Hopper, Thomas, 319, 421, 439
Horeau, Hector, 295
Hornby Castle, Lancashire, 410
Horner family, 81
Hornyold, J. V., 436
Horrocks, Miller & Co., 425
Horsley Towers, Surrey, 307–8, 410, Pls. 402–3
Horsley, John Callcott, 72
Horsted Place, Sussex, 112, 123, 172–8, 237, 429, Fig. 14, Pls. 151–61
Horsted Hall, Norfolk, 440
Hoskins, Flora, 215n.
Hoskyns, H. W., 443
Howard, Henry, 18, 441
Howard, Hon. George James, later 9th Earl of Carlisle, 74, 381
Howell, C. H., 299
Hrádek, Schloss, Czechoslovakia, 432, Pl. 426
Hubbard, J. G., 1st Lord Addington, 393
Hubbard, W. E., 411
Hudson, George, 10
Hughenden Manor, Buckinghamshire, 410
Hughes, Arthur, 214
Hughes, Rev. Edward, 318–9
Hughes, Henry Robert, 319–20, 323, 328n.
Hughes, Thomas, 14, 56, 376
    Tom Brown's Schooldays. Quoted, 14, 56
Humbert, A. J., 419
Hume Dick, see under Dick, W. Wentworth Fitzwilliam Hume
Humewood Castle, Co. Wicklow, 17, 36, 64, 173, 252–62, Fig. 20, Pls. 241–52
Hunloke, Ann, Lady, see under Scarisbrick, Ann, Lady
Huntsham Court, Devon, 438
Hurt, Messrs., 438
Hussey, Edward, 441
Hutchinson, James, 437
Huth family, 11
Huth, Henry, 297
Huth, Louis, 416
Hutton Hall, Yorkshire, 27, 411
Hutton-in-the-Forest, Cumberland, 441

Ibbetson, Sir Henry John Selwin, Bart., 404
Idsworth House, Hampshire, 437
Ilchester, Henry Edward Fox-Strangways, 5th Earl of, 438, 441
Imberhouse, Sussex, 439
Impney Hall (later Château Impney), Worcestershire, 13, 295–6, Col. Pl. XXV
Ingelow, Benjamin, 437
Inglethorpe Hall, Norfolk, 438
Invercauld Castle, Aberdeenshire, 431
Ionides family, 381
Ismay, J. H., 411
Ismay, Thomas Henry, 10, 403
Isaacson, Violet Wooton, wife of Henry Stapleton, 9th Lord Beaumont, 354
Iveagh, Edward Cecil Guinness, 1st Earl of, 405
Ives, Roger, and Son, of Halifax, 208, 210
Iwerne Minster House, Dorset, 10

Jack, George, 389, 418
Jackson, G. and Sons, plasterwork decorators, 416
Jackson Sir Thomas, 225, 401
James family, of Betteshanger, 214–5, 219n.
James, Henry, 79
James, Sir Walter Charles, Bart., later 1st Lord Northbourne, 19n., 214–5
Jeckell, Thomas, 367–70, 397, 419
Jefferson, Rev. J. D., 436
Jekyll, Gertrude, 2
Jennings, Robert, 120
Jephson family, 430
Jerez de la Frontera, Spain, Mansion at, 432
Johnson, Thomas, 408–9
Jones, G. Fowler, 426
Jones, John, Joseph, 392

Jones, Owen, 13, 392, 405, 416
Jowett, Benjamin, 79, 128

Kay, Sir Edward Ebenezer, 436
Kay-Shuttleworth, Sir James Phillips, Bart., 436
Keblas, Chateau at, in Livonia, 432
Keck, Powys, 437
Keele Hall, Staffordshire, 95, 411, Pl. 14
Kelham Hall, Nottinghamshire, 20, 21, 23, 24, 25, 26, 59, 78, 123, 140, 224–35, Fig. 18, Pls. 214–21, Aol. Pl. XIX
Kemp, C. F., 437
Kemp, Edward, 415
Kempe, Charles Eamer, 377–8, 379
Ken Hill, Norfolk, 11, 75, 366–74, Fig. 28, Pls. 349–60, Col. Pl. XXXI
Kenmare, Valentine Augustus Browne, 4th Earl of, 428
Kennard, Adam Steinmetz, 403
Kerr, Robert, 18, 55, 261, 263–4, 269–72, 406, 440, 451
    The Gentleman's House, 18, 29, 35, 37, 48, 52, 60, 69, 150, 263, 271, 293
    Quoted, 30, 33, 34, 50, 54–5, 59, 69, 149, 212, 217
Kew Gardens, Surrey, Nesfield's lodge in, 72, 321
Kiddington Hall, Oxfordshire, 411
Kildale Hall, Yorkshire, 441
Killarney House, Co. Kerry, 222, 428
Killyleagh Castle, Co. Down, 428
Kilmorey, Francis Needham, 2nd Earl of, 442
Kimberley, Albert, 17, 253–4
Kimberley v. Dick & White, Law Suit, 253
Kingsley, Charles, 5, 14, 56, 66, 421
Kingston Hall, Notthinghamshire, 436
Kingston Lacy, Dorset, 436
Kinmel Park, Denbighshire, 37, 74, 85, 318–28, Fig. 24, Pls. 301–15
Kinsett, William, 438
Kinsky, Count, villa for, 432
Kiplin Hall, Yorkshire, 440
Kipling, John Lockwood, 152
Kitchin, Joseph, 440
Knepp Castle, Sussex, 442
Knightley, R., 441
Knightshayes Court, Devon, 61, 411, Pl. 31
Knowle Park, Surrey, 197
Knowles, James Thomas, Senior, 293, 294, 440
Knowles, James Thomas, Junior, 300, 394
Knox, J. Erskine, 352
Knoyle House, Wiltshire, 437

Lainé, French landscape architect, 300
Lamb, Edward Buckton, 58, 65, 410, 414, 440
Lambert, Thomas, 441
Lambourne Place, Berkshire, 438
Landseer, Sir Edwin, 3, 421, 450
Langton, B. R., 438
Langton Hall, Lincolnshire, 438
Lanhydrock House, Cornwall, 411, Col. Pl. II
Lanyon & Lynn, architects, 428
Lapworth Brothers, carpet manufacturers, 242
Largillière, Nicolas de, 242
Lartington Park, Yorkshire, 439
Lascelles, W. H., 452
Latham, J., 394
Latimers, Buckinghamshire, 436
Lauriston, nr. Edinburgh, 35
Lavers, Barraud and Westlake, 352, 416
Lazzerini, Professor G., 240
Leazes, The, Northumberland, 438
Lechlade Manor House, Gloucestershire, 411
Leconfield, Henry Wyndham, 2nd Lord, 441
Lee, E. C., 397
Lee Priory, Kent, 441, 444
Lees, Col. E. B., 422
Legard, Sir Francis Digby, Bart., 437
Le Havre, France, Hotel de Ville, 296
Leicester, Holy Trinity, 199
Leigh, William, 188–9, 193, Pl. 179
Leighton, Frederick, 1st Lord Leighton of Stretton, 290
Leonardslee, Sussex, 411
Leslie, W., of Aberdeen, 430
Lethaby, William Richard, 82, 183, 453

Levaux, decorator, of Paris, 401
Levengrove, Yorkshire, see under Skutterskelf House
Lewis, T. H., 451
Leyland, C. J., 441
Leys, The, Herefordshire, 437
Leys Wood, Kent, 72–4, 78, 308, 312, 359, 382, 416, 418, Pls. 41, 42
Lilford, Thomas Atherton Powys, 3rd Lord, 439
Lillies, The, Buckinghamshire, 438
Lillingstone Dayrell, Buckinghamshire, 437
Limerick, W. H. J. C. Pery, 3rd Earl of, 155, 427
Lindfield Old Hall, Surrey, 377
Lindsay, Sir Coutts, Bart., 423
Lismore Castle, Co. Waterford, 24, 35, 45–6, 170, 174, 429, Pls. 16, 159, 423
Lister family, 81
Little Moreton Hall, Cheshire, 377
Liverpool, 11, 188, 407, 410
Livesey, R. B., 441
Llandogo Priory, Monmouthshire, 442
Llangasty Tal y Llyn, Breconshire, church and school at, 164, 166, Pls. 139–40
Llanover Court, 439
Llantarnam Abbey, Monmouthshire, 442
Lloyd, G., 441
Lloyd, Samuel Jones, Lord Overstone, 415
Llys Dulas, Anglesey, 318, 412, Pl. 405
Lockerley Hall, Hampshire (formerly Oaklands), 437
Locko Park, Derbyshire, 242
Lodsworth, Sussex, 436
Lombe, Edward, 400
London, All Saints', Talbot Road, 253
    Bedford park, 334
    Bridgwater House, 133
    Cadogan Square, House by Ernest George in, 82
    Conservative Club, St. James' St. 142
    Crockford's Club, 292
    Dorchester House, Park Lane, 52
    Harrington Gardens, 82
    Holland Park, 454
    Houses of Parliament, see under Palace of Westminster
    Kensington Palace Green, George Howard's house on, 74
    Law Courts, The, Burges's designs, 275, Pl. 263
    Leighton House, 290
    Lincoln's Inn Fields, house by Philip Webb in, 74
    Lowther Gardens, Makins House in, 370, 374
    Montague House, 292, 293
    New Zealand Chambers, 74
    Palace of Westminster, 56n., 112, 115, 133, 211, 400, 442
    Red House, The, Bayswater, 74, 370
    St Michael's, Paddington, 244
    School Board Offices, 74
    School Board, Schools built by, 74
    St. Andrew's, Wells St., 174
    St. John's Lodge, Regents Park, 452
    St. Pancras Hotel, 225
    St. Saviour's, Aberdeen Park, 258
    Stafford House, 51
    Tower of London, The, 157
    Westminster Hall, 447
Longden & Company, 353
Longford Castle, Wiltshire, 441
Longwood, Hampshire, 438
Lonsdale, H. N., 287, 288
Lorne, Marquess of, see under Argyll, 9th Duke of
Loudon, John Claudius, 23, 93, 94
    Encyclopaedia of Cottage, Farm, and Villa Architecture, 24, 37, 43, 52, 440
Loughton Hall, Essex, 75, 411, Pl. 44
Lovelace, William King, 1st Earl of, 16, 403, 410
Lubbock family, 11
Lucy, Mary, 439
Lugar, Robert, 214
Luscombe Castle, Devonshire, 160
Luttrell, G. F., 441

459

Lutyens, Sir Edwin, 86, 204n.
Lynford Hall, Norfolk, 412
Lyndhurst, Hampshire, the Parish Church, 253
Lyons, Captain, 440
Lytchett Heath, Dorest, 436
Lytton Family, 81
Lytton, Edward George Earle Bulwer-Lytton, 1st Lord, 104, 108–9

Maberley, J. J., 442
Mabey, carver, 420
MacBeth, George, 65
Macclesfield, Thomas Parker, 5th Earl of, 405
Macharoch House, Argyllshire, 438
M'Connochie, John, 274
Macquoid, T. R., 406
'Madame Elise', dress-makers, 354
Madresfield Court, Worcestershire, 412
Magnus Slate Manufactory, 448
Maguire, T. H., 211
Maitland, Rev. J. W., 411
Makins, Colonel Sir William Thomas, Bart., 370
Mallock, William Hurrell, 69
Mallow Castle, Co. Cork, 430
Malpas Court, Monmouthshire, 442
Malwood, Hampshire, 412, Pl. 404
Mamhead, Devon, 33, 44, 62, 94, 123, 173, 441
Manchester, 2, 11, 197, 392, 415
Mander, Theodore, 375–6
Manners family, 81
Manners, Lord John, 90
Manners-Sutton, John Henry, 224–5, 235
Mannington Hall, Norfolk, 115
Manor Heath, Halifax, 207–8, Pl. 196
Mantovani, Alessandro, 394
Manvers, Sydney W. H. Pierrepont, 3rd Earl, 421
Mapleton, Yorkshire, 440
Marks, Murray, 453
Marks, Stacy, 2, 28, 425, 428
Marnock, landscape architect, 416
Marsh, Jones & Crib, 414
Marshall, Major A. W., 438
Marshall, W., 441
Martin, John, 114
Martin, R. B., 411
Martinvast, Chateau de, France, 433
Marton, George, 400
Marton Hall, Yorkshire, 412
Mason family, 405
Mason, G. W., 438
Mason & Barry, 299, 405
Maw and Co., 404
Maxse, Admiral Frederick Augustus, 439
Mayfield, Kent, 412
Maynard, Henry Maynard, 3rd Viscount, 439
Melbury House, Dorset, 438, 441
Melbourne, William Lamb, 2nd Viscount, 36
Melchet Park, Hampshire, 437
Mentmore, Buckinghamshire, 19, 20, 23, 36, 38, 412, Pl. 406
Merevale Hall, Warwickshire, 17, 19, 120–8, 132, 233, Fig. 9, Pls. 92–103
Merrist Wood, Surrey, 398, Pl. 48
Messina, cathedral at, 280
Metcalfe, Charles, 438
Methley Hall, Yorkshire, 441
Mexborough, John Savile, 3rd Earl of, 441
Meynell-Ingram, H. F., 437
Mickleham Manor, Surrey, 440
Micklethwaite, Rev. J. N., 436
Middlesbrough, Yorkshire, 11, 407, 411, 412, 418, 423
Middleton, Lord, 441
Middleton, Sir William Fowle, Bart. 436
Midelney Place, Somerset, 441
Mildmay, Henry Bingham, 405
Millais, Sir John Everett, Bart., 314
Miller Christy family, 359
Millichope Park, Shropshire, 414
Milner, Sir William, Bart., 414
Milner Field, Yorkshire, 10, 37, 414, Pls. 7, 407
Milton Ernest Hall, Bedfordshire, 17, 58, 64, 179–86, Fig. 15, Pls. 162–72, Col. Pl. XVI

Milton Hall, Kent, 437
Milward, George, 411
Minley Manor, Hampshire, 60–61, 74, 292, 414, Pl. 32
Minton tiles, 119, 152, 178, 238, 278
Mitchell, Jasper, 437
Mocatta and Goldsmid, 11
Mochrum, Old Place of, Wigtownshire, 541
Moilliet, James, 392
Monkhams, Essex, 440
Monkshatch, Surrey, 438
Monserrate, Palacio, Portugal, 432
Montefiore family, 27
Montivoli, Giovanni, 394
Montreal, Kent, 440
Moore, Albert, 67, 72, 314
Moore, George, 18, 441
Moor Green, Nottinghamshire, 334
Moorside, Halifax, 212n.
Mordaunt, Sir Charles, Bart., 422
Moreby Hall, Yorkshire, 94, 441
Moreton Hall, Cheshire, 436
Morley family, 13
Morley, Samuel, 19n., 408
Morley, Francis, 398
Morris, William, 67, 68, 80, 86, 314, 321, 378, 418
Morris & Co., 312, 378, 379, 384, 386, 418
Morrison, James, 442
Morton Hall, Nottinghamshire, 438
Mostyn, Hon. Thomas Edward Lloyd, 440
Motcombe, Dorset, 82, 439
Mount Felix, Surrey, see under Walton House, Surrey
Mount Stuart, Isle of Bute, 451
Moxon, marbler and grainer, 421
Muckross House, Co. Kerry, 52, 430, Pls. 422, 427
Muncaster Castle, Cumberland, 414
Muncaster, Josslyn Francis Pennington, 5th Lord, 414
Munro, Alexander, 214
Muntham, Surrey, 442
Muntham, Sussex, 441
Murray, C. Scott, 441
Murray, James, 448
Musker, John, 204
Myddelton-Biddulph, Col. R., 440
Myers, George, 17, 172, 174, 176
Myton Grange, Warwickshire, 439

Narford Hall, Norfolk, 414
Nash, John, 64, 158, 160
Nasmyth, James, 215
Naundorff, decorative artist, 142
Naworth Castle, Cumberland, 441
Nawton Towers, Yorkshire, 436
Neeld, Joseph, 407
Nesbitt, A., 442
Nesfield, William Andrews, 71, 122, 167, 400, 421, 424
Nesfield, William Eden, 11, 18, 19, 20, 35, 46, 66, 67, 70–2, 73, 75, 78, 82, 83–4, 85, 312, 320–8, 376, 440
Netley Abbey, Hampshire, 414
Netley Hall, Shropshire, 439
Newcastle-on-Tyne, 11, 305
Newcastle-under-Lyme, Henry Pelham Archibald Douglas, 7th Duke of, 436
New Lodge, Berkshire, 414
Newman, Sir Ralph, Bart., 441
Newton Hall, Essex, 440
Nicholl, Iltyd, 442
Nicholls, Thomas, 280, 287, 341, 343–5, 414
Nicholson, William Adams, 104–5
Nicholson, Sir William, 67
Noble, John, 297
Norfolk, Henry Howard, 15th Duke of, 394, 439
Normanhurst, Sussex, 26, 43n., 294, 414, 444, Pl. 278
Normanton, J. C. H. W. E. Agar, 3rd Earl of, 437
Norris Castle, Isle of Wight, 147
North, Col. J. T., 43n., 397
North, North, 421

North Perrott Manor, Somerset, 443
North, Susan, Baroness, 439
North Mimms, Hertfordshire, 438
Northampton, Charles Compton, 3rd Marquess of, 329, 401
Northbourne, Lord, see under James, Sir Walter, Bart.
Northesk, George John Carnegie, 9th Earl of, 438
Northumberland, George Percy, 5th Duke of, 394
Norton, John, 18, 53, 66, 245–6, 440
Nucci, architectural sculptor, 394
Nun Appleton Hall, Yorkshire, 58, 65, 414, Pl. 37
Nuneham Paddox, Warwickshire, 294, 443
Nutfield Priory, Surrey, 10, 24, 38, 414

Oaklands, Hampshire now Lockerley Hall), 437
Oatlands House, Surrey, 438, 449
Oakmere Hall, Cheshire, 415
Ockwells, Surrey, 344
Old Warden House, Bedfordshire, 10, 415
Oldlands Hall, Sussex, 442
Orchardleigh House, Somerset, 10, 415
Orwell Park, Suffolk, 437
Osborne House, Isle of Wight, 17, 19, 20, 35, 36, 50, 147–52, 392, Fig. 12, Pls. 12, 120–5, Col. Pls. XII, XIII
Osmaston Hall, Derbyshire, 23, 26
Ossuna, Duchess of, 433
Ottery St. Mary, Devon, see under Chanter's House
Ould, Edward Augustus Lyle, 82, 375–7
Overbury Court, Worcestershire, 441
Overstone, Lord, 415
Overstone Park, Northamptonshire, 25, 26, 415
Oxford, Keble College, 182, 244
Oxhey Grange, Hertfordshire, 443
Oxonhoath, Kent, 292

Packe, Charles William, 138, 142
Paddockhurst, Sussex (now Worth Priory), 441
Page-Turner, Sir Edward, Bart., 292, 396
Paget, Sir Richard Horner, Bart., 443
Pain, James, 426
Pakenham Hall, Co. Westmeath (now Tullynally Castle), 23, 28n., Pl. 15
Paley, Edward Graham, 410, 438, 441
Paley and Austin, 410
Palmella, Duke of, 433
Palmer, Roundell, 1st Earl of Selborne, 397
Palmer, Sir Charles Mark, Bart., 407
Panshanger, Hertfordshire, 453
Pantglas, Carmarthenshire, 449
Paris, the Louvre, 292
Park Place, Oxfordshire, 297
Parker, Admiral George, 441
Parkinson, J., 376
Parnell and Smith, 207, 208
Parris, Edmund Thomas, 448
Parry, Thomas Gambier, 417
Parsons, Henry, 442
Parys Mine Company, The, 318
Patmore, Coventry, 352
Patterdale Hall, Westmorland, 441
Paul, Sir John Dean, Bart., 414
Paxton, Sir Joseph, Bart., 19, 24, 38, 210, 292, 440
Paxton & Stokes, 412
Payne, H. A., 412
Pearson, John Loughborough, 58, 62, 76, 112, 173, 174, 292, 452
Pease family, 11, 27
Pease, J. W., 411
Peckforton Castle, Cheshire, 34, 45, 52, 154–63, Fig. 13, Pls. 126–38
Peek, Sir Henry William, Bart., 13, 418
Peek, William, 449
Pell, Oliver Claude, 424
Pellechet, Jules, 296
Pemberton, Rev. Robert Norgrave, 414
Pembroke, George August Herbert, 11th Earl of, 432
Pencallmick House, Cornwall, 441
Penfold, Captain, 417

Penge Place, Surrey, 436
Penoyre House, Breconshire, 415, 449, Pl. 408
Penrhyn Castle, Carnarvonshire, 157
Penshurst, Kent, 83, 213-4 *and see under* Hammerfield, Redleaf and Swaylands
Penson, T. M., 374
Penzance, John Plaisted Wilde, 1st Lord, 412
Perry & Co., 127
Perry Hall, Staffordshire, 442
Peto, H. E., 439
Peto, Sir Samuel Morton, Bart., 10, 43n. 211-2, 416, 420
Petworth House, Sussex, 52, 441
Phelps, James, 442
Philadelphia, Pavilion, designed by Thomas Jeckell, shown at Philadelphia Exhibition, 1878, 368
Philips family, 11, 20, 392
Philips, Francis, 441
Philips, John Burton, 409
Philips, Mark, 423, 437
Phillipps de Lisle, Ambrose, 45, 113, 440
Phyffers, Theodore, Architectural sculptor, 416
Pickersgill, F. R., 415
Pierrepont, Surrey, 83, 359, 363, 416, Fig. 5
Pilgrim, Charles, 438
Pippbrook House, Surrey, 441
Pippingford Park Sussex, 295
Pite, Alfred Robert, 439
Pite, Beresford, 421
Pitt-Rivers, General, 442
Plas Dinam, Montgomeryshire, 416
Plas Kinmel, Denbighshire, 320, Pls. 301-3
Plas Power, Denbighshire, 439
Pleydell-Bouverie, Hon. Edward, 437
Plucknett of Warwick, furniture-maker, 246, 250
Plymouth, Robert George Windsor-Clive, 1st Earl of, 409
Pochin, H. P., 13, 398
Poland, Mansion in, 432
Poole, G. S., 440
Porcher, Charles, 402
Portland, W. J. A. C. J. Cavendish-Bentinck, 6th Duke of, 423
Portland, W. J. C. B. S. Cavendish-Bentinck, 5th Duke of, 423
Portman, Edward Berkeley Portman, 1st Viscount, 444
Portman, W. H. B. Portman, 2nd Viscount, 399
Possingworth Manor, Sussex, 416
Poundley & Walker, 392
Powell, Rhys D., 442
Powell and Son and Powell Brothers, stained glass makers, 401, 405, 415
Poynter, Sir Edward John, 38
Preen Manor, Shropshire, 441
Preston, Lancashire, 225
Preston Hall, Kent, 10, 416, 444
Preston, Henry, 441
Preston, Major J. W. 438
Preston, William, 404
Prestwold Hall, Leicestershire, 19, 138-42, Fig. 11, Pls. 113-9, Col. Pl. X
Price's Patent Candles, 179
Prichard, John, 58, 339, 405, 440
Prince of Wales, Albert Edward, later Edward VII, 68, 148, 208, 291, 314, 367, 374, 397, 398, 419, 422
Pritchett, J. T., 407
Prothero, Thomas, 442
Prugg in Bruck, Schloss, Austria, 432
Pugh, L. Pugh, 393
Pugin, Augustus Welby, 44-5, 46-8, 52, 58, 59-60, 76, 108, 110-6, 155, 166, 167, 169, 170, 173, 174, 176, 188, 189, 190, 245, 250, 348, 440, 445
True Principles of Pointed or Christian Architecture. Quoted 45, 47, 59, 110
Pugin, Edward Welby, 111, 117-9, 346-51, 353, 441
Pull Court, Worcestershire, 121, 417
Puxley family, 428
Pyrgo Park, Essex, 436, 441, 449

Quantock Lodge, Somerset, 417
Quar Wood, Gloucestershire, 62, 65, 165, 173, 292, 417, Pl. 36
Quy Hall, Cambridgeshire, 417

Radnor, Jacob Pleydell-Bouverie, 4th Earl of, 441
Raikes family, 164-5, 170
Raikes, Robert, 164, 170
Railton, William, 437
Ramsey Abbey, Huntingdonshire, 121, 417
Ramsgate, Granville Hotel, 347
Rawdon House, Hertfordshire, 439
Rebow, John, 425
Red House, The, *see under* Bexley Heath, Kent, and London
Redesdale, Algernon Bertrand Freeman-Mitford, 1st Lord, 396
Redleaf, Penshurst, 214, 450
Redrice House, Hampshire, 417
Rembrandt, 113-4
Rendcomb House, Gloucestershire, 11, 21, 37, 50, 417, 449, Pl. 6
Rendlesham, F. W. B Thellusson, 5th Lord, 236, 437
Rendlesham Hall, Suffolk, 437
Renshaw, Henry, 396
Repton, Humphry, 33
Revelstoke, Edward Charles Baring, 1st Lord, 402, 438
Revesby Abbey, Lincolnshire, 417
Reynolds of Bedford, Builder, 180
Rhinefield, Hampshire, 38, 417, Pls. 17, 409
Riber Castle, Derbyshire, 417
Ricardo, Henry, 439
Ricardo, Mortimer, 411
Richardson, C. J., 432
Richardson, Henry Hobson, 258
Richardson, Slade & Co., 414
Rickman, Thomas, 441
Riddell, F. H., 439
Ridgeway, J., 442
Rigg, Colonel, 441
Rimini, Tempio Malatestiano, 142
Ripley, Sir Henry William, Bart., 439
Robartes, Lord, 411
Robartes, Mr., 437
Robson, Edward Robert, 74, 225, 370
Rockingham Castle, Northamptonshire, 441
Rogers, William R., 302
Rolle, Hon. Mark George Kerr, 294
Rollo, John Rogerson Rollo, 10th Lord, 439
Romaine-Walker, W. H., 417
Rome, The Vatican loggias, 142, 150
Romoli (Pietro?), decorative painter, 242
Rosdohan, Co. Kerry, 440
Rosebery, Archibald Philip Primrose, 5th Earl of, 19n, 438
Rossetti, Dante Gabriel, 19, 67, 68, 275, 312, 314, 321, 453
Rothschild family, 11, 19n., 36n., 300
Rothschild, Alfred Charles de, 43n., 302
Rothschild, Miss Alice de, 438
Rothschild, Baron Alphonse de, 432
Rothschild, Constance de, 300
Rothschild, Baron Ferdinand de, 300
Rothschild, Baron James de, 432
Rothschild, Leo de, 452
Rothschild, Lionel de, 394
Rothschild, Baron Meyer Amschel de 412
Roundwick House, Sussex, 417, Pl. 410
Rounton Grange, Yorkshire, 11, 74, 381, 418, Pl. 411
Rousdon, Devon, 13, 20, 25, 82, 418, Pl. 9
Rowley-Conwy, C. G. H., 398
Royal Institute of British Architects, 16,
Roydon Hall, Kent, 439
Rushford, Norfolk, 198, 199
Rushmore, Wiltshire, 442
Ruskin, John, 58, 60, 86
The Seven Lamps of Architecture, 58, 375, 393
Russell, Matthew, 105, 441
Ruthin Castle, Denbighshire, 17, 419

Saillard, P., 13, 399
St. Alban's Court, Kent, 215, 219-22, Fig. 17, Pls. 209-13
St. Albans, W. A. A. de V. Beauclerk, 10th Duke of, 397
St. Aubyn, James Piers, 392, 419, 441
St. Aubyn, Sir John, Bart., later 1st Lord St. Levan, 419
St. Audries, Somerset, 419
St. Leonard's Hill, Berkshire, 13, 299, 419, Pls. 283-4
St. Margaret's House, Middlesex, 442
St. Michael's Mount, Cornwall, 419
S. Michel, Belgium, Chateau at, 432
Salisbury, Robert Arthur Talbot Cecil, 3rd Marquess of, 25n., 26, 85, 86
Salomons, Sir D. L., Bart., 398
Salt, Sir Titus, Bart., 10, 414
Saltaire, Yorkshire, 10
Salvin, Anthony, 18, 34, 44, 45, 48, 52, 53, 58, 61, 62, 71, 76, 94-5, 96, 98, 99, 105, 154, 157-63, 166, 173, 214, 292, 441
Sandbach, H. R., 11, 408
Sandhoe House, Northumberland, 438
Sandon Hall, Staffordshire, 437
Sandringham House, Norfolk, 368, 374, 419
Sang, Frederick, 142, 400
Sartoris, C., 438
Saunders and Co., 280, 414
Scarisbrick, Ann, Lady, 115-9
Scarisbrick, Charles, 110-19
Scarisbrick Hall, Lancashire, 44, 47, 108, 110-19, 167, 176, 351, Fig. 8, Pls. 80-91, Col. Pls. VII-IX
Schultz, Weir, 451
Scotney Castle, Kent, 44, 52, 62, 174, 441, Pl. 34
Scott, George Gilbert, Junior, 225, 446
Scott, Sir George Gilbert, 6, 11, 18, 21, 48, 59, 67, 71, 74, 78, 224-35, 408, 411, 441
Secular and Domestic Architecture, 18, 69, 224-5
Quoted, 4-5, 21, 46, 53, 60, 78, 154-5, 227, 233
Scott, John, 436
Scott, Sir Walter, 13, 23, 24, 93, 108
Scrivener, Robert, 398
Seacox Heath, Sussex, 419
Sedding, John Dando, 414, 423
Seddon, John Pollard, 393, 440
Sefton, William Philip Molyneux, 4th Earl of, 392
Selborne, 1st Earl of, 176.
Sendholme, Surrey, 438
Seyfsal Asphalt Co., 448
Seymour, Alfred, 437
Sezincote, Gloucestershire, 15, 35
Shabden, Surrey, 297, 299, 420. Pl. 412
Shadwell Park, Norfolk, 17, 30, 58, 64, 65, 112n., 194-204, Fig. 16, Pls. 181-91, Col. Pls. XIV, XV
Sharpe, Edmund, 400, 410, 438, 441
Shaw, Richard Norman, 11, 18, 19, 20, 37, 46, 66, 68, 70-3, 74, 75-7, 78, 79, 80, 82, 83, 84, 85, 86, 305, 307-14, 321, 322, 331, 359-64, 376, 382, 441
Shaw-Savill Shipping Line, The, 70, 72, 74
Shephallbury, Hertfordshire, 442
Shepherd's Spring, Hampshire, 438
Sheringham Hall, Norfolk, 33, 123
Shields, Frederick, 2
Shiplake Court, Oxfordshire, 420, Pl. 413
Shipley Hall, Derbyshire, 320
Shipley, Conway, 442
Shirley, Evelyn Philip, 405
Shobrook House, Devon, 438
Shortlands, Kent, the Corner House, 359
Shotwick Park, Cheshire, 438
Shrewsbury, Henry John Chetwynd Talbot, 18th Earl of, 436
Shrewsbury, John Talbot, 16th Earl of, 44, 113, 176, 394
Shrubb, C. P., 398
Shrubb, J. L., 398, 441
Shrubland Park, Suffolk, 436
Shuffrey, L. A., 379
Shuttleworth, Joseph, 415
Sidbury Manor House, Devon, 436
Silverton Park, Devon, 420
Silwood Park, Buckinghamshire, 442

Simonstone Hall, Yorkshire, 437
Simpson and Son, 278, 343, 420
Singh, Maharajah Bahadur, Sir Duleep, 404
Singh, Bhai Rani, 152
Sitwell, W. Hurt, 440
Skidmore, Francis Alexander, 202, 405
Skipper, Charles, 440
Skutterskelf House, Yorkshire (now Levengrove), 441
Slater, William, 437
Smallwood Manor, Staffordshire, 25, 438, 445
Smeaton, heating and ventilating engineer, 418
Smeaton Manor, Yorkshire, 85, 420, Pl. 57
Smedley, John, 417
Smetham, James, 275
Smirke, Sir Robert, 19, 21, 445
Smith family, bankers, 11, 19n., 407, 438
Smith, Eric C., 438
Smith, George, of Bradford, 401
Smith, George, of Paddockhurst, 441
Smith, H. Lyle, 438
Smith, Lt.-Gen. P., 438
Smith, Raynard, 400
Smith, Robert Abel, 407
Smith, T. Roger, 441
Smith, W. H., 420
Smith, William, 148
Smith-Barry, J. H., 292, 441
Smythe, Rev. W., 440
Snell, W. and E., 127
Sneyd, Ralph, 411
Solomon, Simeon, 67, 275, 322n.
Somerley, Hampshire, 437
Somerleyton Hall, Suffolk, 10, 23, 34, 38, 43, 43n., 50, 211–2, 420, Pls. 18, 201–2
Somerset, Duke of, 438
Sompting Abbots, Sussex, 421
South Park, Kent, 214, 441
South Rauceby Hall, Lincolnshire, 437
Southampton, Charles Fitzroy, 3rd Lord, 437
Southill, Bedfordshire, 33, 35
Southwick Hall, Northamptonshire, 361
Sparrow, Arthur, 441
Spencer-Stanhope, J. R., 374
Spender-Clay Joseph, 271, 406
Spicer, J. G. W., 437
Spiers, R. Phené, 295
Spye Park, Wiltshire, 437
Stalbridge, Lord, 439
Stancliffe Hall, Derbyshire, 26, 421
Standen, Sussex, 381–9, Fig. 30, Pls. 367–77, Col. Pl. XXXII
Stanfield, Clarkson, 421
Stanmore Hall, Shropshire, 24
Stapleton family, 346
Starey family, 179
Starey, Benjamin Helps, 179–81
Stephens, Lyne, 412
Stevens, Alfred, 314
Stevens, H. J., 24
Stevens, J. C. Moore, 424
Stevenson, John J., 67, 70–1, 74, 75, 225, 370–4
House Architecture, 23, 65, 69, 370–1
Stevenstone, Devon, 294
Stewart, J. G., 441
Stewart, W. M., 441
Stoke Rochford Hall, Lincolnshire, 22, 138, 421
Pl. 24
Stokes, G. H., 210, 292, 396, and see under Paxton and Stokes
Stokesay Court, Shropshire, 25, 421, 445
Stoodleigh Court, Devon, 82, 439
Stoughton Grange, Leicestershire, 437
Stourton, Charles Stourton, 19th Lord, 394
Stourton Hall, Yorkshire, see under Allerton Hall
Stow Hall, Norfolk, 436
Stowell Park, Gloucestershire, 421
Stradbroke, J. E. C. Rous, 2nd Earl of, 436
Stratfield Saye House, Hampshire, 23
Stratton Audley Park, Oxfordshire, 442
Strazza, architectural sculptor, 394
Streatfield, Rev. H. W., 215n.
Street, George Edmund, 55, 58, 71, 225, 234, 394
Strutt, Edward, later 1st Lord Belper, 436
Stydd House, Kent, 438

Sudeley Castle, Gloucestershire, 407
Sudeley, Thomas Charles Hanbury Tracy, 2nd Lord, 407
Summers Place, Sussex, 440
Surtees, Lady, 438
Surtees, Robert Smith, quoted, 45
Sutherland, Duchess of, 51, 90, 149
Sutherland, George Granville Leveson-Gower, 2nd Duke of, 51, 90, 149, 402, 422, 430
Sutherland, George Granville William Leveson-Gower, 3rd Duke of, 19n.
Swan, Joseph, 306
Swanbourne, Buckinghamshire, 437
Swaylands, Kent, 17, 438
Swinburne, Algernon Charles, 275
Sykes, Christopher, 398

Taine, Hippolyte, 6
Talbert, Bruce, 75
Talbot Bury, Thomas, 414
Tangley Manor, Surrey, 442
Tankerville, Charles Augustus Bennet, 5th Earl of, 422
Taplow Court, Buckinghamshire, 318, 421
Tarver, Edward John, 422, 433
Taunton family, of Freelands, 164, 165
Taunton, Henry Labouchere, 1st Lord, 417
Taverham Hall, Norfolk, 436
Temple, J. W., 72
Templetown, John Henry Upton, 1st Viscount, 430
Tenerani, Pietro, 134
Tennant family, 81
Tennant, Margot, Asquith, later Margot, Countess of Oxford and Asquith, 79
Tennyson and Tennyson d'Eyncourt families, 103–6
Tennyson, Alfred, 1st Lord, 103, 104, 109, 394
Quoted, 14, 56
Tennyson d'Eyncourt, Charles, 103–9, 115
Teplitz, Elizabethan villa at, 432
Terry, Ellen, 67, 330
Tettenhall, Staffordshire, 26
Teulon family, 203
Teulon, Samuel Sanders, 18, 19, 58, 64–5, 67, 112n., 194, 198–204, 397, 405, 442
Teulon, William Milford, 415
Thellusson, Charles Sabine, 236–7, 242
Thellusson Will, The, 236
Thicket Priory, Yorkshire, 436
Thomas, John, 50, 212, 416, 442
Thomas, William Broderick, 397, 409, 415, 420
Thompson, C. C., 235
Thomson, James, 407
Thoresby Hall, Nottinghamshire, 20, 28, 54, 61, 421, Pls. 27, 414
Thorneycroft, Lt. Colonel, 26
Thorneycroft, Mary, 150
Thornham Hall, Suffolk, 440
Thorpe Abbotts, Norfolk, 436, 449
Thurland Castle, Lancashire, 421
Thurlow, Rev. Thomas, 438
Thurston, Messrs., 150
Tiarks, Henry, 436
Tilston Lodge, Cheshire, 156
Timbrill, Rev. J., 440
Times, The, 263, 268, 272
Toddington Manor, Gloucestershire, 15, 33, 35
Todmorden, Lancashire, 404
Tollemache, John Tollemache, 1st Lord, 154–6, Pl. 127
Tomline, George, 437
Torr, John, 442
Tortworth, Court, Gloucestershire, 23, 24, 26, 64, 422, Pl. 38
Tower, Walter, 377
Tranby Croft, Yorkshire, 10, 374
Travis & Magnall, 393
Treberfydd, Breconshire, 58, 112, 164–70, 174, Pls. 141–50
Tregothnan, Cornwall, Pl. 33
Trelawny, H., 438
Trentham Hall, Staffordshire, 29, 35, 48, 51, 131, 148, 149, 422, Fig. 4, Pl. 22
Treverbyn Vean, Cornwall, 437
Trollope and Sons, 17

Trollope, Anthony, 291n., 299
Tronquois, Auguste, 295
Troyte, C. A. W., 438
Tullynally Castle, Co. Westmeath, see under Pakenham Hall
Turnor, Christopher, 421
Turton, Captain E., 439
Twyford Manor, Hampshire 442
Tyntesfield, Somerset, 13, 17, 24, 26, 36, 243–51, 445, Pls. 8, 229–40

Unwin-Heathcote, U., 442
Upsall Castle, Yorkshire, 439

Vallance, Henry, 405
Van de Weyer, Jean Sylvain, 414
Vane, Lord Harry George, later 4th Duke of Cleveland, 437
Vane, Sir H., Bart., 441
Vaughan family, of Middlesbrough, 11
Vaughan, John, 407, 412
Vaughan, Thomas, architect, 439
Vaughan, Thomas, of Gunnergate Hall, 38, 407
Vaughan-Watkins, Col. Lloyd, 415
Victoria, Queen, 19, 147–152
Viney Hill, Gloucestershire, 437
Viollet-le-Duc, Eugene Emanuel, 71, 189–91
Visconti, Louis Tullius Joachim, 292
Vivian, Mr., 437
Vorontzov family, see under Worontzow
Voysey, Rev. Charles, 84n., 215n.
Voysey, Charles Francis Annesley, 84n. 215n.
Vrams, Gunnarstrop, Sweden, 432
Vulliamy, George, 433
Vulliamy, Lewis, 423, 442

Waddesdon Manor, Buckinghamshire, 300, Pl. 285, Col. Pl. XXIV
Wadhurst Park, Sussex, 26, 422
Wakefield Lodge, Northamptonshire, 440
Wakefield, Yorkshire, 366
Walker, Burges & Cooper, 273, 274
Walmer Castle, Kent, 438, Pl. 54
Walter, John, 17–18, 26, 263–8, 271–2, Pl. 254
Walter-Munro, Lieut. L., 417
Walton Hall, Warwickshire, 422
Walton Hall, Lancasture, 441
Walton House, Surrey, 50, 148, 414, Pl. 23
Ward, James, 242
Ward, Neville, 438
Ward, Robert Edward, 437, 441
Ward, Wilfred, 441
Warlies Park, Essex, 442
Warter Priory, Yorkshire, 10, 423
Warwick Castle, Warwickshire, 441
Washington Hall, Durham, 11, 423
Waterhouse, Alfred, 2, 10, 21, 29, 82, 157, 294
Watkins-Wynn, Sir William, Bart., 426
Watney, H., 442
Watson, J. E. 296
Watson, Hon. R., 441
Watt, W. F., 438
Watts, George Frederick, 3, 214
Watts, James, 393
Wauldby, Yorkshire, 165
Webb, Benjamin, 174
Webb, John, 176, 178
Webb, Philip, 11, 18, 19, 66, 67, 70–1, 74, 79–82, 83, 86, 186, 381–9, 418, 442
Weekes, Decorative artist, 414
Welbeck Abbey, Nottinghamshire, 423
Welby-Gregory, Sir William Earle, Bart., and Lady, Pl. 4
Welcombe, Warwickshire, 423, 437, 444
Wellington, Arthur Wellesley, 1st Duke of, 23
Wellington College, Berkshire, 268n.
Wells, William, 443, 450
Weltz, Livonia, Chateau at, 432
Wemyss, Francis Richard Charteris, 10th Earl of, 431
Wendover Manor, Buckinghamshire, 438
Wenlock, Paul Beilby Lawley, 1st Lord, 121
Wern, The, Caernarvonshire, 438
West, Benjamin, 114
West family, of Ruthin Castle, 17, 419
West Wickham House, Kent, 75, 441

Westlake, N. H. J., 352
Westminster, Hugh Lupus Grosvenor, 1st Duke of, 2–4, 8, 14, 294, Pl. 2
Westminster, Marchioness of, Elizabeth Mary Leveson-Gower, wife of 2nd Marquess, 443
Westminster, Richard Grosvenor, 2nd Marquess of, 52, 406
Weston Manor House, Isle of Wight, 423
Westonbirt House Gloucestershire, 17, 20, 26, 52, 423, Pl. 415
Westroof Hall, Staffordshire, 439
Westwood House, Sydenham, Kent, 452
Westwood House, Staffordshire, 439
Whalley-Tooker, Mr., 437
Wharncliffe, E. M. S. G. Montague-Stuart-Wortley-Mackenzie, 1st Earl of, 437
Whistler, James McNeill, 67, 112n., 367, 416
Whitaker, Henry, 150
Whitbourne Hall, Herefordshire, 424
White, William, 58, 64, 65, 67, 173, 253–62, 397, 417
White, William H., 433
Whitehall, Cumberland, 18, 441
Whitley, J. H. A., 441
Whittlebury, Hampshire, 437
Whitworth, Sir Joseph, 421
Wightwick Manor, Staffordshire, 82, 375–9, 445, Fig. 29, Pls. 361–8, Col. Pl. XXXII
Wilburton Manor House, Cambridgeshire, 424
Wilcote Manor, Oxfordshire, 438
Wildman, Thomas, 447
Wilkins, William, 138
Wilkinson, Philip, 237
Wilkinson, William, 433
Willement, Thomas, 446, 448
Willesley, Kent, 72, 73, 308

Williams, Isaac, 394
Williams, West, & Slade, 394
Willcox, George, of Warwick, 421
Wilshire, William, 436
Wilson family, of Hull, 10, 374
Wilson, Anthony, 437
Wilson, Arthur, 374
Wilson, Charles Henry, 423
Wilson, Henry, 423
Wimperis, J. T., 431
Winchester, John Paulet, 14th Marquess of, 437
Winmarleigh Hall, Lancashire, 441
Winmarleigh, John Wilson Patten, 1st Lord, 441
Winn, Hon. Rowland, 428
Winscott, Devon, 36, 424, Pl. 416
Wise, H. C., 439
Witham, Rev. Thomas, 439
Witley Court, Worcestershire, 176, 424, Pl. 378
Witley Park, Surrey, 38n.
Wivenhoe Hall, Essex, 425
Wokingham, Berkshire, St. Paul's Church, 268
Wollaton Hall, Nottinghamshire, 132, 414, 424
Wolverton, George Grenfell Glyn, 2nd Lord, 10, 411
Wood House, The, Essex, 377
Woodbastwick Hall, Norfolk, 437
Woodchester Park, Gloucestershire, 188–93, Pls. 173–80
Woodcote Hall, Shropshire, 425, 439
Woodcote, Warwickshire, 446
Woodlands Park, Surrey, 445
Woodlands Vale, Isle of Wight 442
Woodward, Benjamin, 412
Woodyer, Henry, 250, 268, 442
Wooldridge, H. E., stained glass designer, 250
Worcester, 424

Worden Hall, Lancashire, 441
Wormleighton & Wise, 404
Woronzow family, 432, 433
Worsley Hall, Lancashire, 51, 121, 424
Worth Park, Sussex, 27
Worth Priory, Sussex (formerly Paddockhurst), 441
Wortley Hall, Yorkshire, 38
Wotton House, Surrey, 442
Wrest Park, Bedfordshire, 100, 292, 425
Wright, Francis, 24, 26
Wright, Whitaker, 38n.
Wroxton Abbey, Oxfordshire, 439
Wyatt, Matthew Digby, 401, 416, 442, 451
Wyatt, Samuel, 318
Wyatt, Thomas Henry, 18, 53, 59, 394, 400, 415, 442
Wyatville, Sir Jeffry, 64, 439
Wyfold Court, Oxfordshire, 10, 425, Pl.5
Wygfair, Flintshire, 438
Wykehurst Park, Sussex, 17, 22, 23, 25, 26, 37, 297–8, 300, 425, Pls. 281–2
Wyndham family, 81
Wyndham, George, 4
Wyndham, Percy Scawen, Hon., 80, 81, 85, 381, 453
Wynnstay, Denbighshire, 292, 426, Pl. 417

Yattendon Court, Berkshire, 426, Pl. 418
Yeates, Alfred B., 439
Yonge, Charlotte M., 14, 15, 38, 52, 244–5
Yonge family, 244
Yorke, John Reginald, 442
Young England, 13, 90, 93, 263
Young, William, 405, 443

Zimdah, Bell supplier, 418

SUBJECT INDEX

Accommodation in the Victorian country house, 27–30; *and see under* Billiard room, Business room, Chapel, Cloakroom, Conservatory, Gun room, Hall, Kitchen, Laundry, Library, Music room, Picture gallery, Saloon, Servants' hall, Serving room, Smoking room; *and see also under* Appurtenances

Agricultural depression in the late 19th century, 9, 86, 204, 235, 354

Americans, appalled by English discomfort, 27n.

Antique fittings, etc., incorporated into Victorian houses, 298, at Bayons, 447, Scarisbrick, 114, Wykehurst and Waddesdon, 298, Mentmore, 414, Revesby, 417, Westonbirt, 424, Adare, 426

Appurtenances to the Victorian country house, *see under* Aviary, Boat-house, Bowling-alley, Dairy, Dove-cot, Farm, Fives-court, Kitchen-garden, Maze, Observatory, Orangery, Roof-garden, Skating-rink, Stable, Temple, Winter-garden

Arabic style, the, at Breadsall, 38, Cardiff, 288, Rhinefield, 417, Jerez, 432

Architects of country houses abroad, employed, 432
  amateurs, 16
  architect as artist, 67–8, 70
  artists' friendships with, 275
  choice of, reasons for, 17–18, 225, 274, 320, 307, 329, 381
  foreign, employed to design English houses, *see in the main index under* Canina, Casentini, Destailleur, Horeau, Montivoli, Pellechet, Tronquois
  furniture designed by Butterfield, 186, Chapple, 345, Godwin, 428, Pearson, 170, Pugin, 170, 393, 429, Shaw, 452–3, 312, Waterhouse, 397, White, 262
  political and social affiliations of, 18–19
  professionalism, increased, of, 16
  social background of, 67, 70–1
  and see under Law suits

Armour, at Bayons, 108, Scarisbrick, 114

Armoury, at Carlton, 353

'Artistic', concept of the, 67–8, 69, 375, 378–9

Artists and craftsmen, *see under* Decorative artists, Furniture makers and designers, Interior decorators, Landscape architects, Metalworkers and designers, Plasterers, Stained glass makers and designers, Stone carvers and architectural sculptors, Tile makers, Woodcarvers

Asphalt, used for roofs at Peckforton, 448

Aviary, at Waddesdon, 300, Chanter's House, 401, Somerleyton, 421

Basements, go out of favour, 31; defended by the architect at Humewood, 258; bathrooms in, at Cragside, 309; unpleasant, at Wykehurst, 298

Bathroom, *see under* Plumbing

Bells: wire-operated, 25; pneumatic, 25, at Cardiff, 280, Rousdon, 418; electric, 25, at Hewell, 409

Billiard room, 35–8, at Highclere, 134, Prestwold, 140, Brodsworth, 237, 242, Tyntesfield, 246, Cragside, 317, Carlton, 352, Standen, 380, Flete, 405; underwater, at Witley, 38n. lined with marble at Avery Hill, 394; modelled on Abbot's Kitchen, Glastonbury, at Hafodunos, 408; billiard table of iron, at Stancliffe, 421

'Blue China', 321–2, 379, 416, 453

Boat-house at Milton Ernest, 181, Tortworth, 422

Bowling alley at Rousdon, 418, Sandringham, 419

Brick, exposed, comes back into fashion, 19, 57–8; brick chimneypiece at Beauvale, 332; brick and terracotta house at Foxwarren, 406, Yattendon, 426; 'Queen-Anne' a red-brick style, 75; white brick at Canford, 400; *and see under* Polychromy, structural

Building contractors, *see in the main index under* Thomas Cubitt, William Cubitt and Co., Estcourt, Hale and Son, Holland and Hannen, Albert Kimberley, George Myers, Reynolds, Trollope and Sons

Building methods, at country houses, 17

Business room, 32, 33, at Horsted, 178, Milton Ernest, 184

Carpet manufacturers, *see in the main index under* Crossleys, Lapworths

Castles, Victorian, 155, 157; Fenians, a pretext for building at Dromore and Humewood, 259, 331

Cavity walls, 26, at Wykehurst, 298, Shabden, 299, Milner Field, 414, Overstone, 415; failure of, at Dromore, 26

Ceramics, decorative use of, at Cragside, 314; Dromore, 428; *and see* 'Blue China'

Chapels, private, at Eaton Hall, 2, Scarisbrick, 110, Peckforton, 158, Woodchester, 191, Tyntesfield, 246, 250, Kinmel, 324, Alton Castle and Towers, 394, Arley, 394, Bedgebury, 397, Bishops-court, 397, Hope End, Horsley, 410, Madresfield, 412, Minley, 414, Tyntesfield, 244, 250, Weston, 423, Killarney, 428, Dunecht, 430

Chivalry, Victorian, 13–14; chivalrous gestures at Killyleagh, 428

Classical styles, losing favour for country houses, 52–3; French high-roof style, the classicists answer to the Gothic revival, 64, 293; classicists infuriated by 'Queen Ann', 75; *and see under* French, Greek, Neo-Georgian

Cloakrooms, 34

Cloisters, at Horsley, 410, Rousdon, 418

Colour in Victorian country houses, 55; Pugin and, 115; at Kelham, 234, Brodsworth, 238, 240, Cardiff, 275–90, Carlton, 353, Castell Coch, 341–5; Webb in reaction against polychromy at Clouds, 81, Standen, 384; *and see* Polychromy, structural

Concrete, 20–1, 407; used for foundations, at Shabden, 299; *and see under* Fireproof construction

Conservatory, 19, 38, 43, at Harlaxton, 96, Prestwold, 138, 140, Treberfydd, 167, 169, Tyntesfield, 246, Normanhurst, 295, Standen, 384, 388, Bestwood, 397, Chanter's House, 401, Hafodunos, 408, Nutfield, 415, Penoyre, 415, Westonbirt, 424; planned but never built at Highclere, 131, Brodsworth, 238, Kelham, 235; *and see* Winter Garden

Construction, *see under* cavity walls, Damp courses, Fireproof construction, half-timbering, Roofs, Vaulting, Windows

Cost of houses, *see under* Wealth

Creeper, deliberate use of, 394

Dairies, specialized in by W. E. Nesfield, 320

Damp course, at Shabden, 299

Decoration, *see under* Artists and craftsmen, Colour, Embroidery, Graining, Heraldry, Inscriptions, Lead, Leather, Lilies, Marble, Marbling, Marquetry and inlay, Metalwork, Mosaics, 'Pies', Plasterwork, Polychromy, Sculpture architectural, Stained glass, Statuary, Sun-flowers, Tiles, Wall and ceiling painting, Wallpapers, Wood carving

Decorative artists, *see in the main index number* Thomas Armstrong, Randolph Caldecott,

Campbell and Smith, J. G. Crace, G. P. Harding, Holzmann, Gertrude Jekyll, Owen Jones, Levaux, H. N. Lonsdale, Mantovani, Stacy Marks, Albert Moore, Naundorff, E. T. Parris, E. J. Poynter, Romoli, Frederick Sang, Weekes

Designs, principles of, in Victorian country houses, *see under* Functionalism, Geometry, Nature, Picturesque, Skyline, Symmetry

Double glazing, at Cranfield, 26, in Poland, 432

Dove-cots at Kinmel, 320, Cloverley, 402

Electricity: electric sewing machine and gongs at Cragside, 307; *see also under* Bells and Lighting

Elizabethan style, the, 52–3, 86, 93–4, muscularity and, 56; Blore and, 121

Embroidery, frieze of at Rounton, 418

Entrances to the country house, 31; luggage entrance, the, 33, at Bear Wood, 271; main entrance at end instead of centre of house, 123

Family suite or wing, the, 28, 33; family suite at Peckforton, 163, Bear Wood, 271; Family wing at Eaton Hall, 4, Osborne, 149, Bryanston, 399, Overstone, 415, Stoke Rochford 421, Worsley, 425

Farm, Roundwick, a manor-farm, 417

Farm buildings: decorative, at Kinmel, 320; impressive, at Quantock, 417; nightmarish, at Foxwarren, 406–7; next to house at Milton Earnest, 186, Kelham, 226, Arisaig, 430

Farm-house, old, incorporated in house at Standen, 383, Broxton, 398

Fire hydrants at Normanhurst, 26,, 295, Bayham, 396, Tyntesfield, 251

Fireproof construction, 20, 26, at Osborne, 152, Kelham, 225, Tyntesfield, 251, Bear Wood, 268, Wykehurst, 298, Berechurch, 397, Dawpool, 403, Grittleton, 407, Heath, 409, Hemsted, 409, Hope End, 410, Millichope, 414, Normanhurst, 414, Rendcomb, 417, Thoresby, 421, at Westonbirt, 424; failures of, 26, at Normanhurst, 414

Fives-court, at Rousdon, 418

Flint, used at Shadwell, 199–200, Bettesshanger, 218, Crawley, 403, Horsley, 410, New Lodge, 414, Rousdon, 418

French high roof style, the, 64, 291–302, 325

Functionalism: external expression of internal uses as a basis for design, 46–8, 59–61, 64, 65

Furniture makers and designers, *see in the main index, under* J. G. Crace, Dowbiggin, Gillows, Aldam Heaton, Hollands, Marsh Jones and Crib, Plucknett, Thurston, W. & E. Snell, John Webb, Henry Whitaker; *and see also under* Architects, furniture designed by

Gas, *see under* Lighting

Gates, *see under* Metalwork

Gate-houses, at Merevale, 122, Possingworth, 416, Quantock Lodge, 417, Killyleagh Castle, 428

Gentleman, the Victorian, 2–6; ideals behind, 13–15, 32–3, 45, 56; kind of house considered suitable for, 15–16, 51, 53, 54, 59; 'Queen Anne' not gentlemanly, 75; Bayons 'so very gentlemanlike', 106; *and see under* Chivalry

Geometry as a basis for design, 56; the diagonal, 62, 174; the triangle, 65; White and the equilateral triangle, 255; 60° roofs at Beauvale, 332

Glass: plate glass, 21–2, 27, at Merevale, 448, Peckforton, 448, Kelham, 226; silvered glass, used decoratively at Elveden, 404–5; glass inlaid in ceiling, at Cardiff, 278; *and see under* Double glazing, Stained glass, and Windows

Gothic style, the 54–5; shift of taste to early
and foreign brands, 55; religious basis of
Gothic revival, 66; reaction against, by
younger Gothic architects, 66–7; Gothic as
stone construction carried to extremes at
Woodchester, 190; Butterfield and Gothic,
181–2; Burges and Gothic, 274–5
Graining, increasingly disapproved of, 48; at
Adcote, 454, Somerleyton, 421
Granite, used at Humewood, 255, St. Michael's
Mount, 419, Winscott, 424, Invercauld, 431
Grates, see under Metalwork
Greek style, the, at Leonardslee, 411, Millichope,
414, Redrice, 417, Silverton, 420,
Whitbourne, 424
Gun room, 37, at Cragside, 317, Hemsted, 409

Half timbering
revival of, by Shaw and Nesfield, 72–3; by
Devey, 83; in Chester, 375; Habershon
family and, 439
with concrete infilling, at the Highlands,
21; imitated in metal and concrete, at
Gregynog. 407
at Cragside, 312, Beauvale, 322, Wightwick,
376–7, Ascott, 394, Broxton, 398, Coombe
Warren, 402, Cowdray, 403, Madresfield,
412, Malwood, 412, Pierrepont, 416,
Roundwick, 418
Hall
used for billiards, 35, 44
Great Hall, revival of the, 43–6, at Harlaxton,
96, Bayons, 45, 105, Scarisbrick, 112,
Peckforton, 162–3, Adcote, 363, Hall, 408,
Horsley, 410, Keele, 411, Knightshayes,
411, Nutfield, 415, Possingworth, 416,
Rousdon, 418, Shiplake, 420, Somerleyton,
421, Thoresby, 421 Wynnstay, 426, Adare,
426, Lismore, 428
living room, used as, 46, 78–9, at
Betteshanger, 218, Ken Hill, 370–1,
Wightwick, 379, Loughton, 411, Plas
Dinam, 416, and see under Saloon
music, used for, at Shadwell, 198, Kelham,
233–4, Standen, 387, Nutfield, 415
sporting tackle hung in, 37
tea, used for, 79, at Standen, 387
Heating, central, 23–4, 27
at Peckforton, 163, Bear Wood, 268,
Bayham, 396, Hope End, 410, Overstone,
415, Possingworth, 416, Rousdon, 418,
Westonbirt, 424
by hot air, 23–4, at Harlaxton, 102, Kelham,
226, Wykehurst, 298, Shabden, 299,
Grittleton, 407, Nutfield, 415, Tortworth,
422, Welbeck, 423
by hot water, 23, at Cragside, 307, Standen,
386, Chanter's House, 401, Mentmore, 414
by steam, 23
English, considered insufficient by Americans,
27n.
centrally heated stables, at Avery Hill, 396
coal and wood brought in by railway at
Harlaxton, 102
and see under Radiators
Heraldry, at Carlton, 353
Hotels, influence on country house design,
293–4
Hydraulic lifts at Alnwick and Cragside, 25,
306, Tyntesfield, 251
Hydraulic machinery at Cragside, 306–7

Indian style, at Osborne, 152, Elveden, 404–5
Inglenooks, 27, 73, 77–8, at Cragside, 312, 314,
Adcote, 364, Wightwick, 378, 379,
Bodrhyddan, 398, Dawpool, 403, Pierrepont,
416, Rousdon, 418, Gosford, 431
Inscriptions, 72, 112n., at Scarisbrick, 112n.,
Shadwell, 202, Cragside and Cloverley, 312,
Hall, 408
Interior decorators, see in the main index under J.
G. Crace, Greenard of Paris, Harland and
Sons, Aldam Heaton, C. E. Kempe,
Lapworths, John Webb; and see also
Decorative artists
Iron, 19–20, 189

iron beams, etc., used at Merevale, 121,
Prestwold, 140, Adcote, 454, Shabden, 420,
Westonbirt, 424; exposed and decorated at
Kelham, 225
iron billiard table, at Stancliffe, 421
and see Fireproof construction

Japanese influence, 70; Shaw and Nesfield and,
76, 321–2; Jeckell, and 369
at Cloverley, 72, Kinmel, 325, Cragside, 312,
Dromore, 427

Kitchen, 30, at Osborne, 152; only place guests
allowed to smoke at St. Alban's Court, 219n.;
next to billiard room at Brodsworth, 237;
modelled on Abbot's Kitchen, Glastonbury,
at Scarisbrick, 116, Hatherop, 408, Milner
Field, 414
Kitchen-garden, romantic, at Castle Ashby, 331,
401

Landscape architects, see in the main index under
Edward Kemp, Marnock, W. A. Nesfield,
W. B. Thomas
Landscape setting, 73; the house in forest as
alternative to house in the park, 74
Laundry, 30; functionally sub-divided at
Humewood, 259
Law suits, over Swaylands, 17, Humewood,
253–4; threatened at Bear Wood, 272,
Glenbegh, 428; E. W. Pugin and, 347
Lead, used ornamentally by Nesfield at
Cloverley, 72, Kinmel, 325, Plas Dinam, 416
Leather, imitated in plaster on walls of Carlton,
353; stamped leather walls at Bodrhyddan,
398
Library: 'a sort of morning room for
gentlemen', 35; used as main family living-
room at Cragside, 312–13; especially elaborate
at Bayons, 105, Cardiff, 288, Chanter's House,
401, Flintham, 406, Madresfield, 412,
Dunecht, 430; little altered at Treberfydd,
169; joke titles on false book-fronts at
Rendcomb, 417
Lifts, at Kelham, 226, Tyntesfield, 251,
Wykehurst, 298, Bayham, 396, Overstone,
415, Tortworth, 422; and see under Hydraulic
Lighting, 24–5;
by electricity, 25, 27; pioneered at Cragside,
306, 314, Hatfield, 25; houses lit by, before
1890, 445; fittings designed by Webb, at
Standen, 386–7; considered vulgar, by upper
classes, 27
by gas, 24, 27, at Kelham, 225–6, Bear Wood,
268, Adcote, 453, Bayham, 396, Flintham,
406, Grittleton, 407, Hemsted, 409, Nutfield,
415, Overstone, 415, Sandringham, 419,
Tortworth, 422, Tyntesfield, 251,
Westonbirt, 424, Welbeck, 423; supplied to
village at Lismore, 24, Kelham, 225–6,
Flintham, 406; gaslights at Flixton, Pl. 13,
Abney, Pl. 379, Dobroyd, Pl. 394
by oil, 25; Argand lights at Merevale, 127;
oil-lamps at Cragside, 314, Thoresby, 421
Local traditions, followed at Woodchester, 191,
Betteshanger, 218, Standen, 383; disregarded
at Cragside, 312; and see Vernacular
architecture
Luxury as a nouveau-riche attribute, 27; Mary
Gladstone oppressed by, at Waddesdon,
300

Male preserve, the, 34–8, and see under Billiard
room and Smoking room
Marble used decoratively at Cardiff, 280,
Kinmel, 328, Cragside, 314, Avery Hill, 394,
Gosford, 431, Jerez de la Frontera, 432
Marbling, increasingly disapproved of, 48; at
Prestwold, 142, Brodsworth, 238,
Somerleyton, 420
Marquetry and inlay at Bear Wood, 271,
Cardiff, 288, Elveden, 404
Materials, see under Asphalt, Brick, Concrete,
Flint, Glass, Granite, Iron, Lead, Leather,
Marble, Pitch-pine, Plaster, Slate, Stone,
Stucco, Terra-cotta, Velvet, Wood;

combinations of, see under Polychromy,
constructional
Maze, at Somerleyton, 420
Metalwork, decorative, at Shadwell, 202,
Carlton, 353, Abney, 393, Elvetham, 405,
Milner Field, 414, Tortworth, 422; metal
gates at Kinmel, 323, Sandringham, 419;
metal grates at Cardiff, 280, Carlton, 353,
Castell Coch, 343, 344, by Jeckell, 368
Metalworkers and designers, see in the main index
under Baily, Barnard Bishop and Barnard,
John Hardman, Hart, Son, Peard and Co.,
Thomas Jeckell, Longden & Co., Perry and
Co., Richardson, Slade and Co.
Middle classes, 5–6, 69–70
'Modern' style, the 293
Moorish style, see under Arabic
Mosaics, at Eaton Hall, 2, Rousdon, 418
'Muscularity', 54–7, 261, 274, 348, 418
Music rooms, at Tettenhall, 26n., Shadwell, 198,
Kelham, 233–4, Flete, 405

Nature as a design source, 59, at Kelham, 234–5
Neo-Georgian style, 85–6; interiors, by Devey,
222; stables by Burn, 319–20

Observatory, at Cragside, 307, 308, Broomhill,
398
'Old English' style, the, 71–3, 331, 359;
anticipated by Devey, 218; modified in the
1890s, 375
Orangery, at Coombe Warren, 402, Heath, 409,
Minley, 414
Organs, at Shadwell, 198, Betteshanger, 218,
Nutfield, 415
Owners of country houses
architects, why chosen by, 17–19 , 225, 274,
307, 320, 329, 381; builders, act as own, at
Swaylands, 17, Bear Wood, 268
art collectors as, at Betteshanger, 214,
Brodsworth, 238, Cragside, 314, Ken Hill,
374, Grittleton, 407, Hafodunos, 408,
Possingworth, 416, Westonbirt, 424,
Wyfold, 425
Building, reasons for, 8; to avoid absenteeism,
at Beauvale, 329; to cater for cricket-
weeks, at Wightwick, 376
Church built by, before house, at Treberfydd,
164–5, Shadwell, 198, Betteshanger, 214,
Bear Wood, 267–8; owner regrets church
not put first at Merevale, 128
financial troubles of, 9, at Treberfydd, 170,
Milton Ernest, 186, Shadwell, 204,
Somerleyton, 212, Kelham, 235, Bear
Wood, 272, Carlton Towers, 354,
Nutfield, 415, Preston, 416, Wadhurst, 422
new families, 10–13, 18–19: case history of
one (Crossleys), 205–12; encouraged by
Prince of Wales, 68, 291; French-roof style
taken up by, 291–304; landed property,
reasons for buying, 6–9, at Milton Ernest,
180, Somerleyton, 212; reactions to
technology, 26–7 and see under Wealth,
origins of
old families, 4–9; reactions to new money,
291; 'French-roof' style, 291–4;
technology, 26; wealth increased by
income from coal, 128, 236, 297, 329, 394,
423, 424, docks, 273–4, iron, 424, town
property, 2, 113, 399, 409, 423, 427;
agricultural depression, effect on, 9, 86, 204,
235, 354

Picture galleries, at Bear Wood, 271, Cragside,
314, Dawpool, 403, Possingworth, 416,
Wyfold, 425
Picturesque tradition, the, 46–8, 61–51, 72;
Barry and 48–50; Salvin and 61–2, 95, 158;
Shaw and, 76; at Bayons, 47, 105
'Pies', used by Shaw and Nesfield, 321–2, at
Kinmel, 322, 325, Cloverley, 322, Cragside,
312
Pitch-pine used at Abermad, 394, Yattendon,
426, Invercauld, 431; used at Treberfydd to
save money for church building, 449
Plan, the Victorian country house, 27–46;

inflexibility of, 31; historical development
of, 31–4, 69–70, 75–8; later Victorian
criticisms of, 69–70
Burn, as planner, 33–4; jealous of revealing
his plans, 33, 264n.
Devey as planner, 84
Shaw as planner, 77–8
and see under Accommodation,
Appurtenances, Basements, Entrances,
Family suite and wing, Male preserve,
Servants' wing
Plasterers, see in the main index under Bernasconi,
Jackson, Shuffrey
Plasterwork, decorative: Adam-style, at Ken
Hill, 374; in the Baroque style, at Harlaxton,
96–8, Revesby, 417; Elizabethan plasterwork
mechanically imitated at Merevale, 127,
skilfully imitated at Wightwick, 378,
especially lavish at Crewe, 403; fibrous
plasterwork, at Possingworth, 416; stamped
to imitate leather, at Carlton, 353; and see
under Rough cast and Stucco
Plumbing, 22–3; internal, at Wykehurst, 298,
Shabden, 299
bathrooms, 22; especially numerous at
Wykehurst, 22, Bear Wood, 268, Byrkley,
400; none at Carlton, 22, Grittleton, 407,
Worsley, 425; richly decorated, at Cardiff,
275, 280; in basement, at Cragside, 309;
misused by upper classes, 27; shower bath
at Osborne, 152, Tyntesfield, 251; Turkish
baths at Tettenhall, 26n., Wightwick, Fig.
29, Avery Hill, 394
hot water supply, 22–3, at Wykehurst, 298
wash-basins, 22, 34
water-closets, 22; self-locking at Batchwood,
26
water-tanks, 23, in a tower at Somerleyton,
23, Clouds, 81, Osborne, 152, Humewood,
259, Bear Wood, 269, Standen, 383,
Broomhill, 398
water pumped by engine, at Somerleyton, 23,
Bear Wood, 269
Polychromy, structural, 27, 58; Butterfield and,
182; at Shadwell, 200, Bishopscourt, 397,
Capel Manor, 59, Crawley, 403, Elvetham,
405, Ettington, 405, Horsley, 410;
polychromatic joinery, at Humewood, 262
Pompeian atrium, at Down Hall, 237
Porte-cochère, at Brodsworth, 237, Humewood,
259, Heath, 409, Rendcomb, 417, Winscott,
424, Wynnstay, 426, Clonghanadfoy, 426;
enlarged, as carriage-court, at Kelham, 233;
paved with rubber, at Enbrook, 26

Quaintness: Nesfield and Shaw and, 73; Ken
Hill described as quaint, 75; deliberately
avoided, at Batsford, 396
'Queen-Anne' style, the 74–5, 83, 370, 396;
country houses, considered unsuitable for, 75;
modified for, 446; Devey and, 83, 218; Kerr
sympathetic to, 263n.

Radiators, designed by Butterfield, at Chanter's
House, 401
Riding school, at Welbeck, 423
Romanesque style, at Grittleton, 407
Roofs, complication of Victorian roof plans, 60,
at Milton Ernest, 185; flat roofs at Osmaston,
24, Peckforton, 163, Osborne, 152; high-
pitched roofs, mid-Victorians keen on, 65,
criticism of, 65; mansard roofs, as a means to
skyline, 64, 292
Roof garden, at Cardiff, 280
Rough-cast at Standen, 383

Saloon, the, as used by Devey, 79, 220–1; at
Ken Hill, 371
Sculptors, see under Stonecarvers
Sculpture, architectural
mid-Victorian vogue for, encouraged by
Ruskin, 58–9
at Shadwell, 202, Kelham, 234–5, Cardiff,
275–90, Cragside, 312, Carlton, 351, Castell
Coch, 340–5, Abermad, 392, Alnwick, 394,
Bylaugh, 400, Dobroyd, 404, Elvetham,

405, Hafodunos, 408, Llys Dulas, 411,
Milner Field, 414, Possingworth, 416,
Shabden, 420, Somerleyton, 421, Wyfold,
425, Wynnstay, 426
and see under Stonecarvers and Architectural
sculptors
Servants, 28–30, 82; their windows not allowed
a view of the gentry, 28; exception at Milton
Ernest, 186; frosted glass for, at Humewood,
258; luxuriously treated at Worth, 27;
bowling-alley for, at Rousdon, 418
Servants hall, 28; given view of the garden at
Milton Ernest, 186
Servants' wing, 29–30, and see under Laundry
and Kitchen
Serving room, the, 33
Skating-rink, at Tettenhall, 26n., Halton, 38
Skyline, importance of, 62–3, 293; Godwin on,
at Dromore, 63; White on, at Humewood,
258; Beresford Hope on, 293
Slate used for chimneypieces, 448; slate-hung
walls, at Plas Dinam, 416
Smoking, 35–6; only allowed in kitchen at St.
Albans, 219n., outside house, at Cragside,
317n.
Smoking room, 35–8, at Ken Hill, 37, Smeaton,
420; in a tower, 36, at Humewood, 259,
Cardiff, 275, 278, Cliffe Castle, 401, Hope
End, 410, Tyntesfield, 250
Souls, the, 81
Stables: especially noteworthy at Scarisbrick,
118, Treberfydd, 169, Shadwell, 200,
Humewood, 257, Kinmel, 319–20, Broom
Hill, 398, Coombe Cottage, 403, Rendcomb,
417, Arisaig, 394; offwind of house, at
Humewood, 259; with covered-ride for
horses at Normanhurst, 295; centrally-heated,
at Avery Hill, 396; and see Riding-school
Stained glass at Eaton Hall, 2, Harlaxton, 447,
Scarisbrick, 119, Merevale, 123, Shadwell,
200, 202, Humewood, 259–60, Tyntesfield,
250, Cardiff, 280, Cragside, 311, Beauvale,
332, Carlton, 352–3, 354, Adcote, 364,
Wightwick, 377–8, Bank Hall, 396, Dobroyd,
404, Elvetham, 405, Milner Field, 414,
Nutfield, 415, Possingworth, 416, Rousdon,
418, Shabden, 429, Somerleyton, 421,
Tortworth, 422, Adare, Clonghanadfoy, 426
Seven Lamps of Architecture in stained glass
at Abermad, 393
Stained-glass makers and designers, see in the
main index under Ballantyne, Clayton and Bell,
Gibbs, John Hardman, C. E. Kempe, Lavers
Barraud and Westlake, Morris and Co., F. R.
Pickersgill, Powell Bros, D. G. Rossetti,
Saunders and Co., Thomas Willement, H. E.
Wooldridge
Statuary, collections of, at Brodsworth, 238–40,
Grittleton, 407, Hafodunos, 408
Stone: mid-Victorian reaction against ashlar, 57,
194; exposed internal stone-walling, at
Peckforton, 163, Adcote, 363, Thoresby,
421; comprehensive use of, at Woodchester,
190; and see Flint, Granite, Vaulting
Stone carvers and architectural sculptors, see in
the main index, under Burke and Co., Thomas
Earp, Farmer and Brindley, James Forsyth,
Fucigna, Halliday Brothers, Mabey, Thomas
Nicholls, Nucci, Phyffers, Raynard Smith,
Strazza, John Thomas
Stucco, increasingly disapproved of, by
Victorians, 19; used externally at Osborne,
149, Carlton, 348–9, Cliveden, 402, Silverton,
420; used internally to imitate stone at
Highclere, 134
Style, see under Arabic, Classical, Elizabethan,
French, Gothic, Greek, Indian, Japanese, Old
English, Pompeian, Queen Anne,
Romanesque, Victorian
Sunflowers, used as decorative motif, 72, 368, at
Kinmel, 321, Cragside, 312
Symmetry, Victorian attitude to, 61

Tea, flourishes in late Victorian days, 79; hall
used for, 79, 387
Technology, 22–7; reactions to, by new and old

families, 26·7; effects on style and plan, 27; see
also under Bells, Electricity, Fire prevention,
Heating, Hydraulic machinery, Lifts,
Lighting, Plumbing, Telephones, Ventilation
Telegraph system, at Tettenhall, 26n.
Telephone systems, at Hatfield, 26, Cragside,
307
Terra-cotta, used at Foxwarren, 406, Yattendon,
426
Temple, at Coombe Warren, 19n., Highclere,
130, Brodsworth, 237
Tile-hanging, revival of, 72, at Beauvale, 332,
Wightwick, 376, Standen, 384, Banstead
Wood, 396, Pierrepont, 416, Rousdon, 418
Tile-makers, see in the main index under Minton,
de Morgan, Simpson and Son
Tiles, decorative, at Scarisbrick, 119, Osborne,
152, Treberfydd, 169, Horsted, 178, Cardiff,
278, Cragside, 312, 314, Carlton, 353, Castell
Coch, 343, Adcote, 364, Greenham, 407,
Shabden, 420; Philip Webb thinks unpleasant
to walk on, 388
Towers, 48; as aid to sky-line, 122; as a corner
accent, 173; Carlton Hall becomes Carlton
Towers, 349; tower containing chapel at
Hope End, 416; ventilation shaft, at
Osmaston, 24; freestanding in park at
Abberley, 392; and see under Smoking room
and Plumbing, water-tank

Unions and strikes at Merevale, 121

Vaulting, in stone or brick, at Highclere, 136,
Peckforton and Alnwick, 163, Woodchester,
190–1, Kelham, 225, Tyntesfield, 250,
Humewood, 259–60, Horsley, 410, Wyfold,
425; and see under Fireproof construction
Velvet, used as a wall-covering at Kelham, 234
Ventilation, 23–4, at Harlaxton, 446, Wykehurst,
298, Shabden, 298, Hope End, 410, Rousdon,
418; especially elaborate at Osmaston, 23–4,
Tettenhall, 26n.
Vernacular architecture, revival of interest in,
68; one source of 'Old English' style, 71–2;
Webb and, 79, 383; Devey and, 83, 213;
Pearson and, 418
'Victorian' style, a, 56,
Visitors' book, at Betteshanger, 215

Wall and ceiling painting
decorative, at Wortley, 38, Bayons, 108,
Scarisbrick, 118–9, Prestwold, 142,
Osborne, 149, Kelham, 234, Brodsworth,
241–2, Tyntesfield, 246, Cardiff, 275, 279,
287, Castell Coch, 341–4, Bylaugh, 400,
Elveden, 404, Milner Field, 414, Penoyre,
Preston, 416, Quy, 417, Shabden, 420,
Clonghanadfoy, 426, Dromore, 427,
Lismore, 429
figurative, at Eaton Hall, 2, Gunnergate, 38,
Scarisbrick, 115, Osborne, 150, Cardiff,
275, 287, Carlton, 352, Castell Coch,
341–4, Bank Hall, 396, Rousdon, 418
and see under Decorative artists
Wallpapers, at Brodsworth, 242, Heath, 409; by
Godwin at Beauvale, 332; by Morris at
Standen, 384
Water-closet, see under Plumbing
Wealth, cost of country houses, at Swaylands,
17, Trentham, 51, Harlaxton, 93, Scarisbrick,
118, Merevale, 120, Peckforton, 156, Horsted,
173, Brodsworth, 242, Humewood, 254,
Bear Wood, 272, Beauvale, 330, Adcote, 454,
Alnwick, 394, Rousdon, 418
Wealth, origins of, in new families, 10–13
architecture, 426
armaments, 306, 421
banking and finance, 11, 164–5, 297, 299–302,
393, 394, 396, 402, 403, 406, 407, 411, 414,
415, 416, 419, 422
biscuits, 13, 418
brewing, 297, 397, 400, 404, 406, 416
bullion broking, 11, 417
candles, 179
carpets, 205–6
chemicals, 423

china clay, 13, 398
coal, 417
contracting, 10, 294, 409, 414, 416, 420
copper, 13, 299, 318, 405, 412, 421
cotton, 10, 393, 404, 415
dressmaking, 354
dyeing, 172
engineering, 11, 305, 366
finance, *see* banking
gloves, 421
guano, 13, 244
hosiery, 13, 408
hatting, 359
hydros, 417
Iron and steel, 10–11, 359, 409, 412, 418, 420
lace, 411
law, 104, 381, 397, 401
linen bleaching, 179

literature, 394, 410
mines, *see under* coal, copper, iron and steel, nitrate, salt
music publishing, 452
newspapers, 263
nitrate, 244, 394
ostrich feathers, 13, 400
paints and varnishes, 297, 375
pianos, 13, 392
politics, 410
printing, 263
railways, 10, 411, *and see* contracting
salt, 13, 295
shipping and shipbuilding, 403, 407, 423
silversmithing, 407
stockbroking, 420
tea, 397
trade with Russia, 393, 411, Spain and S.

America, 244, 422, Portugal, 412
wool, 10, 401, 409, 414
Weather-boarding, at Standen, 383, 384, Coombe Cottage, 403
Windows, 21–2; as used by Salvin, 62, Shaw, 73, 76, Scott, 227; at Merevale, 127; elaborately leaded at Treberfydd, 167; distinctive staircase windows, 65; small-paned sashes revived, 74, used by Butterfield, 181; *and see under* Glass and Double glazing
Winter garden, 38, at Somerleyton, 38, 211, Halton, 302, Avery Hill, 394, Cliffe Castle, 401, Stancliffe, 421
Woodcarvers, *see in the main index under* James Forsyth, J. Erskine Knox, George Willcox
Woodcarving, at Scarisbrick, 114, Cragside, 312, Carlton Towers, 352, Somerleyton, 421